W9-BNR-591

Advanced VBScript for Microsoft® Windows® Administrators

Don Jones and
Jeffery Hicks

PUBLISHED BY
Microsoft Press
A Division of Microsoft Corporation
One Microsoft Way
Redmond, Washington 98052-6399

Copyright © 2006 by Don Jones and Jeffery Hicks

All rights reserved. No part of the contents of this book may be reproduced or transmitted in any form or by any means without the written permission of the publisher.

Library of Congress Control Number 2005937886

Printed and bound in the United States of America.

1 2 3 4 5 6 7 8 9 QWT 9 8 7 6 5

Distributed in Canada by H.B. Fenn and Company Ltd.
A CIP catalogue record for this book is available from the British Library.

Microsoft Press books are available through booksellers and distributors worldwide. For further information about international editions, contact your local Microsoft Corporation office or contact Microsoft Press International directly at fax (425) 936-7329. Visit our Web site at *www.microsoft.com/mspress*. Send comments to *mspinput@microsoft.com*.

Microsoft, Active Directory, ActiveX, Excel, FrontPage, JScript, Microsoft Press, MSDN, Tahoma, Verdana, Visio, Visual Basic, Win32, Windows, the Windows logo, Windows NT, and Windows Server are either registered trademarks or trademarks of Microsoft Corporation in the United States and/or other countries. Other product and company names mentioned herein may be the trademarks of their respective owners.

The example companies, organizations, products, domain names, e-mail addresses, logos, people, places, and events depicted herein are fictitious. No association with any real company, organization, product, domain name, e-mail address, logo, person, place, or event is intended or should be inferred.

This book expresses the author's views and opinions. The information contained in this book is provided without any express, statutory, or implied warranties. Neither the authors, Microsoft Corporation, nor its resellers, or distributors will be held liable for any damages caused or alleged to be caused either directly or indirectly by this book.

Acquisitions Editor: Martin DelRe
Project Editor: Melissa von Tschudi-Sutton
Production: Online Training Solutions, Inc.

Body Part No. X11-89440

Contents at a Glance

Table of Contents

Acknowledgements

I'd like to thank Jeffery, who has easily been one of the best co-authors anyone could ask for. Writing a book can be exceedingly stressful and time-consuming, and a good co-author can really help alleviate a lot of that. Thanks also go out to everyone at SAPIEN Technologies: Jonathan, Alex, and Ferdinand, who provided assistance with tools and technologies that were ancillary to the book's main purpose, making things much smoother. Finally, a big cheer is due all the users at ScriptingAnswers.com, whose persistence and unwavering support of the scripting community were a primary motivation for bringing this book to market.

Don Jones
Las Vegas, NV

Writing your first book can be a daunting and sometimes frightening task. Fortunately, I had a great writing partner. Thanks, Don, for being such a terrific guide in the strange new world of publishing. Thanks, too, to the people at Visory Group. I truly appreciate the flexibility you give me to take on projects like this one. Finally, I want to say an extra big thank-you to Beth, Lucas, and Ellie. Without the love, support, and understanding of my new family ("Daddy has to work again tonight?"), I would never have made it this far. You're the reason I work so hard.

Jeffery Hicks
Syracuse, NY

Introduction

When writing my first scripting book, *Managing Windows with VBScript and WMI* (Addison-Wesley, 2004), I set out to create what was at the time an industry first: a book designed not for developers but specifically for Microsoft Windows administrators with very little VBScript experience who wanted to learn just enough VBScript to be effective. Since that book was published, Windows administrators have become more and more skilled with Windows Script Host, VBScript, Windows Management Instrumentation, and other related technologies. Because administrators attending conferences and viewing my Web site (*http:// www.ScriptingAnswers.com*) are beginning to ask questions about more complex technologies and techniques, the time has come for a book that covers advanced topics.

In this book, my able co-author, Jeffery Hicks, and I try to cover some of the more advanced scripting techniques that we use every day. We certainly aren't pretending that we touch on every topic that might be considered "advanced"; after all, scripting is as varied and complex as Microsoft Windows itself. Instead, we try to cover the most useful advanced technologies, recognizing that our fellow administrators are typically as practical and pragmatic as we are. We also try to cover these technologies in much the same way that we learned about them, by presenting complete solutions and line-by-line walkthroughs, so that you can see the final product as well as a detailed description of how and why it works.

Personally, I'm delighted that Windows is now such a mature, stable product that we have the time and tools to explore automation through scripting. I'm also glad that more administrators are tackling advanced topics, which tells me that Windows has truly become an enterprise operating system, with the level of complexity and scriptability often associated with traditional enterprise-class operating systems such as UNIX.

Jeffery and I both appreciate that you've selected this book for your further scripting education. We certainly hope you find it useful! That said, we want to offer a brief word of caution: This is truly an advanced book. We don't take the time to explain basic scripting concepts, and we assume that you already have medium- to high-level scripting skills. We do cover a few basics at the beginning of the book, but only to provide a quick refresher of techniques you might not use every day.

With that caveat out of the way, I want to wish you the best of luck with your scripting efforts!

Don Jones

Who Is This Book For?

This book is intended for Microsoft Windows administrators who want to take their scripting to the next level. We're assuming readers have intermediate to advanced scripting skills and are looking for new techniques and ideas to expand their scripting toolbox. This book is also for scripting administrators who want to expand their realm into products such as Microsoft Exchange 2003 and Microsoft Virtual Server 2005. If you've never worked with VBScript before, then this book definitely isn't for you. We're not spending much time on the basics, and you'll certainly need those basics to understand what we're covering here. If you'd like a more introductory-level book, consider Don Jones' *Managing Windows with VBScript and WMI* (Addison-Wesley, 2004) or a similar title.

Conventions in This Book

This book is relatively straightforward, and there are no tricky conventions that readers need to be aware of. However, the following reader alerts are used throughout the book to point out useful information:

Reader Alert	Meaning
Tip	Provides a helpful bit of inside information about specific tasks or functions
Note	Alerts you to supplementary information
Caution	Contains important information about possible data loss, breaches of security, or other serious problems
On the CD	Identifies tools or additional information available on the CD that accompanies the book
Best Practice	Identifies techniques or conventions that are recognized as industry standards; while not following these practices won't break anything, they can make things easier and more efficient.

System Requirements

To use the *Advanced VBScript for Microsoft Windows Administrators* companion CD, you'll need a computer equipped with the following configuration:

- Pentium II (or similar) with 266-megahertz (MHz) or higher processor.

- CD-ROM or DVD-ROM drive.

- Microsoft Mouse or compatible pointing device.

- Microsoft Windows Server 2003, Microsoft Windows 2000, or Microsoft Windows XP. We assume you've installed the latest service packs, although in most cases we don't cover information specific to a given service pack (and when we do, we mention it).

- Windows Script Host (WSH) version 5.6 or later. WSH is a core component of Windows 2000 and later versions, so unless you've taken special steps to remove this software, it should already be installed.

- Some scripts—notably the ones dealing with Microsoft Exchange Server 2003, Microsoft Virtual Server 2005, or Microsoft Operations Manager 2005—require additional Microsoft products, as appropriate.

- Microsoft Internet Explorer 5.5 or later.

- Adobe Acrobat or Acrobat Reader.

About the Companion CD

To provide you with quick and easy access to the tools you need to get the most out of this book, we've included the following on the companion CD:

- The scripts presented in the book.

- Links to any of the URLs we mention that are too long to type easily.

- A number of additional tools (or links to them).

Do take a few moments to explore the CD and all it contains. If you'd like to pursue scripting beyond the topics included in this book, we invite you to visit Don's Web site at *http:// www.ScriptingAnswers.com*. You'll find additional script samples, training, discussion forums for questions and answers, and more resources, all designed for Windows administrative scripting.

Support for This Book

Every effort has been made to ensure the accuracy of this book and the contents of the companion CD. Microsoft Press provides general support information for its books and companion CDs at the following Web site:

http://www.microsoft.com/learning/support/books

To search for book and CD corrections for this book by using the book's ISBN, go to

http://www.microsoft.com/mspress/support/search.asp

If you have comments, questions, or ideas regarding this book or the companion CD, please send them to Microsoft Press using either of the following methods:

E-Mail: *mspinput@microsoft.com*

Postal Mail:
Microsoft Press
Attn: *Advanced VBScript for Microsoft Windows Administrators* project editor
One Microsoft Way
Redmond, WA 98052

Please note that Microsoft software product support is not offered through the above addresses.

You are welcome to contact the authors at *http://www.ScriptingAnswers.com* to ask questions or discuss problems that you might have regarding the scripts included on the CD that accompanies this book.

Part I
The Basics of Advanced Windows Scripting

Chapter 1
Getting Started

Before we get started, let's take a few minutes to review some scripting basics. Without a solid foundation in VBScript, Active Directory Services Interface (ADSI), and Windows Management Instrumentation (WMI), many of the topics in this book might frustrate you. We'll cover some of the scripting fundamentals you should understand before proceeding.

Any journey worth taking requires a bit of preparation. In this book, we will be covering a lot of ground. This chapter will help you prepare. We'll go over some of the things you need to already be familiar with to get the most from the material. We'll also spend some time reviewing some scripting fundamentals. If you are new to scripting, this overview should help you get your bearings.

Prerequisite Knowledge

To get the most out of this book, you must have experience with scripting technologies, terminologies, and techniques. Familiarity with the *WSHShell* object and error handling in Microsoft Windows Script Host (WSH) will make your journey quite a bit easier. We include a quick refresher, but if some of this looks new to you, we suggest going through the scripts at the Microsoft TechNet Script Center and reading the *Microsoft Windows 2000 Scripting Guide* (Microsoft Press) or *Managing Windows with VBScript and WMI* (Addison-Wesley). At a minimum, you should download and read the Windows Script Host 5.6 documentation from the Microsoft Web site at

http://www.microsoft.com/downloads/details.aspx?familyid=01592C48-207D-4BE1-8A76-1C4099D7BBB9&displaylang=en

 On the CD   This link, like most of the links referenced in this book, is included on the companion CD. Click *Windows Script 5.6 documentation*.

Understanding Windows Script Host Basics

We assume you have Microsoft Windows Script Host 5.6 installed. If you aren't sure, open a command prompt and type **cscript //logo //?**. You should see something like this.

```
Microsoft (R) Windows Script Host Version 5.6
Copyright (C) Microsoft Corporation 1996-2001. All rights reserved.

Usage: CScript scriptname.extension [option...] [arguments...]

Options:
  //B          Batch mode: Suppresses script errors and prompts from displaying
  //D          Enable Active Debugging
  //E:engine   Use engine for executing script
  //H:CScript  Changes the default script host to CScript.exe
  //H:WScript  Changes the default script host to WScript.exe (default)
  //I          Interactive mode (default, opposite of //B)
  //Job:xxxx   Execute a WSF job
  //Logo       Display logo (default)
  //Nologo     Prevent logo display: No banner will be shown at execution time
  //S          Save current command line options for this user
  //T:nn       Time out in seconds:  Maximum time a script is permitted to run
  //X          Execute script in debugger
  //U          Use Unicode for redirected I/O from the console
```

In the next sections, we'll cover a few key WSH elements that recur in our scripts throughout the book.

> **Note**   Many of the scripts and samples in this book require administrator privileges, either locally or on remote systems. We assume you will be running any scripts as a local or domain administrator. Where appropriate, we will point out how and where to use alternate credentials.

WshShell

The *WshShell* object offers a lot of functionality to scripting administrators. You can use it to send a message to the user through a popup, read and write to the registry, launch other programs, and more. Let's take a quick look at this object.

Popup

The *Popup* method displays a graphical message to the user, complete with buttons and icons. One advantage to using the *Popup* method instead of the similar *MsgBox* function (discussed later in this chapter) is that you can configure the popup window to dismiss itself automatically after a specified number of seconds. This is ideal when you want to display information to a user but you don't want to rely on the user to click OK. Listing 1-1 illustrates the use of the *Popup* method with a sample script.

Listing 1-1 *WshShell Popup* Sample

```
dim wshShell
set wshShell=CreateObject("wscript.shell")
'title for popup window
strTitle="Welcome"

'compose popup message text
strMsg="Thank you for logging in." & VbCrLf
strMsg=strMsg & "It is now " & Now & VbCrLf
strMsg=strMsg & "Have a nice day."

'set time to -1 to never dismiss popup window
wshShell.Popup strMsg,7,strTitle,vbOKOnly+vbInformation
```

On the CD   You will find this script, as well as other scripts listed in this chapter, on the CD that accompanies this book.

Notice that we use some intrinsic constants, *vbOkOnly* and *vbInformation*, as part of our popup parameters. These constants display the OK button and the information icon, respectively. These same constants are also used with the *MsgBox* function. You can find more information about them in the Windows Script Host 5.6 documentation.

Registry Reading

The *WshShell* object is often used to read the local registry. To read or manipulate a remote registry, you must use Windows Management Instrumentation (WMI.) Assuming the user executing the script has the appropriate permissions, you can easily read and write information from the registry. Here is a quick example of reading owner and product information from the local registry.

```
dim objShell
Set objShell=CreateObject("wscript.shell")
strRegisteredUser=objShell.RegRead("HKLM\Software\Microsoft\" &_
"Windows NT\CurrentVersion\RegisteredOwner")
strProduct=objShell.RegRead("HKLM\Software\Microsoft\Windows NT\" &_
"CurrentVersion\ProductName")
WScript.Echo strRegisteredUser & " is running " & strProduct
```

Program Launching

You will often need to call another script or program from your main administrative script. Fortunately, the *WshShell* object makes this possible, as shown in Listing 1-2.

Listing 1-2 *WshShell Run* Sample

```
dim objShell
'Window style
Const WINDOWHIDDEN=0
Const WINDOWNORMAL=1
Const WINDOWMINIMIZE=2
Const WINDOWMAXIMIZE=3
```

```
Set objShell=CreateObject("wscript.shell")

'enter in full path to command or script if not in %Systemroot%
strCommand="Notepad"

objShell.Run strCommand,WINDOWNORMAL,True
'this line won't echo until previous command finishes
WScript.Echo "Script complete"
```

In Listing 1-2, the important parameters are the window style and whether the command should wait before continuing with script execution. In this example, we set up constants for typical window styles. (Again, refer to the Windows Script Host 5.6 documentation for additional window styles.) You will likely want to run a program or script and hide it from the user. Depending on the program or script, you can do this by setting the window type parameter to 0.

If you want execution in your main script to wait for the command to finish, set the *WaitOn-Return* variable to TRUE. In Listing 1-2, the line of code that displays *Script Complete* won't execute until the command launched by the *WshShell* object has completed.

Another way to execute a command is with the *Exec* method. This technique is especially useful for parsing out the results of a command-line tool or utility. Often, you might find yourself developing a script that could use the output of another command for reporting or as parameters. Listing 1-3 takes the output of a *Dir* command that displays all executables, and modifies it so that it displays only the directory name and file information. You must run this script from a command prompt using CScript.

Listing 1-3 *WshShell* **Exec** Sample: *Dir*

```
Dim objShell,objExec
Set objShell=CreateObject("wscript.shell")
'command to Execute
strCommand="cmd /c DIR c:\*.exe /s"
'text to look for in the output
strFind=".exe"

'Create Exec object
Set objExec=objShell.Exec(strCommand)

'parse output and only display lines with
'target text
Do While objExec.StdOut.AtEndOfStream<>True
  strLine=objExec.StdOut.ReadLine
  'parse out lines
  If InStr(strLine,"Directory") Then
    WScript.Echo Trim(strLine)
  Elseif InStr(strLine,strFind) Then
    WScript.Echo vbTab & strLine
  End If
Loop
```

At run time, the script passes the specified command to the *WshShell* object and executes it. The output of that command is then redirected to a new object, called *objExec* in our script. With this object, we can leverage the power of *StdOut* and manipulate the data that would ordinarily be written in the command prompt window. As long as the command is running, the *AtEndOfStream* property will be FALSE. Because we want to display specific information from what would generally be a lengthy output, we set a variable, *strLine*, to the value of the next line of *StdOut*. Then we can use the *InStr* function to find strings of interest. If there is a match, the line is displayed. In Listing 1-3, we want to display the directory name as well as each line that includes the file name.

> **Tip**   With *StdOut*, you can use any text stream property from the *FileSystemObject* library, such as *ReadLine*, *SkipLine*, and *AtEndOfStream*.

Listing 1-4 *WshShell Exec* Sample: *Nslookup*

```
Dim objShell,objExec
Set objShell=CreateObject("wscript.shell")
'command to execute
strCommand="Nslookup www.microsoft.com"

'Create Exec object
Set objExec=objShell.Exec(strCommand)

'skip lines that contain information about our DNS
'server
objExec.StdOut.SkipLine
objExec.StdOut.SkipLine

Do While objExec.StdOut.AtEndOfStream<>True
   strLine=objExec.StdOut.ReadLine
   WScript.Echo strLine
Loop
WScript.Quit
```

Listing 1-4 demonstrates another way to use the *Exec* method: executing an *Nslookup* command. Our script parses out the lines of interest, namely the IP address of the specified name, and neatly displays them. The script simply skips the first two lines of any *Nslookup* output that contains the DNS server name and IP address.

> **Tip**   Although not an absolute requirement, you will find it easier and neater to run scripts that take advantage of *StdOut* and *StdIn* from the command line by using CScript. For example, if you run the script in Listing 1-4 by double-clicking it, you will see a few blank popup windows. If you run the script from a command prompt by using CScript, you will get cleaner looking results.

WshNetwork

The *WshNetwork* object exposes some basic network information for the current user, such as the username or computer name. This object can also be used to manage printer and drive mappings. Let's take a quick look at this object's functionality by incorporating it into the script from Listing 1-1.

Listing1-5 *WshNetwork* Sample

```
dim objShell,objNetwork,collDrives
set objShell=CreateObject("Wscript.shell")
Set objNetwork=CreateObject("WScript.Network")
'title for popup window
strTitle="Welcome"

'enumerate mapped drives
strMappedDrives=EnumNetwork()

'enumerate mapped printers
strMappedPrint=EnumPrint()

'compose popup message text
strMsg=objNetwork.UserName & ", thank you for logging in to " &_
objNetwork.ComputerName & VbCrLf & vbcrlf
strMsg=strMsg & strMappedDrives & VbCrLf & VbCrLf
strMsg=strMsg & strMappedPrint & VbCrLf & VbCrLf
strMsg=strMsg & "It is now " & Now & VbCrLf
strMsg=strMsg & "Have a nice day."

'set time to -1 to never dismiss popup window
objShell.Popup strMsg,10,strTitle,vbOKOnly+vbInformation
WScript.quit

Function EnumNetwork()
On Error Resume Next
  Set colDrives = objNetwork.EnumNetworkDrives

    'If no network drives were enumerated, then inform user, else display
    'enumerated drives
    If colDrives.Count = 0 Then
        ret="There are no network drives to enumerate."
    Else
        ret = "Current network drive connections: " & vbCRLF
        For i = 0 To colDrives.Count - 1 Step 2
            ret = ret & VbCrLf & colDrives(i) & vbTab & colDrives(i + 1)
        Next
    End If
EnumNetwork=ret
End Function


Function EnumPrint()
On Error Resume Next
  Set colPrint = objNetwork.EnumPrinterConnections
```

```
    'If no network printers enumerated, then inform user, else display
    'enumerated printers
    If colPrint.Count = 0 Then
        ret="There are no printers to enumerate."
    Else
        ret = "Current Printer connections: " & vbCRLF
        For i = 0 To colPrint.Count - 1 Step 2
            ret = ret & vbCRLF & colPrint(i) & vbTab & colPrint(i + 1)
        Next
    End If
EnumPrint=ret
End Function
```

In Listing 1-5, we customize the message to display the user name, the computer the user is logging onto, and any mapped drives or printers. We also create an object in our script called *objNetwork*, which is an instance of the *WshNetwork* object. With the *objNetwork* object, we can build a list of mapped drives and printers by calling the *EnumNetwork* and *EnumPrint* functions. These functions use the *EnumNetworkDrives* and *EnumPrinterConnections* methods to create collections of mapped network drives and printers respectively, as follows.

```
For i = 0 To colPrint.Count - 1 Step 2
  ret = ret & vbCRLF & colPrint(i) & vbTab & colPrint(i + 1)
Next
```

The function then loops through the collection and lists the mapped network resources.

Back in the main part of the script, we compose the message. We personalize it by calling the *username* and *computername* properties, as shown here.

```
strMsg=objNetwork.UserName & ", thank you for logging in to " &_
objNetwork.ComputerName & VbCrLf & vbcrlf
```

The only other addition to our display message is the information about mapped drives and printers. The user now sees a personalized message showing all his or her mapped drives and printers. The message appears for 10 seconds and then closes. We raised the time-out value because there's more to read now than in the Listing 1-1 example.

> **Note**   The username property is the user's NT4 style or *sAMAccountName* attribute such as *jhicks* or *donj*. If you want the user's full name or display name from Active Directory, you must add code to search for the account based on the *sAMAccountName* attribute.

Error Handling

Any administrative script should have some degree of error handling. Even if you develop scripts that only you use, error handling makes them easier to develop, debug, and deploy. You certainly don't need to examine every single place where an error could occur, but you should identify sections of code where an error or failure will have a significant and negative effect on your script. For example, if you are creating a log file with the *FileSystemObject* and attempt to write to a drive for which the user lacks proper permissions, that code will fail. The best approach is to catch this kind of error ahead of time and provide some meaningful feedback to the user, as shown in Listing 1-6.

> **Note**   The error handling we are discussing is specific to VBScript. The engine that runs our scripts, Windows Script Host, is language independent. We could have written our scripts in JScript and handled errors in an appropriate manner for that scripting language.

Listing 1-6 Error Handling Sample: *Err*

```
Dim objFSO,objTS
On Error Resume Next
Set objFSO=CreateObject("Scripting.FileSystemObject")
Err.clear
Set objTS=objFSO.CreateTextFile("R:\Logs\auditlog.txt")
If Err.Number<>0 Then
   strMsg="There was an error creating the log file" & VbCrLf
   strMsg=strMsg & "Error #" & Err.Number & " " & Err.Description
   WScript.Echo strMsg
   WScript.Quit
End If
'script continues from here
```

In Listing 1-6, we attempt to create a log file. If this attempt fails, there is no reason to continue with the script. Before we try to capture error information, we make an *Err.Clear* statement. In a short script like this it probably isn't necessary, but in a longer and more complicated script, calling *Err.Clear* removes any errors that occurred earlier in the script and were ignored. For example, you might be creating a user object in Active Directory from new user information stored in a text file. If one of the user attributes you want to populate is *telephonenumber*, but not every new user has this attribute populated, you want the script to continue regardless (hence the *On Error Resume Next* at the beginning of the script). However, when you try to set this attribute in the script, an error is still raised. If you don't call *Err.Clear*, the next time you check for the value of *Err.Number*, it might return the value of the previous error. In Listing 1-6 this is a highly unlikely event—nevertheless, we wanted to be very clear about how and when to use *Err.Clear*.

The actual error checking is looking for the value of *Err.Number*. A value of 0 indicates success. Any value other than 0 indicates some failure or error in the previous command. Depending on what the script was trying to accomplish, you might get a lot of error information or a little. At a minimum, we recommend displaying the *Err.Number* and *Err.Description* information to the user in some sort of error message. Keep in mind that not every error will have a corresponding description. Depending on the nature of your script and the value of *Err.Number*, you might add more sophisticated error handling. First intentionally induce errors that a user might cause and make note of the error numbers and descriptions. Then use a *Select Case* statement to take more sophisticated steps or offer more detailed information based on the error, as follows.

```
Select Case Err.Number
  Case 76
    WScript.Echo "Verify that path is available"
  Case 71
    WScript.Echo "You seem to be attempting to access a drive" &_
" that isn't ready, like a CD"
  Case 70
    WScript.Echo "You don't seem to have permission to write to" &_
" that file."
  Case Else
    WScript.echo "Error #" & Err.Number & " " & Err.Description
End Select
```

Of course, there is more to error handling than just the *Err* object. Some of the objects you might include in your script have their own mechanisms for avoiding or detecting errors. For example, the *FileSystemObject* includes the *FolderExists*, *DriveExists*, and *FileExists* methods. These methods return TRUE if the item in question exists, which means you can write code like that shown in Listing 1-7.

Listing 1-7 Error Handling Sample: *FileSystemObject*
```
On Error Resume Next
Dim objFSO,objTS
strFile="R:\logs\audit.log"
Set objFSO=CreateObject("Scripting.FileSystemObject")
If objFSO.FileExists(strFile) then
   Set objTS=objFSO.OpenTextFile(strFile)
Else
   Wscript.echo "Can't find " & strFile
Wscript.quit
End if
'script continues
```

InputBox

One of the great advantages of VBScript over traditional scripting, such as batch files, is the ability to solicit information or input from the user executing the script. This is typically done with the *InputBox* function, as shown here.

```
Dim objFSO, objTS
strTitle="Select Text File"
strFile=InputBox("What file do you want to open?",strTitle,"C:\boot.ini")
'if value of strFile is blank then either nother was entered
'or Cancel was clicked.  In either case we can't continue
If strFile="" Then WScript.Quit
Set objFSO=CreateObject("Scripting.FileSystemObject")
Set objTS=objFSO.OpenTextFile(strFile)
'script continues
```

As you can see in this brief example, the script asks the user for a file name by using the *Input-Box* function. Although the only parameter required is text to explain what the user should enter, your script will be more user-friendly if you include a title and a default choice. The advantage of offering a default choice is that users have a better idea of exactly what format they should use.

After you get input, you should validate it, as we did in the code just shown. If the user clicks Cancel or doesn't enter anything, there is no reason to continue, so the script silently quits. Depending on the type of information you are seeking, you might want to do further validation, such as checking the length or size of the entry. Or as Listing 1-8 shows, you can validate the value itself.

Listing 1-8 *InputBox* with Menu Sample

```
On Error Resume Next
strTitle="Option Menu"
strMenu="Please select one of the following choices:" & VbCrLf
strMenu=strMenu & "1 - Banana Cream" & VbCrLf
strMenu=strMenu & "2 - Cherry" & VbCrLf
strMenu=strMenu & "3 - Apple Walnut" & VbCrLf
strMenu=strMenu & "4 - Peach"
rc=InputBox(strMenu,strTitle,1)
If rc="" Then WScript.Quit
Select Case rc
  Case "1"
    WScript.Echo "One slice of Banana Cream, coming up!"
  Case "2"
    WScript.Echo "Sorry, we are all out of cherry."
  Case "3"
    WScript.Echo "Do you want ice cream with that?"
  Case "4"
    WScript.Echo "You get the last piece of Peach."
  Case Else
    WScript.Echo Chr(34) & rc & Chr(34) &_
    " is not a valid choice.  Please try again."
    WScript.quit
End Select
'script continues
```

In Listing 1-8, we build a text string in the *strMenu* variable. This variable is passed as the message parameter for the *InputBox* function. Assuming the value returned by the *InputBox* is not blank, we can use *Select Case* to determine the next course of action.

Even though we expect the user to enter a number, he or she might accidentally type some non-numeric character. By enclosing the choices in quotes for the *Case* statement, we treat the value as a literal text value. In this way, we are assured that the error handling code in *Case Else* will work. If the user enters anything other than 1, 2, 3, or 4, the error message is displayed. Entering *A*, which should be invalid, returns the code for Case 1. Copy the script for Listing 1-8 from the companion CD and try it out for yourself.

Alas, the *InputBox* function is the only graphical input option we have, other than using an HTML Application (HTA) (which we cover later in the book) or developing your own input box in a higher-level programming language such as Microsoft Visual Basic 2005 (which is beyond the scope of this book).

MsgBox

Closely related to the *InputBox* function, the *MsgBox* function also displays a message to the user in a graphical dialog box. At its simplest, all you need to code is the *MsgBox* function and text to be displayed.

```
MsgBox "Welcome to the company!"
```

This line displays a message box in which the user must click OK to proceed. Script execution halts until the message box is dismissed. Recall that you use the *WshShell.Popup* method to set a time interval that determines how long to display the message. You can force a popup window to behave like a message box by setting the timeout value to −1, which requires the user to click a button to dismiss it.

You can use a *MsgBox* function to display information or to get information, such as whether the user wants to continue working on the current task. The *MsgBox* function returns a value determined by the button clicked. You can create a message box that offers the button options *OK*, *Yes*, *No*, or *Cancel*.

> **Note**   There are other button types available, but these are the ones you are most likely to use in a script. See the Windows Script Host 5.6 documentation for additional information.

Listing 1-9 displays a code snippet that you can use to let the user control the script.

Listing 1-9 *MsgBox* YesNo Sample
```
strMsg="The file already exists.  Do you want to overwrite it?"
strTitle="File Confirm"
rc=MsgBox(strMsg,vbYesNo,strTitle)
If rc=vbYes Then
   Script.Echo "Overwriting file"
   'insert code here
Else
   strNewName=InputBox("Enter a new filename.",_
   strTitle,"c:\logs\newlog.txt")
   'insert code here
End If
'script continues
```

A *MsgBox* function asks whether the user wants to overwrite the file and uses the constant *vbYesNo* to create Yes and No buttons. We set a *rc* variable to return a value from the *MsgBox* depending on what button the user clicked. We can then add code depending on the returned value. But what if the user has a change of heart and wants to abort the entire script? Take a look at Listing 1-10.

```
Listing 1-10 MsgBox YesNoCancel Sample
strMsg="The file already exists.  Do you want to overwrite it?"
strTitle="File Confirm"

rc=MsgBox(strMsg,vbYesNoCancel,strTitle)
'take next steps based on value returned by
'MsgBox function
Select Case rc
  Case vbYes
    WScript.Echo "Overwriting file"
    'insert code here
  Case vbNo
    strNewName=InputBox("Enter a new filename.",_
    strTitle,"c:\logs\newlog.txt")
    'insert code here
  Case vbCancel
    WScript.Echo "Aborting the script"
    WScript.Quit
End Select

'script continues
```

In Listing 1-10, we use a *Select Case* statement to handle the *MsgBox* value. The code for *vbYes* and *vbNo* is unchanged. All we did was add code to handle *vbCancel*.

> **Tip**   You can also use *vbYesNo*, *vbOKOnly*, and *vbYesNoCancel* as button options in a *WshShell* popup. The value returned is an integer, depending on what button is clicked, but it is easier to use the intrinsic constants like *vbYes*. If you don't use the constants, you have to figure out what the constant equivalent is and use that in your code, and that probably won't be as meaningful unless you comment heavily. Use the constants and make your life easier.

There is one more feature of the *MsgBox* function that also works for the WshShell popup—the ability to add an icon to the dialog box. Table 1-1 shows the icons available.

Table 1-1   *MsgBox* **Icon Constants**

VBScript Constant	Integer Value	Icon Displayed
vbCritical	16	Critical Message
vbQuestion	32	Warning Query
vbExclamation	48	Warning Message
vbInformation	64	Information

To include an icon, simply add it with the appropriate button type, for example, *vbOkOnly+vbInformation*. Take a look at Listing 1-11, which is the script from Listing 1-10 slightly modified to use icons.

Listing 1-11 *MsgBox* with Icon Sample

```
strMsg="The file already exists.  Do you want to overwrite it?"
strTitle="File Confirm"

rc=MsgBox(strMsg,vbYesNoCancel+vbQuestion,strTitle)
'take next steps based on value returned by
'MsgBox Function
Select Case rc
  Case vbYes
    MsgBox "Overwriting file",vbOKOnly+vbInformation,strTitle
    'insert code here
  Case vbNo
    strNewName=InputBox("Enter a new filename.",_
    strTitle,"c:\logs\newlog.txt")
    'insert code here
  Case vbCancel
    MsgBox "Aborting the script",vbOKOnly+vbCritical,strTitle
    WScript.Quit
End Select

'script continues
```

Now our message boxes not only have a little more pizzazz, but they also provide visual rein-
forcement to the user. You can use these icon constants in a *WshShell* popup, but unfortunately, you can't use them with an *InputBox*.

Using the *FileSystemObject* Library

Working with files and directories is an important basic skill for a scripting administrator. You
need to be able to read text files that might contain a list of computers as well as create text
files that might be used as audit or trace logs for your scripts. The *FileSystemObject* library is
fairly extensive and we can't possibly review everything here. We'll focus on a few concepts
that will be used throughout this book.

You can open a text file as follows.

```
strFile="c:\boot.ini"
Set objFSO=CreateObject("Scripting.FileSystemObject")
Set objTS=objFSO.OpenTextFile(strFile)
```

With just two lines of code, we've opened C:\boot.ini. After we create the basic *Scripting.File-
SystemObject*, we create a text stream object that represents the contents of the file. After the
file is open and the text stream object is created, we can read the file line by line. This is accomplished by using a *Do...While* loop and the *AtEndOfStream* property.

```
Do while objTS.AtEndOfStream<>True
Loop
```

As long as we aren't at the end of the text file, we will loop through. We now need to read each line of the file and presumably do something with it. Conveniently, there is a *ReadLine* method. If we simply want to read the file and echo back each line, we would use something like the following code.

```
Do while objTS.AtEndOfStream<>True
  Wscript.echo objTS.ReadLine
Loop
```

More than likely, you will want to do something with the information contained in that line. We prefer to set a temporary variable to hold the line's contents. This makes it easier to clean up, manipulate, or validate the text string.

```
Do while objTS.AtEndOfStream<>True
  r=objTS.ReadLine
  if InStr(r,"XP") then strData=ProcessPC(r)
Loop
```

In this little snippet, we search the read line for *XP* and if it is found, we set *strData* to the value returned from a function in a script called *ProcessPC()*. When we are finished, we should clean up after ourselves by calling *objTS.Close* to close the text file.

Before we leave *OpenTextFile*, we will briefly explain the different modes in which a file can be opened. You can open a file for reading only, for writing, or for appending. You simply specify the mode as one of the *OpenTextFile* parameters. This is generally done by defining constants in your script, as shown here.

```
Const FORREADING=1
Const FORWRITING=2
Const FORAPPENDING=8
strFile="c:\boot.ini"
Set objFSO=CreateObject("Scripting.FileSystemObject")
Set objTS=objFSO.OpenTextFile(strFile,FORREADING)
```

If you open a file for writing, any existing data will be overwritten. If you open a file for appending, any data you write will be added to the end of the file. If you open a file for reading only, no changes can be made to the file. We generally use *OpenTextFile* for reading or appending. If we need to write new data, we use the *CreateTextFile* method, as shown here.

```
strFile="c:\logs\myaudit.log"
Set objFSO=CreateObject("Scripting.FileSystemObject")
Set objTS=CreateTextFile(strFile,TRUE)
objTS.WriteLine "Audit log: " & Now
'script continues
```

With the addition of a *CreateTextFile* parameter, the code is pretty simple. When this parameter is set to TRUE, any existing file with that name will be overwritten. If you don't include a *CreateTextFile* parameter, existing files will not be overwritten, and your script won't get very far unless you add some error handling. But after we've created the text file, we use the

WriteLine method to add whatever data we want. As before, when we are finished, we need to close the file with *objTS.Close*.

The other common use of the *FileSystemObject* is for working with folders and files. Listing 1-12 illustrates some of these techniques.

Listing 1-12 *FileSystemObject* File Sample

```
On Error Resume Next
Dim objFSO,objFldr,objFiles,objTS
strTitle="File Demo"

strDir=InputBox("What folder do you want to examine?",_
strTitle,"c:\files")
If strDir="" Then WScript.quit

Set objFSO=CreateObject("Scripting.FileSystemObject")
If objFSO.FolderExists(strDir) Then
  'open folder
  Set objFldr=objFSO.GetFolder(strDir)

  'get log file information by calling
  'the GetFileName function
  strFile=GetFileName
  If strFile="" Then
    WScript.Quit
  Else
    'call validation subroutine
    ValidateFile strFile
  End If
Else
  WScript.Echo "Can't find " & strDir
  WScript.Quit
End If

objTS.WriteLine "Folder Report for " & strDir
'get files in this folder
'objFiles is a collection
Set objFiles=objFldr.Files

'initialize our counter
i=0
'set variable for total number of files in folder
t=objFiles.Count
'enumerate the collection of files
For Each file In objFiles
  'get file information and write to log file
  objTS.WriteLine file.Name & vbTab & file.size & " bytes" & vbTab &_
  file.DateCreated & vbTab & file.DateLastModified
  i=i+1
  iPer=FormatPercent((i/t))
  WScript.StdOut.Writeline(iPer& " complete")
Next
```

```
'close file
objTS.Close
MsgBox "See " & strFile & " for results.",vbOKOnly+vbInformation,strTitle

WScript.Quit
'////////////////////////////////////////////////////////////////////////
Function GetFileName()
On Error Resume Next

GetFileName=InputBox("What is the name of the audit file you " &_
"want to create?",strTitle,"c:\filelog.txt")

End Function
'////////////////////////////////////////////////////////////////////////
Sub ValidateFile(strFile)
On Error Resume Next
'check if log file exists and if so
  'prompt user if they want to overwrite.
  If objFSO.FileExists(strFile) Then
    rc=MsgBox(strFile & " already exists.  Do you want " &_
    "to overwrite it?",vbYesNoCancel+vbQuestion,strTitle)
    Select Case rc
      Case vbYes
        WScript.Echo "Overwriting file " & strFile
        Err.Clear
        'create our logfile by overwriting
        Set objTS=objFSO.CreateTextFile(strFile,True)
        If Err.Number<>0 Then
          strMsg="There was an error creating " &_
          strFile & VbCrLf & "Error#" & Err.Number &_
          " " & Err.Description
          MsgBox strMsg,vbOKOnly+vbCritical,strTitle
          WScript.Quit
        End If
      Case vbNo
        strFile=GetFileName
        ValidateFile strFile
      Case vbCancel
        WScript.Echo "Aborting the script"
        WScript.Quit
    End Select
  Else
    'create our log file
    Err.Clear
    Set objTS=objFSO.CreateTextFile(strFile)
    If Err.Number<>0 Then
      strMsg="There was an error creating " &_
      strFile & VbCrLf & "Error#" & Err.Number &_
      " " & Err.Description
      MsgBox strMsg,vbOKOnly+vbCritical,strTitle
      WScript.Quit
    End If
  End If
End Sub
```

If you've been reading from the beginning of this chapter, you will notice that Listing 1-12 includes a lot of the suggestions and tips made earlier, plus a little something extra to reward you for getting this far in the chapter.

Listing 1-12 examines all the files in a specified folder and creates a log with specific file information. This common use of the *FileSystemObject* works with any local or mapped drives, as well as Universal Naming Convention (UNC) paths. The script starts by asking the user for the folder path to examine.

```
strDir=InputBox("What folder do you want to examine?",_
strTitle,"c:\files")
```

Assuming the user entered something, we can use the *FolderExists* method to validate the entry.

```
If objFSO.FolderExists(strDir) Then
  'open folder
  Set objFldr=objFSO.GetFolder(strDir)
...
```

We want a log file for the audit results, and now that we know we can continue, we need to create a text file. Recall that typically a function returns a value, and a subroutine is a section of modularized code that you can call as needed. We need to get the name of the log file from the user, so the script has a function called *GetFileName* that works as an *InputBox* wrapper.

```
Function GetFileName()
  On Error Resume Next
  GetFileName=InputBox("What is the name of the audit file you " &_
  "want to create?",strTitle,"c:\filelog.txt")
End Function
```

Again, assuming the user entered something, we need to validate the logfile. We call the *ValidateFile* subroutine that takes a file name as a parameter. If the file already exists, we ask the user if he or she wants to overwrite the file.

```
If objFSO.FileExists(strFile) Then
  rc=MsgBox(strFile & " already exists.  Do you want " &_
    "to overwrite it?",vbYesNoCancel+vbQuestion,strTitle)
```

Depending on the answer, we can either create the text file and overwrite the existing version or prompt the user to specify a new log file name.

```
Select Case rc
    Case vbYes
      WScript.Echo "Overwriting file " & strFile
      Err.Clear
      'create our logfile by overwriting
      Set objTS=objFSO.CreateTextFile(strFile,True)
      If Err.Number<>0 Then
        strMsg="There was an error creating " &_
        strFile & VbCrLf & "Error#" & Err.Number &_
```

```
        " " & Err.Description
        MsgBox strMsg,vbOKOnly+vbCritical,strTitle
        WScript.Quit
    End If
```

Notice the error handling in case there is a problem overwriting the file. If the user clicks No, we call the *GetFileName* function again and then call the *ValidateFile* subroutine, basically rerunning the code.

```
Case vbNo
  strFile=GetFileName
  ValidateFile strFile
```

Of course the user could tire of this and click Cancel, in which case we simply exit the script.

```
Case vbCancel
  WScript.Echo "Aborting the script"
  WScript.Quit
  End Select
```

If the file doesn't exist, we create it and return to the main part of the script. Again notice the error handling and *MsgBox*.

```
'create our log file
  Err.Clear
  Set objTS=objFSO.CreateTextFile(strFile)
  If Err.Number<>0 Then
    strMsg="There was an error creating " &_
    strFile & VbCrLf & "Error#" & Err.Number &_
    " " & Err.Description
    MsgBox strMsg,vbOKOnly+vbCritical,strTitle
    WScript.Quit
  End If
```

Now that we have the audit log taken care of, let's get down to business and use the *FileSystem-Object* to look at the files in the folder. We create a collection object that will represent all the files in the folder by calling the *Files* method.

```
Set objFiles=objFldr.Files
```

We can enumerate this collection with a *For...Each...Next* loop and write information about each file to the log.

```
For Each file In objFiles
  'get file information and write to log file
  objTS.WriteLine file.Name & vbTab & file.size & " bytes" & vbTab &_
  file.DateCreated & vbTab & file.DateLastModified
  i=i+1
  iPer=FormatPercent((i/t))
  WScript.StdOut.Writeline(iPer& " complete")
Next
```

The *FileSystemObject* exposes file properties such as its name; its size; the date it was created, modified, and accessed; and a few others. This script creates a tab-delimited file, but it could easily be a comma-separated value (CSV) log instead.

After we've finished examining every file in the folder, we close the log file and display a completion message to the user.

```
objTS.Close
MsgBox "See " & strFile & " for results.",vbOKOnly+vbInformation,strTitle
```

By the way, the script as written does not recurse through any subfolders. We'll leave that as an exercise for you. But there's one more goody in this script—we added code to provide some progress feedback to the user. The only catch is that you must run the script from a command line using CScript.

There is a *Count* property for our files collection that will show the number of files in the current folder. If we know the total number of files and the number of files processed, we can calculate the percentage complete. We just need some variables.

```
'initialize our counter
i=0
'set variable for total number of files in folder
t=objFiles.Count
```

In the *For...Each* loop, we increment our counter variable and calculate the percent complete. We use the *FormatPercent* function to tidy up the math.

```
i=i+1
iPer=FormatPercent((i/t))
```

All that is left is to display the result. We've decided to use the *StdOut* method of the *Wscript* object to write directly to the command prompt window.

```
WScript.StdOut.Writeline(iPer& " complete")
```

The method will not work if the script is run with WScript. It must be run with CScript at a command prompt by typing **cscript listing1-12.vbs**. The percent complete scrolls down the screen, informing the user about how the script is progressing.

We've reviewed only some of the *FileSystemObject* basics that you're likely to run across in this book. For more information, take a look at the Windows Script Host 5.6 documentation.

> **Best Practices**   There are many opportunities for errors and problems when using the *File-SystemObject*. For example, you might try to create a text file on a nonexistent drive or in a folder where the user lacks the proper permissions. Or you might try to access a folder or drive that doesn't exist. Errors like this are especially common when your script lets users specify files and folders either as run-time parameters or perhaps from an *InputBox*. It is very important that you implement error handling and validation in your scripts. Use the *DriveExists*, *Folder-Exists*, or *FileExists* methods of the *FileSystemObject*. Check for errors when creating new text files, and add code to gracefully handle common errors. You need to think of everything that could reasonably go wrong, such as typing *C;* instead of *C:*, and code accordingly.

Understanding Arrays

One fundamental scripting technique is to store data in an array and then use the data in a script. Arrays can be very complicated and multidimensional, but for our purposes, we keep them simple and basic. Think of an array as a collection of buckets, each bucket holding one piece of information. When we need that piece of information, we retrieve it from its bucket. Each bucket has a number, starting with 0.

There are a few ways to get information into an array. One way is to use the *Array* function.

```
myArray=Array("Elm","Maple","Oak","Walnut","Hickory","Pine")
```

This technique works well when the information to be stored is known ahead of time and there is a relatively small amount of it. For a more dynamic approach, we use the *Split* function.

```
strText="Elm,Maple,Oak,Walnut,Hickory,Pine"
myArray=Split(strText,",")
```

The *Split* function takes the specified text string and splits each element, in this case separated by a comma, into the individual buckets of the array.

After we have data in the array, we can access a bucket directly if we know its number. Thus if we want to use Walnut, we would reference *myArray(3)*. Even though humans would count *Walnut* as the fourth element, because we typically start counting at 1, the array starts counting at 0. Thus the *UBound(myArray)* function, which displays the upper limit of the array, returns 5. If we want to return a human-friendly count of the array elements, we need to use *UBound(myArray)+1*.

To go through every element in the array, we can use a *For...Next* loop, as follows.

```
For i=0 To UBound(myArray)
  WScript.Echo myArray(i)
Next
```

Typically we pass the value from the array to a subroutine or function elsewhere in the script. We'll give you a sample of that later in this chapter.

Dictionary Objects

Like an array, the *Scripting.Dictionary* object can also be used to organize external data, but where the array puts data in buckets starting at 0, the *Dictionary* object stores data in pages called *keys*. The stored data is referred to as an *item*. The *Scripting.Dictionary* object is considered an *associative array*.

Data is stored in the *Dictionary* object by using the *Add* method.

```
Dim objDict
Set objDict=CreateObject("Scripting.Dictionary")
objDict.Add "a","Elm"
objDict.Add "b","Maple"
objDict.Add "c","Oak"
objDict.Add "d","Walnut"
objDict.Add "e","Hickory"
objDict.Add "f","Pine"
```

To reference an individual item, we need to know the corresponding key. The following line of code would return the value for key b or Maple.

```
WScript.Echo objDict.Item("b")
```

If we want to enumerate the keys of the dictionary, we need to use the *Keys* method, as shown here.

```
objKeys=objDict.Keys
wscript.echo "There are " & objDict.Count & " keys"
For x=0 To objDict.Count-1
  WScript.Echo objKeys(x)
Next
```

Some confusion arises with the *Count* method. When used with the *Dictionary* object, the method starts counting at 1 and will return 6 in the example here. However, when we look through the collection of keys, we start counting at 0, which is why we loop from 0 to the *objDict.Count* value minus 1.

To get all the items in the dictionary, we use the *Items* method.

```
objItems=objDict.Items
For x=0 To objDict.Count-1
  WScript.Echo objItems(x)
Next
```

So which is the right technique to use? It depends on your script. If you have a lot of data to shuffle around and keep track of, a *Dictionary* object might be the way to go. There are ways to check if an item exists, delete individual items, and delete all items so that you can start all over again. *Dictionary* objects also make it easier to reference specific elements because you define the key. In an array, each element is stored as a numbered entry, and you have to keep track of what item is in which bucket. However, if you are just going to loop through each element and do something with it, an array is a little easier to manage.

You can also use both in the same script. We have occasionally used code in which the value of the *Dictionary* object is a CSV string that will be put into an array for further handling.

```
Dim objDict,objItems
Set objDict=CreateObject("Scripting.Dictionary")
objDict.Add "user1","John,555-1234,7/7/61"
objDict.Add "user2","Mary,555-1234,12/6/56"
objDict.Add "user3","Mike,555-1234,10/13/76"

wscript.echo "There are " & objDict.Count & " user entries."

objItems=objDict.Items
For x=0 To objDict.Count-1
  tmpArray=Split(objItems(x),",")
  strName=tmpArray(0)
  strPhone=tmpArray(1)
  strBDate=tmpArray(2)
  WScript.Echo "Adding " & strName & "(" & strBdate & ")"
  'insert some code here
Next
```

In short, you should use the technique that works best for you.

Understanding Active Directory Services Interface Fundamentals

Developing scripts to create and manage users and groups is a pretty common administrative task. These types of scripts must interact with a directory service, whether it is the SAM database of Windows NT or Active Directory. Fortunately, Microsoft has a scripting interface called Active Directory Services Interface (ADSI). Don't let the name fool you. You don't need Active Directory to use ADSI in your scripts. If you have a Windows NT 4.0 domain, you can still use ADSI; you just need a different provider.

The provider handles all the dirty work of interacting with a specific directory service type. ADSI has several directory service types, but for our purposes we'll limit our review to the WinNT and LDAP providers.

- The WinNT provider is used when working with legacy Windows domains or systems. The WinNT provider is designed to work with flat namespaces like an NT 4.0 domain. That's not to say that you can't use the WinNT provider with Active Directory—you can, and there might be instances when it is the preferable provider. We'll give you an example later in this chapter.

- The LDAP provider is used for directory services based on the Lightweight Directory Access Protocol (LDAP), such as Active Directory. You can't use the LDAP provider with an NT 4.0 domain because the LDAP provider is expecting a hierarchical directory service like Active Directory.

With Active Directory, you can use the WinNT provider when you want to manage the directory flatly, and use the LDAP provider when you need a more hierarchical approach. Consider this short script that you should run from a command prompt using CScript.

```
Dim objDom,objNetwork
Set objNetwork=CreateObject("WScript.Network")
Set objDom=GetObject("WinNT://" & objNetwork.UserDomain)
WScript.Echo "Listing users in " & objDom.name
objDom.Filter=Array("user")
For Each user In objDom
  WScript.Echo user.name
Next
```

Let's assume your domain is running Active Directory and you run it from a computer in the domain with a domain account. This script lists all the users in your domain, regardless of what organizational unit (OU) they are in. The WinNT provider has no concept of OUs and treats the directory as one big bucket.

> **Tip**   If you find your ADSI scripts mysteriously failing, check the provider. ADSI providers are case sensitive. WinNT works, but WINNT does not work.

We use a *Filter* method to get only the directory objects that are of the *user* class or type. Then we can loop through the list by using a *For...Each...Next* loop, and display the object's name. This name, by the way, is the user's NT 4.0 account name, also known as the *sAMAccountName*. If you have Active Directory and run this script, you won't see a Windows 2003 account name like *Jeffery Hicks*, but rather a pre-Windows 2000 name like *jhicks*. To display the user's common name, you must use the LDAP provider.

> **More Info**   The object the provider uses determines which properties are available. A great source of information on working with ADSI is available from the MSDN Web site at
>
> *http://msdn.microsoft.com/library/default.asp?url=/library/en-us/adsi/adsi/active_directory_service_interfaces_adsi.asp*
>
> (This link is on the companion CD; click *MSDN ADSI*.) We also recommend that you download the ADSI SDK, which contains not only a lot of sample code but also very thorough documentation. You can download the kit from the Microsoft Web site at
>
> *http://download.microsoft.com/download/2/9/7/29720925-faa3-477f-a5cd-beef80adac07/adsrtk.msi*
>
> (This link is on the companion CD; click *ADSI Resource Kit*.)

If we used the LDAP provider, we would have to connect to the root namespace, find all the organizational units and other containers, and enumerate through them all. There are ways of querying LDAP directories, but they are a little more complicated. The WinNT approach for something like this is fast, efficient, and easy to understand.

Another way to use the WinNT provider is to access member servers and desktops. You can use the WinNT provider to query local users, groups, and services. To connect to a remote system, use code like this.

```
strServer="File01"
Set objSrv=GetObject("WinNT://" & strServer)
```

Code like this connects essentially to the entire flat namespace. If you want to connect to a specific object in the namespace, you can use code like the snippet shown in Listing 1-13.

Listing 1-13 WinNT Sample: Change Local Admin Password
```
strServer="File01"
'new password to set for local administrator account
strPass="N3wP@ssw0rd"
set objUser=GetObject("WinNT://" & strServer & "/administrator,user")
objUser.SetPassword strPass
objUser.SetInfo
```

This script connects to the administrator account on *server File01*. It then calls the *SetPassword* method to change the administrator password.

Important   Never, ever hard-code administrator credentials or passwords in a script. Listing 1-13 is for educational purposes only and should not be used in a production environment as written. This information should be passed at run time as script parameters or entered by the user through prompts.

One method we want to emphasize here is *SetInfo*. This method is used for both WinNT and LDAP providers. You've probably noticed that ADSI uses the *GetObject* method as opposed to *CreateObject*. This is because the directory service already exists. ADSI gets a copy of the directory and stores it locally in cache. All the changes you make to objects in the directory are held locally and not committed back to the directory until you call *SetInfo*.

Best Practices   If you find yourself modifying many attributes of a directory object, don't call *SetInfo* after each property change. Wait until you are finished and then call *SetInfo* to commit all the changes at once. Otherwise, you impose unnecessary network traffic and server overhead.

To use the LDAP provider, we must connect the namespace by the *distinguished name* of the object. Suppose we want to create a new user object in the Employees OU that is part of the Company.pri Active Directory domain.

```
Set objDom=GetObject("LDAP://OU=Employees,DC=Company,DC=pri")
```

With this connection, we can use the *Create* method to create a new user object.

```
strUser="Jeffery Hicks"
strSAM="jhicks "
strPass="P@ssw0rd"
Set objUser=objDom.Create("User","CN=" & strUser)
```

After we have the *sAMAccountName* for the new user, we can commit the change to Active Directory, and the user account will essentially exist. We use the *Put* method to set object attributes.

```
objUser.Put "samAccountname",strSAM
objUser.SetInfo
```

Of course, we don't like blank user passwords, so we need to call the *SetPassword* method to specify the user's password and commit the change.

```
objUser.SetPassword(strPass)
objUser.SetInfo
```

Why didn't we just set the password and call *SetInfo* only once? Well, you can't call the *SetPassword* method for an object that doesn't exist yet. Until we call *SetInfo* to commit the new object, it doesn't exist in Active Directory.

We'll end this mini-review with the script in Listing 1-14, which creates a new user account.

Listing 1-14 ADSI Sample: Create User

```
Dim objFSO,objTS
Dim objDom,objUser

Const FORREADING=1

strFile="newusers.csv"
'format of newusers.csv
'givenname,sn,password,telephonenumber,upnsuffix
'example:
'Jeff,Hicks,P@sswordJH,555-1234,@jdhitsolutions.com
'Don,Jones,$cr1pting@nsw3rs,555-1234,@scriptinganswers.com

Set objFSO=CreateObject("Scripting.FileSystemObject")
Set objTS=objFSO.OpenTextFile(strFile,FORREADING)

Set objDom=GetObject("LDAP://OU=Consultants,DC=Company,DC=pri")
```

```
'open text file and process user data on each line
Do while objTS.AtEndofStream<>True
   rline=objTS.readline
   UserArray=Split(rline,",")

   strFirst=UserArray(0)
   strLast=UserArray(1)
   strUser=strFirst & " " & strLast
   strLogon=Left(strFirst,1)&strLast
   strUsername=LCASE(Left(strFirst,1)&strlast)
   strPass=UserArray(2)
   strPhone=UserArray(3)
   strUPN=strUserName & UserArray(4)

  'Create user object
  Set objUser=objDom.Create ("User","cn="&strUser)
  objUser.Put "samAccountName",strUserName
  objUser.SetInfo

  'Now that user object is created, let's set some properties
  objUser.Put "givenname",strFirst
  objUser.Put "sn",strLast
  objUser.Put "displayname",strFirst & " " & strLast
  objUser.Put "UserPrincipalName",strUPN
  objUser.Put "AccountDisabled",FALSE
  objUser.Put "TelephoneNumber",strPhone
  objUser.SetPassword(strPass)
  objUser.SetInfo

  Loop

  objTS.Close

  WScript.Quit
```

In this script we have a text file for each new account. Values for different user attributes are separated by commas.

```
strFile="newusers.csv"
'format of newusers.csv
'givenname,sn,password,telephonenumber,upnsuffix
'example:
'Jeff,Hicks,P@sswordJH,555-1234,@jdhitsolutions.com
'Don,Jones,$cr1pting@nsw3rs,555-1234,@scriptinganswers.com
```

We use the *FileSystemObject* to open and read the file.

```
Set objFSO=CreateObject("Scripting.FileSystemObject")
Set objTS=objFSO.OpenTextFile(strFile,FORREADING)

Set objDom=GetObject("LDAP://OU=Consultants,DC=Company,DC=pri")

'open text file and process user data on each line
Do while objTS.AtEndofStream<>True
rline=objTS.readline
```

You'll notice that we got our connection to the OU where we want to create the user accounts. We create an array of user data using the *Split* function and set some variables based on the data.

```
UserArray=Split(rline,",")
  strFirst=UserArray(0)
  strLast=UserArray(1)
  strUser=strFirst & " " & strLast
  strLogon=Left(strFirst,1)&strLast
  strUsername=LCASE(Left(strFirst,1)&strlast)
  strPass=UserArray(2)
  strPhone=UserArray(3)
  strUPN=strUserName & UserArray(4)
```

After that, it's just a matter of creating the user object specifying the *CN* and *sAMAccountName*.

```
'Create user object
Set objUser=objDom.Create ("User","cn="&strUser)
objUser.Put "samAccountName",strUserName
objUser.SetInfo
```

At this point, all that is left is to set the rest of the user properties and call *SetInfo* to write the changes to Active Directory.

```
'Now that user object is created, let's set some properties
objUser.Put "givenname",strFirst
objUser.Put "sn",strLast
objUser.Put "displayname",strFirst & " " & strLast
objUser.Put "UserPrincipalName",strUPN
objUser.Put "AccountDisabled",FALSE
objUser.Put "TelephoneNumber",strPhone
objUser.SetPassword(strPass)
objUser.SetInfo
```

After that is finished we can loop, read the next line in the text file, and repeat the process. With a script like this, you can create a hundred fully populated user accounts from the comfort of your desk in about the time it takes to read this sentence.

> **Note**   The script in Listing 1-14 is intended as a teaching aid. You could run it in a production environment provided you add some error handling logic. For example, as written, if you try to create a user account that already exists, you will get an error. We recommend you add code to handle that type of error, especially because it is a very foreseeable one.

Understanding Windows Management Instrumentation Fundamentals

One of the more advanced scripting topics an administrator needs to master is how to use Windows Management Instrumentation (WMI). WMI is the technology that Microsoft and many independent software vendors (ISV) use for their management applications and utilities. You can use the same technology and develop your own management scripts, completely customized for your environment. Let's spend a few minutes reviewing some WMI basics. We will explore WMI in much greater detail later in the book.

Winmgmts

Most WMI scripts connect to the WMI namespace using the *Winmgmts* object, which can be used to connect to local or remote WMI namespaces. Usually, the default namespace is root\cimv2, which most Windows management scripts connect to, but that can be changed using the WMI Management Console.

Consider the following line of code.

```
Set objWMI=GetObject("winmgmts://")
```

This will connect to the default WMI namespace on the local computer. Notice we use *Get-Object*, as we do with ADSI. To connect to a remote system, simply add the computer name.

```
strServer="File01"
set objWMI=GetObject("winmgmts://" & strServer)
```

Although it is not required, it is a good practice to specify the namespace you want to connect to, even if it is the default because the default can be changed.

```
set objWMI=GetObject("winmgmts://" & strServer & "\root\cimv2")
```

Using code like this eliminates any doubt about which namespace you are working with, especially if someone changed the default WMI namespace. In later scripts where we connect to different namespaces, we have to specify a namespace; by getting in the habit now, you will make your scripts easier to follow and debug.

So far, all we've done is connect to the WMI namespace—we haven't asked it for any information. Assuming you know the class you want to learn more about, such as *Win32_OperatingSystem*, there are two techniques you can use. The first incorporates the *InstancesOf* method.

```
strServer="File01 "
set objWMI=GetObject("winmgmts://" &_
strServer).InstancesOf("Win32_OperatingSystem")
```

The other technique is to execute a query. We'll review WMI queries in just a moment.

```
strServer="File01"
strQuery="Select * from Win32_OperatingSystem"
set objWMI=GetObject("winmgmts://" & strServer)
set objRef=objWMI.ExecQuery(strQuery)
```

With this technique, we instantiate a new object to hold the results of the query. The data returned is in the form of a collection, so we simply use a *For...Each...Next* loop to do something with the information.

```
For each item in objRef
  wscript.echo item.Name
  wscript.echo item.RegisteredUser
  wscript.echo item.Organization
Next
```

Of course, you need to know the names of the properties. You can get this information from scripting books like *Managing Windows with VBScript and WMI* (Jones, Don, Addison-Wesley, 2004) or from the MSDN Web site at

http://msdn.microsoft.com/library/default.asp?url=/library/en-us/wmisdk/wmi /wmi_reference.asp.

> **On the CD**   This link is included on the companion CD. Click *MSDN WMI Reference.*

> **Tip**   Not every attribute for every class is populated in WMI. WMI provides a repository for the class information, but it is up to the individual vendors to decide what data to store. There can be two servers from two vendors, and one might have information for a particular class and the other might not. Don't assume there is a problem with your script; there just might not be any information. In this situation, use tools like WbemTest and WMI Tools to enumerate classes so that you can verify what information exists.

A quick way to learn the property names is to ask. Use this code in place of the code just shown to get a listing of all properties and values.

```
For each item in objRef
  For Each property in item.Properties_
    WScript.echo property.Name & ": " & Property.Value
  Next
Next
```

WMI Query Language (WQL)

As we just demonstrated, it is very easy to use a query to retrieve information from WMI. WMI has its own query language and syntax that is very similar to SQL. For the purposes of this basic review, there are really only two types of *Select* queries. The first is a query that requests all information about a certain object class.

```
strQuery="Select * from Win32_ComputerSystem"
```

The second query requests information about specified object classes. It is much more selective, so you have to know what information you are looking for.

```
strQuery="Select Manufacturer,Model,Description from Win32_ComputerSystem"
```

Depending on the object class, it might be more efficient to ask only for information you want to use. Using a *Select ** query when you need only one or two property values adds unnecessary overhead to your script.

You can further refine your script by selecting attributes that meet certain criteria. For example, the *Win32_LogicalDisk* class has a property called *DriveType*. The value of this property indicates whether a drive is fixed, like drive C, removable like drive A, or some other kind. Consider the following query, which returns the *DeviceID* and *Size* properties for all fixed drives.

```
strQuery="Select DeviceID,Size from Win32_LogicalDisk Where Drivetype = '3'"
```

We know from experience, and you can tell by testing queries using Wbemtest, that the value for fixed drives is "3". By restricting our query to a specific drive type, we get more useful information faster.

SWbemLocator

One of the principal advantages of the *winmgmts* object is ease of use. You can make secure WMI connections with only a line or two of code. However, there is one situation when this object just doesn't do the job. Usually, when you execute a script, WMI takes the credentials of the user running the script and impersonates that user on the specified computer. But what if you want to run a script with alternate credentials? You could use the *RunAs* command, you could develop a WMI script using Microsoft's WMI scripting application programming interface (API), or you could use the *SWbemObject*.

Using the *SWbemObject* requires more coding than using *winmgmts*, but it allows you to specify alternate credentials. You first need to create a *SWbemLocator* object.

```
Set objLoc=CreateObject("WbemScripting.SwbemLocator")
```

This object has a *Security_* property that you can set. Typically, you can specify the *ImpersonationLevel*, which by default is 3.

```
objLoc.Security_.Impersonation=3
```

This is also where you specify additional privileges that the user might need, such as the ability to shut down a system remotely.

```
Const SHUTDOWNREMOTEPRIVILEGE=23
Set objLoc=CreateObject("WbemScripting.SwbemLocator")
objLoc.Security_.Impersonation=3
objLoc.Security_.Privileges.Add SHUTDOWNREMOTEPRIVILEGE
```

We next connect to the server, either local or remote.

```
Set objCon=objLoc.ConnectServer(strServer,"root\cimv2")
```

This line of code works well for the local system, but if you are connecting to a remote system, you must specify alternate credentials.

```
Set objCon=objLoc.ConnectServer(strServer,"root\cimv2",strUser,strPassword)
```

Remember, you can't specify alternate passwords for a local connection. This connection creates a *SWbemServices* object.

Now that we have a secure connection to a system, we can execute our query.

```
strQuery="Select * from Win32_OperatingSystem"
set objRef=objCon.Execquery(strQuery)
```

Then we can loop through the data in *objRef*. Listing 1-15 illustrates how to use the *SWbemLocator* object to connect to a remote system with alternate credentials.

Listing 1-15 *SWbemLocator* Sample: Get Drive Info

```
Dim objWBEM,objCon,objRef
strServer="FILE01"
strUser="Administrator"
strPassword="$3cret"
strQuery="Select DeviceID,Size,FreeSpace,FileSystem from " &_
"Win32_LogicalDisk where DriveType='3'"
Set objWBEM=CreateObject("WbemScripting.SwbemLocator")
set objCon=objWBEM.ConnectServer(strServer,"root\cimv2",strUser,strPassword)

set objRef=objCon.ExecQuery(strQuery)
For Each drive In objRef
  strMsg=strMsg & "Drive " & drive.DeviceID & "(" & drive.FileSystem &_
   ")" & VbCrLf
  strMsg=strMsg & "Size: " & drive.Size & " bytes"  & VbCrLf
  strMsg=strMsg & "Free Space: " & drive.FreeSpace & " bytes" & VbCrLf
  strMsg=strMsg & FormatPercent(drive.FreeSpace/Drive.size) &_
   " Free" & VbCrLf
  strMsg=strMsg & VbCrLf
Next

WScript.Echo strMsg
WScript.Quit
```

This approach to scripting WMI gives you more precise control and the ability to use alternate credentials. If alternate credentials aren't a requirement, the script in Listing 1-16 on the next page accomplishes the same task as Listing 1-15, but uses *winmgmts*.

Listing 1-16 *Winmgmts* Sample: Get Drive Info

```
dim objWMI, objRef
'enter any computer name
strServer="FILE01"
strQuery="Select DeviceID,Size,FreeSpace,FileSystem from " &_
"Win32_LogicalDisk where drivetype='3'"
set objWMI=GetObject("winmgmts://" & strServer & "\root\cimv2")
set objRef=objWMI.ExecQuery(strQuery)
WScript.Echo "Logical Drive Report for " & strServer
for each drive in objRef
  strMsg=strMsg & "Drive " & drive.DeviceID & "(" & drive.FileSystem &_
  ")" & vbcrlf
  strMsg=strMsg & "Size: " & drive.Size & " bytes" & VbCrLf
  strMsg=strMsg & "Free Space: " & drive.FreeSpace & " bytes" & VbCrLf
  strMsg=strMsg & FormatPercent(drive.FreeSpace/Drive.Size) &_
  " Free" & VbCrLf
  strMsg=strMsg & VbCrLf
Next

WScript.Echo strMsg
```

We will explore WMI quite a bit more throughout this book.

> **More Info**   In addition to the books and links already mentioned, we also recommend *Windows Management and Instrumentation* (Matthew Lavy & Ashley Meggitt, New Riders, 2002) and *WMI Essentials* (Marcin Policht, SAMS, 2002).

Advanced Scripting Goals

Now that we have a foundation, let's take a look at the goals for this book.

Securing Your Scripts

If you are serious about using VBScript as an administrative tool in your enterprise, you must do it securely. In Chapter 2, "Script Security," we take a look at ways to create more secure scripts by using digital signatures and certificates. We also review how to configure your production environment to run scripts securely.

Creating Your Own Script Components and Libraries

One of the hallmarks of a great scripter is the ability to reuse code. In Chapter 3, "Windows Script Files," we spend some time discussing Windows Script Files (.wsf scripts) and how you can build a reusable script library. We also show you how to create your own scripting components in Chapter 4, "Windows Script Components." Using the Script Component Wizard, you'll be able to create your own COM objects.

Running Scripts Remotely

Even though there are numerous ways to remotely manage systems with a script, there might be times when you want a script to run locally on a remote system. In Chapter 6, "Remote Scripting," we show you what you need to know about using the *WshController* object as well as how to properly configure your network.

Retrieving Information from Active Directory

You probably know some ADSI basics. We cover some advanced ADSI and LDAP topics in Chapter 8, "Advanced ADSI and LDAP Scripting," and Chapter 9, "Using ADO and ADSI Together." We demonstrate how to use Microsoft's EZADSomatic and other free tools. These tools not only help with rapid script development, but they can be invaluable when trying to figure out why a script isn't working. We also delve into the mystery of LDAP queries as well as ADSI queries using ActiveX Data Objects (ADO).

Manipulating Information Stored in a Database

For beginning scripting administrators, working with CSV files is a pretty standard practice. To take your scripting to the next level, you must know how to write scripts that use database technology. In Chapter 7, "Database Scripting," we review the various types of databases and how you can connect and manipulate them.

Managing Your Windows Environment with WMI Events

We promised WMI would be a major topic of this book. In Chapter 11, "WMI Events," we explore the world of WMI events, consumers, filters, and timers. We also show you how to use event sinks to closely manage your systems, and include plenty of examples you can use in your environment.

Using New WMI Classes with Windows XP and Windows Server 2003

In Chapter 13, " Advanced Scripting in Windows XP and Windows Server 2003," we cover some of the new WMI classes that are available in Microsoft Windows XP and Microsoft Windows Server 2003. These classes add real power to your script and open new opportunities. We also cover new classes that will help you with DNS, IIS 6.0, printing, quotas, and more. Each new class will include a complete administrative example.

Managing Group Policy Objects with Scripting

If you administer an Active Directory forest, chances are you are using Group Policy. Your Group Policy environment can be managed with VBScript through the Group Policy Management console. We explore the object model in Chapter 14, "Group Policy Management Scripting," and look at how you can use scripts to back up, copy, restore, and set permissions on your Group Policy objects. We also spend a little time discussing how you can script Resultant Set of Policy (RSoP) scenarios.

Managing Your Exchange 2003 Environment

Continuing our exploration of enterprise-level scripting, in Chapter 15, "Exchange Server 2003 Scripting," we cover managing your Exchange 2003 environment. Using new WMI classes, ADSI, Collaboration Data Objects (CDO), and Collaboration Data Objects for Exchange Management (CDOEXM), you will learn how to develop scripts to manage servers, storage groups, and mailstores and mailboxes.

Incorporating Your Scripts into Microsoft Operations Manager

In Chapter 16, "Microsoft Operations Manager 2005 Scripting," we explore how Microsoft Operations Manager 2005 (MOM) uses VBScript. We also explore a new object model. We then look at how to edit existing MOM scripts, and explain how to write new ones from scratch.

Creating a Visual Interface for Your Script with Internet Explorer and HTML Applications (HTAs)

Tired of simple command-line scripts or wishing that there were more to graphical scripting than the *MsgBox* function? In Chapter 5, "HTML Applications: Scripts with a User Interface," we show you how to create richer scripts by using HTAs. You don't have to be a Web developer—we give you enough information and an easy-to-follow example so that you can convert an existing script into an HTA.

What We Won't Cover

Even though this is a book about advanced scripting topics, we can't possibly cover everything an administrator needs to know. We will, however, point you in the right direction for additional information.

- **ASP and Web Scripting**   We're sure that if you visit your favorite bookseller, you will find many, many books on ASP and Web-based scripting. Online, some good places to start are the following:
    - *http://msdn.microsoft.com*
    - *http://www.15seconds.com*
    - *http://www.4guysfromrolla.com/*
    - *http://www.asp.net*

- **.NET Programming**   Even though it might seem like some of our scripts are complex programming exercises in higher languages, they are not. They are scripts meant to be interpreted at run time. We won't spend any time using any of the .NET technologies or any other programming languages.

- **Microsoft Office Automation**   There are quite a few freely available scripts that use Microsoft Word or Microsoft Excel to create nifty reports or to serve as a data source. These scripts use the COM objects for Microsoft Office, essentially taking Visual Basic for Applications (VBA) code and converting it to standalone VBScript. This technique is beyond the scope of this book. If you are interested in this topic, search the Web for "office vbscript," or visit the following Web site:

  http://msdn.microsoft.com/library/default.asp?url=/library/en-us/odc_2003_ta/html /odc_ancoffice.asp

> **On the CD**   This link is included on the companion CD. Click *MSDN Office Automation.*

Finding Information about JScript, Perl, Python, and KiXtart

Certainly, VBScript is not the only scripting language available, but we chose it for this book because we think it is the easiest for novice scripters to learn and read. Other scripting languages have their strengths as well, but VBScript is the dominant scripting language for Microsoft administrators. If you would like to learn more about other scripting languages you might find these sites of interest.

- **JScript**

  - *http://msdn.microsoft.com/library/default.asp?url=/library/en-us/script56/html /js56jsoriJScript.asp*

> **On the CD**   This link is included on the companion CD. Click *MSDN Jscript documentation.*

  The Windows Script Host 5.6 documentation also includes JScript references.

- **Perl**

  - *http://www.perl.com*

  - *http://www.perl.org*

  - *http://www.activestate.com*

  - *http://www.perlmonks.org*

- Python

  - *http://www.python.org*

  - *http://diveintopython.org/*

  - *http://aspn.activestate.com/ASPN/Python/Cookbook/*

- KiXtart

  - *http://www.kixtart.org*

  - *http://www.microsoft.com/technet/scriptcenter/scripts/kixtart/default.mspx*

> **On the CD**   This link is included on the companion CD. Click *Microsoft Technet Script Center - Kix.*

The Right Tool for the Job

If you are going to script professionally, you should invest in professional tools. If you are still using Notepad as a script editor, you are spending more time developing scripts than you need to. At this stage, it's time to buy a commercial-quality script editor.

There are a number of editors on the market, each with a slightly different feature set. What most have in common to one degree or another are features that make the time you spend scripting more efficient. One such feature is inline IntelliSense, which can display objects, methods, and properties in a list. With a quick click, you can save yourself from typing a lot of mistakes. Another feature is the ability to insert snippets or small sections of saved code. Some editors come with a library of code samples and usually let you add your own.

Commercial editors typically also include some form of script color coding. This makes it very easy to identify how your script is constructed and simplifies troubleshooting. Speaking of troubleshooting, most editors allow you to set breakpoints and other debugging features. If an editor has a built-in debugger, so much the better. Some editors also include a variety of script-generating wizards, online help, and links to local tools like RegEdit.

We assembled as many demonstration and evaluation versions of the major scripting editors as we could on the companion CD. We encourage you to try them and find one that meets your needs. You will have to decide which features are important to you and how much you (or your boss) are willing to spend. But even a free editor that provides rudimentary color coding and line numbering will make script development and troubleshooting much easier.

Scripting Techniques

We are firm believers in using the right tool for the right job. One of the great benefits of working with Microsoft technologies is that there is usually more than one way to accomplish a given task. For example, you can get almost the same information using Windows Management Instrumentation Command Line (WMIC) statements in a batch file as you can with WMI in VBScript. Likewise, there might be a resource kit utility that can get a job done almost as well as a script you could write. What makes one tool better than the other?

When you need to develop a solution to a problem, there are several things to consider before opening your script editor. For example, who will be using the solution? How will it be used? Is this something that needs to be scheduled to run in the middle of the night or that is run interactively by someone with domain administrator credentials? Are there environmental, managerial, or security restrictions that might affect your solution?

You also need to take into account your comfort level with the available options. If you can put together a simple batch file that will run a command-line utility more easily than you can write a script from scratch, why bother writing a script? Even if you are an experienced script developer, you need to weigh the time you will invest against the reward. If you can accomplish your goal more easily by using an existing utility and a batch file, there's no need to invest a lot of time writing VBScript. For that matter, even if there is a commercial alternative, you need to weigh the costs. How much time will it take you to develop and test a solution? How much time are you losing because you are not doing other tasks while scripting? How much is the commercial alternative?

We strongly believe that script development in Windows environments is maturing and needs to be more than a temporary solution. Developing scripts or automation solutions should be treated with the same level of professionalism and planning as a Visual Basic .NET project. This means developing a business case, documenting the requirements, and choosing the most economical approach given all the circumstances.

The right tool for the right job is the one that is easy for you to use, lets you develop a working solution in the least amount of time, and makes the most economical sense.

Summary

This chapter was a refresher course in VBScript and many of the scripting technologies we will be using throughout the book. We also gave you an overview of the topics we will be covering, as well as those we won't be covering. Finally, we discussed some scripting philosophy. At this point, you should be ready to take your scripting to the next level. Let's begin.

Chapter 2

Script Security

There's no doubt that scripts can be dangerous; well-publicized viruses such as Melissa and "I Love You" have proven that point. But there's also no doubt that scripts can be useful tools as well. How do you ensure that the good scripts are run and the bad ones aren't? Windows Script Host security, along with other security technologies, can help make scripting safe in any environment. We'll show you how.

We've seen plenty of environments where administrators have taken steps to lock down scripting. Unfortunately, many of those steps aren't effective. For example, simply deleting wscript.exe and cscript.exe doesn't guarantee that scripts can't be run. As a part of the core Microsoft Windows operating system, those files are replaced by Windows File Protection, certain patches and updates, and service packs. Likewise, simply reassigning the script file-name extensions—.vbs and .wsf, for example—also doesn't guarantee safe scripting, because scripts with any filename extension can be executed simply by passing the script filename as a command-line argument to wscript.exe or cscript.exe.

```
WScript.exe MyScript.txt
```

Finally, both of these techniques—and countless variations on them—aren't meant to guarantee *safe* scripting, they're meant to restrict scripting *completely,* thus depriving you of a beneficial administrative tool. There are, however, techniques you can use to make scripting safer.

Script Encoding and Decoding

Script encoding is made possible by the Microsoft Script Encoder, which is available as a free download from the Microsoft Web site.

http://www.microsoft.com/downloads/details.aspx?FamilyId=E7877F67-C447-4873-B1B0-21F0626A6329&displaylang=en

> **On the CD**   This link, like most of the links referenced in this book, is included on the companion CD. Click *Download details- Script Encoder*.

The purpose of the Script Encoder is to prevent your scripts from being easily read. Here is a sample script.

```
'anything here will be left clear-text
'include documentation, comments, etc
'**Start Encode**
'Anything after here is encoded
MsgBox "Hello, world!"
```

After running the Script Encoder, the script will look like this.

```
'anything here will be left clear-text
'include documentation, comments, etc
'**Start Encode**#@~^QQAAAA==@#@&B)XDtk o,COD+.P4+.n,k/,nx1WN[@#@&t/
TAG6~E_+SVKSPSW.s9"J@#@&zxIAAA==^#~@
```

You might think that this would be a valuable tool for certain types of script security issues, such as writing scripts that have hard-coded administrator credentials. For example, such a script might allow an assistant to reset user passwords without giving him or her the ability to perform other administrative tasks. It's not entirely true, however, that this is a safe way to script, and it is important to clear up this misconception as early as possible.

The fact of the matter is that the Script Encoder is not a script *encrypter*. Technically, the Encoder does perform a type of encryption, by using what's called a *symmetric key*. This is a single encryption key that is used to both encrypt and decrypt the password, but because every copy of Windows Script Host has the same key built into it, the Encoder has long since been rendered useless as a security tool. There are a number of readily available tools that can decode scripts back into their plain-text versions, revealing any sensitive information in them. Some of these tools include the following:

- *http://www.virtualconspiracy.com/index.php?page=scrdec/intro*, a downloadable tool
- *http://www.greymagic.com/security/tools/decoder/*, an online tool that decodes scripts right in a Web page with no download required
- *http://www.password-crackers.com/crack/scrdec.html*, which is not free, although it more or less the same as the free utilities

We aren't publishing these URLs to reward the tools' authors, but rather to draw your attention to the fact that the Script Encoder cannot be relied upon to protect security-sensitive information. Indeed, that was never the Script Encoder's purpose. It was originally meant to obscure the code in Web pages, thereby reducing (but not eliminating) the possibility of intellectual property theft. The ease with which scripts can be decoded means you should *never* consider the Script Encoder a security tool, because it's too easy for a decoder to reveal the sensitive information you were trying to protect.

Script Signing and the Windows Script Host TrustPolicy

Windows Script Host (WSH) 5.6 includes a new feature called TrustPolicy. Because WSH 5.6 is installed with the latest versions of the Windows operating systems (including the latest service packs) and is available as a free download, there's no reason not to utilize TrustPolicy to provide a safer scripting environment. TrustPolicy uses advanced, certificate-based technologies to help determine which scripts can be trusted and which cannot.

Understanding Digital Certificates and Script Signing

TrustPolicy is based on the concept of *code signing*, which uses digital certificates to uniquely sign a piece of code, such as a script or an executable. The code-signing process calculates a *checksum*, which is a unique value created by a complex mathematical algorithm. Any given piece of code has only one checksum, and no two pieces of code have the same checksum. The checksum is encrypted by using a certificate's private key, and decrypted by using the certificate's public key. Microsoft, for example, signs the executables and DLLs for much of their software. Figure 2-1, for example, shows the signature applied to the main executable for Microsoft Excel 2003.

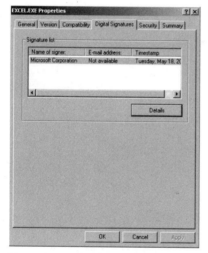

Figure 2-1   The signature for Excel.exe

To verify a signature, Windows uses the certificate's public key to decrypt the signature. If the decryption is successful, Windows knows that the signature is valid, because only the signer would have the private key that created the signature. Windows then calculates a checksum on the code, and compares it to the checksum in the decrypted signature. If the two match, the code is unmodified. If the two do not match, the code has been modified since it was signed. And if that's the case, the code is considered *untrusted*.

Simply having a proper signature doesn't guarantee that code is considered trusted, however, because the certificate used to create the digital signature must also have been issued by a trusted certification authority (CA). Figure 2-2 shows the details for the certificate used to sign Excel.exe. As you can see, the certificate was issued by Microsoft Code Signing PCA.

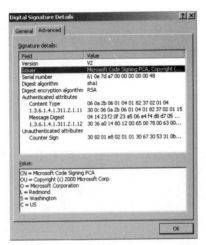

Figure 2-2   Reviewing the details of a code signing certificate

Figure 2-3 shows the certification path for the certificate, which lists the Microsoft Root Authority as the root CA that authorized this certificate.

Figure 2-3   Reviewing the certification path of a code signing certificate

A Matter of Trust

Why is Microsoft Root Authority a trusted CA? Why are *any* of the CAs listed in Internet Options trusted? Generally, it's because Microsoft included them with Windows when it shipped, or because you've added them as trusted root CAs on your own. But what does being trusted entail?

The purpose of a digital certificate is to uniquely identify the certificate holder. In the case of Microsoft, the certificate represents Microsoft Corporation. If someone other than Microsoft were to obtain a Microsoft certificate, that person could sign malicious software as though he or she were Microsoft, fooling you into thinking it was safe. The purpose of a CA, then, is to ensure that certificates are given *only* to the proper individuals. When you say that you trust a CA, you're saying that you trust them to verify individual or corporate identities before issuing certificates.

Chances are, you probably have no idea how many of the CAs listed in the Certificates dialog box are trustworthy. For maximum security, you should remove any CAs whose business practices you're not familiar with from the Trusted Root Certification Authorities list until you've verified that their business practices with regard to security are satisfactory. Note that removing one or more CAs can result in warnings in applications like Internet Explorer, because you might try to connect through https to a Web site that has a certificate issued by one of the CAs you removed. However, if you don't trust the CA, you shouldn't trust the https connection either.

Recognizing many administrators' concerns in this regard, Microsoft has published a Knowledge Base article at

http://support.microsoft.com/default.aspx?scid=kb;en-us;293819

that describes how to remove a CA from the list.

On the CD   This link is included on the companion CD. Click *How to Remove a Root Certificate from the Trusted Root Store*.

To check if this CA is trusted on a Microsoft Windows 2000, Microsoft Windows XP, or Microsoft Windows Server 2003 computer, open Control Panel, double-click the Internet Options icon, and click the Content tab. In the Internet Properties dialog box, on the Root Certification Authorities tab, click the Publishers button to see a list of trusted root certification authorities, as shown in Figure 2-4 on the next page. As you can see, the Microsoft Root Authority is in this list, meaning it—and all certificates it authorizes or issues, and that its subordinate CAs authorize or issue—is trusted.

Therefore, because the certificate used to sign Excel.exe ultimately comes from a trusted root CA, and because the signature is intact and correct, Excel.exe is trusted code.

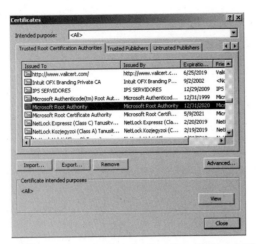

Figure 2-4 Reviewing the list of trusted root CAs

This idea of trust works exactly the same way for scripts. You can obtain a code-signing certificate, either from a commercial CA or from an internal CA, and use that certificate to sign your scripts. If the CA that issued the scripts is trusted and the scripts remain unmodified, the scripts will be trusted.

Now you need a way to stop untrusted scripts from running, which is where WSH TrustPolicy comes into play.

Understanding WSH TrustPolicy

WSH TrustPolicy defaults to an essentially neutral condition in which both trusted and untrusted scripts are allowed to run. You can, however, reconfigure WSH through specific registry settings. There are two main configurable sections; one section configures computer-wide settings for all users, and the other configures user-specific preferences.

The user-specific settings are located at HKEY_CURRENT_USER\SOFT-WARE\Microsoft\Windows\Windows Script Host\Settings. There is one major REG_DWORD value you can create under this registry key:

■ **TrustPolicy**   Set this to 0 to run both trusted and untrusted scripts, or to 2 to run only trusted scripts. If you set this value to 1, the user will be prompted before untrusted scripts are allowed to run.

The computer-wide settings are located at HKEY_LOCAL_MACHINE\SOFT-WARE\Microsoft\Windows\Windows Script Host\Settings, and there are several REG_DWORD values you can specify:

■ **TrustPolicy**   This is configured in the same way as the per-user value of the same name. Usually, the per-user setting takes precedence over the computer-wide setting.

- **IgnoreUserSettings**   If set to 1, the computer-wide TrustPolicy setting will override any per-user settings. The default is 0.

- **SilentTerminate**   If set to 1, any attempt to run untrusted scripts will not result in a warning message. If set to 0 (the default), running untrusted scripts (with TrustPolicy set to 2, that is) will result in a warning message.

- **UseWINSAFER**   This value applies only to Windows XP and later. If set to 0, which is the default, WSH TrustPolicy is disabled in favor of Software Restriction Policies (which we'll discuss later in this chapter). Setting this value to 1 enables WSH TrustPolicy.

We generally recommend enabling WSH TrustPolicy and setting it to 2 for all users, unless you're using Software Restriction Policies, which are more flexible.

Configuring WSH TrustPolicy in Your Environment

If you've decided to implement WSH TrustPolicy in your environment (and why wouldn't you?), you could make the necessary registry changes manually through a logon script or through some other utility, but Group Policy is by far the most effective means for deploying these settings. Listing 2-1 is an administrative template (.adm file) that can be imported into a Group Policy object (GPO) to centralize configuration of WSH TrustPolicy.

Listing 2-1 WSH TrustPolicy Template

```
#if version >= 3
CLASS USER

  CATEGORY "Windows Script Host"

    POLICY "Windows Script Host trust policy"
      EXPLAIN "Configure the behavior of Windows Script Host 5.6 or later with regard to
unsigned or untrusted scripts. This interacts with Windows Script Host settings in
Computer Configuration. On WinXP and higher, this setting is only active if WSH Software
Restriction Policies are turned off."
      KEYNAME "Software\Microsoft\Windows Script Host\Settings"
      PART "Allow untrusted scripts" DROPDOWNLIST REQUIRED
        VALUENAME "TrustPolicy"
        ITEMLIST
          NAME "Always" VALUE 0
          NAME "Prompt user" VALUE 1
          NAME "Never" VALUE 2
        END ITEMLIST
      END PART
    END POLICY

  END CATEGORY


CLASS MACHINE

  CATEGORY "Windows Script Host"
```

```
       POLICY "Windows Script Host trust policy"
           EXPLAIN "Configure the behavior of Windows Script Host 5.6 or later with regard to
unsigned or untrusted scripts. This interacts with Windows Script Host settings in User
Configuration. On WinXP and higher, this setting is only active if WSH Software
Restriction Policies are turned off."
           KEYNAME "Software\Microsoft\Windows Script Host\Settings"
           PART "Allow untrusted scripts" DROPDOWNLIST REQUIRED
             VALUENAME "TrustPolicy"
             ITEMLIST
               NAME "Always" VALUE 0
               NAME "Prompt user" VALUE 1
               NAME "Never" VALUE 2
             END ITEMLIST
           END PART    END POLICY


       POLICY "Ignore User Configuration settings for WSH security"
           EXPLAIN "when enabled, causes Computer Configuration setting for WSH trust policy
to override User Configuration setting"
           KEYNAME "Software\Microsoft\Windows Script Host\Settings"
           PART "Ignore User Configuration" CHECKBOX
             VALUENAME "IgnoreUserSettings"
             VALUEON 1
             VALUEOFF 0
           END PART
       END POLICY


       POLICY "Use Software Restriction Policies"
           EXPLAIN "when enabled, Software Restriction Policies overrides WSH trust policy
setting"
           KEYNAME "Software\Microsoft\Windows Script Host\Settings"
           PART "Use Software Restriction Policies" CHECKBOX
             VALUENAME "UseWINSAFER"
             VALUEON 1
             VALUEOFF 0
           END PART
       END POLICY


       POLICY "Warn User"
           EXPLAIN "when enabled, displays a warning when WSH cannot execute an untrusted
script"
           KEYNAME "Software\Microsoft\Windows Script Host\Settings"
           PART "Warn user that untrusted scripts won't execute" CHECKBOX
             VALUENAME "SilentTerminate"
             VALUEON 0
             VALUEOFF 1
           END PART
       END POLICY



     END CATEGORY
#endif
```

On the CD   You'll also find this ADM template, Wsh.adm, on the CD that accompanies this book.

Note that the WSH TrustPolicy settings aren't contained under the \SOFTWARE\Policies section of the registry, which means they're not considered true policies. Instead, Microsoft refers to them as *preferences,* and there are some important differences between a policy and a preference:

- To remove preferences, you have to configure a GPO that reconfigures the preferences to their original, default values. Simply removing the settings or unlinking the GPO won't remove preferences.

- The GPO editor doesn't usually display preferences. Right-click the Administrative Templates folder and click Properties to force the GPO editor to display them.

These differences aside, GPOs are a great way to deploy consistent WSH TrustPolicy settings throughout your enterprise.

Signing Scripts by Using a Digital Certificate

After you obtain a code-signing certificate and install it on your computer, you'll be ready to start signing scripts. Typically, you'll install the certificate to the store named Personal Certificates, which is the default. You'll need to know the name of the certificate, which appears in the Internet Properties dialog box after the certificate is installed. To sign a script, simply write a VBScript script that contains the following:

```
Set objSigner = CreateObject("Scripting.Signer")
objSigner.SignFile "MyScript.vbs","MyCert"
```

Where Do You Get a Certificate?

There are a couple ways to obtain a code-signing certificate, and the one you use depends largely on your specific needs. Remember, any computer expected to run your scripts has to trust the CA that issued your certificate, so that'll place some limitations on where you can obtain a certificate. For example, a number of tools exist that will create *self-signed certificates*. These are essentially certificates that you issue to yourself, meaning you're the CA. There's no real way to configure computers to trust you as a CA, though, so these certificates are primarily useful only for testing purposes on your local computer.

If you have an internal CA in your company, you might be able to obtain a code-signing certificate from it. However, you will need to make sure that all your computers are configured to trust that CA. Commercial CAs are also an option—VeriSign, Thawte, Cyber-Trust, among others—because most Windows computers are already configured to trust the major commercial CAs. A commercial CA has one big advantage over an internal CA: portability. If you intend to share signed scripts outside of your environment, a commercial CA is probably required. That's because it's unlikely that anyone trusts your internal CA outside of your own network. However, the organizations you work with are likely to trust the same commercial CAs that you do.

Of course, substitute the path and filename of the script you want to sign for *MyScript.vbs*, and the name of the certificate you're using to sign the script for *MyCert*. This short script can be used to sign other scripts.

The signed script will have a special signature block at the end of the file.

```
On Error Resume Next
Dim objSet

If WScript.arguments.count>0 Then
  strSrv=WScript.arguments(0)
Else
  strSrv="LOCALHOST"
End If

Set objSet=GetObject("winmgmts://" & strSrv).InstancesOf("Win32_OperatingSystem")
If Err.Number Then
  strErrMsg= "Error connecting to WINMGMTS on " & UCase(strSrv) & vbCrlf
  strErrMsg= strErrMsg & "Error #" & err.number & " [0x" & _
   CStr(Hex(Err.Number)) &"]" & vbCrlf
  If Err.Description <> "" Then
    strErrMsg = strErrMsg & "Error description: " & _
     Err.Description & "." & vbCrlf
  End If
  Err.Clear
  WScript.echo strErrMsg
  WScript.quit
End If

For Each obj In objSet
  currtime=obj.LastBootUptime
Next

curryr=Left(currtime,4)
currmo=Mid(currtime,5,2)
currdy=Mid(currtime,7,2)
currtm=Mid(currtime,9,6)

LastBoot= currmo & "/" & currdy & "/" & curryr & " " & _
FormatDateTime(Left(currtm,2)&":"&Mid(currtm,3,2)&":"&Right(currtm,2),3)
WScript.echo UCase(strSrv) & " Last Boot: " & LastBoot

Set objSet=Nothing


'' SIG '' Begin signature block
'' SIG '' MIID7AYJKoZIhvcNAQcCoIID3TCCA9kCAQExDjAMBggq
'' SIG '' hkiG9w0CBQUAMGYGCiSGAQQBgjcCAQSgWDBWMDIGCiSG
'' SIG '' AQQBgjcCAR4wJAIBAQQQTVApFpkntU2P5azhDxfrqwIB
'' SIG '' AAIBAAIBAAIBAAIBADAgMAwGCCqGSIb3DQIFBQAEECJJ
'' SIG '' dGPYS4TpW1/NYibcd/mgggIVMIICETCCAXqgAwIBAgIQ
'' SIG '' 3zX2vaMlcZVHykons8ASeTANBgkqhkiG9w0BAQQFADAW
'' SIG '' MRQwEgYDVQQDEwtQZXJzb25hbCBJVDAeFw0wNTAxMDEw
'' SIG '' NDAwMDBaFw0xMTAxMDEwNDAwMDBaMBYxFDASBgNVBAMT
'' SIG '' C1BlcnNvbmFsIElUMIGfMA0GCSqGSIb3DQEBAQUAA4GN
```

```
'' SIG '' ADCBiQKBgQCsFHTjlxN8p8imHhQMrnIGCcrr+F9uyk2r
'' SIG '' n4eb/APZFFgJS7dAVPWycgbNoy6UR4aWY94Xo/f4sA6L
'' SIG '' czUxoJbbgTo33/O/MOy2AAuUBk3hDfzllaQ9S9k7Coyu
'' SIG '' oYT3di0y4Nm4nJ5E+RQ5xD1Nf4s2uLDU6gGFded+6aa7
'' SIG '' 9BaMgwIDAQABo2AwXjATBgNVHSUEDDAKBggrBgEFBQcD
'' SIG '' AzBHBgNVHQEEQDA+gBAZxXwZaG1kHAAb42VQV5xmoRgw
'' SIG '' FjEUMBIGA1UEAxMLUGVyc29uYWwwgSVSCEN819r2jJXGV
'' SIG '' R8pKJ7PAEnkwDQYJKoZIhvcNAQEEBQADgYEANIL//6LJ
'' SIG '' euOk8a4NdbmvLSSs4tujkf4chm6TxzLEQcOcH8IvkaxP
'' SIG '' l+9vshoJul6ngYWZa2H5mT5opc1FIDmWwlEoZXv2qGiQ
'' SIG '' +aTFEOSAVbG6LpmqjVkFYWmyhP1piL9QWi4sGENVTdOn
'' SIG '' JntdaQJVl2txOLFOA2RVVS37qAsFVl8xggFBMIIBPQIB
'' SIG '' ATAqMBYxFDASBgNVBAMTC1BlcnNvbmFsIElUAhDfNfa9
'' SIG '' oyVxlUfKSiezwBJ5MAwGCCqGSIb3DQIFBQCgbDAQBgor
'' SIG '' BgEEAYI3AgEMMQIwADAZBgkqhkiG9w0BCQMxDAYKKwYB
'' SIG '' BAGCNwIBBDAcBgorBgEEAYI3AgELMQ4wDAYKKwYBBAGC
'' SIG '' NwIBFTAfBgkqhkiG9w0BCQQxEgQQlpHc1iO9Yobzitac
'' SIG '' Rx2eRjANBgkqhkiG9w0BAQEFAASBgBvylURhAFtNNN9j
'' SIG '' UT3NQAjfAO9Md5kEClsDiPXIkMtWloucEJO/f2wZ4iYB
'' SIG '' sX6kJUZFu2logH2ZhZQFPYtokpJsw3q15oETYTL65YmI
'' SIG '' U7stVz/pp4mIL4tBxbLFwKGlXth+R+Fi8btGFOaUOsfb
'' SIG '' pZwKmYUlkAWOd4HbFNQjMual
'' SIG '' End signature block
```

Be careful not to modify this signature block (which begins with the line " *SIG* " *Begin signature block*), or any portion of your script. Any modification will render the signature invalid.

Another way to sign scripts is to use SAPIEN PrimalScript (*www.primalscript.com*), a commercial script editor, and the only one we're aware of that includes built-in script signing. As shown in Figure 2-5, you can provide PrimalScript with the name of your certificate (leave the store name blank if your certificate is in the default store), and the tool can sign scripts each time you save them, ensuring that they'll run correctly afterward. You can also configure the HKEY_LOCAL_USER version of the TrustPolicy value, so you can test the TrustPolicy settings with your newly signed scripts.

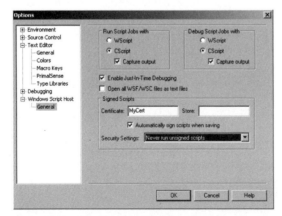

Figure 2-5   Configuring PrimalScript to sign scripts

Using Software Restriction Policies

Software Restriction Policies (SRP) were introduced in Windows XP and Windows Server 2003 as a way to better control the software that is allowed to run in a Windows environment. Configured and deployed through GPOs, SRP allows administrators to define a set of exceptions that identify various pieces of permitted software, and specify a default security rule that prevents all other software from being executed. SRP uses digital signatures to identify software, much like WSH TrustPolicy does, although SRP can also use a variety of other methods. Initially configuring SRP can be time consuming, because you need to identify and define an exception for each authorized piece of software in your environment. However, after it is configured, SRP can virtually eliminate malware and other unauthorized software, making for a great return on the initial investment of time.

> **Note**   A complete discussion of SRP is beyond the scope of this book. However, you can read more about SRP in the Windows XP or Windows Server 2003 documentation, and in any number of good books, including *Windows Server 2003 Weekend Crash Course* (Don Jones, 2003, Wiley) and *Introducing Microsoft Windows Server 2003* (Jerry Honeycutt, 2003, Microsoft).

Alternate Credentials

From time to time, you'll need to run scripts using alternate credentials. Perhaps you need to run an administrative script and aren't logged on with administrative credentials, or perhaps you're connecting to a remote service and need to specify appropriate credentials for that service. Whatever the reason, scripting provides a number of ways to use alternate credentials.

> **Note**   Keep in mind that security isn't always as simple as alternate credentials. For example, any script that is intended to modify portions of a user's profile usually must run under that user's security context to gain access to the profile. Chapter 6 covers this type of remote scripting in more detail.

Using the *RunAs* Command

The RunAs.exe command-line tool can be used to execute scripts by using alternate credentials. This is useful if, for example, your organization practices the Principle of Least Privilege (or Access), and you log on to your computer using a non-administrative account. Using *RunAs* will allow you to execute the script with the necessary administrative credentials. From a command prompt window, type **Runas /?** to see the command's proper syntax.

Using Scheduled Tasks Credentials

For scripts that must be run on a regular basis, or that you want to schedule to run while you're away, you can use the Windows Task Scheduler. The Task Scheduler allows you to specify alternate credentials under which a script is run.

This technique can often be used as a workaround when you need a script run on another computer under alternate credentials, but you have no direct means for doing so. Use the Schtasks.exe command-line tool (included with Windows Server 2003) to create a task on a remote computer. Have the task use alternate credentials and execute whatever script is necessary. In a command prompt window, type **Schtasks /create /?** to see the correct syntax for creating tasks on remote computers and for specifying credentials for the task to use.

Using ADSI Alternate Credentials

Active Directory Services Interface (ADSI) scripts use the security context of the user running the script. In some instances, you might want to provide alternate credentials for the actual ADSI connection, for example, when the account running the script doesn't have permission to perform whatever tasks you need the script to perform. Listing 2-2 shows an example of using alternate credentials to connect to Active Directory through an LDAP query.

Listing 2-2 ADSI Alternate Credentials

```
Const ADS_SECURE_AUTHENTICATION = 1

'Specify alternate credentials
strUserDN = "cn=Administrator,cn=Users,dc=company,dc=com"
strPassword = InputBox("Enter password for Administrator@company.com")

'Connect to the domain
Set objRoot = GetObject("LDAP:")
Set objDomain = _
  objRoot.OpenDSObject("LDAP://dc=company,dc=com", _
    strUserDN, strPassword, ADS_SECURE_AUTHENTICATION)
```

On the CD   You will find this script, as well as other scripts listed in this chapter, on the CD that accompanies this book.

This example connects to the domain. You could, of course, specify any legal LDAP query to return any object, such as a user, group, organizational unit, contact, and so forth. Also note that this technique works with the ADSI WinNT provider, which would allow you to specify alternate credentials for connections to Microsoft Windows NT domains, to standalone computers, or domain-member computers.

Using WMI Alternate Credentials

Using alternate credentials with WMI queries is similar to using them in ADSI queries, as shown in Listing 2-3. Note that you cannot use the winmgmts: moniker technique to connect to WMI if you are using alternate credentials; you must use the object-based connection method shown here. Additionally, Windows does not permit the specification of alternate credentials to the local computer. If you specify alternate credentials for a local connection, you'll get an error.

```
Listing 2-3 WMI Alternate Credentials
Const wbemImpersonationLevelImpersonate = 3

'specify credentials
strComputer = "server1"
strUser = "Administrator"
strPassword = InputBox("Enter password for " & strUser & _
 " on " & strComputer)

'connect to WMI
Set objSWbemLocator = _
 CreateObject("WbemScripting.SWbemLocator")
objSWbemLocator.Security_.ImpersonationLevel = _
 wbemImpersonationLevelImpersonate
Set objSWbemServices = _
 objSWbemLocator.ConnectServer(strComputer, _
 "root\cimv2", strUser, strPassword)
```

You can then, of course, use the *ExecQuery* method of the *objSWbemServices* object to execute a WMI query.

Summary

In this chapter, we presented an overview of common scripting security issues. We discussed ways to make scripting safer and more secure by using WSH TrustPolicy and SRP. We also showed you some techniques for running scripts under alternate credentials, and gave you ideas for how these techniques might be used. These are techniques you'll use again and again with the scripting techniques in this book, so be sure to refer back to this chapter from time to time to refresh your memory of these security options.

Part II
Packaging Your Scripts

Chapter 3
Windows Script Files

VBScript can be used in a variety of ways, including as a Windows Script File (WSF). These XML-formatted scripts offer many benefits and features that we'll explore in this chapter.

A standard VBScript contains one script per file, plus supporting functions and subroutines, so if you have many related scripts, you have to manage them individually. If you have a collection of code you use frequently, you probably cut and paste between scripts. A Windows Script File (WSF) makes it easier to manage scripts and reuse code, and it can even make scripts easier to write.

Defining Windows Script Files

A Windows Script File is a standard Microsoft Visual Basic script that has been formatted in an XML structure. This XML structure defines various sections of the script and allows you to *package* scripts. Each WSF can have as many scripts, or *jobs*, as you like. They can even be written in different scripting languages. For example, one WSF can contain a script written in VBScript that calls another script written in JScript.

The XML formatting might appear daunting at first, but after you gain some experience with it, you'll see how all the pieces work. Each section is defined by a *tag,* similar to an HTML tag. The tags define the various elements. Each element has an opening and closing tag. For example, *<comment></comment>* tags define the comment element. There is an opening *<comment>* tag and a closing *</comment>* tag for each element. The text between the tags is referred to as the *body.* You've probably seen WSF scripts with many tags and what looks like complicated formatting. Not to worry. Much of the XML format is not required. All you really need are *<job>* and *<script>* tags.

```
<job>
<script language="vbscript">
MsgBox "Hello World!"
</script>
</job>
```

Because this is an advanced scripting book, we'll explore WSF scripts in greater detail.

Understanding XML

Let's examine the tags in the order you would use them in a WSF script. Remember, each tag must be closed with a corresponding ending tag that includes the slash (/) character, for example *<comment>* and *</comment>*. In the following sample, the *<object>* tag doesn't have a body, so you can close it with just a slash and closing angle bracket (/>).

```
<object id="objShell" progid="WScript.Shell"/>
```

WSF scripts can be configured to use strict XML formatting. If you start the WSF with the tag *<?XML version="1.0" ?>*, you are specifying that the script parser should enforce XML rules. (There is no other version than 1 for scripting purposes.) Forcing strict XML parsing is a matter of preference, and to some degree, experience. Strict enforcement will ensure that all your tags are properly formatted and prevent run-time errors. In fact, enforcement is so strict that tags are case sensitive. If you enter *<comment>This is a practice script.</Comment>* in your WSF, you will get an error at run time about a tag mismatch.

When you use strict formatting, you will also want to place your script code between a *CDATA* tag like this.

```
<script language="VBScript">
<![CDATA[
On Error Resume Next
MsgBox "<100> Perfect Score!"
]]>
</script>
```

If you don't include this tag, anything that looks like a tag, in this case the text *<100>*, will generate a run-time error.

Let's take a quick look at the tags.

The *package* Tag

This tag is the wrapper for all the jobs in the script file. There should be only one *package* tag per file. If you specify *<?XML version="1.0" ?>* in your script, this tag is required, unless you have only one job in your WSF.

The *comment* Tag

If you want to add some metadata or other notes about the script, use the *comment* tag. You use this tag at the beginning of the script, after the *package* tag. Anything between *<comment>* and *</comment>* will be treated as a comment and not processed in any way. The tag body is never displayed to the user at run time. The only way to view the comment is to open the script in a text or script editor. Also, don't use this tag to add comments to the body of your script. Use the apostrophe as you would in any other VBScript.

> **Note**   You can also use the <!–and --> tags to define a comment anywhere outside of the <script> tag.

The *job* Tag

The *job* tag is used to group everything related to a specific task, such as *description*, *example*, *named*, *object* and *script*. You can have as many jobs as you want in a single WSF file but if you have more than one job, you must set the tag's *id* attribute.

```
<package>
<job id="Backup">
...
</job>
<job id="Restore">
...
</job>
</package>
```

To execute a specific job in a WSF script that includes more than one, you must use the *//Job* switch with CScript. For example, to run the *Backup* job in ServerJobs.wsf at a command prompt, you would type **cscript serverjobs.wsf //job:Backup**. If you have multiple jobs defined and don't specify which one to run, only the first job will run. Jobs do not run sequentially in the script.

The *runtime* Tag

One of the benefits of using the WSF format is a richer set of run-time features, such as named arguments and detailed help information. These features are defined by tags that are enclosed in a set of *runtime* tags.

```
<runtime>
<description>…</description>
<named>…</named>
<example>…</example>
</runtime>
```

The *description* Tag

This tag is similar to the *comment* tag, except the body is displayed to the user at run time if the *wscript.ShowUsage* method is called. You can use this tag to provide a description of the scripts, version information, contact information, or anything else you like. You don't have to supply examples or syntax information; that can be handled by other tags. The tag body can be as long as you want, but it will be displayed as formatted in the file.

```
<description>
 BigEasy.wsf
 -----------------------------------------
 This is the first line of my description.
 This script will make your life very easy
 and make your morning coffee.
</description>
```

If you have a lengthy description, you will need to test the script and adjust the line lengths accordingly.

The *example* Tag

If the *wscript.ShowUsage* method is called, the body of the *example* tag can be used to give syntax examples to the user.

```
<example>
 cscript wsfdemo.wsf /dir:directorypath /file:filename
 cscript wsfdemo.wsf /dir:c:\temp /file:c:\results.txt
</example>
```

As with the *comment* tag, formatting is retained, so in the code snippet just shown, a blank line appears before the sample commands are displayed. You will need to test your help message to make sure the formatting is correct.

The *named* Tag

The *named* tag is used to specify run-time arguments. If your script needs a server name as a parameter, you could use a *named* tag to define the parameter.

```
<named name="server" />
```

At run time, the user would type **cscript myscript.wsf /server:File01** to execute the script using *File01* as the server name parameter. I'm sure you noticed that there is no *</named>* closing tag. Remember, if the tag doesn't have a body, you can use a single tag element, as we've done here.

> **Note**   You might have noticed that sometimes a run-time parameter is specified as */server*, like the example just shown. Other times, we've used a parameter like the pervious example, *//job*. This is because CScript uses two forward slashes (//) for its run-time parameters so that it knows which parameters apply to CScript and which apply to your script. The following command is correct, even though it might look a little odd.
>
> ```
> Cscript myscript.wsf //job:Backup /server:File01
> ```

> **Best Practices**   By the way, the best practice is to put all the CScript options first followed by any parameters for your script.

The *object* Tag

The *object* tag is used to create objects for your script without using the *CreateObject* method. As an added bonus, when you use the *object* tag, you can access the object's type library. This is helpful because with full access to the type library, you can access all the object's constants without having to define them. A traditional script might contain code like this.

```
Dim objFSO
Const FORREADING=1
Const FORWRITING=2
Const FORAPPENDING=8

Set objFSO=CreateObject("Scripting.FileSystemObject")
```

In a WSF script, this can be replaced with a single line of code.

```
<object id="objFSO" progid="Scripting.FileSystemObject" reference="TRUE"/>
```

You don't have to call *CreateObject* or define any constants. You still need to know the name of the constant within the type library, but you can find that by searching the Internet, studying related scripts, or by using an object browser utility. By the way, you still have to explicitly create any child objects. For example, based on the *object* tag just shown, you would still need to write the following in the script section.

```
Set objFile=objFSO.OpenTextFile("MyLog.txt",FORAPPENDING)
```

You can't define *objFile* with an *object* tag. You also can't use the tag for objects you *get*, like *winmgmts*.

Let's take a look at the *object* tag in a bit more detail:

- Every *object* tag has an *id* property. The value of this property is the name of the *object* variable that you want to use in your script. In this example, it is *objFSO*.

- Every *object* tag must have a defined *progid* property. This value is the same as the value you would use in a traditional *CreateObject* statement. In our example, it is *Scripting.File-SystemObject*. If you need to create an object that doesn't have a *progid*, use the object's *guid* property.

- The *reference* property is optional, but we usually set it to TRUE. When set to TRUE, you have full access to the object's type library. There is no performance penalty for enabling this attribute. If you don't set it to TRUE, you must explicitly define any type library constants in your script.

The *script* Tag

The main part of any WSF file is the script section. You can have as many scripts as you want within each job. If you have multiple scripts, they will be executed sequentially. Most administrators use a single *script* tag for each job, but the functionality for multiple jobs is there should you need it.

The only property you need to define for a script is the scripting language, typically VBScript or JScript. This is accomplished by using the *language* attribute. You can have multiple script languages within one job.

```
<job id="Main">
<script language="vbscript">
...
</script>
<script language="jscript">
...
</script>
</job>
```

Creating Script Jobs

Most WSF files have a single job with a single script element, although there is nothing wrong with multiple jobs containing multiple scripts. In the example just shown, the scripts would run sequentially when the *Main* job is executed. Keep in mind that variables defined in the first script are available to the second script, but variables defined in the second script are not available to the first.

To create a script job, simply use a set of *script* tags, and put your VBScript code between them. Remember that if you are using strict XML parsing, you need to put your code between *<![CDATA[* and *]]>* tags.

```
<script language="vbscript">
<![CDATA
'your vbscript code here
]]>
</script>
```

Including Other Scripts

When you create a script job, you are not limited to code within the WSF file itself. You can create a script element that references an external script by using the *src* property.

```
<script language="VBScript" src="ScriptFunctionLibrary.vbs"/>
```

Notice that there is no closing *</script>* tag because there is no code body. You can include as many external scripts as you want.

```
<script language="VBScript" src="ScriptFunctionLibrary.vbs"/>
<script language="JScript" src="E:\scripts\MathFunctions.js"/>
<script language="VBScript" src="\\file01\scripts\Corporate.vbs"/>
```

As you can see, we still need to define the language of the referenced script. The *src* property can be the script name if the reference file is in the same directory as the WSF script. If not, you must specify the full path to the external script, as we did in the example. This is an excellent way to reuse existing code. Create a VBScript file that contains your commonly used functions and subroutines, and include it in your WSF file. Then you can call any function or subroutine in the external file as though it were written directly in the WSF file. If you need to revise a function or subroutine, you can change it in one file, and all the WSF scripts that call it will automatically use the updated code.

Adding Resources

The body of a *resource* tag is used in the same way as a traditional constant, but whereas a constant usually contains a single value, a *resource* tag can contain as many lines of information as you would like. The tag's body is also available to all scripts within a given job. You might use this tag to store script version and contact information. Use the *getResource* method to retrieve the resource value.

```
<job>
<resource id="strAbout">
version 1.0
JDH Information Technology Solutions
http://www.jdhitsolutions.com
</resource>
...
<script language="VBScript">
'if user passes version as the first parameter then display version information
'stored in the resource tag
If InStr(Lcase(wscript.arguments.item(0)), "version") then
  MsgBox getResource("strAbout")
  wscript.quit
End if
'script continues
</script>
</job>
```

> **Troubleshooting**   The *resource* ID is case sensitive, so if your script fails, compare the case of the *resource* ID to the parameter of the *getResource* method.

Creating Examples and Help Text

As mentioned previously, you can use the *example* and *description* tags to display helpful information to the user. The bodies of these tags are displayed when the *ShowUsage* method is called. This is especially helpful when validating run-time syntax. If the user doesn't specify the correct number of parameters, you can display usage information. Let's assume your script needs four parameters. You might use code like this.

```
If wscript.arguments.count<4 then
  Wscript.echo "Missing Parameter"
  Wscript.arguments.ShowUsage.
  Wscript.quit
End if
```

Many command-line utilities have a /? switch to show help information. You can use this switch with a WSF file without having to add any code. Using /? as a run-time parameter will automatically call the *ShowUsage* method.

Using Named Parameters

One advantage of a WSF script over a traditional script is the ease of passing parameters at run time. Of course, you can pass run-time parameters with a traditional script, but processing the values takes some extra coding, especially if there are more than two or three of them. In a traditional script, run-time parameters generally must be passed in a specific order. For example, a script might expect the first parameter to be a server name, the second to be a username, and the third to be a password. If the user gets these out of order, the script will probably fail. Using named parameters with a WSF file simplifies the process and provides a few added benefits that we'll show you later in this chapter.

The *<named>* tag goes inside the *<runtime></runtime>* tags. Here is an example.

```
<named helpstring="The NetBIOS name of the server to query"_
 name="Server" required="true" type="string"/>
```

There are several properties that you can set inside the *named* tag. We'll examine them one by one.

The *name* Property

The *name* property is self-explanatory. At run time, the administrator would type **cscript CheckServer.wsf /server:DC01**. The value of the *server* parameter can then be used in the script. It is also easy set an internal variable with the value of the named argument.

```
strServer=wscript.arguments.named("Server")
```

> **Troubleshooting**   If the value you need to pass has spaces, enclose the value in quotation marks. For example, a parameter passed as */user:Jeff Hicks* will fail. The correct entry is */user: "Jeff Hicks"* You cannot include quotation marks as part of a named argument.

The *helpstring* Property

Any text you enter for the *helpstring* property will be displayed whenever the *ShowUsage* method is called. This provides an easy way to document the script's parameters. Here is a set of named parameters.

```
<named helpstring="The name of the server to query"_
 name="Server" required="true" type="string"/>
<named helpstring="The username for alternate credentials"
 name="user" required="false" type="string"/>
<named helpstring="Alternate credentials password"_
 name="pass" required="false" type="string"/>
<named helpstring="Save results to a text file (True/False)._
 Default is FALSE." name="Log" required="false"type="boolean"/>
```

When the *ShowUsage* method is called, part of the help message will be the *helpstring* property you specified for each named attribute. Using the named parameters just shown, this is what part of the help message looks like.

```
Options:

Server : The name of the server to query
user   : The user for alternate credentials
pass   : Alternate credentials pass.
Log    : Save results to a text file (True/False).
         Default is FALSE.
```

The *helpstring* property is required.

The *type* Property

The optional *type* property is also self-explanatory. You can use named values of type *string*, *Boolean*, or *simple*. When you use the *string* type, the parameter is entered as */named:value*. A *simple* type will pass just the named argument, such as */Trace*. You can then check for the existence of this parameter.

```
<named name="Trace" helpstring: "Turn on tracing" type=simple/>
...
If wscript.arguments.named.exists("Trace") then
  Wscript.echo "Turning on code tracing"
  'code tracing
End if
...
```

A *Boolean* type is a value like plus (+) or minus (-), or true or false. For example, examine the following parameter.

```
<named name="Debug" helpstring: "Turn on debugging" type="Boolean"/>
```

At run time, the user would specify /**debug:+** or /**debug:true** to return a positive value.

The *required* Property

As odd as it sounds, *required* is an optional property. Contrary to what you might think, setting *required* to *true* won't automatically enforce the requirement or even notify the user if the parameter is omitted. If the script requires the parameter, you must add code to validate run-time parameters. This property is for display purposes only.

Let's look at this set of named parameters again.

```
<named helpstring="The name of the server to query"_
 name="Server" required="true" type="string"/>
<named helpstring="The username for alternate credentials"_
 name="user" required="false" type="string"/>
<named helpstring="Alternate credentials password"_
```

```
name="pass"_ required="false" type="string"/>
<named helpstring="Save results to a text file (True/False)._
 Default is FALSE." name="Log" required="false"type="boolean"/>
```

Only the *Server* parameter is required. When the *ShowUsage* method is called, a usage line is displayed showing all the parameters. Optional parameters are indicated by brackets, just like any other command-line utility.

```
Usage: osinfo.wsf /Server:value [/user:value] [/pass:value] [/Log[+|-]]
```

Viewing a Windows Script File in Action

Let's put it all together with a modified version of the *HelloWorld* script from the beginning of the chapter. Listing 3-1 has a basic WSF script.

Listing 3-1 HelloUser.wsf

```
<?xml version="1.0" ?>
<package>
<comment>Demo WSF File</comment>
<job>
<runtime>
<description>
HelloUser.wsf
--------------------------
This is a sample WSF script

</description>
<example>
cscript hellouser.wsf /user:Username [/date]
</example>
<named name="user" helpstring="Your name" type="string" _
required="True"/>
<named name="date" helpstring="Use to display current date" type="simple" _
required="False"/>
</runtime>
<script language="vbscript">
<![CDATA[

if wscript.arguments.named.Exists("user") then
  strUser=wscript.arguments.named("user")
else
  wscript.echo "Missing Parameter!"
  wscript.arguments.ShowUsage
  wscript.quit
end if
if wscript.arguments.named.Exists("date") then strMsg=" It is now " & Now
wscript.echo "Hello " & strUser & "." & vbcrlf & strMsg

]]>
</script>
</job>
</package>
```

On the CD   You will find this script, as well as other scripts listed in this chapter, on the companion CD.

This script uses strict XML parsing by including a *<?xml version="1.0" ?>* tag, which requires that we include the *<![CDATA[* tag. We defined the *<runtime>* tag with *<description>* and *<example>* tags. When the *ShowUsage* method is called, the user will see usage information like this.

```
HelloUser.wsf
-------------------------
This is a sample WSF script

Usage: hellouser.wsf /user:value [/date]

Options:

user : Your name
date : Use to display current date

cscript hellouser.wsf /user:Username [/date]
```

The named parameter *date* is optional, so notice how it is displayed. The body of the script is pretty simple. We validate the parameters to verify that a user name was passed; if not, we display an error message and call the *ShowUsage* method.

```
if wscript.arguments.named.Exists("user") then
  strUser=wscript.arguments.named("user")
else
  wscript.echo "Missing Parameter!"
  wscript.arguments.ShowUsage
  wscript.quit
end if
```

We use a similar line of code to check if the *date* parameter was passed. Because this named parameter is simple, we are only checking for its existence. If it exists, we set a variable.

```
if wscript.arguments.named.Exists("date") then strMsg=" It is now " & Now
```

We reach the main part of the script and display a personalized message to the user. The file then ends with the closing tags.

```
]]>
</script>
</job>
</package>
```

It's worth pointing out that you don't have to figure out all the XML tags yourself. Many commercial script editors have some sort of support for Windows Script File. Some, like OnScript by XLNow and Sapien's PrimalScript, include wizards that will generate the XML-formatted script.

Figure 3-1 displays the first screen of the PrimalScript WSF Wizard, in which we specify the location for the script file.

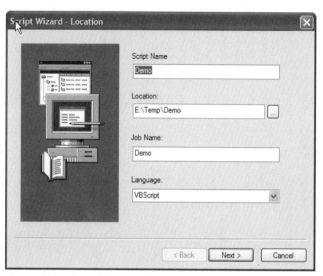

Figure 3-1   Specifying the location

The next step, shown in Figure 3-2, is where we specify all the objects we want to add. Primal-Script offers a few common choices, but we can add any object we want.

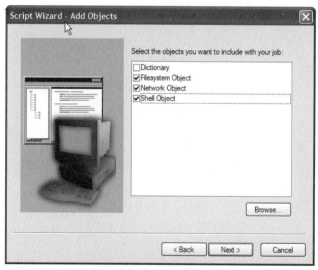

Figure 3-2   Adding the objects

Figure 3-3 shows where to add references to external type libraries.

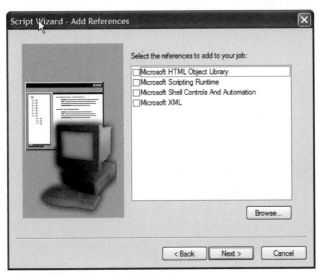

Figure 3-3   Adding the references

Figure 3-4 displays where to add other scripts. This is the same as using the *src* attribute in a *script* tag.

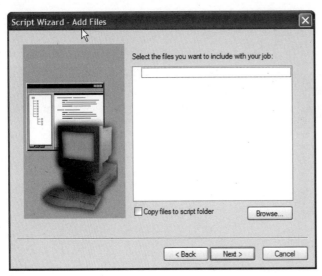

Figure 3-4   Adding the scripts

Figure 3-5 is the last screen of the wizard.

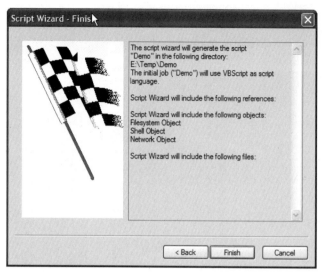

Figure 3-5   Finishing the wizard

PrimalScript will completely shield you from having to write any XML code. The editor displays the file in a workspace. The right pane is reserved for VBScript code and the left pane, as shown in Figure 3-6, is an interface to the XML tags.

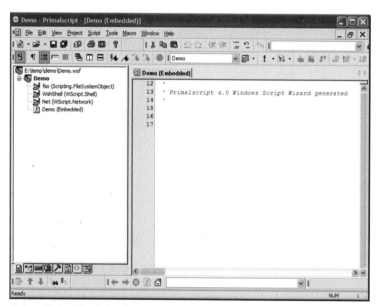

Figure 3-6   The PrimalScript workspace

You can set tags such as *example*, *description*, and *named* through the properties of WSF. Figure 3-7 shows a dialog box for the properties of the named arguments of the HelloUser.wsf file from Listing 3-1.

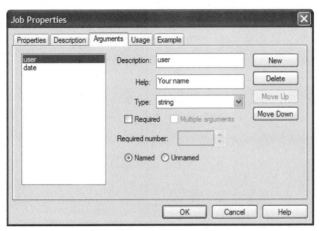

Figure 3-7   Named arguments properties

With the right editor, you can create WSF files without ever having to touch a single XML tag.

Converting an Existing Script to a WSF Utility

Hopefully by now you are intrigued and excited by the benefits of using a WSF script. You likely have a number of scripts in your library that might be easier to use if they were WSF files. Now we'll show you how to take an existing script and turn it into a WSF script.

Listing 3-2 contains a script that queries WMI on a user-specified computer and displays operating system information. We won't go through the script details, but we will show you what parts of the script can be converted to WSF elements.

Listing 3-2 OSInfo.vbs

```
'OSINFO.VBS
'v3.0 July 2004
'USAGE: cscript|wscript OSINFO.VBS
'DESCRIPTION: Using WMI get operating system info for specified computer.
'Includes code to display uptime.
'NOTES: You must have admin rights on the queried system.  You will be
'prompted for alternate credentials. But they can't be used on the local
'system.

On Error Resume Next

Dim objLocator,objService,objRet
Dim objShell,objNetwork

Const wbemFlagReturnImmediately=&h10
Const wbemFlagForwardOnly=&h20
```

```
strTitle="OS Info"

strQuery="Select CSName,BootDevice,Caption,ServicePackMajorVersion," &_
"FreePhysicalMemory,FreeVirtualMemory,InstallDate,LastBootUpTime," &_
"Status,SystemDevice,TotalVirtualMemorySize,TotalVisibleMemorySize," &_
"Version,WindowsDirectory FROM Win32_OperatingSystem"

Set objShell=CreateObject("WScript.Shell")
Set objNetwork=CreateObject("wscript.network")

strSrv=InputBox("What computer do you want to query?",strTitle,_
objNetwork.ComputerName)
If strSrv="" Then WScript.Quit

'if not local system, then prompt for alternate credentials
If UCase(strSrv)<>UCase(objNetwork.ComputerName) Then
  strUser=InputBox("Enter an alternate credential account, or leave " &_
   "blank to use the current credentials.",strTitle,"")
  'if something was entered for strUser, then prompt for password

  If strUser<>"" Then
    strPass=GetIEPassword()
  End If
End If


'if computer is accessible then get information
If TestPing(strSrv) Then
  Set objLocator = CreateObject("WbemScripting.SWbemLocator")
  If Err.Number <>0 then
    strMsg= "Error " & err.number & " [0x" & CStr(Hex(Err.Number)) &_
     "] occurred in creating a locator object."

    If Err.Description <> "" Then
      strMsg=strMsg &vbCrLf & "Error description: " & Err.Description & "."
    End If
    objShell.Popup strMsg,10,strTitle,vbOKOnly+vbCritical
    Wscript.quit
End If

Set objService = objLocator.ConnectServer (strSrv,"root\cimv2",_
 strUser,strPass)
ObjService.Security_.impersonationlevel = 3

Set objRet=objService.ExecQuery(strQuery,"WQL",wbemFlagForwardOnly+_
 wbemFlagReturnImmediately)
If Err.Number<>0 Then
  strErrMsg= "Error executing query on " & UCase(strSrv) & VbCrLf
  strErrMsg= strErrMsg & "You might not have valid credentials." & VbCrLf
  strErrMsg= strErrMsg & "Error #" & err.number & " [0x" &_
   CStr(Hex(Err.Number)) &"]" & VbCrLf
  If Err.Description <> "" Then
    strErrMsg = strErrMsg & "Error description: " & Err.Description & "."
  End If
```

```
      objShell.Popup strErrMsg,10,strTitle,vbOKOnly+vbExclamation
      wscript.quit
   End If

   For each item in objRet
     strInfo=item.CSNAME & vbCrlf
     strInfo=strInfo & item.Caption & " (" & item.Version & ")" & vbCrlf
     strInfo=strInfo & "Service Pack " & item.ServicePackMajorVersion & VbCrLf
     strInfo=strInfo & "Windows Directory: " & item.WindowsDirectory & vbCrlf
     strInfo=strInfo & "Boot Device: " & item.BootDevice & vbCrlf
     strInfo=strInfo & "System Device: " & item.SystemDevice & vbCrlf
     strInfo=strInfo & "Physical Memory: " &_
     FormatNumber(item.TotalVisibleMemorySize/1024,0) & "MB" & _
     " Total/" & FormatNumber(item.FreePhysicalMemory/1024,0) & "MB Free" &_
     " (" &_
     FormatPercent(item.FreePhysicalMemory/item.TotalVisibleMemorySize,0) &_
     ")" & VbCrLf

     strInfo=strInfo & "Virtual Memory: " & _
     FormatNumber(item.TotalVirtualMemorySize/1024,0) & "MB" & _
     " Total/" & FormatNumber(item.FreeVirtualMemory/1024,0) & "MB Free" & _
     " (" & FormatPercent(item.FreeVirtualMemory/item.TotalVirtualMemorySize,0)_
     & ")" & VbCrLf

     strInfo=strInfo & "Install Date: " & ConvWMITime(item.InstallDate) &_
     vbCrlf
     strInfo=strInfo & "Last Boot: " & ConvWMITime(item.LastBootUpTime) &_
     VbCrLf
     iDays=DateDiff("d",ConvWMITime(item.LastBootUpTime),Now)
     iHours=DateDiff("h",ConvWMITime(item.LastBootUpTime),Now)
     iMin=DateDiff("n",ConvWMITime(item.LastBootUpTime),Now)
     iSec=DateDiff("s",ConvWMITime(item.LastBootUpTime),Now)
     strUptime=iDays & " days " & (iHours Mod 24) & " hours " &_
     (iMin Mod 60) & " minutes " & (iSec Mod 60) & " seconds"
     strInfo=strInfo & "Uptime: " & strUptime & VbCrLf
     strInfo=strInfo & "Status: " & item.Status

   Next

   objShell.Popup strInfo,30,strTitle,vbOKOnly+vbInformation
   strMsg="Do you want to save results to text file " & GetCurDir() &_
   UCase(strSrv) & "_OSInfo.txt?" & VbCrLf &_
   " Any existing file will be overwritten."
   rc=MsgBox(strMsg,vbYesNo+vbQuestion,strTitle)
   If rc=vbYes Then
      Dim objFSO,objFile
      Set objFSO=CreateObject("Scripting.FileSystemObject")
      Set objFile=objFSO.CreateTextFile(UCase(strSrv) & "_OSInfo.txt",True)
      objFile.Write strInfo
      objFile.WriteBlankLines(1)
      objFile.WriteLine "recorded " & Now
      objFile.Close
      objShell.Popup "Results saved to " & strSrv &_
         "_OSInfo.txt",10,strTitle,vbOKOnly+vbinformation
   End If
```

```
     Else
         strMsg="Failed to ping " & UCase(strSrv) & "."
         objShell.Popup strMsg,10,strTitle,vbOKOnly+vbExclamation

     End If

Wscript.quit
'End of main script
'////////////////////////////////
' Convert WMI Time Function
'////////////////////////////////
On Error Resume Next
Function ConvWMITime(wmiTime)
yr = left(wmiTime,4)
mo = mid(wmiTime,5,2)
dy = mid(wmiTime,7,2)
tm = mid(wmiTime,9,6)

ConvWMITime = mo&"/"&dy&"/"&yr & " " & FormatDateTime(left(tm,2) & _
":" & Mid(tm,3,2) & ":" & Right(tm,2),3)

End Function


'//////////////////////////////////////////
'Ping target system using WMI. Requires XP
' or Windows 2003 locally
'//////////////////////////////////////////
Function TestPing(strName)
On Error Resume Next
'this function requires Windows XP or 2003
Dim cPingResults, oPingResult
strPingQuery="SELECT * FROM Win32_PingStatus WHERE Address = '" &_
 strName & "'"

Set cPingResults = GetObject("winmgmts://./root/cimv2").ExecQuery(strPingQuery)
For Each oPingResult In cPingResults
  If oPingResult.StatusCode = 0 Then
    TestPing = True
  Else
    TestPing = False
  End If
Next
End Function


'////////////////////////////////
'Use IE Password prompt
'to securely get a password
'////////////////////////////////
Function GetIEPassword()
Dim ie
On Error Resume Next
set ie=Wscript.CreateObject("internetexplorer.application")
ie.width=400
ie.height=150
```

```
ie.statusbar=True
ie.menubar=False
ie.toolbar=False

ie.navigate ("About:blank")
ie.visible=True
ie.document.title="Password prompt"

strHTML=strHTML & "<Font color=RED><B>Enter password: <br>"_
&"<input id=pass type=Password></B></Font>  "
strHTML=strHTML & "<input type=checkbox id=Clicked size=1>"_
&"click box when finished"

ie.document.body.innerhtml=strHTML

Do While ie.busy<>False
  wscript.sleep 100
Loop

'loop until box is checked
 Do While ie.Document.all.clicked.checked=False
  wScript.Sleep 250
Loop

GetIEPassword=ie.Document.body.all.pass.value

ie.Quit
set ie=Nothing
End Function


'////////////////////////////////////////////////////
'Get current path script is running in
'////////////////////////////////////////////////////
Function GetCurDir()
On Error Resume Next
  GetCurDir=Left(WScript.ScriptFullName,Len(WScript.ScriptFullName)_
-Len(WScript.ScriptName))
End Function

'EOF
```

To convert this to a WSF script, start by creating the tags you know you will need. We can fill in the rest as we progress.

```
<?xml version="1.0" ?>
<package>
<job>
<script language="vbscript>
<![CDATA[
]]>
</script>
</job>
</package>
```

The first thing we can do is take the comment section at the beginning of the script and use it as the body of a *<comment>* tag.

```
<package>
  <comment>
OSINFO.VBS
v3.0  July 2004
Jeffery Hicks
jhicks@jhditsolutions.com  http://www.jhditsolutions.com
USAGE: cscript|wscript WMIOSINFO.VBS
DESCRIPTION: Using WMI get operating system info.  Includes code to
display uptime.
NOTES: You must have admin rights on the queried system.  You will be
prompted for alternate credentials. But they can't be used on the local
system.
  </comment>
```

Next, we can take the description and notes from the comments and put them in a *<description>* tag. This will be useful information to the administrator running the script.

```
<description>
Using WMI get operating system info.
You must have admin rights on the queried system.  You will be
prompted for alternate credentials. But they can't be used on the local
system.
</description>
```

The existing script prompts the user for a server name. We can easily make this a named parameter.

```
<named helpstring="The name of the server to query"_
 name="Server"  required="true" type="string"/>
```

Because we can pass parameters, we can also improve the original script. Let's ask for alternate credentials, but we won't make them required.

```
<named helpstring="The user namefor alternate credentials"
name="user" required="false" type="string"/>
<named helpstring="Alternate credentials password"_
 name="pass" required="false" type="string"/>
```

Finally, let's also add a parameter to save the results to a text file. We could use a simple named parameter, but let's use a Boolean parameter to make it more interesting.

```
<named helpstring="Save results to a text file (True/False).
Default is FALSE." name="Log" required="false" type="boolean"/
```

The original script has a simple usage example, but we can improve on that with the *<example>* tag.

```
<example>
Examples:
cscript wmiosinfo.wsf /server:FILE01
cscript wmiosinfo.wsf /server:FILE01 /user:Admin /pass:P@ssw0rd
cscript wmiosinfo.wsf /server:FILE01 /user:* /pass:*
cscript wmiosinfo.wsf /server:FILE01 /user:Admin /pass:P@ssw0rd /log:TRUE
cscript wmiosinfo.wsf /?

If you use * for /server, /user or /pass, you will be prompted
You cannot use alternate credentials for local systems.
Existing log files with the same name will be overwritten.
</example>
```

Between the description and examples, the user will get excellent help information.

Now let's look at the objects in the original script and think about what we might need in the WSF script. We first need to add the *Scripting.FileSystemObject*, because it wasn't in the original file and we will need it for the log file. The other objects can be created by using *object* tags. We use the same ID we used in the original script.

```
<object id="objFSO" progid="Scripting.FileSystemObject" reference="true"/>
<object id="objShell" progid="WScript.Shell"/>
<object id="objNetwork" progid="WScript.Network"/>
<object id="objLocator" progid="WbemScripting.SWbemLocator" _ reference="true"/>
```

In the original script, we had to define constants that are part of the *WbemScripting.SWbemLocator* object. In a WSF script, however, if we set the reference property to TRUE, we have full access to the object's type library and all constants.

The original script had several functions that are also used in other scripts. We can plan for future scripts by building a script function library. By including this script, we have full access to all the functions.

```
<script language="VBScript" src="ScriptFunctionLibrary.vbs"/>
```

Now we can simply copy and paste the script body from the original script into the new file after *<![CDATA[*.

Because we are using *object* tags, we can delete the lines of code that instantiate these objects. We can also delete the lines of code related to the *InputBox* prompt, because that is now handled with named arguments.

We have to add code to validate the arguments.

```
if WScript.Arguments.Named.exists("Server") then
   strSrv=wscript.arguments.named("Server")
else
   wscript.echo "No Server Parameter specified!"
```

```
   wscript.arguments.showusage
   wscript.quit
end if

if WScript.Arguments.Named.exists("user") then _ strUser=WScript.Arguments.Named("user")
if WScript.Arguments.Named.exists("pass") then _ strPass=WScript.Arguments.Named("pass")
if WScript.Arguments.Named.exists("log") then _ blnLog=WScript.Arguments.Named("Log")
```

The remaining edits are enhancements, such as the use of alternate credentials and logging. Listing 3.3 shows the updated and converted script.

Listing 3-3 OSInfo.wsf

```
<?xml version="1.0" ?>
<package>
  <comment>
OSINFO.WSF
v3.0  July 2004
Jeffery Hicks
jhicks@jhditsolutions.com  http://www.jhditsolutions.com
USAGE: cscript|wscript WMIOSINFO.VBS
DESCRIPTION: Using WMI get operating system info for specified computer.
Includes code to display uptime.
NOTES: You must have admin rights on the queried system.  You will be
prompted for alternate credentials. But they can't be used on the local
system.
  </comment>
  <job>
    <runtime>
    <description>
Using WMI get operating system info.
You must have admin rights on the queried system.  You will be
prompted for alternate credentials. But they can't be used on the local
system.
    </description>
      <named helpstring="The name of the server to query" _
      name="Server" required="true" type="string"/>
      <named helpstring="The user for alternate credentials"
      name="user" required="false" type="string"/>
      <named helpstring="Alternate credentials pass." name="pass"_
      required="false" type="string"/>
      <named helpstring="Save results to a text file (True/False).
      Default is FALSE." name="Log" required="false"_
      type="boolean"/>
<example>
Examples:
cscript wmiosinfo.wsf /server:FILE01
cscript wmiosinfo.wsf /server:FILE01 /user:Admin /pass:P@ssw0rd
cscript wmiosinfo.wsf /server:FILE01 /user:* /pass:*
cscript wmiosinfo.wsf /server:FILE01 /user:Admin /pass:P@ssw0rd /log:TRUE
cscript wmiosinfo.wsf /?

If you use * for /server, /user or /pass, you will be prompted
You cannot use alternate credentials for local systems.
Existing log files with the same name will be overwritten.
```

```
</example>
    </runtime>
    <object id="objFSO" progid="Scripting.FileSystemObject" _
    reference="true"/>
    <object id="objShell" progid="WScript.Shell"/>
    <object id="objNetwork" progid="WScript.Network"/>
    <object id="objLocator" progid="WbemScripting.SwbemLocator" _
    reference="true"/>
    <script language="VBScript" src="ScriptFunctionLibrary.vbs"/>
    <script language="VBScript">
<![CDATA[
 On Error Resume Next

If WScript.Arguments.Count<1 Then
  wscript.Arguments.ShowUsage
  WScript.Quit
End If
strTitle="OS Info"
'verify user is running Windows XP
If InStr(GetOS,"XP Professional")=False Then
  objShell.Popup "This script requires Windows XP Professional",10,_
  strTitle,vbOKOnly+vbExclamation
  WScript.Quit
End If

strQuery="Select CSName,BootDevice,Caption,ServicePackMajorVersion," &_
"FreePhysicalMemory,FreeVirtualMemory,InstallDate,LastBootUpTime," &_
"Status,SystemDevice,TotalVirtualMemorySize,TotalVisibleMemorySize," &_
"Version,WindowsDirectory FROM Win32_OperatingSystem"

if WScript.Arguments.Named.exists("Server") then
  strSrv=wscript.arguments.named("Server")
else
  wscript.echo "No Server Parameter specified!"
  wscript.arguments.showusage
  wscript.quit
end if

if WScript.Arguments.Named.exists("user") then _ strUser=WScript.Arguments.Named("user")
if WScript.Arguments.Named.exists("pass") then _ strPass=WScript.Arguments.Named("pass")
if WScript.Arguments.Named.exists("log") then _ blnLog=WScript.Arguments.Named("Log")

If strSrv="*" Then
  strSrv=InputBox("What computer do you want to query?",strTitle,_
  objNetwork.ComputerName)
  If strSrv="" Then WScript.Quit
End If

'skip getting alternate credentials if Server is local system
If UCase(strSrv)<>UCase(objNetwork.Computername) Then
  If strUSer="*" Then
    strUSer=InputBox("Enter alternate credentials, or leave " &_
    "blank to use the current credentials.",strTitle,"")
  End If
```

```
    If strPass="*" Then
        strPass=GetIEpassword()
    End If
End If

'if local system, then set any alternate credentials to blank
If UCase(strSrv)=UCase(objNetwork.ComputerName) Then
    strUSer=""
    strPass=""
End If

'if computer is accessible then get information
If TestPing(strSrv) Then

Set objService = objLocator.ConnectServer (strSrv,"root\cimv2",_
strUSer,strPass)
ObjService.Security_.impersonationlevel = 3

Set objRet=objService.ExecQuery(strQuery,"WQL",wbemForwardOnly+_
wbemFlagReturnImmediately)
If Err.Number<>0 Then
    strErrMsg= "Error executing query on " & UCase(strSrv) & VbCrLf
    strErrMsg= strErrMsg & "You might not have valid credentials." & VbCrLf
    strErrMsg= strErrMsg & "Error #" & err.number & " [0x" &_
    CStr(Hex(Err.Number)) &"]" & VbCrLf
    If Err.Description <> "" Then
        strErrMsg = strErrMsg & "Error description: " & Err.Description & "."
    End If
    objShell.Popup strErrMsg,10,strTitle,vbOKOnly+vbExclamation
    wscript.quit
End If

For each item In objRet
    strInfo=item.CSNAME & vbCrlf
    strInfo=strInfo & item.Caption & " (" & item.Version & ")" & VbCrLf
    strInfo=strInfo & "Service Pack " & item.ServicePackMajorVersion & VbCrLf
    strInfo=strInfo & "Windows Directory: " & item.WindowsDirectory & vbCrlf
    strInfo=strInfo & "Boot Device: " & item.BootDevice & vbCrlf
    strInfo=strInfo & "System Device: " & item.SystemDevice & vbCrlf
    strInfo=strInfo & "Physical Memory: " &_
    FormatNumber(item.TotalVisibleMemorySize/1024,0) & "MB" & _
    " Total/" & FormatNumber(item.FreePhysicalMemory/1024,0) & "MB Free" &_
    " (" &_
    FormatPercent(item.FreePhysicalMemory/item.TotalVisibleMemorySize,0) &_
    ")" & vbCrLf

    strInfo=strInfo & "Virtual Memory: " & _
    FormatNumber(item.TotalVirtualMemorySize/1024,0) & "MB" & _
    " Total/" & FormatNumber(item.FreeVirtualMemory/1024,0) & "MB Free" & _
    " (" &FormatPercent(item.FreeVirtualMemory/item.TotalVirtualMemorySize,0)_
    & ")" & vbCrLf

    strInfo=strInfo & "Install Date: " & ConvWMITime(item.InstallDate) &_
    VbCrLf
    strInfo=strInfo & "Last Boot: " & ConvWMITime(item.LastBootUpTime) &_
```

```
    VbCrLf
    iDays=DateDiff("d",ConvWMITime(item.LastBootUpTime),Now)
    iHours=DateDiff("h",ConvWMITime(item.LastBootUpTime),Now)
    iMin=DateDiff("n",ConvWMITime(item.LastBootUpTime),Now)
    iSec=DateDiff("s",ConvWMITime(item.LastBootUpTime),Now)
    strUptime=iDays & " days " & (iHours Mod 24) & " hours " &_
    (iMin Mod 60) & " minutes " & (iSec Mod 60) & " seconds"
    strInfo=strInfo & "Uptime: " & strUptime & VbCrLf
    strInfo=strInfo & "Status: " & item.Status

Next

objShell.Popup strInfo,30,strTitle,vbOKOnly+vbInformation

If blnLog Then
    Set objFile=objFSO.CreateTextFile(UCase(strSrv) & "_OSInfo.txt",True)
    objFile.Write strInfo
    objFile.WriteBlankLines(1)
    objFile.WriteLine "recorded " & Now
    objFile.Close
    objShell.Popup "Results saved to " & strSrv &_
    "_OSInfo.txt",10,strTitle,vbOKOnly+vbInformation
End If

Else
strMsg="Failed to ping " & UCase(strSrv) & "."
objShell.Popup strMsg,10,strTitle,vbOKOnly+vbExclamation

End If

Wscript.quit
'End of main script

]]>
    </script>
  </job>
</package>
```

As you can see, with just a little work, you can turn an existing script into a full-fledged command-line utility. But what if you would prefer a graphical interface?

In the new WSF script, we added code to prompt the user for a password if the passed argument value is a wildcard (*). We did this primarily so we could use a password dialog box for extra security, but we can also use this technique to display a graphical interface. But how can the user get prompted if he or she has to type a wildcard character to begin with? We use another script.

Listing 3-4 is a regular VBScript. The sole function of this script is to launch our new WSF script by using WScript and pass named arguments.

Listing 3-4 RunOSInfo.vbs

```
Dim objShell

strCmd="wscript"
strScript="listing3-3.wsf"
strParams="/server:* /username:* /password:* /log:True"

Set objShell=CreateObject("WScript.Shell")
objShell.Run strCmd & " " & strScript & " " & strParams,1,False

WScript.Quit
```

When the administrator double-clicks this script, the WSF script is called with the wildcard character for argument values. The WSF script follows its code and prompts the user for all the necessary values.

```
If strSrv="*" Then
  strSrv=InputBox("What computer do you want to query?",strTitle,_
  objNetwork.ComputerName)
  If strSrv="" Then WScript.Quit
End If

'skip getting alternate credentials if Server is local system
If UCase(strSrv)<>UCase(objNetwork.Computername) Then
  If strUser="*" Then
   strUser=InputBox("Enter alternate credentials, or leave " &_
   "blank to use the current credentials.",strTitle,"")
  End If

  If strPass="*" Then
    strPass=GetIEpassword()
  End If
End If
```

We get the best of both worlds. We can use a command-line utility, or we can wrap the utility in another script and use a graphical utility.

Creating and Using a Wrapper WSF

Let's now look at how to use a WSF file as a wrapper script. Let's say you have some code that you would like to run against a list of computers. You might have the list in a text file, or perhaps you'd like to query an Active Directory organizational unit. The wrapper script handles the details of getting computer names. All you have to so is insert the code that will execute against each remote machine.

The script in Listing 3-5 uses named arguments to indicate whether to read computer names from a text file, an organizational unit, or to use a single computer name. Here's that section of code.

```
<named helpstring="Text file to pull computer names from" name="list"_
 required="false" type="string"/>
<named helpstring="OU to pull computer names from" name="container"_
 required="false" type="string"/>
<named helpstring="Run command against single specified computer" _
name="computer" required="false" type="string"/>
```

The wrapper script also has optional named arguments for verbose information, recursion, and pinging the remote computer to verify availability and logging.

```
<named helpstring="Use for verbose output" name="verbose" _
required="false" type="simple"/>
<named helpstring="Use with /container to include sub-OUs" _
name="recurse" required="false" type="simple"/>
<named helpstring="File to log names which can't be reached" _
name="log" required="false" type="string"/>
<named helpstring="Reduce timeout wait by pinging before connecting" _
name="ping" required="false" type="simple"/>
```

```
Listing 3-5 MultiComputer Wrapper.wsf
<?xml version="1.0" ?>
<package>
  <job id="MultiComputer" prompt="no">
    <?job error="false" debug="false" ?>
    <runtime>
      <description>
ScriptingAnswers.com - Where Windows Administrators Go To Automate
----------------------------------------------------------------------
The shell script upon which this command is built was written by Don Jones
for ScriptingAnswers.com, and provides the following command-line arguments:

Use only one of the following:
  /list:filename    : text file containing one computer name per line
  /container:ouname : name of an OU containing computer accounts
  /computer:name    : run command against single specified computer

Optionally, use one or more of the following:
  /verbose          : display detailed status messages
  /recurse          : used with /container to include sub-OUs
  /log:filename     : write unreachable computer names to specified file
  /ping             : pre-test connectivity to each computer
Note that /ping argument is only available on Windows XP and later.
----------------------------------------------------------------------
This command adds the following (if any) command-line arguments:
  (none)
----------------------------------------------------------------------
SYNOPSIS (see above for more detailed descriptions):
      </description>
      <named helpstring="Text file to pull computer names from" _
name="list" required="false" type="string"/>
```

```
      <named helpstring="OU to pull computer names from" name="container" _
required="false" type="string"/>
      <named helpstring="Use for verbose output" name="verbose"_
required="false" type="simple"/>
      <named helpstring="Use with /container to include sub-OUs"_
name="recurse" required="false" type="simple"/>
      <named helpstring="File to log names which can't be reached"_
 name="log" required="false" type="string"/>
      <named helpstring="Reduce timeout wait by pinging before connecting"_
 name="ping" required="false" type="simple"/>
      <named helpstring="Run command against single specified computer" _
name="computer" required="false" type="string"/>
    </runtime>
    <object id="fso" progid="Scripting.FileSystemObject"/>
    <script id="MultiComputer" language="VBScript">
<![CDATA[
'------------------------------------------------------------
' ScriptingAnswers.com Gold        www.scriptinganswers.com
'          MEGA-MULTICOMPUTER WRAPPER SCRIPT
'                   by Don Jones
'------------------------------------------------------------
'
' SYNOPSIS
' --------
' Accepts a list of computer names from a file, or computer
' names in specified AD organizational units, or a single
' computer name. Executes your code against each computer.
' Includes functions for logging data to a file, querying
' WMI, and querying ADSI. Also has options to ping computers
' before trying to connect, to speed up timeouts. Designed
' to be run from the command-line; run command with /?
' argument for command-line argument assistance.
'
' SUPPORT
' -------
' Support for this script is provided online ONLY in the
' forums at www.scriptinganswers.com. This script is Not
' intended to run without modification; it is a "shell,"
' or "template" script.
'
'' WARRANTY
' --------
' This script is provided AS-IS without warranty
' of any kind. Author and ScriptingAnswers.com further
' disclaims all implied warranties including, without limit,
' any implied warranties of merchantability or of fitness
' for a particular purpose. The entire risk arising out of
' the use or performance of this script remains with you,
' the user of this script. In no event shall the author,
' ScriptingAnswers.com, Don Jones, or BrainCore Nevada, Inc.
' be liable for any damages whatsoever (including, without
' limitation, damages for loss of business profits, business
' interruption, loss of business information, or other
' pecuniary loss) arising out of the use or inability to use
' this script, even if aforementioned parties have been
' advised of the possibility of such damages.
```

```
'
' COPYRIGHT
' ---------
' This script is copyrighted by the above-named
' author and is distributed by ScriptingAnswers.com under
' license. You may use this script in your own environment
' and use it to create derivative scripts. You may distribute
' any derivative scripts, provided this text block remains
' intact and unmodified. You may not distribute this script
' as-is (e.g., not as part of a derivative script) or with
' any modifications to the code included with this script.
' In other words, you may ADD your code to this wrapper
' script, but you may not remove or modify any of the code
' that was published with this wrapper script. You may Not
' distribute the wrapper as-is, but you may distribute any
' scripts that you create using this wrapper.
'
'-----------------------------------------------------------

'make sure we're running from CScript, not WScript
If LCase(Right(WScript.FullName,11)) <> "cscript.exe" Then
  If MsgBox("This script is designed to work with CScript, but you are" _
"running it under WScript. " & _
    "This script may produce a large number of dialog boxes when running" _
"under WScript, which you may find to be inefficient. Do you want to" _
"continue anyway?",4+256+32,"Script host warning") = 7 Then
  WScript.Echo "Tip: Run ""Cscript //h:cscript"" from a command-line to" _
"make CScript the default scripting host."
  WScript.Quit
  End If
End If

'count arguments
Dim iArgs
If WScript.Arguments.Named.exists("computer") Then iArgs = iArgs + 1
If WScript.Arguments.Named.exists("container") Then iArgs = iArgs + 1
If WScript.Arguments.Named.exists("list") Then iArgs = iArgs + 1
If iArgs <> 1 Then
  WScript.Echo "Must specify either /computer, /container, or /list arguments."
  WScript.Echo "May not specify more than one of these arguments."
  WScript.Echo "Run command again with /? argument for assistance."
  WScript.Quit
End If

'if ping requested, make sure we're on XP or later
Dim bPingAvailable, oLocalWMI, cWindows, oWindows
bPingAvailable = False
Set oLocalWMI = GetObject("winmgmts:\\.\root\cimv2")
Set cWindows = oLocalWMI.ExecQuery("Select BuildNumber from " &_
"Win32_OperatingSystem",,48)
For Each oWindows In cWindows
  If oWindows.BuildNumber >= 2600 Then
    bPingAvailable = True
  End If
Next
```

```
'was ping requested?
If WScript.Arguments.Named.Exists("ping") Then
  If bPingAvailable Then
    Verbose "will attempt to ping all connections to improve performance"
  Else
    WScript.Echo "*** /ping not supported prior to Windows XP"
  End If
End if


'either /list, /computer, or /container was specified:
Dim sName
If WScript.Arguments.Named("list") <> "" Then
  'specified list - read names from file
  Dim oFSO, oTS
  Verbose "Reading names from file " & WScript.Arguments.Named("list")
  Set oFSO = WScript.CreateObject("Scripting.FileSystemObject")
  On Error Resume Next
  Set oTS = oFSO.OpenTextFile(WScript.Arguments.Named("list"))
  If Err <> 0 Then
    WScript.Echo "Error opening " & WScript.Arguments.Named("list")
    WScript.Echo Err.Description
    WScript.Quit
  End If
  Do Until oTS.AtEndOfStream
    sName = oTS.ReadLine
    TakeAction sName
  Loop
  oTS.Close


Elseif WScript.Arguments.Named("container") <> "" Then
  'specified container - read names from AD
  Dim oObject, oRoot, oChild
  Verbose "Reading names from AD container " & _
WScript.Arguments.Named("container")
  On Error Resume Next
  Set oRoot = GetObject("LDAP://rootDSE")
  If Err <> 0 Then
    WScript.Echo "Error connecting to default Active Directory domain"
    WScript.Echo Err.Description
    WScript.Quit
  End If
  Set oObject = GetObject("LDAP://ou=" & WScript.Arguments.Named("container") & _
    "," & oRoot.Get("defaultNamingContext"))
  If Err <> 0 Then
    WScript.Echo "Error opening organizational unit " & _
WScript.Arguments.Named("container")
    WScript.Echo Err.Description
    WScript.Quit
  End If
  WorkWithOU oObject


Elseif WScript.Arguments.Named("computer") <> "" Then
  'specified single computer
```

```
     Verbose "Running command against " & WScript.Arguments.Named("computer")
     TakeAction WScript.Arguments.Named("computer")

  End If

  'display output so user will know script finished
  WScript.Echo "Command completed."

  ' -------------------------------------------------------------------
  ' Sub WorkWithOU
  '
  ' Iterates child objects in OU; calls itself to handle sub-OUs If
  ' /recurse argument supplied
  ' -------------------------------------------------------------------
  Sub WorkWithOU(oObject)
    For Each oChild In oObject
      Select Case oChild.Class
        Case "computer"
          TakeAction Right(oChild.Name,len(oChild.name)-3)
        Case "user"
        Case "organizationalUnit"
          If WScript.Arguments.Named.Exists("recurse") Then
            'recursing sub-OU
            Verbose "Working In " & oChild.Name
            WorkWithOU oChild
          End If
      End Select
    Next
  End Sub

  ' -------------------------------------------------------------------
  ' Sub TakeAction
  '
  ' Makes connection and performs command-specific code
  ' -------------------------------------------------------------------
  Sub TakeAction(sName)

    'verbose output?
    Verbose "Connecting to " & sName

    'ping before connecting?
    If WScript.Arguments.Named.Exists("ping") Then
      If Not TestPing(sName,bPingAvailable) Then
        LogBadConnect(sName)
        Exit Sub
      End If
    End If

    '-------------------------------------------
    '        INSTRUCTIONS & REFERENCE
    '-------------------------------------------
    ' sName contains the current name to work with
    '
    ' If /ping argument supplied, name has already
    ' been verified as reachable at this point.
```

```
'
' Otherwise, need to trap for connection error
' and call LogBadConnect(sName) to log bad
' connections, if necessary.
'
' To output status messages:
'   Verbose "Message"
'
' To append to a text file:
'   LogFile "filename","text",False
'
' To write to a new text file, overwriting previous file:
'   LogFile "filename","text",True
'
' To query WMI (simple queries): See example 1.
' To query ADSI (using LDAP or WinNT): See example 2.
'
'-----------------------------------------------
'                    EXAMPLE 1
'-----------------------------------------------
' Example WMI query, will prompt for password:
' Echoes OS build number for specified computers
' Uncomment lines below to try it.
'
'   Dim obj, oItem
'      Set obj = QueryWMI(sName,"root/cimv2","Select * from" &_
'      " win32_operatingsystem","administrator","")
'      If IsObject(obj) Then
'        For Each oItem In obj
'        WScript.Echo sName & " is at Windows build " & oItem.BuildNumber
'        Next
'         Else
'          WScript.Echo "Couldn't get build info for " & sName
'         End If


'-----------------------------------------------
'                    EXAMPLE 2
'-----------------------------------------------
' Example ADSI query
'  ' Echoes password age for the
'  ' local Administrator account from a specified
'  ' list of computers. Uncomment lines below to
'  ' try it. See description of function, below,
'  ' for more detail.
'  '
'   Dim obj
'   Set obj = QueryADSI(sName,"WinNT://%computer%/Administrator,user","%computer%")
'   If IsObject(obj) Then
'       WScript.Echo "Administrator password on " & sName & _
'       " is " & obj.Get("PasswordAge") & " days old."
'   Else
'       WScript.Echo "Couldn't get password age from " & sName
'   End If
```

```
'##########################################
'#       COMMAND-SPECIFIC CODE GOES HERE      #
'#----------------------------------------#
'#                                        #
' "your code here" - see examples above
'#                                        #
'#----------------------------------------#
'#          END COMMAND-SPECIFIC CODE         #
'##########################################
End Sub


' -------------------------------------------------------------------
' Sub LogBadConnect
'
' Logs failed connections to a log file. Will append if file already exists.
' -------------------------------------------------------------------
Sub LogBadConnect(sName)
If WScript.Arguments.Named.Exists("log") Then
  Dim oLogFSO, oLogFile
  Set oLogFSO = WScript.CreateObject("Scripting.FileSystemObject")
  On Error Resume Next
  Set oLogFile = oLogFSO.OpenTextFile(WScript.Arguments.Named("log"),8,True)
  If Err <> 0 Then
    WScript.Echo " *** Error opening log file to log an unreachable computer"
    WScript.Echo " " & Err.Description
  Else
    oLogFile.WriteLine sName
    oLogFile.Close
    Verbose " Logging " & sName & " as unreachable"
  End If
End If
End Sub


' -------------------------------------------------------------------
' Function TestPing
'
' Tests connectivity to a given name or address; returns true or False
' -------------------------------------------------------------------
Function TestPing(sName,bPingAvailable)
If Not bPingAvailable Then
  WScript.Echo " Ping functionality not available prior to Windows XP"
Exit Function
End If
Dim cPingResults, oPingResult
Verbose " Pinging " & sName
Set cPingResults = GetObject("winmgmts://./root/cimv2").ExecQuery_
("SELECT * FROM Win32_PingStatus WHERE Address = '" & sName & "'")
  For Each oPingResult In cPingResults
    If oPingResult.StatusCode = 0 Then
      TestPing = True
      Verbose "  Success"
    Else
      TestPing = False
      Verbose "  *** FAILED"
    End If
```

```
Next
End Function


' -------------------------------------------------------------------
' Sub Verbose
'
' Outputs status messages if /verbose argument supplied
' -------------------------------------------------------------------
Sub Verbose(sMessage)
If WScript.Arguments.Named.Exists("verbose") Then
  WScript.Echo sMessage
End If
End Sub


' -------------------------------------------------------------------
' Sub LogFile
'
' Outputs specified text to specified logfile. Set Overwrite=True To
' overwrite existing file, otherwise file will be appended to.
' Each call to this sub is a fresh look at the file, so don't Set
' Overwrite=True except at the beginning of your script.
' -------------------------------------------------------------------
Sub LogFile(sFile,sText,bOverwrite)
Dim oFSOOut,oTSOut,iFlag
If bOverwrite Then
  iFlag = 2
Else
  iFlag = 8
End If
Set oFSOOut = WScript.CreateObject("Scripting.FileSystemObject")
On Error Resume Next
Set oTSOut = oFSOOut.OpenTextFile(sFile,iFlag,True)
If Err <> 0 Then
  WScript.Echo "*** Error logging to " & sFile
  WScript.Echo "    " & Err.Description
Else
  oTSOut.WriteLine sText
  oTSOut.Close
End If
End Sub


' -------------------------------------------------------------------
' Function QueryWMI
'
' Executes WMI query and returns results. User and Password may be
' passed as empty strings to use current credentials; pass just a blank
' username to prompt for the password
' -------------------------------------------------------------------
Function QueryWMI(sName,sNamespace,sQuery,sUser,sPassword)
Dim oWMILocator, oWMIService, cInstances
On Error Resume Next

'create locator
Set oWMILocator = CreateObject("WbemScripting.SWbemLocator")
```

```
If sUser = "" Then

'no user - connect w/current credentials
Set oWMIService = oWMILocator.ConnectServer(sName,sNamespace)
If Err <> 0 Then
  WScript.Echo "*** Error connecting to WMI on " & sName
  WScript.Echo "    " & Err.Description
  Set QueryWMI = Nothing
  Exit Function
End If

Else

  'user specified
  If sUser <> "" And sPassword = "" Then

    'no password - need to prompt for password
    If LCase(Right(WScript.FullName,11)) = "cscript.exe" Then

      'cscript - attempt to use ScriptPW.Password object
      Dim oPassword
      Set oPassword = WScript.CreateObject("ScriptPW.Password")
        If Err <> 0 Then
        WScript.Echo " *** Cannot prompt for password " &_
        "prior to Windows XP"
          WScript.Echo "     Either ScriptPW.Password " &_
          "object not present on system, Or"
          WScript.Echo "     " & Err.Description
          WScript.Echo "     Will try to proceed with" &_
          "blank password"
        Else
          WScript.Echo "Enter password for user '" & _
          sUser & "' on '" & sName & "'."
          sPassword = oPassword.GetPassword()
        End If
      Else

        'wscript - prompt with InputBox()
        sPassword = InputBox("Enter password for user '" &
        sUser & "' on '" & sName & "'." & vbcrlf & vbcrlf & _
         "WARNING: Password will echo to the screen. Run " &_
        "command with CScript to avoid this.")
      End if
    End If

    'try to connect using credentials provided
    Set oWMIService = _
    WMILocator.ConnectServer(sName,sNamespace,sUser,sPassword)
    If Err <> 0 Then
      WScript.Echo " *** Error connecting to WMI on " & sName
      WScript.Echo "     " & Err.Description
      Set QueryWMI = Nothing
      Exit Function
    End If
  End If
```

```
'execute query
  If sQuery <> "" Then
    Set cInstances = oWMIService.ExecQuery(sQuery,,48)
    If Err <> 0 Then
      WScript.Echo "*** Error executing query "
      WScript.Echo "      " & sQuery
      WScript.Echo "      " & Err.Description
      Set QueryWMI = Nothing
      Exit Function
    Else
      Set QueryWMI = cInstances
    End If
  Else
    Set QueryWMI = oWMIService
  End If

End Function


' --------------------------------------------------------------------
' Function QueryADSI
'
' Executes ADSI query. Expects variable sQuery to include a COMPLETE
' query beginning with the provider LDAP:// or WinNT://. The query String
' may include a placeholder for the computer name, such as "%computer%".
' Include the placeholder in variable sPlaceholder to have it replaced
' with the current computer name. E.g.,
'   sQuery = "WinNT://%computer%/Administrator,user"
'   sPlaceholder = "%computer%"
' will query each computer targeted by the script and query their local
' Administrator user accounts.
' --------------------------------------------------------------------
Function QueryADSI(sName,sQuery,sPlaceholder)

Dim oObject
sQuery = Replace(sQuery,sPlaceholder,sName)
On Error Resume Next
Verbose " Querying " & sQuery
Set oObject = GetObject(sQuery)
If Err <> 0 Then
  WScript.Echo " *** Error executing ADSI query"
  WScript.Echo "      " & sQuery
  WScript.Echo "      " & Err.Description
  Set QueryADSI = Nothing
Else
  Set QueryADSI = oObject
End If

End Function
]]>
    </script>
  </job>
</package>
```

The script processes each computer in the appropriate list and sets a variable with the current computer name. You insert your code in the *TakeAction* subroutine. The wrapper script includes a few examples.

```
' Example WMI query, will prompt for password:
' Echoes OS build number for specified computers
' Uncomment lines below to try it.
'
'    Dim obj, oItem
'    Set obj = QueryWMI(sName,"root/cimv2","select * from " &_
'    "win32_operatingsystem","administrator","")
'    If IsObject(obj) Then
'      For Each oItem In obj
'   WScript.Echo sName & " is at Windows build " & oItem.BuildNumber
'  Next
'    Else
'      WScript.Echo "Couldn't get build info for " & sName
'    End If
```

You'll notice that this WSF script contains all its functions and subroutines as part of the script, even though they could have been relegated to an included library script. However, whenever you include a library script, you have to make sure that the included script is in the appropriate directory. This is especially problematic if you are sharing your scripts with people outside your organization.

But there is nothing preventing you from adding your own script library. In fact, you might find it easier to put the code you want to call in a separate script as a standalone subroutine or function. In the wrapper script, all you need to do is call your subroutine or function.

The advantage of using a WSF wrapper script is that you use it as a command-line utility, which makes it very easy to set up as a scheduled task The wrapper script handles all the list processing, error handling, and logging. You simply plug in your existing code.

Summary

In this chapter, we gave you a quick overview of XML and demonstrated the features and benefits of a Windows Script File. We showed you a WSF in action and walked you through converting an existing VBScript file to a WSF. These types of scripts take a little longer to develop and can be daunting at first; but with a little experience, you will learn where you can exploit this script format. It isn't the right solution for every problem, but it's another tool for your administrative scripting toolbox.

More Info   For more information visit the Microsoft Web site at

http://msdn.microsoft.com/library/default.asp?url=/library/en-us/script56/html /wsorixmlelements.asp

(This link is on the companion CD; click *MSDN XML Elements*.) ScriptingAnswers.com also offers a training video, *Windows Script Files Unmasked*, that covers this topic in detail.

Chapter 4
Windows Script Components

If you've developed complex VBScript code that you want to use in other scripts, packaging it into a Windows Script Component is a good way to do that. By turning your code into a component, you can use it as you would any other COM object. The Windows Script Component is packaged in an XML format, but there is an easy way to generate an XML skeleton, which we'll walk you through. We will also give you an overview on COM. Finally, we'll show you a Windows Script Component in action.

Like many developers, you probably have some complex scripts, or perhaps just a few functions, that you'd like to use in other scripts. You could copy and paste, but this just adds to the length and complexity of the new script. You could create your script as a Windows Script File and reference external scripts, but you might not need a WSF. One solution is to create your own Component Object Model (COM) object out of the reusable code, and use that new object in your script. You don't run a component like script, but rather instantiate the component within your script in the same way you instantiate an object like *WshShell*.

Understanding COM Objects, Methods, and Properties

Traditional COM programming is beyond the scope of this book, but we will provide a brief overview on the topic, which you might know more about than you realize.

Think of a COM object as a black box full of programming that accomplishes a set of related tasks. We don't need to know what's in the box, just how to use it. To use the code in the box, the programmer first assigns a name, or *progid*, to the object so he can tell WScript to create, or *instantiate*, an instance of that object. The programmer also assigns a globally unique identifier (*GUID*) called the *classid*. These values are stored in the registry when the object is registered on the computer.

Next, the programmer creates interfaces on the outside of the box to manipulate the code inside. You use these interfaces when you work with an object's properties or methods. A property is a value, such as the *Username* property of the *Wscript.Network* object. Some properties are read-only, but others you can change. Most COM objects also expose a method that calls internal code to perform a task, for example, to map a network drive. We aren't interested in the code that creates the drive mapping; it might be very complex. The COM object simplifies it and gives us an uncomplicated method; for example, *MapNetworkDrive*.

Typically, COM objects are compiled into a dynamic link library (.dll) file. This file must be registered on a computer before it can be used. The registration usually occurs as part of an application installation, but you can use regsvr32.exe to manually register a file. Type **regsvr32 /?** in a command prompt window to see the help information about this utility.

ActiveX, COM, and OLE

When you hear about ActiveX, it often brings to mind Internet Explorer ActiveX controls, but that is just a specific implementation. ActiveX actually refers to all of Microsoft's application component programming technologies, including OLE and COM. These technologies allow applications to share information.

OLE (Object Linking and Embedding) is a legacy approach. If you've ever embedded a Microsoft Excel spreadsheet in a Microsoft Word document, you used OLE. The OLE object connects the embedded spreadsheet to its application, Microsoft Excel.

COM was introduced in the early 1990s as part of Microsoft's approach to object-oriented programming. COM objects provide interfaces and communication mechanisms that programmers can manipulate to build larger applications. ActiveX is the latest incarnation of COM.

Understanding Windows Script Components

A Windows Script Component (WSC) file is a type of script file that can be used as a COM object in VBScript or JScript scripts. A script component takes complex code and provides a simpler interface. For example, you might have a subroutine that connects to a SQL database and returns information about a specific computer. With a script component, you can simplify the functionality by creating a COM object and utilizing the object's interfaces to execute the code.

The script component isn't a true COM object because it is not compiled. It is actually a specially formatted XML file that you can create and edit with any text or script editor. The WSC is used like a COM object, but the script component library, Scrobj.dll, does all the hard work of translating the WSC into standard COM interfaces. You don't have to worry about developing a complex, compiled COM object; you can just take advantage of COM features by using a WSC file.

The XML file consists of the following tags:

- The *package* tag is used much the same way it is used in a Windows Script File—as the wrapper tag. If you have only one component, this tag is optional; with multiple components, your file will start and end with *package* tags.

- The *component* tag, like the *job* tag in a Windows Script File, contains all the elements of your component. You can have more than one component in your file, but as a practical matter, we think you'll find it easier to have a single component per file. This tag has an *id* property that you should set.

  ```
  <component id="JDHIT.Demo">
  ```

  Setting this is required if you have more than one component or if you plan on generating a type library. We recommend making it the same as the script component's *progid*.

- The *?component* tag has *error* and *debug* flags that are set as either TRUE or FALSE. In production, COM objects, including WSC files, run silently. However, during development, you might want to use the *?component* tag to facilitate debugging and troubleshooting. If you set *error* to TRUE, script errors within the component file that generate messages will be displayed to the user. If you are using a script debugger, you can set *debug* to TRUE as well.

  ```
  <?component error="true" debug="false" ?>
  ```

  Notice the use of a question mark instead of a slash character to close the tag. Before putting your component into production, we recommend setting these flags to FALSE.

- The *registration* tag contains all the information needed to register your component. Even though all the tag properties are optional, from a practical standpoint, you really should define most of them.

  ```
  <registration progid="JDHDemo.WSC"
  classid="{443fdeb9-7d32-4331-b289-dd3b8da3d9d5}"
  description="JDHDemo" remotable="yes" version="1.00">
  </registration>
  ```

  The *registration* tag's properties include the following:

  - The *progid* property is the name you will use when you create an instance of the object in your script.

  - The *classid* property reflects the GUID of your new object. Don't just type in any number. You need to use a utility like uuidgen.exe or a script component wizard to generate a proper value.

❑ The *description* property is used in the registry to describe your object. You can see this value when you use a COM object browser. Keep this value short.

❑ The *remoteable* property is a Boolean flag that dictates whether the COM object can be instantiated on a remote system through Distributed COM (DCOM). The object must be installed and registered on the remote system before you can use it. When you create a remote instance, the script treats the object as though it were running locally. However, all properties and methods are executed from the remote system, depending on credentials and security settings.

❑ The *version* property is used for internal version information. This data is stored in the registry.

■ The *public* tag is used to identify the publicly available methods and properties of an object.

```
<public>
 <property name="size">
   <get/>
 </property>
 <property name="modified">
  <get/>
 </property>
 <property name="linecount">
   <get/>
 </property>
 <method name="view">
 </method>
</public>
```

■ The *event* tag is used to define events that you can call, or *fire*, from within your script component. An event is some action that occurs while the script is running, such as a file changing size. You define what that action is. When the action is detected, you fire the event. The fired event essentially raises a flag that something happened. You can add code to take further steps depending on the nature of the event. You must define the *name* property.

```
<event name="sizechanged"/>
```

■ The *script* tag has the same role as the tag with this name in a Windows Script File. The body of this tag contains all the functions and subroutines that are called to execute the object's properties and methods. The script code is hidden within the black box and exposed through the object's properties and methods.

> **Important**   Even though we talk about code being "hidden," we don't mean it literally. Unlike a traditional COM object that is compiled, a WSC file is plain text that anyone can view with a text editor. Don't hard-code administrator credentials, passwords, or any other information you don't want made public.

- The *object* tag, like the tag with this name in a WSF script, is used to make the external object globally available. Without this tag, you would have to use *CreateObject* throughout your script.

```
<object id=objFSO progid="Scripting.FileSystemObject"/>
```

- The *resource* tag, like the tag with this name in a WSF script, is used to define constants that you want to use throughout the component. The *id* property is used to identify the resource body in your script.

```
<resource id="version">JDHIT Demo v1.0</resource>
...
<script language="VBScript">
...
Function ShowVersion()
  strVer=getResource("version")
  ShowVersion=MsgBox(strVer,vbokonly+vbinformation,"Version")
End Function
...
```

- The *comment* tag is used within other script elements to provide comments or documentation.

```
<public>
  <comment>
   Get the file size of the specified file. Data returned is in bytes.
  </comment>
  <property name="size">
    <get/>
  </property>
</public>
```

Best Practices   We encourage you to use comment blocks liberally throughout your script component file. You might understand what every property and method is supposed to do right now, but you might not recall next year. In addition, comments make it easier for other people to understand and troubleshoot the file.

Listing 4-1 is a skeleton outline for a WSC file.

Listing 4-1 WSC Skeleton
```
<?XML version="1.0"?>
<package>
<?component error="true" debug="true"?>

    <comment>
        This skeleton shows how script component elements are
        assembled into a .wsc file.
    </comment>

<component id="MyScriptlet">
    <registration
```

```
        progid="progID"
        description="description"
        version="version"
        clsid=" {00000000-0000-0000-000000000000}" />

    <reference object="progID">

    <public>
        <property name="propertyname" />
        <method name="methodname" />
        <event name="eventname" />
    </public>

    <script language="VBScript">
        <![CDATA[
        dim propertyname
        Function methodname()
        ' Script here.
        End Function
        ]]>
    </script>

    <object id="objID" progId="some.object">
    <resource ID="resourceID1">string or number here</resource>
    <resource ID="resourceID2">string or number here</resource>
</component>
</package>
```

On the CD   You will find this script, as well as other scripts listed in this chapter, on the CD that accompanies this book.

Keep in mind that if your formatting is incorrect, the script component will fail. Fortunately, Microsoft offers a free utility called the Script Component Wizard that will create a framework on which to build your component. You can download the wizard at

http://www.microsoft.com/downloads/details.aspx?FamilyId=408024ED-FAAD-4835-8E68-773CCC951A6B&displaylang=en

On the CD   This link, like most of the links referenced in this book, is included on the companion CD. Click *Script Component Wizard*.

You can also search for information at the following Web site.

http://msdn.microsoft.com/scripting

Using the Script Component Wizard

The Script Component Wizard creates a WSC file in a user-specified location. It will prompt you for the names of properties, methods, and events to expose, and then create the appropriate registration information, including a GUID.

As an example, we will build a script component that will make it easier to work with a user object in Active Directory. We want an object that will get the user's distinct name, given the *sAMAccountName*, as well as the other way around. We'd also like to be able to set a user's password with a single line of code. Finally, we want to get the date when the user object was created, when it was last modified, and the organizational unit to which it belongs. We'll use the Script Component Wizard to build an XML skeleton. The wizard (scriptwz.exe) is installed by default in C:\Program Files\Microsoft Windows Script\Component Wizard.

In Figure 4-1, the wizard prompts us for information about the new WSC file.

Figure 4-1   Defining the script component

On Step 2 of the wizard, shown in Figure 4-2 on the next page, we specify component characteristics, such as scripting language and whether to enable error checking or debugging.

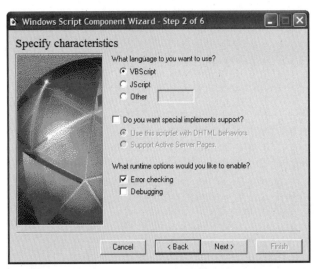

Figure 4-2   Defining script component characteristics

We now define the properties we want to expose. We will specify the names and type of our properties. The values we are returning from Active Directory are read-only, so that is the type we will select. Figure 4-3 shows all the options. Don't worry if you forget a property. You can always edit the file and add the appropriate XML tags later.

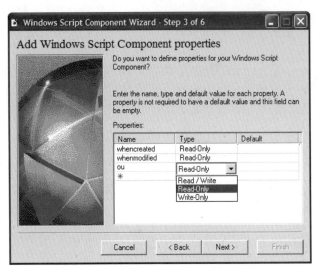

Figure 4-3   Defining script component properties

On Step 4 of the wizard, shown in Figure 4-4, we define the component's methods. We create a method called *getsam* that takes a variable called *strDN* as a parameter that returns the DN. The *getDN* method returns the *sam* for the passed DN. We also create a *changepassword* method.

Figure 4-4   Defining script component methods

If we had any events to add, we would define them on Step 5 of the wizard, as shown in Figure 4-5.

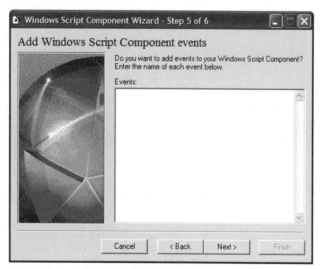

Figure 4-5   Defining script component events

The wizard's last step, shown in Figure 4-6 on the next page, is a summary of what we have specified. We can click Back to make any corrections, or click Finish to create the WSC file. Our finished WSC shell is shown in Listing 4-2, also on the next page.

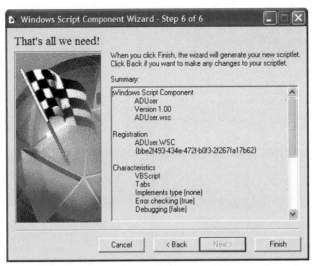

Figure 4-6   Finishing the Windows Script Component Wizard

Listing 4-2 Script Component Wizard Shell

```xml
<?xml version="1.0"?>
<component>

<?component error="true" debug="false"?>

<registration
  description="ADUser"
  progid="ADUser.WSC"
  version="1.00"
  classid="{bbe2f493-434e-472f-b0f3-2f267fa17b62}"
>
</registration>

<public>
  <property name="whencreated">
    <get/>
  </property>
  <property name="whenmodified">
    <get/>
  </property>
  <property name="ou">
    <get/>
  </property>
  <method name="getsam">
    <PARAMETER name="strDN"/>
  </method>
  <method name="getdn">
    <PARAMETER name="strSAM"/>
  </method>
  <method name="changepassword">
    <PARAMETER name="strSAM"/>
    <PARAMETER name="strPassword"/>
```

```
      <PARAMETER name="BlnChangeNextLogon"/>
   </method>
</public>

<script language="VBScript">
<![CDATA[

dim whencreated
dim whenmodified
dim ou

function get_whencreated()
   get_whencreated = whencreated
end function

function get_whenmodified()
   get_whenmodified = whenmodified
end function

function get_ou()
   get_ou = ou
end function

function getsam(strDN)
   getsam = "Temporary Value"
end function

function getdn(strSAM)
   getdn = "Temporary Value"
end function

function changepassword(strSAM,strPassword,BlnChangeNextLogon)
   changepassword = "Temporary Value"
end function

]]>
</script>

</component>
```

All that remains is to add documentation comments and the VBScript code that will execute our functions.

Working with Properties

In a WSC, you can work with properties in two ways. First, you can have a simple, preset property name defined like this.

```
<property name="user" />
```

In the script section, you can then define values for this property, assuming you defined the property as read/write.

```
<script language="VBScript">
<![CDATA[
'define user property
User="Test User 98"
...
```

The other way to work with properties is to return a value from a function. In Listing 4-2, the property values are calculated by functions.

```
<property name="whencreated">
  <get/>
</property>
...
function get_whencreated()
  get_whencreated = whencreated
end function
```

The Script Component Wizard produces an outline. We need to develop the script code in the functions and modify the property tags. For the *whencreated* property, we will enter a user's distinct name as a parameter. We can modify the property element to reflect this change, and update the function with the necessary code.

```
<property name="whencreated">
  <get/>
</property>
...
Function get_whencreated(strDN)
On Error Resume Next
  Set objUser=GetObject("LDAP://" & strDN)
  If Err.Number<>0 Then
  get_whencreated="Not Found"
  Else
  get_whencreated = ObjUser.whencreated
  End If
end Function
```

We add *strDN* as a parameter for the function. You probably also noticed the *get* tag. This tag identifies the property as read-only. To make a property read/write, add a *put* tag. These actions, *get* and *put*, are standard COM commands for dealing with properties. You'll notice that the associated function for the *whencreated* property is *get_whencreated*. This helps us remember that we are reading a property value.

> **Tip**   The *get* tag can use an attribute called *internalname*. You can use the *internalname* attribute for the name of an internal function.
>
> ```
> <property name="size">
>   <get internalname="readsize"/>
> </property>
> ...
> Function readsize(strFile)
>   'function code here to read file size
>   readsize="some value"
> End function
> ```
>
> If you don't specify an internal name, the associated function will use the property name. You should use an internal name for longer or more complex WSC files to make it easy to remember what a particular function is supposed to do. The *name* attribute of the *property* tag is for the user. You might want to use something simpler and more meaningful for internal use.

Working with Methods

Using methods in a WSC file is very similar to working with properties. Generally, the method name is the name of a function or subroutine that is executed. You can also use the *internalname* attribute if you want to use a different name for the function or subroutine.

```
<method name="changepassword">
  <PARAMETER name="strSAM"/>
  <PARAMETER name="strPassword"/>
  <PARAMETER name="BlnChangeNextLogon"/>
</method>
function changepassword(strSAM,strPassword,BlnChangeNextLogon)
  'code to run goes here
  changepassword = "Temporary Value"
end function
```

The *changepassword* method in this example requires three parameters. Anyone who uses this object needs to know what the parameters are to use the method. You can document this information within the WSC file, or you can generate a type library. If you want to generate a type library for your WSC file, you must add the *parameter* tags for the method.

Type Libraries

A type library provides information about an object's automation properties and methods. Type libraries are included with most good script editors and are used by COM object browsers so you can learn how to use an object. If your script editor offers Intellisense, the type library is used to populate the Intellisense drop-down menus with object information. Some script editors, like PrimalScript, will generate the type library for you when you right-click the component and click Generate Type Library. You can also right-click the WSC file in Windows Explorer and click Generate Type Library. There are a few other methods; see the Windows Script Component section of the Windows Script Host documentation for more information.

Working with Events

Depending on your component, you might want to include support for events. An event is an action such as a window closing, or a change in state like a saved file. In a WSC file, you determine what the event is and when to call it. An event is defined within the public section along with properties and methods.

```
<event name="UserAdded" />
```

You use the *fireevent* method to fire the event in your WSC code. For example, you might have a method called *AddUser*, and you want to fire the *UserAdded* event when this method is completed.

```
<method name="adduser" internalname="NewUser">
  <parameter name=""strSAM"/>
</method>
<script language="VBScript">
<![CDATA[

function NewUser(strSAM)
  'code to create to new user goes here
  fireEvent "UserAdded"
End function
]]>
</script>
```

The WSC file doesn't do anything with the event other than define and fire it. The script using the object determines what to do, if anything. To facilitate this decision, include a *sink* in the script that is connected to the event. A sink is an object that attracts external interactions, much like a kitchen sink attracts water. The sink waits for something to happen, and when it does, it is contacted by external sources. This is part of DCOM programming, but you don't have to know much more than that. When the event fires, the code in the sink is executed. You might have something like this.

```
Dim objWSC
Set objWSC=CreateObject("MyObject.wsc","sink_")
objWSC.AddUser("jhicks")
'insert other code here
Wscript.disconnectObject objWSC
wscript.quit
Function sink_UserAdded()
  MsgBox "A new user was added."
End function
```

When you instantiate the object, you also define a prefix that is tied to the event name. These actions create the sink. When the event fires, the code in the corresponding function or subroutine, in this example *obj_UserAdded*, is executed. Events are useful because they can occur at any time in the script. You can start a long process, run other code, and wait for the event to happen. However, if you exit the script before the event fires, you'll never know if it fired. If you want the event code sink to run, you'll need to add code that prevents the script from ending until the event occurs. One way of doing this is to create a message box. As long as you don't dismiss the message box, the script is running. After the event fires, you can dismiss the message box and exit the script.

You can also have an event return information by defining one or more parameters.

```
<event name="UserAdded">
  <parameter name="strSAM">
  <parameter name="strDN">
</event>
```

When you call *fireevent*, you pass the parameters at that time.

```
function NewUser(strSAM)
  'code to create to new user goes here
  'code to define strDN
  fireEvent "UserAdded",strSAM,strDN
End function
```

You can then use this information in your sink code.

```
Function sink_UserAdded(strSAM,strDN)
  MsgBox "User " & strSAM & " is " & strDN & "."
End function
```

We don't have any events in our ADUser.wsc example, but the finished file is shown in Listing 4-3.

Listing 4-3 ADUser.wsc

```
<?xml version="1.0" ?>
<component>
  <?component error="true" debug="false" ?>
  <registration progid="ADUser.WSC"
  classid="{bbe2f493-434e-472f-b0f3-2f267fa17b62}"
  description="ADUser" version="1.00">
  </registration>
  <public>
    <property name="whencreated">
      <get/>
    </property>
    <property name="whenmodified">
      <get/>
    </property>
    <property name="ou">
      <get/>
    </property>
    <method name="getsam">
      <parameter name="strDN"/>
    </method>
    <method name="getdn">
      <parameter name="strSAM"/>
    </method>
```

```
    <method name="changepassword">
      <parameter name="strUser"/>
      <parameter name="strPassword"/>
      <parameter name="blnChangeNextLogon"/>
    </method>
  </public>
  <object id="cmd" progid="ADODB.Command" events="true" reference="false"/>
  <object id="conn" progid="ADODB.Connection" events="true" reference="false"/>
  <script language="VBScript">
<![CDATA[
dim whencreated
dim whenmodified
dim ou

Function get_whencreated(strDN)
On Error Resume Next
  Set objUser=GetObject("LDAP://" & strDN)
  If Err.Number<>0 Then
    get_whencreated="Not Found"
  Else
    get_whencreated = ObjUser.whencreated
  End If
end Function

function get_whenmodified(strDN)
On Error Resume Next
 Set objUser=GetObject("LDAP://" & strDN)
  If Err.Number<>0 Then
    get_whenmodified="Not Found"
  Else
    get_whenmodified = ObjUser.whenchanged
  End If
end function

function get_ou(strSAM)
On Error Resume Next
strDN=getdn(strSAM)
Set objUser=GetObject("LDAP://" & strDN)
  If Err.Number<>0 Then
     get_ou="Not Found"
     Exit function
  Else
    strParent=objUser.Parent
    set objParent=GetObject(strParent)
    get_ou=objParent.name
  End If

end function

function getsam(strDN)
On Error Resume Next
Set RootDSE=GetObject("LDAP://RootDSE")
Set myDomain=GetObject("LDAP://"&RootDSE.get("DefaultNamingContext"))
```

```
strQuery="Select SAMAccountname,cn,distinguishedname from '" & _
myDomain.AdsPath & "' where objectcategory='person' AND objectclass=" _
"'user'" & " AND distinguishedname='" & strDN & "'"

set cat=GetObject("GC:")
for each obj In cat
  set GC=obj
Next

conn.Provider="ADSDSOObject"
conn.Open "Active Directory Provider"
cmd.ActiveConnection=conn
cmd.Properties("Page Size") = 100
cmd.Properties("asynchronous")=True
cmd.Properties("Timeout") =30
cmd.Properties("Cache Results") = False
cmd.CommandText=strQuery

set RS=cmd.Execute

Do While not RS.EOF
  GetSAM=rs.Fields("samAccountname")
  rs.movenext
Loop

If GetSAM="" Then GetSAM="Not Found"

rs.Close
conn.Close

end function

function getdn(strSAM)
On Error Resume Next
Set RootDSE=GetObject("LDAP://RootDSE")
Set myDomain=GetObject("LDAP://"&RootDSE.get("DefaultNamingContext"))

strQuery="Select SAMAccountname,cn,distinguishedname from '" & _
myDomain.AdsPath & "' where objectcategory='person' AND objectclass=" _
"'user'" & " AND SAMAccountName='" & strSAM & "'"

set cat=GetObject("GC:")
for each obj In cat
  set GC=obj
Next

conn.Provider="ADSDSOObject"
conn.Open "Active Directory Provider"
cmd.ActiveConnection=conn
cmd.Properties("Page Size") = 100
cmd.Properties("asynchronous")=True
cmd.Properties("Timeout") =30
cmd.Properties("Cache Results") = False
cmd.CommandText=strQuery

set RS=cmd.Execute
```

```
Do While not RS.EOF
  GetDN=rs.Fields("distinguishedname")
  rs.movenext
Loop

If GetDN="" Then GetDN="Not Found"

rs.Close
conn.Close

end Function

function changepassword(strSAM,strPassword,BlnChangeNextLogon)
'returns TRUE if successful
On Error Resume Next
strDN=getdn(strSAM)
Set objUser=GetObject("LDAP://" & strDN)
If Err.number<>0 Then
  changepassword=MsgBox("Failed to find user " & _
  strSAM,vbOKOnly+vbInformation,"Change Password Error")
  changepassword=False
  Exit Function
else
  objUser.setPassword strPassword
  objUser.SetInfo
  If Err.Number<>0 Then
    strMsg="Failed to set password For " & strSAM & VbCrLf & _
    "Error #" & Err.Number & " " & Err.Description
    MsgBox strMsg,vbOKOnly+vbCritical,"Password Failure"
    changepassword=False
    Exit Function
  Else
    If BlnChangeNextLogon then
      objUser.put "pwdLastSet", 0
      objUser.SetInfo
    End If
  changepassword = True
  End If
End If

end Function

]]>
  </script>
</component>
```

Creating a Windows Script Component with a Script Editor

The Script Component Wizard is not the only way to create a WSC file. Some commercial script editors such as OnScript by XLNow and PrimalScript by SAPIEN include their own versions of the Script Component Wizard. Editors also have their own approaches to editing a WSC file. Let's walk through the PrimalScript 4.0 wizard.

Figure 4-7 displays the first page of the wizard, in which we define our script location.

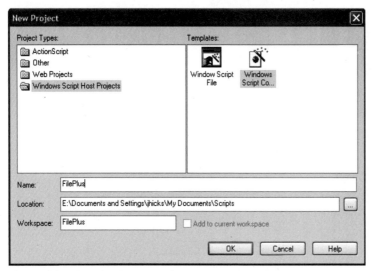

Figure 4-7   Creating a new project

On the wizard's next page, shown in Figure 4-8, we fill in some general information about the component such as name, location, and primary script language.

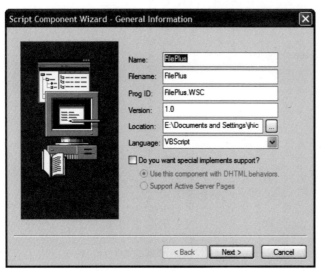

Figure 4-8   Filling in general information

On the wizard's next page, we are prompted to specify the objects we want to include, shown in Figure 4-9. PrimalScript offers a list of commonly used objects, and you can click Browse to add any other registered object.

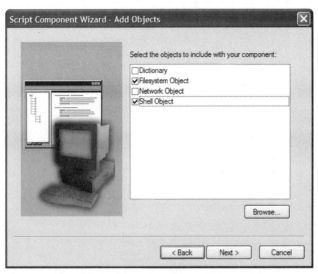

Figure 4-9   Adding objects

If we want to add any references, we can do so on the wizard's next page, shown in Figure 4-10.

Figure 4-10   Adding references

On the wizard's next page, shown in Figure 4-11, we can add any function libraries or other scripts.

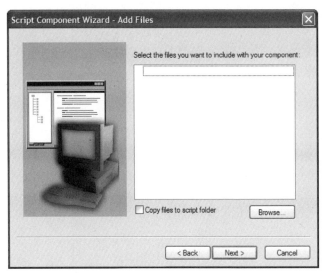

Figure 4-11   Adding files

The wizard's last page is a summary, shown in Figure 4-12.

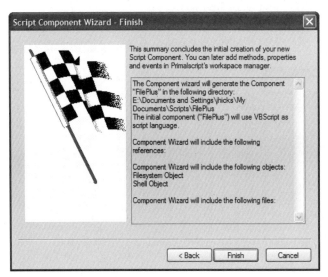

Figure 4-12   Wizard summary

PrimalScript opens the file in a workspace, much the same way it handles WSF script. The editor masks all the XML code and leaves the main editing pane open for your VBScript. To add methods and properties, right-click Interface in the left pane, and click the appropriate menu choice, as shown in Figure 4-13 on the next page.

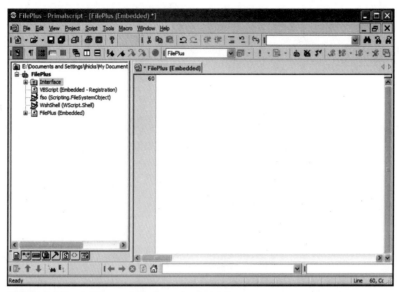

Figure 4-13 Adding methods and properties

In Figure 4-14, we add and define a property. In this example, the internal and external names are different. The external name will be used in the generated type library, so it is more user friendly. We'll use the internal name for our functions.

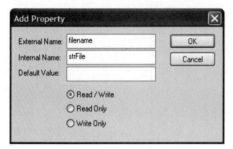

Figure 4-14 Adding a property

We follow a similar process in Figure 4-15 to add methods to the script file.

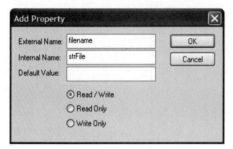

Figure 4-15 Adding a method

After you add the component's methods, properties, and events, all you need to do is write the underlying code. When you are finished, right-click the component in the left pane, and register the component. PrimalScript will also generate a type library. Now your component is ready to use. The finished script component is in Listing 4-4.

Listing 4-4 FilePlus.wsc

```
<?xml version="1.0" ?>
<package>
    <comment>
    Use this component for easy file operations such as returning
    file size and modified date. Includes functions to return linecount,
    the first X number of lines in the file or the last X number of
    lines in the file. Also a view method to open the file in Notepad.
    </comment>
    <component id="FilePlus">
        <?component error="true" debug="false" ?>
        <registration progid="FilePlus.WSC"
        classid="{DB619F63-768F-4746-BCDC-88F5DA1EBB42}"
        description="FilePlus" remotable="no" version="1.0">
            <script language="VBScript">
<![CDATA[
                Function Register()
                    Dim TypeLib
                    Set TypeLib = CreateObject("Scriptlet.TypeLib")
                    TypeLib.AddURL "FilePlus.WSC"
                    TypeLib.Path = "FilePlus.tlb"
                    TypeLib.Doc = "FilePlus"
                    TypeLib.Name = "FilePlus.tlb"
                    TypeLib.MajorVersion = 1
                    TypeLib.MinorVersion = 0
                    TypeLib.Write
                End Function

                Function Unregister()

                End Function

]]>
            </script>
        </registration>
        <public>
            <property internalname="strFile" name="filename">
                <get/>
                <put/>
            </property>
            <property name="linecount">
                <get/>
            </property>
            <property internalname="readsize" name="size">
                <get/>
            </property>
            <property internalname="readmodified" name="modified">
                <get/>
```

```
                </property>
                <method name="view">
                </method>
                <method name="head">
                    <parameter name="numLines"/>
                </method>
                <method name="tail">
                    <parameter name="numLines"/>
                </method>
        </public>
<object id="objFSO" progid="Scripting.FileSystemObject"
events="false" reference="TRUE"/>
<object id="objShell" progid="WScript.Shell" events="false" reference="TRUE"/>
        <script id="FilePlus" language="VBScript">
<![CDATA[

Dim linecount
dim strFile
Dim readsize
Dim readmodified

strFile = 0
linecount = 0
readsize = 0
readmodified = 0

Function get_strFile()
    get_strFile = strFile
End Function

Function put_strFile(newValue)
    strFile = newValue
End Function

Function view()
On Error Resume Next
'open file in Notepad

If objFSO.FileExists(strFile) Then
    view = objShell.Run("Notepad " & strFile,1,False)
Else
    view=MsgBox("File " & strFile & " not found!",vbOKOnly+vbCritical,"Error!")
End If
End Function

Function get_linecount()
On Error Resume Next
If objFSO.FileExists(strFile) Then
    Set objFile=objFSO.OpenTextFile(strFile,ForReading)
    i=0
    Do While objFile.AtEndOfStream<>True
        objFile.ReadLine
        i=i+1
    Loop
    objFile.Close
```

```
        get_linecount=i
Else
        get_linecount =0
End If
End Function


Function get_readsize()
On Error Resume Next
If objFSO.FileExists(strFile) Then
        Set objFile=objFSO.GetFile(strFile)
        get_readsize = objFile.size
Else
        get_readsize=0
End If
        'get_readsize = readsize
End Function


function get_readmodified()
On Error Resume Next
If objFSO.FileExists(strFile) Then
        Set objFile=objFSO.GetFile(strFile)
        get_readmodified = objFile.DateLastModified
Else
        get_readmodified=0
End If
end function

function head(numLines)
On Error Resume Next
'Display X number of lines from beginning of file
If objFSO.FileExists(strFile) Then
        Set objFile=objFSO.OpenTextFile(strFile,ForReading)
        i=0
        Do While i<numLines
                strData=strData & objFile.ReadLine & VbCrLf
                i=i+1
        Loop
        objFile.Close
        head = strData
Else
        head=MsgBox("File " & strFile & _
 " not found!",vbOKOnly+vbCritical,"Error!")
End If
end Function

function tail(numLines)
On Error Resume Next
If objFSO.FileExists(strFile) Then
        Set objFile=objFSO.OpenTextFile(strFile,ForReading)
        strText=objFile.ReadAll
        objFile.Close
        tmpArray=Split(strText,VbCrLf)
        iCount=get_linecount()
```

```
    iLimit=iCount-numLines
    For x= iLimit To iCount
        strData=strData & tmpArray(x) & VbCrLf
    Next
    tail = strData
Else
    tail=MsgBox("File " & strFile & _
    " not found!",vbOKOnly+vbCritical,"Error!")
End If

end Function
]]>
        </script>
    </component>
</package>
```

Viewing a Windows Script Component in Action

Let's go through the FilePlus component and see it in action. The first thing to look at is the comment section, which gives a broad overview of the component's functionality.

```
<comment>
Use this component for easy file operations such as returning
file size and modified date. Includes functions to return linecount,
the first X number of lines in the file or the last X number of
lines in the file. Also a view method to open the file in Notepad.
</comment>
```

The name of the component is FilePlus and it will be registered as FilePlus.WSC.

```
<component id="FilePlus">
<?component error="true" debug="false" ?>
<registration progid="FilePlus.WSC"
classid="{DB619F63-768F-4746-BCDC-88F5DA1EBB42}"
description="FilePlus" remotable="no" version="1.0">
```

The component has a read/write property called *filename* and read-only properties called *linecount*, *size*, and *modified*.

```
<property internalname="strFile" name="filename">
    <get/>
    <put/>
</property>
<property name="linecount">
    <get/>
</property>
<property internalname="readsize" name="size">
    <get/>
</property>
<property internalname="readmodified" name="modified">
    <get/>
</property>
```

Notice that *size* and *modified* have internal names defined because we want a friendly name for the external property name, and a more meaningful name for internal use.

The component has three methods, *view*, *head*, and *tail*. The last two methods require a parameter to indicate the number of lines of text to return.

```
<method name="view">
</method>
<method name="head">
  <parameter name="numLines"/>
</method>
<method name="tail">
  <parameter name="numLines"/>
</method>
```

Because we are relying on the *Scripting.FileSystemObject* so much, it makes sense to define it with an *object* tag at the beginning of the component. After it is included, we won't have to define it in every function. We will do the same thing with *WshShell* object.

```
<object id="objFSO" progid="Scripting.FileSystemObject" events="false" reference="TRUE"/>
<object id="objShell" progid="WScript.Shell" events="false" reference="TRUE"/>
```

The rest of the component is the VBScript that supports the properties and methods. Each property and method has its own function. We won't go through the details of each function, but we do want to point out that the external name is *filename*, and the internal name is the more meaningful *strName*. Also, if you are reusing code with the *strName* variable, as we did here, you don't have to modify anything.

After the code is complete and the component is registered, it's time to use the component in a script. The script in Listing 4-5 on the next page is a short demonstration of how the File-Plus.wsc component is used.

> **Note**   You must register a script component before you can use it. Do this by right-clicking the component in Windows Explorer, and clicking Register. Some scripting editors also offer a shortcut menu command. You can also register a component by running Regsvr32 mycomponent.wsc. You'll need to use the full path to the file. Registering the component makes it available through the registry. If you add or remove any properties, method, or events, you must un-register the component and re-register it for the changes to take effect. There is an Unregister switch you can use with Regsvr32. The syntax is *regsvr32 /u mycomponent.wsc*. By the way, you don't have to un-register and re-register your component when you modify the underlying VBScript, only when the component's structure changes. Remember, the component file must be copied and registered on any computer where you intend to use it.

Listing 4-5 FilePlusDemo.vbs

```vbs
'Use CSCRIPT
Dim objFP
Set objFP=CreateObject("fileplus.wsc")
objFP.filename=InputBox("What file do you want to look at?","FilePlus","c:\boot.ini")

strData="Properties for " & objFP.filename & vbcrlf
strData=strData & "modified: " & objFP.modified & vbcrlf
strData=strData & "size: " & objFP.size & " bytes" & VbCrLf

strData=strData & "#lines: " & objFP.linecount

WScript.Echo strData
WScript.Echo String(10,"*")
iHead=CInt(InputBox("How many lines do you want to see from head?","FilePlus",5))

'view first 5 lines of file
strHead=objFP.head(iHead)
WScript.Echo strHead
WScript.Echo String(10,"*")

iTail=CInt(InputBox("How many lines do you want to see from tail?","FilePlus",5))

'view last 5 lines of file
strTail=objFP.tail(iTail)
WScript.Echo strTail

rc=MsgBox("Do you want to view file?",vbYesNo+vbQuestion,"FilePlus")

'open file in Notepad
if rc=vbYes Then objFP.view

WScript.Quit
```

The component can be used like any other object. We instantiate an object by using the *CreateObject* method. Use the component's registered name for the *progid*.

```vbs
Set objFP=CreateObject("fileplus.wsc")
```

This object needs to have a filename defined for all the other properties and methods to work. In Listing 4-5, we set the object's *filename* property to a prompted value by using the *InputBox* function.

```vbs
objFP.filename=InputBox("What file do you want to look at?","FilePlus","c:\boot.ini")
```

The *internalname* variable, *strFile*, has this same value and will be used in the functions when necessary. With this variable defined, we can get the *size*, *modified*, and *linecount* properties and display the results.

```
strData="Properties for " & objFP.filename & vbcrlf
strData=strData & "modified: " & objFP.modified & vbcrlf
strData=strData & "size: " & objFP.size & " bytes" & VbCrLf
strData=strData & "#lines: " & objFP.linecount
WScript.Echo strData
```

When the object's property is invoked, a function is called to return a value. For example, to get the *modified* property, this function is called.

```
function get_readmodified()
On Error Resume Next
If objFSO.FileExists(strFile) Then
  Set objFile=objFSO.GetFile(strFile)
  get_readmodified = objFile.DateLastModified
Else
  get_readmodified=0
End If
end function
```

Here is another instance in which we use different names for the internal and external property. The function name, *get_readmodified*, reflects that we are reading a property value, although in actuality we are calculating the value with VBScript and the file system object. This function is essentially a wrapper for the file system object, and it returns the file's *datelast-modified* property.

To use the object's *head* and *tail* methods, we need a value for the number of lines to read. The sample script prompts the user.

```
iHead=CInt(InputBox("How many lines do you want to see" & _
" from head?","FilePlus",5))
```

Because the *head* method returns data, we'll set it to a variable and display the results.

```
strHead=objFP.head(iHead)
WScript.Echo strHead
```

The same process holds true for the *tail* method.

```
iTail=CInt(InputBox("How many lines do you want to see" & _
" from tail?","FilePlus",5))
```

```
strTail=objFP.tail(iTail)
WScript.Echo strTail
```

The last method, *view*, opens the file in Notepad if the user running the script so chooses.

```
rc=MsgBox("Do you want to view file?",vbYesNo+vbQuestion,"FilePlus")
'open file in Notepad
if rc=vbYes Then objFP.view
```

We could have defined the method to get the specified number of lines, or to view the entire file and display the results in a popup window, Notepad, or Internet Explorer. That's the benefit of this technique—you can hide complex code in a Windows Script Component. The scripts that use the component only have to deal with simple properties and methods.

Summary

In this chapter, we showed you how to create your own COM objects by creating a Windows Script Component. Using a WSC file, you can take existing code that accomplishes a specific task and package it as part of a component. This component is utilized in your administrative scripts and simplifies script development. We demonstrated how to use the Windows Script Component Wizard as well as outlined the benefits of using a script editor to develop script components. Finally, we showed you how a WSC operates and how to use it in a script. Windows Script Components take time to develop and deploy, but the power, flexibility, and ease they provide make them well worth the effort.

Chapter 5

HTML Applications: Scripts with a User Interface

HTML applications (HTAs) combine the flexibility of a Web page with the functional power of VBScript. With HTAs, you can build scripts that look and feel in many respects like Windows applications, but without needing to learn a complex language like VB.NET or use a complex development tool like Microsoft Visual Studio. We'll show you a step-by-step conversion method to take an existing VBScript and wrap it in an HTA, turning it into a graphical script.

A regular VBScript doesn't offer much in the way of user interface elements—the *MsgBox* and *InputBox* functions are nearly the limit of what VBScript offers intrinsically, and that's not a lot. Sometimes, you might want to create a script that includes more robust user interface elements, perhaps offering users a way of entering data into a Windows-style dialog box. You might want to produce formatted output, such as a status report. Many third-party products can give you this kind of flexibility, but Windows offers a built-in option: HTML applications (HTA).

Understanding HTML Applications

An HTA is a type of HTML page that combines standard HTML elements and formatting with VBScript. HTAs are executed by Mshta.exe, an executable file that's a core part of the Microsoft Windows operating system. Mshta.exe instantiates Microsoft Internet Explorer's

HTML rendering engine (even if Internet Explorer is not the user's default Web browser) and allows Internet Explorer to display the page and execute its scripts. This arrangement has some distinct differences from both Web pages and regular Windows scripting.

- The usual Internet Explorer security model doesn't apply to HTAs. HTAs can instantiate ActiveX controls and other Component Object Model (COM) objects, such as the *FileSystemObject* object, without displaying warning messages to the user. Typically, Internet Explorer will only execute HTAs that are located on the hard drive of the user's computer. Internet Explorer displays warnings when downloading an HTA from the Internet because HTAs can bypass most of the security features built into Internet Explorer. This security bypass allows an HTA to behave more like a Windows application—which typically has few restrictions on what it can do—than a Web page.

- You have much more control over the appearance of the window. Unlike a standard Web page, where Internet Explorer usually displays several toolbars, an address bar, a menu, and so forth, you decide which elements an HTA displays. To make the HTA look more like a Windows application than a Web page, you'd hide all the Internet Explorer user interface elements such as toolbars and menus. (These elements are collectively referred to as *chrome* by developers.) You can also specify the text that appears in the window's title bar, whether it has standard minimized and maximize buttons, and even whether the application icon is displayed in the title bar and the Windows taskbar.

- Because the script is executed by Mshta.exe rather than wscript.exe or cscript.exe, you won't have intrinsic access to the WScript objects, as you would in a ordinary VBScript. In other words, you won't be able to use methods like *WScript.Echo*. However, in an HTA, most of the intrinsic WScript properties and methods are replaced by something more suitable for a graphical application. You can, for example, use VBScript's built-in *MsgBox* statement to display simple pop-up dialog boxes within your HTA.

> **Note**   By default, the HTA filename extension is associated with Mshta.exe, which allows Windows to automatically execute HTAs when you double-click them. Some corporate environments, however, might modify or remove this filename extension association, so HTAs won't execute when you double-click them. If that's the case, you can manually execute Mshta.exe, passing it the name of the HTA as a command-line argument.

You might have already run an HTA without realizing it because they can look almost exactly like a "real" Windows application. For example, the Microsoft Scripting Guys' Scriptomatic tool, shown in Figure 5-1, is an HTA, yet it has the look and feel of a traditional Windows application.

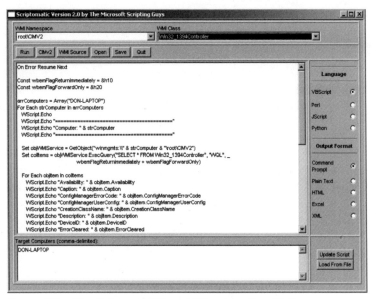

Figure 5-1   The Scriptomatic is an HTA written in VBScript.

If you haven't run an HTA before, download the Scriptomatic and try it out. You'll get a better feel for how an HTA works and what it can look like. Then open the HTA in a script editor (or Microsoft Notepad, if you don't have a script editor) and see how VBScript and HTML work together to make the HTA function. You can download the Scriptomatic at

http://www.microsoft.com/technet/scriptcenter/tools/scripto2.mspx

On the CD   This link, like most of the links referenced in this book, is included in the Links folder on the companion CD. Click *Scriptomatic 2.0.*

The following are some specific points to notice about the Scriptomatic.

- The window's title bar is customized. Notice that the window's icon isn't the standard Internet Explorer icon, but rather the default icon used by Mshta.exe. The authors could have specified a custom icon, but that icon graphic would have to have been distributed along with the HTA itself.

- The HTA can be distributed simply by copying the HTA file. Try copying it to another computer and running it, and it should work fine. As a Web site download, the Scriptomatic is packaged in an installer, but that's mainly because some corporate firewalls block the downloading of HTA files for security reasons. (Remember, HTAs bypass the Internet Explorer security model.) Because you'll usually be creating and using HTAs entirely on your intranet (or even just on your own computer), you won't need to create an installer.

- The HTA uses standard Windows user interface elements such as drop-down list boxes, radio buttons, and so forth. These elements can be dynamically changed at run time. Notice how the WMI Class drop-down list populates itself after you select an item from the WMI Namespace drop-down list.

- The HTA is built with HTML. For example, the entire page layout is contained within an HTML table, which is how the dividing lines between the various sections were created (they're just table borders).

If looking at the Scriptomatic HTA in a script editor is confusing, don't worry! This HTA was written by gurus who practically do it for a living. We'll be working with much simpler techniques to generate HTAs, and we'll walk you through it step-by-step. Before we get started with the essentials of creating a new HTA, however, we need to spend a little time reviewing some background material.

Our earlier statement that HTAs bypass most of the security restrictions in Internet Explorer might seem alarming, but you shouldn't worry. First, strictly speaking, HTAs don't run in Internet Explorer. Internet Explorer is actually composed of several distinct parts. One part provides the visual user interface: the window's title bar, the toolbars, the spinning *e* icon, and so forth. Another part is the HTML rendering engine, which interprets text-based HTML instructions and creates the final, fully laid-out page. That engine is instantiated within the Internet Explorer application, making the two work as a single unit. Other applications also instantiate the rendering engine—you've no doubt run across a few Microsoft Management Console (MMC) snap-ins that display HTML. They use the Internet Explorer HTML rendering engine. HTAs are executed by Mshta.exe, which also instantiates the Internet Explorer HTML rendering engine. It might seem like whether or not Internet Explorer runs HTAs is a tiny detail, but it's an important one.

From a security standpoint, HTAs will usually only execute without warning if they're launched from the local computer or from a Web site that's in the Internet Explorer trusted security zone. HTAs downloaded from other Web sites are treated as executables, so Internet Explorer will display the appropriate warning dialog boxes, and typically prompt the user to save, rather than to directly execute, the HTA. Many commercial firewalls that include software-filtering capabilities will filter HTAs right along with executables, which is perfectly reasonable because the two application types can have similar capabilities and risks. In short, you should probably think of HTAs as equal to regular executables in terms of both functionality and security risks. Windows treats them as such, so you're as protected from rogue HTAs as you are from rogue executables.

Understanding the Internet Explorer Document Object Model

When you're working with an HTA, you can write VBScript that interacts with and modifies the HTML content of the application. You can see this interaction in the Scriptomatic. As you click buttons or make selections, the HTA responds by changing its content. List boxes are populated with new choices, text boxes fill with script code, and so forth–all in response to your interaction with the HTA's interactive elements. All the visual elements within an HTA are defined by HTML code, or *tags*. Let's look at the Scriptomatic (version 2) again for a demonstration. (If you haven't already downloaded this handy tool, do so now.)

Notice that the user interface includes buttons labeled *Run*, *CIMv2*, and so forth. Examining the HTML code–use Notepad if you don't have an HTML or script editor–you'll find the following code.

```
    <tr>
        <td VALIGN=TOP WIDTH=700 COLSPAN=2>
            <table BORDER=0>
                <tr>
                    <td><input id=runbutton  class="button" type="button" value="Run"
name="run_button"  onClick="RunScript()"></td>
                    <td><input id=cimv2button  class="button" type="button" value="CIMv2"
name="cimv2_button"  onClick="SetNamespaceToCIMV2()"></td>
                    <td><input id=wmisourcebutton class="wmibutton" type="button" value="WMI Source"
name="wmisource_button" onClick="SetWMIRepository()" title="Change computer used for WMI
namespace and class information"></td>
                    <td><input id=openbutton class="button" type="button" value="Open"
name="open_button" onClick="OpenScript()"></td>
                    <td><input id=savebutton class="button" type="button" value="Save"
name="save_button" onClick="SaveScript()"></td>
                    <td><input id=quitbutton class="button" type="button" value="Quit"
name="quit_button" onClick="QuitScript()"></td>
                </tr>
            </table>
        </td>
    </tr>
```

> **Note** These long lines of code will look a lot better in an editor like Notepad, Microsoft FrontPage, or SAPIEN PrimalScript, where they won't wrap to multiple lines. However, HTML doesn't differentiate between wrapped and unwrapped lines, so even if you typed this exactly as it's shown in this book, it would still work.

Take a look at the six *<input>* tags. Each tag defines a button. The button labels are contained in the value attribute of each tag. Each button also has an *id* and a *name* attribute, which allow the buttons to be uniquely identified.

Understanding the HTML Document Hierarchy

In the sample code just shown, the buttons' tags are nested within several other tags. (This is much easier to see in an HTML editor.) Each *<input>* tag is contained within a *<td>* tag, which defines a table cell. The *<td>* tags are nested within a *<tr>* tag, which defines a table row. The *<tr>*tag is nested within a *<table>* tag that, as you might guess, defines a table. All the tags that comprise the page are contained within a *<body>* tag that itself is contained within a top-level *<html>* tag. All this nesting forms a hierarchy of tags. An editing environment like SAPIEN PrimalScript 4 (*http://www.primalscript.com*) displays this hierarchy in a tree view, as shown in Figure 5-2.

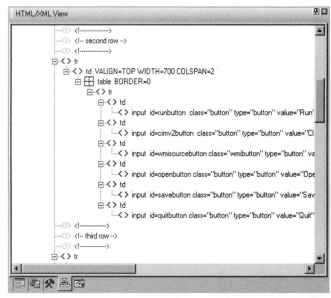

Figure 5-2   The hierarchy of the HTML tags

This hierarchy forms the Internet Explorer Document Object Model (DOM). The DOM provides a way to programmatically work with complex, hierarchical documents in HTML format by defining relationships between the tags. In our example, you can say that each of the *<td>* tags are parents of the *<input>* tags; conversely, the *<input>* tags are children of the *<td>* tags. The *<td>* tags, in turn, are children of the *<tr>* tag, and are siblings of the other *<td>* tags (meaning they have the same parent tag). If you think of tags as programming objects—like the Component Object Model (COM) objects you've worked with before—the following would be true.

- Each tag has a *parentElement* property, which refers to that tag's parent tag.

- Each tag has a *children* collection, which refers to any child tags.

- Each tag has an *innerHTML* property, which refers to any HTML text contained within the tag. For example, the *<tr>* tag would have an *innerHTML* property that includes everything between *<tr>* tags.

HTML tags are treated as programmable objects that have these, and other, properties and collections. The various attributes of an HTML tag—such as the *value* attribute of the *<input>* tags—are also exposed as properties. That means that you can, for example, change the label of the Run button simply by writing script that modifies the button's *value* property.

To make changes to HTML tags by using a script, you need to first find a way to refer to specific tags within your script. The DOM hierarchy provides one way. We've already pointed out that tags have a *children* collection that contains references to all of the tag's child tags. We've also told you that the document has a single top-level tag representing the document itself, and a *<body>* tag that contains all the visual HTML elements. You could conceivably refer to the Run button in the Scriptomatic like this.

```
Document.Body.Chilen(0).Children(1).Children(0).Children(0).Children(0).
Children(0).Children(0).Value = "Execute"
```

This line starts with the *Document* object, the top level of the DOM. The *Document* object includes a *Body* property that refers to the *<body>* HTML tag. Next is the first child of the *<body>* tag. (DOM collections are zero-based, meaning the first child has an index of zero, the second an index of one, and so forth.) Next is the second child, that tag's first child, and so on. We end the line with the *<input>* tag, and we set its *value* property to have a fancier-sounding label for the button.

This is, of course, ridiculous. If you actually had to script this way, you'd rip your hair out within five minutes. The DOM provides a *much* simpler way—the *id* attribute. The Scriptomatic's HTML code doesn't define an *id* attribute for every tag; instead, it defines an *id* attribute only for those tags that we're likely to use. In the case of the Run button, the tag has an *id* attribute of *runbutton*. We can avoid that earlier nonsense and just change the button's label.

```
Runbutton.value = "Execute"
```

The *id* attribute is your key to quickly and easily accessing HTML elements throughout the document, without having to navigate through a complicated hierarchy of tags. However, it's important to understand that this hierarchy exists, because you'll have to use it from time to time.

Understanding HTML Events

In addition to properties and collections, HTML tag objects also have events. Events occur whenever something happens to a tag. For example, button tags—as defined by *input type="button"*—can be clicked by a user, and can therefore have an *onClick* event. Carefully examine the HTML for the Run button.

```
<input id=runbutton  class="button" type="button" value="Run"  name="run_button"
onClick="RunScript()">
```

This tag defines a button and tells the HTA to execute the *RunScript* subroutine when the *onClick* event occurs. You'll find the *RunScript* subroutine elsewhere in the HTA—at line 885, in fact. The HTML tag also defined an *event handler*, meaning it identified a subroutine that will respond to the *onClick* event.

You can also define an event handler by creating a specially named subroutine. For example, the authors of the Scriptomatic could have created the Run button's HTML tag as follows.

```
<input id=runbutton  class="button" type="button" value="Run"  name="run_button">
```

There's no event handler included in this example. We've specified a subroutine that's named after the default event handler. Instead of having a subroutine named *RunScript*, as the HTA does now, it could have a subroutine named *runbutton_onClick*. The first few lines of the subroutine would look like this.

```
Sub runbutton_onClick
   Const ForReading = 1
   Const ForWriting = 2
   Const PERMISSION_DENIED = &h46
...
```

This event handler's name comes from the button's *id* attribute, *runbutton*, and the name of the event, *onClick*. It's up to you which of the two types—the default event handler or the specially named one—you use. You might prefer the technique used in the Scriptomatic because it lets you use more sensible names, such as *RunScript*, for your subroutines. Or you might think that *runbutton_onClick* is more intuitive and easier to remember. The choice is yours.

Putting the DOM to Work

At this point, you've learned how to refer to HTML tags within your HTA (by using the *id* attribute), and how to respond to interactive events like button clicks (by defining and writing event handlers). Essentially, building an HTA requires these steps.

1.   Create the graphical user interface in HTML.

2.   Assign an *id* attribute to any tags you'll need to access from your script.

3.   Define event handlers to react to users' actions, such as clicking buttons.

4.   Write the event handlers to do whatever your script needs to do.

We'll spend the rest of this chapter looking into these four steps in greater detail.

Preparing Your HTA

A lot of administrators become frustrated with HTAs because they're so complex to debug. With so much interaction between VBScript and HTML, it can sometimes be difficult to figure out where bugs are. That's why we strongly encourage you to write the majority of your functional code as a regular VBScript file before you start using HTAs. Doing this will let you debug the most complex portion of an HTA more easily, by focusing entirely on the VBScript. In this section, we'll walk you through an example.

Using a Script Rather than an HTA

We'll start with a simple script that reads computer names from a file (one computer name per line), connects to each computer by using Windows Management Instrumentation (WMI), and then displays the computer's name, operating system build number (such as 2600 for Microsoft Windows XP), and the version number of the latest installed service pack. The script is shown in Listing 5-1.

Listing 5-1 Service Pack Inventory
```
Dim objFSO, objTS, strComputer, objWMIService, colItems, objItem
Set objFSO = CreateObject("Scripting.FileSystemObject")
Set objTS = objFSO.OpenTextFile("c:\computers.txt")
Do Until objTS.AtEndOfStream
 strComputer = objTS.ReadLine
 Set objWMIService = GetObject("winmgmts:\\" & strComputer & _
  "\root\cimv2")
 Set colItems = objWMIService.ExecQuery("SELECT * " & _
  "FROM Win32_OperatingSystem")
 For Each objItem In colItems
  WScript.Echo strComputer & ": " & _
   objItem.BuildNumber & ", " & _
   objItem.ServicePackMajorVersion & "." & _
   objItem.ServicePackMinorVersion
 Next
Loop
objTS.Close
```

> **On the CD**   You will find this script, as well as other scripts listed in this chapter, on the CD that accompanies this book.

This script performs a fairly common and useful function. We'd like the HTA to have the following features.

- It should provide a text box where computer names can be entered. It should also provide a button that reads an existing file of computer names and adds those names to the current list in the text box.

- It should provide options to read several properties of each computer.

- It should display the information in a new Internet Explorer window, formatted in an HTML table so that we can save the file (in HTML format, by using the Save As command), or copy and paste the data into a Microsoft Excel workbook.

- It should continue with the next computer in the list instead of crashing when one of the listed computers can't be contacted.

Specifying the goals ahead of time will help clarify the HTA's design and spot potential trouble points. We already have two potential trouble spots in our list. We specified two functional changes to be incorporated into the script *prior* to starting our HTA work. Two of our goals are directly related to the graphical HTA environment: providing a text box for computer names and providing options (perhaps check boxes) for different properties to query. The other two goals are not directly related to HTAs, so they can be incorporated into our script right away. Incorporating the changes in the script now, before adding it to the HTA, will make the final HTA easier to debug.

> **Tip**   Regular scripts are easier to debug than HTAs largely because HTAs add a lot of distraction in the way of HTML tags. By getting your script working before pasting it into an HTA, you'll be starting with functionality that you know works. Then you can focus on the HTML to get it looking right. In addition, using script debuggers can save a lot of time, so you should use them if you can. Many (such as the Microsoft Script Debugger or SAPIEN PrimalScope) work better with plain VBScript than they do with HTAs.

Listing 5-2 is the revised script. We've added some comments to help you follow what's going on.

Listing 5-2 Revised Service Pack Inventory

```
Dim objFSO, objTS, strComputer, objWMIService, colItems, objItem, strHTML

'open the text file
Set objFSO = CreateObject("Scripting.FileSystemObject")
Set objTS = objFSO.OpenTextFile("c:\computers.txt")

'create the starting HTML
strHTML = "<table border=1>" & VbCrLf
strHTML = strHTML & "<tr>" & VbCrLf
strHTML = strHTML & "<td>Computer</td>" & VbCrLf
strHTML = strHTML & "<td>Build</td>" & VbCrLf
strHTML = strHTML & "<td>Service Pack</td>" & VbCrLf
strHTML = strHTML & "</tr>" & VbCrLf

'read through the text file
Do Until objTS.AtEndOfStream

 'add a table row to the HTML
 strHTML = strHTML & "<tr>" & VbCrLf
```

```
'get the next computer name
strComputer = objTS.ReadLine

'query the computer
On Error Resume Next
Set objWMIService = GetObject("winmgmts:\\" & strComputer & _
 "\root\cimv2")
If Err = 0 Then
 'no error connecting - query the info
 Set colItems = objWMIService.ExecQuery("SELECT * " & _
  "FROM Win32_OperatingSystem")

 'build the output HTML cells
 For Each objItem In colItems
  strHTML = strHTML & "<td>" & strComputer & "</td>" & VbCrLf
  strHTML = strHTML & "<td>" & objItem.BuildNumber & "</td>" & VbCrLf
  strHTML = strHTML & "<td>" & objItem.ServicePackMajorVersion & _
   "." & objItem.ServicePackMinorVersion & "</td>" & VbCrLf
 Next

 'finish the HTML row
 strHTML = strHTML & "</tr>"
Else
 'error connecting
 strHTML = strHTML & "<tr>" & VbCrLf
 strHTML = strHTML & "<td>" & strComputer & "</td>" & VbCrLf
 strHTML = strHTML & "<td>?</td>" & VbCrLf
 strHTML = strHTML & "<td>?</td>" & VbCrLf
 strHTML = strHTML & "</tr>" & VbCrLf
End If
On Error GoTo 0

Loop

'close the text file
objTS.Close

'close the table
strHTML = strHTML & "</table>" & VbCrLf

'display the table
Dim objIE
Set objIE = CreateObject("InternetExplorer.Application")
objIE.Navigate "about:blank"
objIE.Document.body.innerhtml = strHTML
objIE.Visible = True
```

Figure 5-3 on the next page shows the final output in Internet Explorer.

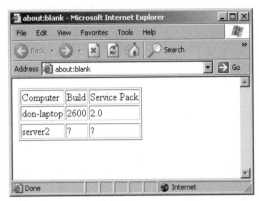

Figure 5-3   The revised script produces its output in Internet Explorer.

This script can be used entirely on its own. Because we'll be working with it so much throughout this chapter, we'll briefly run through what it's doing. The first part simply instantiates the *FileSystemObject* library and opens a text file.

```
Dim objFSO, objTS, strComputer, objWMIService, colItems, objItem, strHTML
'open the text file
Set objFSO = CreateObject("Scripting.FileSystemObject")
Set objTS = objFSO.OpenTextFile("c:\computers.txt")
```

Next, the script creates a variable to hold the final output. Because we want to display that output in Internet Explorer, the output needs to be formatted in HTML. The script starts by defining the beginning of an HTML table, including a header row that contains labels for each of three columns.

```
'create the starting HTML
strHTML = "<table border=1>" & VbCrLf
strHTML = strHTML & "<tr>" & VbCrLf
strHTML = strHTML & "<td>Computer</td>" & VbCrLf
strHTML = strHTML & "<td>Build</td>" & VbCrLf
strHTML = strHTML & "<td>Service Pack</td>" & VbCrLf
strHTML = strHTML & "</tr>" & VbCrLf
```

The script then begins reading through the text file, one line at a time.

```
'read through the text file
Do Until objTS.AtEndOfStream
```

For each line in the text file, we create a new row in the HTML table. This row will hold the information for a single computer listed in the text file.

```
'add a table row to the HTML
strHTML = strHTML & "<tr>" & VbCrLf
```

We read the next computer name from the text file into a variable.

```
'get the next computer name
strComputer = objTS.ReadLine
```

Now we direct WMI to connect to that computer. Notice that we've enabled error checking by using *On Error Resume Next*. That'll let the script continue to run even if the WMI connection fails.

```
'query the computer
On Error Resume Next
Set objWMIService = GetObject("winmgmts:\\" & strComputer & _
  "\root\cimv2")
```

After attempting the connection, we check the error status by using the built-in *Err* object. If it's zero, no error occurred and we're connected to WMI on the remote computer. We can then direct WMI to retrieve the WMI class we want to examine.

```
If Err = 0 Then
  'no error connecting - query the info
  Set colItems = objWMIService.ExecQuery("SELECT * " & _
    "FROM Win32_OperatingSystem")
```

The WMI query will return a collection of instances, so we use a *For Each...Next* loop to enumerate each instance in turn. In reality, because of the class we're querying, this collection will only ever contain one instance.

```
'build the output HTML cells
For Each objItem In colItems
```

We want each computer to be listed in a row of the HTML table, so we build that HTML now, and add it to the *strHTML* variable.

```
    strHTML = strHTML & "<td>" & strComputer & "</td>" & VbCrLf
    strHTML = strHTML & "<td>" & objItem.BuildNumber & "</td>" & VbCrLf
    strHTML = strHTML & "<td>" & objItem.ServicePackMajorVersion & _
      "." & objItem.ServicePackMinorVersion & "</td>" & VbCrLf
  Next
  'finish the HTML row
  strHTML = strHTML & "</tr>"
```

Here's the code that executes if the *Err* object isn't equal to zero, meaning an error occurred connecting to WMI on the remote computer. We're still adding an HTML table row to the *strHTML* variable, but we're populating it with question marks so that it'll be obvious in the final output which computers weren't contacted.

```
Else
  'error connecting
  strHTML = strHTML & "<tr>" & VbCrLf
  strHTML = strHTML & "<td>" & strComputer & "</td>" & VbCrLf
  strHTML = strHTML & "<td>?</td>" & VbCrLf
```

```
    strHTML = strHTML & "<td>?</td>" & VbCrLf
    strHTML = strHTML & "</tr>" & VbCrLf
 End If
 On Error GoTo 0
Loop
```

Finally, when we've read through each computer, we close the text file and finish the table HTML.

```
'close the text file
objTS.Close
'close the table
strHTML = strHTML & "</table>" & VbCrLf
```

Here's the code that displays the table. We instantiate Internet Explorer, direct it to display a blank page (by using the URL *about:blank*), and then set the inner HTML of the document's body to the HTML table stored in the *strHTML* variable.

```
'display the table
Dim objIE
Set objIE = CreateObject("InternetExplorer.Application")
objIE.Navigate "about:blank"
objIE.Document.body.innerhtml = strHTML
objIE.Visible = True
```

Try the final script for yourself. Create a text file named *c:\computers.txt*, and populate it with a couple of computer names from your network. Those computers must be running Windows 2000 or later, and you will need to be an administrator on the computers to query them.

Getting the Script Ready for an HTA

HTAs are, by nature, fairly modular. Remember that the functionality provided by your script is built into event handlers, each of which is basically a standalone subroutine. As it is, our HTA would probably have a button labeled *Execute*, and the event handler for that button would contain the entire script we've written thus far. However, some of the functionality in the existing script is self-contained, and we might want to separate it into its own subroutine. Doing so won't make the HTA any easier to write, but it will make it easier to reuse standalone functionality, for example, the part of the script that opens Internet Explorer and displays output. Listing 5-3 is the slightly-modified script, which now makes the Internet Explorer handling a standalone subroutine.

Listing 5-3 Modularized Inventory Script

```
Dim objFSO, objTS, strComputer, objWMIService, colItems, objItem, strHTML

'open the text file
Set objFSO = CreateObject("Scripting.FileSystemObject")
Set objTS = objFSO.OpenTextFile("c:\computers.txt")

'create the starting HTML
strHTML = "<table border=1>" & VbCrLf
```

```
strHTML = strHTML & "<tr>" & VbCrLf
strHTML = strHTML & "<td>Computer</td>" & VbCrLf
strHTML = strHTML & "<td>Build</td>" & VbCrLf
strHTML = strHTML & "<td>Service Pack</td>" & VbCrLf
strHTML = strHTML & "</tr>" & VbCrLf

'read through the text file
Do Until objTS.AtEndOfStream

  'add a table row to the HTML
  strHTML = strHTML & "<tr>" & VbCrLf

  'get the next computer name
  strComputer = objTS.ReadLine

  'query the computer
  On Error Resume Next
  Set objWMIService = GetObject("winmgmts:\\" & strComputer & _
   "\root\cimv2")
  If Err = 0 Then
   'no error connecting - query the info
   Set colItems = objWMIService.ExecQuery("SELECT * " & _
    "FROM Win32_OperatingSystem")

   'build the output HTML cells
   For Each objItem In colItems
    strHTML = strHTML & "<td>" & strComputer & "</td>" & VbCrLf
    strHTML = strHTML & "<td>" & objItem.BuildNumber & "</td>" & VbCrLf
    strHTML = strHTML & "<td>" & objItem.ServicePackMajorVersion & _
     "." & objItem.ServicePackMinorVersion & "</td>" & VbCrLf
   Next

   'finish the HTML row
   strHTML = strHTML & "</tr>"
  Else
   'error connecting
   strHTML = strHTML & "<tr>" & VbCrLf
   strHTML = strHTML & "<td>" & strComputer & "</td>" & VbCrLf
   strHTML = strHTML & "<td>?</td>" & VbCrLf
   strHTML = strHTML & "<td>?</td>" & VbCrLf
   strHTML = strHTML & "</tr>" & VbCrLf
  End If
  On Error GoTo 0

Loop

'close the text file
objTS.Close

'close the table
strHTML = strHTML & "</table>" & VbCrLf

'display the table
DisplayOutputInIE(strHTML)
```

```
Sub DisplayOutputInIE(strHTML)
  Dim objIE
  Set objIE = CreateObject("InternetExplorer.Application")
  objIE.Navigate "about:blank"
  objIE.Document.body.innerhtml = strHTML
  objIE.Visible = True
End Sub
```

Now if we ever want another HTA that displays information in a pop-up Internet Explorer window, we can just copy and paste the *DisplayOutputInIE* subroutine. It's already debugged and working, so we'll have saved ourselves a considerable amount of time.

Best Practices   Administrative scripting—indeed, the very word *VBScript*—is often looked down upon by many software developers and even IT managers. This is because too many administrators fail to follow basic best practices when creating their scripts, and the administrators earn reputations as rogues. One way to avoid that stigma is to follow industry best practices for software development in your scripts, particularly for modularization. The general rule is that if a piece of script can be used more than once, either in the same script or in a different one, break that piece into a function or subroutine of its own. We won't always do that with the scripts in this book, and when we do, we won't always modularize as much as we could. We've made that decision for this book to help keep the scripts clearer and simpler to follow. We firmly believe that you, however, should modularize whenever possible.

Now we can begin working on the HTA itself. There are a few basics you'll need to pick up before you can start working on your HTA. In the next few sections, we'll cover this background material and provide some snippets. We'll pick up in the last section, *Viewing HTAs in Action*, by taking all of this disparate knowledge and bringing it together with our original VBScript example to create the final, functional HTA.

Understanding HTA Requirements and Essentials

In the next few sections, we'll discuss some of the basic rules for building an HTA and introduce some of the design decisions you'll need to make before you start working in an editor.

Tip   A lot of the things we show you in the next several sections can be tough to remember, especially HTML tag formatting. There are tools to help make these easier, though. The freely available HTA Helpomatic is a Microsoft tool that produces samples of various HTML and HTA-related formatting for you. (Download at *http://www.microsoft.com/technet/scriptcenter/hubs/htas.mspx*. This link is included on the CD; click *HTA Helpomatic*.) If you use a commercial tool as your development environment, contact Scripting Outpost (*http://www.scriptingout-post.com*) about their HTA Snippets Pack. These snippets integrate into the PrimalScript environment and allow you to drag HTML and HTA elements into your script.

Using HTA Tags

Only two things really differentiate an HTA from a Web page. First, HTAs use the filename extension .hta. It's this filename extension that tells Windows to execute the file in Mshta.exe rather than directly in Internet Explorer. Second, HTAs contain a special tag, called the *HTA* tag, that tells Mshta.exe a number of details about how the HTA should look, how it should execute, and so forth.

The *HTA* tag must appear within the *head* tags of an HTML page. The *head* section of an HTML page doesn't contain regular HTML tags intended for viewing; instead, it contains a number of other types of tags—including the tags in which your VBScript code will be stored—that provide background information and supporting functionality for the application. The complete *HTA* tag looks like this.

```
<hta:application
applicationname="MyHTA"
border="dialog"
borderstyle="normal"
caption="My HTML Application"
contextmenu="false"
icon="myicon.ico"
maximizebutton="false"
minimizebutton="true"
navigable="false"
scroll="false"
selection="false"
showintaskbar="true"
singleinstance="true"
sysmenu="true"
version="1.0"
windowstate="normal"
/>
```

Almost everything there is optional. At a minimum, your *HTA* tag needs to contain the following information.

```
<hta:application />
```

By using the many optional attributes, you can significantly customize how your HTA looks and behaves. The complete set of attributes are as follows.

- The *applicationname* attribute assigns a name to your application.

- The *border* attribute determines the type of border that the HTA window will have. The default is a thick border, which includes resizable edges and a size grip graphical element in the lower-right corner. You can also specify the following:

    - Thin. A resizable border lacking the size grip element

    - None. No border

    - Dialog. A fixed (non-resizable) border

- The *borderstyle* attribute controls the appearance of the window border. It defaults to normal, but you can also specify the following:

  - ❑ Complex. A raised and sunken border

  - ❑ Raised. A raised 3-D border

  - ❑ Static. A 3-D border usually used for windows that don't accept user input

  - ❑ Sunken. A sunken 3-D border

- The *caption* attribute specifies the text that appears in your HTA window's title bar.

- The *contextmenu* attribute, set to TRUE or FALSE, indicates whether right-clicking the HTA will display the Internet Explorer context menu. Because traditional Windows applications don't do this, setting *ContextMenu="false"* will better mimic the behavior of a Windows application.

> **Tip** HTA attributes can generally accept *true* or *yes* for true, and *false* or *no* for false. The HTA documentation in MSDN Library prefers *yes* and *no*.

- The *icon* attribute sets the name of a .ico file that will be the application's window and taskbar icon. If you omit this, the standard Mshta.exe icon will be used. A downside to this attribute is that there's no way to bundle the icon file with the HTA file. You're better off specifying an icon file that is accessible through UNC (perhaps on a file server) or URL (perhaps on an intranet Web server), than an icon on the local hard disk.

- The *innerborder* attribute displays a 3-D inner border around the HTA. Setting it to *No* suppresses the inner border. The default is *Yes*.

- The *maximizebutton* attribute, when set to TRUE displays a button that maximizes the HTA window. We prefer setting this to FALSE because the layout of the HTA doesn't usually look as good in a full screen as it does at whatever size it was created.

- The *minimizebutton* attribute, when set to TRUE, displays a button that will minimize the HTA to the taskbar. Setting this to FALSE hides the button.

- The *navigable* attribute, when set to TRUE, specifies that any hyperlinks in your HTA will be opened in the HTA, navigating away from your HTA content. We recommend setting this to FALSE so that any hyperlinks will open in a new Internet Explorer window, leaving your HTA open.

- The *scroll* attribute, when set to TRUE, shows scrollbars in your HTA's main area. Setting it to FALSE hides the scrollbars.

- The *scrollflat* attribute, when set to TRUE, displays flat or 3-D scroll bars. Setting it to FALSE hides the scrollbars.

- The *selection* attribute, when set to TRUE, allows selection of text within the HTA. We recommend setting it to FALSE to mimic the behavior of a traditional Windows application. Setting this to FALSE will not prevent text in text boxes and other input controls from being selected, just the static text that you create within the HTA.

- The *showintaskbar* attribute, when set to TRUE, allows the HTA to be displayed in the Windows taskbar. Setting this to FALSE prohibits the HTA from being displayed in the taskbar.

- The *singleinstance* attribute, when set to TRUE, allows only one copy of the HTA to run at a time. If set to FALSE, multiple copies can run. When set to TRUE, if a user double-clicks the HTA file while the HTA is already running, the currently running instance will come to the foreground rather than launching a new copy of the HTA.

- The *sysmenu* attribute, when set to TRUE, shows the system menu, usually in the upper-left of the window's title bar. If you set this to FALSE, the minimize, maximize, and restore buttons will also be hidden.

- The *version* attribute sets the version number of the HTA. This can be whatever value you like.

- The *windowstate* attribute specifies the initial window state for the HTA. The default, *normal*, uses the default specified by Internet Explorer. You can also specify the following:

  - Minimize. The window is displayed only in the taskbar. If, however, the *showInTaskBar* attribute is FALSE, the window will not be displayed and the user will be unable to access it.

  - Maximize. The window will be maximized, covering the full screen.

> **Note**   Technically, the *application* attribute can have a value, too. Specifying *hta:application* is the same as *hta:application="no"*, which applies the default HTA security model. This model prevents untrusted content within a frame from accessing the HTA or being accessed by it. Specify *hta:application="yes"* to force all frame content to be trusted. This is a pretty rare requirement, usually something you'd do only if your HTA were implementing a frame that included content from another intranet Web server. Because it's so rare, we won't cover that situation in this book.

The *HTA* tag allows you to exercise considerable control over the initial appearance and behavior of your HTA.

Sizing an HTA

One thing you can't do with the *HTA* tag is specify the initial size of the HTA window. The only way to force the HTA window to a specific size is to do so at run time. The *onLoad* event of the *window* object always runs when an HTA loads, even before the user can begin interacting with the HTA. The *window* object represents the window in which the HTA runs, and you can control its *height*, *width*, *left*, and *top* properties to size and position it on the screen.

```
Sub window_onLoad()
 window.moveTo(10,10)
 window.resizeTo(640,480)
End Sub
```

This will force the window to position itself to 10 pixels from the left edge of the screen and 10 pixels from the top edge of the screen, and to size itself to 640 pixels wide by 480 pixels high. This event handler runs automatically; you don't need to do anything special other than include it in your HTA.

> **Tip**   The *window_onLoad* event is also a good place to put any script code that sets up your HTA. For example, you could dynamically populate list boxes, set defaults for options, and so forth.

Using *<div>* and *<span>* Tags

In an earlier example, we showed you the code used to change a button's text label. That's not something you'll probably do a lot in your scripts. However, what you probably *will* do a lot is display dynamic messages. For instance, in our example, we might want to display a message like *Now inventorying computers* while the inventory portion of the script runs. Then we might want to change that message to *Inventory complete* when the inventory is finished. Displaying that type of dynamic message in an HTA is easy, provided you leave room for it in your initial layout or design.

Division, or *<div>*, tags, let you make that room for dynamic messages. A *<div>* tag simply defines a region of the HTML document. Because you can give the *<div>* tag an *id* attribute, you can refer to it from your script code. The *<div>* tag has an *innerHTML* property, so you can control what appears between the opening and closing *<div>* tags. Internet Explorer also supports a similar tag, called *<span>*. For the purposes of writing HTAs, there is not a lot of difference between the two. What differences there are date back to the days when Microsoft and Netscape were exploring ways of extending HTML's usefulness. One company came up with *<div>* tags; the other came up with *<span>* tags. Use whichever one you prefer. There are some slight differences in how the two are displayed: a *<div>* tag creates line breaks, for example. For the purposes of writing an HTA, however, you probably won't notice the differences much. In the Scriptomatic code, you'll notice two *<span>* tags near line 1403.

```
<span id="wmi_namespaces"></span>
<span id="wmi_classes"></span>
```

Notice that these have no inner text or HTML to start with, so when the HTA first loads, they'll be completely invisible. They do, however, have *id* attributes, allowing them to be modified by the script code. The first reference to the *wmi_classes* span is on line 194.

```
wmi_classes.innerHTML = "<div style=""font-size:8pt;color:red;"">Please wait, trying to load
WMI Classes in namespace " & namespacespulldown.value & " ...</div>"
```

This is modifying the span's *innerHTML* property, which starts out empty. The script inserts a *<div>* tag (which contains formatting to display red text) and a message.

> **Note**   You'll find that many HTA developers use *<span>* tags as placeholders for dynamic text, like this *Please wait* message, and use *<div>* tags to apply formatting. That's a perfectly acceptable practice, and if it's one you find convenient and understandable, we encourage you to use it.

Creating areas for dynamic messages is that easy. Simply define the location of the message by using a *<span>* or *<div>* tag that has an ID, and then display the message by modifying the *innerHTML* property of the tag.

Using Inline Frames

If you haven't worked with HTML a lot, inline frames—or IFrames, as the Web folks like to call them—can seem unintuitive. Essentially, an IFrame defines a rectangular region that displays the content of a Web page. Figure 5-4 shows an inline frame in action, and Listing 5-4 is the HTML that makes it happen.

Figure 5-4   A page with an inline frame

Listing 5-4 Inline Frame

```
<p>This is the main page.</p>
<p><iframe name="I1" src="http://www.scriptinganswers.com">
Your browser does not support inline frames or is currently configured not to display
inline frames.
</iframe></p>
<p>This is the main page.</p>
```

The *<iframe>* tag is doing the work of creating the inline frame. Like other tags, it can have an *id* attribute (although it does not have one in this simple example), and a *src* attribute that tells the IFrame what to display within the inline frame area. Additional attributes can be specified to control the IFrame's size, whether it has scroll bars, whether it has a border around it, and so forth.

You can think of an IFrame as a miniature Internet Explorer browser entirely contained within a rectangular area that you define. As we explained earlier, your HTA won't generally have access to the contents of the IFrame, but you can control the *<iframe>* tag itself, which means you can control what the IFrame displays. For example, you can place the following inside an HTA.

```
<p>This is the main page.</p>
<p><iframe id="myiframe" name="I1" src="http://www.scriptinganswers.com">
Your browser does not support inline frames or is currently configured not to display inline
frames.
</iframe></p>
<p>This is the main page.</p>
```

Elsewhere, you might have script that reads as follows.

```
myiframe.src = "http://www.microsoft.com"
```

This would cause the IFrame to display the Microsoft.com home page. Your script would not, however, be able to access the Internet Explorer DOM of the Microsoft home page unless you used the *<hta:application="true">* tag we described earlier, which disables cross-frame security precautions.

> **Important**   Disabling cross-frame security means that your code can access the contents of the IFrame, and also that the IFrame—and any scripts it might contain—can access the contents of your HTA. If you're going to do this, make absolutely certain that you trust whatever content is loaded into the IFrame.

Inline frames can also be useful for displaying information. For example, in our sample HTA, we want the output to be displayed in a pop-up window. However, we could just as easily design an inline frame into the HTA, and display the output there instead. Inline frames are simply another option for displaying information within your HTA.

Working with Forms and Fields

One of the main reasons most administrators use HTAs is to gain more robust input capabilities. After all, VBScript's intrinsic *InputBox* function—the sole means of graphically collecting user input—is a bit limiting. HTML forms and input controls (or *fields*) provide much more flexibility.

Perhaps the most basic input control is the text box, and HTML includes three kinds.

- A *text box* is a simple, one-line entry field.

- A *text area* is a box for typing multiple lines of text.

- A *password box* mimics a text box in functionality but masks whatever is typed in it.

The text box and password box are implemented by using HTML *<input>* tags, whereas the text area has its own special *<textarea>* tag. Here's what they look like.

```
<input type="text" id="txtName">
<input type="password" id="txtPassword">
<textarea id="txtStory"></textarea>
```

Notice that each carries an *id* attribute, allowing it to be referred to from within your scripts.

As a general rule, we believe that manually typing HTML tags is a bad idea. There are a number of excellent commercial What You See Is What You Get (WYSIWYG) HTML editors on the market, and there's no reason not to use them. Microsoft FrontPage is one you might be familiar with and be able to access easily. One problem with FrontPage, however, at least from an HTA standpoint, is that it goes a bit overboard. Here's a snippet of HTML that FrontPage created. It includes the three types of input controls.

```
<form method="POST" action="--WEBBOT-SELF--">
<!--webbot bot="SaveResults" U-File="fpweb:///_private/form_results.csv" S-Format="TEXT/CSV"
S-Label-Fields="TRUE" -->
<p><input type="text" name="T1" size="20"></p>
<p><input type="password" name="T2" size="20"></p>
<p><textarea rows="2" name="S1" cols="20"></textarea></p>
<p><input type="submit" value="Submit" name="B1"><input type="reset" value="Reset"
name="B2"></p>
</form>
```

You'll need to work on this code a bit to make it more suitable for use in an HTA. There's only a few steps to take.

1. Remove the *<form>* tags.

2. Remove the *<!–webbot –>* tag.

3. Add a unique *id* attribute to each input control. For clarity, change the *name* attribute to match your *id* attribute.

4. Delete the Submit or Reset buttons, and add regular buttons for your application.

FrontPage or another WYSIWYG HTML editor can make creating complex, professional-looking applications much easier, so we think it's worth the trouble to go in and clean up the HTML they create and make it more suitable for an HTA. Actually working with the input controls—reading their values in your script, and modifying them at run time—can be a bit complicated. In the next few sections, we'll cover everything you'll need to know.

Populating a List Box

Creating drop-down list boxes (or regular, scrolling list boxes) is easy with FrontPage (or whatever editor you're using). You can use the tools the editor provides to add selections to your list boxes. However, there will be situations when you want to dynamically add items to a list. When you select a WMI namespace, for example, the Scriptomatic HTA figures out what classes are in that namespace, and adds them to a drop-down list box. Both types of list box are defined by using *<select>* tags. Here's a drop-down list with two options.

```
<select size="1" name="lstOptions">
<option>Option 1</option>
<option>Option 2</option>
</select>
```

Making this into a scrolling list box involves changing only one thing.

```
<select size="3" name="lstOptions">
<option>Option 1</option>
<option>Option 2</option>
</select>
```

Can you see the difference? In the second example, the list box has a size of 3, making it three lines high. In the first option, the list box has a size of 1, which forces it to be a drop-down list box. Options—that is, items in the list—are defined by *<option>* tags, which are contained within the list box's *<select>* tags. The text between the *<option>* tags appears in the list box. You can specify a value that will represent that option. If you don't specify a value, the option's text is used as its value. Here's an example.

```
<option value="1">Option 1</option>
<option>Option 2</option>
```

To dynamically add an option to the list box, add a new *<option>* tag. Here's an example.

```
Dim objOption
Set objOption = document.createElement("OPTION")
objOption.Text = "Option 3"
objOption.Value = "3"
lstOptions.Add(objOption)
```

This adds a third option to our list, with text that reads *Option 3* and a value of 3.

Creating Buttons

We've already mentioned that you don't want to use the Submit and Reset button types. The Submit button is designed to send a form's contents to a Web server for processing. HTAs are typically self-contained and don't rely on a Web server, so the Submit button is useless. Reset buttons are used to clear form fields, and you might find a use for that, but having mistakenly clicked a few of these buttons, we suggest just leaving them out.

You're going to need buttons, though; the Scriptomatic HTA has several, in fact. Fortunately, buttons are among the easiest HTML elements to create.

```
<input type="button" value="OK" name="btnOK">
```

This is straight from FrontPage, and you'll notice that it lacks an *id* attribute, which you'll need to add. The *value* attribute determines the label that appears on the face of the button, and the *type* attribute indicates that this is a regular button, not a Submit or Reset button.

Connecting a Button to a Script

Generally, your HTA will only do things when someone clicks a button, so connecting buttons to the script is very important. We've briefly discussed event handlers already—they're how you write script to react to button clicks. There are two main ways to connect an event handler. The first way is to simply write a subroutine with the special event handler name.

```
Sub btnOK_onClick()
  'your code goes here
End Sub
```

This would need to appear between a *<script language="vbscript">* tag and a *</script>* tag, which would in turn be located within the *head* section of the HTA. This method generally works well for most buttons. However, you might want more than one button connected to an event handler. Perhaps, for example, you have two buttons that will do something very similar. An easy way to do that is to create the buttons as follows.

```
<input type="button" value="OK" name="btnOK" id="btnOK1" onClick="DoButton">
<input type="button" value="OK" name="btnOK" id="btnOK2" onClick="DoButton">
```

This will connect both buttons' *onClick* event to the *DoButton* subroutine. Write that subroutine as follows.

```
Sub DoButton()
  Select Case window.event.srcElement.id
    Case "btnOK1"
      'your code for btnOK1 goes here
    Case "btnOK2"
      'your code for btnOK2 goes here
End Sub
```

The special *window.event.srcElement* object is a reference to whatever object—in this case, one of the two buttons—generated the last event. By checking the object's *id* property, you can quickly determine which button was clicked, and act accordingly.

Using Check Boxes and Radio Buttons

Check boxes and radio buttons are useful ways to display options to your HTA's users. They're easy to create in a WYSIWYG editor, or manually by using this HTML.

```
<input type="checkbox" name="chkCheckbox" value="ON" checked>My Checkbox
<input type="radio" value="Value1" checked name="optButton">My Radio
Button 1
<input type="radio" name="optButton" value="Value2">My Radio Button 2
```

Notice a few things here.

- FrontPage didn't add the *id* attributes to these elements, so you'll need to do that manually. As always, try to keep the *id* and *name* attributes identical for ease of use.

- Both the check box and radio button (also called an *option button*) elements only create the actual check box or radio button; the text accompanying the element is inserted separately.

- The *checked* attribute, if present in a check box, makes the default state of the check box selected. To make the default state cleared, omit the *checked* attribute.

- The two radio buttons have the same *name* attribute. This makes them part of the same group, meaning that only one of them can be selected at a time. They should also have the same *id* attribute to make them scriptable.

- One of the radio buttons has a *checked* attribute, meaning it's the one selected by default.

Checking the value of these elements from within your script is straightforward. For the radio button, simply access the element's *value* property. Although multiple elements with the same *id* attribute will exist, the *value* property will correspond to the *value* attribute of whichever radio button is selected by the user. In this brief example, if the user selects the second radio button, *optButton.Value* would equal *Value2*.

Check boxes work similarly. When selected, their *value* property will return whatever you set the *value* attribute to (*ON*, in this case). When not selected, the *value* property will contain an empty string. You can examine the value like this.

```
If chkCheckbox.Value = "ON" Then
  'checked
Else
 'not checked
End If
```

Adding Graphics

Graphics are easy to add to an HTA. Obviously, a WYSIWYG editor makes it easy to insert images, but you can also manually build the HTML tag.

```
<img src="mygraphic.gif">
```

By default, a graphic must be contained within the same folder as the HTA itself. As with referencing external scripts, you'll need to be sure you distribute the graphic along with your HTA. To make your HTA easier to distribute, you can put the graphic on a file server or a Web server, and let the HTA pull it from there. Because of this extra bit of complexity, we try to minimize our use of graphics in HTAs.

Adding Subroutines and Functions

All your script code—event handlers as well as any other subroutines and functions you write—must appear within special tags that tell Windows what script language you're using. The beginning of an HTA that contains no script code (yet) would therefore look something like this.

```
<html>
<head>
<script language="vbscript">

</script>
<hta:application>
</head>
<body>
```

After the *<body>* tag, you insert the HTML that creates your HTA's visual interface. First, you specify the language you're using (which can be VBScript or JScript). JScript is the default language, so if you don't specify VBScript, you'll run into errors.

Second, you can use multiple script sections. If you plan to include all your code within the HTA file itself (as the Scriptomatic and many other HTAs do), there's no need for multiple script sections. The Scriptomatic HTA contains all its code in a single script section. However, suppose you want to include a file full of standard subroutines that you use in several HTAs. You might have one script section that contains event handlers for the particular HTA you're working on, and a second script section that includes an external file containing those standard subroutines.

```
<script language="vbscript">
Sub btnOK_onClick()
End Sub

Sub btnCancel_onClick()
End Sub
</script>
<script language="vbscript" src="c:\scripts\standard.vbs" />
```

> **Best Practices**   Keeping commonly used subroutines in an external file is a good idea because any changes you make to those subroutines (such as bug fixes) will only need to be made once. If you get into the habit of copying and pasting code into multiple HTAs, any changes will have to be made multiple times, opening the door to errors, missed HTAs, and other potential problems.

The second script section includes an external file named C:\Scripts\Standard.vbs. One downside to this technique is that your HTA is no longer self-contained; to run properly, it must have access to that external file. If you'll be distributing your HTA, you'll either need to distribute this extra file along with it, or keep that external file in an accessible area, such as a file server.

> **Caution**   Including an external file does not prevent someone from seeing your script code. To run the HTA, a user must have read permission to the HTA file and to any external scripts referenced by the HTA. Users can utilize those read permissions to directly open the external scripts, and read them at will.

Viewing HTAs in Action

Now we'll show you how to build an HTA from scratch. We'll use Listing 5-3, because it's debugged and has most of the functionality we want. We begin by using an editor like Front-Page to design the HTA's visual interface. There are a few additional features we want in the HTA, so we can design those into the interface. Figure 5-5 shows the interface in FrontPage, and Listing 5-5 on the next page is the HTML. Note that this HTML is straight from FrontPage; we haven't touched it up or made it into an HTA yet.

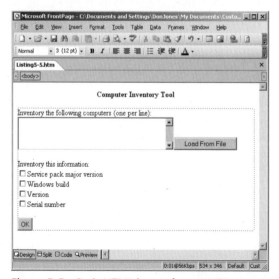

Figure 5-5   Basic HTML layout for our HTA

Listing 5-5 Basic HTML

```
<html>

<head>
<meta http-equiv="Content-Language" content="en-us">
<meta http-equiv="Content-Type" content="text/html; charset=windows-1252">
<title>Computer Inventory Tool</title>
</head>

<body>

<p align="center"><b>Computer Inventory Tool</b></p>
<form method="POST" action="--WEBBOT-SELF--">
<!--webbot bot="SaveResults" U-File="C:\Documents and Settings\DonJones\My
Documents\Customer Files\MSPress\AdvancedScripting\Manuscript and CD\On The
CD\Scripts\Chap5\_private\form_results.csv" S-Format="TEXT/CSV" S-Label-Fields="TRUE" --
>
<p align="left">Inventory the following computers (one per line):<br>
<textarea rows="4" name="txtComputers" cols="40"></textarea><input type="button"
value="Load From File" name="btnLoadFromFile"></p>
<p align="left">Inventory this information:<br>
<input type="checkbox" name="chkServicePack" value="ON">Service pack major
version<br>
<input type="checkbox" name="chkBuild" value="ON">Windows build<br>
<input type="checkbox" name="chkVersion" value="ON">Version<br>
<input type="checkbox" name="chkSerialNumber" value="ON">Serial number</p>
<p align="left"><input type="button" value="OK" name="btnOK"></p>
</form>

</body>

</html>
```

Now we need to convert this to an HTA. In addition to changing the filename, we'll remove the FrontPage form tags, add a script section, add the *HTA* tag, and add *id* attributes. Listing 5-6 shows the changes.

Listing 5-6 HTA Modifications

```
<html>

<head>
<meta http-equiv="Content-Language" content="en-us">
<meta http-equiv="Content-Type" content="text/html; charset=windows-1252">
<title>Computer Inventory Tool</title>
<script language="vbscript">

</script>
<hta:application>
</head>

<body>

<p align="center"><b>Computer Inventory Tool</b></p>
```

```
<p align="left">Inventory the following computers (one per line):<br>
<textarea id="txtComputers" rows="4" name="txtComputers" cols="40"></textarea><input
type="button" value="Load From File" id="btnLoadFromFile" name="btnLoadFromFile"></p>
<p align="left">Inventory this information:<br>
<input type="checkbox" id="chkServicePack" name="chkServicePack" value="ON">Service pack
major
version<br>
<input type="checkbox" id="chkBuild" name="chkBuild" value="ON">Windows build<br>
<input type="checkbox" id="chkVersion" name="chkVersion" value="ON">Version<br>
<input type="checkbox" id="chkSerialNumber" name="chkSerialNumber" value="ON">Serial
number</p>
<p align="left"><input id="btnOK" type="button" value="OK" name="btnOK"></p>

</body>

</html>
```

Best Practices   Notice that we used prefixes for the various control types: *chk* for check boxes, *btn* for buttons, and so forth. This naming convention, called *Hungarian notation*, is a best practice because it helps identify the type of object you're referring to in your script. It's very similar to the naming convention used for variable names, such as using *str* to prefix variables which will contain string data.

Now we just need to add functionality. We have only two buttons, and much of the code for the OK button is already taken care of in Listing 5-3. We need to make the following modifications to the code.

- Pull the contents of *txtComputers* into a string array rather than reading names from a text file.

- Add output based on the selected check boxes.

- Add appropriate column headers based on the selected check boxes.

- Add an event handler for *btnLoadFromFile* that prompts for a filename and then reads the file into the computer names text area.

Listing 5-7 is the completed HTA.

Listing 5-7 Completed Inventory HTA
```
<html>

<head>
<meta http-equiv="Content-Language" content="en-us">
<meta http-equiv="Content-Type" content="text/html; charset=windows-1252">
<title>Computer Inventory Tool</title>
<script language="vbscript">
```

```vbscript
Sub btnOK_onClick
    Dim arrComputers, strComputer, objWMIService, colItems, objItem, strHTML

    'get the computer names into a string
    'and split it into an array
    arrComputers = Split(txtComputers.InnerText,vbcrlf)

    'create the starting HTML
    strHTML = "<table border=1>" & VbCrLf
    strHTML = strHTML & "<tr>" & VbCrLf
    strHTML = strHTML & "<td>Computer</td>" & VbCrLf
    if chkBuild.value = "ON" Then
       strHTML = strHTML & "<td>Build</td>" & VbCrLf
    end if
    if chkServicePack.value = "ON" Then
       strHTML = strHTML & "<td>Service Pack</td>" & VbCrLf
    end if
    if chkVersion.value = "ON" Then
       strHTML = strHTML & "<td>Version</td>" & VbCrLf
    end if
    if chkSerialNumber.value = "ON" Then
       strHTML = strHTML & "<td>Serial Number</td>" & VbCrLf
    end if

    'read through the array
    For Each strComputer in arrComputers

      'add a table row to the HTML
      strHTML = strHTML & "<tr>" & VbCrLf

      'query the computer
      On Error Resume Next
      Set objWMIService = GetObject("winmgmts:\\" & strComputer & _
       "\root\cimv2")
      If Err = 0 Then
       'no error connecting - query the info
       Set colItems = objWMIService.ExecQuery("SELECT * " & _
        "FROM Win32_OperatingSystem")

      'build the output HTML cells
      For Each objItem In colItems
        strHTML = strHTML & "<td>" & strComputer & "</td>" & VbCrLf
        if chkBuild.value = "ON" Then
          strHTML = strHTML & "<td>" & objItem.BuildNumber & "</td>" & VbCrLf
        end if
        if chkServicePack.value = "ON" Then
          strHTML = strHTML & "<td>" & objItem.ServicePackMajorVersion & "</td>" & VbCrLf
        end if
        if chkVersion.value = "ON" Then
          strHTML = strHTML & "<td>" & objItem.Version & "</td>" & VbCrLf
        end if
        if chkSerialNumber.value = "ON" Then
          strHTML = strHTML & "<td>" & objItem.SerialNumber & "</td>" & VbCrLf
        end if
      Next
```

```
        'finish the HTML row
        strHTML = strHTML & "</tr>"
      Else
        'error connecting
        strHTML = strHTML & "<tr>" & VbCrLf
        strHTML = strHTML & "<td>" & strComputer & "</td>" & VbCrLf
        strHTML = strHTML & "<td>?</td>" & VbCrLf
        strHTML = strHTML & "</tr>" & VbCrLf
      End If
      On Error GoTo 0

    Next

    'close the table
    strHTML = strHTML & "</table>" & VbCrLf

    'display the table
    DisplayOutputInIE(strHTML)
End Sub

Sub DisplayOutputInIE(strHTML)
 Dim objIE
 Set objIE = CreateObject("InternetExplorer.Application")
 objIE.Navigate "about:blank"
 objIE.Document.body.innerhtml = strHTML
 objIE.Visible = True
End Sub

Sub btnLoadFromFile_onClick()
    Dim objFSO, objTS, strFile
    Set objFSO = CreateObject("Scripting.FileSystemObject")
    strFile = InputBox("Path and filename to load?")
    If objFSO.FileExists(strFile) Then
        Set objTS = objFSO.OpenTextFile(strFile)
        txtComputers.innerText = objTS.ReadAll
        objTS.Close
    Else
        MsgBox("File does not exist.")
    End If
End Sub

</script>
<hta:application>
</head>

<body>

<p align="center"><b>Computer Inventory Tool</b></p>
<p align="left">Inventory the following computers (one per line):<br>
<textarea id="txtComputers" rows="4" name="txtComputers" cols="40"></textarea><input
type="button" value="Load From File" id="btnLoadFromFile" name="btnLoadFromFile"></p>
<p align="left">Inventory this information:<br>
<input type="checkbox" id="chkServicePack" name="chkServicePack" value="ON">Service pack
major
version<br>
```

```
<input type="checkbox" id="chkBuild" name="chkBuild" value="ON">Windows build<br>
<input type="checkbox" id="chkVersion" name="chkVersion" value="ON">Version<br>
<input type="checkbox" id="chkSerialNumber" name="chkSerialNumber" value="ON">Serial
number</p>
<p align="left"><input id="btnOK" type="button" value="OK" name="btnOK"></p>

</body>
</html>
```

That's all there is to it! Our work was made easier by the fact that we had a debugged script ready to go that contained the majority of the functionality we needed. By tweaking some minor portions of that code and merging it into a simple HTML page developed in FrontPage, we created a complete HTA.

Summary

In this chapter, you learned that HTAs are a type of script that combines VBScript and HTML formatting to create applications that resemble Windows applications. We showed you a methodology that will help you quickly convert standalone VBScripts into full HTAs, and explained ways to help troubleshoot and debug your HTAs more effectively. Remember, however, that HTAs aren't the perfect solution for every situation. Sometimes, especially for scripts that you'll be using yourself, the effort of creating a fancy-looking HTA is more than it's worth. But for scripts that you plan to share with others, especially users who are less technically savvy, HTAs can make scripts much friendlier usable by incorporating the familiar Windows user interface elements.

More Info   As you work with HTAs, you'll find both the official HTA documentation as well as the Internet Explorer dynamic HTML (DHTML) documentation to be useful. The HTA documentation is located at

http://msdn.microsoft.com/library/default.asp?url=/workshop/author/hta/hta_node_entry.asp

(This link is on the companion CD; click *HTML Applications*.) The DHTML documentation is allocated at the following Web site.

http://msdn.microsoft.com/library/default.asp?url=/workshop/author/dhtml/reference/dhtml_reference_entry.asp

(This link is on the companion CD; click *HTML and DHTML Reference*.)

Because those locations change, you should also know how to get to these sites manually. Go to *http://msdn.microsoft.com/library*, click Web development in the left tree, click either HTML And DHTML in the right pane or HTML And CSS in the left pane, and then click HTML Applications.

Part III
Advanced Scripting Techniques, Tools, and Technologies

Chapter 6

Remote Scripting

There are two main types of remote scripting. The first type involves running a script that connects to a remote computer and then performs tasks on that remote computer. The second type involves deploying scripts to remote computers that then run on the remote computers. In this chapter, we'll look at both kinds of remote scripting, including the security concerns and difficulties you can encounter, the techniques and technologies you'll use, and the benefits you can expect to enjoy.

One of the benefits of administrative scripting is having the ability to write scripts that perform tasks on other computers. Windows Management Instrumentation (WMI) and Active Directory Services Interfaces (ADSI) are perhaps two of the best remote-scripting technologies currently available. WMI, for example, can be used to write scripts that obtain information about remote computers, or even modify the configuration of those computers. Remote scripting comes with certain difficulties and challenges, though, and we'll help you understand and address them in this chapter.

Before we start, let's clarify our terminology. Unfortunately, the term *remote scripting* is a bit ambiguous because it refers to two distinct techniques that involve completely different technologies. To avoid confusing the two, we'll invent some new terms. We'll use the term *deployed scripts* to refer to the type of remote scripting in which a script is physically copied from your computer to a remote computer, and then executed on that remote computer. We'll use the term *connectivity scripts* to refer to scripts that are executed on your computer, but connect to remote computers to perform tasks on them. These aren't industry-standard terms that you're likely to run across elsewhere; we're simply using these terms in this chapter to help keep the two different kinds of remote scripting clear and distinct.

Understanding Remote Scripting and Security

As Microsoft Windows becomes a more secure operating system, the difficulty of performing administrative tasks on remote computers becomes more complex. In addition, the underlying architecture of the Windows operating system—which includes capabilities such as multiple user profiles on a single computer—can make remote scripting somewhat more complex. Any kind of remote scripting typically requires you to navigate through a few security elements.

- Connectivity
- Identity
- Permissions
- Context

We'll discuss each of these elements in this chapter. Keep in mind, though, that Windows is an operating *system*, comprised of many tightly integrated subsystems. As a result, these security elements often interact with one another. This interaction can sometimes make remote scripting problems more difficult. For example, you might connect to a remote computer by using domain administrator credentials that provide you with connectivity, a specific identity, and valid permissions—in other words, a *security context*. However, the user profile you'd have access to through that connection might not be what you expected. For example, if you're trying to access the profile of the computer's primary user, your script wouldn't work properly, because that's not the user profile to which the script's security context would be connected. Whenever you're troubleshooting remote scripting, therefore, it's important to think about what the script is doing and what it's encountering in the context of each of these security elements.

Connectivity

The first task in any kind of remote scripting is to connect to the remote computer. Generally, connectivity issues are caused by low-level network problems like an inability to resolve a name to an IP address. These are problems that any experienced administrator should have no problem troubleshooting. Other connectivity problems can be caused by local firewall software on the remote computer, or even on your computer. We will examine firewall problems later in this chapter.

After network and firewall issues have been resolved, the next step is connecting to the proper services and components on the remote computer. For example, WMI requires a connection to the remote computer's Windows Management Instrumentation service. If that service isn't running, you won't be able to make a connection, and your script won't run properly. Other types of remote scripting might require Distributed Component Object Model (DCOM) connectivity. If a connection to the correct DCOM object on the remote computer can't be established—perhaps because the object isn't properly installed or registered—your script will not function properly.

The key to solving this type of connectivity issue is to clearly understand what type of connection is required by the scripting task you're trying to perform.

- WMI queries typically require access to the remote computer's WMI service. This requires a Remote Procedure Call (RPC) connection to the service, as well as the ability to instantiate certain DCOM objects that are installed as part of Windows.

- ADSI queries connect to a service of some kind. In the case of ADSI's LDAP provider, the connection is to an LDAP server using the LDAP protocol, such as Active Directory. In the case of a WinNT provider, ADSI connects to the service using the RPC protocol.

- *FileSystemObject* queries to a remote computer's files and folders require a file-sharing connection that uses Server Message Blocks (SMB), just as though you were connecting to the remote computer's file system by using Windows Explorer.

In addition to the physical connection, some form of permissions can also be required. There are two types of permissions involved in most forms of remote scripting. The first permission that a script might need is *connectivity permission*—the permission to connect to a service or object and ask it to perform a task. The second permission is *execution permission*—the permission to execute the task. There's a subtle difference between these two.

For example, suppose you install a DCOM object on a computer named Server2, and the object is capable of deleting user accounts from that computer's local Security Accounts Manager (SAM). You then write a script on Client1 that attempts to utilize Server2's DCOM object. The first permission issue you'll run into is when your script tries to instantiate the DCOM object. Permissions are governed by Windows' Component Services security layer, which can be configured through the Component Services console. As shown in Figure 6-1 on the next page, these permissions can be left at their default settings, or they can be customized.

Customizing the launch permissions allows you to see what DCOM can control. As shown in Figure 6-2 on the next page, DCOM can be configured with permissions that control a *local launch* (an application running on the local computer that needs to use the object), or a *remote launch* (an application, such as your script, running on a different computer trying to remotely instantiate the object).

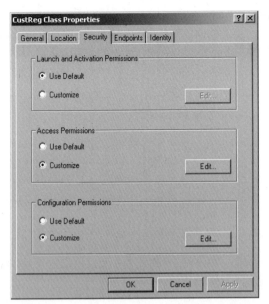

Figure 6-1 Configuring the security for a specific DCOM object or application

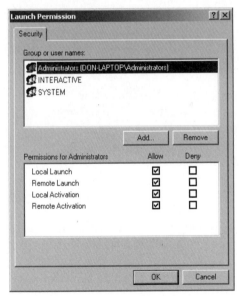

Figure 6-2 Customizing launch permissions for a DCOM object

You can configure similar permissions for activation. The account you're using to run your script must have remote launch and activation permissions. This can be difficult on a standalone computer, or one that isn't a member of a domain, because your script might not be able to provide the necessary credentials to obtain remote launch and activation permissions to the object.

You can also configure permissions to control access to the DCOM object after it has been launched and activated. By default, only the local Administrators group can be assured of having the necessary permissions, although obviously you can reconfigure the permissions as needed.

These are just the permissions necessary to get started on the remote computer. After that DCOM object is up and running, it'll still need permissions to perform the task you want it to do. We'll discuss execution permissions later in this chapter.

Identity

The tasks you can perform on a remote computer are governed by your (or your script's) *identity* on that remote computer. You can think of your identity in this context as the user account that represents you on the remote computer. Your scripts will often use Windows' ability to pass along authentication and identity information. For example, when you use Windows Explorer to open a shared folder on a remote computer, Windows authenticates you by using the account you used to log on to your computer. Were you to use a script to remotely access files on a computer, the same process would occur. The only way for the script to access the files using alternate credentials is to use the *RunAs* command. When you use the *RunAs* command, the script is executed under a different account, and uses that account to connect to the shared folder.

Only a few scripting technologies support the easy use of alternate credentials without *RunAs*. For example, both WMI and ADSI connections can be created using alternate credentials, but this is the exception, not the rule. Most of the time, the account used to execute the script is the account used for all connections and tasks that the script performs.

> **Caution** Although some scripting technologies—such as WMI and ADSI—provide a means to pass alternate credentials, don't make the mistake of hard-coding those credentials directly into your scripts. Instead, prompt for those credentials when the script runs. As we discussed in Chapter 2, "Script Security," there's no way to ensure that hard-coded credentials will remain confidential, making them a significant security risk.

The reason that your identity is so important is that the remote computer will grant you permissions based on your identity. In other words, your identity controls what you can do on the remote computer.

Permissions

We've already talked about the permission necessary to connect to various scripting-related technologies and services. After you are connected, however, you'll need the proper permissions to perform whatever task your script is trying to perform.

Almost every area of Windows has its own unique security layer. For example, files and folders utilize NTFS permissions. If you're logged into your computer using a domain account named *Jeff*, and you connect to a shared folder on a remote computer in the same domain, you'll only be able to access the files and folders to which the Jeff account has permission. It's the same as using a non-scripted means, such as Windows Explorer, of accessing those files and folders. There's no special layer of permissions for scripts; they are subject to the same rules as everyone else.

WMI has its own layer of security, which you can administer through the WMI Control MMC snap-in. As shown in Figure 6-3, the snap-in provides access to each WMI namespace installed on a computer.

Figure 6-3   Managing WMI security through the WMI Control snap-in

Modifying the permissions on a namespace is done through a dialog box that's similar to the NTFS permissions dialog box. As shown in Figure 6-4, permissions can be applied to execute WMI methods, write full or partial WMI properties, enable accounts, remotely enable accounts, and much more. As indicated by the gray check boxes, permissions on a namespace can be inherited from a parent namespace or from the WMI root namespace.

Figure 6-4   Configuring security

ADSI also deals with permissions. Connecting to an LDAP-based directory, such as Active Directory, means you'll be dealing with that directory's permissions. Connecting to a standalone or member computer through the WinNT provider means you'll be dealing with local permissions on that computer. Those permissions are often applied through the use of user rights assignments.

As with many other potential scripting problems, the best way to understand remote scripting security is to think about how security would work if you were performing the task manually, without using a script. For example, if you wanted to open Active Directory and delete a user account, what permissions would a user account need to do that? Would the account you use to log onto your workstation have those permissions? If not, a script executed by that same account won't have permissions, either.

Context

Context can be one of the most confusing aspects of remote scripting. It involves identity, and the fact that Windows is a multi-user operating system. Think about this: if Jeff and Don both share a Microsoft Windows XP Professional computer, both of them can log on and have a different desktop configuration, different My Documents contents, and different application preferences saved in the registry. All these user-specific items are stored in the *user profile*, which is made up of both a file system–based profile (a hierarchy of folders that resides under the top-level Documents and Settings folder) and a registry hive (which resides under HKEY_USERS in the registry).

Suppose that Don writes a script that copies several files to the special My Documents folder, and modifies several registry keys under HKEY_CURRENT_USER. Don tests this script on his own, unshared computer, where he's logged in to his usual domain account. The script works fine. Then Don modifies the script slightly to perform the same tasks remotely, through a connection to the computer that Don and Jeff share. Don's goal is to copy several files into Jeff's My Documents folder, and to modify registry keys in HKEY_CURRENT_USER so that they'll affect Jeff's logon session. When Don runs the script, it is completed without error, but Jeff can't see any changes. Figure 6-5 illustrates what happened.

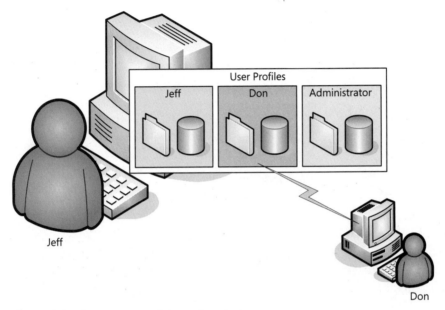

Figure 6-5   Remote connectivity and context

When Don runs the script on his computer, it connects to the shared computer. The script is authenticated by using Don's user account, because that's the account Don used to execute the script. When you log on to a computer using a specific account, your profile loads, so Don's script modified My Documents and HKEY_CURRENT_USER—but it did it for *Don's* profile on that computer, not Jeff's. If Don had never logged on to that computer, the computer would have created a new profile, just as it does any time a user logs on for the first time. Jeff didn't see any of the changes made by the script because none of the changes were made to his profile.

This example illustrates one of the most common problems administrators have: trying to write a script that modifies the profile for the so-called "primary user" of a computer. Windows doesn't designate a "primary user"; it simply stores user accounts and profiles. User A logs on, and has access to User A's profile; if User B logs on, he or she has access to User B's profile. Simple, but frustrating when you're trying to remotely modify a user's profile. As administrators, we commonly think of a computer as belonging to a single, "primary" user, and when we want to perform administrative tasks on a computer, we typically want to do so in a way that will affect that primary user. However, because Windows doesn't support the designation of a single user as the primary one, we need to keep in mind that the user account—or *context*—used by a script might be connected to a different profile than the one we'd prefer.

The next question, of course, is how to write a script that remotely modifies a user's profile. As with most scripting problems, the easiest way to answer this question is to ask another question: How would you copy files into another user's My Documents folder, or modify registry keys in another user's HKEY_CURRENT_USER hive manually? For the files, you'd probably open the remote computer's administrative share (such as \\Client1\C$), navigate to the Documents and Settings folder, and then look for the user's name on a profile folder. From there, you'd navigate to the My Documents folder. The complete file path would look something like \\Client1\C$\Documents and Settings\Jeff\Jeff's Documents. That is exactly what you'd design your script to do. Rather than trying to access the special My Documents folder, which will also provide access to the current profile's My Documents folder, you design your script to navigate through the folder hierarchy to the folder you want to modify.

Modifying the registry is similar, but it's more difficult. Each user's HKEY_CURRENT_USER hive is really just a shortcut to a specific registry tree under HKEY_USERS. However, rather than listing users by name, users' individual trees are identified by Security Identifier, or SID. Figure 6-6 shows the Windows registry editor opened to the HKEY_USERS hive. Each user's personal tree is identified by SID.

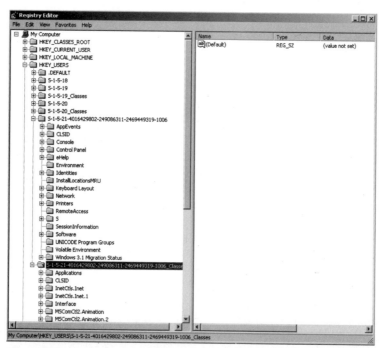

Figure 6-6   Each user has a SID-identified tree under HKEY_USERS

Modifying a user's HKEY_CURRENT_USER hive requires your script to start in HKEY_USERS and to know the SID of the user whose hive you want to modify. This is obviously more complex than just knowing the computer's name, which is why you might want to investigate alternate means of making the modification.

An alternate method might, for example, provide a way for your script to access a specified user's profile. The only way to do this to is if the script is running under that user's security context. In other words, if that user ran the script, the script would have access to that user's full profile, including HKEY_CURRENT_USER. Although asking users to run scripts isn't usually practical, one type of script that always runs under the user's context is a logon script. Because users generally have full permissions to their own profiles, a logon script should have permission to make whatever changes you need to the user's profile. A logon script is therefore an alternate means of executing script code under a specified user's security context, for the purpose of modifying that user's profile.

Working with Windows Firewall

The Windows Firewall, introduced in Microsoft Windows XP Professional Service Pack 2 and Microsoft Windows Server 2003 Service Pack 1, provides a high level of local security for computers on which the Firewall is enabled. However, by default, the Firewall blocks most incoming connections, making remote administration of any kind—including scripting—impossible. That's no reason to turn the Firewall off, of course; you simply need to modify it to allow the necessary incoming connections.

- For file and folder access, enable a Firewall exception for file sharing.

- For WMI access, enable remote management and DCOM connections.

- For other scripting technologies, enable incoming DCOM connections and possibly RPC connections.

Because the configuration and management of the Windows Firewall can involve significant planning and security issues, a more in-depth discussion of it is beyond the scope of this book. Keep in mind that the Firewall can be configured and managed centrally, through Active Directory and Group Policy, meaning you can easily and efficiently create, deploy, and enforce a Windows Firewall policy throughout your enterprise.

More Info   For more information about configuring the Firewall for use with WMI and other remote scripting technologies, see the article at

*http://msdn.microsoft.com/library/default.asp?url=/library/en-us/wmisdk/wmi
/connecting_through_windows_firewall.asp*

(This link is included on the companion CD; click *Connecting through Windows Firewall.*)

Understanding Remote Scripting Objects

To this point, everything we've discussed applies to both types of remote scripting. From now on, however, we're going to focus on deployment scripting. (Much of the rest of this book, especially the chapters about WMI and ADSI, covers the techniques used in connectivity scripting.)

Windows Script Host (WSH) 5.6 includes objects designed for remote scripting. These objects take a script from your computer, copy it to a remote computer, and then execute it on the remote computer. Some objects can transfer script errors back to your computer, where you can have your original script deal with them appropriately. Remote scripting involves two scripts.

- The *deployment script*, which runs on your computer, deploys scripts to one or more remote computers, and can deal with errors raised from the remote computers.

- The *deployed script*, which is copied to and runs on the remote computer, can send errors back to your computer.

Essentially, a simple deployment script looks something like this.

```
Dim objController, objRemoteScript
Set objController = CreateObject("WshController")
Set objRemoteScript = objController.CreateScript( _
  "C:\MyScript.vbs", "Client1")
objRemoteScript.Execute
Do While objRemoteScript.Status <> 1
  WScript.Sleep 1000
Loop
MsgBox "Script complete"
```

We'll discuss each of these objects and methods in the following sections. The core objects here are *WshController*, which copies the script, and *WshRemote*, which represents the remote script and provides methods for controlling it (to a limited degree).

Keep in mind that two restrictions that apply when using the *WshController* object.

- You must be a local administrator on the remote computer.

- The script you deploy to the remote computer must not attempt to interact with the user interface by using *WScript.Echo*, *MsgBox*, *InputBox*, or similar functions. The deployed script will not run in an interactive desktop, so there will be no way for someone to respond to dialog boxes.

Using Other Kinds of Remote Scripting

The *WshController* object is the only object built into the Windows Script Host specifically intended for remote scripting, but that doesn't mean it's the only kind of remote scripting available. Some third-party manufacturers have produced robust and flexible technologies for remote scripting. For example, iTriopoli's AdminScript-Editor (*http://www.adminscripteditor.com*) includes Script Packager, which you use to bundle scripts into a standalone executable file and deploy it. SAPIEN PrimalScript (*http://www.primalscript.com*) has a similar feature, the Evolved Script Packager, which offers a great deal of deployment flexibility.

Another script editor, OnScript (*http://www.onscript.com*) includes remote script-management capabilities. You can use OnScript to manage and execute a repository of scripts on a remote computer. The scripts will run on the remote computer and send status information back to your OnScript console. PrimalScript incorporates a feature roughly similar in purpose, Remote Script Execution Engine, which provides enhanced flexibility for running remote scripts, monitoring their status, and so forth.

Because each of these features is associated with a specific commercial product, we won't cover them in this book. However, if remote scripting of this kind is a common need in your environment, we recommend that you check out one or all of these tools (each is available in a trial version) to see which one best meets your needs.

Understanding Remote Scripting Methods

The *WshController* object has no properties, and one method, *CreateScript*. This method accepts only two arguments: the full path and filename of the script to deploy, and the computer name where the script should be copied. The *CreateScript* method copies the script (the remote computer must also have WSH 5.6 installed), returns a *WshRemote* object that represents the remote script, and provides properties and methods for working with it.

- The *Error* property represents a *WshRemoteError* object, which holds information about any errors that caused the remote script to terminate unexpectedly.

- The *Status* property can have a value of 0, meaning the script is running, or a value of 1, meaning the script has completed.

- The *Execute* method runs the remote script. When the script completes, it is generally removed from the computer. (There are a few very rare circumstances in which it might be left behind, such as when connectivity to the remote computer was interrupted before the script completed.)

- The *Terminate* method cancels the remote script. It first tries to end the script by sending an appropriate *close* message, but if that doesn't work, it simply terminates the remote script's process.

Use the *WshController.CreateScript* object to create your remote script, use the *WshRemote.Execute* object to run it, and check the *WshRemote.Status* object to see when the script is done. Using the *WshRemoteError* object is a bit more complicated because there's no status that tells you whether an error occurred. Instead, when an error occurs, an event is raised. Because events aren't something that are usually dealt with in VBScript, they can seem strange. Essentially, there are two steps for working with events.

1. Create a subroutine that handles the event.

2. Direct the object that might raise the event to use your subroutine.

To react to an error raised by a remote script, for example, you might write a short subroutine that simply displays the remote error.

```
Sub remote_Error
    Dim objError
    Set objError = objRemote.Error
    WScript.Echo "Error - Line: " & theError.Line & _
        ", Char: " & theError.Character & vbCrLf & _
        "Description: " & theError.Description
    WScript.Quit -1
End Sub
```

You would add this subroutine to the earlier script that declared the *objRemote* object. With the subroutine in place, you just need to tell the *objRemote* object to use the new *remote_Error* subroutine if its *Error* event occurs.

```
WScript.ConnectObject objRemote, "remote_"
```

This command tells the *objRemote* object that any events will be handled by subroutines whose names are prefixed with *remote_*. In other words, the *Error* event will be handled by *remote_Error*. The *objRemote* object also has a *Start* event and an *End* event, which would be handled by *remote_Start* and *remote_End*, respectively. The whole script, in one piece, is shown in Listing 6-1 on the next page.

Listing 6-1 Remote Scripting with Error Handling

```
Dim objController, objRemoteScript
Set objController = CreateObject("WshController")
Set objRemoteScript = objController.CreateScript( _
  "C:\MyScript.vbs", "Client1")
WScript.ConnectObject objRemoteScript, "remote_"
objRemoteScript.Execute
Do While objRemoteScript.Status <> 1
  WScript.Sleep 1000
Loop
MsgBox "Script complete"

Sub remote_Error
    Dim objError
    Set objError = objRemoteScript.Error
    WScript.Echo "Error - Line: " & objError.Line & _
        ", Char: " & objError.Character & vbCrLf & _
        "Description: " & objError.Description
    WScript.Quit -1
End Sub
```

 On the CD   You will find this script, as well as other scripts listed in this chapter, on the CD that accompanies this book.

Troubleshooting the *WshController* Object

Unfortunately, *WshController* has a few known problems, and because WSH 5.6 is considered a "mature" product by Microsoft, we're unlikely to see outright fixes to them. There are, however, workarounds.

One known problem is that an error message, "ActiveX component can't create object," appears when you try to use the *CreateScript* method. The bug occurs when the WSH remote scripting setup wasn't done correctly. Microsoft's official resolution is to register the WScript object by typing **wscript –regserver** in a command-line window.

However, that might not always solve the problem. You might also need to add a value to HKEY_LOCAL_MACHINE\SOFTWARE\Microsoft\Windows Script Host\Settings. This should be a string value, its name must be *Remote*, and the data should be the number *1* (even though it's a string value). You'll need to add this value to the remote computer to enable remote scripting functionality. You must have local Administrator privileges on the remote computer to enact this.

Viewing Remote Scripting in Action

Listing 6-2 is a script that deploys C:\Deployed.vbs to each computer listed in C:\Computers.txt. Results are logged to C:\Log.txt.

Listing 6-2 Remote Scripting with Logging

```
Dim objController, objRemoteScript, objFSO
Dim objTSIn, objTSOut, strComputer

'Create objects
Set objController = CreateObject("WshController")
Set objFSO = CreateObject("Scripting.FileSystemObject")

'Read computer names from file
Set objTSIn = objFSO.OpenTextFile("C:\computers.txt")

'Open output file for log
Set objTSOut = objFSO.CreateTextFile("C:\log.txt", True)

Do Until objTSIn.AtEndOfStream

    'Deploy script to remote computer
    strComputer = objTSIn.ReadLine

    objTSOut.WriteLine strComputer & ": Deploying at " & Now

    Set objRemoteScript = objController.CreateScript( _
     "C:\Deployed.vbs", strComputer)
    WScript.ConnectObject objRemoteScript, "remote_"
    objRemoteScript.Execute

    Do Until objRemoteScript.Status = 1
        WScript.Sleep 1000
    Loop

    objTSOut.WriteLine strComputer & " Completed at " & Now

    Set objRemoteScript = Nothing

Loop

objTSIn.Close
objTSOut.Close
WScript.Echo "Deployment script complete."

Sub remote_Error
    Dim objError
    Set objError = objRemote.Error
    objTSOut.WriteLine strComputer & ": Error at " & Now
    objTSOut.WriteLine "  Line: " & objError.Line & _
      ", Char: " & objError.Character & vbCrLf & _
      "Description: " & objError.Description
    WScript.Quit -1
End Sub
```

Let's go through each section of this script and examine what it's doing. The script begins by declaring a *FileSystemObject* object and a *WshController* object.

```
Dim objController, objRemoteScript, objFSO
Dim objTSIn, objTSOut, strComputer

'Create objects
Set objController = CreateObject("WshController")
Set objFSO = CreateObject("Scripting.FileSystemObject")
```

Next, the script opens C:\Computers.txt, which lists one computer name per line. The script also opens a text file for output, which is where we'll write remote script status information.

```
'Read computer names from file
Set objTSIn = objFSO.OpenTextFile("C:\computers.txt")

'Open output file for log
Set objTSOut = objFSO.CreateTextFile("C:\log.txt", True)
```

The script will now read through each line of C:\computers.txt, entering each computer name into the variable *strComputer*.

```
Do Until objTSIn.AtEndOfStream

    'Deploy script to remote computer
    strComputer = objTSIn.ReadLine
```

Note that the script's log messages include the computer name, what happened, and a date and time stamp.

```
    objTSOut.WriteLine strComputer & ": Deploying at " & Now
```

Now the script creates a *WshRemote* object and connects the object's events to an event handler subroutine. Because we don't care about the *Start* or *End* events, we didn't include subroutines for those. When those events are raised, nothing will happen because no matching subroutine exists.

```
    Set objRemoteScript = objController.CreateScript( _
      "C:\Deployed.vbs", strComputer)
    WScript.ConnectObject objRemoteScript, "remote_"
    objRemoteScript.Exceute
```

Next, the deployment script pauses until the deployed script finishes executing. Upon its completion, we'll write another log entry, and then release the *WshRemote* object so that it can be reused in the next iteration of the loop.

```
Do Until objRemoteScript.Status = 1
    WScript.Sleep 1000
Loop

objTSOut.WriteLine strComputer & " Completed at " & Now

Set objRemoteScript = Nothing

Loop
```

When the script concludes, we'll close the text files and display a completion message.

```
objTSIn.Close
objTSOut.Close
WScript.Echo "Deployment script complete."
```

Here's the *WshRemote Error* event handler. It's simply writing error information to our log file.

```
Sub remote_Error
    Dim objError
    Set objError = objRemote.Error
    objTSOut.WriteLine strComputer & ": Error at " & Now
    objTSOut.WriteLine "  Line: " & objError.Line & _
        ", Char: " & objError.Character & vbCrLf & _
        "Description: " & objError.Description
    WScript.Quit -1
End Sub
```

This is a basic script, but it can be easily expanded to perform additional logging or error handling.

Summary

In this chapter, we covered two kinds of remote scripts: those that connect to remote computers to perform a task, and those that deploy scripts to remote computers and execute them there. We discussed the security issues that are involved in remote scripting, and explained how the underlying security layers work, which will help you better analyze and troubleshoot remote scripting security problems when they occur. With this information, you will be prepared to use the scripting techniques in this book and elsewhere.

Chapter 7
Database Scripting

Databases can seem like one of the most difficult technologies to work with from within a script. However, the topic seems more complicated than it really is, largely because most of the documentation for it is written for professional software developers. We'll give you the information you need about database scripting without overloading you with unnecessary details, so you can quickly master the core concepts to make databases an integral part of your scripts.

Database scripting, at first glance, seems difficult, overly complex, and error prone. All that can be true if you're writing a major database-driven application. Fortunately, if you're a Windows administrator trying to automate tasks and keep track of information, databases can be very easy to use. You simply need to focus on the core database technologies, without getting distracted by all the features that only a professional developer would use.

You can use database scripting to perform tasks such as, for example, producing a simple Microsoft Access application with which users could enter information about new accounts. The script would read the new account information from the Access database and create the necessary accounts. This kind of automation helps reduce a somewhat boring and error-prone task into an easy, one-click operation.

Understanding ActiveX Data Objects

The technology that scripts use to access databases is called ActiveX Data Objects (ADO). Don't confuse this with ADO.NET, which is unique to the Microsoft .NET Framework, and isn't designed to be used from VBScript. ADO is the slightly older, just as functional counterpart to ADO.NET that's readily accessible to your scripts.

It's important to understand that ADO is not the only means of accessing data. For example, Microsoft Excel and Access are both capable of storing data, and both can be manipulated through Microsoft Office's built-in Component Object Model (COM) automation interfaces. Text files, another type of data storage, can be easily accessed through the *FileSystemObject* library that you've no doubt used. The great thing about ADO, however, is that it can access *all* these data sources—and many others—through a single, standardized interface. ADO's ability to access multiple data sources is illustrated in Figure 7-1. Your script uses ADO, which provides a single, standardized set of programming interfaces to access any kind of database. ADO, in turn, translates that set of interfaces into the specific interfaces needed by whatever data source you're accessing. In other words, by taking the time to learn ADO, you'll have access to dozens of different types of databases with no additional effort—you won't have to learn separate techniques to access SQL Server databases, Access databases, text files, and so forth.

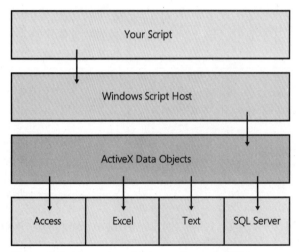

Figure 7-1   Accessing databases through ADO

Before we continue our discussion of databases, however, let's define our terminology.

■ A *database* is a file or other storage mechanism that contains data. A single SQL Server computer can hold multiple databases, whereas a single Access .mdb file is a single database.

■ A *table* is the organizational unit inside a database; most databases can contain one or more tables. Tables are also referred to as *entities*, because they usually contain information about a single type of object, or entity, such as people or computers. Each table consists of the following:

   ❑ *Columns* (also called *fields*) contain the attributes about the entity represented by a table. In a table containing information about people, for example, a column might contain a person's name or address.

❑ *Rows* (also called *records*) contain all the information about a single entity. For example, in a table containing information about computers, a row would include all the columns that contain that computer's name, IP address, and so forth.

An Excel file is a great way to visualize this structure. A single Excel workbook represents a database, with each worksheet, or tab, representing a table, and the rows and columns representing records and fields, as shown in Figure 7-2.

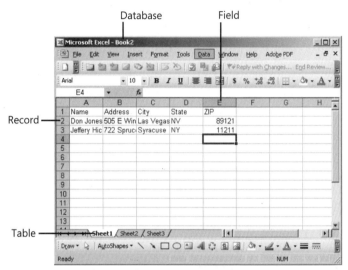

Figure 7-2   Using an Excel file as a database

By and large, working with databases is as easy as working with an Excel workbook. However, before you can begin working with a database, you first have to connect to it.

Understanding *Connection* Objects

In ADO, a *Connection* object is used to represent an electronic connection between your script and a specific database. The *Connection* object tells ADO where the database can be found, how to open it, what user name and password to use (if necessary), and so forth. Creating a new *Connection* object is straightforward.

```
Dim objConn
Set objConn = CreateObject("ADODB.Connection")
```

You call the *Connection* object's *Open* method, and pass it the information needed to connect to the database. This is where most administrators start to get worried, because the so-called *connection strings* can look amazingly complex. But they're not—we'll cover them in the next two sections. When you're done using your database (such as at the end of your script), you call the *Connection* object's *Close* method.

```
objConn.Close
```

This ensures that all database files are properly closed, any server connections (such as those used with SQL Server) are released, and so forth.

ODBC DSN Connections

ADO is capable of making a couple of different types of connections. One type is made through Microsoft's Open Database Connectivity (ODBC) technology. The main benefit of using ODBC is that it offers easy configuration for *Connection* objects. This is technically an outdated technology (it has since been replaced with OLE DB), but it still works, and because your scripts aren't likely to need super fast performance, ODBC does a great job.

You begin by creating an ODBC Data Source Name, or DSN. If you click Administrative Tools on the Start menu and then click Data Sources (ODBC), you'll see a list of existing DSNs, much like the list shown in Figure 7-3. There are two types of DSNs: *User* DSNs, which are configured on the local computer and are only accessible to you; and *System* DSNs, which are configured on the local computer and are accessible to all users of that computer. You can create whichever type is appropriate by clicking the Add button.

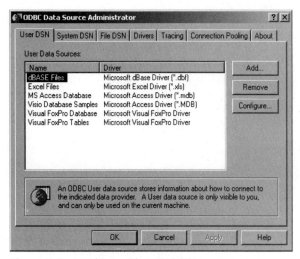

Figure 7-3   Working with ODBC DSNs

Figure 7-4 shows the Create New Data Source dialog box, which appears when you click Add. In it, you select a driver for the DSN. Pick the driver that matches the type of database you want to access: Access, Excel, dBase, FoxPro, Oracle, Paradox, Text files, SQL Server, and so forth.

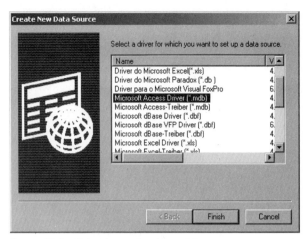

Figure 7-4   Selecting a database driver

When you click Finish, another dialog box appears that is specific to the type of database you selected. For example, Figure 7-5 shows the dialog box for an Access database. You must specify a DSN, which is the name of your data source. For an Access database or an Excel file, you'll also specify the file to which you want to connect.

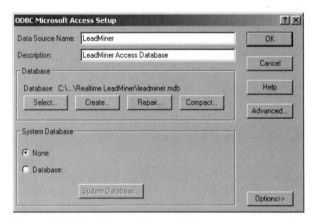

Figure 7-5   Creating an Access DSN

For SQL Server, you must complete a short wizard, which prompts you for the name of the server, the database, login credentials, and so forth. Figure 7-6 on the next page shows a screen from the SQL Server ODBC DSN wizard.

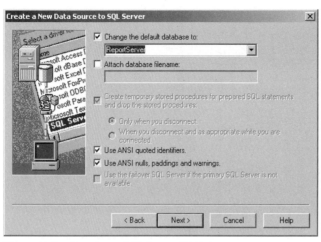

Figure 7-6   Creating a SQL Server DSN

Regardless of the type of database you will connect to, when you're finished, you'll have a new DSN and you'll know its name. Activating the DSN is as simple as calling your *Connection* object's *Open* method, and giving it the DSN.

```
objConn.Open "MyDSN"
```

The downside of connecting in this fashion is that your script now requires that the DSN exist on the computer. In other words, your script won't run properly on other computers until you set up the DSN, which can be a bit difficult to deploy automatically. However, for scripts that you will only run from your own computer, DSNs are a convenient, easy-to-configure way of connecting to databases.

> **Best Practices**   Whenever you use a DSN in your scripts, be sure to include some comment lines describing to what the DSN is connected. These comments will help you, or another administrator, re-create the DSN in the future. You should also document where the database resides, and briefly describe its structure. With these comments in place, everything your script needs will be documented right in the script, so it will be self-contained and easy to maintain.

Connection Strings

Connection strings can seem intimidating, but they provide a more flexible connection option than DSNs. Unlike a DSN, a connection string doesn't require any special configuration on the computer where the script will run. The connection string itself contains everything the *Connection* object needs to find the database. Another advantage is that connection strings can utilize newer OLE DB database drivers (called *providers*), which will make any developers in your environment happier (you probably won't notice any differences). Connection strings can vary widely between databases; the following are examples of the most common. Note that the elements in *italics* are placeholders intended to be replaced with your own information, such as database names. Information in [square brackets] is optional; you can omit those elements if you don't need them in your environment.

- The connection string to Microsoft Access is:

```
Provider=Microsoft.Jet.OLEDB.4.0;Data Source=database path and filename;
```

- The connection string to Microsoft Excel is:

```
Provider=Microsoft.Jet.OLEDB.4.0;Data Source=database path and filename;Extended
Properties=Excel 8.0;
```

- The connection string to Microsoft SQL Server is:

```
Provider=SQLOLEDB;Data Source=server name;Initial Catalog=database name; [User ID=user
name;Password=password]
```

- The connection string to text files (such as CSV, which includes the column names in the first row) is:

```
Provider=Microsoft.Jet.OLEDB.4.0;Data Source=database path;Extended
Properties=Text;HDR=Yes;FMT=Delimited;
```

> **Caution**   Don't hard-code passwords into your scripts. If you need to provide a password in a connection string, prompt for it by using the *InputBox* function or some other technique, and then append the password into the connection string.

Using the connection string is straightforward—simply pass it as the argument of the *Open* method.

```
objConn.Open "Provider=Microsoft.Jet.OLEDB.4.0;Data Source=C:\MyDB.mdb;"
```

Note that when you're using the text file connection string, you're providing only the *path* to the text file; you'll specify the *filename* in your query, which we'll cover next.

Understanding *Recordset* Objects

A database table is simply a set of rows, or *records*. The word *recordset*, then, means pretty much the same thing as the word *table*. That's certainly the case in ADO, where a *Recordset* object represents all, or part, of a database table. When you query information from a database, ADO stores the data in a *Recordset* object so that you can work with it. Suppose you have a database table named *Users* that contains columns named *UserID*, *UserName*, and *UserDescription*. You could query all the rows from that table like this.

```
Dim objRS
Set objRS = CreateObject("ADODB.Recordset")
Set objRS = objConn.Execute("SELECT * From Users")
```

Here are some things to note about querying a database.

- This code snippet just shown assumes that a *Connection* object named *objConn* has been created and opened already.

- The second line in the block just shown is technically unnecessary. The *Execute* method of the *Connection* object returns an *ADODB.Recordset* object, so you don't specifically have to tell VBScript that it's coming. However, including this line makes it easier for script editors to provide assistance specific to the *Recordset* object, which is why we included it.

- We cover the query syntax—called Structured Query Language (SQL)—later in this chapter. However, for now you need to know that the *SELECT * FROM Users* statement retrieves all rows and columns from the Users table.

> **Best Practices**   Professional software developers dislike statements like *SELECT * FROM Users* because it doesn't perform well. A developer would prefer a *SELECT UserID,User-Name,UserDescription FROM Users* statement because it returns the same results and explicitly lists the columns to be retrieved. Performance considerations aside, we also prefer the second method because it makes the script self-documenting. The statement clearly lists the column names being retrieved, so you don't have to hunt around in the database to figure it out later.

Forward-Only Recordsets

Recordsets provide access to a single row, or record, at a time. They use an internal *pointer* to keep track of the current row. By default, they start with the pointer on the first row. You can use one of four statements to move the pointer around.

- *MoveNext*

- *MovePrevious*

- *MoveFirst*

- *MoveLast*

However, the example we just showed you—using the *Connection* object's *Execute* method to return a recordset—returns a special type of recordset called a *forward-only recordset*. These are fast performers, but they only support the *MoveNext* statement, meaning after you've moved on to the next row, you can't go back. In a lot of cases, such as enumerating through a list of users to be added to Active Directory, forward-only functionality is all you need.

The *Recordset* object also supports a property called *EOF*, which stands for end of file. This property is set to TRUE when the recordset pointer is positioned past the last row of data. An easy way to enumerate through each row is to use the *EOF* property in a loop.

```
Do Until objRS.EOF = True
    objRS.MoveNext
Loop
```

Of course, just looping through all the records isn't terribly useful—you need to somehow get to the data inside those records. You do this by referring to the column name you want.

```
Do Until objRS.EOF = True
    strUser = objRS("UserName")
    strID = objRS("UserID")
    strDesc = objRS("Description")
    objRS.MoveNext
Loop
```

This pulls the contents of each row into a set of string variables, which can then be used in other statements to add the new user to Active Directory.

> **Tip**   Don't forget that *MoveNext* statement inside the loop. Without it, the recordset pointer is never moved, so it never reaches the end. The loop continues indefinitely, or until you press Ctrl+Break to terminate the script.

When you're finished using the recordset, it's a good idea to close it, releasing any resources it had been using.

```
Do Until objRS.EOF = True
    strUser = objRS("UserName")
    strID = objRS("UserID")
    strDesc = objRS("Description")
    objRS.MoveNext
Loop
objRS.Close
```

Other Types of Recordsets

There are several other types of recordset are available to you. After forward-only (which is the default), the most useful type is *dynamic*. To open a dynamic recordset, you have to explicitly declare a new *Recordset* object and use its *Open* method.

```
Dim objRS
Set objRS = CreateObject("ADODB.Recordset")
objRS.Open "SELECT Column FROM Table", objConn, 2
```

Note that the *Open* method requires a SQL statement, a reference to an open *Connection* object, and the number 2, which indicates that you want a dynamic recordset. If you forget the 2, the default is 0, which opens a forward-only recordset.

Note   Not all database providers support dynamic recordsets. If you get an error trying to open one, try opening a forward-only recordset. If that works, your database provider doesn't support a dynamic recordset.

With a dynamic recordset, you can use the full range of the *Recordset* object's navigation methods to move the recordset pointer forward and backward. You can also modify a dynamic recordset.

```
Dim objRS
Set objRS = CreateObject("ADODB.Recordset")
objRS.Open "SELECT Birthday FROM Table WHERE [Name] = 'Don'", objConn, 2
objRS("Birthday") = "11/22/71"
objRS.Update
```

Note   Sometimes, a database provider will give you a dynamic recordset, but won't support the *Update* method. You won't know this is the case until you try it and get an error on the update attempt. Later in this chapter, we'll show you other ways to add and change data.

In the example just shown, a *WHERE* clause was added to the SQL statement, so the only rows returned are those in which the *Name* column contains the value *Don*. The query selected only one column, *Birthday*, and we can assign a new value to that column. Calling the *Update* method saves the change back to the database. Remember to call the *Update* method before calling a statement such as *MoveNext*, which moves the recordset pointer. Failing to call *Update* first could result in your changes being lost, depending on the type of database to which you're connected.

Note   Notice that the *Name* column is listed inside square brackets. That's because the word *Name* has a specific meaning in most database systems. By enclosing it in square brackets, we can ensure that it'll be treated as a column name, and not as something else.

You can also use dynamic recordsets to add new records.

```
Dim objRS
Set objRS = CreateObject("ADODB.Recordset")
objRS.Open "SELECT * FROM Table", objConn, 2
objRS.AddNew
objRS.("UserName") = "Don"
objRS("Birthday") = "11/22/71"
objRS.Update
```

This is similar to changing data. You call the *AddNew* method to create a new, blank record, and move the recordset pointer to it. Then you populate the table's columns with data, and call the *Update* method to save your changes.

> **Note**   Many databases contain internal rules about what type of data is allowed. For
> example, if the *Birthday* column is defined as a date field, and you try to insert a name,
> the database will reject your change. That rejection probably won't occur until you call the
> *Update* method, which is when data is saved back to the database. When failures occur on
> the *Update* method, carefully check the changes you've made, because one of them is proba-
> bly causing the problem.

Another less common type of recordset is *static* (its number is 1 in the *Recordset* object's *Open*
method). It's a combination of the forward-only and dynamic recordset types. You can use it
to move back and forth through a static recordset, but you can't make changes.

Recordset Tips and Tricks

There are a few handy tips and tricks for working with recordsets. First, the *Recordset* object
has a *RecordCount* property, which you'd think would provide the number of records inside
the recordset. Unfortunately, the recordset doesn't know how many records there are until
you've moved the pointer to the last record. With a forward-only recordset, that's pretty useless, but with a dynamic recordset you can move back and forth between records, as shown in
this snippet.

```
Dim objRS
Set objRS = CreateObject("ADODB.Recordset")
objRS.Open "SELECT * FROM Table", objConn, 2
objRS.MoveLast
objRS.MoveFirst
WScript.Echo objRS.RecordCount & " records queried."
```

This usually provides an accurate count (depending on the database type) and ends with the
recordset pointer positioned on the first row, right where it started.

You might want to check if a recordset is completely empty when, for example, your query
doesn't return any results. If you run the following when *Table* is empty, you'll get an empty
recordset.

```
Dim objRS
Set objRS = CreateObject("ADODB.Recordset")
objRS.Open "SELECT *FROM Table", objConn, 2
```

An easy way to check is to see if the recordset's *EOF* and *BOF* (beginning of file) properties are
TRUE. *BOF* is only TRUE when the recordset pointer is positioned on the first record. If both
BOF and *EOF* are TRUE, the recordset is empty.

```
Dim objRS
Set objRS = CreateObject("ADODB.Recordset")
objRS.Open "SELECT *FROM Table", objConn, 2
If objRS.EOF And objRS.BOF Then
    'empty recordset
End If
```

Recordset objects have a few other useful properties and methods, including the following:

- The *Bookmark* property can be used to store the position of any record and then quickly return to that record. As you might expect, this property isn't useful in forward-only recordsets, because the recordset can't move backward to a bookmark's location. To use a bookmark, position the recordset—by using *MoveFirst*, *MoveNext*, or whatever—in the record you want to remember. Assign a variable to the *Bookmark* property (*myVar = objRS.Bookmark*). To later return to the bookmark, simply assign the *Bookmark* property to that variable (*objRS.Bookmark = myVar*). You can have multiple bookmarks in effect at once, provided you have a unique variable to hold each one.

- The *State* property can be used to check whether a recordset is open. The *State* property will be zero when a recordset is closed, and 1 when it is opened. Other states—2 for connecting, 4 for executing a query, and 8 for fetching data—exist, but typically change rapidly.

- The *Sort*, *Filter*, and *MaxRecords* properties can be used to sort the recordset, filter it so that only specific rows are accessible, and limit the number of rows returned by a query. However, it's more efficient to perform these operations in the original SQL query used to populate the recordset. We'll show you how to do that later in this chapter.

- The *Find* method is used to locate matching records. Execute something like *objRS.Find "Column = Value"* (or *objRS.Find "Column = 'Value'"* if the column contains string values) to immediately move the recordset pointer to the first matching column. You can also execute *objRS.Find "Column = Value", 5* to skip 5 rows (or any other number you specify) before beginning the search. Executing *objRS.Find "Column = Value",,-1* will search backward (in a dynamic or static recordset) rather than forward. The *Seek* method works similarly, but isn't quite as flexible.

- The *Delete* method deletes the current row in a dynamic recordset.

- The *Supports* method can be used to determine the capabilities of a given recordset, based on its type and the database provider. *Supports* accepts a number, which specifies how many capabilities you're checking. It returns TRUE if all the capabilities specified are supported, FALSE if not. For example, *objRS.Supports(16778240)* will return TRUE if *objRS* supports the *AddNew* method. The following list provides values for most of the available recordset capabilities. To check for multiple capabilities, use *Supports* once per capability, or combine capabilities by using the Boolean *Or* operator (for example, execute *objRS.Supports(16778240 Or 512)* to check for *AddNew* and *MovePrevious* support).

  - *AddNew* = 16778240
  - *Bookmark* = 8192
  - *Delete* = 16779264
  - *Find* = 524288
  - MovePrevious = 512
  - *Update* = 65536

There are a lot more things that you can do with a recordset, but these are the techniques you'll use most when writing administrative scripts.

> **Tip**   You can find the full ADO documentation in the Microsoft MSDN Library if you're using the CD-based or DVD-based Library (ask the developers in your organization for an old copy). To navigate through the Table of Contents click Data Access, click Reference, click ADO, click ADO Programmer's Reference, click ADO API Reference, and finally click ADO Objects and Interfaces. An online version of the Library is available at *http://msdn.microsoft.com/library*. Because the URLs and organization of the online Library changes from time to time, we can't guarantee that the ADO information will be in the same location, or even available, but at press time, to navigate to the topic, click Win32 and COM Development, click Data Access and Storage, click ADO, click ADO, click ADO Programmer's Reference, click ADO API Reference, and finally click ADO Objects and Interfaces. The current URL to this location is
>
> *http://msdn.microsoft.com/library/default.asp?url=/library/en-us/ado270/htm /mdmscadoapireference.asp*
>
> (This link is included on the companion CD; click *ADO API Reference*.)

The following best practices apply to accessing any database by using code or a script.

- Always specify a column list in *SELECT* statements, and only specify the columns you plan to use.

- Unless you actually need *all* the data in a table, specify a *WHERE* clause to help reduce the amount of data returned.

- Dynamic recordsets require more computing resources than forward-only recordsets, so use a forward-only recordset whenever possible.

There are ways to add and change data other than the methods available to a dynamic recordset—we'll cover them later in this chapter.

Understanding *Command* Objects

Most scripters ignore ADO *Command* objects. In fact, if you have no plans to work with SQL Server-based databases, you can safely skip this section. If you intend to work with SQL Server, however (or other relational database management systems like Oracle, Sybase, or DB2), *Command* objects provide better performance and help you better utilize the capabilities built into the server software.

A *Command* object is a way of passing a query to the server in a way that allows the server to execute the command more efficiently. The biggest benefit is seen when you're accessing a stored procedure, which is a special type of script contained and executed on the server. Creating stored procedures is beyond the scope of this book, but if there are stored procedures on your server, we encourage you to use them through the *Command* object. Even without stored procedures, however, the *Command* object is useful in conjunction with database servers, because it allows queries to be executed more efficiently, especially if the query will be executed more than once. You create a *Command* object in much the same way as other database objects.

```
Dim objCmd
Set objCmd = CreateObject("ADODB.Command")
```

There are three required properties that must be set for the *Command* object to function properly.

```
objCmd.ActiveConnection = objConn
objCmd.CommandText = "SELECT Column1 FROM Table2"
objCmd.CommandType = 1
```

The *objConn* property must represent a declared, opened *Connection* object. You can then use the *Command* to open a *Recordset* object.

```
Set objRS = objCmd.Execute
```

These six lines of code submit a query to the server and return a forward-only recordset. You wouldn't use this format if you were executing a stored procedure, however. Most stored procedures are *parameterized*, that is, they accept one or more input arguments and might even provide output through an output argument—not unlike a command-line utility. Using a stored procedure with a *Command* object requires some special setup. First, you set the *CommandText* property to be the name of the stored procedure, and then you set the *CommandType* property to the appropriate value for stored procedures.

```
objCmd.ActiveConnection = objConn
objCmd.CommandText = "sp_MyProc"
objCmd.CommandType = 4
```

Next you need to add the parameters. Suppose your stored procedure has three parameters, *Parm1*, *Parm2*, and *Parm3*. *Parm1* is a SQL Server *varchar* data type with a length of 10, *Parm2* is a SQL Server *bigint* data type, and *Parm3* is another *bigint* that will contain the stored procedure's output.

```
objCmd.NamedParameters = True
objCmd.Parameters.Add(objCmd.CreateParameter("Parm1",200,1,10,MyVal1))
objCmd.Parameters.Add(objCmd.CreateParameter("Parm2",20,1,,MyVal2))
objCmd.Parameters.Add(objCmd.CreateParameter("Parm3",20,2,,MyVal3))
```

Setting the *NamedParameters* property to TRUE allows you to add parameters in any order, regardless of the order in which they're defined in the stored procedure. ADO matches parameters based on the names you provide. Here's how the *CreateParameter* method works.

- The method's first argument is the name of the parameter.

- The second argument is the data type of the parameter. Common values for data types include the following:

  - *Bigint* = 20

  - *Char* = 129

  - *Currency* = 6

  - *Date* = 7

  - *Decimal* = 14

  - *Single* = 4

  - *Double* = 5

  - *Empty* = 0

  - *Int* (integer) = 3

  - *Smallint* = 2

  - *Tinyint* = 16

  - *Varchar* = 200

  - *VarWChar* (SQL Server *nvarchar* type) = 202

- The third argument specifies the direction of the parameter: 1 for input, 2 for output.

- The fourth argument is optional, and is only required for variable-length data types such as *varchar*, *char*, and so forth. This argument specifies the length of the data field. In this example, *Parm1* was declared with a length of 10 characters, so this length is passed in the *CreateParameter* argument. If you're not using this argument—it isn't required for any of the *int* data types, for example—leave it blank, but be sure to include the extra comma as shown in the example just shown.

- The final argument is the value you're passing to the parameters, or the variable in which an output parameter's value will be stored.

If you're having trouble figuring out what goes where, talk to the developer who created the stored procedure, if possible.

> **Note**   You can use tools such as SQL Server Query Analyzer (in SQL Server 2000), SQL Management Studio (in SQL Server 2005), or SQL Express Manager (for SQL Server 2005 Express Edition) to examine stored procedures and find their input and output parameters and data types.

Listing 7-1 lists all stored procedures in a database, and their parameters (including name, type, direction, and so forth). This script was written using an extension to ADO called ADOX. Although ADOX is beyond the scope of this book, this short script will make it easier to figure out how to use any stored procedures you might have available. Note that system-stored procedures (those built into SQL Server) are not listed. Also note that you need to modify the connection string to match your environment (server name, database name, and so on). This connection string includes additional parameters to utilize SQL Server's Windows-integrated security.

> **Note**   For Listing 7-1 to run properly, you must have appropriate permissions, and the database server must support the ADOX library. If your results include procedure names but not parameters, you might not have sufficient permissions, or your database server might not be configured to enumerate parameters through ADOX.

Listing 7-1 List Stored Procedures

```
Dim objConn
Set objConn = CreateObject("ADODB.Connection")
objConn.ConnectionString = "Provider=SQLOLEDB.1;Integrated " & _
  "Security=SSPI;" & _
  "Persist Security Info=False;Initial " & _
  "Catalog=database-name;Data Source=server-name"
objConn.Open

Dim objCatalog
Set objCatalog = CreateObject("ADOX.Catalog.2.8")
objCatalog.ActiveConnection = objConn

Dim objProcedure, objParameter
Set objProcedure = CreateObject("ADODB.Command")
Set objParameter = CreateObject("ADODB.Parameter")

'show procedure count
objCatalog.Procedures.Refresh
WScript.Echo objCatalog.Procedures.Count & " procedures"
WScript.Echo ""

'set the procedure name
For Each objProcedure In objCatalog.Procedures
 WScript.Echo "Procedure " & objProcedure.Name
 WScript.Echo "Parameters: "

 'show parameters
 On Error Resume Next
 For Each objParameter In objProcedure.Parameters
  WScript.Echo " " & objParameter.Name & _
   ", type=" & objParameter.Type & _
   ", direction=" & objParameter.Direction & _
   ", size=" & objParameter.Size
 Next
 On Error GoTo 0

 WScript.Echo String(40,"-")

Next
```

On the CD   You will find this script, as well as other scripts listed in this chapter, on the CD that accompanies this book.

Understanding the Differences Between Databases

Although ADO provides fairly uniform access to a variety of data sources, some data sources have slightly different requirements than others. To prevent you from becoming stuck because of these different requirements, we're going to explain as many of them as we can, focusing on the ones that caused problems for us when we were first working with ADO.

Text Files

The issue with text files is that the connection strings don't specify the file.

```
Provider=Microsoft.Jet.OLEDB.4.0;Data Source=C:\Data\;Extended
Properties=Text;HDR=Yes;FMT=Delimited;
```

The connection string simply specifies the *path* where the file is located. You specify the file when you write your query, substituting the name of the file for the table name.

```
SELECT Column1,Column2 FROM MyTextData.csv
```

The text file also must contain column headers. In other words, the first row of the file must be the names of each column. Text files can be delimited by using commas, tabs, or other common characters. In a comma-separated values (CSV) file, any values that contain commas must be further delimited inside double quotation marks.

Tip   Because text files are so picky about formatting, we often find it's easier to load an existing CSV or other text file into Excel, save it as an Excel workbook, and then work with it directly in that format.

Excel Workbooks

Excel workbooks use most of the techniques we've already shown you. One thing that sometimes causes problems, however, is the worksheet names, which act as table names in ADO. For example, if you have a sheet named *Sheet1*, you'd need to write your queries like this.

```
SELECT Column1, Column2 FROM [$Sheet1]
```

Also note that the Excel database provider uses the values in the first row of the worksheet as the column names. Although you can also use column labels as names, we don't recommend this technique.

```
SELECT A, B, C FROM [$Sheet1]
```

When you're reading your script six months later, it's going to be difficult to remember what A, B, and C were supposed to represent. Instead, create column names that describe the data in the column. *UserName*, *UserPassword*, *ComputerName*, *ServicePackVersion*, and so forth are all good examples of column names that'll be easy and clear when you need to work on your script months down the line.

Access Databases

The biggest difference between Access and other providers is Access' date delimiters. Most databases allow you to treat dates as a string.

```
SELECT Column1, Column2 FROM Table WHERE DateField = '1/1/2005'
```

However, Access requires dates to be delimited with the hash or pound sign (#) character.

```
SELECT Column1, Column2 FROM Table WHERE DateField = #1/1/2005#
```

Other than this, you use Access in largely the same way you use the other techniques we've showed you.

> **Tip**   If you execute a query and your script returns an error indicating that one or more parameters is incorrect, check the spelling of your column names. That type of error is usually Access' way of telling you that it didn't recognize one of the column names you specified.

> **Tip**   Whenever you're debugging queries, one trick is to open the database directly in Access. There, you can create a new query, switch to SQL view, and paste whatever query you're debugging. You can execute the query by clicking the Run Query (!) button, and Access will immediately display any errors, often with more detail than the errors you get through ADO. After your query is debugged, you can move it back into your script.

SQL Server Databases

SQL Server databases are essentially the standard around which ADO was built, so they don't have any differences from the examples and techniques we've shown you so far. However, because a SQL Server is a true *back-end* database, rather than just a file like Access, Excel, or a text file, SQL Server provides less support for some dynamic recordset capabilities. You also need to be more careful when using SQL Server, and understand that others might be using the server to work with data in the same or other databases. You should always specify the columns to retrieve, retrieve as few rows and columns as possible, and use forward-only or static recordsets (which help reduce overhead on the SQL Server computer).

Tip   As with Access, debugging queries can be easier through SQL Server itself. Simply open SQL Server's Query Analyzer tool (which is installed as part of the SQL Server administrative tools, and you need a license to run it). For SQL Server 2005, use Management Studio (Query Analyzer was only a separate tool prior to SQL Server 2005). There, you can create a new query and execute it. As with Access, you'll get immediate and detailed feedback about any problems with your query, and after your query is debugged, you can move it back into your script.

Understanding SQL

SQL is the universal language of databases, and ADO is built around it. Although you can use ADO without using SQL, you'll get the most power and flexibility from ADO when it is used in conjunction with the SQL language. In the next couple of sections, we'll introduce you to the SQL language as it's used to query and change data, and we'll provide you with a complete toolset for database scripting.

Queries that Return Results

The most common SQL query is the *SELECT* query, which is used to retrieve data from a database. The simplest form of a *SELECT* query retrieves all columns and rows from a given table.

```
SELECT * FROM MyTable
```

You can improve the performance and the maintainability of your script by specifying the columns that you're querying, even if you're querying all the columns in the table.

```
SELECT UserName, UserID, Description FROM MyTable
```

Best Practices   SQL is not case-sensitive. However, as a general rule, SQL keywords—like *SELECT* and *FROM*—are in all uppercase, whereas object names—such as column and table names—are in camel case.

The *WHERE* Clause

You can and should limit the rows returned by a query to just those you need. A *WHERE* clause can provide a filter mechanism and limit the number of rows.

```
SELECT UserName, UserID, Description
FROM MyTable
WHERE UserName = 'DonJ'
```

The *WHERE* clause can contain any type of column-to-value comparison, much like a VBScript *If...Then* construct. The following are some examples of comparisons.

- A string comparison:

  ```
  WHERE UserName = 'DonJ'
  ```

- A wildcard string comparison:

  ```
  WHERE UserName LIKE 'Don%'
  ```

  This will match any string beginning with *Don*.

  ```
  WHERE UserName LIKE '%on%'
  ```

  This will match any string containing *on*.

- A numeric comparison:

  ```
  WHERE ServicePackVer > 2
  ```

- A comparison from a list:

  ```
  WHERE ServicePackVer In (1,2,3)
  ```

  This will match any rows where the *ServicePackVer* column contains 1, 2, or 3.

- A range comparison:

  ```
  WHERE StartDate BETWEEN '1/1/2000' AND '1/1/2001'
  ```

- Multiple comparisons:

  ```
  WHERE (UserName Is Null) Or (UserName = '')
  ```

  This will match rows where the *UserName* column contains the special *Null* value, or where it contains an empty string.

The *TOP* Clause

Another way to limit the number of rows returned is to use the *TOP* clause. This clause works with SQL Server and Access, and it can work with other database providers as well. You can choose to return a specific number of rows, or a specific percentage of rows.

```
SELECT TOP 5 UserName FROM Users
SELECT TOP 5 PERCENT ComputerName FROM Computers
```

Of course, *TOP* can be combined with *WHERE* to further limit the results returned by the query. You can also add an *ORDER BY* clause to sort the results by a specified column. When *WHERE* is combined with *TOP*, the records are first sorted, and then the *TOP* clause is executed, so you're getting the first of however many rows based on the sort criteria. Here are some examples of *TOP* and *ORDER BY* in use.

```
SELECT UserName, UserID FROM Users ORDER BY UserName
SELECT TOP 5 ComputerName FROM Computers ORDER BY InstallDate
SELECT UserName FROM Users ORDER BY DateAdded DESC
```

> **Note** Exactly how the *TOP* clause works can be very confusing. For example, suppose you have a table that includes a column named *Version*. Within your table, the *Version* column contains either the value 1 or the value 2, but no other values. Were you to execute a query such as *SELECT TOP 5 Version FROM MyTable*, the query would return all the rows in the table, because it would be trying to select the first 5 values for the *Version* column. With only two values available, all the rows would fit into the *TOP* clause's criteria. This is true for most SQL-compliant databases, including Access. Some databases might behave differently, and not every database supports the *TOP* clause.

The *ORDER BY* Clause

The *ORDER BY* clause sorts in ascending order by default. In the previous example, we added the *DESC* operator to force a reverse (descending) sort, so that the largest *DateAdded* value (the most recent date) would appear first.

> **Note** Each database provider supports a specific version and dialect of SQL. The techniques we cover here should work on almost any database, but the database you're working with might have additional query capabilities.

The *JOIN* Clause

A *JOIN* clause connects two database tables on some related column, producing a set of query results that combine data from the two joined tables. Say, for example, that you have a database with two tables, *Computers* and *Hotfixes*. The Computers table contains basic information about computers, and the Hotfixes table contains information about installed hotfixes. Each hotfix installed on a computer is represented by a single row in the Hotfixes table. The Computers table might be laid out something like this.

ComputerID	ComputerName	InstallDate	WindowsVer	ServicePackVer
2	GS77834	1/1/2001	5.1	2
3	RM88167	2/14/2001	5.1	1
4	ZW85839	3/15/2001	5/1	2

The Hotfixes table might look like this.

HotfixID	ComputerID	HFInstallDate
2	2	4/1/2004
3	2	4/13/2004
4	2	5/11/2005
5	3	4/1/2004

The *ComputerID* column links, or *joins* the tables. By querying all rows in the Hotfixes table that have a Computer ID of 2, you'll find all the hotfixes installed on computer GS77834. It's possible to query all the information from each table in a single recordset. The resulting recordset might look something like this.

Computer-ID	Hotfix-ID	HFInstallDate	Computer-Name	InstallDate	Windows-Ver	Service-PackVer
2	2	4/1/2004	GS77834	1/1/2001	5.1	2
2	3	4/13/2004	GS77834	1/1/2001	5.1	2
2	4	5/11/2005	GS77834	1/1/2001	5.1	2

Here's the query that will create this recordset.

```
SELECT c.ComputerID, c.ComputerName, c.InstallDate, c.WindowsVer, c.ServicePackVer,
hf.HotfixID, hf.HFInstallDate
FROM Computers c INNER JOIN Hotfixes hf
ON c.ComputerID = hf.ComputerID
```

Note the following about how this query works.

- The column names are prefixed with *c* or *hf*, indicating the table where each column is located. Notice that the tables names—in the *FROM* portion of the query—are given the *c* and *hf* alias.

- The column aliases are necessary because the tables share one common column name: *ComputerID*. The aliases allow ADO to determine to which column you're referring.

- The *INNER JOIN* clause in the *FROM* section specifies the tables that will be joined.

- The *ON* clause specifies the columns that join the two tables.

- You could also add *TOP*, *WHERE*, or *ORDER BY* clauses to further filter or sort the result set.

Queries that include *JOIN* clauses can become quite complicated, especially when more than two tables are involved. We find it's easier to use a tool like Microsoft Access, which provides a visual query builder, to create these complicated queries. After building your query graphically in Access, you can switch to SQL view, copy the SQL query syntax to the Clipboard, and then paste it into your script.

Queries that Make Changes

We mentioned earlier that the dynamic recordset methods—*Update*, *Delete*, and *AddNew*—can be used to add and change data. The dynamic recordset methods can also be used with the *SQL INSERT*, *UPDATE*, and *DELETE* queries, which change data but don't return any rows into a recordset. You execute these queries by using the *Connection* or *Command* object's *Execute* method. However, unlike previous examples, you don't set a *Recordset* object as the result, because these queries don't return any results.

```
objConn.Execute "DELETE FROM MyTable WHERE Column = 'Value'"
```

> **Note**   Notice that there are no parentheses around the query. The *Execute* method is being used as a statement, not as a function, because it isn't returning any results.

The *DELETE* Query

To delete data, specify the table name in your query. This query will delete everything in the Users table.

```
DELETE FROM Users
```

Notice that no column list is included; none is needed, because entire rows are being deleted. There's no way to delete just a single column, so there's no need to specify a column list. Most of the time, you'll add a WHERE clause to limit the scope of the deletion.

```
DELETE FROM Users WHERE UserDeactivated = 1
```

Keep in mind that there's no "undo" function with the *DELETE* query. After records are deleted, they're gone forever unless you have a made backup.

The *UPDATE* Query

You use the *UPDATE* query to change data within existing rows of a table. The basic form of the query looks like this.

```
UPDATE MyTable SET Column1 = 'Value1', Column2 = 'Value2'
WHERE Column = 'Value'
```

Omitting the WHERE clause causes the changes to be applied to all rows of the database, so be sure to specify a valid WHERE clause unless you want to modify every row. You can change any number of columns in the SET section by separating each *column=value* pair with a comma.

The *INSERT* Query

You use the *INSERT* query to add new rows to the database. You must specify the table to insert the rows into, the columns that you're providing values for, and the values for those columns. The basic form of the query looks like this.

```
INSERT INTO Table (Column1,Column2,Column3)
VALUES ('Value1', 'Value2', 'Value3')
```

> **Note**   Notice that string values are included in single quotation marks. Numeric values are not. Date values, in SQL Server and most other database systems, are also included in single quotation marks. An exception is Access, which requires date value to be enclosed within hash marks (#).

As a best practice, you should provide a value for every column. One of the most common *INSERT* query errors is caused by not providing a required value for a column. For example, a database might define a column named *Description*, and allow that column to be *Null* or empty. In that case, you can legally omit *Description* from the column list. In other circumstances, the database might define default values for a column, meaning the database will provide values for the column if you don't do so. In that case, if you're okay with the default value, you can omit the column from your *INSERT* query. In all other cases—when there's no default value, and the column doesn't allow empty or *Null* values, you must include the column in your query and provide a value for it.

The other common error is providing an incorrect data type, such as a string value for a column that can only store numeric data. If that happens, your *INSERT* query will typically return an error indicating a *type mismatch*. The exact error depends, of course, on the type of database you're using.

Viewing ActiveX Data Objects

Listing 7-2 connects to each computer in Active Directory and queries its current service pack version. That information is then added to an Access database. Note that this script is connecting to the database by means of an ODBC DSN named *ServicePackDB*, which you'll need to manually create.

> **On the CD**   A sample Access database with the appropriate table is included on this book's companion CD, along with Listing 7-2.

Listing 7-2 Create Service Pack Inventory

```
'update an Access database with all AD computers
'and their current service pack version

'NOTE: See UpdateDB subroutine; expects an ODBC DSN
'to be defined.

'connect to the root of AD
Dim rootDSE, domainObject
Set rootDSE=GetObject("LDAP://RootDSE")
domainContainer = rootDSE.Get("defaultNamingContext")
Set oDomain = GetObject("LDAP://" & domainContainer)

'start with the domain root
WorkWithObject(oDomain)

Sub WorkWithObject(oContainer)
 Dim oADObject
 For Each oADObject in oContainer
  Select Case oADObject.Class
```

```
       Case "computer"
        'oADObject represents a COMPUTER object;
        'get the service pack version and log
        'it to the database
        Dim strComputer
        strComputer = oADObject.cn
        WScript.Echo strComputer
        UpdateDB strComputer, GetSPVer(strComputer)
       Case "organizationalUnit" , "container"
        'oADObject is an OU or container...
        'go through its objects
        WorkWithObject(oADObject)
     End select
  Next
End Sub


Sub UpdateDB(strComputer, strSPVer)
  Dim objConn, objRS, strSQL
  Set objConn = CreateObject("ADODB.Connection")
  objConn.Open "ServicePackDB"

  'see if computer exists in database
  Set objRS = objConn.Execute("SELECT ComputerName FROM Computers " & _
    "WHERE ComputerName = '" & strComputer & "'")
  If objRS.EOF And objRS.BOF Then
     'computer not in database = add
     strSQL = "INSERT INTO Computers (ComputerName," & _
      "ServicePackVersion,LastCheck) VALUES(" & _
      "'" & strComputer & "'," & _
      "'" & strSPVer & "'," & _
      "#" & FormatDateTime(Now,2) & "#)"
  Else
     'computer in database = update
     strSQL = "UPDATE Computers SET " & _
      "ServicePackVersion = '" & strSPVer & "', " & _
      "LastCheck = #" & FormatDateTime(Now,2) & "# " & _
      "WHERE ComputerName = '" & strComputer & "'"
  End If
  objRS.Close
  objConn.Execute strSQL
  objConn.Close
End Sub


Function GetSPVer(strComputer)
  On Error Resume Next
  Dim objWMIService
  Dim propValue
  Dim objItem
  Dim SWBemlocator
  Dim colItems
  Dim strSPVer
  Set SWBemlocator = CreateObject("WbemScripting.SWbemLocator")
  Set objWMIService = SWBemlocator.ConnectServer(strComputer, _
    "\root\CIMV2")
  Set colItems = objWMIService.ExecQuery("Select * " & _
```

```
  "from Win32_OperatingSystem",,48)
 For Each objItem in colItems
   strSPVer= objItem.ServicePackMajorVersion & "." & _
   objItem.ServicePackMinorVersion
 Next
 GetSPVer = strSPVer
End Function
```

Let's take a more detailed look at what this script is doing. Notice that the script's initial comment lines include a reminder about the ODBC DSN, so anyone running the script in the future can easily see the DSN they need to set up for the script to function.

```
'update an Access database with all AD computers
'and their current service pack version

'NOTE: See UpdateDB subroutine; expects an ODBC DSN
'to be defined.
```

The script continues by connecting to the root of the default domain. That means the script needs to run on a computer that is in the domain with which you want to work. Incidentally, you'll need to be a local administrator on each computer in the domain for the script to function. Ideally, you'll run the script as a member of the Domain Admins group.

```
'connect to the root of AD
Dim rootDSE, domainObject
Set rootDSE=GetObject("LDAP://RootDSE")
domainContainer = rootDSE.Get("defaultNamingContext")
Set oDomain = GetObject("LDAP://" & domainContainer)
```

The *WorkWithObject* subroutine is called, and it passes a reference to the root of the domain.

```
'start with the domain root
WorkWithObject oDomain
```

The subroutine is designed to enumerate each object in the current container. A *Select...Case* construct handles both *Computer* and other container objects. In the case of a *Computer* object, the *GetSPVer* function is used to query the service pack version, and the *UpdateDB* subroutine is used to write the information to the database. For a container or organizational unit (OU), the script recursively calls the *WorkWithObject* subroutine, ensuring that every object, no matter how deeply nested in the directory, is processed.

```
Sub WorkWithObject(oContainer)
 Dim oADObject
 For Each oADObject in oContainer
  Select Case oADObject.Class

   Case "computer"
    'oADObject represents a COMPUTER object;
    'get the service pack version and log
    'it to the database
```

```
    Dim strComputer
    strComputer = oADObject.cn
    WScript.Echo strComputer
    UpdateDB strComputer, GetSPVer(strComputer)

  Case "organizationalUnit" , "container"
    'oADObject is an OU or container...
    'go through its objects
    WorkWithObject(oADObject)
  End select
 Next
End Sub
```

The *UpdateDB* subroutine adds information to the database, or updates existing information. It starts by opening the ADO connection to the ODBC DSN, which represents an Access database.

```
Sub UpdateDB(strComputer, strSPVer)
 Dim objConn, objRS, strSQL
 Set objConn = CreateObject("ADODB.Connection")
 objConn.Open "ServicePackDB"
```

Next, the subroutine queries the database for the current computer name to see whether it exists in the database. By checking the recordset's *EOF* and *BOF* properties, the script can determine if the queried computer is already in the database.

```
 'see if computer exists in database
 Set objRS = objConn.Execute("SELECT ComputerName FROM Computers " & _
   "WHERE ComputerName = '" & strComputer & "'")
 If objRS.EOF And objRS.BOF Then
```

If the computer isn't found, an *INSERT* query is constructed in the *strSQL* variable.

```
  'computer not in database = add
  strSQL = "INSERT INTO Computers (ComputerName," & _
    "ServicePackVersion,LastCheck) VALUES(" & _
    "'" & strComputer & "'," & _
    "'" & strSPVer & "'," & _
    "#" & FormatDateTime(Now,2) & "#)"
```

If the computer is located in the database, an *UPDATE* query is constructed and stored in the *strSQL* variable.

```
 Else
  'computer in database = update
  strSQL = "UPDATE Computers SET " & _
    "ServicePackVersion = '" & strSPVer & "', " & _
    "LastCheck = #" & FormatDateTime(Now,2) & "# " & _
    "WHERE ComputerName = '" & strComputer & "'"
 End If
```

The query in *strSQL* is executed, either updating the computer or adding its information to the database. Notice that both of the queries use the hash mark or pound sign (#) as a delimiter for the date column. If you were working with a SQL Server or an Excel database, you'd change that to a single quotation mark.

```
objRS.Close
objConn.Execute strSQL
objConn.Close
End Sub
```

Last is a simple *GetSPVer* function, which uses WMI to query the service pack from the computer. This is where the most errors can occur. If the script can't connect to the computer, for example, it'll return an empty string. (It shouldn't crash, thanks to *On Error Resume Next*.) Inadequate permissions, the Windows Firewall, or simple connectivity problems can result in the target computer being unreachable.

```
Function GetSPVer(strComputer)
 On Error Resume Next
 Dim objWMIService
 Dim propValue
 Dim objItem
 Dim SWBemlocator
 Dim colItems
 Dim strSPVer
 Set SWBemlocator = CreateObject("WbemScripting.SWbemLocator")
 Set objWMIService = SWBemlocator.ConnectServer(strComputer, _
  "\root\CIMV2")
 Set colItems = objWMIService.ExecQuery("Select * " & _
  "from Win32_OperatingSystem",,48)
 For Each objItem in colItems
  strSPVer= objItem.ServicePackMajorVersion & "." & _
   objItem.ServicePackMinorVersion
 Next
 GetSPVer = strSPVer
End Function
```

This useful tool can serve as a template for other homemade inventory tools.

Summary

Although database scripting might look complicated, it can actually be quite straightforward. The flexibility you gain from being able to store complex data in Access, Excel, SQL Server, and other databases is well worth the effort needed to get started in database scripting. In this chapter, we gave you several examples of how to use various types of databases, and we explained all the major ADO objects and techniques to supplement almost any Windows administrative script. If problems occur with your database scripts, remember to test your technique outside the context of a script. Try queries directly in the appropriate tool, for example, or write a smaller test script that's less complicated. That'll help you spot the problem more quickly and get your script up and running as quickly as possible.

Chapter 8

Advanced ADSI and LDAP Scripting

ADSI is one of the most powerful—and sometimes most intimidating—tools that your scripts can use. ADSI can interact with Active Directory, any LDAP directory, the Security Accounts Manager, and other services. The capabilities of ADSI are broad, so we'll introduce you to some tools and techniques that make ADSI scripting a bit easier and more accessible.

If you've been scripting for a while, you've probably worked with Active Directory Services Interface (ADSI). In our experience, however, most administrators are using only a fraction of ADSI's power and flexibility, and often they're not using it at all because it looks so confusing and complex. We're going to introduce you to tools that make writing ADSI scripts easier, so you can get the most out of ADSI.

> **Note** We're deliberately omitting material that's considered basic, or that a scripter with a bit of experience would have already encountered. However, if you'd like a refresher of ADSI's essentials, we suggest reading Don's book, *Managing Windows with VBScript and WMI* (Addison-Wesley, 2004), which includes several chapters on ADSI scripting.

Using the ADSI Scriptomatic

Microsoft's Scripting Guys created an HTML application (HTA) to help make writing ADSI scripts a bit easier. Similar to their popular Scriptomatic, which writes WMI scripts, the ADSI Scriptomatic (also called the EZ-AD Scriptomatic) writes LDAP-based scripts that create, modify, and delete various types of Active Directory objects. As shown in Figure 8-1 on the next page, the scripts produced by this tool are fairly short.

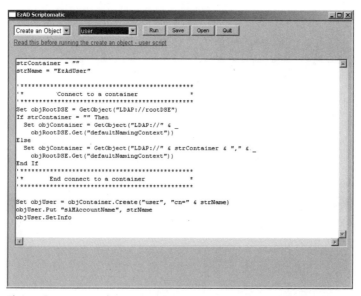

Figure 8-1   Using the ADSI Scriptomatic to create a user account

Selecting a new task from the first drop-down list changes the script. However, notice in Figure 8-2, which now shows the task as deleting a user account, that the script doesn't change very much.

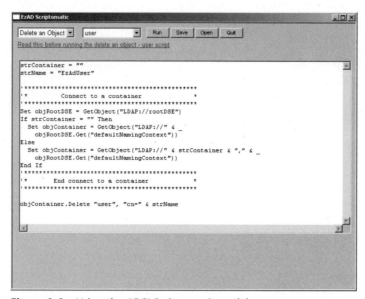

Figure 8-2   Using the ADSI Scriptomatic to delete a user account

Now change the type of object from *user* to *computer*, and you'll see that the script still doesn't change very much. In fact, just the last couple of lines have a significant change, as shown in Figure 8-3. The second line also changes, but that's just a string variable defining the name of the object to, in this case, *delete*.

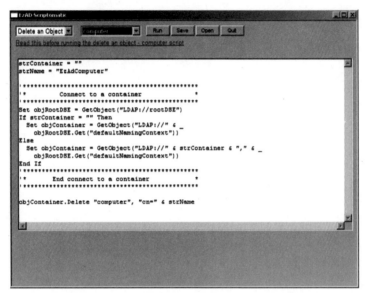

Figure 8-3   Using the ADSI Scriptomatic to delete a computer account

The fact that much of the Scriptomatic's code is boilerplate (it doesn't change no matter what you ask the tool to do) makes the code easier to reuse in your own scripts, which gives you a head start on your ADSI scripts.

Note   If you haven't already done so, download the Scriptomatic at

http://www.microsoft.com/technet/scriptcenter/tools/admatic.mspx

(This link is included on the companion CD; click *ADSI (Active Directory Service Interfaces) Scriptomatic*.)

Connecting to a Domain

The Scriptomatic uses a basic block of code to connect to the domain. Actually, the code connects to a *container,* which can include the domain itself, an organizational unit (OU), or an OU-like container such as the built-in Users container. The code that does the work is on the next page.

```
strContainer = ""
strName = "EzAdUser"

'**************************************************
'*          Connect to a container               *
'**************************************************
Set objRootDSE = GetObject("LDAP://rootDSE")
If strContainer = "" Then
  Set objContainer = GetObject("LDAP://" & _
    objRootDSE.Get("defaultNamingContext"))
Else
  Set objContainer = GetObject("LDAP://" & strContainer & "," & _
    objRootDSE.Get("defaultNamingContext"))
End If
```

The code attempts to connect to whatever is specified in the *strContainer* variable. By default, the variable is an empty string, and you can see the *If...Else...End If* construct that connects to the default naming context of the domain. However, if you populate the variable with something like *ou=Sales* or *cn=Users*, both of which specify a container, the script will connect to that container to retrieve the default naming context.

Obviously, the *strName* variable should be populated with the name of the object you're going to use. After the connection to the domain or container is made, there is a variable named *objContainer* that represents that container. You use that container object's methods to create, delete, and modify objects.

Creating Objects

Creating an object involves directing the container that will store the object—typically an OU—to create the object. The container has a *Create* method for this purpose, and you need only specify the class of object you want to create and the canonical name (*cn*) that the new object will use. The container will create the object and return a reference to it. For most Active Directory objects, you also have to specify a Security Accounts Manager (SAM) name, which is typically just the account name. You can set this name by using the *Put* method of the new object, and then using its *SetInfo* method to save the information back to the directory. Here's what a user account looks like.

```
Set objUser = objContainer.Create("user", "cn=" & strName)
objUser.Put "sAMAccountName", strName
objUser.SetInfo
```

A computer account doesn't need a SAM name.

```
Set objComputer = objContainer.Create("computer", "cn=" & strName)
objComputer.SetInfo
```

A contact object doesn't need a SAM name either. In fact, notice that only the variable name—*objContact*—and the class passed to the *Create* method are different. The variable name doesn't even *have* to be different, but it does make the script clearer. Even an account for an organizational unit is almost identical.

```
Set objOrganizationalunit = objContainer.Create("organizationalUnit", _
  "ou=" & strName)
objOrganizationalunit.SetInfo
```

There are bigger differences in a group account. In addition to longer code at the end of the script, constants are added to the beginning. The main code to create the group looks like this.

```
Set objGroup = objContainer.Create("group", "cn=" & strName)
objGroup.Put "sAMAccountName", strName
objGroup.Put "groupType", ADS_GROUP_TYPE_GLOBAL_GROUP Or _
  ADS_GROUP_TYPE_SECURITY_ENABLED
objGroup.SetInfo
```

Not only must your script specify a SAM account name for the group, but you also have to specify the type of group you're creating. That's done by setting the *groupType* property. The constants at the beginning of the script provide your options.

```
ADS_GROUP_TYPE_GLOBAL_GROUP = &h2
ADS_GROUP_TYPE_LOCAL_GROUP = &h4
ADS_GROUP_TYPE_UNIVERSAL_GROUP = &h8
ADS_GROUP_TYPE_SECURITY_ENABLED = &h80000000
```

Select one of the first three options to make a distribution list (or group). To make a security group, use the Boolean *Or* operator and append the *SECURITY_ENABLED* constant. The sample just shown, which is the default script produced by the Scriptomatic when creating a group, would create a new global security group.

Retrieving Object Information

Using the Scriptomatic to read an object produces a fairly long script. This is one of the most useful scripts you'll from the tool because it displays so many properties for each of the object classes it supports. The following is the portion of the user script that retrieves the object's information. It assumes the boilerplate that connects to the domain has already executed.

```
WScript.Echo VbCrLf & "** General Properties Page**"
WScript.Echo "** (Single-Valued Attributes) **"
strname = objItem.Get("name")
WScript.Echo "name: " & strname
strgivenName = objItem.Get("givenName")
WScript.Echo "givenName: " & strgivenName
strinitials = objItem.Get("initials")
WScript.Echo "initials: " & strinitials
strsn = objItem.Get("sn")
WScript.Echo "sn: " & strsn
strdisplayName = objItem.Get("displayName")
WScript.Echo "displayName: " & strdisplayName
```

```
strdescription = objItem.Get("description")
WScript.Echo "description: " & strdescription
strphysicalDeliveryOfficeName = objItem.Get("physicalDeliveryOfficeName")
WScript.Echo "physicalDeliveryOfficeName: " & strphysicalDeliveryOfficeName
strtelephoneNumber = objItem.Get("telephoneNumber")
WScript.Echo "telephoneNumber: " & strtelephoneNumber
strmail = objItem.Get("mail")
WScript.Echo "mail: " & strmail
strwWWHomePage = objItem.Get("wWWHomePage")
WScript.Echo "wWWHomePage: " & strwWWHomePage

WScript.Echo VbCrLf & "** General Properties Page**"
WScript.Echo "** (MultiValued Attributes) **"
strotherTelephone = objItem.GetEx("otherTelephone")
WScript.Echo "otherTelephone:"
For Each Item in strotherTelephone
 WScript.Echo vbTab & Item
Next
strurl = objItem.GetEx("url")
WScript.Echo "url:"
For Each Item in strurl
 WScript.Echo vbTab & Item
Next

WScript.Echo VbCrLf & "** Address Properties Page**"
WScript.Echo "** (Single-Valued Attributes) **"
strstreetAddress = objItem.Get("streetAddress")
WScript.Echo "streetAddress: " & strstreetAddress
strl = objItem.Get("l")
WScript.Echo "l: " & strl
strst = objItem.Get("st")
WScript.Echo "st: " & strst
strpostalCode = objItem.Get("postalCode")
WScript.Echo "postalCode: " & strpostalCode
strc = objItem.Get("c")
WScript.Echo "c: " & strc

WScript.Echo VbCrLf & "** Address Properties Page**"
WScript.Echo "** (MultiValued Attributes) **"
strpostOfficeBox = objItem.GetEx("postOfficeBox")
WScript.Echo "postOfficeBox:"
For Each Item in strpostOfficeBox
 WScript.Echo vbTab & Item
Next

WScript.Echo VbCrLf & "** Account Properties Page**"
WScript.Echo "** (Single-Valued Attributes) **"
struserPrincipalName = objItem.Get("userPrincipalName")
WScript.Echo "userPrincipalName: " & struserPrincipalName
strdc = objItem.Get("dc")
WScript.Echo "dc: " & strdc
strsAMAccountName = objItem.Get("sAMAccountName")
WScript.Echo "sAMAccountName: " & strsAMAccountName
struserWorkstations = objItem.Get("userWorkstations")
WScript.Echo "userWorkstations: " & struserWorkstations
```

```
WScript.Echo VbCrLf & "** Account Properties Page**"
WScript.Echo "** (The userAccountControl attribute) **"
Set objHash = CreateObject("Scripting.Dictionary")
objHash.Add "ADS_UF_SMARTCARD_REQUIRED", &h40000
objHash.Add "ADS_UF_TRUSTED_FOR_DELEGATION", &h80000
objHash.Add "ADS_UF_NOT_DELEGATED", &h100000
objHash.Add "ADS_UF_USE_DES_KEY_ONLY", &h200000
objHash.Add "ADS_UF_DONT_REQUIRE_PREAUTH", &h400000
intuserAccountControl = objItem.Get("userAccountControl")
For Each Key in objHash.Keys
  If objHash(Key) And intuserAccountControl Then
    WScript.Echo Key & " is enabled."
  Else
    WScript.Echo Key & " is disabled."
  End If
Next
If objItem.IsAccountLocked = True Then
  WScript.Echo "ADS_UF_LOCKOUT is enabled"
Else
  WScript.Echo "ADS_UF_LOCKOUT is disabled"
End If

If err.Number = -2147467259 OR _
  objItem.AccountExpirationDate = "1/1/1970" Then
  WScript.Echo "Account doesn't expire."
Else
  WScript.Echo "Account expires on: " & objItem.AccountExpirationDate
End If

WScript.Echo VbCrLf & "** Profile Properties Page**"
WScript.Echo "** (Single-Valued Attributes) **"
strprofilePath = objItem.Get("profilePath")
WScript.Echo "profilePath: " & strprofilePath
strscriptPath = objItem.Get("scriptPath")
WScript.Echo "scriptPath: " & strscriptPath
strhomeDirectory = objItem.Get("homeDirectory")
WScript.Echo "homeDirectory: " & strhomeDirectory
strhomeDrive = objItem.Get("homeDrive")
WScript.Echo "homeDrive: " & strhomeDrive

WScript.Echo VbCrLf & "** Telephone Properties Page**"
WScript.Echo "** (Single-Valued Attributes) **"
strhomePhone = objItem.Get("homePhone")
WScript.Echo "homePhone: " & strhomePhone
strpager = objItem.Get("pager")
WScript.Echo "pager: " & strpager
strmobile = objItem.Get("mobile")
WScript.Echo "mobile: " & strmobile
strfacsimileTelephoneNumber = objItem.Get("facsimileTelephoneNumber")
WScript.Echo "facsimileTelephoneNumber: " & strfacsimileTelephoneNumber
stripPhone = objItem.Get("ipPhone")
WScript.Echo "ipPhone: " & stripPhone
strinfo = objItem.Get("info")
WScript.Echo "info: " & strinfo
```

```
WScript.Echo VbCrLf & "** Telephone Properties Page**"
WScript.Echo "** (MultiValued Attributes) **"
strotherHomePhone = objItem.GetEx("otherHomePhone")
WScript.Echo "otherHomePhone:"
For Each Item in strotherHomePhone
 WScript.Echo vbTab & Item
Next
strotherPager = objItem.GetEx("otherPager")
WScript.Echo "otherPager:"
For Each Item in strotherPager
 WScript.Echo vbTab & Item
Next
strotherMobile = objItem.GetEx("otherMobile")
WScript.Echo "otherMobile:"
For Each Item in strotherMobile
 WScript.Echo vbTab & Item
Next
strotherFacsimileTelephoneNumber = objItem.GetEx("otherFacsimileTelephoneNumber")
WScript.Echo "otherFacsimileTelephoneNumber:"
For Each Item in strotherFacsimileTelephoneNumber
 WScript.Echo vbTab & Item
Next
strotherIpPhone = objItem.GetEx("otherIpPhone")
WScript.Echo "otherIpPhone:"
For Each Item in strotherIpPhone
 WScript.Echo vbTab & Item
Next

WScript.Echo VbCrLf & "** Organization Properties Page**"
WScript.Echo "** (Single-Valued Attributes) **"
strtitle = objItem.Get("title")
WScript.Echo "title: " & strtitle
strdepartment = objItem.Get("department")
WScript.Echo "department: " & strdepartment
strcompany = objItem.Get("company")
WScript.Echo "company: " & strcompany
strmanager = objItem.Get("manager")
WScript.Echo "manager: " & strmanager

WScript.Echo VbCrLf & "** Organization Properties Page**"
WScript.Echo "** (MultiValued Attributes) **"
strdirectReports = objItem.GetEx("directReports")
WScript.Echo "directReports:"
For Each Item in strdirectReports
 WScript.Echo vbTab & Item
Next

WScript.Echo VbCrLf & "** Environment Properties Page**"
WScript.Echo "** (The ADSI Extension for Terminal Services interface) **"
WScript.Echo "TerminalServicesInitialProgram: " & _
  objItem.TerminalServicesInitialProgram
WScript.Echo "TerminalServicesWorkDirectory: " & _
  objItem.TerminalServicesWorkDirectory
```

```
WScript.Echo "ConnectClientDrivesAtLogon: " & _
  objItem.ConnectClientDrivesAtLogon
WScript.Echo "ConnectClientPrintersAtLogon: " & _
  objItem.ConnectClientPrintersAtLogon
WScript.Echo "DefaultToMainPrinter: " & _
  objItem.DefaultToMainPrinter

WScript.Echo VbCrLf & "** Sessions Properties Page**"
WScript.Echo "** (The ADSI Extension for Terminal Services interface) **"
WScript.Echo "MaxDisconnectionTime: " & _
  objItem.MaxDisconnectionTime
WScript.Echo "MaxConnectionTime: " & _
  objItem.MaxConnectionTime
WScript.Echo "MaxIdleTime: " & _
  objItem.MaxIdleTime
WScript.Echo "BrokenConnectionAction: " & _
  objItem.BrokenConnectionAction
WScript.Echo "ReconnectionAction: " & _
  objItem.ReconnectionAction

WScript.Echo VbCrLf & "** Remote Control Properties Page**"
WScript.Echo "** (The ADSI Extension for Terminal Services interface) **"
WScript.Echo "EnableRemoteControl: " & _
  objItem.EnableRemoteControl

Select Case objItem.EnableRemoteControl
  Case 0
    WScript.Echo "Remote Control disabled"
  Case 1
    WScript.Echo "Remote Control enabled"
    WScript.Echo "User permission required"
    WScript.Echo "Interact with the session"
  Case 2
    WScript.Echo "Remote Control enabled"
    WScript.Echo "User permission not required"
    WScript.Echo "Interact with the session"
  Case 3
    WScript.Echo "Remote Control enabled"
    WScript.Echo "User permission required"
    WScript.Echo "View the session"
  Case 4
    WScript.Echo "Remote Control enabled"
    WScript.Echo "User permission not required"
    WScript.Echo "View the session"
End Select

WScript.Echo VbCrLf & "** Terminal Services Profile Properties Page**"
WScript.Echo "** (The ADSI Extension for Terminal Services interface) **"
WScript.Echo "TerminalServicesProfilePath: " & _
  objItem.TerminalServicesProfilePath
WScript.Echo "TerminalServicesHomeDirectory: " & _
  objItem.TerminalServicesHomeDirectory
WScript.Echo "TerminalServicesHomeDrive: " & _
  objItem.TerminalServicesHomeDrive
```

```
WScript.Echo "AllowLogon: " & _
  objItem.AllowLogon

WScript.Echo VbCrLf & "** COM+ Properties Page**"
WScript.Echo "** (Single-Valued Attributes) **"
WScript.Echo "msCOM-UserPartitionSetLink: "
WScript.Echo " " & objItem.Get("msCOM-UserPartitionSetLink")

WScript.Echo VbCrLf & "** Member Of Properties Page**"
WScript.Echo "** (Single-Valued Attributes) **"
strprimaryGroupID = objItem.Get("primaryGroupID")
WScript.Echo "primaryGroupID: " & strprimaryGroupID

WScript.Echo VbCrLf & "** Member Of Properties Page**"
WScript.Echo "** (MultiValued Attributes) **"
strmemberOf = objItem.GetEx("memberOf")
WScript.Echo "memberOf:"
For Each Item in strmemberOf
 WScript.Echo vbTab & Item
Next

WScript.Echo VbCrLf & "** Object Properties Page**"
WScript.Echo "** (Single-Valued Attributes) **"
strwhenCreated = objItem.Get("whenCreated")
WScript.Echo "whenCreated: " & strwhenCreated
strwhenChanged = objItem.Get("whenChanged")
WScript.Echo "whenChanged: " & strwhenChanged

objItem.GetInfoEx Array("canonicalName"), 0
WScript.Echo VbCrLf & "** Object Properties Page**"
WScript.Echo "** (MultiValued Attributes) **"
strcanonicalName = objItem.GetEx("canonicalName")
WScript.Echo "canonicalName:"
For Each Item in strcanonicalName
 WScript.Echo vbTab & Item
Next
```

As you can see, there's an incredible amount of useful information here. You can see nearly every major property of the object, as well as how to retrieve information from each one. Examining this code is a great way to explore the properties that are available and learn what they do and what values they contain for a typical user in your domain. In fact, you can copy and paste enough code out of the Scriptomatic to create a script that automates the creation of new user accounts. Add some database code, for example, and you could retrieve new user information from an Access database.

Tip   To change any of these properties, use the *Put* or *PutEx* methods instead of *Get* or *GetEx*.

Using Other ADSI Tools

Exploring Active Directory is a great way to expand your scripting repertoire. When you encounter a property that you aren't familiar with, you can examine its values by looking at several existing users. You can also enter the property name into a search engine, and you'll often find examples of how it's used. (Add the term *VBScript* to your search for more script-specific examples.) In the next few sections, we'll look at a few tools that are particularly useful for exploring Active Directory and that make ADSI scripting easier.

Using the ADSI Software Development Kit

The ADSI Software Development Kit (SDK) is a free download from Microsoft's Web site. The SDK is used mainly by professional software developers, but it includes three tools that we've found useful for writing ADSI scripts: ADSVW, ADSCmd, and ADSIDump.

> **On the CD**   We've included a link to the SDK on the CD that accompanies this book. You can also link to the SDK from the Microsoft TechNet Script Center at *http://www.microsoft.com /technet/scriptcenter*.

ADSVW

The Active Directory Browser (ADSVW) is a great tool for exploring Active Directory. Unlike the Scriptomatic, which produces fairly generic scripts, you use ADSVW to browse your domain itself, meaning you can view sample data from objects in your domain to see what's in use. When you first launch the tool, select ObjectViewer, as shown in Figure 8-4.

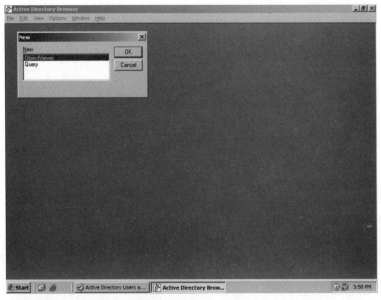

Figure 8-4   Launching ADSVW

Next, you'll be prompted to connect to a specific object, as shown in Figure 8-5. We usually prefer to connect to the root of the domain. That way, the entire domain is available for browsing. To do so, enter **LDAP:** in the Enter ADs Path box. Be sure to clear the Use OpenObject check box to connect to your client computer's default domain.

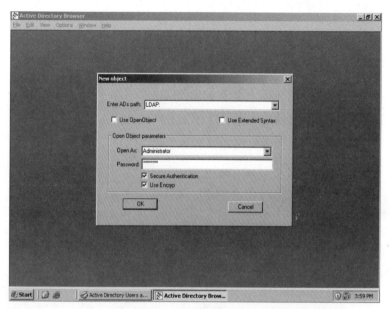

Figure 8-5   Using ADSVW to connect to your default domain

Figure 8-6 shows the browser connected to a domain. Notice that containers such as OUs aren't expandable until you click them in the tree view in the left panel. In Figure 8-6, a user object has been selected. In the Properties drop-down list in the right panel, we selected the *nTSecurityDescriptor* property. The browser recognizes that this is a special property and displays the security descriptor specifics. Also notice that two buttons—SetPassword and Change-Password—are displayed, offering functionality specific to this type of object.

If you select a computer from the domain, the view changes. In Figure 8-7, we selected a simpler property, so the right pane displays general information about the object. Because the object in question is a computer, the password buttons are replaced with a Shutdown button.

The ADSVW graphical interface makes it easier to explore the objects in your domain and see their properties from the same viewpoint that a developer—or a scripter such as yourself—would use. You'll see property names, their values, and so forth, and you can even modify the properties. In fact, ADSVW can be a great development tool because you can use it to verify your property names, object classes, and even the values you place into properties, all before you start writing your script. By testing these things first, your script will be much less likely to run into trouble.

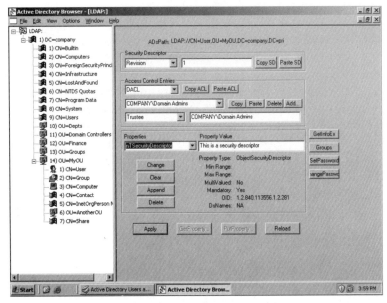

Figure 8-6   Working with users in ADSVW

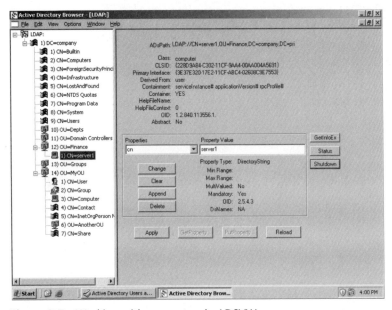

Figure 8-7   Working with computers in ADSVW

ADSCmd

ADSCmd is, as its name implies, a command-line tool. You can use it to list objects in a domain, including objects that aren't usually available to graphical tools. ADSCmd works with any ADSI provider. Remember, ADSI stands for Active Directory Services Interface, but that doesn't mean it's designed only for Active Directory. In fact, rather than thinking of it as *Active Directory* Services Interface, think of it as *Active* Directory Services Interface, meaning it's a generic directory services interface. (ADSI existed before Active Directory itself.) Here's an example of running ADSCmd against a laptop computer using the WinNT provider.

```
adscmd list WinNT://Don-laptop
  __vmware_user__(User)
  Administrator(User)
  ASPNET(User)
  DonJones(User)
  Guest(User)
  HelpAssistant(User)
  IUSR_DON-LAPTOP(User)
  IWAM_DON-LAPTOP(User)
  SQLDebugger(User)
  SUPPORT_388945a0(User)
  testuser(User)
  VUSR_DON-LAPTOP(User)
  WADM_DON-LAPTOP(User)
  Administrators(Group)
  Backup Operators(Group)
  Guests(Group)
  Network Configuration Operators(Group)
  Power Users(Group)
  Remote Desktop Users(Group)
  Users(Group)
  Debugger Users(Group)
  ESR_Administrator(Group)
  ESR_Reporter(Group)
  HelpServicesGroup(Group)
  VS Developers(Group)
  __vmware__(Group)
  ACS(Service)
  Adobe LM Service(Service)
  AdobeVersionCue(Service)
  Alerter(Service)
  ALG(Service)
  AppMgmt(Service)
  aspnet_admin(Service)
  aspnet_state(Service)
  Ati HotKey Poller(Service)
  AudioSrv(Service)
  BITS(Service)
  Browser(Service)
  BthServ(Service)
  CeEPwrSvc(Service)
```

```
CFSvcs(Service)
CiSvc(Service)
ClipSrv(Service)
COMSysApp(Service)
CryptSvc(Service)
DcomLaunch(Service)
Dhcp(Service)
...
W3SVC(Service)
WebClient(Service)
winmgmt(Service)
WmcCds(Service)
WmcCdsLs(Service)
WMDM PMSP Service(Service)
WmdmPmSN(Service)
Wmi(Service)
WmiApSrv(Service)
wscsvc(Service)
wuauserv(Service)
WZCSVC(Service)
xmlprov(Service)
Total Number of Objects enumerated is 143
```

> **Note**   We snipped some lines out of the middle of this listing to keep it short, but 143 total objects were listed when we ran it.

You'll notice that in addition to users and groups, the WinNT provider can connect to services. (The LDAP provider, when used with Active Directory, can't connect to services.) You can start and stop services by using the WinNT provider to connect to these service objects (which we'll demonstrate later in this chapter). Here's an example of using ADSCmd with the LDAP provider to connect to a domain's root.

```
adscmd list LDAP://company.pri
  CN=Builtin(builtinDomain)
  CN=Computers(container)
  OU=Depts(organizationalUnit)
  OU=Domain Controllers(organizationalUnit)
  OU=Finance(organizationalUnit)
  CN=ForeignSecurityPrincipals(container)
  OU=Groups(organizationalUnit)
  CN=Infrastructure(infrastructureUpdate)
  CN=LostAndFound(lostAndFound)
  OU=MyOU(organizationalUnit)
  CN=NTDS Quotas(msDS-QuotaContainer)
  CN=Program Data(container)
  CN=System(container)
  CN=Users(container)
Total Number of Objects enumerated is 14
```

Notice that only the objects in the root—which is what we queried—are listed. If you wanted to see what was in a specific OU, such as *MyOU*, you'd do this.

```
adscmd list LDAP://dc/OU=MyOU,DC=company,DC=pri
  OU=AnotherOU(organizationalUnit)
  CN=Computer(computer)
  CN=Contact(contact)
  CN=Group(group)
  CN=InetOrgPerson No idea(inetOrgPerson)
  CN=Share(volume)
  CN=User(user)
Total Number of Objects enumerated is 7
```

ADSCmd is a useful tool for quickly determining what is in a particular container. It's also useful for testing LDAP queries that are intended to retrieve a container. ADSCmd can also retrieve other objects. For example, the listing just shown indicates that *MyOU* contains a user account named *User*. Here's how you'd retrieve that.

```
adscmd dump LDAP://company.pri/CN=User,OU=MyOU,dc=company,
  DC=pri
cn                              : User
instanceType                    : 4
nTSecurityDescriptor            : Data type is 9

objectCategory                  : CN=Person,CN=Schema,CN=Configuration,DC=compan
y,DC=pri
objectClass                     : top, person, organizationalPerson, user
objectSid                       : Data type is 8209

SAMAccountName                  : User
```

The *dump* keyword shows the properties of the object, rather than its child objects, because in this case, the object, a user, doesn't have child objects. This is a great way to test an LDAP query before adding it to your script, or to test LDAP queries generated by your script as part of a troubleshooting process.

ADSIDump

This powerful command-line utility lists every object, and most of their attributes, from the domain. The information is output to a file for easier review. Here's a portion of a file generated by ADSIDump. (Note that the output shown onscreen is less complete that what's sent to the output file you specify.)

```
==========================================================

***  DC=company  ***
  ROOT OBJECT
  Full ADs path: "LDAP://DC=company,dc=pri"
  Class: domainDNS
  Schema: LDAP://schema/domainDNS
  Attributes ------------------
    dc : (BSTR) "company"
    instanceType : (INT) 5
    nTSecurityDescriptor : (Unknown variant type)
    objectCategory : (BSTR) "CN=Domain-DNS,CN=Schema,CN=Configuration,DC=company,DC=pri"
    objectClass : (ARRAY) [ "top" "domain" "domainDNS"]
    auditingPolicy : (Unknown variant type)
    creationTime : (Unknown variant type)
    distinguishedName : (BSTR) "DC=company,DC=pri"
    forceLogoff : (Unknown variant type)
    fSMORoleOwner : (BSTR) "CN=NTDS Settings,CN=DC,CN=Servers,CN=Default-First-Site-
Name,CN=Sites,CN=Configuration,DC=company,DC=pri"
    gPLink : (BSTR) "[LDAP://CN={31B2F340-016D-11D2-945F-
00C04FB984F9},CN=Policies,CN=System,DC=company,DC=pri;0]"
    isCriticalSystemObject : (BOOL) TRUE
    lockoutDuration : (Unknown variant type)
    lockOutObservationWindow : (Unknown variant type)
    lockoutThreshold : (INT) 0
    masteredBy : (BSTR) "CN=NTDS Settings,CN=DC,CN=Servers,CN=Default-First-Site-
Name,CN=Sites,CN=Configuration,DC=company,DC=pri"
    maxPwdAge : (Unknown variant type)
    minPwdAge : (Unknown variant type)
    minPwdLength : (INT) 7
    modifiedCount : (Unknown variant type)
    modifiedCountAtLastProm : (Unknown variant type)
    ms-DS-MachineAccountQuota : (INT) 10
    msDS-AllUsersTrustQuota : (INT) 1000
    msDS-Behavior-Version : (INT) 0
    msDs-masteredBy : (BSTR) "CN=NTDS Settings,CN=DC,CN=Servers,CN=Default-First-Site-
Name,CN=Sites,CN=Configuration,DC=company,DC=pri"
    msDS-PerUserTrustQuota : (INT) 1
    msDS-PerUserTrustTombstonesQuota : (INT) 10
    name : (BSTR) "company"
    nextRid : (INT) 1003
    nTMixedDomain : (INT) 1
    objectGUID : (Unknown variant type)
    objectSid : (Unknown variant type)
    pwdHistoryLength : (INT) 24
    pwdProperties : (INT) 1
    rIDManagerReference : (BSTR) "CN=RID Manager$,CN=System,DC=company,DC=pri"
    serverState : (INT) 1
    subRefs : (ARRAY) [ "DC=ForestDnsZones,DC=company,DC=pri"
"DC=DomainDnsZones,DC=company,DC=pri" "CN=Configuration,DC=company,DC=pri"]
    systemFlags : (INT) -1946157056
    uASCompat : (INT) 1
    uSNChanged : (Unknown variant type)
    uSNCreated : (Unknown variant type)
    wellKnownObjects : (ARRAY) []
    whenChanged : (Unknown variant type)
    whenCreated : (Unknown variant type)
```

That's just the domain itself; each object within the domain is broken down in a similar fashion. (If you're running ADSIDump in a large domain, be prepared to wait a while for the file to finish!). Here's another section of the output, this time for the built-in container.

```
*** CN=Builtin  ***
  Child of DC=company
  Full ADs path: "LDAP://CN=Builtin,DC=company,dc=pri"
  Class: builtinDomain
  Schema: LDAP://schema/builtinDomain
  Attributes ------------------
    instanceType : (INT) 4
    nTSecurityDescriptor : (Unknown variant type)
    objectCategory : (BSTR) "CN=Builtin-Domain,CN=Schema,CN=Configuration,DC=company,DC=pri"
    objectClass : (ARRAY) [ "top"  "builtinDomain"]
    cn : (BSTR) "Builtin"
    creationTime : (Unknown variant type)
    distinguishedName : (BSTR) "CN=Builtin,DC=company,DC=pri"
    forceLogoff : (Unknown variant type)
    isCriticalSystemObject : (BOOL) TRUE
    lockoutDuration : (Unknown variant type)
    lockOutObservationWindow : (Unknown variant type)
    lockoutThreshold : (INT) 0
    maxPwdAge : (Unknown variant type)
    minPwdAge : (Unknown variant type)
    minPwdLength : (INT) 0
    modifiedCount : (Unknown variant type)
    modifiedCountAtLastProm : (Unknown variant type)
    name : (BSTR) "Builtin"
    nextRid : (INT) 1000
    objectGUID : (Unknown variant type)
    objectSid : (Unknown variant type)
    pwdHistoryLength : (INT) 0
    pwdProperties : (INT) 0
    serverState : (INT) 1
    showInAdvancedViewOnly : (BOOL) FALSE
    systemFlags : (INT) -1946157056
    uASCompat : (INT) 1
    uSNChanged : (Unknown variant type)
    uSNCreated : (Unknown variant type)
    whenChanged : (Unknown variant type)
    whenCreated : (Unknown variant type)
```

You can use this technique to get a reference of every object in your domain, along with those objects' key attributes. This output file can be an invaluable reference as you write scripts, because it contains property names, sample data straight from your actual domain, and so forth. Notice that it also lists the full Active Directory path for every object, which can help you fine-tune your LDAP queries. Here's the built-in Account Operators group.

```
*** CN=Account Operators  ***
  Child of CN=Builtin
  Full ADs path: "LDAP://CN=Account Operators,CN=Builtin,DC=company,dc=pri"
  Class: group
  Schema: LDAP://schema/group
```

```
Attributes ------------------
  cn : (BSTR) "Account Operators"
  groupType : (INT) -2147483643
  instanceType : (INT) 4
  nTSecurityDescriptor : (Unknown variant type)
  objectCategory : (BSTR) "CN=Group,CN=Schema,CN=Configuration,DC=company,DC=pri"
  objectClass : (ARRAY) [ "top" "group"]
  objectSid : (Unknown variant type)
  sAMAccountName : (BSTR) "Account Operators"
  adminCount : (INT) 1
  description : (BSTR) "Members can administer domain user and group accounts"
  distinguishedName : (BSTR) "CN=Account Operators,CN=Builtin,DC=company,DC=pri"
  isCriticalSystemObject : (BOOL) TRUE
  name : (BSTR) "Account Operators"
  objectGUID : (Unknown variant type)
  sAMAccountType : (INT) 536870912
  systemFlags : (INT) -1946157056
  uSNChanged : (Unknown variant type)
  uSNCreated : (Unknown variant type)
  whenChanged : (Unknown variant type)
  whenCreated : (Unknown variant type)
```

Included in the full Active Directory path is the LDAP query you need to execute to connect to this group. If LDAP queries seem complex or intimidating, just borrow them from the ADSI-Dump output file, rather than trying to write them yourself.

Using the PrimalScript Professional ADSI Wizard

Most commercial script editors include ADSI wizards similar to the ADSI Scriptomatic. Primal-Script Professional (*http://www.primalscript.com*) takes a different approach, however, and we like how easy it makes ADSI scripting. You start by selecting the types of Active Directory objects you want to script, as shown in Figure 8-8. Notice that for each object type, the wizard can produce sample code showing how to add an item of that type, delete an item, or modify an item.

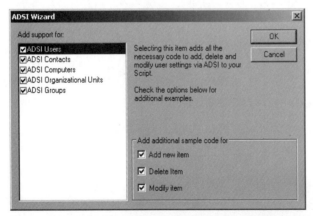

Figure 8-8   Using the PrimalScript Professional ADSI Wizard

The wizard generates a series of new classes that represent the object types you selected. These classes are supported by PrimalScript's PrimalSense feature (which displays menus that list the members of a class, a feature generically referred to as *code hinting*), as shown in Figure 8-9. We think this is a great feature because it helps you script without having to refer to documentation. Rather than working with plan object variables, you work with objects that behave like users, groups, and so forth, and that have all the properties and methods you'd expect.

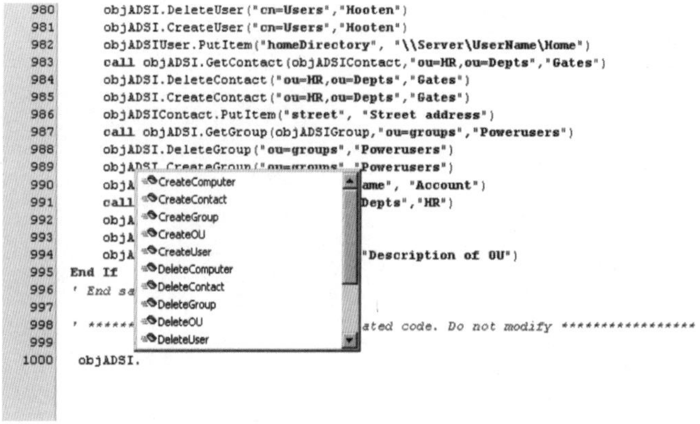

```
980    objADSI.DeleteUser ("cn=Users","Hooten")
981    objADSI.CreateUser ("cn=Users","Hooten")
982    objADSIUser.PutItem("homeDirectory", "\\Server\UserName\Home")
983    call objADSI.GetContact(objADSIContact,"ou=HR,ou=Depts","Gates")
984    objADSI.DeleteContact ("ou=HR,ou=Depts","Gates")
985    objADSI.CreateContact ("ou=HR,ou=Depts","Gates")
986    objADSIContact.PutItem("street", "Street address")
987    call objADSI.GetGroup(objADSIGroup,"ou=groups","Powerusers")
988    objADSI.DeleteGroup ("ou=groups","Powerusers")
989    objADSI.CreateGroup ("ou=groups", "Powerusers")
990    objA  CreateComputer          ame", "Account")
991    call  CreateContact           Depts","HR")
992    objA  CreateGroup
993    objA  CreateOU
994    objA  CreateUser              "Description of OU")
995    End If  DeleteComputer
996    ' End sa DeleteContact
997          DeleteGroup
998    ' ***** DeleteOU              ated code. Do not modify ******************
999          DeleteUser
1000   objADSI.
```

Figure 8-9   Using code hinting with the PrimalScript ADSI Wizard

Adding a new user is straightforward. You connect to ADSI with a single line of code, and use one more line to create a new user. Here's the code we wrote, based on the classes added by the ADSI Wizard.

```
Dim objADSI, objADSIUser
Set objADSI = New ADSIConnection
Set objADSIUser = New ADSIUser
objADSI.CreateUser("cn=Users","JHicks")
```

That definitely makes it easier to write ADSI scripts!

Writing Active Directory Queries

Writing basic LDAP queries like this one is easy.

```
LDAP://CN=Account Operators,CN=Builtin,DC=company,dc=pri
```

But this isn't always the most efficient way to work with LDAP, and sometimes—especially if you're querying a large number of objects—simple queries won't do what you need them to. In the next two sections, we'll explore some advanced techniques for writing LDAP queries.

Using Search Filters

The LDAP query language includes filtering capabilities that can help refine your searches. For example, you can add filters that restrict the object classes or categories that a search returns.

```
(objectCategory=person)
```

This example only returns objects whose *objectCategory* property is *person*. Using it in a complete LDAP query might look like this.

```
<LDAP://dc=company,dc=pri>;(objectClass=User)
```

That would return all user objects from the *company.pri* domain. Setting search filters in this fashion can help make your result sets smaller, easier to work with, and more specific.

How you use these filters in VBScript depends on how you're connecting to ADSI. For example, here's an LDAP connection that retrieves all objects and then filters them so that only user objects are accessible.

```
Set colUsers = GetObject ("LDAP://CN=Users,DC=company,DC=pri")
colUsers.Filter = Array("user")
```

A downside to this technique is that more data is being transmitted to the client than necessary, because the client is adding the filter. In the next chapter, we'll use ActiveX Data Objects (ADO) to connect to Active Directory, where full LDAP filtering and searching is an option for more efficient queries.

Using Data Return Limits

One tricky part about ADSI is that it's designed to minimize negative impact in terms of performance, which can sometimes cause it to produce results that aren't what you expect. For example, if you try to execute a query that would return a million objects, ADSI will limit you to about 1,000 objects, so you won't overtax the computer you're querying. Getting around this limit can be annoying and confusing if you don't know that the limit is in effect.

The best way to work with the limit is to access ADSI through its ActiveX Data Object (ADO) provider (a topic we cover in detail in the next chapter). For example, suppose you want to find the distinguished name for a user account, but you only know its NetBIOS account name. You first create an ADO *Connection* object and a *Command* object.

```
Dim objConn,objCmd,objRS
Set objConn=Createobject("ADODB.Connection")
Set objCmd=Createobject("ADODB.Command")
```

Next, set a string variable to *NotFound*. This will be the default value returned in case the user account you specified isn't located.

```
strGetDN="NotFound"
```

Use an LDAP query to connect to the domain root and retrieve the default naming context for the domain.

```
Set objRoot=Getobject("LDAP://RootDSE")
Set objDomain=Getobject("LDAP://"& objRoot.get("DefaultNamingContext"))
```

Now comes the query. Select the *sAMAccountName*, *cn*, and *distinguishedName* properties from the domain, specifying the object category to be person, the object's class to be user, and the *sAMAccountName* to be contained in the variable *samAccount* (which must be set to a value).

```
strQuery="Select sAMAccountname,cn,distinguishedname from '" & _
  objDomain.AdsPath & "' where objectCategory='person' " & _
  "AND " & "objectclass='user'" & _
  " AND sAMAccountName='" & samAccount & "'"
```

Global catalogs (GCs) have all the information you need, so you'll connect to one. This query gets connects to the GCs, and the loop runs through them. At the end, *objGC* represents a GC server.

```
set objCatalog=Getobject("GC:")
for each objItem In objCatalog
    Set objGC=objItem
Next
```

Now you can set up the connection to Active Directory through ADO.

```
objConn.Provider="ADSDSOobject"
objConn.Open "Active Directory Provider"
```

After the connection is open, you assign it to a *Command* object. Notice that the *Command* object's page size property is set to 100. That's the maximum number of records we'll get back at a time. We set the *CommandText* property to our query, which is in the *strQuery* variable.

```
objCmd.ActiveConnection=objConn
objCmd.Properties("Page Size") = 100
objCmd.Properties("asynchronous")=True
objCmd.Properties("Timeout") =30
objCmd.Properties("Cache Results") = False
objCmd.CommandText=strQuery
```

Now execute the *Command* object and specify that its results of the query are placed in an ADO *Recordset* object—into the variable *objRS*.

```
set objRS=objCmd.Execute
```

Run through the recordset until you reach its end. As we pass 100 records, ADO will automatically requery for the next 100 records.

```
do while not objRS.EOF
    strGetDN=objRS.Fields("distinguishedname")
    objRS.movenext
Loop
```

When finished, close both the recordset and the connection.

```
objRS.Close
objConn.Close
```

That's the easiest way to avoid the record query limit. Listing 8-1 is the complete script, written as a function so that it can be added into your scripts.

Listing 8-1 Avoid the Record Query Limit

```
Function strGetDN(samAccount)

    'Given NT4 account name, find the distinguished name for the user account
    On Error Resume Next
    Dim objConn,objCmd,objRS
    Set objConn=Createobject("ADODB.Connection")
    Set objCmd=Createobject("ADODB.Command")

    strGetDN="NotFound"

    Set objRoot=Getobject("LDAP://RootDSE")
    Set objDomain=Getobject("LDAP://"& objRoot.get("DefaultNamingContext"))

    strQuery="Select SAMAccountname,cn,distinguishedname from '" & _
     objDomain.AdsPath & "' where objectCategory='person' AND " & _
     "objectclass='user'" & _
     " AND SAMAccountName='" & samAccount & "'"

    set objCatalog=Getobject("GC:")
    for each objItem In objCatalog
        Set objGC=objItem
    Next

    objConn.Provider="ADSDSOobject"
    objConn.Open "Active Directory Provider"
    objCmd.ActiveConnection=objConn
    objCmd.Properties("Page Size") = 100
    objCmd.Properties("asynchronous")=True
    objCmd.Properties("Timeout") =30
    objCmd.Properties("Cache Results") = False
    objCmd.CommandText=strQuery

    set objRS=objCmd.Execute

    do while not objRS.EOF
        strGetDN=objRS.Fields("distinguishedname")
        objRS.movenext
    Loop

    objRS.Close
    objConn.Close

    set objConn=Nothing
    set objCmd=Nothing
    set objRoot=Nothing
```

```
    set objCatalog=Nothing
    set objRS=Nothing

End Function
```

> **On the CD** You will find this script, as well as other scripts listed in this chapter, on the CD that accompanies this book.

Scripting the WinNT Provider

The WinNT provider is too often overlooked by administrators who don't realize that ADSI is capable of working with more than just Active Directory, or who believe that the WinNT provider is useful only with Microsoft Windows NT. Nothing could be further from the truth.

Remember that the WinNT provider can connect to services on a computer. One such service is the Server service, which is responsible for handling all shared folders and the files within them. Say, for example, that you wrote this short piece of code that connects to a server's Server service.

```
sServerName = InputBox ("Server name to check")
sFilename= InputBox ("Full path and filename of the file on the" & _
 "server (use the local path as if you were " & _
 "at the server console)")
' bind to the server's file service
set oFileService = GetObject("WinNT://" & sServerName & _
 "/lanmanserver,fileservice")
```

The code returns a server name and a filename. There is also a reference to that server's *lanmanserver* service, which is just another name for the Server service. This service maintains a *Resources* collection, and each item in that collection represents an open resource—a file, for example. The following code runs through each resource and checks whether its path matches the filename you specified.

```
bFoundNone = True
For Each oResource In oFileService.Resources
 If oResource.Path = sFilename Then
  bFoundNone = False
  WScript.Echo oResource.Path & " is opened by " & oResource.User
 End If
Next
```

If it matches, the name of the user who has that file open is displayed. Listing 8-2 shows the entire script, including comments to help you follow along.

Listing 8-2 Find Open Files

```
' first, get the server name we want to work with
sServerName = InputBox ("Server name to check")

' get the local path of the file to check
sFilename= InputBox ("Full path and filename of the file on the" & _
 " server (use the local path as if you were " & _
 "at the server console)")

' bind to the server's file service
set oFileService = GetObject("WinNT://" & sServerName & _
 "/lanmanserver,fileservice")

' scan through the open resources until we
' locate the file we want
bFoundNone = True

' use a FOR...EACH loop to walk through the
' open resources
For Each oResource In oFileService.Resources

  does this resource match the one we're looking for?
 If oResource.Path = sFilename Then

  ' we found the file - show who's got it
  bFoundNone = False
  WScript.Echo oResource.Path & " is opened by " & oResource.User
 End If
Next

' if we didn't find the file open, display a msg
If bFoundNone = True Then
 WScript.Echo "Didn't find that file opened by anyone."
End If
```

Note that this script won't run in all circumstances. We tested it on Microsoft Windows XP, but it might not work on file servers. Nonetheless, it's a useful illustration of how the WinNT provider remains relevant even though Windows NT is largely a thing of the past.

Listing 8-3, which starts on the next page, is a Windows Script File (WSF) designed to be run as a command-line tool. It'll change any local account password (such as the local Administrator account) on a batch of computers. It works on a list of computers from a text file, or you can target computer accounts in your domain or an OU.

Note   This script is excerpted from Don's book *Microsoft Windows Administrator's Automation Toolkit* (Microsoft Press, 2005), which includes over eighty scripts designed to automate Windows administration. The listing here is just the code portion of the script. On the CD that accompanies this book, you'll find the complete, XML-formatted script in WSF format.

Listing 8-3 Change Local Password

```
<?xml version="1.0" ?>
<package>
        <job id="ChangeLocalPassword" prompt="no">
                <?job error="false" debug="false" ?>
                <runtime>
                            <description>
Changes a local account password on one or more computers.

Use only one of the following:
  /list:filename    : text file containing one computer name per line
  /container:ouname : name of an OU containing computer accounts
  /computer:name    : run command against single specified computer

Other arguments are optional.
                        </description>
                            <named helpstring="Text file to pull computer names from"
name="list" required="false" type="string"/>
                            <named helpstring="OU to pull computer names from" name="container"
required="false" type="string"/>
                            <named helpstring="Run command against single specified computer"
name="computer" required="false" type="string"/>
                            <named helpstring="Display detailed messages" name="verbose"
required="false" type="simple"/>
                            <named helpstring="Use with /container to include sub-OUs"
name="recurse" required="false" type="simple"/>
                            <named helpstring="File to log names which can't be reached"
name="log" required="false" type="string"/>
                        <named helpstring="Reduce timeout wait by pinging before attempting"
name="ping" required="false" type="simple"/>
                            <named helpstring="User account to change" name="user"
required="true" type="string"/>
                            <named helpstring="New password for user account" name="password"
required="true" type="string"/>
                    </runtime>
                    <object id="fso" progid="Scripting.FileSystemObject"/>
                    <script id="MultiComputer" language="VBScript">
<![CDATA[
'-------------------------------------------------------
' Change local password
'-------------------------------------------------------
' supported: 2003,XP,2000,NT4

'make sure we're running from CScript, not WScript
If LCase(Right(WScript.FullName,11)) <> "cscript.exe" Then
        If MsgBox("This script is designed to work with CScript, but you are running it
under WScript. " & _
            "This script may produce a large number of dialog boxes when running under
WScript, which you may " & _
            "find to be inefficient. Do you want to continue anyway?",4+256+32,"Script
host warning") = 7 Then
                WScript.Echo "Tip: Run ""Cscript //h:cscript"" from a command-line to
make CScript the default scripting host."
        WScript.Quit
```

```
                End If
End If


'count arguments
Dim iArgs
If WScript.Arguments.Named.exists("computer") Then iArgs = iArgs + 1
If WScript.Arguments.Named.exists("container") Then iArgs = iArgs + 1
If WScript.Arguments.Named.exists("list") Then iArgs = iArgs + 1
If iArgs <> 1 Then
        WScript.Echo "Must specify either /computer, /container, or /list arguments."
        WScript.Echo "May not specify more than one of these arguments."
        WScript.Echo "Run command again with /? argument for assistance."
        WScript.Quit
End If


'if ping requested, make sure we're on XP or later
Dim bPingAvailable, oLocalWMI, cWindows, oWindows
bPingAvailable = False
Set oLocalWMI = GetObject("winmgmts:\\.\root\cimv2")
Set cWindows = oLocalWMI.ExecQuery("Select BuildNumber from Win32_OperatingSystem",,48)
For Each oWindows In cWindows
        If oWindows.BuildNumber >= 2600 Then
                bPingAvailable = True
        End If
Next


'was ping requested?
If WScript.Arguments.Named.Exists("ping") Then
        If bPingAvailable Then
                Verbose "will attempt to ping all connections to improve performance"
        Else
                WScript.Echo "*** /ping not supported prior to Windows XP"
        End If
End If



'check required arguments
If Not WScript.Arguments.Named.Exists("password") Or Not
        WScript.Arguments.Named.Exists("user") Then
        WScript.Echo "One or more required arguments are missing."
        WScript.Arguments.ShowUsage
        WScript.Quit
End If


'either /list, /computer, or /container was specified:
Dim sName
If WScript.Arguments.Named("list") <> "" Then
        'specified list - read names from file
        Dim oFSO, oTS
        Verbose "Reading names from file " & WScript.Arguments.Named("list")
        Set oFSO = WScript.CreateObject("Scripting.FileSystemObject")
        On Error Resume Next
        Set oTS = oFSO.OpenTextFile(WScript.Arguments.Named("list"))
        If Err <> 0 Then
                WScript.Echo "Error opening " & WScript.Arguments.Named("list")
                WScript.Echo Err.Description
```

```
                    WScript.Quit
            End If
            Do Until oTS.AtEndOfStream
                    sName = oTS.ReadLine
                    TakeAction sName
            Loop
            oTS.Close

    ElseIf WScript.Arguments.Named("container") <> "" Then
            'specified container - read names from AD
            Dim oObject, oRoot, oChild
            Verbose "Reading names from AD container " & WScript.Arguments.Named("container")
            On Error Resume Next
            Set oRoot = GetObject("LDAP://rootDSE")
            If Err <> 0 Then
                    WScript.Echo "Error connecting to default Active Directory domain"
                    WScript.Echo Err.Description
                    WScript.Quit
            End If
            Set oObject = GetObject("LDAP://ou=" & WScript.Arguments.Named("container") & _
              "," & oRoot.Get("defaultNamingContext"))
            If Err <> 0 Then
                    WScript.Echo "Error opening organizational unit " & _
    WScript.Arguments.Named("container")
                    WScript.Echo Err.Description
                    WScript.Quit
            End If
            WorkWithOU oObject

    ElseIf WScript.Arguments.Named("computer") <> "" Then
            'specified single computer
            Verbose "Running command against " & WScript.Arguments.Named("computer")
            TakeAction WScript.Arguments.Named("computer")

    End If

    'display output so user will know script finished
    WScript.Echo "Command completed."

    ' ----------------------------------------------------------------------
    ' Sub WorkWithOU
    '
    ' Iterates child objects in OU; calls itself to handle sub-OUs If
    ' /recurse argument supplied
    ' ----------------------------------------------------------------------
    Sub WorkWithOU(oObject)
            For Each oChild In oObject
                    Select Case oChild.Class
                            Case "computer"
                                    TakeAction Right(oChild.Name,len(oChild.name)-3)
                            Case "user"
                            Case "organizationalUnit"
                                    If WScript.Arguments.Named.Exists("recurse") Then
                                            'recursing sub-OU
                                            Verbose "Working In " & oChild.Name
```

```
                            WorkWithOU oChild
                        End If
                End Select
        Next
End Sub


' -----------------------------------------------------------------------
' Sub TakeAction
'
' Makes connection and performs command-specific code
' -----------------------------------------------------------------------
Sub TakeAction(sName)

        'verbose output?
        Verbose "Connecting to " & sName

        'ping before connecting?
        If WScript.Arguments.Named.Exists("ping") Then
                If Not TestPing(sName,bPingAvailable) Then
                        LogBadConnect(sName)
                    Exit Sub
                End If
        End If



        '#########################################
        '#          COMMAND CODE GOES HERE       #
        '#---------------------------------------#
        '#                                       #
    Dim oUser
    On Error Resume Next
    Set oUser = QueryADSI(sName,"WinNT://" & sName & "/" & WScript.Arguments.Named("user")
& ",user", "")
    If Not IsObject(oUser) Then
        WScript.Echo " *** Couldn't retrieve user from " & sName
    Else
        On Error Resume Next
        oUser.setpassword WScript.Arguments.Named("password")
        If Err <> 0 Then
            WScript.Echo " *** Couldn't change password on " & sname
            WScript.Echo " " & Err.Description
        Else
            Verbose " Changed password on " & sName
        End If
    End If


    '#                                       #
    '#---------------------------------------#
    '#          END COMMAND CODE             #
    '#########################################


End Sub
```

```
' -------------------------------------------------------------------
' Sub LogBadConnect
'
' Logs failed connections to a log file. Will append if file already exists.
' -------------------------------------------------------------------
Sub LogBadConnect(sName)
        If WScript.arguments.Named.Exists("log") Then
                Dim oLogFSO, oLogFile
                Set oLogFSO = WScript.CreateObject("Scripting.FileSystemObject")
                On Error Resume Next
                Set oLogFile = oLogFSO.OpenTextFile(WScript.Arguments.Named("log"),8,True)
                If Err <> 0 Then
                        WScript.Echo " *** Error opening log file to log an unreachable
computer"
                        WScript.Echo " " & Err.Description
                Else
                        oLogFile.WriteLine sName
                        oLogFile.Close
                        Verbose " Logging " & sName & " as unreachable"
                End If
        End If
End Sub


' -------------------------------------------------------------------
' Function TestPing
'
' Tests connectivity to a given name or address; returns true or False
' -------------------------------------------------------------------
Function TestPing(sName,bPingAvailable)
        If Not bPingAvailable Then
                WScript.Echo " Ping functionality not available prior to Windows XP"
                Exit Function
        End If
        Dim cPingResults, oPingResult
        Verbose " Pinging " & sName
        Set cPingResults = GetObject("winmgmts://./root/cimv2").ExecQuery("SELECT * FROM
Win32_PingStatus WHERE Address = '" & sName & "'")
        For Each oPingResult In cPingResults
                If oPingResult.StatusCode = 0 Then
                        TestPing = True
                        Verbose "  Success"
                Else
                        TestPing = False
                        Verbose "  *** FAILED"
                End If
        Next
End Function


' -------------------------------------------------------------------
' Sub Verbose
'
' Outputs status messages if /verbose argument supplied
' -------------------------------------------------------------------
Sub Verbose(sMessage)
```

```
                If WScript.Arguments.Named.Exists("verbose") Then
                        WScript.Echo sMessage
                End If
        End Sub


' -------------------------------------------------------------------
' Sub LogFile
'
' Outputs specified text to specified logfile. Set Overwrite=True To
' overwrite existing file, otherwise file will be appended to.
' Each call to this sub is a fresh look at the file, so don't Set
' Overwrite=True except at the beginning of your script.
' -------------------------------------------------------------------
Sub LogFile(sFile,sText,bOverwrite)
        Dim oFSOOut,oTSOUt,iFlag
        If bOverwrite Then
                        iFlag = 2
        Else
                        iFlag = 8
        End If
        Set oFSOOut = WScript.CreateObject("Scripting.FileSystemObject")
        On Error Resume Next
        Set oTSOUt = oFSOOut.OpenTextFile(sFile,iFlag,True)
        If Err <> 0 Then
                WScript.Echo "*** Error logging to " & sFile
                WScript.Echo "    " & Err.Description
        Else
                oTSOUt.WriteLine sText
                oTSOUt.Close
        End If
End Sub


' -------------------------------------------------------------------
' Function QueryWMI
'
' Executes WMI query and returns results. User and Password may be
' passed as empty strings to use current credentials; pass just a blank
' username to prompt for the password
' -------------------------------------------------------------------
Function QueryWMI(sName,sNamespace,sQuery,sUser,sPassword)
        Dim oWMILocator, oWMIService, cInstances
        On Error Resume Next

        'create locator
        Set oWMILocator = CreateObject("WbemScripting.SwbemLocator")

        If sUser = "" Then

                'no user - connect w/current credentials
                Set oWMIService = oWMILocator.ConnectServer(sName,sNamespace)
                If Err <> 0 Then
                        WScript.Echo "*** Error connecting to WMI on " & sName
                        WScript.Echo "    " & Err.Description
                        Set QueryWMI = Nothing
                        Exit Function
                End If
```

```
        Else

                'user specified
                If sUser <> "" And sPassword = "" Then

                        'no password - need to prompt for password
                        If LCase(Right(WScript.FullName,11)) = "cscript.exe" Then

                                'cscript - attempt to use ScriptPW.Password object
                                Dim oPassword
                                Set oPassword = WScript.CreateObject("ScriptPW.Password")
                                If Err <> 0 Then
                                        WScript.Echo " *** Cannot prompt for password prior
to Windows XP"
                                        WScript.Echo "      Either ScriptPW.Password object
not present on system, Or"
                                        WScript.Echo "      " & Err.Description
                                        WScript.Echo "    Will try to proceed with blank password"
                                Else
                                        WScript.Echo "Enter password for user '" & sUser & "' on
'" & sName & "'."
                                        sPassword = oPassword.GetPassword()
                                End If
                        Else

                                'wscript - prompt with InputBox()
                                sPassword = InputBox("Enter password for user '" & sUser & "' on
'" & sName & "'." & vbcrlf & vbcrlf & _
                                        "WARNING: Password will echo to the screen. Run command with
CScript to avoid this.")
                                End if
                        End If

                        'try to connect using credentials provided
                        Set oWMIService =
oWMILocator.ConnectServer(sName,sNamespace,sUser,sPassword)
                        If Err <> 0 Then
                                WScript.Echo " *** Error connecting to WMI on " & sName
                                WScript.Echo "      " & Err.Description
                                Set QueryWMI = Nothing
                                Exit Function
                        End If
                End If

                'execute query
                If sQuery <> "" Then
                        Set cInstances = oWMIService.ExecQuery(sQuery,,48)
                        If Err <> 0 Then
                                WScript.Echo "*** Error executing query "
                                WScript.Echo "      " & sQuery
                                WScript.Echo "      " & Err.Description
                                Set QueryWMI = Nothing
                                Exit Function
                        Else
                                Set QueryWMI = cInstances
                        End If
```

```
        Else
                Set QueryWMI = oWMIService
        End If

End Function

' -----------------------------------------------------------------------
' Function QueryADSI
'
' Executes ADSI query. Expects variable sQuery to include a COMPLETE
' query beginning with the provider LDAP:// or WinNT://. The query String
' may include a placeholder for the computer name, such as "%computer%".
' Include the placeholder in variable sPlaceholder to have it replaced
' with the current computer name. E.g.,
'   sQuery = "WinNT://%computer%/Administrator,user"
'   sPlaceholder = "%computer%
' Will query each computer targeted by the script and query their local
' Administrator user accounts.
' -----------------------------------------------------------------------
Function QueryADSI(sName,sQuery,sPlaceholder)

        Dim oObject
        sQuery = Replace(sQuery,sPlaceholder,sName)
        On Error Resume Next
        Verbose " Querying " & sQuery
        Set oObject = GetObject(sQuery)
        If Err <> 0 Then
                WScript.Echo " *** Error executing ADSI query"
                WScript.Echo "       " & sQuery
                WScript.Echo "       " & Err.Description
                Set QueryADSI = Nothing
        Else
                Set QueryADSI = oObject
        End If

End Function
]]>
                </script>
        </job>
</package>
```

The main part of the script uses the WinNT provider.

```
Dim oUser
On Error Resume Next
Set oUser = QueryADSI(sName,"WinNT://" & _
 sName & "/" & WScript.Arguments.Named("user") & ",user", "")
If Not IsObject(oUser) Then
    WScript.Echo " *** Couldn't retrieve user from " & sName
Else
    On Error Resume Next
    oUser.setpassword WScript.Arguments.Named("password")
    If Err <> 0 Then
        WScript.Echo " *** Couldn't change password on " & sname
        WScript.Echo " " & Err.Description
    Else
        Verbose " Changed password on " & sName
    End If
End If
```

The script simply connects to the current computer, retrieves the specified user account, and changes its password.

Scripting Active Directory Security

Security can be one of the toughest things to script in Active Directory, mainly because security itself is complicated. Trustees are the users and groups to which permissions are assigned. Discretionary access control lists (DACL) are applied to each Active Directory object. DACLs consist of one or more access control entries (ACE), each of which assigns specific permissions to a specific trustee. Scripting all that can be a mess.

Active Directory also includes extended rights. These are permissions that don't apply specifically to an attribute, but rather govern a specific action, such as the permission to reset a user's password, or to send messages as a user. Extended rights are stored as discrete objects within Active Directory. To script with these objects, start by defining a few constants for the values you'll need to use.

```
Const ADS_ACETYPE_ACCESS_ALLOWED_OBJECT = &H5
Const ADS_FLAG_OBJECT_TYPE_PRESENT = &H1
Const ADS_RIGHT_DS_CONTROL_ACCESS = &H100
```

Next connect to a specific user—the one to whom you want to grant permissions. For our example, we're going to give user JHicks permission to reset the password for DJones' account. Use a regular LDAP query.

```
Set objUser = GetObject("LDAP://CN=DJones,OU=MIS,DC=company,DC=pri")
```

Next you need to find the user's *ntSecurityDescriptor* property (we discussed this property in the discussion on ADSVW, earlier in this chapter). From that security descriptor, you'll retrieve the set of DACLs.

```
Set objSD = objUser.Get("ntSecurityDescriptor")
Set objDACL = objSD.DiscretionaryACLSet
```

You now add a new ACE to the DACL, giving JHicks the necessary permission. First, create a new ACE object.

```
objAce = CreateObject("AccessControlEntry")
```

Then add the new trustee. You can use in the old-fashioned *domain\username* format.

```
objAce.Trustee = "company\jhicks"
```

Set the ACE's flags to zero. These flags govern aspects like inheritance, which we aren't config-uring. You'll use the constants you declared earlier to give the ACE *object allowed* permission.

```
objAce.AceFlags = 0
objAce.AceType = ADS_ACETYPE_ACCESS_ALLOWED_OBJECT
objAce.Flags = ADS_FLAG_OBJECT_TYPE_PRESENT
```

The ACE is granting permission on an object, and the object type is present in the ACL. You now have to specify *which* object, and you do that by using the object's globally unique iden-tifier (GUID). This identifies the object type in the ACL.

```
objAce.ObjectType = "{00299570-246d-11d0-a768-00aa006e0529}"
```

GUIDs are tough to remember (you can declare them in constants within your script to make them more readable), so here's a list.

- Change Password: {ab721a53-1e2f-11d0-9819-00aa0040529b}
- Reset Password: {00299570-246d-11d0-a768-00aa006e0529}
- Receive As: {ab721a56-1e2f-11d0-9819-00aa0040529b}
- Send As: {ab721a54-1e2f-11d0-9819-00aa0040529b}

We've already specified that we are granting permission, so we now need to indicate which specific permissions are being granted. Because this is an extended right, only the *CONTROL_ACCESS* permission makes sense.

```
objAce.AccessMask = ADS_RIGHT_DS_CONTROL_ACCESS
```

Add the new ACE to the DACL.

```
objDACL.AddAce objAce
```

Add the revised DACL to the security descriptor.

```
objSD.DiscretionaryAcl = objDACL
```

Now save the revised security descriptor back to the user account.

```
objUser.Put "ntSecurityDescriptor", Array(objSD)
objUser.SetInfo
```

Listing 8-4 is the complete script.

Listing 8-4 Add Extended Rights in Active Directory

```
Const ADS_ACETYPE_ACCESS_ALLOWED_OBJECT = &H5
Const ADS_FLAG_OBJECT_TYPE_PRESENT = &H1
Const ADS_RIGHT_DS_CONTROL_ACCESS = &H100
Set objUser = GetObject("LDAP://CN=DJones,OU=MIS,DC=company,DC=pri")
Set objSD = objUser.Get("ntSecurityDescriptor")
Set objDACL = objSD.DiscretionaryACLSet
objAce = CreateObject("AccessControlEntry")
objAce.Trustee = "company\jhicks"
objAce.AceFlags = 0
objAce.AceType = ADS_ACETYPE_ACCESS_ALLOWED_OBJECT
objAce.Flags = ADS_FLAG_OBJECT_TYPE_PRESENT
objAce.ObjectType = "{00299570-246d-11d0-a768-00aa006e0529}"
objAce.AccessMask = ADS_RIGHT_DS_CONTROL_ACCESS
objDACL.AddAce objAce
objSD.DiscretionaryAcl = objDACL
objUser.Put "ntSecurityDescriptor", Array(objSD)
objUser.SetInfo
```

To grant the permission for an entire OU, instead of retrieving the DJones user account in the initial LDAP query, retrieve an OU. However, the permission applied to the OU must be inherited by its child objects, so the permission applies to the users *within* the OU, and not just to the OU itself. Listing 8-5 is the revised script, with the changes in bold italic.

Listing 8-5 Grant Permissions to an OU

```
Const ADS_ACETYPE_ACCESS_ALLOWED_OBJECT = &H5
Const ADS_FLAG_OBJECT_TYPE_PRESENT = &H1
Const ADS_FLAG_INHERITED_OBJECT_TYPE_PRESENT = &H2
Const ADS_RIGHT_DS_CONTROL_ACCESS = &H100
Const ADS_ACEFLAG_INHERIT_ACE = &H2

Set objOU = GetObject("LDAP://OU=MIS,DC=company,DC=pri")
Set objSD = objOU.Get("ntSecurityDescriptor")
Set objDACL = objSD.DiscretionaryACL
Set objAce = CreateObject("AccessControlEntry")

objAce.Trustee = "company\jhicks"
objAce.AceFlags = ADS_ACEFLAG_INHERIT_ACE
objAce.AceType = ADS_ACETYPE_ACCESS_ALLOWED_OBJECT
objAce.Flags = ADS_FLAG_OBJECT_TYPE_PRESENT OR _
 ADS_FLAG_INHERITED_OBJECT_TYPE_PRESENT
objAce.ObjectType = "{00299570-246d-11d0-a768-00aa006e0529}"
objACE.InheritedObjectType = "{BF967ABA-0DE6-11D0-A285-00AA003049E2}"
objAce.AccessMask = ADS_RIGHT_DS_CONTROL_ACCESS
objDACL.AddAce objAce
objSD.DiscretionaryAcl = objDACL
objOU.Put "ntSecurityDescriptor", Array(objSD)
objOU.SetInfo
```

There are only a few changes here. First, we added two constants to handle the inherited rights. Next, we set the *AceFlags* property to indicate that this ACE, applied to an OU, should be inherited. The *Flags* property still gets the *OBJECT_TYPE_PRESENT* flag, indicating that the object is in the ACE itself. The *INHERITED_OBJECT_TYPE_PRESENT* flag is added as well. As a result, we needed to add the *InheritedObjectType* property, which is the GUID of the user account object class. This is not a GUID for a specific account, it is for the user account class itself. This means the permission will be inherited only by user accounts, and not by computers or whatever else might be in the OU. We found the GUID at the following Web site. (Scroll down, click User, and the Schema-Id-Guid is displayed near the top of the page.)

*http://msdn.microsoft.com/library/default.asp?url=/library/en-us/adschema/adschema
/classes_all.asp*

> **On the CD**   This link is included on the companion CD. Click *Schema Reference (User)*.

> **More Info**   Check out the Scripting Guys' articles about scripting Active Directory security at
>
> *http://www.microsoft.com/technet/scriptcenter/topics/security/propset.mspx*
>
> (This link is on the companion CD; click *Using Scripts to Manage Active Directory Security*.)

Summary

In this chapter, we showed you new ways of exploring Active Directory and the WinNT provider. We covered some advanced scripting techniques, including the Active Directory security model. We also introduced techniques for using the WinNT ADSI provider to perform various computer-management tasks. Hopefully, this will give you some ideas for writing ADSI-based scripts to help automate Windows management in your organization.

Chapter 9

Using ADO and ADSI Together

Microsoft's database access technology, ActiveX Data Objects (ADO), can be used to efficiently work with Active Directory. We'll explore how this integration of database and directory works, and how it can provide some great capabilities to your scripts. Although it might seem strange to have two completely different means—ADO and Active Directory Services Interface (ADSI)—to work with Active Directory, you'll find that ADO has its own strengths and weaknesses, making it well worth the time to learn how to use it.

In Chapter 8, "Advanced ADSI and LDAP Scripting," we briefly discussed connecting to ADSI by using ADO as a means to overcome the 1000-record limit in ADSI queries. Whereas the standard Lightweight Directory Access Protocol (LDAP) provider isn't intended to return large query result sets, ADO is designed to work with billion-record databases. ADO includes a paging mechanism that allows large result sets to be retrieved in smaller, more manageable chunks called *pages*. To illustrate this concept, we used a function like the one in the following example, which is capable of scanning through a very large result set to locate an object's distinguished name.

```
Function strGetDN(samAccount)
    'Given NT4 account name, find the distinguished name
    On Error Resume Next
    Dim objConn,objCmd,objRS
    Set objConn=Createobject("ADODB.Connection")
    Set objCmd=Createobject("ADODB.Command")
    strGetDN="NotFound"
    Set objRoot=Getobject("LDAP://RootDSE")
    Set objDomain=Getobject("LDAP://"& objRoot.get("DefaultNamingContext"))
    strQuery="Select sAMAccountname,distinguishedname from '" & _
      objDomain.AdsPath & "' where objectCategory='person' AND " & _
      "objectclass='user'" & _
      " AND SAMAccountName='" & samAccount & "'"
```

```
        set objCatalog=Getobject("GC:")
        for each objItem In objCatalog
            Set objGC=objItem
        Next
        objConn.Provider="ADSDSOobject"
        objConn.Open "Active Directory Provider"
        objCmd.ActiveConnection=objConn
        objCmd.Properties("Page Size") = 100
        objCmd.Properties("asynchronous")=True
        objCmd.Properties("Timeout") =30
        objCmd.Properties("Cache Results") = False
        objCmd.CommandText=strQuery
        set objRS=objCmd.Execute
        do while not objRS.EOF
            strGetDN=objRS.Fields("distinguishedname")
            objRS.movenext
        Loop
        objRS.Close
        objConn.Close
        set objConn=Nothing
        set objCmd=Nothing
        set objRoot=Nothing
        set objCatalog=Nothing
        set objRS=Nothing
End Function
```

In this chapter, we're going to examine this example in detail and show you how ADO provides access to information inside Active Directory.

More Info   If you're not already comfortable working with ADO, we suggest that you read Chapter 7, "Database Scripting," before continuing with this chapter. Chapter 7 explains the basic concepts behind database scripting and ADO, and we'll be building on those concepts.

Understanding the ADSI Provider for ADO

A *connection string* is one way to tell ADO what type of database to use and where to find it. For example, the following connection string connects to a Microsoft Access database located at C:\MyDB.mdb.

```
Provider=Microsoft.Jet.OLEDB.4.0;Data Source=C:\MyDB.mdb;
```

A critical part of a connection string is the *provider*. In this example, the provider is *Microsoft.Jet.OLEDB.4.0*, which is the OLE DB provider used by Access databases. To treat Active Directory as a database, we need to use a provider that allows ADO to connect to Active Directory. The Microsoft OLE DB Provider for Microsoft Active Directory Service (ADSI Provider, for short) is bundled into Microsoft Windows. The simplest way to start using the ADSI Provider is to create a new ADO *Connection* object, and pass the ADSI Provider's name, *ADSDSOObject*, to it in the *ConnectionString* property.

```
Dim objConn
Set objConn = CreateObject("ADODB.Connection")
objConn.ConnectionString = "ADSDSOobject"
objConn.Open
```

This uses your current credentials to open a connection to the domain to which your computer belongs. Notice that we're using the *ConnectionString* property, as opposed to the *Provider* property that we used in the original example. For the most part, the two properties are interchangeable when it comes to ADSI connectivity.

The ADSI Provider–like other parts of ADSI–can connect to more than just Active Directory. In fact, it can connect to Windows NT directory services, non-Microsoft LDAP directories, and more, including Novell Directory Services (NDS).

Connecting to ADSI by Using ADO

It might seem like we've gotten ahead of ourselves by showing you how to connect to Active Directory through ADO, but we haven't. There's much more to ADO and ADSI than a basic connection that utilizes your current credentials. For example, one of the most common variations of the connection string we showed you allows you to specify alternate credentials for your connection.

```
Dim objConn
Set objConn = CreateObject("ADODB.Connection")
objConn.ConnectionString = "Provider=ADSDSOObject;" & _
 "User ID=MyUserID;Password=MyPassword;"
objConn.Open
```

This can be a tremendously useful technique because it can be used to specify alternate credentials when creating an ADO connection to Active Directory.

> **Important**   This technique does not mean you should hard-code credentials into your scripts. As we discussed in Chapter 2, "Script Security," there's no safe way to hard-code any credentials in your scripts safely. Instead, use a function like *InputBox* to prompt for the alternate username or password, store them in variables, and then pass the contents of those variables in your connection string. Of course, you could always just run your script by using the RunAs command-line utility, which allows you to enter alternate credentials.

You also need to pass commands, or queries, to the database, and then you need to take care of the results that are returned. The same holds true when the database is Active Directory.

Treating Active Directory as a Database

Let's put together a query to send to Active Directory. In the example at the beginning of this chapter, we built the query in a string variable.

```
strQuery="Select sAMAccountname,cn,distinguishedname from '" & _
    objDomain.AdsPath & "' Where objectCategory='person' AND " & _
    "objectclass='user'" & _
    " AND sAMAccountName='" & samAccount & "'"
```

Assuming our domain is named *company.pri*, and the variable, *samAccount*, contains the string *DONJ*, this query will look something like this.

```
Select sAMAccountname,distinguishedname from
 'dc=company,dc=pri' where objectCategory = 'person' AND
 objectclass='user' AND sAMAccountName='DONJ'
```

This is a pretty straightforward SQL query. Here's what it's doing.

- Querying the *sAMAccountName* and *distinguishedName* properties from Active Directory objects that match the query criteria. Active Directory properties (*attributes*, as they're more properly called) serve in place of the columns you'd find in a traditional database like Access or Microsoft SQL Server.

> **Tip** We often need to map an individual attribute to a particular check box, text field, or some other graphical element within Active Directory. Microsoft maintains a complete list of the GUI-to-attribute mappings at
>
> *http://msdn.microsoft.com/library/default.asp?url=/library/en-us/ad/ad /mappings_for_the_active_directory_users_and_computers_snap-in.asp*
>
> (This link, like most of the links referenced in this book, is included on the companion CD; click *Mappings for the Active Directory Users and Computers Snap-in*.)

- Specifying the source of the records that we want to query, which is the *company.pri* domain.

- Specifying three query criteria, so only objects meeting all three criteria (because the *And* operator was used) will be returned as results of the query. The specified criteria are the following:

    - The *objectCategory* attribute must contain *person*.

    - The *objectClass* attribute must contain *user*.

    - The *sAMAccountName* attribute must contain *DONJ*.

> **Tip**   In most SQL queries, anything outside quotation marks isn't case-sensitive. The attribute name *objectclass* works just as well as *objectClass*. However, values inside single quotation marks (which are used to delimit string literals) *are* case-sensitive. Therefore, *user* must be written in all lowercase letters because that's how Active Directory stored the value.

Next, the query is assigned to the *CommandText* property of an ADO *Command* object. The *Command* object also needs to be connected to the open *Connection* object.

```
Dim objCmd
Set objCmd = CreateObject("ADODB.Command")
objCmd.ActiveConnection=objConn
objCmd.CommandText=strQuery
```

Now the command can be executed; doing so returns an ADO *Recordset* object.

```
Set objRS = objCmd.Execute
```

As we explained in Chapter 7, there are various types of ADO *Recordset* objects. The *Execute* method of a *Connection* or *Command* object returns a static, forward-only *Recordset* object. With ADSI, the *Command* object's *Execute* method will always return static *Recordset* objects. It's useful to understand how some of the *Recordset* object's properties are affected by the fact that only static recordsets are available. Here's a list of all the *Recordset* object's properties and how they are used in an ADSI connection.

- *AbsolutePage*   This property is read/write.

- *AbsolutePosition*   This property is read/write.

- *ActiveConnection*   This property is read only.

- *BOF*   This property is read only.

- *Bookmark*   This property is read/write.

- *CacheSize*   This property is read/write.

- *CursorLocation*   This property must always use the *adUseServer* constant (which is the default).

- *CursorType*   This property must always be set to *adOpenStatic* (which is the default).

- *EditMode*   This property will always be set to *adEditNone*, meaning you can't edit the recordset directly.

- *EOF*   This property is read only.

- *Filter*   This property is read/write.

- *LockType*   This property is read/write.

- *MarshalOptions*   This property is not supported.

- *MaxRecords*   This property is read/write.

- *PageCount*   This property is read only.

- *PageSize*   This property is read/write. If you don't set this property, as we did in our original example, paging will be disabled and you'll get a maximum of about 1000 records for any query. To enable automatic paging, you must set this property.

- *RecordCount*   This property is read only.

- *Source*   This property is read/write.

- *State*   This property is read only.

- *Status*   This property is read only.

Probably the most important property to set is the *PageSize* property. We set it by specifying the property name in the *Command* object's *Properties* collection.

```
objCmd.Properties("Page Size") = 100
```

This sets a page size of 100 records and forces ADO to query the next 100 records when you navigate to near the end of the current page. Remember that you use the standard ADO methods—primarily the *MoveNext* method—to navigate through the recordset. Here's a complete list of the methods that are supported in an ADSI recordset.

- *Clone*

- *Close*

- *GetRows*

- *Move*

- *MoveFirst*

- *MoveLast*

- *MoveNext*

- *MovePrevious*

- *NextRecordset*

- *Open*

- *Requery*

- *Resync*

- *Supports*

To be clear, the following methods are *not* available.

- *AddNew*

- *Cancel*

- *CancelBatch*

- *CancelUpdate*

- *Delete*

- *Update*

- *UpdateBatch*

Notice that the methods that aren't available are all associated with making changes to the recordset. Because only static recordsets are available, making changes isn't allowed.

You can explore the Active Directory schema to see a complete list of available Active Directory attributes for the various classes. We suggest using the Active Directory Schema console to do so. Simply open a new Microsoft Management Console (MMC) session and add the Active Directory Schema snap-in.

> **Tip**   The Active Directory Schema snap-in isn't available by default, so you'll need to register it the first time so that it will be in the list of available snap-ins. To register it, open a command-line window and type **regsvr32 schmmgmt.dll** (you might need to use the System32 folder to do this correctly). You should see a dialog box indicating a successful registration, and the next time you open the MMC, the snap-in should be listed.

Writing ADSI Queries to Retrieve Information

We've already explained how to query Active Directory through ADO by using a SQL query. As an alternative to the SQL syntax, however, you can use a special query syntax that's unique to ADSI. It's a four-part query specification.

```
Root; Filter; Attributes [; Scope]
```

The last part, *Scope*, is optional, which is why it's typically shown in square brackets. The *Root* portion of the query is an LDAP reference to the starting point of your query. This might be targeted at a Global Catalog server.

```
<GC://dc=company,dc=pri>
```

It could also be a simple LDAP reference to an organizational unit (OU).

```
<LDAP://ou=Sales,dc=company,dc-pri>
```

The *Filter* portion of the query limits the types of objects that are returned by the query. You can specify a filter that is, in effect, no filter at all, allowing all objects to be retrieved.

```
(objectClass=*)
```

Filters are contained in parentheses and take the basic format of *attribute=value*. For example, this will only return user objects.

```
(objectCategory=user)
```

This will query groups that have a particular user as a member.

```
(&(objectCategory=Group)(member=cn=TestUser,ou=it,dc=company,dc=pri))
```

Let's look at this filter in detail. Notice that there are two criteria specified: one for *object-Category* and one for *member*. Both are contained within an outer set of parentheses, and an ampersand (a Boolean *And*) indicates that both criteria must be true for all returned results. A pipe character (located above the backslash key on most keyboards) would indicate a Boolean *Or*, allowing either of the criteria to be met for the object to be included in the query result set.

> **Note**   This filter format is an industry standard, specified in RFC 1960.

The *Attributes* portion of the query is a comma-delimited list of the attributes you want the query to return.

```
ADsPath, sn, givenName
```

The *Scope* portion of the query limits the depth of the query in the Active Directory tree. You can specify *Base* to search only the object specified as the base, *OneLevel* to search the base and one level down, or *Subtree* to specify the base and anything below it. An entire query might look something like this.

```
<LDAP://dc=company,dc=pri>;(objectClass=*);distinguishedName;subtree
```

This connects to the *company.pri* domain, queries all objects, returns only their *distinguished-Name* attribute, and includes the entire tree below the domain root. We prefer to specify the four parts of the query in individual string variables, and to concatenate them to make an entire query—it makes the script a bit easier to read.

As an example, we will query all users from Active Directory and display their backward-compatible NT name as well as their Active Directory canonical name (*cn*). We start by connecting to Active Directory through ADO, and setting up an ADO *Command* object.

```
Set objCmd = CreateObject("ADODB.Command")
Set objCn = CreateObject("ADODB.Connection")
objCn.Provider = "ADsDSOObject"
objCn.Open "Active Directory Provider"
objCmd.ActiveConnection = objCn
```

Next we specify the base portion of our query—an LDAP reference to the domain root.

> **Tip**   The only case-sensitive part of this is the LDAP, GC, or other protocol or provider name.

```
strBase = "<LDAP://dc=company,dc=pri>"
```

We specify the filter as anything with an *objectCategory* of *person* and an *objectClass* of *user*. Note the ampersand, which specifies that both filter criteria must be true.

```
strFilter = "(&(objectCategory=person)" & _
 "(objectClass=user))"
```

We specify our attributes listed as the NT-style *sAMAccountName* and the Active Directory-style *cn*.

```
strAttributes = "sAMAccountName,cn"
```

Now we build the query and specify a scope of *Subtree*.

```
strQuery = strBase & ";" & strFilter & ";" & _
 strAttributes & ";subtree"
```

This could easily return more than 1,000 records, so we set up the *Command* object to return the results in paging blocks of 100.

```
objCmd.CommandText = strQuery
objCmd.Properties("Page Size") = 100
objCmd.Properties("Timeout") = 30
objCmd.Properties("Cache Results") = False
```

Now we execute the command to retrieve a recordset.

```
Set objRS = objCmd.Execute
```

We run through the recordset one record at a time, displaying the *sAMAccountName* and *cn*.

```
Do Until objRS.EOF
  strName = objRS.Fields("sAMAccountName").Value
  strCN = objRS.Fields("cn").value
  Wscript.Echo "NT Name: " & strName & _
   ", AD Name: " & strCN
  objRS.MoveNext
Loop
```

Finally, we close the connection when we're finished.

```
objCn.Close
```

Listing 9-1 is the script in its entirety.

Listing 9-1 Query All Users

```
Dim objCmd, objCn
Dim strBase, strFilter, strAttributes
Dim strQuery, objRS, strName, strCN
Set objCmd = CreateObject("ADODB.Command")
Set objCn = CreateObject("ADODB.Connection")
objCn.Provider = "ADsDSOObject"
objCn.Open "Active Directory Provider"
objCmd.ActiveConnection = objCn
strBase = "<LDAP://dc=company,dc=pri>"
strFilter = "(&(objectCategory=person)" & _
  "(objectClass=user))"
strAttributes = "sAMAccountName,cn"
strQuery = strBase & ";" & strFilter & ";" & _
  strAttributes & ";subtree"
objCmd.CommandText = strQuery
objCmd.Properties("Page Size") = 100
objCmd.Properties("Timeout") = 30
objCmd.Properties("Cache Results") = False
Set objRS = objCmd.Execute
Do Until objRS.EOF
  strName = objRS.Fields("sAMAccountName").Value
  strCN = objRS.Fields("cn").value
  Wscript.Echo "NT Name: " & strName & _
    ", AD Name: " & strCN
  objRS.MoveNext
Loop
objCn.Close
```

On the CD   You will find this script, as well as other scripts listed in this chapter, on the CD that accompanies this book.

Writing ADSI Queries to Make Changes

You can only use ADO to read information from Active Directory; you can't use ADO to make changes to Active Directory. However, you can use ADO to query information and then use regular ADSI interfaces to make changes to that information. Here's a walk-through.

1. Execute an ADO query to retrieve one or more results into a recordset.

2. The *ADsPath* property, which you can query, contains the complete LDAP path to each Active Directory object about which you retrieve information.

3. Pass the *ADsPath* to a regular *GetObject* function to retrieve the Active Directory objects.

4. Make changes to the information you retrieved.

Keep in mind that ADO isn't retrieving actual Active Directory objects—it's simply retrieving certain properties of those objects, which is why you can't really make any changes. To query information with ADO and make changes, you have to do it in several steps. First, declare an ADO *Connection* object and open a connection to Active Directory. We've shown you how to do this by using the *ConnectionString* property and the *Open* method; here's a shortcut that passes the connection string directly to the *Open* method.

```
Set objConnection = CreateObject("ADODB.Connection")
objConnection.Open "Provider=ADsDSOObject;"
```

Second, write a query and pass it to an ADO *Command* object. Be sure to set the *Command* object's *ActiveConnection* property to the *Connection* object.

```
Set objCommand = CreateObject("ADODB.Command")
objCommand.ActiveConnection = objConnection
objCommand.CommandText = _
 "<LDAP://dc=company,dc=pri>;" & _
 "(&(objectCategory=person)(objectClass=user));" & _
 "ADsPath;subtree"
```

In this example, we are querying all user objects from the *company.pri* domain. Next, we execute the *Command* object to return a static (that is, read-only) recordset.

```
Set objRecordSet = objCommand.Execute
```

Now we can loop through the recordset and work with one user at a time.

```
Do Until objRecordset.EOF
```

We now pull the *ADsPath* property into a string variable.

```
 strADsPath = objRecordset.Fields("ADsPath")
```

We use a regular ADSI query to retrieve the user object.

```
 Set objUser = GetObject(strADsPath)
```

We can use the *Put* method to modify one or more properties. We'll modify *postalCode*.

```
 objUser.Put "postalCode", "89123"
```

When we're done, the *SetInfo* method saves the information back to Active Directory, and the *MoveNext* method of the recordset brings up the next user account.

```
 objUser.SetInfo
 objRecordset.MoveNext
Loop
```

Close the ADO connection to Active Directory.

```
objConnection.Close
```

Listing 9-2 is the entire script.

Listing 9-2 Query and Modify

```
Set objConnection = CreateObject("ADODB.Connection")
objConnection.Open "Provider=ADsDSOObject;"
Set objCommand = CreateObject("ADODB.Command")
objCommand.ActiveConnection = objConnection
objCommand.CommandText = _
 "<LDAP://dc=company,dc=pri>;" & _
 "(&(objectCategory=person)(objectClass=user));" & _
 "ADsPath;subtree"
Set objRecordSet = objCommand.Execute
Do Until objRecordset.EOF
 strADsPath = objRecordset.Fields("ADsPath")
 Set objUser = GetObject(strADsPath)
 objUser.Put "postalCode", "89123"
 objUser.SetInfo
 objRecordset.MoveNext
Loop
objConnection.Close
```

Note   The recordset you query with ADO is static. That means it won't usually reflect any changes that were made after the recordset was built. (There are some exceptions to this, especially in large result sets where data is retrieved in pages. Each page will be up to date at the time it's queried and sent to your computer.) In this example, checking the ADO recordset for the *postalCode* property would return the *old* property value, not the new value just specified.

Viewing ADO and ADSI in Action

You can use ADO and ADSI to test for group membership, including nested group membership. This capability is very useful in a login script for mapping drives and printers to user groups, for example. However, ADSI doesn't contain many built-in ways to check nested group membership, so you'll have to build your own function. We built one called *IsMember*. The function first checks whether a VBScript *Dictionary* object named *objGroupList* exists, and if it doesn't, the function creates it. Note that we're using the *objGroupList* variable across functions, so it must be declared globally—outside the function itself—so that it'll be globally available.

```
Dim strUser, objGroupList, strGroup
Dim objRootDSE, strDNSDomain, objCmd, objCn
Dim strBase, strAttributes
Function IsMember(strGroup)
  If IsEmpty(objGroupList) Then
    Set objGroupList = CreateObject("Scripting.Dictionary")
```

We set a comparison option for the *Dictionary* object to help ensure that comparison details, such as capitalization differences, don't matter. The option we're specifying, for example, ensures that the string *Sample* is treated the same as the string *sample*.

```
objGroupList.CompareMode = vbTextCompare
```

Now we retrieve the DNS name of the domain.

```
Set objRootDSE = GetObject("LDAP://RootDSE")
strDNSDomain = objRootDSE.Get("DefaultNamingContext")
```

To search Active Directory, we create and open an ADO *Connection* object, and create an ADO *Command* object. We connect the *Command* object to the *Connection* object and specify a base query that queries the base domain from a Global Catalog server.

```
Set objCmd = CreateObject("ADODB.Command")
Set objCn = CreateObject("ADODB.Connection")
objCn.Provider = "ADsDSOObject"
objCn.Open "Active Directory Provider"
objCmd.ActiveConnection = objCn
strBase = "<GC://" & strDNSDomain & ">"
```

We want to query the *distinguishedName* property, so we put that property name into a string variable.

```
strAttributes = "distinguishedName"
```

To help avoid a huge result set, we specify the properties that set up paging.

```
objCmd.Properties("Page Size") = 100
objCmd.Properties("Timeout") = 30
objCmd.Properties("Cache Results") = False
```

Finally, we call a *LoadGroups* function that loads all groups to which the user belongs into our *Dictionary* object. Notice that we pass the distinguished name of the user account. When we're finished, we close the ADO connection. Note that our call to *LoadGroups* passes filter criteria, so only groups containing our user's distinguished name are returned.

```
    Call LoadGroups("(member=" & strUser & ")")
    objCn.Close
End If
```

At this point, every group the user belongs to is in the *objGroupList Dictionary* object. We use the *Dictionary* object's *Exists* method to query if the group we're looking for is in the list. The *Exists* method returns a TRUE or FALSE value as the result of the *IsMember* function.

```
    IsMember = objGroupList.Exists(strGroup)
End Function
```

We then created a function named *LoadGroups* that starts by declaring several variables.

```
Sub LoadGroups(strUserFilter)
  Dim strFilter, strQuery, strDN, objRecordSet
  Dim strNextFilter, blnRecurse
```

A string variable is constructed to filter the ADO query results. This filter will query only objects with the *Group* category, and only groups that have a *member* property equal to our user's distinguished name.

```
  strFilter = "(&(objectCategory=Group)" & strUserFilter & ")"
```

Here's the full query assembled from the base query, the filter, and the list of attributes.

```
  strQuery = strBase & ";" & strFilter & ";" & strAttributes & ";subtree"
```

Now we assign the query text to the *Command* object and execute it. The results are returned in a *Recordset* object.

```
  objCmd.CommandText = strQuery
  Set objRecordSet = objCmd.Execute
  strNextFilter = "(|"
  blnRecurse = False
```

We go through each result in the recordset and pull the distinguished name of the group into a string variable.

```
  Do Until objRecordSet.EOF
    strDN = objRecordSet.Fields("DistinguishedName")
```

If a group isn't already in our dictionary, we add it. Because we also want to include nested groups, we add the group to our filter criteria and set a variable to TRUE, indicating that we need to recursively query this group's membership.

```
    If Not objGroupList.Exists(strDN) Then
      objGroupList(strDN) = True
      strNextFilter = strNextFilter & "(member=" & strDN & ")"
      blnRecurse = True
    End If
    objRecordSet.MoveNext
  Loop
```

When we recursively process a nested group, the *LoadGroups* function calls itself, so the nested group membership is also processed.

```
  If blnRecurse = True Then
    strNextFilter = strNextFilter & ")"
    Call LoadGroups(strNextFilter)
  End If
End Sub
```

You use the function by simply specifying a user account's distinguished name (DN), and the group you want to check.

```
' Get a user object.
strUser = "cn=TestUser,ou=it,dc=company,dc=pro"

' Specify group DN and check for membership.
strGroup = "cn=Admins,ou=it,dc=company,dc=pri"
If IsMember(strGroup) Then
  'is a member
Else
  'is not a member
End If
```

Listing 9-3 contains the entire script, including code that demonstrates the use of the *IsMember* function.

Listing 9-3 Test for Group Membership

```
Dim strUser, objGroupList, strGroup
Dim objRootDSE, strDNSDomain, objCmd, objCn
Dim strBase, strAttributes

' Get a user object.
strUser = "cn=TestUser,ou=it,dc=company,dc=pri"

' Specify group DN and check for membership.
strGroup = "cn=Admins,ou=it,dc=company,dc=pri"
If IsMember(strGroup) Then
  'is a member
Else
  'is not a member
End If

Function IsMember(strGroup)
' Function to test group membership.
' strGroup is the Distinguished Name of the group.
  If IsEmpty(objGroupList) Then
    Set objGroupList = CreateObject("Scripting.Dictionary")
    objGroupList.CompareMode = vbTextCompare

    ' Get DNS domain name.
    Set objRootDSE = GetObject("LDAP://RootDSE")
    strDNSDomain = objRootDSE.Get("DefaultNamingContext")

    ' Search Active Directory.
    Set objCmd = CreateObject("ADODB.Command")
    Set objCn = CreateObject("ADODB.Connection")
    objCn.Provider = "ADsDSOObject"
    objCn.Open "Active Directory Provider"
    objCmd.ActiveConnection = objCn
    strBase = "<GC://" & strDNSDomain & ">"
    strAttributes = "distinguishedName"
    objCmd.Properties("Page Size") = 100
```

```
    objCmd.Properties("Timeout") = 30
    objCmd.Properties("Cache Results") = False

    Call LoadGroups("(member=" & strUser & ")")
    objCn.Close
  End If
  IsMember = objGroupList.Exists(strGroup)
End Function

Sub LoadGroups(strMemberFilter)
  Dim strFilter, strQuery, strDN, objRecordSet
  Dim strNextFilter, blnRecurse

  strFilter = "(&(objectCategory=Group)" & strMemberFilter & ")"
  strQuery = strBase & ";" & strFilter & ";" & strAttributes & ";subtree"
  objCmd.CommandText = strQuery
  Set objRecordSet = objCmd.Execute
  strNextFilter = "(|"
  blnRecurse = False

  Do Until objRecordSet.EOF
    strDN = objRecordSet.Fields("DistinguishedName")
    If Not objGroupList.Exists(strDN) Then
      objGroupList(strDN) = True
      strNextFilter = strNextFilter & "(member=" & strDN & ")"
      blnRecurse = True
    End If
    objRecordSet.MoveNext
  Loop
  If blnRecurse = True Then
    strNextFilter = strNextFilter & ")"
    Call LoadGroups(strNextFilter)
  End If
End Sub
```

Summary

Although ADSI can be used directly to access Active Directory, using ADO has several advantages. ADO can query larger result sets, and it uses a syntax that some administrators find easier to remember. The syntax ADO uses to access Active Directory is also easily adapted to other types of databases, making the time spent learning ADO well worth it.

Chapter 10
Advanced WMI Scripting

Windows Management Instrumentation (WMI) is a staple of administrative scripting; it provides an amazing amount of access into configuration parameters, Windows capabilities, and much more. In fact, WMI is largely responsible for the surge of interest in administrative scripting over the past few years. However, most administrators are aware of only a fraction of what WMI can do. In this chapter, we look at WMI's often-overlooked advanced capabilities.

WMI is a powerful technology for Microsoft Windows administration. Tools like the Scriptomatic and the WMI wizards built into some commercial script editors have made WMI more accessible, and they help administrators take advantage of the technology's capabilities. Even a simple script like this one, which lists all the local user accounts on the local computer, can be a valuable administrative tool.

```
Dim strComputer
Dim objWMIService
Dim propValue
Dim objItem
Dim SWBemlocator
Dim UserName
Dim Password
Dim colItems

strComputer = "."
UserName = ""
Password = ""
Set SWBemlocator = CreateObject("WbemScripting.SWbemLocator")
Set objWMIService = SWBemlocator.ConnectServer(strComputer, _
 "\root\CIMV2",UserName,Password)
Set colItems = objWMIService.ExecQuery("Select * from Win32_Account")
For Each objItem in colItems
    WScript.Echo "Caption: " & objItem.Caption
    WScript.Echo "Description: " & objItem.Description
    WScript.Echo "Domain: " & objItem.Domain
    WScript.Echo "InstallDate: " & objItem.InstallDate
    WScript.Echo "LocalAccount: " & objItem.LocalAccount
```

```
    WScript.Echo "Name: " & objItem.Name
    WScript.Echo "SID: " & objItem.SID
    WScript.Echo "SIDType: " & objItem.SIDType
    WScript.Echo "Status: " & objItem.Status
Next
```

However, WMI is capable of much more than basic configuration inventory. It can be used to change configuration settings, cause remote computers to take specific actions, and even respond to events that occur within Windows.

Understanding Advanced WQL

WMI uses a fairly sophisticated query language, modeled after the Structured Query Language (SQL) used by relational database management systems such as SQL Server. This query language is called the WMI Query Language (WQL), and it is something you've doubtless already encountered. The example shown at the beginning of this chapter includes a short WQL query.

```
Select * from Win32_Account
```

Most WMI queries consist of simply the *Select* keyword, an asterisk, the *From* keyword, and a WMI class name. The query just shown will select all available properties from the designated class.

Selecting Specific Properties

If you've ever written a script that queries an entire WMI class from a group of computers, you might have wondered if there was a way to speed up the process. Listing 10-1 opens a text file named C:\Computers.txt, which is expected to contain one computer name per line. The script then connects to each computer, queries all properties of the *Win32_OperatingSystem* class, and displays each computer's name and current service pack version number.

Listing 10-1 Service Pack Inventory

```
Set objFSO = CreateObject("Scripting.FileSystemObject")
Set objTS = objFSO.OpenTextFile("c:\computers.txt")
Do Until objTS.AtEndOfStream
    objTS.ReadLine
    Set SWBemlocator = CreateObject("WbemScripting.SWbemLocator")
    Set objWMIService = SWBemlocator.ConnectServer(strComputer,"\root\CIMV2")
    Set colItems = _
     objWMIService.ExecQuery("Select ServicePackMajorVersion " & _
     " from Win32_OperatingSystem Where Primary = True")
    For Each objItem in colItems
        WScript.Echo strComputer & "="
        WScript.Echo objItem.ServicePackMajorVersion
    Next
Loop
objTS.Close
```

> **On the CD**   You will find this script, as well as other scripts listed in this chapter, on the CD that accompanies this book.

> **Note**   Listing 10-1 assumes that each computer is available and can be contacted by WMI; it doesn't include any error handling if a computer can't be reached.

This script queries all properties of the *Win32_OperatingSystem* class, but it uses only one of them, *ServicePackMajorVersion*. The other two dozen or so properties are transmitted across the network but not used, creating waste both on the computer running the script and on the computer being queried. Because the script might be connecting to hundreds of computers, this slight inefficiency can be compounded into a major slowdown. One way to speed it up is to query only what you need.

```
Select ServicePackMajorVersion from Win32_OperatingSystem
```

It's that easy. Simply specify a comma-separated list of the properties you want to query, and you'll make your script more efficient, because only the queried properties need to be assembled and transmitted over the network.

Including a *WHERE* Clause

Just as querying too many properties can cause your script to be inefficient, querying too many instances can have the same effect. For example, in Listing 10-1, we query *all* instances of the *Win32_OperatingSystem* class. Usually a computer has only one operating system, so only one instance of the class would be returned. A computer could contain multiple operating systems, though (when virtual computing becomes more common, that will become more likely), so that query could, in theory, return multiple instances. If we want the service pack information for only the primary operating system, we'd be querying and displaying too much information. Including a WHERE clause in your WQL query can correct that. Listing 10-2 on the next page is an updated version of Listing 10-1.

In Listing 10-2 on the next page, a WHERE clause limits the query to those instances where the *Primary* property has a value of TRUE. This clause—which always takes the form property comparison value, as in *Primary = True*—is evaluated by the remote computer, which then returns only those instances of the class that meet the WHERE clause's conditions.

Listing 10-2 Revised Service Pack Inventory

```
Set objFSO = CreateObject("Scripting.FileSystemObject")
Set objTS = objFSO.OpenTextFile("c:\computers.txt")
Do Until objTS.AtEndOfStream
    strComputer = objTS.ReadLine
    Set SWBemlocator = CreateObject("wbemScripting.SWbemLocator")
    Set objwMIService = SWBemlocator.ConnectServer(strComputer,"\root\CIMV2")
    Set colItems = _
     objwMIService.ExecQuery("Select ServicePackMajorVersion " & _
     " from Win32_OperatingSystem WHERE Primary = True")
    For Each objItem in colItems
        WScript.Echo strComputer & "="
        WScript.Echo objItem.ServicePackMajorVersion
    Next
Loop
objTS.Close
```

> **Note**   When comparing string values, be sure to include the comparison value in single quotation marks. For example, *WHERE Property = 'Value'*. Numeric values, as well as the Boolean values TRUE and FALSE, are not enclosed in quotation marks. If you need to include a backslash character—in a file path, for example—you have to type double backslashes. For example, *WHERE Property = '\\\\Server\\Share'* for the path \\Server\Share. If you don't use double backslashes, WQL interprets them as a type of data delimiter.

Suppose you want to retrieve all event log entries with an ID of 1073741925 (which on our systems indicates that the SQL Server agent service was started). You then want to list the time the event was generated. Listing 10-3 is one way to accomplish this task.

Listing 10-3 Event Log Scanner

```
strComputer = "."
Set SWBemlocator = CreateObject("wbemScripting.SWbemLocator")
Set objwMIService = SWBemlocator.ConnectServer(strComputer, _
 "\root\CIMV2",UserName,Password)
Set colItems = _
 objwMIService.ExecQuery("Select * from Win32_NTLogEvent")
For Each objItem in colItems
    If objItem.EventIdentifier = 1073741925 Then
        WScript.Echo "TimeGenerated: " & objItem.TimeGenerated
        WScript.Echo "TimeWritten: " & objItem.TimeWritten
        WScript.Echo "User: " & objItem.User
    End If
Next
```

On our test system, which has three pretty full event logs, this script takes about three minutes to complete. Imagine running this on a dozen servers—it would take a significant amount of time. Including a *WHERE* clause can restrict the query so only those events matching our needs are returned. It's a simple change, as shown in Listing 10-4. This alternate version of the script completes in just a few seconds—a marked improvement.

Listing 10-4 Revised Event Log Scanner

```
strComputer = "."
Set SWBemlocator = CreateObject("WbemScripting.SWbemLocator")
Set objWMIService = SWBemlocator.ConnectServer(strComputer, _
 "\root\CIMV2",UserName,Password)
Set colItems = _
objWMIService.ExecQuery("Select * from Win32_NTLogEvent " & _
  "WHERE LogFIle = 'Application' AND " & _
  "EventIdentifier = 1073741925",,48)
For Each objItem in colItems
    WScript.Echo "TimeGenerated: " & objItem.TimeGenerated
    WScript.Echo "TimeWritten: " & objItem.TimeWritten
    WScript.Echo "User: " & objItem.User
Next
```

In this modified version, only events with the *EventIdentifier* value are queried, so our script doesn't have to run through all the events to find the right ones. Were this to run against a remote computer, it'd save considerably more time because all the extraneous events wouldn't be transmitted across the network and then processed by our script.

A *WHERE* clause can contain more than one condition. Simply join conditions together with Boolean operators. You can use parentheses to specify the order in which conditions are evaluated (the conditions nested deepest are evaluated first). For example, here's another revision that'll make our event log scanner work a bit faster.

```
objWMIService.ExecQuery("Select * from Win32_NTLogEvent " & _
  "WHERE LogFile = 'Application' AND " & _
  "EventIdentifier = 1073741925",,48)
```

We specified that only events listed in the Application event log and that have the *Event-Identifier* value should be returned. This allows the computer processing the query to eliminate all event logs except the one specified because no other event log's entries could match the *LogFile = 'Application'* criteria. The more specific you can be in your WQL query, the faster your query will execute, and the more efficiently your script will run.

Using the *LIKE* Operator

If you don't know which value to include in a *WHERE* clause, Microsoft Windows XP and later versions of Windows (including Microsoft Windows Server 2003) support a special operator called *LIKE*. It takes the place of the equal sign (=) or other comparison operator in a *WHERE* clause, and it allows you to specify wildcards in your criteria. The *LIKE* operator executes very rapidly, making it an excellent choice for reducing query result set sizes even if you don't have specific criteria.

For example, suppose you want to return a list of installed software (that is, products) with the word *Microsoft* in the name. That would be difficult to do with the equals operator because it requires a precise match. However, the *LIKE* operator can be used with the wildcard character (%). Listing 10-5 is a sample that shows the *LIKE* operator in action. Note that the wildcard character is included both before and after the search term *Microsoft*, allowing products with *Microsoft* anywhere in the name to be retrieved. That is, the first wildcard character will match any number of characters prior to the word *Microsoft*, and the second wildcard character will match any number of character after the word *Microsoft*.

Listing 10-5 Wildcard Query

```
strComputer = "."
Set SWBemlocator = CreateObject("WbemScripting.SWbemLocator")
Set objWMIService = SWBemlocator.ConnectServer(strComputer,"\root\CIMV2")
Set colItems = _
 objWMIService.ExecQuery("Select * from Win32_Product " & _
 "WHERE Caption LIKE '%Microsoft%'")
For Each objItem in colItems
        WScript.Echo "Caption: " & objItem.Caption
        WScript.Echo "Description: " & objItem.Description
        WScript.Echo "Name: " & objItem.Name
        WScript.Echo
Next
```

Note   This script will work only on Windows XP computers and Windows Server 2003 computers where the optional Installed Applications WMI provider (included on the Windows Server 2003 product CD) has been installed.

Our results from this script look, in part, like this.

```
Caption: Microsoft IntelliType Pro 5.2
Description: Microsoft IntelliType Pro 5.2
Name: Microsoft IntelliType Pro 5.2

Caption: Microsoft .NET Framework 1.1
Description: Microsoft .NET Framework 1.1
Name: Microsoft .NET Framework 1.1

Caption: Microsoft Visio Viewer 2002
Description: Microsoft Visio Viewer 2002
Name: Microsoft Visio Viewer 2002

Caption: HighMAT Extension to Microsoft Windows XP CD Writing Wizard
Description: HighMAT Extension to Microsoft Windows XP CD Writing Wizard
Name: HighMAT Extension to Microsoft Windows XP CD Writing Wizard
```

Notice that products with *Microsoft* at the start of the name are retrieved, as well as products that include the word *Microsoft* in the middle of the name.

> **Note**   Remember that only Windows XP and later versions of Windows support the *LIKE* operator. You'll receive an error if you try to use it with unsupported operating systems. Also remember that the computer executing the query must also support the *LIKE* operator. Therefore, if you're running the script on a Windows XP computer, and connecting to a Microsoft Windows NT computer, the *LIKE* operator won't be supported.

The *LIKE* operator also uses the underscore character (_) as a wildcard. Unlike the % wildcard, which matches any number of characters, the underscore matches only one character. For example, the expression *LIKE '_icrosoft'* would match *Microsoft* as well as *microsoft* and *dicrosoft*, but it would not match *Microsoft Office* or *Update for Microsoft Office*.

Understanding the *LIKE* operator and the *WHERE* clause will help you produce more efficient and flexible WMI scripts.

Using Queries and *associator* Classes

WMI has many *associator* classes. These classes don't typically provide information in and of themselves; instead, they are used in conjunction with two or more other classes. In the next two sections, we'll show you how *associator* classes work and how to use them.

Understanding Associations

The *Win32_DependentService* class represents the dependencies between various Windows system services. The class itself has three properties:

- The antecedent class, which is the service on which the service depends.
- The dependent class, which is the service that depends upon the antecedent.
- The type of dependency, which can be a value representing an unknown dependency, other dependency, or a value indicating that the antecedent service must have completed, started, or been stopped.

One instance of the *Win32_DependentService* class exists for each service dependency in the system. Figure 10-1 on the next page illustrates this relationship to the *Win32_Service* class. In Figure 10-1, ServiceB depends on ServiceA. The instance of the *Win32_DependentService* class codifies this relationship by listing ServiceB's instance of the *Win32_Service* class as dependent, and listing ServiceA's instance of the *Win32_Service* class as antecedent. Other instances of the *Win32_Service* class—such as ServiceC—can exist and have no relationship to either ServiceA or ServiceB.

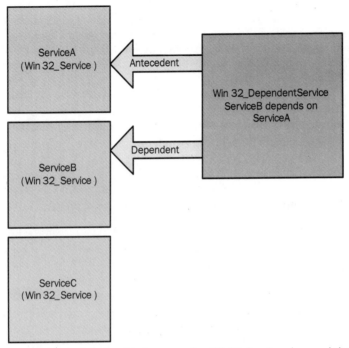

Figure 10-1   Relationship between the Win32_Service class and the Win32_DependentService class

Each instance of the *Win32_Service* class represents an installed service. When one service depends upon another, an instance of the *Win32_DependentService* class represents that dependency and associates the two classes with one another.

Writing Association Queries

The *ASSOCIATORS OF* query replaces the standard *SELECT* query. This special query is designed to find all *associator* classes for a given class. To continue using the *Win32_DependentService* class as an example, you might write a query like this.

```
ASSOCIATORS OF {Win32_Service.Name='MSSQLSERVER'}
WHERE AssocClass = Win32_DependentService
```

This query is asking for all classes that associate with the instance of *Win32_Service* where the *Name* property is *MSSQLSERVER*, specifically those associated classes of the *Win32_DependentService* class. This is a good query to test in Wbemtest.

1.   Run Wbemtest.exe by typing **wbemtest** at the Start menu's Run prompt or a command-line prompt.

2.   Click Connect and type **root\cimv2** in the Namespace text box of the dialog box that appears.

3.   Click Connect again to close the dialog box.

4. Click Query and enter the *ASSOCIATORS OF* query.

5. Click Apply to see the results, as shown in Figure 10-2.

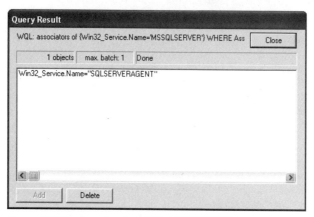

Figure 10-2   Results of a WMI ASSOCIATORS OF query

> **Note**   The *ASSOCIATORS OF* query in the previous example does, of course, assume that you're running an instance of Microsoft SQL Server, or the Microsoft SQL Server Desktop Engine (MSDE). To further explore this concept, however, you should try substituting other service names to see what results the query returns.

The results of the query are all the *Win32_Service* classes that, through *Win32_DependentService*, associate with the specified *Win32_Service* class (that is, the one with the name *MSSQLSERVER*). Of course, this query only works on systems that have Microsoft SQL Server installed. The query asks for all classes associated with a specific instance of *Win32_Service*, where the association is made by the *Win32_DependentService* class. This particular query returns all dependent and antecedent services of the *Win32_Service* instance specified.

The *Win32_DiskDriveToDiskPartition* class associates instances of *Win32_DiskDrive* with instances of *Win32_DiskPartition*. For example, suppose you were to execute a simple WMI query that returned the caption and device ID for all disk drives attached to your system. You'd start with something like this.

```
ComputerName = "."
Set wmiServices  = GetObject ( _
    "winmgmts:{impersonationLevel=Impersonate}!//" _
    & ComputerName)

' Get physical disk drive
Set wmiDiskDrives =  wmiServices.ExecQuery ( _
    "SELECT Caption, DeviceID FROM Win32_DiskDrive")
```

The *wmiDiskDrives* variable is a collection of *Win32_DiskDrive* instances, so you can use a *For...Each* loop to enumerate through the collection. For each *Win32_DiskDrive* instance, you could retrieve the partition associated with the drive by using an *ASSOCIATORS OF* query.

```
Set wmiDiskPartitions = wmiServices.ExecQuery _
    ("ASSOCIATORS OF {Win32_DiskDrive.DeviceID='" _
    & strEscapedDeviceID & "'} WHERE " & _
    "AssocClass = Win32_DiskDriveToDiskPartition")
```

This would return a collection of matching *Win32_Partition* instances, because *Win32_DiskDriveToDiskPartition* associates *Win32_DiskDrive* with *Win32_Partition*. Yet another *associator* class associates *Win32_Partition* with *Win32_LogicalDisk*, and you might use the following query to retrieve those associated instances.

```
Set wmiLogicalDisks = wmiServices.ExecQuery _
    ("ASSOCIATORS OF " _
        & "{Win32_DiskPartition.DeviceID='" & _
    wmiDiskPartition.DeviceID & "'} WHERE " & _
    "AssocClass = Win32_LogicalDiskToPartition")
```

Listing 10-6 utilizes these three queries. It starts by listing every drive letter in your system, then it lists each drive's associated partitions, and then it lists each partition's associated logical disks.

Listing 10-6 *associator* Query

```
ComputerName = "."
Set wmiServices  = GetObject ( _
    "winmgmts:{impersonationLevel=Impersonate}!//" _
    & ComputerName)

' Get physical disk drive
Set wmiDiskDrives = wmiServices.ExecQuery ( _
    "SELECT Caption, DeviceID FROM Win32_DiskDrive")

For Each wmiDiskDrive In wmiDiskDrives
    WScript.Echo "Disk drive Caption: " _
        & wmiDiskDrive.Caption _
        & VbCrLf & "DeviceID: " _
        & " (" & wmiDiskDrive.DeviceID & ")"

    'Backslash in disk drive deviceid
    ' must be escaped by "\"
    strEscapedDeviceID = Replace( _
        wmiDiskDrive.DeviceID, "\", "\\")

    'Use the disk drive device id to
    ' find associated partition
    Set wmiDiskPartitions = wmiServices.ExecQuery _
        ("ASSOCIATORS OF {Win32_DiskDrive.DeviceID='" _
        & strEscapedDeviceID & "'} WHERE " & _
        "AssocClass = Win32_DiskDriveToDiskPartition")
```

```
For Each wmiDiskPartition In wmiDiskPartitions

    'Use partition device id to find logical disk
    Set wmiLogicalDisks = wmiServices.ExecQuery _
        ("ASSOCIATORS OF " _
            & "{Win32_DiskPartition.DeviceID='" & _
        wmiDiskPartition.DeviceID & "'} WHERE " & _
        "AssocClass = Win32_LogicalDiskToPartition")

    For Each wmiLogicalDisk In wmiLogicalDisks
        WScript.Echo "Drive letter associated" _
            & " with disk drive = " _
            & wmiDiskDrive.Caption _
            & wmiDiskDrive.DeviceID _
            & VbCrLf & " Partition = " _
            & wmiDiskPartition.DeviceID _
            & VbCrLf & " is " _
            & wmiLogicalDisk.DeviceID
    Next
Next
Next
```

Note   Listing 10-6 is adapted from a sample in the Microsoft MSDN Library Platform SDK, which includes developer documentation for WMI. Note that the script might not work consistently on all systems, because drive-to-partition mapping is not always consistent.

Listing 10-7 is a version of Listing 10-6 that doesn't include the *Win32_LogicalDisk* associator queries. This more clearly illustrates the original association between *Win32_DiskDrive* and *Win32_Partition*.

Listing 10-7 Revised *associator* Query

```
ComputerName = "."
Set wmiServices  = GetObject ( _
    "winmgmts:{impersonationLevel=Impersonate}!//" _
    & ComputerName)

' Get physical disk drive
Set wmiDiskDrives =  wmiServices.ExecQuery ( _
    "SELECT Caption, DeviceID FROM Win32_DiskDrive")

For Each wmiDiskDrive In wmiDiskDrives
    WScript.Echo "Disk drive Caption: " _
        & wmiDiskDrive.Caption _
        & VbCrLf & "DeviceID: " _
        & " (" & wmiDiskDrive.DeviceID & ")"

Next
```

Notice that the *WHERE* clause of an *ASSOCIATORS OF* query is a bit different from a *WHERE* clause in a *SELECT* query. In Listing 10-7, the *WHERE* clause is restricted to some very specific values. We used the *AssocClass* property, which indicates the name of the associator class we want the query to use; you'll almost always use that in an *ASSOCIATORS OF* query. Some of the other keywords that you can specify include:

- *ClassDefsOnly* This keyword specifies that only class definitions, rather than instances, are returned by the query. Note that this keyword is specified by itself, and not as part of a comparison that uses the equal sign or another comparison operator.

- *RequiredAssocQualifier=qualifier* This keyword indicates that the returned instances must be associated with the source object through an association class that includes the specified qualifier. For example, the following would require the association class to include a qualifier named *Association*.

```
ASSOCIATORS OF {Win32_LogicalDisk.DeviceID='C:'}
  WHERE RequiredAssocQualifier = Association
```

- *RequiredQualifier=qualifier* This keyword specifies that the returned instances include the specified qualifier. For example, the following would return only the classes that include a property named *Locale*.

```
ASSOCIATORS OF {Win32_LogicalDisk.DeviceID='C:'}
  WHERE RequiredQualifier = Locale
```

- *ResultClass=classname* This keyword (which can't be used in conjunction with *Class-DefsOnly*) allows you to specify the class you want to retrieve. For example, the following query would return instances in the *Win32_Directory*, *Win32_ComputerSystem*, and *Win32_DiskPartition* classes.

```
ASSOCIATORS OF {Win32_LogicalDisk.DeviceID='C:'}
```

  However, the following revision would return instances only from *Win32_Directory*, which derives from the generic *CIM_Directory* class.

```
ASSOCIATORS OF {Win32_LogicalDisk.DeviceID='C:'}
  WHERE ResultClass = CIM_Directory
```

These keywords, when used in a query, aren't separated by commas when you use more than one.

```
ASSOCIATORS OF {Win32_LogicalDisk.DeviceID='C:'}
  WHERE ClassDefsOnly AssocClass=Win32_LogicalDiskToPatition
```

> **Note** You can consult the WMI documentation to see the generic Computer Information Model (CIM) class from which any *Win32_* class is derived.

Using References Queries

The *REFERENCES OF* statement can also be used in place of standard *SELECT* queries. You use the *REFERENCES OF* statement similarly to the way you use *ASSOCIATORS OF* statements, but in reverse. The *REFERENCES OF* statement retrieves all association instances that refer to a particular source instance. Like *ASSOCIATORS OF* queries, it can use keywords in a *WHERE* clause, although the available keywords are more limited: *ClassFedsOnly*, *RequiredQualifier*, and *ResultClass*.

```
REFERENCES OF {Adapter="AHA-294X"} WHERE ResultClass = AdapterDriver
```

This returns all instances of *Win32_AdapterDriver* (with the specified *ResultClass*) associated with the class where the adapter is *AHA-294X*. Here's another example.

```
REFERENCES OF {Win32_NetworkAdapter.DeviceID="0"}
WHERE resultclass = Win32_NetworkAdapterSetting
requiredQualifier = Dynamic
```

This returns all instances of the *Win32_NetworkAdapterSetting* class that are set to *Dynamic*, and that reference the instance of *Win32_NetworkAdapter* with a device ID of 0.

Using Advanced WMI Security Techniques

WMI has default settings for authentication, authentication service (NTLM or Kerberos), and impersonation (which allows the WMI service on the remote computer to impersonate your credentials execute your queries). In Chapter 2, we explained how to supply alternate credentials for a WMI connection. However, WMI provides additional security options for specific types of WMI activity. To use these security and impersonation options, it's often easier to use the *SWBemLocator* object, rather than connecting to WMI through the *winmgmts://* moniker. This is because the *SWBemLocator* object syntax is often easier to read, especially when using multiple options at once. A simple connection and query would look like this.

```
strComputer = "."
Set SWBemlocator = CreateObject("wbemScripting.SwbemLocator")
Set objWMIService = SWBemlocator.ConnectServer(strComputer,"\root\CIMV2")
Set colItems = objWMIService.ExecQuery( _
 "Select * from Win32_OperatingSystem")
```

Before calling the *ExecQuery* method, however, you can modify the *Security_* property of the *SWBemLocator* object. The property is an *SWbemSecurity* object, and it has three properties: *AuthenticationLevel*, *ImpersonationLevel*, and *Privileges*.

Using the *AuthenticationLevel* Property

The *AuthenticationLevel* property determines the level of authentication performed by WMI. The available authentication levels are:

- **0: Default**   Authentication is set to whatever Windows uses as its default.
- **1: None**   Authentication is not used.
- **2: Connect**   Authentication occurs only during the initial connection.
- **3: Call**   Authentication occurs for each call to a remote computer.
- **4: Packet**   Authentication occurs for each packet sent or received.
- **5: Packet Integrity**   Authentication is performed on each packet, and the integrity of packets is verified to ensure they haven't changed.
- **6: Packet Privacy**   Authentication is performed on each packet; they are authenticated, checked for integrity, and encrypted to help ensure privacy.

Note that you can also specify the *AuthenticationLevel* property when using a moniker to connect to WMI.

```
Set objinst = GetObject("WinMgmts:{ "& _
                        "authenticationLevel=pktPrivacy}" & _
                        "!root/cimv2:Win32_LogicalDisk='c:'")
```

Using the *ImpersonationLevel* Property

Specifying an impersonation level allows the remote WMI service to use your credentials to execute your queries. The available impersonation levels are:

- **1: Anonymous**   Doesn't allow impersonation of your credentials. WMI usually will not work with this level.
- **2: Identify**   Identifies you but doesn't allow impersonation of your credentials. WMI usually will fail with this level.
- **3: Impersonate**   Allows the remote WMI service to impersonate your credentials. This is the default on Windows 2000 and later versions.
- **4: Delegate**   Allows the remote computer to impersonate you and gives your credentials to other services, which can also impersonate you. This is generally unnecessary and can be a security risk.

Note that you can also specify the *AuthenticationLevel* property when using a moniker to connect to WMI.

```
Set objinst = GetObject("WinMgmts:{ "& _
                        "impersonationLevel=Impersonate}" & _
                        "!root/cimv2:Win32_LogicalDisk='c:'")
```

Using the *Privileges* Property

Sometimes it's not enough to have permissions to do whatever you want with WMI. For safety reasons, certain security-sensitive privileges are restricted, even if your current user account has permissions. These privileges must be specifically enabled.

The *Privileges* property is a *SWbemPrivilegeSet* object. To add a privilege, use the object's *Add-AsString* method to add a specific privilege name.

```
wmiService.Security_.Privileges.AddAsString "SeDebugPrivilege", True
```

Here are the available security privileges. Many of these privileges aren't used frequently in administrative scripts, but we list them all for completeness. The privileges in bold are used most commonly.

- *SeCreateTokenPrivilege*
- *SeAssignPrimaryTokenPrivilege*
- *SeLockMemoryPrivilege*
- *SeIncreaseQuotaPrivilege*
- **SeMachineAccountPrivilege**–required to create a computer account
- *SeTcbPrivilege*
- **SeSecurityPrivilege**–required to perform tasks such as clearing the Security event log and other security-sensitive tasks
- **SeTakeOwnershipPrivilege**–required to take ownership of an object without having specific permissions for the object
- *SeLoadDriverPrivilege*
- **SeSystemProfilePrivilege**–required to gather system profile and performance information
- **SeSystemtimePrivilege**–required to set the system time
- *SeProfileSingleProcessPrivilege*
- *SeIncreaseBasePriorityPrivilege*
- *SeCreatePageFilePrivilege*
- *SePermanentPrivilege*
- **SeBackupPrivilege**–required to perform backup operations
- **SeRestorePrivilege**–required to perform restore operations
- **SeShutdownPrivilege**–required to shut down a system locally
- *SeDebugPrivilege*

- *SeAuditPrivilege*

- *SeSystemEnvironmentPrivilege*

- *SeChangeNotifyPrivilege*

- **SeRemoteShutdownPrivilege**–required to remotely shut down a system

- *SeUndockPrivilege*

- *SeSyncAgentPrivilege*

- *SeEnableDelegationPrivilege*

> **Note**   You must use the exact privilege string shown when using the *Add* method and the *SWbemPermissionSet* object. For example, *wmiService.Security_.Privileges.AddAsString "SeDebugPrivilege"*, *True*

Note that you can also specify privileges when using a moniker-style connection.

```
Set Service = GetObject("winmgmts:{impersonationLevel=impersonate, (Debug)}")
```

> **Tip**   Note that in the example just shown, the privilege is *Debug*, not *SeDebugPrivilege*. When using the moniker, you use the simplest version of the privilege string. Drop the *Se* and *Privilege* portions of the string.

Viewing Advanced WMI Scripting in Action

We'll end this chapter by covering one of the most requested and complex tasks that you can perform with WMI: managing file permissions. The association between a file, its discretionary access control list (DACL), the access control entries (ACEs) on that DACL, and the trustees listed on the ACEs, can be complicated. WMI provides some shortcuts so you don't have to execute a half a dozen *ASSOCIATORS OF* queries to get a single file permission, but navigating the hierarchy of classes can still be confusing. For our example, we'll write a script that accepts a filename or folder path, and then displays the permissions associated with it. We start by prompting for that file or folder name. Note that we're using the *Replace* method to replace any single backslashes with double backslashes. That's a general requirement of WMI because it uses the backslash as a special character.

```
Dim objFileSecuritySetting
Dim strFile
strFile = Replace(InputBox("File path and name?"),"\","\\")
```

Next we query the *Win32_LogicalFileSecuritySetting* class instance that has the specified *Path* property. Note that although this class's name says *File*, it works for both files and folders.

> **Tip**   There's a similar *Win32_LogicalShareSecuritySetting* class that handles shared folder permissions. You could use it to modify the following example relatively easily to work with shared folders instead of files and folders.

```
Set objFileSecuritySetting = _
 GetObject("winmgmts:Win32_LogicalFileSecuritySetting.path='" _
  & strFile & "'")
```

Now we display the description of the returned instance, as well as its *ControlFlags* property. That property is simply a set of bit flags, so we write a series of *If...Then* statements that check whether a particular flag is on.

```
'FileSecuritySetting Basics
WScript.Echo objFileSecuritySetting.Description
If objFileSecuritySetting.ControlFlags And 1 Then _
 WScript.Echo " Default owner"
If objFileSecuritySetting.ControlFlags And 2 Then _
 WScript.Echo " Default group"
If objFileSecuritySetting.ControlFlags And 4 Then _
 WScript.Echo " DACL exists"
If objFileSecuritySetting.ControlFlags And 8 Then _
 WScript.Echo " Default DACL"
If objFileSecuritySetting.ControlFlags And 16 Then _
 WScript.Echo " SACL exists"
If objFileSecuritySetting.ControlFlags And 32 Then _
 WScript.Echo " Default SACL"
If objFileSecuritySetting.ControlFlags And 256 Then _
 WScript.Echo " DACL auto-inherit req"
If objFileSecuritySetting.ControlFlags And 512 Then _
 WScript.Echo " SACL auto-inherit req"
If objFileSecuritySetting.ControlFlags And 1024 Then _
 WScript.Echo " DACL auto-inherited"
If objFileSecuritySetting.ControlFlags And 2048 Then _
 WScript.Echo " SACL auto-inherited"
If objFileSecuritySetting.ControlFlags And 4096 Then _
 WScript.Echo " DACL Protected"
If objFileSecuritySetting.ControlFlags And 8192 Then _
 WScript.Echo " SACL Protected"
If objFileSecuritySetting.ControlFlags And 32768 Then _
 WScript.Echo " Self-relative"
WScript.Echo
```

> **Tip**   This is an excellent example of how to use VBScript's Boolean operators. Each bit in a byte has a value: the first bit has a value of 1, the second is 2, continuing to 4, 8, 16, 32, and so forth, incrementing in powers of 2. To see whether the first bit is turned on, use the *FlagVariable And 1* expression. This will return TRUE if the bit is on, or FALSE if it isn't. Similarly, *FlagVariable And 4* will tell you whether the third bit is on (TRUE) or off (FALSE).

Next, we ask the security setting instance to return the security descriptor (DACL) for itself. This is a *Win32_SecurityDescriptor* class, and we retrieved it by using the security setting's *GetSecurityDescriptor* method.

```
'security descriptor specifics
'working with a Win32_SecurityDescriptor instance
Dim intReturn, objSecDesc
intReturn = objFileSecuritySetting.GetSecurityDescriptor(objSecDesc)
```

The DACL also has a bit-based flag property, so we run through each bit to see which ones are on.

```
WScript.Echo "Security Descriptor:"
If objSecDesc.ControlFlags And 1 Then _
 WScript.Echo " Default owner"
If objSecDesc.ControlFlags And 2 Then _
 WScript.Echo " Default group"
If objSecDesc.ControlFlags And 4 Then _
 WScript.Echo " DACL exists"
If objSecDesc.ControlFlags And 8 Then _
 WScript.Echo " Default DACL"
If objSecDesc.ControlFlags And 16 Then _
 WScript.Echo " SACL exists"
If objSecDesc.ControlFlags And 32 Then _
 WScript.Echo " Default SACL"
If objSecDesc.ControlFlags And 256 Then _
 WScript.Echo " DACL auto-inherit req"
If objSecDesc.ControlFlags And 512 Then _
 WScript.Echo " SACL auto-inherit req"
If objSecDesc.ControlFlags And 1024 Then _
 WScript.Echo " DACL auto-inherited"
If objSecDesc.ControlFlags And 2048 Then _
 WScript.Echo " SACL auto-inherited"
If objSecDesc.ControlFlags And 4096 Then _
 WScript.Echo " DACL Protected"
If objSecDesc.ControlFlags And 8192 Then _
 WScript.Echo " SACL Protected"
If objSecDesc.ControlFlags And 32768 Then _
 WScript.Echo " Self-relative"
WScript.Echo String(25,"-")
```

The security descriptor's DACL property provides the actual DACL, which consists of one or more ACEs. We assign the DACL to a variable so that we can work with it.

```
Dim objDACL, objTrustee, strAccount
objDACL = objSecDesc.DACL
```

We now go through each ACE one at a time.

```
'go through the ACEs on the DACL
'each is an instance of Win32_ACE
Dim objACE
For Each objACE In objDACL
```

Each ACE has a trustee, which is the security account (a user or group) assigned to it. For each trustee, we display the domain and name.

```
'get trustee for this ACE - Win32_Trustee instance
Set objTrustee = objACE.Trustee
strAccount = objTrustee.Domain & "\" & objTrustee.Name
```

Then we display the type of ACE: *Allow*, *Deny*, or *Audit*.

```
'write ACE type
Select Case objACE.AceType
    case 0
        WScript.Echo strAccount & _
         " Allowed to:"
    Case 1
        WScript.Echo strAccount & _
         " Denied to:"
    Case 2
        WScript.Echo strAccount & _
         " Audit for:"
End Select
```

The permissions being allowed, denied, or audited are stored in another bit flag, so once again we run through each bit and display the names of the bits that are turned on, or assigned, to the ACE.

```
'write permissions
If objACE.AccessMask And 1 Then _
 WScript.Echo " File: List Dir"
If objACE.AccessMask And 2 Then _
 WScript.Echo " File: Add file"
If objACE.AccessMask And 4 Then _
 WScript.Echo " File: Add Subdir"
If objACE.AccessMask And 8 Then _
 WScript.Echo " File: Read EA"
If objACE.AccessMask And 16 Then _
 WScript.Echo " File: Write EA"
If objACE.AccessMask And 32 Then _
 WScript.Echo " File: Traverse"
If objACE.AccessMask And 64 Then _
 WScript.Echo " File: Delete child"
If objACE.AccessMask And 128 Then _
 WScript.Echo " File: Read attrs"
If objACE.AccessMask And 256 Then _
 WScript.Echo " File: Write attrs"
If objACE.AccessMask And 65536 Then _
 WScript.Echo " Delete"
If objACE.AccessMask And 131072 Then _
 WScript.Echo " Read-control"
If objACE.AccessMask And 262144 Then _
 WScript.Echo " Write-DACL"
If objACE.AccessMask And 524288 Then _
 WScript.Echo " Write-owner"
If objACE.AccessMask And 1048576 Then _
 WScript.Echo " Synchronize"
```

The ACE also holds flags that describe the ACE's inheritance behavior, which we display.

```
'write flags
If objACE.AceFlags And 1 Then _
 WScript.Echo " (Non-container child objects will inherit)"
If objACE.AceFlags And 2 Then _
 WScript.Echo " (Container child objects will inherit)"
If objACE.AceFlags And 4 Then _
 WScript.Echo " (ACE does not propagate inheritance)"
If objACE.AceFlags And 8 Then _
 WScript.Echo " (Inherit-only ACE)"
If objACE.AceFlags And 16 Then _
 WScript.Echo " (Inherited ACE)"
```

We end by displaying a line between this ACE and the next ACE.

```
'separator
WScript.Echo String(25,"-")
Next
```

Listing 10-8 is the entire script.

Listing 10-8 File Permissions

```
Dim objFileSecuritySetting
Dim strFile
strFile = Replace(InputBox("File path and name?"),"\","\\")
Set objFileSecuritySetting = _
 GetObject("winmgmts:Win32_LogicalFileSecuritySetting.path='" _
  & strFile & "'")


'FileSecuritySetting Basics
WScript.Echo objFileSecuritySetting.Description
If objFileSecuritySetting.ControlFlags And 1 Then _
 WScript.Echo " Default owner"
If objFileSecuritySetting.ControlFlags And 2 Then _
 WScript.Echo " Default group"
If objFileSecuritySetting.ControlFlags And 4 Then _
 WScript.Echo " DACL exists"
If objFileSecuritySetting.ControlFlags And 8 Then _
 WScript.Echo " Default DACL"
If objFileSecuritySetting.ControlFlags And 16 Then _
 WScript.Echo " SACL exists"
If objFileSecuritySetting.ControlFlags And 32 Then _
 WScript.Echo " Default SACL"
If objFileSecuritySetting.ControlFlags And 256 Then _
 WScript.Echo " DACL auto-inherit req"
If objFileSecuritySetting.ControlFlags And 512 Then _
 WScript.Echo " SACL auto-inherit req"
If objFileSecuritySetting.ControlFlags And 1024 Then _
 WScript.Echo " DACL auto-inherited"
If objFileSecuritySetting.ControlFlags And 2048 Then _
 WScript.Echo " SACL auto-inherited"
If objFileSecuritySetting.ControlFlags And 4096 Then _
 WScript.Echo " DACL Protected"
```

```
If objFileSecuritySetting.ControlFlags And 8192 Then _
 WScript.Echo " SACL Protected"
If objFileSecuritySetting.ControlFlags And 32768 Then _
 WScript.Echo " Self-relative"
WScript.Echo

'security descriptor specifics
'working with a Win32_SecurityDescriptor instance
Dim intReturn, objSecDesc
intReturn = objFileSecuritySetting.GetSecurityDescriptor(objSecDesc)
WScript.Echo "Security Descriptor:"
If objSecDesc.ControlFlags And 1 Then _
 WScript.Echo " Default owner"
If objSecDesc.ControlFlags And 2 Then _
 WScript.Echo " Default group"
If objSecDesc.ControlFlags And 4 Then _
 WScript.Echo " DACL exists"
If objSecDesc.ControlFlags And 8 Then _
 WScript.Echo " Default DACL"
If objSecDesc.ControlFlags And 16 Then _
 WScript.Echo " SACL exists"
If objSecDesc.ControlFlags And 32 Then _
 WScript.Echo " Default SACL"
If objSecDesc.ControlFlags And 256 Then _
 WScript.Echo " DACL auto-inherit req"
If objSecDesc.ControlFlags And 512 Then _
 WScript.Echo " SACL auto-inherit req"
If objSecDesc.ControlFlags And 1024 Then _
 WScript.Echo " DACL auto-inherited"
If objSecDesc.ControlFlags And 2048 Then _
 WScript.Echo " SACL auto-inherited"
If objSecDesc.ControlFlags And 4096 Then _
 WScript.Echo " DACL Protected"
If objSecDesc.ControlFlags And 8192 Then _
 WScript.Echo " SACL Protected"
If objSecDesc.ControlFlags And 32768 Then _
 WScript.Echo " Self-relative"
WScript.Echo String(25,"-")

Dim objDACL, objTrustee, strAccount
objDACL = objSecDesc.DACL

'go through the ACEs on the DACL
'each is an instance of Win32_ACE
Dim objACE
For Each objACE In objDACL
    'get trustee for this ACE - Win32_Trustee instance
    Set objTrustee = objACE.Trustee
    strAccount = objTrustee.Domain & "\" & objTrustee.Name

    'write ACE type
    Select Case objACE.AceType
        case 0
            WScript.Echo strAccount & _
             " Allowed to:"
```

```
        Case 1
            WScript.Echo strAccount & _
             " Denied to:"
        Case 2
            WScript.Echo strAccount & _
             " Audit for:"
    End Select

    'write permissions
    If objACE.AccessMask And 1 Then _
     WScript.Echo " File: List Dir"
    If objACE.AccessMask And 2 Then _
     WScript.Echo " File: Add file"
    If objACE.AccessMask And 4 Then _
     WScript.Echo " File: Add Subdir"
    If objACE.AccessMask And 8 Then _
     WScript.Echo " File: Read EA"
    If objACE.AccessMask And 16 Then _
     WScript.Echo " File: Write EA"
    If objACE.AccessMask And 32 Then _
     WScript.Echo " File: Traverse"
    If objACE.AccessMask And 64 Then _
     WScript.Echo " File: Delete child"
    If objACE.AccessMask And 128 Then _
     WScript.Echo " File: Read attrs"
    If objACE.AccessMask And 256 Then _
     WScript.Echo " File: Write attrs"
    If objACE.AccessMask And 65536 Then _
     WScript.Echo " Delete"
    If objACE.AccessMask And 131072 Then _
     WScript.Echo " Read-control"
    If objACE.AccessMask And 262144 Then _
     WScript.Echo " Write-DACL"
    If objACE.AccessMask And 524288 Then _
     WScript.Echo " Write-owner"
    If objACE.AccessMask And 1048576 Then _
     WScript.Echo " Synchronize"

    'write flags
    If objACE.AceFlags And 1 Then _
     WScript.Echo " (Non-container child objects will inherit)"
    If objACE.AceFlags And 2 Then _
     WScript.Echo " (Container child objects will inherit)"
    If objACE.AceFlags And 4 Then _
     WScript.Echo " (ACE does not propagate inheritance)"
    If objACE.AceFlags And 8 Then _
     WScript.Echo " (Inherit-only ACE)"
    If objACE.AceFlags And 16 Then _
     WScript.Echo " (Inherited ACE)"

    'separator
    WScript.Echo String(25,"-")
Next
```

This technique is used for almost all permissions in WMI. Most security-related classes—including *Win32_LogicalFileSecuritySetting* as well as certain Active Directory classes—offer a *GetSecurityDescriptor* method that can be used as we've shown here. There's also a *SetSecurity-Descriptor* method, which you use to change permissions. Simply get the security descriptor, modify it, and then pass it back to the *SetSecurityDescriptor* method to apply permission changes.

> **Caution**   Just because you *can* do a thing with a script doesn't necessarily mean you *should* do that thing with a script. File permissions are an excellent example. Although WMI provides everything you need to manage file permissions, using it to do so is a lot more complicated than using a command-line tool such as Cacls.exe or Xcacls.exe, both of which can also be scripted if you need to automate their operation.

Summary

We covered a lot of ground in this chapter. You learned how to use both *ASSOCIATORS OF* and *REFERENCES OF* statements, as well as about some of the advanced and flexible security techniques supported by WMI. You also learned how to refine and limit your WMI query results by using *WHERE* clauses and by specifying the properties you want the query to return. Finally, you learned how to tackle one of WMI's toughest tasks, managing NTFS file permissions. Hopefully, the examples in this chapter will help your WMI scripts become more powerful and efficient.

Chapter 11
WMI Events

Managing events in Windows Management Instrumentation (WMI) is an important skill that will take your administrative scripting to the next level. Microsoft Windows is an event-driven operating system. By using WMI and VBScript, we can monitor events and take action when they occur. We'll show you how to create WMI scripts that you can use as monitoring utilities.

Servers and desktops are dynamic systems: files are created and modified, services are started and stopped, processes are created and destroyed, and event logs are written. As an administrator, you might want to do something when one of these actions takes place. For example, you might want to detect when a service is started or stopped. The way a program is informed of these actions is through *events*. An event is any interesting action to which a program might want to respond. Operating system programmers and application developers determine which events to define and how they occur. For example, a stop event is generated when a service is stopped. When an event occurs, it is said to have *fired*. We can use WMI to monitor many types of events.

Understanding WMI Events

In WMI, an event is a WMI object, so when an event fires, we can use the resulting object. This event object is a system object, so it is prefixed with two underscores (__). Event objects derive their base functionality from the *__Event* class. Because the *__Event* class is abstract, event objects will be children of the *__Event* class. There are several types of *__Event* classes, but from a scripting perspective, we will most likely use the following child classes of *__InstanceOperationEvent*.

- *__InstanceCreationEvent* is fired when something is created, such as a new process or an event log entry.

- *__InstanceModificationEvent* is fired when something is modified, such as a file.

■ ___InstanceDeletionEvent_ is fired when something is deleted, such as a file. This event would also be fired as a process is destroyed.

Understanding Consumers

Objects that use the information from the fired events are called *consumers*. Without an event consumer, events would go unnoticed. A consumer object is derived from the *EventViewer-Consumer* class, which in turn is derived from the ___EventConsumer_ system class. WMI includes temporary and permanent consumers. A temporary consumer receives events only as long as the consumer is running. For example, a VBScript monitoring WMI events would generally be considered a temporary consumer. As soon as the script is terminated, event processing ends even though events continue to fire. We will be using temporary consumers.

A permanent consumer is an application or Component Object Model (COM) object that receives specific types of events. Developing permanent consumers is outside the scope of this book, but there is a permanent consumer application you can run on Microsoft Windows XP called eventtriggers.exe. You can use this consumer to monitor events written to an event log on local or remote systems. Type **eventtriggers /?** and **eventtriggers /create /?** at a command prompt for more information.

> **Tip**   When using *eventtriggers /create* with the */TK* parameter, remember that it will run in the context of the user credentials you supply. If you don't specify any credentials, the utility will use the System account. You can specify the credentials of the currently logged on user when creating triggers for the local system. This is very useful when you want to have user interaction or intervention when a specific event occurs.

Permanent event consumers need to be registered on the system to receive event notifications. We don't mean every remote system, just the system from which you will be monitoring. This requires that you define a consumer instance and an event filter, which we'll cover in a moment. Using WMI events in VBScript doesn't require any registration.

Understanding Notification Queries

A notification query is a query written in WMI Query Language (WQL) that specifies which event to monitor and what information to return. These queries are called notification queries, because you will be notified when the event occurs.

```
Select * from __InstanceCreationEvent
```

In this notification query statement, we specify to monitor the ___InstanceCreationEvent_ type. The query will return all properties from the ___InstanceCreationEvent_ system class when a new instance of any type is created.

We can create a notification query, but for it to do anything, we need to execute the query, also called *subscribing* to the event. We can execute a notification query synchronously, semi-synchronously, or asynchronously. We'll discuss these concepts in more detail later in the chapter.

Understanding Filters

Filter instances are used to define or limit the type of events to monitor. A filter is derived from the __EventFilter system class. Typically, filters are defined as part of the notification query statements.

```
Select * from __InstanceCreationEvent WHERE TargetInstance ISA 'Win32_NTLogEvent'
```

In this notification query statement, we are returning all properties from the __InstanceCreationEvent system class. However, we don't want every instance, only a specific type, called the *TargetInstance*. In this example, we want all the information when an instance of the *Win32_NTLogEvent* class is created. You might think we need to use the equal sign (=) operator and construct a filter like this.

```
TargetInstance='Win32_NTLogEvent'
```

However, in the world of WMI events, this won't work because we are comparing class instances. Instead, WQL provides a different operator, *ISA*.

```
TargetInstance ISA 'Win32_NTLogEvent'
```

This filter indicates to only perform the query when the instance *is a Win32_NTLogEvent* type.

Understanding Polling

To check for an event at a specific time, we can create event timers. Absolute timers check for events at a specified date and time. This has some value, but in most cases, *polling* is more useful. Polling is not a type of timer event, but it is timing related. Polling means checking for some action at regular intervals, and it is accomplished by using the *WITHIN* clause in the WQL statement.

```
Select * from __InstanceCreationEvent WITHIN 5 where TargetInstance ISA 'CIM_DATAFILE' AND
TargetInstance.drive='e:' AND TargetInstance.Path='\\temp\\'
```

In this query, we ask WMI to check every five seconds if any new files have been created in E:\Temp.

> **Tip**   When setting a polling interval by using WMI Tools (discussed later in the chapter), the value you specify is in milliseconds. In VBScript and WBEMTest, the value is in seconds.

Some classes, such as *CIM_DataFile* and *Win32_Process*, require you to use the *WITHIN* clause. If you don't use it and it is required, you will get an error message.

> **Best Practices**   Setting a polling interval is as much an art as it is a science. If you poll every few seconds, you get more information, but polling too often can introduce a lot of overhead. How frequently to poll depends on your query. Because a poorly crafted query can seriously degrade system performance, test all polling queries on non-production systems. Testing and experience will help determine an adequate polling interval.

Using Notification Queries

Let's start putting some of this information about WMI events together. First, we experiment with a notification query using the WBEMTest tool. Then, we examine a script that executes a notification query semisynchronously. Finally, we examine a script that executes a notification query asynchronously.

Using WBEMTest

Let's use WBEMTest to look at a notification query. We cover WBEMTest in more detail in Chapter 12. Start WBEMTest, and click Enable All Privileges, as shown in Figure 11-1.

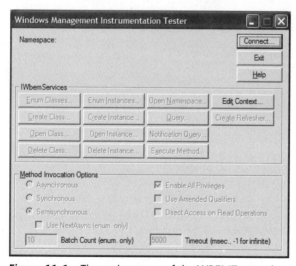

Figure 11-1   The main screen of the WBEMTest tool

Click the Connect button, and change the namespace to **root\cimv2**.

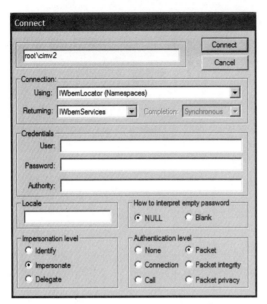

Figure 11-2   Specifying connection information in WBEMTest

Click the Connect button again to redisplay the main WBEMTest screen. Notice the available options: Asynchronous, Synchronous, and Semisynchronous. We cover asynchronous queries later in this chapter. For now, accept the default of Semisynchronous.

Click the Notification Query button. In the Query dialog box, enter the following, as shown in Figure 11-3:

*Select * from __InstanceCreationEvent WHERE TargetInstance ISA 'Win32_NTLogEvent'*

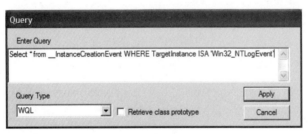

Figure 11-3   Entering a notification query

Click Apply to display the Query Result dialog box, as shown in Figure 11-4 on the next page.

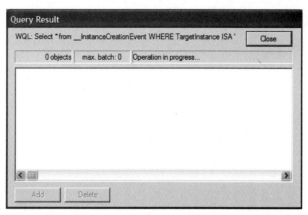

Figure 11-4   Query results for a notification query

In a command-prompt window, use the **net stop** command to stop a service. For example, stop the alerter service or another running service. As soon as the service stops, you should see a few entries in the Query Result dialog box, as shown in Figure 11-5.

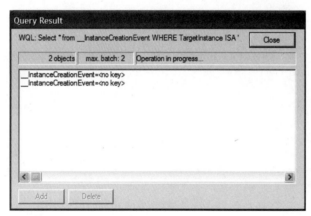

Figure 11-5   Win32_NTLogEvent creation events detected when a service is stopped

Double-click the second entry in the list. Select the Hide System Properties check box to make it easier to view the properties of _InstanceCreationEvent. Figure 11-6 shows the details of _InstanceCreationEvent.

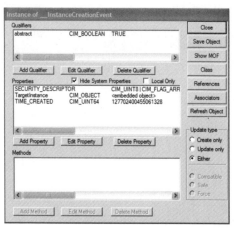

Figure 11-6 Properties of _*InstanceCreationEvent*

Notice that the *TargetInstance* property is shown as an embedded object. This is the *Win32_NTEventLog* object. Double-click *TargetInstance* to display the Property Editor dialog box, and then click View Embedded. You should see the Object Editor for the *Win32_NTEventLog* object, shown in Figure 11-7.

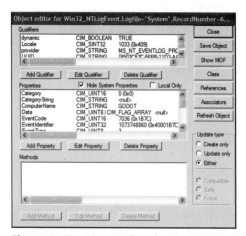

Figure 11-7 Object Editor for the *Win32_NTEventLog* object

As you explore the *Win32_NTEventLog* object, you will see some familiar event log properties, such as Logfile, SourceName, Type, and Message. When you are finished exploring, close or cancel all the open windows, and exit WBEMTest.

Executing a Notification Query Semisynchronously

As you saw in WBEMTest, the default query method is semisynchronous, which means the query is executed and then control returns to the user pretty quickly. To execute a notification query semisynchronously in a script, a call is made to the *ExecNotificationQuery* method.

Using the semisynchronous method in a script allows any code following the query method to execute. When using this method, we need to use a WMI scripting technique called *blocking*. When blocking is used, the script blocks (pauses) until an event occurs. When a notification query is executed, the query returns an *SWbemEventSource* object. The *SWbemEventSource* object has a method called *NextEvent*. When the *NextEvent* method is called, the script will block until the next event occurs.

```
Set oWMI=GetObject("winmgmts:{(security)}")
strQuery="Select * from __InstanceCreationEvent WHERE TargetInstance " &_
"ISA 'Win32_NTLogEvent'"
Set oEventSrc=oWMI.ExecNotificationQuery(strQuery)
'start blocking
Set NTEvent=oEventSrc.NextEvent()
'script continues after event fires
```

In this snippet, a notification query is executed and returns a *SWbemEventSource* object. The script pauses when the *NextEvent* method is called and waits for a new entry to be added to the event log. When the event fires, it returns an object that corresponds to the *TargetInstance* property in the query, in this case, a *Win32_NTLogEvent*. As written, the snippet will wait until an event occurs before continuing and exiting the script.

If we wanted to detect additional event log creation events, we could add a loop to run continuously or for a specified number of times. To abort the script, press Ctrl+C if you are using CScript.exe, or end the WScript.exe task in Task Manager.

If you want to wait a specific length of time for an event, you can specify a timeout parameter with the *NextEvent* method in milliseconds.

```
Set NTEvent=oEventSrc.NextEvent(60000)
```

This snippet will wait 60 seconds for the next event before timing out and continuing with the rest of the script. Listing 11-1 demonstrates using blocking as we wait for new entries to be written to the event log.

Listing 11-1 Block for Events

```
Dim oWMI,oEventSrc,NTEvent
On Error Resume Next
strComputer="."
strQuery="Select * from __InstanceCreationEvent WHERE TargetInstance " &_
"ISA 'Win32_NTLogEvent'"
'you need the security privilege to read any security events
Set oWMI=GetObject("winmgmts:{(security)}!\\"&strComputer)
If Err.number<>0 Then
  strErrMsg= strErrMsg & "Error #" & err.number & " [0x" &_
  CStr(Hex(Err.Number)) &"]" & VbCrLf
    If Err.Description <> "" Then
      strErrMsg = strErrMsg & "Error description: " & Err.Description & "."
    End If
  Err.Clear
```

```
 wscript.echo strErrMsg
 wscript.quit
End If

Set oEventSrc=oWMI.ExecNotificationQuery(strQuery)

'start blocking and timeout after one minute
Set NTEvent=oEventSrc.NextEvent(60000)
logtime=NTEvent.TargetInstance.TimeGenerated
logyr = left(logtime,4)
logmo = mid(logtime,5,2)
logdy = mid(logtime,7,2)
logtm = mid(logtime,9,6)

strMsg=NTEvent.TargetInstance.ComputerName & vbcrlf

strMsg=strMsg & "Event ID: " & NTEvent.TargetInstance.EventCode &_
" Source: " & NTEvent.TargetInstance.SourceName & vbTab & logmo & "/" &_
 logdy & "/" & logyr & " [" & FormatDateTime(left(logtm,2) & ":" &_
 Mid(logtm,3,2) & ":"&Right(logtm,2),3) & "]" & VbCrLf &_
 NTEvent.TargetInstance.Message

wscript.echo strMsg
```

> **On the CD**   You will find this script, as well as other scripts listed in this chapter, on the CD that accompanies this book.

This script waits for the next entry to be written in the event log. Because it could be a security event, we need to explicitly add the security privilege.

```
Set oWMI=GetObject("winmgmts:{(security)}!\\"&strComputer)
```

If we want to be more selective about the types of events to monitor, we can modify the query to filter by logfile.

```
strQuery="Select * from __InstanceCreationEvent WHERE TargetInstance " &_
"ISA 'Win32_NTLogEvent' AND TargetInstance.LogFile='Security'"
```

In this script, we are monitoring for any event. We use the *ExecNotificationQuery* method to create an event subscription.

```
Set oEventSrc=oWMI.ExecNotificationQuery(strQuery)
```

We have to make sure the script doesn't end, or we'll never know when an event occurs. We set up blocking by invoking the *NextEvent* method with a timeout value of 60,000 milliseconds or 1 minute.

```
'start blocking and timeout after one minute
Set NTEvent=oEventSrc.NextEvent(60000)
```

When the event occurs, the script continues to execute and an instance of a *Win32_NTEventlog* object is available. We can use any of the properties of the object to create a message for the user. In this script, we report back the computer name, the event ID, the event source, a time stamp, and the event message.

```
strMsg=NTEvent.TargetInstance.ComputerName & vbcrlf
strMsg=strMsg & "Event ID: " & NTEvent.TargetInstance.EventCode &_
" Source: " & NTEvent.TargetInstance.SourceName & vbTab & logmo & "/" &_
 logdy & "/" & logyr &  " [" & FormatDateTime(left(logtm,2) & ":" &_
 Mid(logtm,3,2) & ":"&Right(logtm,2),3) & "]" & VbCrLf &_
 NTEvent.TargetInstance.Message
wscript.echo strMsg
```

Executing a notification query semisynchronously and using the blocking technique is fairly easy, but there are some limitations. Script execution is halted until the next event occurs. If you want to capture more than one event, you must construct a loop. If you want to capture different types of events or if you want the script to be more responsive, you need to execute the notification query asynchronously.

Executing a Notification Query Asynchronously

Scripts and tools that make calls asynchronously are much more responsive. To see for yourself, run through the WBEMTest steps from earlier in the chapter, but select the Asynchronous option. WBEMTest is much more responsive because it isn't waiting, and doing very little else, for the next event.

To execute a notification query asynchronously, a call is made to the *ExecNotificationQueryAsync* method. When a notification query is executed asynchronously, the script does not block (pause) waiting for the next event to occur. Instead, WMI calls your script when the event you subscribed to occurs. But how does your script know how to handle the call? The answer lies with event sinks.

Using Event Sinks

An event sink, or *sink*, for short, is an object that gets called when an asynchronous operation is completed. In WMI, sinks are implemented with the *WbemScripting.SWbemSink* object. Creating and using a sink is not especially difficult. In the following script, we create a sink and give it a name, which traditionally ends with an underscore. You'll see why in a moment.

```
Set SINK = WScript.CreateObject("WbemScripting.SWbemSink","SINK_")
```

We pass the name of the sink as a parameter when executing the notification query by using *ExecNotificationQueryAsync*.

```
strQuery="Select * from __InstanceCreationEvent WHERE " &_
"TargetInstance ISA 'Win32_NTLogEvent'"
Set oWMI=GetObject("winmgmts:{(security)}")
oWMI.ExecNotificationQueryAsync SINK, strQuery
```

This links the results of the query to a sink—any information returned will be sent to the sink. But how does the script know when something comes back? This is accomplished by using standard COM events such as *OnObjectReady*. We create a subroutine that will be called when the specified COM event occurs. In event-based programming, when your code is informed of the completion of some event, this is known as a *callback*.

```
'callback subroutine
'this is code to happen when we get a return from the async call
Sub SINK_OnObjectReady(NTEvent,refContext)

logtime=NTEvent.TargetInstance.TimeGenerated
logyr = Left(logtime,4)
logmo = mid(logtime,5,2)
logdy = mid(logtime,7,2)
logtm = mid(logtime,9,6)

 WScript.Echo "  Event ID: " & NTEvent.TargetInstance.EventCode &_
 "   Source: " & NTEvent.TargetInstance.SourceName & vbTab & logmo & _
 "/" & logdy & "/" & logyr & " [" & FormatDateTime(left(logtm,2) &_
 ":"&Mid(logtm,3,2) & ":"&Right(logtm,2),3) & "]" & vbCrlf &_
 NTEvent.TargetInstance.message

End Sub
```

In this subroutine, when the WMI event fires, it also fires the *OnObjectReady* event. The subroutine includes the names of the sink, *SINK_*, and the COM event, *OnObjectReady*. The COM object returns the WMI object (remember the embedded object from WBEMTest?). The COM object also returns a context reference (which isn't used now but we included it for completeness).

You'll probably use the *OnObjectReady* event most often. You might also use one of the following:

- The *OnCompleted* event is fired when the asynchronous call is finished. This event returns an integer indicating success (0) or failure (an error number), or a reference to the WMI *ERR* object if the call failed.

- The *OnProgress* event is fired when the asynchronous call returns an in-progress status message. Not every object or class will support this event method; you must request it in your asynchronous query by setting the *iFlags* parameter of the asynchronous call to the *wbemFlagSendStatus* value. The required parameters are an integer to describe the total number of tasks to be completed, an integer to describe the current item being processed, a string that describes the status of the current task, and the context reference object.

- The *Cancel* event cancels the sink and any connections to the asynchronous query. It has no parameters.

- The *OnObjectPut* event is fired if the object *puts* or sets a value asynchronously. The required parameters are the WMI object and the context reference object.

Listing 11-2 uses the same event log query we've worked with before, but in an asynchronous manner.

Listing 11-2 Monitor an Event Log Asynchronously

```
Dim oWMI,oEventSrc,NTEvent,objSINK
strComputer="."
strQuery="Select * from __InstanceCreationEvent WHERE TargetInstance " &_
"ISA 'Win32_NTLogEvent'"

'need security privilege
Set oWMI=GetObject("winmgmts:{(security)}\\" & strComputer & "\root\cimv2")
Set objSINK = wscript.CreateObject("WbemScripting.SWbemSink","SINK_")

oWMI.ExecNotificationQueryAsync objSINK, strQuery

'The script has to continue long enough for the async operation to complete.
'One way to accomplish this is to use a msgbox.  If you click ok, the
'script will finish before the async operation completes and it won't
'have anywhere to display its results.
 MsgBox "Waiting for an event to happen.  Do NOT press OK until you " & _
 "get your results or you won't see anything.",vbokonly+vbinformation, _
 "WMI Sink Demo"

'Cancel SINK since we no longer need it around to receive information.
objSINK.Cancel

wscript.quit

'callback subroutine
'this is code to happen when we get a return from the async call
Sub SINK_OnObjectReady(NTEvent,refContext)

logtime=NTEvent.TargetInstance.TimeGenerated
logyr = Left(logtime,4)
logmo = mid(logtime,5,2)
logdy = mid(logtime,7,2)
logtm = mid(logtime,9,6)

 WScript.Echo "  Event ID: " & NTEvent.TargetInstance.EventCode &_
 "   Source: " & NTEvent.TargetInstance.SourceName & vbTab & logmo & _
 "/" & logdy & "/" & logyr & " [" & FormatDateTime(left(logtm,2) &_
 ":"&Mid(logtm,3,2) & ":"&Right(logtm,2),3) & "]" & vbCrlf &_
 NTEvent.TargetInstance.message

End Sub
```

Like semisynchronous queries, if the script ends before the notification is received, you'll never get it. You need something to keep the script alive—even something as simple as a message box will work. This script displays a message box to keep the script running, but there is a drawback. It's hard to resist clicking OK much in the same way we can't ignore a ringing telephone.

An asynchronous query to the local system is helpful if your script has other work to do or if you want to keep your system as responsive as possible. An asynchronous query is also easier to work with when you want to monitor several remote systems. You can connect to each remote system and execute the asynchronous notification query. Each system will respond to the same sink.

There's nothing saying you can't have multiple sinks and multiple queries in the same script. Take a look at the script in Listing 11-3. This script checks CPU utilization every 30 seconds. If the processor load is greater than 70 percent, a message is displayed. The script also checks every 10 seconds to see if the Character Map program has been launched. When the Character Map program is detected, the script terminates.

Listing 11-3 Create a Processor Query

```
'USAGE: cscript|wscript wmiprocessorquery.vbs server

Dim CPUSink,ProcSink,objShell
On error Resume Next

If (wscript.arguments.count=0) Then
 strMsg="Usage: " & VbCrLf
 strMsg=strMsg & "cscript|wscript processorquery.vbs server" & VbCrLf
 strMsg=strMsg & "example: cscript processorquery.vbs File02"
 wscript.echo strMsg
 wscript.quit
Else
 strSrv=wscript.arguments(0)
End If


'check every 30 seconds for processor load > 70%.
strCPUQuery="Select * from __InstanceModificationEvent WITHIN 30 WHERE " &_
"TargetInstance ISA 'Win32_Processor' AND " &_
"TargetInstance.LoadPercentage >70"

'check every 10 seconds for existence of charmap.exe process
strProcQuery="Select * from __InstanceCreationEvent WITHIN 10 WHERE " &_
"TargetInstance ISA 'Win32_Process' AND " &_
"TargetInstance.Name='charmap.exe'"

Set objShell=CreateObject("wscript.Shell")
Set CPUSink=wscript.CreateObject("WBemScripting.SWbemSink","CPUSINK_")
Set ProcSink=wscript.CreateObject("WBemScripting.SWbemSink","PROCSINK_")

Set oWMILocal=GetObject("winmgmts://")
oWMILocal.ExecNotificationQueryAsync ProcSink,strProcQuery
If err.number<>0 Then
 objShell.Popup "Oops! There was an error creating process event sink " &_
 "locally." & vbCrlf & "Error #" &err.number & vbCrlf &_
 "Description (if available): " & vbCrlf & " " & err.description &_
  vbCrlf & "Source (If available): " & VbCrLf & " " &_
   err.source,-1,"CPU Monitoring",vbOKOnly+vbCritical
 WScript.quit
Else
```

```
   Err.Clear
 End If

 Set oWMIRemote=GetObject("winmgmts://" & strSrv)
 If err.number<>0 Then
  objShell.Popup "Oops!  There was an error connecting to " &_
   UCASE(strSrv) & vbCrlf & "Error #" &err.number & VbCrLf &_
   "Description (if available): " & VbCrLf & " " &_
   err.description & VbCrLf & "Source (If available): " & _
   vbCrlf & " " & Err.source,-1,"CPU Monitoring",vbOKOnly+vbCritical
  wscript.quit
 Else
  oWMIRemote.ExecNotificationQueryAsync CPUSink,strCPUQuery
   If err.number<>0 Then
    objShell.Popup "Oops! There was an error creating CPU sink for " &_
     UCASE(strSrv) & vbCrlf & "Error #" &err.number & vbCrlf &_
      "Description (if available): " & vbCrlf & " " &_
      err.description & vbCrlf & "Source (If available): " & _
    vbCrlf & " " & err.source,-1,"CPU Monitoring",vbOKOnly+vbCritical
    wscript.quit
   Else
    err.Clear
   End If
 End If

 objShell.popup "Launch CHARMAP to stop monitoring",3,"CPU Monitoring",0+32

 blnLoop=True
 'Check if trigger process has been run, sleeping every 5 seconds.
 While blnLoop
  wscript.sleep 5
 Wend

 objShell.Popup "Cancelling monitoring.  You can go ahead and close " &_
 "the trigger application.",3,"CPU Monitoring",vbOKOnly+vbInformation
 objShell.AppActivate("Character Map")

 CPUSink.Cancel()
 ProcSink.Cancel()
 wscript.DisconnectObject(CPUSink)
 wscript.DisconnectObject(ProcSink)

 Set oWMILocal=Nothing
 Set oWMIRemote=Nothing
 Set CPUSink=Nothing
 Set ProcSink=Nothing
 wscript.quit

 '****************************************************************
 Sub CPUSINK_OnObjectReady(objEvent,objContext)
 strSystem=objEvent.Path_.Server
 'wscript.echo "fired " & NOW
 objShell.popup "Processor load is " &_
  objEvent.TargetInstance.LoadPercentage & "%" & _
 vbCrlf & NOW,-1,"System - " & strSystem,vbOKOnly+vbInformation
```

```
End Sub

Sub PROCSINK_OnObjectReady(objEvent,objContext)
'trigger has been detected to close out this script
  blnLoop=False
End Sub

'EOF
```

Important   The script in Listing 11-3 requires that queried servers be running at least Microsoft Windows 2000 SP3. Running it on older versions might not work, and it could cause memory leaks.

Listing 11-3 uses two asynchronous queries and event sinks. The first query and sink is for the main part of the script, which monitors CPU utilization.

```
'check every 30 seconds for processor load > 70%.
strCPUQuery="Select * from __InstanceModificationEvent WITHIN 30 WHERE " &_
"TargetInstance ISA 'Win32_Processor' AND " &_
"TargetInstance.LoadPercentage >70"
```

Tip   Depending on your system, to get the CPU utilization event to fire, you might need to decrease the load percentage.

The second query and sink is used to monitor for the existence of a process that can be used to trigger script termination.

```
'check every 10 seconds for existence of charmap.exe process
strProcQuery="Select * from __InstanceCreationEvent WITHIN 10 WHERE " &_
"TargetInstance ISA 'Win32_Process' AND " &_
"TargetInstance.Name='charmap.exe'"
```

Note   Credit for this clever technique goes to Matthew Lavy and Ashley Meggitt who suggest it in their excellent book *Windows Management Instrumentation* (New Riders, 2002).

After the sinks are created and the queries executed, the script executes a loop until the value for *blnLoop* is TRUE.

```
blnLoop=True
'Check if trigger process has been run, sleeping every 5 seconds.
While blnLoop
  wscript.sleep 5
Wend
```

If the charmap.exe process is detected, the event for the process-monitoring sink fires and calls back to the corresponding subroutine.

```
Sub PROCSINK_OnObjectReady(objEvent,objContext)
'trigger has been detected to close out this script
  blnLoop=False
End Sub
```

The value for *blnLoop* is set to FALSE, which will exit the loop and complete the script. We then cancel the sinks and call the *DisconnectObject* method.

> **Best Practices**   It is always a good idea to cancel the sink and call *DisconnectObject*, especially when querying remote systems. VBScript and Windows Script Host do a pretty good job of cleaning up, but it doesn't hurt to clean up after yourself.

You can use any program you want as a trigger—you can even create your own, as Lavy and Meggitt did. We chose Character Map because it is a little-used program that is almost universally available in all versions of Microsoft Windows.

> **Important**   Although asynchronous queries are useful, they are not without risk. The callback mechanism that WMI uses to connect to the sink entails that your script is waiting to hear from somebody. It is theoretically possible for COM communication to be intercepted over the network, and for malicious code to be inserted. We recommend setting the WMI authentication level to *wbemAuthenticationLevelPktPrivacy*.

Using WMI Tools

If you don't want to create a script or don't have time, you can use the WMI Event Registration and WMI Event Viewer utilities that come with WMI Tools.

> **More Info**   You can download WMI Tools at Microsoft's Web site.
> *http://www.microsoft.com/downloads/details.aspx?displaylang=en&FamilyID=6430F853-1120-48DB-8CC5-F2ABDC3ED314*
>
> (This link is on the companion CD; click *WMI Tools*.)

Using WMI Event Registration

You use the WMI Event Registration tool to define the consumer and filter objects. When an event fires, you can use the WMI Event Viewer to view the details of the event. Let's walk through an event registration. In this example, we'll set up an event registration to detect when new files are added to the C:\downloads folder.

To start WMI Event Registration, click the WMI Event Registration shortcut on the Programs menu. This tool must be run in Internet Explorer. If you are running Windows XP with SP2 installed, make sure that you have specified that you allow blocked content. Then you will be prompted to connect to namespace root\CIMV2, as shown in Figure 11-8.

Figure 11-8   Connecting to a namespace in WMI Event Registration

If you want to connect to a remote machine, click the computer button and enter the machine's name, as shown in Figure 11-9. Be sure to change the starting namespace to **root\cimv2**.

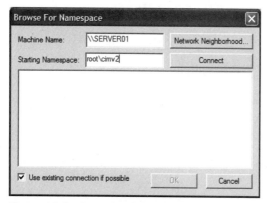

Figure 11-9   Browsing for a namespace on a remote computer

The default setting uses the current credentials, as shown in Figure 11-10.

Figure 11-10   Login credentials when connecting to WMI Event Registration

If you want to specify alternate credentials, clear the Login As Current User check box. If you are connecting to the local system, the check box is grayed out, because you can only specify alternate credentials for remote systems. If you click the Options button, additional authentication and privilege options are displayed, as shown in Figure 11-11 on the next page.

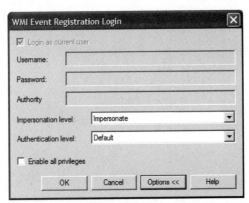

Figure 11-11 Expanded login credentials when connecting to WMI Event Registration

If you are querying remote systems asynchronously, we recommend setting authentication level to Packet Privacy. Depending on the object class you are querying, or if you will be querying security logs, you must enable all privileges. After you specify your connection options, the start page of WMI Event Registration appears, as shown in Figure 11-12.

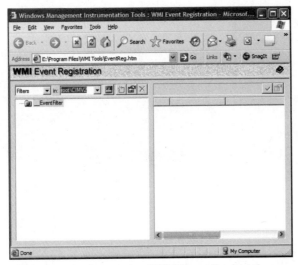

Figure 11-12 Start page of WMI Event Registration

We are ready to create our event filter and consumer. Right-click __EventFilter, and click New Instance. The Edit New Instance Properties dialog box appears, as shown in Figure 11-13.

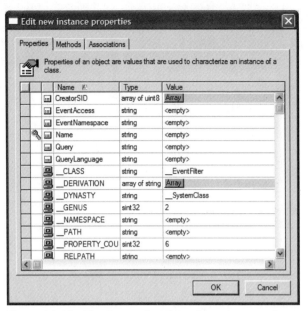

Figure 11-13   The Properties dialog box when creating a new filter

In the dialog box, set the following properties. Remember, the filter is really our notification query. In this query, the C:\downloads folder is monitored every 30 seconds to see if a new file is added.

- Name: NewFileAdded
- Query: Select * from __InstanceCreationEvent WITHIN 30 where TargetInstance ISA 'CIM_DATAFILE' AND TargetInstance.drive='C:' AND TargetInstance.Path='\\downloads\\'
- QueryLanguage: WQL

Click OK to create the *NewFileAdded* filter. You can edit the instance at any time by right-clicking the filter and selecting Edit Instance Properties.

> **Tip**   Look through the WMI Tools' help documentation for more examples of event filters.

Now that we have a filter, we need a consumer. In the drop down box in the upper-left panel, click Consumers. There are two types of consumers that can be created, *CmdTriggerConsumer* and *EventViewerConsumer*, as shown in Figure 11-14 on the next page.

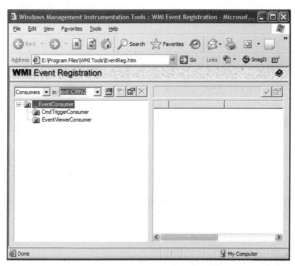

Figure 11-14   Viewing consumers in WMI Event Registration

Right-click EventViewerConsumer, and select New Instance to display the Edit New Instance Properties dialog box shown in Figure 11-15.

Figure 11-15   The Properties dialog box when creating a new event viewer consumer

Set these properties as follows.

- Description: consumer for new file events
- Name: NewFileConsumer
- Severity: 1

Because the local system will be receiving the event notification, the MachineName field is left empty. Click OK to create the *NewFileConsumer* consumer. As shown in Figure 11-16, the *New-FileAdded* filter created earlier is displayed in the right pane. Now we will bind the consumer and filter together. Until we do so, event notification won't happen.

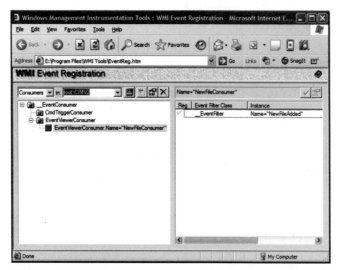

Figure 11-16   Newly created consumer named NewFileConsumer

To register the *NewFileAdded* filter with the *NewFileConsumer* consumer, right-click the New-FileAdded filter and click Register. To register, you can also click the Register (green check mark) button in the menu bar. Figure 11-16 shows the result after the filter has been registered. From this point on, we have a permanent event consumer until we unregister the filter from the consumer. To view the events, we will use the WMI Event Viewer utility.

Using WMI Event Viewer

To start the WMI Event Viewer, locate and click the WMI Event Viewer shortcut on the Programs menu. When you first open the WMI Event Viewer, you see an empty screen, as shown in Figure 11-17 on the next page, unless an event is being registered at the time.

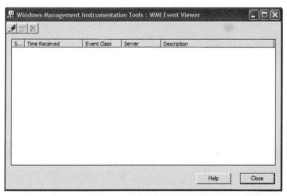

Figure 11-17   An empty WMI Event Viewer

> **Tip**   You can launch the WMI Event Registration tool from the WMI Event Viewer by clicking the pen button.

Create a folder named *downloads* on your C:\ drive. Add a file to this folder. When a new file is detected, the event fires and appears in the WMI Event Viewer, as shown in Figure 11-18.

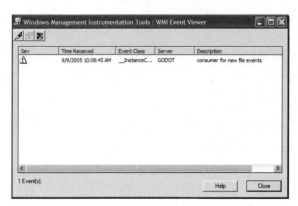

Figure 11-18   WMI Event Viewer displaying information about a detected registered event

The yellow warning icon appears because we set the severity in the consumer to 1. If we had set it to 0, a red critical icon would appear. Setting the severity to 2 means no icon is displayed. To display event properties, double-click the event. As you can see in Figure 11-19, the target instance is an embedded object.

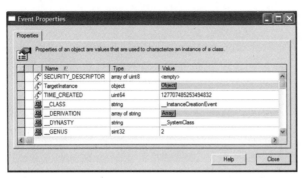

Figure 11-19   Properties for an event in WMI Event Viewer

To display the properties of the target instance, click the Object button. Figure 11-20 shows the *CIM_DataFile* properties for the new file added to the downloads folder.

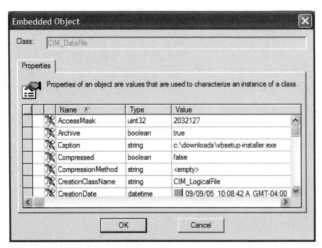

Figure 11-20   Properties for an embedded object in an event in WMI Event Viewer

Using the WMI Event Registration and WMI Event Viewer tools is a great way to monitor events, and a useful prototyping technique for script development. You can see what type of object is returned as well as the property values, making it much easier to create your own scripts.

Tip   You can define as many consumers and filters as you like. They will all be displayed in the WMI Event Viewer, which is why a good consumer description is important.

Viewing WMI Events in Action

Let's finish this chapter by putting everything we've covered so far into a full-fledged script. Listing 11-4 is a WSF script that monitors specific types of events from a specific log file and displays the results in an Internet Explorer window. The script reads a list of computers and creates asynchronous queries to each.

> **Note**   If you need a refresher on WSF scripts, review Chapter 3, "Windows Script Files."

Listing 11-4 EventAlert.wsf

```
<?xml version="1.0" ?>
<package>
<comment>
!!!!Test in a non-production environment!!!!
</comment>
<job id="EventAlert">
  <?job error="false" debug="false" ?>
<runtime>
<description>
EVENTALERT.WSF
Monitor event logs on remote computers. You can specify the event log to
monitor, such as application or system, as well as they type of event such
as error or warning. The polling interval specifies how often to check.

This script uses WMI asynchronous notifications and will display events as
they are detected as popups.
</description>
<named helpstring="List of computers to monitor" name="File"_ required="true"
type="string"/>
<named helpstring="The number of seconds to poll" name="Poll"_
required="true" type="string"/>
<named helpstring="The log file to monitor, ie application, or security" _
name="Log" required="true" type="string"/>
<named helpstring="The event type to monitor such as warning or error"_
name="Type" required="true" type="string"/>
<named helpstring="alternate credential username" name="User"_
required="false" type="string"/>
<named helpstring="alternate credentials password" name="Password"_
required="false" type="string"/>
<example>cscript EventAlert.wsf /File:servers.txt /Poll:20 /Log:Application /Type:Error
cscript EventAlert.wsf /File:servers.txt /Poll:60 /Log:System /Type:Warning /User:Admin /
Password:P@ssw0rd
</example>
</runtime>
<object id="ie" progid="InternetExplorer.Application" events="true" _
reference="true"/>
<object id="objFSO" progid="Scripting.FileSystemObject" reference="TRUE"/>
```

```
<object id="WshShell" progid="WScript.Shell" reference="TRUE"/>
<object id="objLocator" progid="WbemScripting.SWbemLocator" _
reference="TRUE"/>
<object id="objSink" progid="WBemScripting.SWbemSink" events="TRUE" _
reference="TRUE"/>
<object id="objProcSink" progid="WBemScripting.SWbemSink" events="TRUE" _
reference="TRUE"/>
<script id="Main" language="VBScript">
<![CDATA[
On Error Resume Next
If WScript.Arguments.Count<4 Then
  WScript.Arguments.ShowUsage
  WScript.Quit
End If


If WScript.Arguments.Named.Exists("File") Then
  strFile=WScript.Arguments.Named("File")
  If objFSO.FileExists(strFile)<>True Then
    WScript.Echo "Can't find " & strFile
    WScript.Quit
  End If
End If


If WScript.Arguments.Named.Exists("Poll") Then
  iPoll=WScript.Arguments.Named("Poll")
Else
  WScript.Echo "You forgot to specify a polling interval."
  WScript.Arguments.ShowUsage
  WScript.Quit
End If


If WScript.Arguments.Named.Exists("Log") Then
  strLog=WScript.Arguments.Named("Log")
Else
  WScript.Echo "You forgot to specify an event log."
  WScript.Arguments.ShowUsage
  WScript.Quit
End If


If WScript.Arguments.Named.Exists("Type") Then
  strType=WScript.Arguments.Named("Type")
Else
  WScript.Echo "You forgot to specify an event type."
  WScript.Arguments.ShowUsage
  WScript.Quit
End If


If WScript.Arguments.Named.Exists("User") Then
  strUser=WScript.Arguments.Named("User")
End If


If WScript.Arguments.Named.Exists("Password") Then
  strPassword=WScript.Arguments.Named("Password")
End If
```

```
strQuery="Select * from __InstanceCreationEvent WITHIN " & iPoll &_
" where TargetInstance ISA " & "'Win32_NTLogEvent' AND " &_
"TargetInstance.Logfile='" & strLog & "' AND " &_
"TargetInstance.Type='" & strType & "'"

'check every 10 seconds for existence of charmap.exe process
strProcQuery="Select * from __InstanceCreationEvent WITHIN 10 WHERE " &_
"TargetInstance ISA 'Win32_Process' AND " &_
"TargetInstance.Name='charmap.exe'"

'uncomment for debugging
' WScript.Echo strQuery
'wscript.echo "connecting as " & strUser & " " & strPassword

'connect to local system and create
Set objWMILocal=GetObject("winmgmts://")
objWMILocal.ExecNotificationQueryAsync objProcSink,strProcQuery

Dim objFile
Set objFile=objFSO.OpenTextFile(strFile,ForReading)
Do While objFile.AtEndOfStream<>True
 strComputer=Trim(objFile.ReadLine)
 If TestPing(strComputer,True) Then
   'add security privilege if querying security logs
   If UCase(strLog)="SECURITY" Then
    objLocator.Security_.Privileges.AddAsString "SeSecurityPrivilege",True
   End If
   Err.Clear
  set objWMI=objLocator.ConnectServer(strComputer,"root\cimv2",_
  strUser,strPassword)
   If Err.Number<>0 Then
    WScript.Echo "Failed to connect to " & UCase(strComputer) &_
    " [Error #" & Hex(Err.Number) &" " & err.Description & "]"
   End If
  Err.Clear
  objWMI.Security_.authenticationLevel = WbemAuthenticationLevelPktPrivacy
  WScript.Echo "Connecting sink to " & strComputer
  Err.clear
  objWMI.ExecNotificationQueryAsync objSink, strQuery
   If Err.Number<>0 Then
    WScript.Echo "Asynch Query failed To " & UCase(strComputer) &_
    " [Error #" & Hex(Err.Number) & " " & err.Description & "]"
   End If
 Else
  WScript.Echo "Failed to ping " & UCASE(strComputer)
  Err.Clear
 End If
Loop
objFile.close

strTitle="Monitoring"
ie.width=630
ie.height=530
ie.top=10
ie.left=10
```

```
ie.menubar=False
ie.statusbar=False
ie.resizable=True
ie.toolbar=False
ie.navigate ("About:blank")
ie.document.title=strTitle

do while ie.ReadyState<>4
Loop
ie.visible=True

ie.document.body.InnerHTML="<font face=Tahoma Size=1 Color=Blue>" &_
 strQuery & "</font><br><HR>"

 blnFlag=True

wscript.echo "Monitoring...launch CHARMAP.EXE to end."
blnLoop=True
'Check if trigger process has been run, sleeping every 5 seconds.
while blnLoop
  wscript.sleep 5
Wend

WScript.Echo "Cancelling and disconnecting sink"
objSink.Cancel
objProcSink.Cancel
wscript.DisconnectObject(objSINK)
wscript.DisconnectObject(objPROCSINK)
ie.Quit
WScript.Quit


' -----------------------------------------------------------------
'callback subroutines
'this is code to happen when we get a return from the async call
' -----------------------------------------------------------------
Sub objSINK_OnObjectReady(NTEvent,refContext)
On Error Resume Next

'define background color variables to alternate
if blnFLAG then
  strColor="#FFFFFF"
  blnFlag=False
Else
  strColor="#CCFF66"
  blnFlag=True
End If

logtime=NTEvent.TargetInstance.TimeGenerated
logyr = Left(logtime,4)
logmo = Mid(logtime,5,2)
logdy = Mid(logtime,7,2)
logtm = Mid(logtime,9,6)

strMsg=NTEvent.TargetInstance.ComputerName & "  Event ID: " &_
  NTEvent.TargetInstance.EventCode &_
```

```
"   Source: " & NTEvent.TargetInstance.SourceName & vbTab & logmo & _
"/" & logdy & "/" & logyr & " [" & FormatDateTime(left(logtm,2) &_
":"&Mid(logtm,3,2) & ":"&Right(logtm,2),3) & "]" & vbCrlf &_
NTEvent.TargetInstance.message
'you can use a popup if you'd like
' WshShell.Popup strMsg,45,NTEvent.TargetInstance.ComputerName &_
' " Event Log Alert",vbOKOnly

ie.document.body.InsertAdjacentHTML "beforeEnd","<Table border=0 " &_
"Cellpadding=0 cellspacing=2><TR><TD BGColor=" & strColor &_
"><font face=tahoma size=1>" & strMsg & "</TD><TR>"
End Sub

Sub OBJPROCSINK_OnObjectReady(objEvent,objContext)
'trigger has been detected to close out this script
  blnLoop=False
End Sub


' --------------------------------------------------------------------
' Function TestPing
'
' Tests connectivity to a given name or address; returns true or False
' --------------------------------------------------------------------
Function TestPing(sName,bPingAvailable)
On Error Resume Next
If Not bPingAvailable Then
  TestPing=False
  Exit Function
End If
Dim cPingResults, oPingResult
Set cPingResults = GetObject("winmgmts://./root/cimv2")._
ExecQuery("SELECT * FROM Win32_PingStatus WHERE Address = '" & sName & "'")
For Each oPingResult In cPingResults
  If oPingResult.StatusCode = 0 Then
    TestPing = True
    'wscript.echo "  Success"
  Else
    TestPing = False
    'WScript.Echo "  *** FAILED"
  End If
Next
End Function
]]>
</script>
</job>
</package>
```

The script takes several parameters, as defined in the run time section.

```
<named helpstring="List of computers to monitor" name="File"_ required="true" type="string"/>
<named helpstring="The number of seconds to poll" name="Poll"_
required="true" type="string"/>
<named helpstring="The log file to monitor, ie application, or security" _
name="Log" required="true" type="string"/>
<named helpstring="The event type to monitor such as warning or error"_
```

```
name="Type" required="true" type="string"/>
<named helpstring="alternate credential username" name="User"_
required="false" type="string"/>
<named helpstring="alternate credentials password" name="Password"_
required="false" type="string"/>
```

The *username* and *password* parameters are optional. To run the script using current credentials, you would type a command such as this.

```
cscript Listing11-4.wsf /File:servers.txt /Poll:20 /Log:System /Type:Error.
```

The script will connect to every server listed in servers.txt, establish an asynchronous query,
and check every 20 seconds for any new entries in the system log that are errors. The script
will continue to run until the charmap.exe process is detected. We first define the objects we
need for the script.

```
<object id="ie" progid="InternetExplorer.Application" events="true" _
reference="true"/>
<object id="objFSO" progid="Scripting.FileSystemObject" reference="TRUE"/>
<object id="WshShell" progid="WScript.Shell" reference="TRUE"/>
<object id="objLocator" progid="WbemScripting.SWbemLocator" _
reference="TRUE"/>
<object id="objSink" progid="WBemScripting.SWbemSink" events="TRUE" _
reference="TRUE"/>
<object id="objProcSink" progid="WBemScripting.SWbemSink" events="TRUE" _
reference="TRUE"/>\
```

We are using the *WbemScripting.SWbemLocator* object so that we can specify alternate credentials. Notice that we can define the sink objects here by instantiating the *WbemScript-
ing.SWbemSink* object. You do not need to add an underscore character as part of the object
ID, but the *OnObjectReady* subroutine should include it.

```
Sub OBJPROCSINK_OnObjectReady(objEvent,objContext)
'trigger has been detected to close out this script
  blnLoop=False
End Sub
```

After we validate the parameters and define the variables, we define our queries. The first
query is the main one that is monitoring for new events.

```
strQuery="Select * from __InstanceCreationEvent WITHIN " & iPoll &_
" where TargetInstance ISA " & "'Win32_NTLogEvent' AND " &_
"TargetInstance.Logfile='" & strLog & "' AND " &_
"TargetInstance.Type='" & strType & "'"
```

The second query monitors the creation of the trigger process, charmap.exe, which will terminate the script.

```
'check every 10 seconds for existence of charmap.exe process
strProcQuery="Select * from __InstanceCreationEvent WITHIN 10 WHERE " &_
"TargetInstance ISA 'Win32_Process' AND " &_
"TargetInstance.Name='charmap.exe'"
```

For this query to work, we connect to the local machine and establish the asynchronous query.

```
'check every 10 seconds for existence of charmap.exe process
strProcQuery="Select * from __InstanceCreationEvent WITHIN 10 WHERE " &_
"TargetInstance ISA 'Win32_Process' AND " &_
"TargetInstance.Name='charmap.exe'"
```

You should already know how to open a text file and read lines, so we won't review that code. Each computer name is read and passed to a ping function to verify network connectivity. If the computer is "pingable," we can create the sink.

If the user specified the security log, we need to add the security privilege to the locator object.

```
If UCase(strLog)="SECURITY" Then
  objLocator.Security_.Privileges.AddAsString "SeSecurityPrivilege",True
End If
```

The script connects to the remote server, sets the WMI authentication level to Packet Privacy, and executes the asynchronous notification query. We've emphasized these lines for clarity.

```
set objWMI=objLocator.ConnectServer(strComputer,"root\cimv2",_
strUser,strPassword)
If Err.Number<>0 Then
    WScript.Echo "Failed to connect to " & UCase(strComputer) &_
    " [Error #" & Hex(Err.Number) &" " & err.Description & "]"
    End If
  Err.Clear
objWMI.Security_.authenticationLevel = WbemAuthenticationLevelPktPrivacy
WScript.Echo "Connecting sink to " & strComputer
Err.clear
objWMI.ExecNotificationQueryAsync objSink, strQuery
  If Err.Number<>0 Then
    WScript.Echo "Asynch Query failed To " & UCase(strComputer) &_
    " [Error #" & Hex(Err.Number) & " " & err.Description & "]"
  End If
```

> **Best Practices**   We included error handling at critical points in the script. It is very important to provide feedback to the user when problems occur.

Even though we are running the script from a command line, it would be nice to have a graphical event viewer. We can use Internet Explorer by creating a new instance, navigating to a blank page, and then inserting HTML text.

```
strTitle="Monitoring"
ie.width=630
ie.height=530
ie.top=10
ie.left=10
ie.menubar=False
```

```
ie.statusbar=False
ie.resizable=True
ie.toolbar=False
ie.navigate ("About:blank")
ie.document.title=strTitle

do while ie.ReadyState<>4
Loop
ie.visible=True

ie.document.body.InnerHTML="<font face=Tahoma Size=1 Color=Blue>" &_
 strQuery & "</font><br><HR>"
```

The script now runs while checking every ten seconds if charmap.exe is running. If it is, then code in the corresponding sink (explained in a moment) will execute. In order to keep the script alive we have a simple loop.

```
wscript.echo "Monitoring...launch CHARMAP.EXE to end."
blnLoop=True
'Check if trigger process has been run, sleeping every 5 seconds.
While blnLoop
  wscript.sleep 5
Wend
```

When an event fires, the *objSink_OnObjectReady* subroutine is called. The code in this subroutine takes the properties of the returned object and creates a message string. This string is then included in HTML code and inserted into the Internet Explorer window.

```
' ------------------------------------------------------------
'callback subroutines
'this is code to happen when we get a return from the async call
' ------------------------------------------------------------
Sub objSINK_OnObjectReady(NTEvent,refContext)
On Error Resume Next

'define background color variables to alternate
if blnFLAG then
  strColor="#FFFFFF"
  blnFlag=False
Else
  strColor="#CCFF66"
  blnFlag=True
End If

logtime=NTEvent.TargetInstance.TimeGenerated
logyr = Left(logtime,4)
logmo = Mid(logtime,5,2)
logdy = Mid(logtime,7,2)
logtm = Mid(logtime,9,6)

strMsg=NTEvent.TargetInstance.ComputerName & "  Event ID: " &_
  NTEvent.TargetInstance.EventCode &_
  "   Source: " & NTEvent.TargetInstance.SourceName & vbTab & logmo & _
  "/" & logdy & "/" & logyr & " [" & FormatDateTime(left(logtm,2) &_
```

```
    ":"&Mid(logtm,3,2) & ":"&Right(logtm,2),3) & "]" & vbCrlf &_
    NTEvent.TargetInstance.message
'you can use a popup if you'd like
' WshShell.Popup strMsg,45,NTEvent.TargetInstance.ComputerName &_
' " Event Log Alert",vbOKOnly

ie.document.body.InsertAdjacentHTML "beforeEnd","<Table border=0 " &_
"Cellpadding=0 cellspacing=2><TR><TD BGColor=" & strColor &_
 "><font face=tahoma size=1>" & strMsg & "</TD><TR>"
End Sub
```

Each entry is written as an HTML table with one column and one row. We added some code so that tables will alternate in color, making it easier to read. Figure 11-21 illustrates the result of this script.

Figure 11-21   Sample HTML output for the script in Listing 11-4

To terminate the script, we launch Character Map. The process will be detected and code in the corresponding sink will be executed.

```
Sub OBJPROCSINK_OnObjectReady(objEvent,objContext)
'trigger has been detected to close out this script
  blnLoop=False
End Sub
```

In this case, the *blnLoop* variable is set to FALSE, which will halt the *While* loop. We then cancel and disconnect the sinks and close Internet Explorer.

```
While blnLoop
  wscript.sleep 5
Wend

WScript.Echo "Cancelling and disconnecting sink"
objSink.Cancel
```

```
objProcSink.Cancel
wscript.DisconnectObject(objSINK)
wscript.DisconnectObject(objPROCSINK)

ie.Quit
WScript.Quit
```

The EventAlert.wsf script combines just about everything we've covered in this chapter. We have multiple asynchronous queries and sinks, a trigger application to end the script, and a graphical event viewer.

> **Note**   We're often asked about running scripts as a service, as you might be tempted to do. We don't recommend it. First of all, the script could not include any user interaction or feedback such as message boxes or even *wscript.echo* commands because there's no user to interact with. Second, if there are problems during run time, a script has very limited recovery capabilities. However, almost everything we've covered about WMI events can be used for developing a compiled application in a higher-level programming language like Microsoft Visual Basic .NET, where it is much easier to create an application that can run as a service.
>
> You might want to use the WMI scripts we've been discussing as monitoring and management tools to run interactively on your desktop. Depending on your needs, you might find it beneficial to have a dedicated XP desktop devoted to monitoring and management logged on with administrative credentials. Just be sure it is physically secure.

Summary

WMI events can produce powerful results. We showed you how to filter or query for different types of WMI events. We also showed you how to set up event notification by using VBScript, WMI Tools, and WBEMTest. Spend a little time with these tools, work with the sample scripts on the CD, and see for yourself what information can be used on your servers and desktops.

> **More Info**   For additional information on WMI events, we recommend *Windows Management Instrumentation* by Matthew Lavy and Ashley Meggitt (New Riders 2002). For information about WMI events online, visit the following Web site.
>
> *http://msdn.microsoft.com/library/default.asp?url=/library/en-us/wmisdk/wmi/ receiving_a_wmi_event.asp*
>
> (This link is on the companion CD; click *Receiving WMI Events*.)

Chapter 12
Better Scripting with WMI Tools

There are many freely available tools, such as WBEMTest and Scriptomatic, that can greatly reduce the amount of time it takes to develop administrative scripts. We'll discuss how to use a variety of Windows Management Instrumentation (WMI)-related tools to increase your scripting efficiency.

Most administrators are always pressed for time and have a dozen things to accomplish before lunch. Taking time to develop scripts is often a low priority, even when the need for administrative scripts is high. Fortunately, with a few good tools, the time it takes to develop a script, even a complicated WMI script, can be dramatically reduced. You might even find that these applications can be valuable diagnostic and troubleshooting tools.

Using Tools as a Scripting Shortcut

The tools and utilities we cover in this chapter can reduce the amount of time it takes to create administrative scripts in the following ways:

- You can generate VBScript code that can be used as is, or as a foundation for your scripts.

- You can learn about WMI classes, objects, and properties to quickly identify the information you need for your scripts.

- You can test and debug WMI queries. After you know a query works, it is a simple matter to plug it into your scripts.

- You can test alternate credentials and privileges. If you suspect a permission or privilege problem in your script, you can use some of these tools to validate your script's security context.

Using Scriptomatic

One of the most popular scripting tools is Scriptomatic, available free from the Microsoft Scripting Guys. With this tool, you can do the following:

- Browse WMI namespaces
- Browse WMI classes
- Connect to remote systems
- Generate script code in VBScript and other scripting languages
- Choose the format of your script output
- Save generated scripts

Even if your scripting ability is limited and you understand only the basics of WMI, you can create fully functioning administrative scripts in seconds with Scriptomatic. If you are an experienced script developer, Scriptomatic-generated code can serve as a foundation for your own script development. Copying and pasting code saves time and reduces typos.

> **Note**   If you don't have the Scriptomatic tool, download it from the Microsoft Web site at
>
> *http://www.microsoft.com/downloads/details.aspx?FamilyID=09dfc342-648b-4119-b7eb-783b0f7d1178&DisplayLang=en*
>
> (This link is on the companion CD; click *Scriptomatic v2.0*.)

Listing Classes and Namespaces

The primary function of Scriptomatic is to enumerate WMI namespaces and classes. After you've found the WMI class you want, Scriptomatic will generate a script based on that class. When you start Scriptomatic, it connects to the default WMI namespace, *root\cimv2*, as shown in Figure 12-1.

As you can see in Figure 12-2, when you click the WMI Class down arrow, all the available object classes within this namespace are displayed.

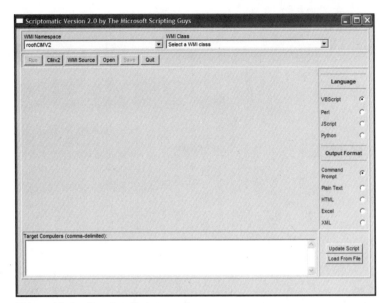

Figure 12-1   Starting Scriptomatic

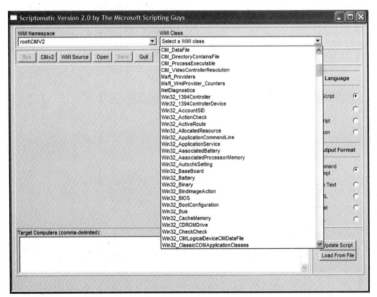

Figure 12-2   Displaying the WMI classes

You can also connect to other WMI namespaces by clicking the WMI Namespace down arrow, as shown in Figure 12-3 on the next page. Depending on the system, you might see other namespaces listed. For example, Microsoft Exchange 2003 will have the *root\MicrosoftExchangeV2* namespace.

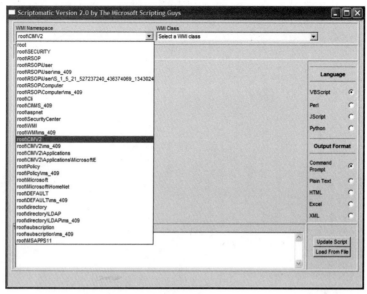

Figure 12-3   Listing WMI Namespaces

For most administrators, the Win32 objects in *root\cimv2* are of most interest. In Figure 12-4, the *Win32_OperatingSystem* class has been selected in the WMI Class drop-down list, and a script automatically generated. Scriptomatic will generate code in several programming languages. We used the VBScript default.

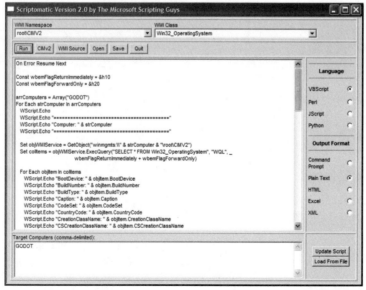

Figure 12-4   Displaying Win32_OperatingSystem script

Scriptomatic also includes options for handling the output of the script, which essentially enumerates all the properties and values for all the instances of a particular class of object. Selecting the Plain Text option will send the script output to a text file that automatically opens in Notepad, as shown in Figure 12-5.

Figure 12-5   Displaying Win32_OperatingSystem script in Notepad

Output in HTML is shown in Figure 12-6.

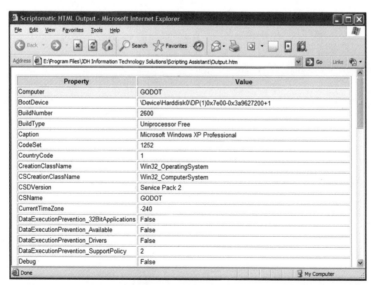

Figure 12-6   Displaying Win32_OperatingSystem script in HTML

> **Note**   The WMI Source button is used to connect to a remote system. After you are connected to the remote system, you can enumerate all the WMI namespaces and objects on the remote computer. This is very useful for exploring WMI classes that are not installed locally. For example, Exchange 2003 has many WMI classes. By connecting to an Exchange 2003 server, you can explore these classes without having to install Exchange 2003 locally. However, in Scriptomatic v2.0, there is a bug in this feature. When you connect to the remote system, the computer name changes in the generated script, but the tool is still querying the local WMI database. The Microsoft Scripting Guys are aware of this bug and will correct it in the next release of the tool.

Generating Scripts

Of course, you can still edit the script directly within the utility. Scriptomatic's scripts are really enumeration scripts. That is, they report on defined properties for a specified WMI class. This type of reporting probably constitutes the bulk of most administrative scripting libraries. Scriptomatic can make this easy by running a script against a list of computers.

The generated script is basically a wrapper that defaults to the local computer. At the bottom of the tool's interface, there is a Target Computers pane. You can manually enter a list of computer names and click the Update Script button to add the names to the array defined by *arrComputers*. Alternatively, if you click the Load from File button, you can specify a text file with all the computer names you want to use. The list of target computers can be separated by commas or returned as a simple list, as shown in Figure 12-7.

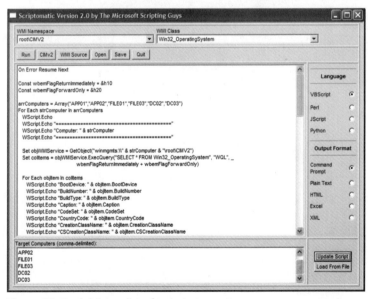

Figure 12-7   Adding a list of target computers

Saving Scripts

After you have the script the way you like it, click the Save button. You will be prompted for the script name and location. One thing Scriptomatic won't do is add the formatting code it uses to generate the HTML page or text file when the script is run from Scriptomatic itself. The saved script is exactly what you see in the window. If you want to save the output to an HTML page, a Microsoft Excel workbook, or an XML file, you have to add that code yourself.

Scriptomatic can create a fully functional WMI script that queries multiple remote systems in literally a minute. In fact, you might find it easier to use Scriptomatic to run the script and handle the special formatting like HTML. You could take a generated script, add a list of computers, and strip out all the WMI attributes you don't want, or add a WMI query to limit the amount of data returned. You could then save the script as we just showed you. When you are ready to run it, start Scriptomatic and click Open. Then find your script, and click OK. Use Scriptomatic to execute the script and generate the desired output.

Using WMIC

If you prefer to access WMI from a command prompt, WMI Command Line (WMIC) is the tool for you. WMIC isn't a scripting tool like Scriptomatic. In fact, Microsoft intended WMIC to be a tool for administrators who want to leverage the power of WMI without having to write complex VBScript code. However, because this is a command-line tool, you can still script it with an old-fashioned batch file. We provide an example later in this chapter.

Note   WMIC is available only on Microsoft Windows XP and Microsoft Windows Server 2003. You can, however, use it to remotely connect to Microsoft Windows 2000 or even Microsoft Windows NT 4.0 servers, if the WMI core files are installed on the target computer.

You can use WMIC to perform the following tasks:

- Manage the local system.
- Manage a remote system.
- Manage multiple remote systems.
- Use alternate credentials.
- Format output.

Like *NSLookup*, you can use WMIC in interactive mode or as a single command. However, before you can use WMIC, it must be installed. To do so, at a command prompt, type **WMIC**, and press Enter. WMIC will be installed and configured in less than a minute, after which the WMIC command prompt, *wmic:root\cli>*, will appear. To get WMI help from the command prompt window, type /?.

Connecting to Namespaces

Namespace paths are relative to the current namespace. When you launch WMIC, it connects to the default WMI namespace, typically *root\cimv2*. However, you can connect to a different namespace by typing /**namespace:**<namespace>. Unless you extend WMIC (a topic beyond the scope of this book), you probably won't need to change namespaces. We expect the default configuration to satisfy 99 percent of your scripting needs. Plus, if you have the technical expertise to extend WMIC, you probably have the expertise to develop a script by using VBScript.

Using Aliases

WMIC can be confusing at first because it doesn't use the standard *Win32* class names. Instead, WMIC uses *aliases* that define WMI classes by function rather than by class name. Remember, WMIC was designed for administrators who might not know the WMI class name for an operating system (*Win32_OperatingSystem*), but who recognize something like *OS*. Typing *WMIC /?* in a command prompt lists the available aliases.

- *ALIAS*   Access to the aliases available on the local system
- *BASEBOARD*   Base board (also known as a motherboard or system board) management
- *BIOS*   Basic input/output services (BIOS) management
- *BOOTCONFIG*   Boot configuration management
- *CDROM*   CD-ROM management
- *COMPUTERSYSTEM*   Computer system management
- *CPU*   CPU management
- *CSPRODUCT*   Computer system product information from SMBIOS
- *DATAFILE*   Data file management
- *DCOMAPP*   DCOM Application management
- *DESKTOP*   User's desktop management
- *DESKTOPMONITOR*   Desktop monitor management
- *DEVICEMEMORYADDRESS*   Device memory addresses management
- *DISKDRIVE*   Physical disk drive management
- *DISKQUOTA*   Disk space usage for NTFS volumes
- *DMACHANNEL*   Direct memory access (DMA) channel management
- *ENVIRONMENT*   System environment settings management
- *FSDIR*   File system directory entry management
- *GROUP*   Group account management

- *IDECONTROLLER*   IDE Controller management
- *IRQ*   Interrupt request line (IRQ) management
- *JOB*   Access to the jobs scheduled by using the schedule service
- *LOADORDER*   Management of system services that define execution dependencies
- *LOGICALDISK*   Local storage device management
- *LOGON*   LOGON sessions
- *MEMCACHE*   Cache memory management
- *MEMLOGICAL*   System memory management (configuration layout and availability of memory)
- *MEMPHYSICAL*   Computer system's physical memory management
- *NETCLIENT*   Network client management
- *NETLOGIN*   Network login information (of a particular user) management
- *NETPROTOCOL*   Protocols (and their network characteristics) management
- *NETUSE*   Active network connection management
- *NIC*   Network Interface Controller (NIC) management
- *NICCONFIG*   Network adapter management
- *NTDOMAIN*   NT domain management
- *NTEVENT*   Entries in the NT event log
- *NTEVENTLOG*   NT event log file management
- *ONBOARDDEVICE*   Management of common adapter devices built into the motherboard (system board)
- *OS*   Installed operating system management
- *PAGEFILE*   Virtual memory file swapping management
- *PAGEFILESET*   Page file settings management
- *PARTITION*   Management of partitioned areas of a physical disk
- *PORT*   I/O port management
- *PORTCONNECTOR*   Physical connection ports management
- *PRINTER*   Printer device management
- *PRINTERCONFIG*   Printer device configuration management
- *PRINTJOB*   Print job management
- *PROCESS*   Process management
- *PRODUCT*   Installation package task management

- *QFE*   Quick fix engineering
- *QUOTASETTING*   Setting information for disk quotas on a volume
- *RECOVEROS*   Information gathered from memory when the operating system fails
- *REGISTRY*   Computer system registry management
- *SCSICONTROLLER*   SCSI controller management
- *SERVER*   Server information management
- *SERVICE*   Service application management
- *SHARE*   Shared resource management
- *SOFTWAREELEMENT*   Management of the elements of a software product installed on a system
- *SOFTWAREFEATURE*   Management of software product subsets of *SOFTWAREELEMENT*
- *SOUNDDEV*   Sound device management
- *STARTUP*   Management of commands that run automatically when users log onto the computer system
- *SYSACCOUNT*   System account management
- *SYSDRIVER*   Management of the system driver for a base service
- *SYSTEMENCLOSURE*   Physical system enclosure management
- *SYSTEMSLOT*   Management of physical connection points including ports, slots and peripherals, and proprietary connection points
- *TAPEDRIVE*   Tape drive management
- *TEMPERATURE*   Data management of a temperature sensor (electronic thermometer)
- *TIMEZONE*   Time zone data management
- *UPS*   Uninterruptible power supply (UPS) management
- *USERACCOUNT*   User account management
- *VOLTAGE*   Voltage sensor (electronic voltmeter) data management
- *VOLUMEQUOTASETTING*   Associates the disk quota setting with a specific disk volume
- *WMISET*   WMI service operational parameters management

Ironically, experienced WMI users are more likely to be confused by the aliases because it's not always clear to which *Win32* class the alias is referring. Table 12-1 lists each alias and the corresponding *Win32* object class target.

Table 12-1   Aliases and Target Classes

Alias	Where	Target Class
Alias	WHERE FriendlyName = '#'	Select * from Msft_CliAlias
BaseBoard		Select * from Win32_BaseBoard
BIOS		Select * from Win32_BIOS
BootConfig		Select * from Win32_BootConfiguration
CDROM	WHERE Drive='#'	Select * from Win32_CDRomDrive
ComputerSystem		Select * from Win32_ComputerSystem
CPU	WHERE DeviceID='#'	Select * from WIN32_Processor
CSProduct		Select * from Win32_ComputerSystemProduct
DataFile	WHERE Name = '#'	Select * from CIM_DataFile
DCOMAPP	WHERE Name='#'	Select * from WIN32_DCOMApplication
Desktop	WHERE Name='#'	Select * from WIN32_Desktop
DesktopMonitor	WHERE DEVICEID='#'	Select * from WIN32_Desktopmonitor
DeviceMemoryAddress	ss	Select * from Win32_DeviceMemoryAddress
DiskDrive	WHERE Index=#	Select * from Win32_DiskDrive
DiskQuota		Select * from Win32_DiskQuota
DMAChannel	WHERE DMAChannel=#	Select * from Win32_DMAChannel
Environment		Select * from Win32_Environment
FSDir	WHERE Name='#'	Select * from Win32_Directory
Group		Select * from Win32_Group
IDEController		Select * from Win32_IDEController
IRQ	WHERE IRQNumber=#	Select * from Win32_IRQResource
Job	WHERE jobid=#	Select * from Win32_ScheduledJob
LoadOrder		Select * from Win32_LoadOrderGroup
LogicalDisk	WHERE Name='#'	Select * from Win32_LogicalDisk
LOGON		Select * from Win32_LogonSession
Memcache	WHERE DeviceID='#'	Select * from WIN32_Cachememory

Table 12-1 Aliases and Target Classes

Alias	Where	Target Class
MemLogical		Select * from Win32_LogicalMemoryConfiguration
MemPhysical		Select * from Win32_PhysicalMemoryArray
NetClient	WHERE Name='#'	Select * from WIN32_NetworkClient
NetLogin	WHERE Name='#'	Select * from Win32_NetworkLoginProfile
NetProtocol		Select * from Win32_NetworkProtocol
NetUse	WHERE LocalName='#'	Select * from Win32_NetworkConnection
NIC	WHERE DeviceID=#	Select * from Win32_NetworkAdapter
NICConfig	WHERE Index=#	Select * from Win32_NetworkAdapterConfiguration
NTDomain	WHERE DomainName='#'	Select * from Win32_NTDomain
NTEvent		Select * from Win32_NTLogEvent
NTEventLog	WHERE LogfileName='#'	Select * from Win32_NTEventlogFile
OnBoardDevice		Select * from Win32_OnBoardDevice
OS		Select * from Win32_OperatingSystem
PageFile		Select * from Win32_PageFileUsage
PageFileSet		Select * from Win32_PageFileSetting
Partition	WHERE Index=#	Select * from Win32_DiskPartition
Port		Select * from Win32_PortResource
PortConnector	WHERE ExternalReferenceDesignator='#'	Select * from Win32_PortConnector
Printer	WHERE Name='#'	Select * from Win32_Printer
PrinterConfig	WHERE Name='#'	Select * from Win32_PrinterConfiguration
PrintJob	WHERE JobId=#	Select * from Win32_PrintJob
Process	WHERE ProcessId='#'	Select * from Win32_Process
Product	WHERE Name='#'	Select * from Win32_Product
QFE		Select * from Win32_QuickFixEngineering
QuotaSetting		Select * from Win32_QuotaSetting

Table 12-1   Aliases and Target Classes

Alias	Where	Target Class
RecoverOS		Select * from Win32_OSRecoveryConfiguration
Registry		Select * from Win32_Registry
SCSIController		Select * from Win32_SCSIController
Server		Select * from Win32_PerfRawData_PerfNet_Server
Service	WHERE Name='#'	Select * from Win32_Service
Share	WHERE Name='#'	Select * from Win32_Share
SoftwareElement		Select * from Win32_SoftwareElement
SoftwareFeature		Select * from Win32_SoftwareFeature
SoundDev	WHERE Name='#'	Select * from WIN32_SoundDevice
Startup	WHERE Caption='#'	Select * from Win32_StartupCommand
SysAccount	WHERE Name='#'	Select * from Win32_SystemAccount
SysDriver	WHERE Name='#'	Select * from Win32_SystemDriver
SystemEnclosure		Select * from Win32_SystemEnclosure
SystemSlot		Select * from Win32_SystemSlot
TapeDrive		Select * from Win32_TapeDrive
Temperature		Select * from Win32_TemperatureProbe
TimeZone		Select * from Win32_TimeZone
UPS		Select * from Win32_UninterruptiblePowerSupply
UserAccount		Select * from Win32_UserAccount
Voltage		Select * from Win32_VoltageProbe
VolumeQuotaSetting	WHERE Element = # and Setting = #	Select * from Win32_VolumeQuotaSetting
WMISet		Select * from Win32_WMISetting

To get more information about a particular alias, open a command prompt window, and type
wmic \<alias> **/?**. For example, typing *wmic share /?* displays the information shown on the
next page.

```
SHARE - Shared resource management.

HINT: BNF for Alias usage.
(<alias> [WMIObject] | <alias> [<path where>] | [<alias>]
<path where>) [<verb clause>].

USAGE:

SHARE ASSOC [<format specifier>]
SHARE CALL <method name> [<actual param list>]
SHARE CREATE <assign list>
SHARE DELETE
SHARE GET [<property list>] [<get switches>]
SHARE LIST [<list format>] [<list switches>]
```

Most WMIC commands follow the pattern WMIC *<connection options> <alias> <alias options>*
<wmic verb> <wmic verb options>. We cover the WMIC syntax in more detail later in this
chapter.

Connecting to Remote Systems

You connect to remote systems with WMIC by using the */node* switch. If you don't specify a
node, WMIC defaults to the local system. You specify a single computer like this.

```
wmic /node:Server03
```

Specify a comma-separated list of computers like this.

```
wmic /node:Server03,App01,File02,Print01
```

In a text file with computer names, the names can be either comma-separated values, or in a
columnar list.

```
wmic /node:@servers.txt
```

WMIC will process your query against each system in the list.

Passing Credentials

If you want to use alternate credentials when connecting to a remote system, you can use the
/user and */ password* switches. The username value should be in the form of *domain\user*. The
value you type as a password will be displayed. There is no option for a password prompt.
Combining this feature with the previous example would produce this code snippet.

```
wmic /node:@servers.txt /user:"company\j-admin" /password:P@ssw0rd
```

Notice that we put the user name in quotation marks. If the value for any switch includes a
special character like a dash or a slash, it must be enclosed in quotation marks. If in doubt,
include quotation marks.

Making Queries with *list* and *get*

Of course, the whole purpose of WMIC is to learn about a system. This is accomplished by using the verbs *list* or *get*. Both verbs return values for the specified alias, but the information they return and how it is returned often differs, depending on how the aliases are defined. For example, here is the output from the *wmic pagefile list* command.

```
AllocatedBaseSize  CurrentUsage  Description       InstallDate
Name              PeakUsage  Status  TempPageFile
1535              223         C:\pagefile.sys 20050906105923.788062-240 C:\pagefile.sys  261
```

The output will have wrapped lines. Here is the output from the *wmic pagefile get* command.

```
AllocatedBaseSize  Caption            CurrentUsage  Description
InstallDate            Name           PeakUsage  Status
TempPageFile  1535               C:\pagefile.sys 223
C:\pagefile.sys  20050906105923.788062-240  C:\pagefile.sys  261
```

WMIC is looking at the same object in both commands but presenting slightly different information. You use *get* to specify the properties for which you want to display values. Running the command *wmic os get caption, csdversion* will return the following result.

```
Caption                          CSDVersion
Microsoft Windows XP Professional  Service Pack 2
```

If you want to know what properties will be returned by the *get* command for a given alias, type **wmic <alias> get /?**. The default is to return all property values.

You can find the same information for the *list* command by typing **wmic <alias> list /?**. The results will vary, depending on the alias you specify. For example, the help output for *wmic os list /?* includes the formatting options of *Brief*, *Full*, *Free*, and several others. Entering *wmic cpu list /?* shows formatting options of *Brief*, *Config*, *Full*, and a few others. The primary difference between *get* and *list* is that the *get* verb returns every property for the alias, and the *list* verb uses a predefined list of properties defined by a name, such as *Brief*, *Full*, *Config*, *Free*, or whatever is appropriate to the alias.

You can also use a WMI *WHERE* query as part of your WMIC command. Simply put the conditional clause in parentheses.

```
wmic process where (name="spoolsv.exe") list brief
```

This command will produce the following output.

```
HandleCount  Name        Priority  ProcessId  ThreadCount  WorkingSetSize
180          spoolsv.exe  8         1344       13           6262784
```

Both *get* and *list* also have a */every* switch that will run the query at scheduled intervals. The interval you specify is in seconds.

```
wmic process where (name="spoolsv.exe") list brief /every:10
```

This will run the command every 10 seconds and display the output to the screen. You can press any key to end the command. You can also use the */repeat* switch to execute the command every *x* seconds for a specified number of times.

```
wmic process where (name="spoolsv.exe") list brief /every:10 /repeat:6
```

Formatting Output

If you've been testing WMIC as you've been reading the chapter, you probably noticed how difficult it is to read some of the output. Fortunately, there are several options for producing more user friendly output or reports. If you are using the *get* verb, the easiest way to do this is by adding */value* to the end of the command.

```
wmic os get /value
```

This command will produce an easy-to-read columnar list of properties and values. If you want only certain values to be displayed, use a command like this.

```
wmic os get caption,csdversion,version /value
```

This command will produce the following type of output.

```
Caption=Microsoft Windows XP Professional
CSDVersion=Service Pack 2
Version=5.1.2600
```

Saving Output to the Command Prompt Window

All the commands we've run so far have been implicitly using another global switch, */output*. This switch determines how the output is handled. The default value is *StdOut*, which means that data is written to the command prompt window. If we wanted to be explicit, we could use the command like this.

```
wmic /output:stdout OS get /value
```

Saving Output to the Clipboard

There are a few other formatting choices. Note for example, the following command, which uses the *clipboard* value.

```
wmic /output:clipboard OS get /value
```

This command specifies that nothing is displayed on the screen. However, we can view the output of the operation by opening Notepad and pasting the data stored on the clipboard.

Saving Output to a File

Of course if you want to save yourself a step, you can send output directly to a file. All you have to do is specify a filename in the command.

```
wmic /output:"e\logs\os audit\local.txt" OS get /value
```

Obviously, you will need to put any file paths that include spaces in quotation marks. When using */output,* any existing files will be overwritten. If you want to append to an existing file, you can use */append* instead of */output.*

```
wmic /append:"e\logs\os audit\local.txt" OS get /value
```

Using XSL Files

Creating a file is only half the story. WMIC includes a number of transform files (.xsl) that you can use to format the output. You will find these files at %SystemRoot%\System32\wbem. You can specify one of these files by using the */format* switch, and the resulting output will be formatted according to the file. The following XSL files are used most commonly:

- **Textvaluelist**   Creates a list of properties and their values.
- **Htable**   Creates a horizontal HTML table that displays properties and their values.
- **Hform**   Creates a vertical HTML table that displays properties and their values.
- **CSV**   Creates a comma-separated list of properties and their values.
- **RAWXML**   Formats the output in XML. This is very useful when building your own XSL files because WMIC natively uses the XML format.

These format options work with either *list* or *get.* Here are some examples you might want to try.

```
wmic cpu list brief /format:textvaluelist
wmic /output:processreport.csv process list brief /format:csv
wmic /output:bios.xml bios get /format:rawxml
wmic /output:osinfo.html os list full /format:hform
wmic /output:test.html process list brief /format:htable
```

Figure 12-8 on the next page illustrates the result of the last command.

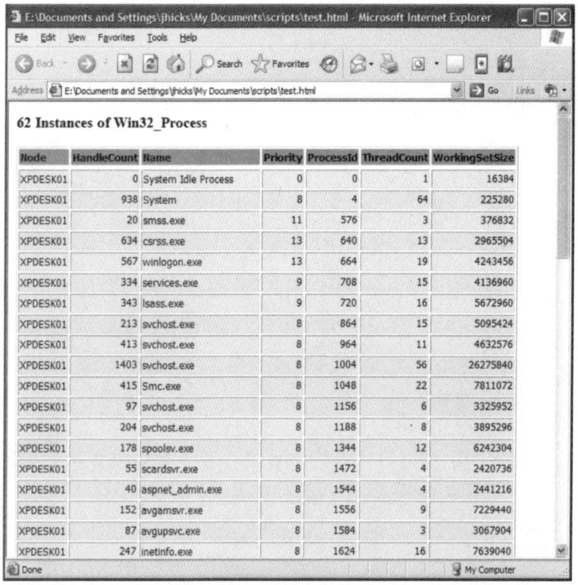

62 Instances of Win32_Process

Node	HandleCount	Name	Priority	ProcessId	ThreadCount	WorkingSetSize
XPDESK01	0	System Idle Process	0	0	1	16384
XPDESK01	938	System	8	4	64	225280
XPDESK01	20	smss.exe	11	576	3	376832
XPDESK01	634	csrss.exe	13	640	13	2965504
XPDESK01	567	winlogon.exe	13	664	19	4243456
XPDESK01	334	services.exe	9	708	15	4136960
XPDESK01	343	lsass.exe	9	720	16	5672960
XPDESK01	213	svchost.exe	8	864	15	5095424
XPDESK01	413	svchost.exe	8	964	11	4632576
XPDESK01	1403	svchost.exe	8	1004	56	26275840
XPDESK01	415	Smc.exe	8	1048	22	7811072
XPDESK01	97	svchost.exe	8	1156	6	3325952
XPDESK01	204	svchost.exe	8	1188	8	3895296
XPDESK01	178	spoolsv.exe	8	1344	12	6242304
XPDESK01	55	scardsvr.exe	8	1472	4	2420736
XPDESK01	40	aspnet_admin.exe	8	1544	4	2441216
XPDESK01	152	avgamsvr.exe	8	1556	9	7229440
XPDESK01	87	avgupsvc.exe	8	1584	3	3067904
XPDESK01	247	inetinfo.exe	8	1624	16	7639040

Figure 12-8 Displaying the output as an HTML table

Creating Your Own XSL File

This topic is outside the scope of this book, but if you have any experience with XML and XSL, you can create your own formatting files. You can also make a copy of one of the existing files and then customize it to better suit your needs. In any event, the XSL file you create or modify must be located in the %Systemroot%\System32\wbem folder. Listing 12-1 is a very simple XSL file that we put together as a demonstration.

Listing 12-1 Demo XSL File

```
<?xml version="1.0"?>
<xsl:stylesheet version="1.0" xmlns:xsl="http://www.w3.org/1999/XSL/Transform">
<xsl:template match="/">
<html>
<body bgcolor="#FFFF99">
<img src="http://www.jdhitsolutions.com/images/JDHITSolutionsBtn.jpg" alt="logo"/>
<xsl:for-each select="COMMAND/REQUEST/COMMANDLINECOMPONENTS">
 <h3>COMPUTER SYSTEM - <xsl:value-of select="NODELIST/NODE"/></h3>
 <HR></HR>
 <I><FONT COLOR="BLUE"><xsl:value-of select="RESULTANTQUERY"/></FONT></I>
</xsl:for-each>

<br></br><br></br>

 <table border="1"><tr style="background-color:6666ff;font:10pt Tahoma;">
 <xsl:for-each select="COMMAND/REQUEST/COMMANDLINECOMPONENTS/PROPERTIES/PROPERTY">
 <th><xsl:value-of select="NAME"/></th>
 </xsl:for-each>
 </tr>
```

```
<xsl:for-each select="COMMAND/RESULTS/CIM/INSTANCE">
<tr style="font:8pt Tahoma;">
<xsl:for-each select="PROPERTY">
  <td><xsl:value-of select="VALUE"/></td>
  </xsl:for-each>
</tr>
  </xsl:for-each>
 </table>
</body>
</html>

</xsl:template>

</xsl:stylesheet>
```

On the CD   You will find this script, as well as other scripts listed in this chapter, on the CD that accompanies this book.

To use this file, save it to the WBEM folder with a name like basichtml.xsl. Then run a command like the following:

```
wmic /output:computersystem.html OS list full /format:basichtml
```

Open the computersystem.html file in your browser to view the results.

Note   The XSL file in Listing 12-1 is designed for WMIC commands running on a single node and using *list /brief*. It has not been fully tested for formatting compatibility with other WMIC commands and aliases.

Scripting with WMIC

Because WMIC is a command-line tool, it can be incorporated into a batch file. Listing 12-2 is an example of a batch file that uses WMIC.

Listing 12-2 WMIC in a Batch File
```
@echo off
::SysPeek.bat
::USAGE- syspeek [computer]

::DESC- Build HTML page of system resource usage for specified computer.
::Default html filename is computernameInfo.htm and it is created in the
::same directory you run the script from. If you don't specify a
::computer, script will default to local host.

::Information gathered:
::  Processor
::  OS
::  pagefile
```

```
::  memory
::  logical drives
::  services
::  processes

::IMPORTANT NOTES- This script uses a command line version of WMI that is
::only available on Windows XP and 2003 platforms. Before you can run the
::script you must install WMIC. Open a command prompt and type 'WMIC'
::which will start the installation. When it is finished you will have an
::interactive prompt (wmic:root\cli>). Type 'exit'. You can now run this
::script. The computer you are querying doesn't need WMIC but it must be
::WMI-enabled.

::You must have appropriate credentials on the target computer. You can
::specify alternate credentials, but you will need to use the /USER and
:://PASSWORD global switches. Run wmic /? at a command prompt to see help
::screens.

::You can build your own format files (.xsl) if you understand XML. The
::files are found in %systemroot%\system32\wbem.

:Top
::script version used in output
set zver=v2.0

 if "%1"=="" goto :Local
 set zSrv=%1
 goto :Main

:Local
 set zSrv=%computername%

:Main
 echo Getting system resource information for "%zSrv%"

::Define file for html output
 set zOutput=%zSrv%-Info.htm

::delete file if it already exists
 if exist %zOutput% del %zOutPut% >NUL
::delete error log if it previously exists
 if exist %zSrv%-Error.log del %zSrv%-Error.log >NUL

::build a shell html file.  Not required but I wanted to try.
 echo ^<html^> >> %zOutput%
 echo ^<body^> >> %zOutput%
 echo ^<H3^>^<Font Face=Verdana Color=Blue^>^<P align=Center^>%zSrv%^<BR^>
 >>%zOutput%
 echo System Resources Information^</Font^>^</H3^>^</P^> >>%zOutput%
 echo ^<HR^> >>%zOutput%
 echo ^</html^> >> %zOutput%
 echo ^</body^> >> %zOutput%

::verify connectivity and WMI compatibility
wmic /node:"%zSrv%" os list brief 1>NUL 2>> %zSrv%-Error.log
 if errorlevel=0 goto :Gather
```

```
echo ^<Font Color=Red^>^<B^> OOPS!! ^</P^>>> %zOutPut%
echo Can't verify connectivity to or WMI compatibility with "%zSrv%" ^</P^>
 >> %zOutPut%
for /f "tokens=*" %%i in (%zSrv%-Error.log) do @echo %%i ^<br^> >>%zoutput%
echo ^</Font^>^</B^> ^</P^> >> %zOutPut%
goto :Cleanup

:Gather
::start gathering information.  WMIC command must be on one line.
 echo  OS...
 echo ^<Font Color=Green^>^<H3^>^<B^>^<I^>Operating System^</Font^>
^</H3^>^</B^>^</I^> >> %zOutPut%
 wmic /node:"%zSrv%" /append:"%zOutPut%" OS get Caption,Version,
 CSDVersion,installDate,LastBootUpTime,Status,WindowsDirectory
/format:hform.xsl >NUL

 echo  processor...
 echo ^<Font Color=Green^>^<H3^>^<B^>^<I^>Processors^</Font^>
^</H3^>^</B^>^</I^> >> %zOutPut%
 wmic /node:"%zSrv%" /append:"%zOutPut%" cpu get deviceID,name,
 addresswidth,currentclockspeed,l2cachesize,loadpercentage
/format:htable.xsl >NUL

 echo  memory...
 echo ^<Font Color=Green^>^<H3^>^<B^>^<I^>Memory^</Font^>
 ^</H3^>^</B^>^</I^> >> %zOutPut%
 wmic /node:"%zSrv%" /append:"%zOutPut%" memlogical get
AvailableVirtualMemory, TotalVirtualMemory, TotalPhysicalMemory,
TotalPageFileSpace /format:hform.xsl >NUL

 echo  pagefile...
 echo ^<Font Color=Green^>^<H3^>^<B^>^<I^>PageFile^</Font^>
^</H3^>^</B^>^</I^> >> %zOutPut%
 wmic /node:"%zSrv%" /append:"%zOutPut%" pagefileset get name, initialsize,
 maximumsize /format:hform.xsl >NUL
 wmic /node:"%zSrv%" /append:"%zOutPut%" pagefile get Caption,
CurrentUsage, PeakUsage, InstallDate /format:hform.xsl >NUL

 echo  logical drives...
 echo ^<Font Color=Green^>^<H3^>^<B^>^<I^>Drive
Information^</Font^>^</H3^>^</B^>^</I^> >> %zOutPut%
 wmic /node:"%zSrv%" /append:"%zOutPut%" logicaldisk where drivetype=3 get
 name, size, freespace, compressed, filesystem /format:htable.xsl >NUL

 echo  process...
 echo ^<Font Color=Green^>^<H3^>^<B^>^<I^>Processes^</Font^>^</H3^>^</B^>^</I^> >>
%zOutPut%
 wmic /node:"%zSrv%" /append:"%zOutPut%" process list brief
/format:"htable.xsl":"sortby=Name" >NUL

 echo  service...
 echo ^<Font Color=Green^>^<H3^>^<B^>^<I^>Services^</Font^>
^</H3^>^</B^>^</I^> >> %zOutPut%
 wmic /node:"%zSrv%" /append:"%zOutPut%" service where
startmode!="disabled" get pathname, state, startmode, displayname,
processid /format:"htable.xsl":"sortby=State" >NUL
```

```
:Cleanup
 echo ^<I^>^<Font Size=-1^>^<BR^>%zver% >>%zOutput%
 date /t >>%zOutput%
 time /t >>%zOutput%
 echo - %username% ^</I^>>>%zOutput%

 echo Open %zOutPut% to view results
 Start %zOutPut%

 if exist %zSrv%-Error.log del %zSrv%-Error.log >NUL

 set zSrv=
 set zOutput=
 set zVer=

::EOF
```

Note In this batch file, each *echo* and *wmic* command is on a single line. For code listing purposes some lines break. The script file on the CD is properly formatted.

This batch file builds an HTML page with WMI information about a single computer. You can specify a computer name as a parameter at run time. If you don't, the script defaults to the local system. The script uses the */output* and */append* switches to build a file. It then runs a series of WMIC commands, appending the results to the file. We use the htable.xsl file to format the results. Figure 12-9 gives you an idea of the output from the script.

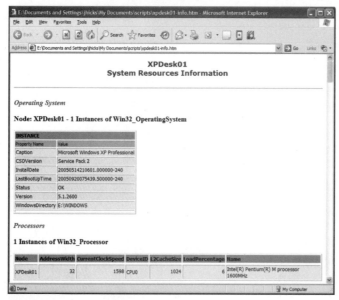

Figure 12-9 Viewing the Listing 12-2 output

As you can see, you can produce a fairly complete system report with WMI information, without writing a single line of VBScript. There is much, much more to WMIC, but we'll leave that for you to discover on your own.

> **More Info**   You can learn more about WMIC by searching in the Help and Support Center on a Windows XP desktop. There is also a help file, wmic.chm, located in the Windows\Help folder. You can also visit the following Web sites:
>
> *http://www.microsoft.com/technet/prodtechnol/windows2000serv/maintain/featusability /wmic.mspx*
>
> *http://support.microsoft.com/kb/290216/EN-US/*
>
> (These links can be found on the companion CD; click *WMIC Introduction* and *A Description of WMIC*, respectively.)

Using WBEMTest

In Chapter 11, we demonstrated how to use WBEMTest to work with WMI event notification. We believe WBEMTest's primary purpose is as a query validation tool. If your WMI query works in WBEMTest and returns the information you are expecting, it should work in your script.

Connecting to a Namespace

Start WBEMTest by clicking the Start menu, clicking Run, and then typing **wbemtest** in the command prompt window. You will need to connect to a namespace by clicking the Connect button. Even though you might be tempted to accept the default, you must change it to **root\cimv2** if you want to work with the Win32 object classes.

> **Tip**   If you want to connect to a remote system, enter \\servername**root\cimv2**.

Enabling Privileges

As we explained in Chapter 11, "WMI Events," to enable privileges to, for example, read security logs or shut down remote systems, you must select the Enable All Privileges check box *before* you click the Connect button. If you encounter errors running a WBEMTest query, you might need to select that check box and then reconnect.

Enabling Impersonation

The Connect dialog box includes an option to specify an impersonation level. Remember, WMI works by impersonating the user and executing commands. This means a user can't access any system resources or information without the appropriate permissions. You should accept the default setting.

Enabling Authentication

The authentication level refers to how communication is handled between systems. If you are only connecting to the local system, you can accept the default because no packets are leaving the computer. Otherwise, you can select an appropriate level of security. Packet privacy provides the highest level.

> **More Info** You can learn more about authentication levels, including how to set them in VBScript, at *http://msdn.microsoft.com/library/default.asp?url=/library/en-us/wmisdk/wmi/setting_the_default_process_security_level_using_vbscript.asp*. (This link is also on the companion CD; click *WMI Authentication Levels*.)

Enabling Authority

If you specify alternate credentials, WMI will use NTLM for user authentication. Don't confuse this with the authentication level we just discussed. If you leave the Authority field blank and need to enter alternate credentials, use the form *domain\username*. If you want to explicitly use NTLM, you need only the username. WMI will assume that the computer you are running WBEMTest on and the remote system are in the same domain.

Alternatively, you can use Kerberos, in which case the format for authority is *Kerberos: <domain>\computername*. The domain name should be the fully qualified name of your Active Directory domain, and the computer name should be the name of the remote system. Figure 12-10 shows a WBEMTest Connect dialog box connecting to a remote system, APP01, using alternate credentials and Kerberos authentication.

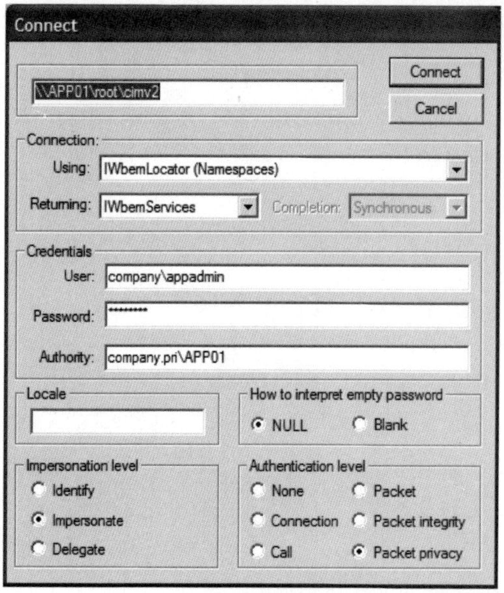

Figure 12-10 Connecting to a remote system with WBEMTest Connect

Enumerating Instances

After you are connected, click the Query button, enter a WMI query like *Select * from win32_physicalmemory*, and click Apply. WBEMTest will execute the query and return a list of all instances. Double-click one of the instances to open the object editor window and display all the object properties and values for that instance. This verifies that your query syntax is correct and shows you what type of information is available. You might want to refine your query to something like *Select DeviceLocator,Capacity,Speed from win32_physicalmemory* and run it in WBEMTest to verify you have the right WMI property names.

> **Tip**   When reviewing object properties, select the Hide System Properties check box. This will hide the class and system properties and display only the object properties.

As you begin to write more complex WMI queries and scripts, you will find that WBEMTest is a valuable tool in administrative script development.

> **Tip**   Some queries, like *Select DeviceLocator,Capacity,Speed from win32_physicalmemory* will return results like *Win32_PhysicalMemory=<no key>*. When you double-click the instance, the object editor window still opens. This type of result simply reflects that the query did not include the key index property. The lack of a key index has no effect on your query or the results.

Using WMI Tools

We discussed the Event Viewer and Registration Tool in Chapter 11, so in this chapter, we give you an overview of two more WMI tools: CIM Studio and the WMI Object Browser.

Using CIM Studio

CIM Studio is a Web page with ActiveX components that allow you to view information in and about the CIM repository, where all WMI information is stored or generated. You must open CIM Studio in Internet Explorer and allow blocked content if running Windows XP Service Pack 2.

Connecting to a Namespace

When you first launch CIM Studio, you are prompted for a namespace. Unless you are working with a special WMI namespace, such as for Exchange 2003, you should accept the default of root*cimv2*, as shown in Figure 12-11 on the next page.

Figure 12-11   Connecting to a namespace

If you want to connect to a different namespace, click the computer icon next to the namespace field in the connection dialog box. Make sure that *root* is entered as the starting namespace, and click Connect. The Browse for Namespace dialog box appears, as shown in Figure 12-12.

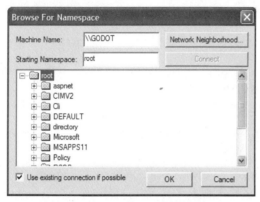

Figure 12-12   Browsing to namespaces

Double-clicking a namespace will connect you to that namespace.

Connecting to Remote Computers

We typically use CIM Studio to work with the local CIM repository. You can also connect to remote machines and view their CIM repository and WMI objects. When you browse to the namespace, you can enter a remote computer name. CIM Studio defaults to the local system.

Using Alternate Credentials

If you specify a remote system, you have the option of using alternate credentials. After you click **Connect**, clear the Login as Current User check box.

> **Note**   When connecting to the local system, the Login as Current User check box is dimmed because you can't specify alternate credentials for the local system, and CIM Studio is smart enough to not let you try. WBEMTest will let you enter alternate credentials for a local connection, and then give you an error when you try to connect.

If you want to specify additional connection properties, such as authentication level, authority, and privileges, click the Options button. Then follow the same guidelines that we outlined for WBEMTest earlier. If your connection succeeds, a page similar to the one shown in Figure 12-13 will appear.

Figure 12-13   Connecting with CIM Studio

Searching for Classes

Click or expand an element in the left pane to display its classes, properties, methods, and associations in the right pane. To search for WMI classes, click the binoculars button at the top of the left pane. You don't have to enter the full name of the class in the Search for Class dialog box. Figure 12-14 shows the results returned on a search for any class with the word "display" in the name.

Figure 12-14   Searching for a class

Click the class you want, and click OK. The CIM Studio page is redisplayed with the selected class highlighted. As usual, the right pane shows the classes' properties, methods, and associations.

Returning Instances

Now that you know property names that can help you develop a script, you might also want to know what instances of the class exist on the computer to which you're connected. To return all the instances of a particular class, click the Instances button, which is immediately to the right of the disk button in the right pane. If you position your mouse pointer over a button, a ScreenTip will appear informing you of each button's name.

When you click the Instances button, all the instances of that class that exist on the computer you are connected to will be listed in the right pane. Double-click one of the instances to display the instance with populated values, as shown in Figure 12-15.

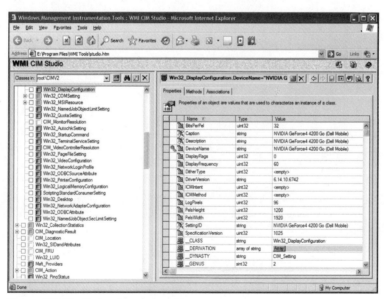

Figure 12-15   Returning an instance

Click the Associations tab in the right pane to see the relationship between associated classes. Double-click one of the connected graphics to display that class instance in CIM Studio.

Running Queries

CIM Studio also includes a WMI query feature. To run a query, click the WQL (WMI Query Language) button to the left of the question mark button. In the Query dialog box, enter any type of WMI query in the Query pane, just as you would in WBEMTest. Click the Execute button to run the query. If any instances are found, double-click them to view details. One advantage with CIM Studio is that you can save your queries.

Using WMI Object Browser

CIM Studio is used to browse WMI classes, although you can also use it to return class instances on a specified computer. To simplify the process and explore all the WMI objects on a computer, use the WMI Object Browser.

You connect to local and remote systems and change namespaces the same way you do in CIM Studio. When you use the WMI Object Browser to connect to the default namespace on the local computer, a page similar to the one shown in Figure 12-16 will appear.

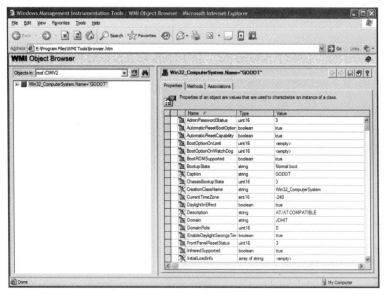

Figure 12-16   Launching WMI Object Browser

Notice that you don't have to look for instances; they are immediately apparent. If you expand the tree in the left pane, you will see all the WMI components, which you can further expand to see the underlying WMI object.

For example, expand *Win32_SystemServices.PartComponent* to reveal *Win32_Service*. When you attempt to expand *Win32_Service*, a WMI query is launched to return all instances of the selected class, as shown in Figure 12-17 on the next page.

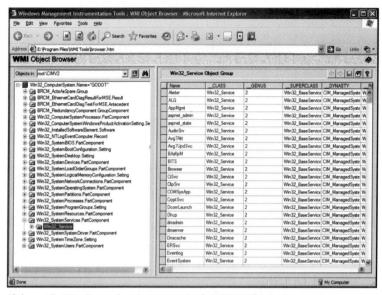

Figure 12-17   Returning instances in the WMI Object Browser

As with CIM Studio, you can double-click an instance in the right pane to display WMI properties for that specific instance. Click the binoculars button at the top of the left pane to browse for instances of other classes. Figure 12-18 shows the result of searching for *Win32_Processor*.

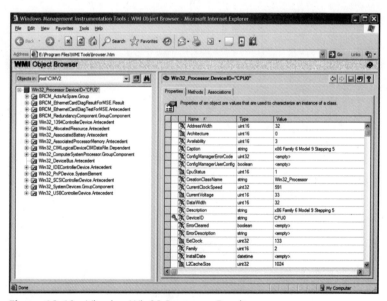

Figure 12-18   Viewing Win32 Processor Results

The WMI Object Browser is an excellent tool for seeing how all the various elements and components of WMI work together. Keep in mind that just because a class is listed, that doesn't mean there is an instance on your computer. A message of *No Instances Available* is not unusual.

Comparing WMI Wizards

A few commercial script editors include a WMI wizard to help speed code development. Even with minimal WMI experience, these wizards can help you produce fully functioning scripts, much as Scriptomatic does. Let's take a look at the WMI wizards in AdminScriptEditor by iTripoli and Sapien's PrimalScript. We don't intend to pass judgment on which is the better product, only to demonstrate these features and point out some differences.

AdminScriptEditor's WMI Wizard is located in the right pane of the application. To use the wizard, first create a blank VBScript file. The WMI Wizard lets you browse all the available Win32 classes on the local computer. There doesn't appear to be a way to connect to a remote system, or a way to connect to any namespace other than root\cimv2. When you select a class, the appropriate properties are displayed in the middle of the panel. Figure 12-19 shows the WMI Wizard and its generated code.

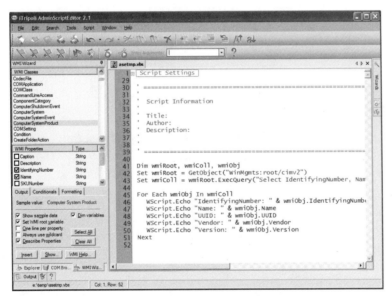

Figure 12-19   Viewing the AdminScriptEditor WMI Wizard

Specify which properties you want reported by selecting the appropriate check box in the left pane. AdminScriptEditor displays a sample value when you select a property. If you want more information about a specific class, clicking the WMI Help button launches your Web browser and loads the MSDN WMI page about the selected class.

The wizard uses the *winmgmt* moniker and a *select* query. If you want a more selective query, clear the Always Use Wildcard check box. Usually, the generated code will echo the WMI property and its value, but if you just want the value, clear the Describe Properties check box.

On the Conditionals tab, you can build a conditional *WHERE* clause for the query based on the selected properties. You don't have to do much typing, simply select the property and an operator, and type in your constraint. Figure 12-20 illustrates this with the *Win32_Process* class. You can also see the finished script in the left pane.

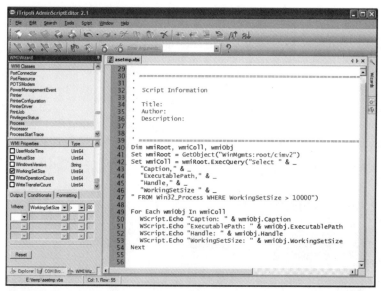

Figure 12-20   Creating a conditional clause

When you are satisfied with your selections, click the Show button on the Output tab to display a code preview. Clicking Insert will generate your script which you can run as-is, or modify further.

You can use the AdminScriptEditor WMI Wizard to produce some very specific WMI code, although there is no support for remote systems or remote credentials. You could easily modify the code to connect to a remote system, but adding alternate credentials would require major revisions.

PrimalScript takes a slightly different approach to their WMI Wizard. You access the wizard from the Script menu. Like AdminScriptEditor, the wizard defaults to the Win32 classes in the local root\cimv2 namespace. However, you can specify a server name or a different namespace at the bottom of the WMI Wizard. There are also options to enter an alternate username and password.

Selecting a class will generate a script that enumerates all the properties of that class. You can specify whether you want to use JScript of VBScript. You'll notice that PrimalScript uses the

WbemScripting.SWbemLocator object instead of the *winmgmt* moniker. Not only does this allow for alternate credentials, it also provides PrimalSense support for the object, which is Sapien's version of Intellisense. Figure 12-21 shows the PrimalScript WMI Wizard and its generated code for the *Win32_DiskPartition* class.

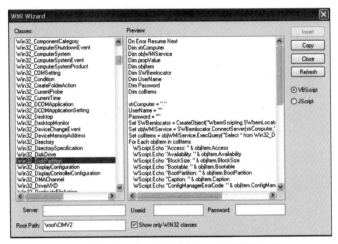

Figure 12-21   Viewing the PrimalScript WMI Wizard

You can make simple script edits in the wizard, such as deleting or adding commenting to lines. Click the Copy button to copy the script to the clipboard, or if you have a file open in PrimalScript, you can use the Insert button to insert the code directly into your script. As with AdminScriptEditor, you have a fully functioning script or the basis for your own work all within minutes without having to type a single line of code.

The PrimalScript wizard lacks the granularity of the AdminScriptEditor, but it allows for connections to remote systems and other namespaces. In either case, WMI script development time and effort can be reduced dramatically.

Summary

To truly advance your scripting, you need to have a well-equipped toolbox. Fortunately there are many WMI-related tools that you can add for free or for a small investment. In this chapter, we reviewed a number of WMI-related tools that can help educate you about WMI and dramatically improve your scripting efficiency. We showed you how to use Scriptomatic to create WMI scripts and execute them as wrappers for multiple machines. We introduced you to WMIC, which lets you execute WMI queries from a command line. We showed you how WBEMTest can be used for query testing, and demonstrated how to use WMI Tools to explore the CIM repository. Although WMI Tools don't generate any code, they will help you better understand how WMI works. Finally, we explored the WMI wizards in a few commercial script editors. These wizards can cut your script development time to literally a minute and require almost no typing.

Chapter 13

Advanced Scripting in Windows XP and Windows Server 2003

Microsoft Windows XP and Microsoft Windows Server 2003 introduced a wide variety of new management capabilities, particularly through new WMI classes. We'll take a look at some of the most useful of these, and show you some sample scripts that can make administrative tasks faster and easier.

Microsoft Windows 2000 created an enormous surge of interest in Windows administrative scripting. It was the first version of Windows to include Windows Management Instrumentation (WMI), and that created tremendous new capabilities for scripting languages like VBScript. Microsoft responded to administrators' newfound enthusiasm for scripting by including even more capabilities in Windows XP and Windows Server 2003.

> **Note** Some of the topics we'll cover in this chapter—such as Active Directory and Internet Information Services scripting—could easily fill a book on their own. We're not trying to provide comprehensive coverage of them here; instead, we're simply showing you what's available.

It's important to note that the scripts in this chapter aren't all intended to be complete administrative scripts. In fact, most of them are as short as possible to make as clear as possible how the capabilities work. However, most of the scripts in this chapter can easily be made more useful by adding them into a wrapper. For example, Listing 13-1 shows a wrapper script that reads computer names from a text file.

Listing 13-1 Read Names from a File

```
'Create a FileSystemObject
Set oFS = _
  CreateObject("Scripting.FileSystemObject")

'Open a text file of computer names
'with one computer name per line
Set oTS = oFS.OpenTextFile("c:\computers.txt")
Set oTSOut = oFS.CreateTextFile("c:\errors.txt")

'go through the text file
Do Until oTS.AtEndOfStream

  'get next computer
  sComputer = oTS.ReadLine

On Error Resume Next
'***MAKE CONNECTION***
If Err <> 0 Then
    oTSOut.WriteLine "Error on " & sComputer & _
    ":" & Err.Number & ", " & Err.Description
Else
    On Error Goto 0
    '***REST OF CODE HERE
End If

Loop

oTS.Close
oTSOut.Close
```

On the CD   You will find this script, as well as other scripts listed in this chapter, on the CD that accompanies this book.

You'd insert your code in place of the *REST OF CODE HERE* placeholder. This wrapper can take a basic script that queries a single DNS server's *A* records, for example, and turn it into a complete inventory script that documents the records in all your DNS servers. We use this wrapper in examples later in this chapter. You can also incorporate a wrapper to read computer names from Active Directory, and then target each computer for some scripted administrative task. That's what Listing 13-2 does.

Listing 13-2 Read Names from Active Directory

```
'connect to the root of AD
Dim rootDSE, domainObject
Set rootDSE=GetObject("LDAP://RootDSE")
domainContainer = rootDSE.Get("defaultNamingContext")
Set oDomain = GetObject("LDAP://" & domainContainer)

'start with the domain root
WorkWithObject(oDomain)

Sub WorkWithObject(oContainer)
 Dim oADObject
 For Each oADObject in oContainer
  Select Case oADObject.Class
   Case "computer"
    'oADObject represents a COMPUTER object;
    'do something with it
    '** YOUR CODE HERE**
   Case "organizationalUnit" , "container"
    'oADObject is an OU or container...
    'go through its objects
    WorkWithObject(oADObject)
  End select
 Next
End Sub
```

Again, just insert your code in place of the *YOUR CODE HERE* placeholder. The variable *oADObject* represents a computer object. You can access the *oADObject.cn* property to get the computer's name, and then you can add, for example, inventory Windows Update configuration settings to make sure that all your client computers are consistently configured. These wrappers can make scripting against multiple computers easier and more efficient, and we encourage you to use them.

Using New and Discontinued WMI Classes

Windows XP and Windows Server 2003 introduced a wide variety of new WMI classes. One of the biggest challenges in scripting is remembering which classes aren't supported in Windows 2000 and older versions of Windows. It can be frustrating to write a script that runs perfectly on one computer, but that doesn't run at all on another.

We've found that the best resource for figuring out what WMI classes will work on a particular operating system is the MSDN Library, available at *http://msdn.microsoft.com/library*.

To access the Library's information about WMI classes, follow these steps.

1. On the Library's main page, click the Win32 and COM Development link in the left pane to expand the list.

2. Click each of these links to further expand the list and display information in the right pane: click Administration and Management, click Windows Management Instrumentation, click SDK Documentation, click Windows Management Instrumentation, click WMI Reference, click WMI Classes, and finally, click Win32 Classes.

> **Note** The path to this information is somewhat different on the CD or DVD versions of the Library, and this path to the Web-based Library is also subject to change.

Within each class' description—usually at the bottom of a WMI class' description—you'll find a list of requirements for client and server operating systems. Older classes will list the client requirement as, for example. *Requires Windows XP, Windows 2000 Professional, or Windows NT Workstation 4.0 SP4 and later.* A newer class might simply specify *Requires Windows XP*. The classes that aren't supported on older versions of Windows won't list the older versions as a requirement in the class description. For example, the *Win32_Ping* class lists Windows XP and Windows Server 2003, but not older versions of Windows.

One interesting fact about Windows Server 2003 is that it actually *omits* a set of WMI classes, and discontinues several others. These classes are still supported, but you have to specifically install them. One set of classes provides support for working with installed software packages, whereas another provides WMI with the capability to work with Simple Network Management Protocol (SNMP). To install the WMI SNMP provider on a Windows Server 2003 server, follow these steps.

1. Open Control Panel.
2. Click Add or Remove Programs.
3. Click the Add/Remove Windows Components icon in the left pane.
4. Click Management and Monitoring Tools Details, and then click the Details button.
5. Select the WMI SNMP Provider check box, and click OK.

The Windows Installer provider, which provides support for installed software, is located on the Windows Server 2003 product CD. Note that this provider might not be directly available in future versions of Windows. Windows Server 2003 also discontinues the WMI ADSI extension and the ODBC WMI adapter, although both might still be present on Windows XP systems.

Using the *Win32_PingStatus* Class

One of the neatest new WMI classes added in Windows XP and Windows Server 20030 is *Win32_PingStatus*. Unlike most WMI classes, which represent some portion of the operating system or a computer's hardware, this class executes a network ping command and returns the results as properties of a class instance. Listing 13-3 shows this new class in its basic format.

Listing 13-3 View the *Win32_PingStatus* Class Results

```
Set cPingResults = _
 GetObject("winmgmts://./root/cimv2").ExecQuery("SELECT * " & _
 "FROM Win32_PingStatus WHERE Address = 'don-laptop'")
For Each oPingResult In cPingResults
    If oPingResult.StatusCode = 0 Then
        WScript.Echo "Responds"
    Else
        WScript.Echo "Doesn't respond"
    End If
Next
```

As you can see, you simply add a *WHERE* clause and specify the address you want to ping. The address can be a network-resolvable name or an IP address, whichever you prefer. The instance that comes back will have a *StatusCode* property, which is 0 if the specified address responded, and nonzero if it didn't. This is a great tool to add to scripts that connect to remote computers. Rather than letting the script fail when it can't connect, or adding error trapping and then waiting through a lengthy timeout, you can proactively ping the computer to see if it's available before attempting any other type of connection. Listing 13-4 wraps the ping capability into an easy-to-use function that you can paste into your scripts.

Listing 13-4 Ping the Network

```
Function Ping(strComputer)
    Set cPingResults = _
     GetObject("winmgmts://./root/cimv2").ExecQuery("SELECT * " & _
     "FROM Win32_PingStatus WHERE Address = '" & strComputer & "'")
    For Each oPingResult In cPingResults
        If oPingResult.StatusCode = 0 Then
            Ping = True
        Else
            Ping = False
        End If
    Next
End Function
```

With this function in a script, you can perform a basic test by adding something like the following:

```
WScript.Echo Ping("192.168.0.1")
```

Of course, the *Win32_PingStatus* class has properties besides *Status*, and they can provide useful information about the computer you're pinging. Consider Listing 13-5 on the next page, which uses some of the additional properties of this new class.

Listing 13-5 Get Ping Information

```
strComputer = "www.sapien.com"
Set cPingResults = _
 GetObject("winmgmts://./root/cimv2").ExecQuery("SELECT * " & _
 "FROM Win32_PingStatus WHERE Address = '" & strComputer & "'")
For Each oPingResult In cPingResults
    If oPingResult.StatusCode = 0 Then
        WScript.Echo strComputer & " Responds from "
        WScript.Echo oPingResult.ProtocolAddress
        WScript.Echo "Response time " & oPingResult.ResponseTime
        WScript.Echo "Source routes " & oPingResult.SourceRoute
    Else
        WScript.Echo strComputer & " Doesn't respond"
    End If
Next
```

This script will check the availability of a computer and then display the address that was resolved from the name, the response time for the ping, and any source routing information that's available. For example, you might check the response time to a remote computer before launching into some particularly intensive administrative task. A computer returning a slow response time might not be an ideal target for that task. Listing 13-6 is a function that returns a computer's response time.

Listing 13-6 Return Ping Response Time

```
Function PingResponse(strComputer)
    Dim t, intResponse
    intResponse = -1
    For t = 1 To 5
        Set cPingResults = _
         GetObject("winmgmts://./root/cimv2").ExecQuery("SELECT * " & _
         "FROM Win32_PingStatus WHERE Address = '" & strComputer & "'")
        For Each oPingResult In cPingResults
            If oPingResult.StatusCode = 0 Then
                If intResponse = -1 Then intResponse = 0
                intResponse = intResponse + oPingResult.ResponseTime
            End If
        Next
    Next
    If intResponse = -1 Then
        PingResponse = -1
    Else
        PingResponse = Int(intResponse/5)
    End If
End Function
```

You can test this as follows.

```
WScript.Echo PingResponse("192.168.0.1")
```

The function will ping the remote computer five times, and then list its average response time in milliseconds, much like the command-line *Ping* command does. Your script can then take appropriate action.

```
If PingResponse(strComputer) < 75 Then
     'Perform Tasks
Else
     'Don't perform tasks
End If
```

Although it's fairly simple, the new *Win32_PingStatus* class has terrific functionality. Keep in mind that the computer being pinged does not need this class. Only the computer running the script needs to have the *Win32_PingStatus* class (meaning it must be Windows XP or later).

Configuring the Windows Firewall

The Windows Firewall, introduced in Windows XP Service Pack 2 and Windows Server 2003 Service Pack 1, provides per-system firewall capabilities. The Windows Firewall is completely configurable by using either its local graphical user interface, or the centrally configured Group Policy objects in Active Directory. The latter is our preferred method for configuring the Windows Firewall, because it's easier and fits well into most organizations' administrative models.

However, in the event that you want to script the Windows Firewall, there is a complete set of interfaces for doing so. Unlike many of the topics we cover in this chapter, the Windows Firewall isn't exposed through a set of WMI classes. Instead, you'll work with a set of COM objects from the Home Networking Configuration (HNetCfg) library. Specifically, you'll work with the *HNetCfg.FwMgr* object, which provides most firewall management functions. For example, Listing 13-7 is a basic script that lists the globally open ports in the firewall.

Listing 13-7 List Open Firewall Ports

```
Set objFirewall = CreateObject("HNetCfg.FwMgr")
Set objPolicy = objFirewall.LocalPolicy.CurrentProfile

Set colPorts = objPolicy.GloballyOpenPorts

For Each objPort in colPorts
    Wscript.Echo "Port name: " & objPort.Name
    Wscript.Echo "Port number: " & objPort.Port
    Wscript.Echo "Port IP version: " & objPort.IPVersion
    Wscript.Echo "Port protocol: " & objPort.Protocol
    Wscript.Echo "Port scope: " & objPort.Scope
    Wscript.Echo "Port remote addresses: " & objPort.RemoteAddresses
    Wscript.Echo "Port enabled: " & objPort.Enabled
    Wscript.Echo "Port built-in: " & objPort.Builtin
Next
```

The script starts by instantiating the Windows Firewall's manager object. Note that the script instantiates the local object by using this.

```
Set objFirewall = CreateObject("HNetCfg.FwMgr","\\Client23")
```

You can instantiate the object on a remote computer (if you have permission to do so and the Windows Firewall isn't blocking the Distributed COM traffic). This object is physically implemented in Hnetcfg.dll, which is located in the System32 folder.

The script then accesses the local firewall policy for the current profile (the firewall profile, not the current user profile). Last, the script enumerates the ports in the current profile's *GloballyOpenPorts* list, and displays them.

The local policy of the current profile is what you'll use for most Windows Firewall manipulation. Listing 13-8 configures the Windows Firewall to permit remote administration traffic, including remote WMI scripting.

Listing 13-8 Enable Remote Administration
```
Set objFirewall = CreateObject("HNetCfg.FwMgr")
Set objPolicy = objFirewall.LocalPolicy.CurrentProfile

Set objAdminSettings = objPolicy.RemoteAdminSettings
objAdminSettings.Enabled = True
```

You'll deploy this simple script often in a login script, because the Windows Firewall blocks administrative traffic. This is one of the first things we put into a login script in some environments, because it ensures that users can't block administrative traffic. (Note that a Group Policy object can prevent this script from working, but if you have a Group Policy object in place, you're already capable of centrally controlling this setting.)

Because Group Policy can be used to effectively control the Windows Firewall, you might wonder why you would bother with scripts. Sometimes you might need to make a change that's difficult to walk a user through when the user's computer—such as a laptop—isn't connected to the corporate network. In a circumstance like that, e-mailing a short script can provide a temporary quick fix. For example, suppose a remote employee needs a particular application authorized in the Windows Firewall. Listing 13-9 is a script that can do the job.

Listing 13-9 Authorize Applications
```
Set objFirewall = CreateObject("HNetCfg.FwMgr")
Set objPolicy = objFirewall.LocalPolicy.CurrentProfile

Set objApplication = CreateObject("HNetCfg.FwAuthorizedApplication")
objApplication.Name = "Corp App"
objApplication.IPVersion = 2
objApplication.ProcessImageFileName = "c:\myapp1.exe"
objApplication.RemoteAddresses = "*"
objApplication.Scope = 0
```

```
objApplication.Enabled = True

Set colApplications = objPolicy.AuthorizedApplications
colApplications.Add(objApplication)
```

This script is working with the current profile from the local policy. However, notice that it's also working with a second object, *HNetCfg.FwAuthorizedApplication*, which represents an authorized application in the Windows Firewall. The script begins by assigning a display name to the application, and setting the IP version to 2.

```
objApplication.Name = "Corp App"
objApplication.IPVersion = 2
```

It then specifies the executable, or image, of the application. This is what the Windows Firewall will use to identify the application.

```
objApplication.ProcessImageFileName = "c:\myapp1.exe"
```

Next, the script indicates the remote addresses that will be allowed to connect to the application. In this example, we specified the wildcard character (*) to indicate that all remote addresses are allowed to connect. We also specified a local scope for the connection, and set the new application to be enabled.

```
objApplication.RemoteAddresses = "*"
objApplication.Scope = 0
objApplication.Enabled = True
```

Finally, we retrieve the current list of authorized applications from the current profile's firewall policy. We use the connection's *Add* method to add our newly created application to the collection, making it an officially authorized application in the Windows Firewall.

```
Set colApplications = objPolicy.AuthorizedApplications
colApplications.Add(objApplication)
```

Not all changes to the Windows Firewall have to be this complex (although this is a pretty straightforward example). Listing 13-10 is an even simpler example that opens a single port (port 9999) in the globally open ports list.

Listing 13-10 Open a Globally Open Port

```
Set objFirewall = CreateObject("HNetCfg.FwMgr")
Set objPolicy = objFirewall.LocalPolicy.CurrentProfile
Set colPorts = objPolicy.GloballyOpenPorts

Set objPort = colPorts.Item(9999,6)
objPort.Enabled = TRUE
```

The *HNetCfg* object library contains a number of object categories that can be useful, including the following:

- *LocalPolicy*   This object represents the local firewall policy, as opposed to a domain firewall policy. You've seen this type of object in action earlier in this chapter, as well as how to retrieve it by using the *HNetCfg.FwMgr* object's *LocalPolicy* property.

- *Profile*   These objects for manipulating the Windows Firewall profiles include:

  - *AuthorizedApplications*   This object is a collection of authorized applications in the firewall. You can retrieve this collection through any profile object.

  - *CurrentProfile*   This object represents the current firewall profile. Using the *HNetCfg.FwMgr.LocalPolicy.CurrentProfile* command is one way to retrieve a profile object, specifically, the current profile.

  - *CurrentProfileType*   This property indicates the type of Windows Firewall profile that's currently in effect. This property will be 0 (zero) if the current profile is a domain profile, or 1 if it's a standard profile.

  - *ExceptionsNotAllowed*   This property, which can be TRUE or FALSE, tells the Windows Firewall whether to allow firewall exceptions. It's a part of any profile object.

  - *FirewallEnable*   This property, which can be TRUE or FALSE indicates whether the firewall is enabled. It is accessible through a profile object.

  - *GetProfileByType*   This method retrieves the Windows Firewall of the specified type. Aside from the *CurrentProfile* object, using this method is the only way to retrieve a profile object. For example, the *HNetCfg.FwMgr.GetProfileByType* command will retrieve the domain firewall profile.

  - *GloballyOpenPorts*   This is a collection of globally opened ports in the profile. It is accessible through a profile object.

  - *IcmpSettings*   This is a read-only property that details the ICMP settings in a profile. It is accessible though a profile object.

  - *NotificationsDisabled*   This property, which can be TRUE or FALSE indicates whether interactive user notifications are turned on or off. This property is accessed through a profile object.

  - *RemoteAdminSettings*   This is a child object that represents the remote administration settings of the firewall profile. It is accessible though a profile object.

  - *Services*   This is a collection of the services in a profile. It is accessible through a profile object.

  - *Type*   This indicates the type of a profile (0 for domain, 1 for standard). It is accessed as a property of a profile object.

> **Tip**   All this business about profiles can be confusing. Just remember that you can choose to work with the *CurrentProfile*, or you can specifically retrieve the domain or standard profile. All the other profile-related properties and collections are accessed through a profile object. If *HNetCfgMgr.LocalPolicy.CurrentProfile* returns the firewall's domain profile object, *HNetCfgMgr.LocalPolicy.GetProfileBy-Type(0)* returns the same profile object.

- **RemoteAdministration**   These objects affect how the firewall treats remote administration traffic. *RemoteAdministration* is a child object of a profile object, as discussed earlier, and it has the following members:

  - **Enabled**   This property, which can be TRUE or FALSE indicates whether remote administration is allowed.

  - **IpVersion**   This indicates the version of IP for which remote administration is enabled.

  - **RemoteAddresses**   This is a list of remote IP addresses that are allowed to send administrative traffic (can be * for all).

  - **Scope**   This indicates the network scope from which network administration is allowed.

> **Tip**   Remote administration is an excellent example of why the firewall offers two profiles. When the domain profile is current, you might want remote administration enabled, but when the standard profile is current, you might not, because the user might not be connected to the corporate network while the standard profile is active.

Other objects include *IcmpSettings*, *Port*, *Application*, and *Service*. You can read more about them at

http://www.microsoft.com/technet/prodtechnol/windowsserver2003/library/TechRef /47f25d7d-882b-4f87-b05f-31e5664fc15e.mspx

> **On the CD**   This link is included on the companion CD. *Click Windows Firewall Tools and Settings (Scripting Reference).*

> **More Info**   You'll find more scripts for working with the Windows Firewall in the Microsoft TechNet Script Center, at
>
> *http://www.microsoft.com/technet/scriptcenter/scripts/network/firewall/default.mspx*
>
> (This link is included on the companion CD; click *Windows Firewall*.) The listings in this section were adapted from samples in the Script Center.

Using Disk Quota Management

Although Windows 2000 introduced built-in disk quotas to the Windows operating system, WMI-based management of disk quotas is included for the first time in Windows Server 2003. A new class, *Win32_DiskQuota*, represents an individual disk quota entry. Listing 13-11 lists all the quotas from a file server named *FILES1*.

Listing 13-11 List Quota Entries

```
Set objWMIService = GetObject("winmgmts:" _
    & "{impersonationLevel=impersonate}!\\FILES1\root\cimv2")

Set colDiskQuotas = objWMIService.ExecQuery( _
 "Select * from Win32_DiskQuota")

For each objQuota in colDiskQuotas
    Wscript.Echo "Disk Space Used: " & objQuota.DiskSpaceUsed
    Wscript.Echo "          Limit: " & objQuota.Limit
    Wscript.Echo "   Quota Volume: " & objQuota.QuotaVolume
    Wscript.Echo "         Status: " & objQuota.Status
    Wscript.Echo "           User: " & objQuota.User
    Wscript.Echo "  Warning Limit: " & objQuota.WarningLimit
    WScript.Echo "-------------------------------------------"
Next
```

The *Win32_DiskQuota* class supports several properties that make it easy to see current quota entries. You might find, however, that the *User* property takes a bit of getting used to. It's actually a reference to a *Win32_Account* class instance, so you'll have to work with that class to obtain user property information. Similarly, the *QuotaVolume* property is a reference to an instance of the *Win32_LogicalDisk* class. For example, consider this alternate query that retrieves the quota entry for a particular user on a volume.

```
Set objQuota = objWMIService.Get _
  ("Win32_DiskQuota.QuotaVolume= " & _
  "'Win32_LogicalDisk.DeviceID=""C:""'," & _
  "User='Win32_Account.Domain=""company"",Name=""donj""'")
```

Here, the WMI service's *Get* method, rather than the *ExecQuery* method, is used to retrieve a class instance. Specifically, the instance for the user *donj*, on the server's *C* volume, is being retrieved.

After you retrieve an instance of the class, you can make modifications to it. Most likely, you'll want to modify the *Limit* property.

```
objQuota.Limit = 10000
objQuota.Put_
```

This modifies the limit to 10,000KB, or 10MB.

A second class, *Win32_QuotaSetting*, provides access to the quota configuration settings for an entire server. This class has several properties; Listing 13-12 displays them all.

Listing 13-12 List Quota Settings

```
Set objWMIService = GetObject("winmgmts://FILES1/root/cimv2")
Set colItems = objWMIService.ExecQuery("Select * from Win32_QuotaSetting",,48)
For Each objItem in colItems
    WScript.Echo "Caption: " & objItem.Caption
    WScript.Echo "DefaultLimit: " & objItem.DefaultLimit
    WScript.Echo "DefaultWarningLimit: " & objItem.DefaultWarningLimit
    WScript.Echo "Description: " & objItem.Description
    WScript.Echo "ExceededNotification: " & objItem.ExceededNotification
    WScript.Echo "SettingID: " & objItem.SettingID
    WScript.Echo "State: " & objItem.State
    WScript.Echo "VolumePath: " & objItem.VolumePath
    WScript.Echo "WarningExceededNotification: " & _
      objItem.WarningExceededNotification
Next
```

You can modify many of these settings. For example, to change the default quota limit, assuming you've queried a quota setting instance into the variable *objQuotaSetting*, you would enter the following:

```
objQuotaSetting.DefaultLimit = 10000000
objQuotaSetting.Put_
```

> **More Info**   You can find additional sample scripts for managing disk quotas in the TechNet Script Center at
>
> *http://www.microsoft.com/technet/scriptcenter/scripts/storage/quotas/default.mspx*
>
> (This link is included on the companion CD; click *Disk Quotas*.)

Using the DNS Provider

The new DNS provider for WMI included in Windows Server 2003 exposes much of the Windows DNS server functionality to WMI, and therefore to your scripts. Keep in mind that this provider only exists on Windows Server 2003 computers that have the DNS Server software installed and running. Although you can run the scripts in this section on any Windows computer, they'll need to target a server that has the DNS software.

> **Note**   A version of this provider was released for Windows 2000 Server. You'll find it in the Windows 2000 Server Resource Kit.

The provider exposes two distinct categories of WMI classes: one for DNS record management, and the other for DNS server management. As an example of the first category, Listing 13-13 on the next page shows how to clear a DNS server's name resolution cache by using the *MicrosoftDNS_Cache* class.

Listing 13-13 Clear DNS Server Cache

```
Set objWMIService = GetObject("winmgmts:" _
 & "{impersonationLevel=impersonate}!\\DNS1" & _
 "\root\MicrosoftDNS")
Set colItems = objWMIService.ExecQuery("Select * From MicrosoftDNS_Cache")
For Each objItem in colItems
    objItem.ClearCache()
Next
```

The most notable feature of this script is that it isn't querying the commonly used *root\cimv2* WMI namespace. Instead, the DNS provider is accessible through a new namespace, *root\MicrosoftDNS*. Also notice that the class names, unlike most of those in *root\cimv2*, don't start with *Win32_*. Listing 13-13 is a short, simple script, but it still offers the flexibility of most WMI scripts. For example, Listing 13-14 repurposes the script to run against several DNS servers whose names are listed in a text file, C:\Dnsservers.txt.

Listing 13-14 Clear Multiple DNS Servers' Caches

```
Set objFSO = CreateObject("Scripting.FileSystemObject")
Set objTS = objFSO.OpenTextFile("c:\dnsservers.txt")
Do Until objTS.AtEndOfStream
    strComputer = objTS.ReadLine
    Set objWMIService = GetObject("winmgmts:" _
     & "{impersonationLevel=impersonate}!\\" & strComputer & _
     "\root\MicrosoftDNS")
    Set colItems = objWMIService.ExecQuery( _
     "Select * From MicrosoftDNS_Cache")
    For Each objItem in colItems
        objItem.ClearCache()
    Next
Loop
objTS.Close
```

The following classes provide other server-management capabilities.

- *MicrosoftDNS_Zone*   This class represents a DNS zone. You can use it to age records, pause the zone, change the zone type, and so forth.

- *MicrosoftDNS_Server*   This class represents the server itself. You can use it to start record scavenging, start and stop the DNS Server service, and access server configuration properties. Listing 13-15 lists all the properties of the class.

- *MicrosoftDNS_Domain*   This class provides access to a DNS domain's configuration settings.

- *MicrosoftDNS_RootHints*   This class provides access to a server's root hints.

- *MicrosoftDNS_Statistic*   This class provides access to a variety of performance statistics.

Listing 13-15 List DNS Server Properties

```
strComputer = "."
Set objWMIService = GetObject("winmgmts:" _
    & "{impersonationLevel=impersonate}!\\" & strComputer & _
        "\root\MicrosoftDNS")

Set colItems = objWMIService.ExecQuery("Select * from MicrosoftDNS_Server")

For Each objItem in colItems
    Wscript.Echo "Name: " & objItem.Name
    Wscript.Echo "Address Answer Limit: " & objItem.AddressAnswerLimit
    Wscript.Echo "Allow Update: " & objItem.AllowUpdate
    Wscript.Echo "Autocache Update: " & objItem.AutoCacheUpdate
    Wscript.Echo "Autoconfig File Zones: " & objItem.AutoConfigFileZones
    Wscript.Echo "Bind Secondaries: " & objItem.BindSecondaries
    Wscript.Echo "Boot Method: " & objItem.BootMethod
    Wscript.Echo "Default Aging State: " & objItem.DefaultAgingState
    Wscript.Echo "Default No-Refresh Interval: " & _
        objItem.DefaultNoRefreshInterval
    Wscript.Echo "Default Refresh Interval: " & objItem.DefaultRefreshInterval
    Wscript.Echo "Disable AutoReverse Zones: " & _
        objItem.DisableAutoReverseZones
    Wscript.Echo "Disjoint Nets: " & objItem.DisjointNets
    Wscript.Echo "Directory Service Available: " & objItem.DsAvailable
    Wscript.Echo "Directory Service Polling Interval: " & _
        objItem.DsPollingInterval
    Wscript.Echo "Directory Service Tombstone Interval: " & _
        objItem.DsTombstoneInterval
    Wscript.Echo "EDNS Cache Timeout: " & objItem.EDnsCacheTimeout
    Wscript.Echo "Enable Directory Partitions: " & _
        objItem.EnableDirectoryPartitions
    Wscript.Echo "Enable DNSSec: " & objItem.EnableDnsSec
    Wscript.Echo "Enable EDNS Probes: " & objItem.EnableEDnsProbes
    Wscript.Echo "Event Log Level: " & objItem.EventLogLevel
    Wscript.Echo "Forward Delegations: " & objItem.ForwardDelegations
    If Not IsNull(objItem.Forwarders) Then
        strForwarders = Join(objItem.Forwarders, ",")
        Wscript.Echo "Forwarders: " & strForwarders
    Else
        Wscript.Echo "Forwarders:"
    End If
    Wscript.Echo "Forwarding Timeout: " & objItem.ForwardingTimeout
    Wscript.Echo "Is Slave: " & objItem.IsSlave
    If Not IsNull(objItem.ListenAddresses) Then
        strListenAddresses = Join(objItem.ListenAddresses, ",")
        Wscript.Echo "Listen Addresses: " & strListenAddresses
    Else
        Wscript.Echo "Listen Addresses:"
    End If
    Wscript.Echo "Local Net Priority: " & objItem.LocalNetPriority
    Wscript.Echo "Logfile Maximum Size: " & objItem.LogFileMaxSize
    Wscript.Echo "Logfile Path: " & objItem.LogFilePath
    Wscript.Echo "Log Level: " & objItem.LogLevel
    Wscript.Echo "Loose Wildcarding: " & objItem.LooseWildcarding
    Wscript.Echo "Maximum Cache Time-to-Live: " & objItem.MaxCacheTTL
    Wscript.Echo "Maximum Negative Cache Time-to-Live: " & _
        objItem.MaxNegativeCacheTTL
```

```
    Wscript.Echo "Name Check Flag: " & objItem.NameCheckFlag
    Wscript.Echo "No Recursion: " & objItem.NoRecursion
    Wscript.Echo "Recursion Retry: " & objItem.RecursionRetry
    Wscript.Echo "Recursion Timeout: " & objItem.RecursionTimeout
    Wscript.Echo "RoundRobin: " & objItem.RoundRobin
    Wscript.Echo "Rpc Protocol: " & objItem.RpcProtocol
    Wscript.Echo "Scavenging Interval: " & objItem.ScavengingInterval
    Wscript.Echo "Secure Responses: " & objItem.SecureResponses
    Wscript.Echo "Send Port: " & objItem.SendPort
    If Not IsNull(objItem.ServerAddresses) Then
        strServerAddress = Join(objItem.ServerAddresses, ",")
        Wscript.Echo "Server Addresses: " & strServerAddress
    Else
        Wscript.Echo "Server Addresses:"
    End If
    Wscript.Echo "Started: " & objItem.Started
    Wscript.Echo "Start Mode: " & objItem.StartMode
    Wscript.Echo "Strict File Parsing: " & objItem.StrictFileParsing
    Wscript.Echo "Update Options: " & objItem.UpdateOptions
    Wscript.Echo "Version: " & objItem.Version
    Wscript.Echo "Write Authority NS: " & objItem.WriteAuthorityNS
    Wscript.Echo "Xfr Connect Timeout: " & objItem.XfrConnectTimeout
Next
```

> **Tip**   Listing 13-15 was generated by a WMI code wizard like those found in Scriptomatic v2.0 and SAPIEN PrimalScript. You can see how useful these wizards are for quickly generating scripts that list all the properties of a given class, including array-style properties such as the *Forwarders* property. Note that this script, as written, must be run on a server that has the DNS server software installed.

Additionally, a huge list of classes provides access to DNS record management. Essentially, one class exists for each type of record that the DNS server can contain: *A*, *MX*, *CNAME*, *TXT*, *NS*, *SRV*, and so forth. Listing 13-16 shows how to list all the *A* records from the server. (Here again, WMI code wizards save a great deal of time by quickly generating simple scripts like this.)

Listing 13-16 List All *A* Records

```
Set objWMIService = GetObject("winmgmts:" _
 & "{impersonationLevel=impersonate}!\\DNS1" & _
  "\root\MicrosoftDNS")
Set colItems = objWMIService.ExecQuery("Select * from MicrosoftDNS_AType")
For Each objItem in colItems
    Wscript.Echo "IP Address: " & objItem.IPAddress
    Wscript.Echo "Owner Name: " & objItem.OwnerName
    Wscript.Echo "Container Name: " & objItem.ContainerName
    Wscript.Echo "DNS Server Name: " & objItem.DnsServerName
    Wscript.Echo "Domain Name: " & objItem.DomainName
    Wscript.Echo "Record Class: " & objItem.RecordClass
    Wscript.Echo "Record Data: " & objItem.RecordData
    Wscript.Echo "Text Representation: " & objItem.TextRepresentation
    Wscript.Echo "Time-to-Live: " & objItem.TTL
    Wscript.Echo
Next
```

Notice that the WMI class name is *MicrosoftDNS_AType*. You can easily figure out the class name for other record types based on that pattern. For example, *CNAME* records are exposed through the *MicrosoftDNS_CNAMEType* class. As shown in Listing 13-17, working with a different class doesn't require many changes to a script.

Listing 13-17 List All *CNAME* Records

```
Set objWMIService = GetObject("winmgmts:" _
 & "{impersonationLevel=impersonate}!\\DNS1" & _
 "\root\MicrosoftDNS")
Set colItems = objWMIService.ExecQuery("Select * from MicrosoftDNS_CNAMEType")
For Each objItem in colItems
    Wscript.Echo "Owner Name: " & objItem.OwnerName
    Wscript.Echo "Primary Name: " & objItem.PrimaryName
    Wscript.Echo "Container Name: " & objItem.ContainerName
    Wscript.Echo "DNS Server Name: " & objItem.DnsServerName
    Wscript.Echo "Domain Name: " & objItem.DomainName
    Wscript.Echo "Record Class: " & objItem.RecordClass
    Wscript.Echo "Record Data: " & objItem.RecordData
    Wscript.Echo "Text Representation: " & objItem.TextRepresentation
    Wscript.Echo "Time-to-Live: " & objItem.TTL
    Wscript.Echo
Next
```

Notice the slight change in properties between *A* and *CNAME*. Because those two record types are so similar, their listing of properties is equally similar. Records like *MX*, however (accessible through the *MicrosoftDNS_MXType* class), have much different properties, corresponding with the different properties you find in an *MX* record. These WMI classes are good for listing records and creating new records. Scripting the creation of new static records is an excellent way to ensure that they're created consistently across multiple servers, and to automate the tedious process of creating multiple new records. Listing 13-18 is an example of using the *MicrosoftDNS_MXType* class to create a new record.

Listing 13-18 Create an *MX* Record

```
strDNSServer = "dns1.company.com"
strContainer = "company.com"
strOwner = "mail1.company.com"
intRecordClass = 1
intTTL = 600
intPreference = 0
strMailExchanger = "mail1.company.com"

Set objWMIService = GetObject("winmgmts:" _
 & "{impersonationLevel=impersonate}!\\DNS1" & _
 "\root\MicrosoftDNS")

Set objItem = objWMIService.Get("MicrosoftDNS_MXType")
errResult = objItem.CreateInstanceFromPropertyData _
 (strDNSServer, strContainer, strOwner, intRecordClass, intTTL, _
 intPreference, strMailExchanger)
```

> **Note**   You will need to modify this and other DNS-related examples to include appropriate values. For example, if your domain isn't company.com, this script won't work, because mail1.company.com wouldn't be valid for your domain.

Here, string variables are used to set up the properties for the new record. Then the DNS provider itself is queried, rather than a particular class.

```
Set objWMIService = GetObject("winmgmts:" _
 & "{impersonationLevel=impersonate}!\\DNS1" & _
 "\root\MicrosoftDNS")
```

Next, the script asks the DNS provider to return the desired record type. No specific instance is being retrieved here; instead, the provider is returning what's referred to as the *class proto-type,* which is essentially just a description of the class.

```
Set objItem = objWMIService.Get("MicrosoftDNS_MXType")
```

With that class description available, the script can create a new instance—that is, a new record—by using the class' own *CreateInstanceFromPropertyData* method. The method requires that the script provide values for all the class' properties.

```
errResult = objItem.CreateInstanceFromPropertyData _
 (strDNSServer, strContainer, strOwner, intRecordClass, intTTL, _
 intPreference, strMailExchanger)
```

This technique can be used to create a new instance of any DNS record class. Listing 13-19, for example, uses the technique to create a new *TXT* record, populated with a Sender Policy Framework (SPF) description.

Listing 13-19 Create a *TXT* Record

```
strDNSServer = "dns1.company.com"
strContainer = "company.com"
strOwner = "dns1.company.com"
intRecordClass = 1
intTTL = 600
strText = "v=spf1 a ~all"

Set objWMIService = GetObject("winmgmts:" _
 & "{impersonationLevel=impersonate}!\\DNS1" & _
 "\root\MicrosoftDNS")

Set objItem = objWMIService.Get("MicrosoftDNS_TXTType")
errResult = objItem.CreateInstanceFromPropertyData _
 (strDNSServer, strContainer, strOwner, intRecordClass, intTTL, strText)
```

Again, the new instance's property values are assigned to variables. The script connects to the DNS provider and asks for the class prototype for the *MicrosoftDNS_TXTType* class. The script uses that information to create a new instance of the class, passing in the variables to populate the new instance's properties.

More Info   Additional DNS record management sample scripts can be found at

http://www.microsoft.com/technet/scriptcenter/scripts/network/dns/records/default.mspx

(This link is included on the companion CD; click *DNS Records*.) Scripts for managing the DNS Server itself can be found at

http://www.microsoft.com/technet/scriptcenter/scripts/network/dns/manage/default.mspx

(This link is included on the companion CD; click *DNS Server Management Tasks*.)

Using Active Directory Replication and Trusts

Windows Server 2003 domain controllers expose a new set of classes for managing Active Directory. Like the DNS classes, these classes are installed into their own name-space, *root\MicrosoftActiveDirectory*. From an administrative viewpoint, some of the most useful classes relate to Active Directory replication. For example, Listing 13-20 uses the *MSAD_ReplPendingOp* class, which lists pending replication operations, to display the number of replication jobs pending on a given domain controller.

Listing 13-20 List Pending Replication Jobs

```
strComputer = "DC1"
Set objWMIService = GetObject("winmgmts:" _
 & "{impersonationLevel=impersonate}!\\" & _
 strComputer & "\root\MicrosoftActiveDirectory")

Set colReplicationOperations = objWMIService.ExecQuery _
 ("Select * from MSAD_ReplPendingOp")

If colReplicationOperations.Count = 0 Then
    WScript.Echo "There are no replication jobs pending."
Else
    Dim intCount
    For each objReplicationJob in colReplicationOperations
        intCount = intCount + 1
    Next
    WScript.Echo "There are " & intCount & " replication" & _
    " job(s) pending."
End If
```

> **Tip**   At the beginning of this chapter, we provided two wrappers designed to target multiple computers. If you had a text file that listed the names of all domain controllers in your domain, and then inserted Listing 13-20 into the wrapper that reads names from a text file (Listing 13-1), you'd have a tool that showed pending replication for every domain controller in your environment. That would be a handy tool for various troubleshooting tasks or for routine monitoring.

Each domain controller also includes a class named *MSAD_DomainController*, which represents the domain controller and provides access to various pieces of status information. Listing 13-21 shows how to query this class, and displays several of its properties.

Listing 13-21 Display Domain Controller Properties

```
strComputer = "DC"
Set objWMIService = GetObject("winmgmts:" _
 & "{impersonationLevel=impersonate}!\\" & _
 strComputer & "\root\MicrosoftActiveDirectory")

Set colDC = objWMIService.ExecQuery _
 ("Select * from MSAD_DomainController")

For Each objDC In colDC
    WScript.Echo "Common name: " & objDC.CommonName
    WScript.Echo "Is a GC: " & objDC.IsGC
    WScript.Echo "Next RID pool available?: " & _
     objDC.IsNextRIDPoolAvailable
    WScript.Echo "In DNS?: " & objDC.IsRegisteredInDNS
    WScript.Echo "Sysvol ready?: " & objDC.IsSysVolReady
    WScript.Echo "% RIDs left: " & objDC.PercentOfRIDsLeft
    WScript.Echo "Site: " & objDC.SiteName
    WScript.Echo "Oldest add: " & objDC.TimeOfOldestReplAdd
    WScript.Echo "Oldest delete: " & objDC.TimeOfOldestReplDel
    WScript.Echo "Oldest mod: " & objDC.TimeOfOldestReplMod
    WScript.Echo "Oldest sync: " & objDC.TimeOfOldestReplSync
Next
```

This script could also be a useful tool for quickly displaying vital statistics for the domain controllers in your environment. Other classes include *MSAD_ReplNeighbor*, which provides access to all of a domain controller's replication neighbors, as well as exposing information about the last synchronization and the number of synchronization failures.

There are also WMI classes that work with domain trust relationships. For example, the *Microsoft_LocalDomainInfo* class (also in the *root\MicrosoftActiveDirectory* namespace) provides trust-related information about the local domain (that is, the domain to which the queried domain controller belongs). Listing 13-22 illustrates this class and its properties.

Listing 13-22 List Domain Properties

```
Set objWMIService = GetObject("winmgmts:" _
 & "{impersonationLevel=impersonate}!\\" & _
 "DC1\root\MicrosoftActiveDirectory")

Set colDomainInfo = objWMIService.ExecQuery _
 ("Select * from Microsoft_LocalDomainInfo")

For each objDomain in colDomainInfo
    Wscript.Echo " DNS name: " & objDomain.DNSName
    Wscript.Echo "Flat name: " & objDomain.FlatName
    Wscript.Echo "      SID: " & objDomain.SID
    Wscript.Echo "Tree name: " & objDomain.TreeName
    Wscript.Echo "  DC name: " & objDomain.DCName
Next
```

Somewhat more interesting—and useful—is the *Microsoft_DomainTrustStatus* class, which provides information about all trust relationships within the domain. The script in Listing 13-23 is an excellent tool for getting a quick snapshot of the domain's trusts and their current status.

Listing 13-23 List Trusts Status

```
Set objWMIService = GetObject("winmgmts:" _
 & "{impersonationLevel=impersonate}!\\" & _
 "DC1\root\MicrosoftActiveDirectory")

Set colTrustList = objWMIService.ExecQuery _
 ("Select * from Microsoft_DomainTrustStatus")

For each objTrust in colTrustList
    Wscript.Echo "  Trusted domain: " & objTrust.TrustedDomain
    Wscript.Echo " Trust direction: " & objTrust.TrustDirection
    Wscript.Echo "      Trust type: " & objTrust.TrustType
    Wscript.Echo "Trust attributes: " & objTrust.TrustAttributes
    Wscript.Echo " Trusted DC name: " & objTrust.TrustedDCName
    Wscript.Echo "    Trust status: " & objTrust.TrustStatus
    Wscript.Echo "    Trust is OK: " & objTrust.TrustIsOK
    WScript.Echo "-------------------------------------------"
Next
```

As with many other WMI classes, you can modify instance properties to reconfigure Active Directory. For example, a class named *Microsoft_TrustProvider* exposes configuration information for the portion of Active Directory that manages domain trusts. By modifying its properties, you can change the way this portion of Active Directory behaves. Listing 13-24, starting on the next page, shows how to change the trust provider's *TrustListLifetime*, *TrustStatusLifetime*, and *TrustCheckLevel* properties.

> **Caution** Modifying the way the trust provider works can create problems in your domain if you're not careful. Make sure you know the ramifications of changing these properties before doing so.

Listing 13-24 Modify the Trust Provider

```
Set objWMIService = GetObject("winmgmts:" _
 & "{impersonationLevel=impersonate}!\\" & _
 "DC1\root\MicrosoftActiveDirectory")

Set colTrustList = objWMIService.ExecQuery _
 ("Select * from Microsoft_TrustProvider")

For Each objTrust in colTrustList
    objTrust.TrustListLifetime = 25
    objTrust.TrustStatusLifetime = 10
    objTrust.TrustCheckLevel = 1
    objTrust.Put_
Next
```

Note that the modifications here follow a pattern that should be familiar to you: new values are assigned to the properties, and the *Put* method is called to save the changes.

> **More Info** You'll find more Active Directory trust and replication sample scripts at
>
> *http://www.microsoft.com/technet/scriptcenter/scripts/ad/monitor/default.mspx*
>
> (This link is included on the companion CD; click *AD Trust and Replication*.)

Using Internet Information Services 6.0

Internet Information Services (IIS) 6.0 exposes nearly all its administrative information and capabilities through WMI, by using classes in a new *root\MicrosoftIISv2* namespace. (Note that the *v2* in the name refers to the namespace's version, not the IIS version.) Working with this namespace is distinctly different from working with other WMI namespaces, so you need to understand a bit about how IIS' XML configuration metabase is built. The metabase consists of a hierarchy, at the top of which is the *IIsComputer* class. Below it are services for Web, FTP, NNTP, and so forth. Of course, IIS supports multiple Web sites per server, so the Web service can include multiple child sites. This hierarchy is typically represented in a path format not unlike a file path. For example, *W3SVC/1/ROOT* refers to the Web service (W3SVC), the first child site (typically the default Web site), and then the root virtual directory of that site.

The IIS namespace is divided into two sets of classes. One set of classes provides access to read-only properties, and the other set provides access to read/write properties. For example, a virtual directory—the *IisWebVirtualDir* class—consists of read-only properties, and its companion class—*IisWebVirtualDirSettings*—contains properties that can be read and written (changed). Listing 13-25 shows how a particular virtual directory can be queried and all its properties displayed.

Listing 13-25 List IIS Virtual Directory Properties

```
On Error Resume Next
set oProvider = GetObject("winmgmts://localhost/root/MicrosoftIISv2")
set oVirtualDir = oProvider.get("IIsWebVirtualDir='W3SVC/1/ROOT'")
set oVirtualDirSetting = oProvider.get("IIsWebVirtualDirSetting='W3SVC/1/ROOT'")

WScript.Echo "Read only properties of W3SVC/1/Root:"
For Each Property in oVirtualDir.Properties_
  WScript.Echo Property.Name & " = " & Property.Value
Next
WScript.Echo
WScript.Echo "Read/Write properties of W3SVC/1/Root:"
For Each Property in oVirtualDirSetting.Properties_
  WScript.Echo Property.Name & " = " & Property.Value
Next
```

Let's quickly walk through how this works. The script starts by connecting to the *MicrosoftIISv2* namespace. Notice that it doesn't query a particular class; instead, it asks the namespace—through use of the *Get* method—to return a particular class (*IisWebVirtualDir*) that matches a specified path.

```
On Error Resume Next
set oProvider = GetObject("winmgmts://localhost/root/MicrosoftIISv2")
set oVirtualDir = oProvider.get("IIsWebVirtualDir='W3SVC/1/ROOT'")
set oVirtualDirSetting = oProvider.get("IIsWebVirtualDirSetting='W3SVC/1/ROOT'")
```

The script then enumerates through the class' properties collection, displaying each property's name and value.

```
WScript.Echo "Read only properties of W3SVC/1/Root:"
For Each Property in oVirtualDir.Properties_
  WScript.Echo Property.Name & " = " & Property.Value
Next
```

The same technique is used to display the read/write settings from the companion *IisWebVirtualDirSettings* class.

```
WScript.Echo "Read/Write properties of W3SVC/1/Root:"
For Each Property in oVirtualDirSetting.Properties_
  WScript.Echo Property.Name & " = " & Property.Value
Next
```

The IIS WMI namespace is often used to consistently configure IIS servers. For example, manually creating a new Web site in a Web farm of 20 servers can be boring and error-prone. Using a script is faster and includes far less possibility of typos and other errors. Listing

13-26 creates a new Web site on a single computer. You could add this into a wrapper script to target multiple computers.

Listing 13-26 Create a New Web Site

```
set oLocator = CreateObject("WbemScripting.SWbemLocator")
set oProvider = oLocator.ConnectServer("Server2", "root/MicrosoftIISv2")
set oService = oProvider.Get("IIsWebService='W3SVC'")

oBindings = Array(0)
Set oBindings(0) = oProvider.Get("ServerBinding").SpawnInstance_()
oBindings(0).IP = ""
oBindings(0).Port = "8383"
oBindings(0).Hostname = ""

Dim sSiteObjectPath
sSiteObjectPath = oService.CreateNewSite("NewWebSite", oBindings, "C:\Inetpub\wwwroot")
If Err Then
WScript.Echo "*** Error Creating Site: " & Hex(Err.Number) & _
  ": " & Err.Description & " ***"
WScript.Quit(1)
End If

Set oPath = CreateObject("WbemScripting.SWbemObjectPath")
oPath.Path = sSiteObjectPath
sSitePath = oPath.Keys.Item("")

Set oVirtualDir = oProvider.Get("IIsWebVirtualDirSetting='" & _
  sSitePath & "/ROOT'")
oVirtualDir.AuthFlags = 5 ' AuthNTLM + AuthAnonymous
oVirtualDir.EnableDefaultDoc = True
oVirtualDir.DirBrowseFlags = &H4000003E ' date, time, size, _
  extension, longdate
oVirtualDir.AccessFlags = 513 ' read, script
oVirtualDir.AppFriendlyName = "Root Application"

oVirtualDir.Put_()

Set oServer = oProvider.Get(sSiteObjectPath)
oServer.Start

WScript.Echo "Complete"
```

Again, we'll walk through what this script is doing. It starts by connecting to the namespace, and retrieving the *IIsWebService* class.

```
set oLocator = CreateObject("WbemScripting.SWbemLocator")
set oProvider = oLocator.ConnectServer("Server2", "root/MicrosoftIISv2")
set oService = oProvider.Get("IIsWebService='W3SVC'")
```

The script then sets up the *bindings* for a new Web site. A binding is a unique combination of IP address, port, and host header on which this site will be accessed. Here, the script is getting a new instance of the *ServerBinding* class to populate it.

```
oBindings = Array(0)
Set oBindings(0) = oProvider.Get("ServerBinding").SpawnInstance_()
```

The script next sets a blank IP address (meaning all unassigned IP addresses will be used), a blank hostname, and a specific port. This information is represented as an array.

```
oBindings(0).IP = ""
oBindings(0).Port = "8383"
oBindings(0).Hostname = ""
```

Next the script asks the Web service to create a new Web site. It passes the name for the site, the bindings array, and the file system path to the new site's root folder. Error handling ends the script if this operation isn't completed. The variable *sSiteObjectPath* will contain the WMI path to the newly created Web site.

```
Dim sSiteObjectPath
sSiteObjectPath = oService.CreateNewSite("NewWebSite", _
 oBindings, "C:\Inetpub\wwwroot")
If Err Then
WScript.Echo "*** Error Creating Site: " & Hex(Err.Number) & _
 ": " & Err.Description & " ***"
WScript.Quit(1)
End If
```

The script now creates a new WMI object path object, and sets it to equal the newly created site. This is used to retrieve the IIS metabase path of the site.

```
Set oPath = CreateObject("WbemScripting.SWbemObjectPath")
oPath.Path = sSiteObjectPath
sSitePath = oPath.Keys.Item("")
```

Using the new metabase path, the script asks the IIS WMI provider to get the *IisWebVirtual-DirSetting* class of the new site. Specifically, it retrieves the site's roto folder. Remember that this class contains writable properties, so we can configure the site's properties.

```
Set oVirtualDir = oProvider.Get("IIsWebVirtualDirSetting='" & _
 sSitePath & "/ROOT'")
```

A number of properties are set, including authentication level, default document, directory browsing flags, access flags, and the site's application name. The *Put* method saves the changes.

```
oVirtualDir.AuthFlags = 5 ' AuthNTLM + AuthAnonymous
oVirtualDir.EnableDefaultDoc = True
oVirtualDir.DirBrowseFlags = &H4000003E ' date, time, size, _
 extension, longdate
oVirtualDir.AccessFlags = 513 ' read, script
oVirtualDir.AppFriendlyName = "Root Application"
oVirtualDir.Put_()
```

Finally, the provider is asked to retrieve the newly created and configured Web site so that it can be started.

```
Set oServer = oProvider.Get(sSiteObjectPath)
oServer.Start
WScript.Echo "Complete"
```

It's a lot to do, but when you break it down, the script follows the same process that you'd go through to manually create a new Web site.

Now we will focus on backing up the metabase. The metabase backup functionality has several options; for example, you can include child keys of the backed-up portion of the metabase, or include inherited properties. We usually define these values as named constants to make them easier to use.

```
Const EXPORT_CHILDREN = 0
' Adds properties of child keys to the export file.

Const EXPORT_INHERITED = 1
' Adds inherited properties of the exported keys to the export file.

Const EXPORT_NODE_ONLY = 2
' Does not add subkeys of the specified key to the export file.
```

You can also assign a password to the metabase backup.

```
sPassword = "ExportingPassw0rd"
```

This password will be used to later import the configuration, if you need to do so. You must tell IIS which portion of the metabase you want to export. You'll use a metabase path to do so. For example, here's how to export the custom logging portion of the metabase configuration.

```
sMetabasePath = "/lm/logging/custom logging"
```

In this example, *lm* is the root name of the IIS computer, which is why it appears at the beginning of the path. Performing the backup is just a matter of connecting to the IIS WMI namespace, retrieving the *IisComputer* instance that represents IIS, and asking IIS to export the selected portion of the metabase.

```
set oLocator = CreateObject("WbemScripting.SWbemLocator")
set oProvider = oLocator.ConnectServer("Server2", "root/MicrosoftIISv2")
Set oComputer = oProvider.get("IIsComputer='LM'")
oComputer.Export sPassword, sFilePath, sMetabasePath, iFlags
```

Listing 13-27 is the entire, completed script.

Listing 13-27 Export IIS Metabase

```
Const EXPORT_CHILDREN = 0
' Adds properties of child keys to the export file.

Const EXPORT_INHERITED = 1
' Adds inherited properties of the exported keys to the export file.

Const EXPORT_NODE_ONLY = 2
' Does not add subkeys of the specified key to the export file.

Dim sPassword, sFilePath, sMetabasePath, iFlags
sPassword = "ExportingPassw0rd"
' Use this password to import the configuration.

sFilePath = "C:\exported.xml"

sMetabasePath = "/lm/logging/custom logging"
' As represented in the metabase.xml file.

iFlags = EXPORT_NODE_ONLY OR EXPORT_INHERITED

set oLocator = CreateObject("WbemScripting.SWbemLocator")
set oProvider = oLocator.ConnectServer("Server2", "root/MicrosoftIISv2")
Set oComputer = oProvider.get("IIsComputer='LM'")

oComputer.Export sPassword, sFilePath, sMetabasePath, iFlags

WScript.Echo "Exported the node at " & sMetabasePath & " to " & sFilePath
```

Imagine being able to run a script like this on a regular basis—perhaps as a scheduled task—to regularly save portions of the IIS metabase for use in a disaster recovery scenario. That's just one use for a script like this, and it's a good illustration of how scripting can make IIS easier to manage.

Of course, you can do plenty of scripted IIS management without writing a line of VBScript code. That's because Windows Server 2003 includes a handful of command-line utilities, such as *iisweb*, *iisftp*, and so forth, which can be used to automate the configuration of IIS. (These utilities are, in fact, written in VBScript, illustrating the power of the language.) As a bonus, we offer Listing 13-28 on the next page. This script creates a text file containing the names of IIS servers, inserts an IIS command-line string, and executes that command against each IIS server listed in the file. This provides mass administration of Web farms without having to learn any VBScript whatsoever.

Listing 13-28 Create Multi-IIS Administration Template

```
Dim sCommand
sCommand = "INSERT IIS COMMAND HERE"

Dim sFile
sFile = "c:\ListOfIISservers.txt"

Dim oFSO, oTS
Set oFSO = CreateObject("Scripting.FileSystemObject")
On Error Resume Next
Set oTS = oFSO.OpenTextFile(sFile)
If Err <> 0 Then
    WScript.Echo Err.Description
    WScript.Echo "** Couldn't open " & sFile
    WScript.Quit
End If

Dim sServer, oShell, oExex, sCmd
Set oShell = CreateObject("WScript.Shell")
Do Until oTS.AtEndOfStream
    sServer = oTS.ReadLine
    sCmd = Replace(sCommand,"%name%",sServer)
    WScript.Echo "Running against " & sServer
    Set oExec = oShell.Exec(sCmd & " /s " & sServer)
    Do While oExec.Status = 0
        WScript.Sleep 100
    Loop
    WScript.Echo "  Completed with exit code " & oExec.ExitCode
Loop
oTS.Close
WScript.Echo "Completed."
```

Note   This script is excerpted from Don's book *Windows Administrator's Automation Toolkit* (Microsoft Press, 2005), which explains how to automate over 100 common Windows administrative tasks by using readymade tools and scripts.

The trick to using this script is to first test your IIS command-line tasks on a single computer. Then substitute *%name%* for the server name in the command-line text. Paste the command-line text into this script where indicated (on line 2). Then create a text file (C:\ListOfIISservers.txt, by default), and you're ready to go.

More Info   More IIS management scripts, including scripts for IIS 5.0, can be found at

http://www.microsoft.com/technet/scriptcenter/scripts/iis/default.mspx

(This link is included on the companion CD; click *Script Repository-Internet Information Server*.)

Managing Printing

Windows XP and Windows Server 2003 include a new *Win32_Printer* class that provides some great administrative capabilities for managing print queues, print jobs, and so forth. The class exposes methods that can pause and resume a print queue. For example, Listing 13-29 pauses a print queue (or *printer*, to use the correct Windows terminology).

Listing 13-29 Pause a Print Queue

```
Dim strServer, objWMI, strQueue, colPrinters, objPrinter
strServer = "."
strQueue = "HP LaserJet 5"
Set objWMI = GetObject("winmgmts:\\" & _
 strServer & "\root\cimv2")
Set colPrinters = objWMI.ExecQuery _
 ("SELECT * FROM Win32_Printer WHERE Name = '" & _
 strQueue & "'")
For Each objPrinter In colPrinters
    objPrinter.Pause
Next
```

The *WHERE* clause in the WQL query specifies the queue to retrieve. Then, the *colPrinters* collection would contain only one instance of the class to be paused. Of course, if you needed to pause every queue on the targeted server, you'd simply remove the *WHERE* clause. As written, this script affects the local computer, but you could change the *strComputer* variable to target a server. Listing 13-30 resumes a print queue by simply changing the method call from *Pause* to *Resume*.

Listing 13-30 Resume a Print Queue

```
Dim strServer, objWMI, strQueue, colPrinters, objPrinter
strServer = "."
strQueue = "HP LaserJet 5"
Set objWMI = GetObject("winmgmts:\\" & _
 strServer & "\root\cimv2")
Set colPrinters = objWMI.ExecQuery _
 ("SELECT * FROM Win32_Printer WHERE Name = '" & _
 strQueue & "'")
For Each objPrinter In colPrinters
    objPrinter.Resume
Next
```

You can also cancel all jobs in a print queue. This can be especially useful if you're experiencing problems with a server. Listing 13-31 on the next page is similar to Listing 13-29 and 13-30, but it uses a different method call. Additionally, Listing 13-31 has been modified to prompt for a server and queue name, making it a more immediately useful administrative tool.

Listing 13-31 Cancel Jobs in a Print Queue

```
Dim strServer, objWMI, strQueue, colPrinters, objPrinter
strServer = InputBox("Server name to target?")
strQueue = InputBox("Name of queue?",,"HP LaserJet 5")
Set objWMI = GetObject("winmgmts:\\" & _
 strServer & "\root\cimv2")
Set colPrinters = objWMI.ExecQuery _
 ("SELECT * FROM Win32_Printer WHERE Name = '" & _
 strQueue & "'")
For Each objPrinter In colPrinters
    objPrinter.CancelAllJobs
Next
```

Tip   You might ask yourself why you'd need a script to do this when Windows has a perfectly good graphical user interface that does the same thing. (In fact, Windows Server 2003 Release 2 provides an entire printer management console.) Suppose you want your help desk to be able to delete jobs in a print queue, but you don't want to give them direct permissions to do so. You can take a script such as the one in Listing 13-31, package it (by using a script packager available in products like iTripoli AdminScriptEditor or SAPIEN PrimalScript 4 Professional), and include alternate credentials in the package. By running the package (a standalone executable), the help desk can access the script to perform this task without the necessary permissions.

The *Win32_Printer* class also exposes a number of properties that describe the capabilities of a print device. For example, Listing 13-32 displays a print device's resolution, collation capabilities, duplication capabilities, and name.

Listing 13-32 Check Print Device Capabilities

```
Dim strServer, objWMI, strQueue, colPrinters, objPrinter
strServer = "."
strQueue = "HP LaserJet 5"
Set objWMI = GetObject("winmgmts:\\" & _
 strServer & "\root\cimv2")
Set colPrinters = objWMI.ExecQuery _
 ("SELECT * FROM Win32_Printer WHERE Name = '" & _
 strQueue & "'")
For Each objPrinter In colPrinters
 Script.Echo "  Printer: " & objPrinter.Name
 WScript.Echo "Collation: " & objPrinter.Collate
 WScript.Echo "Duplexing: " & objPrinter.Duplex
 WScript.Echo "Horiz res: " & _
  objPrinter.HorizontalResolution
 WScript.Echo " Vert res: " & _
  objPrinter.VerticalResolution
Next
```

You can also redirect a print job from one device to another. To do this, you'll need to know the name of both the original device and the target device. Specify the original queue name and the port where the job should be redirected.

```
strQueue = "HP LaserJet 5"
strNewPort = "IP_192.168.0.25"
```

Then simply set the *PortName* property of the queue, and call the *Put* method to save the change.

```
objPrinter.PortName = strNewPort
objPrinter.Put_
```

Listing 13-33 is the complete script. This is a very useful tool; we've used it to temporarily redirect the queue to a different device of the same make and model, keeping users printing while the original device was offline.

Listing 13-33 Redirect a Print Queue
```
Dim strServer, objWMI, strQueue, colPrinters
Dim objPrinter, strNewPort
strServer = "."
strQueue = "HP LaserJet 5"
strNewPort = "IP_192.168.0.25"
Set objWMI = GetObject("winmgmts:\\" & _
  strServer & "\root\cimv2")
Set colPrinters = objWMI.ExecQuery _
  ("SELECT * FROM Win32_Printer WHERE Name = '" & _
  strQueue & "'")
For Each objPrinter In colPrinters
    objPrinter.PortName = strNewPort
    objPrinter.Put_
Next
```

Windows also has a WMI class named *Win32_TCPIPPrinterPort*, which allows you to create, delete, and modify TCP/IP printer ports on the system. This can be useful for automating the configuration of new print servers in your organization. A third class, *Win32_PrinterDriver*, exposes print device driver functionality and allows you to enumerate installed drivers, install a new driver, and remove unnecessary drivers. This class requires some special handling, so we'll give you a quick example of installing a new driver.

You first make a standard WMI connection to the WMI service on the server where you want to install the driver. Use the *Get* method rather than a query so that you can retrieve the *Win32_PrinterDriver* class itself and not an existing instance.

```
Set objWMIService = GetObject("winmgmts:" _
 & "{impersonationLevel=impersonate}!\\SERVER1\root\cimv2")
Set objDriver = objWMIService.Get("Win32_PrinterDriver")
```

Note that the impersonation directive probably isn't necessary because it's the default, but installing a printer driver is a security-sensitive task, so it's best to make sure. To activate the *LoadDriver* security privilege, add it to the WMI services' *Security* object (specifically, the *Privileges* property).

```
objWMIService.Security_.Privileges.AddAsString _
  "SeLoadDriverPrivilege", True
```

Next, specify a name and version for the driver. This must be the name of a driver that's already physically installed or accessible on the server—the software must be physically present. This is easy for drivers that are included with Windows; for others you'll need to copy them first. This script we're building won't run a setup executable; it expects the software to already be in the proper place.

```
objDriver.Name = "HP LaserJet 5"
objDriver.SupportedPlatform = "Windows NT x86"
objDriver.Version = "3"
```

Also notice that we specified a *SupportedPlatform* property. Keep in mind that Windows supports the installation of multiple drivers for a print device; this allows a print server to host the drivers that will be needed by clients. Here, we specified *Windows NT x86*, which covers most versions of Windows back to Windows NT and Windows 2000. We could also specify *Windows IA64*, for example, to specify the drivers for an Itanium 64-bit system.

We finish by using the *AddPrinterDriver* method. Essentially, we're asking the new instance we've created to add itself to the system. It looks funny, but works great.

```
errResult = objDriver.AddPrinterDriver(objDriver)
```

Listing 13-34 is the complete script.

Listing 13-34 Add a Printer Driver

```
Set objWMIService = GetObject("winmgmts:" _
  & "{impersonationLevel=impersonate}!\\SERVER1\root\cimv2")
Set objDriver = objWMIService.Get("Win32_PrinterDriver")
objWMIService.Security_.Privileges.AddAsString _
  "SeLoadDriverPrivilege", True
objDriver.Name = "HP LaserJet 5"
objDriver.SupportedPlatform = "Windows NT x86"
objDriver.Version = "3"
errResult = objDriver.AddPrinterDriver(objDriver)
```

More Info   Additional client-side print management script samples can be found at

http://www.microsoft.com/technet/scriptcenter/scripts/printing/client/default.mspx

(This link is included on the companion CD; click *Client-Side Printing*.)

Using Windows Update Services

Windows XP Service Pack 2 and Windows Server 2003 Service Pack 1 introduced Automatic Updates software. (A newer version is available from the Microsoft Update Web site at *http:/ /update.microsoft.com*.) This new software corresponds with the Windows Software Update Services (WSUS) server software. Although the server software is primarily built for use by managed code (such as VB.NET and C#), the Automatic Updates client is now exposed through a set of COM objects, which are readily accessible to scripts. The practical upshot of this is that you can write a VBScript that manages the Automatic Updates client on Windows XP and Windows Server 2003 computers.

At its simplest, you might use this new capability as shown in Listing 13-35. This listing simply changes the settings of the Automatic Updates client to install downloaded updates on Tuesdays at 4:00 AM local time.

```
Listing 13-35 Configure Automatic Updates Settings
Set objAutoUpdate = CreateObject("Microsoft.Update.AutoUpdate")
Set objSettings = objAutoUpdate.Settings
objSettings.ScheduledInstallationDay = 3
objSettings.ScheduledInstallationTime = 4
objSettings.Save
```

Of course, because this information is exposed through a COM object and not WMI, performing this task from a remote computer can be complicated. You can specify a remote computer in the *CreateObject* call.

```
Set objAutoUpdate = _
 CreateObject("Microsoft.Update.AutoUpdate", "\\Client2")
```

You might just as easily place this short script into a login script that's assigned to all your computers. That way, you're assured of these settings always being in effect. Of course, the Automatic Updates client can also be configured through Group Policy, so you have a number of ways to deploy these settings and ensure that your client computers are being automatically updated.

Listing 13-36 on the next page shows how the *CreateObject* function can be used to instantiate COM objects on remote computers. This script is designed to connect to every computer in Active Directory and display its Automatic Updates configuration, including notification level, installation date and time, and so forth. (This was built by using the wrapper script at the beginning of this chapter.)

Listing 13-36 Display Automatic Updates Inventory

```
' requires Windows XP Service Pack 2 or later
'connect to the root of AD
Dim rootDSE, domainObject
Set rootDSE=GetObject("LDAP://RootDSE")
domainContainer = rootDSE.Get("defaultNamingContext")
Set oDomain = GetObject("LDAP://" & domainContainer)

'start with the domain root
WorkWithObject(oDomain)

Sub WorkWithObject(oContainer)
 Dim oADObject
 For Each oADObject in oContainer
  Select Case oADObject.Class
   Case "computer"
    'oADObject represents a COMPUTER object;
    'do something with it
    WScript.Echo String(40,"-")
    WScript.Echo oADObject.cn
    On Error Resume Next
    Set objWU = CreateObject("Microsoft.Update.AutoUpdate", _
     "\\" & oADObject.cn)
    If Err <> 0 Then
        WScript.Echo Err.Description
    Else
        Set objSetting = objWU.Settings
        WScript.Echo "Notification: " & objSetting.NotificationLevel
        WScript.Echo "Read-only: " & objSetting.ReadOnly
        WScript.Echo "Required: " & objSetting.Required
        WScript.Echo "Install time: " & _
         objSetting.ScheduledInstallationDay
        WScript.Echo "Install day: " & _
         objSetting.ScheduledInstallationTime
    End If
 Case "organizationalUnit" , "container"
    'oADObject is an OU or container...
    'go through its objects
    WorkWithObject(oADObject)
  End Select
 Next
End Sub
```

Of course, this script isn't terribly efficient, because it can only connect to one computer at a time. Also, the Windows Firewall might keep this script from working at all. To help resolve both problems, we created Listing 13-37. It is designed to be deployed as a login script, bypassing the Windows Firewall by eliminating the need for an incoming remote connection. Also, performance is improved because each computer performs its own inventory, writing the information to a Microsoft Access database located on a file server. (The default location is \\fileserver\share\wuinventory.mdb; you should change that to something appropriate.)

> **On the CD**   We've included an empty Access database named wuinventory.mdb with the proper table and column layouts. You'll find it on the CD along with the script.

Listing 13-37 Display Automatic Updates Database Inventory

```
'assumes Access drivers installed on all clients
'assumes Access database has a table named Updates
'assumes table has columns for Name,Required,ReadOnly,
' Day, and Time. All columns are assumed to be text.

On Error Resume Next
Dim strCN, objWU, objSet, objNet, strComputer
Dim strSQL, objCN

'set connection String
strCN = "Provider=Microsoft.Jet.Oledb.4.0;" & _
 "Data Source=\\fileserver\share\wuinventory.mdb;"

'open WU objects
Set objWU = CreateObject("Microsoft.Update.AutoUpdate")
Set objSet = objWU.Settings
Set objNet = CreateObject("WScript.Network")

'get computer name
strComputer = objNet.ComputerName

'open database
Set objCN = CreateObject("ADODB.Connection")
objCN.Open strCN

'delete existing row
strSQL = "DELETE FROM Updates WHERE Name = '" & _
 strComputer & "'")
objCN.Execute strSQL

'build new row
strSQL = "INSERT INTO Updates (Name,Required,ReadOnly" & _
 ",Day,Time) VALUES("
strSQL = strSQL & "'" & strComputer & "',"
strSQL = strSQL & "'" & objSet.Required & "',"
strSQL = strSQL & "'" & objSet.ReadOnly & "',"
strSQL = strSQL & "'" & objSet.ScheduledInstallationDay & "',"
strSQL = strSQL & "'" & objSet.ScheduledInstallationTime & "')"

'insert new row
objCN.Execute strSQL
objCN.Close
```

The script starts by connecting to the database by using an OLE DB connection string.

```
strCN = "Provider=Microsoft.Jet.Oledb.4.0;" & _
 "Data Source=\\fileserver\share\wuinventory.mdb;"
```

The script then instantiates the Automatic Updates client's COM object and retrieves its settings. It also gets the local computer name from the *WshNetwork* object.

```
Set objWU = CreateObject("Microsoft.Update.AutoUpdate")
Set objSet = objWU.Settings
Set objNet = CreateObject("WScript.Network")
strComputer = objNet.ComputerName
```

The database connection is opened, and any existing rows with the same computer name is deleted. This ensures that each computer will be listed only once in the database.

```
Set objCN = CreateObject("ADODB.Connection")
objCN.Open strCN

strSQL = "DELETE FROM Updates WHERE Name = '" & _
 strComputer & "'")
objCN.Execute strSQL
```

A SQL *INSERT* statement containing the computer name and values from the Automatic Updates settings is placed in a string variable.

```
strSQL = "INSERT INTO Updates (Name,Required,ReadOnly" & _
 ",Day,Time) VALUES("
strSQL = strSQL & "'" & strComputer & "',"
strSQL = strSQL & "'" & objSet.Required & "',"
strSQL = strSQL & "'" & objSet.ReadOnly & "',"
strSQL = strSQL & "'" & objSet.ScheduledInstallationDay & "',"
strSQL = strSQL & "'" & objSet.ScheduledInstallationTime & "')"
```

Finally, the SQL statement is executed to add the computer to the database, and the database connection is closed.

```
objCN.Execute strSQL
objCN.Close
```

A script like this can help "close the loop" on patch management; that is, it can help ensure that the settings are, in fact, configured the way you want on each computer. If you've centrally configured these settings, they should be consistent across your network. You can quickly spot any anomalous settings by opening the Access database and scrolling through the table.

> **More Info**   The TechNet Script Center includes additional Windows Update management scripts at
>
> *http://www.microsoft.com/technet/scriptcenter/scripts/sus/client/default.mspx*
>
> (This link is included on the companion CD; click *Windows Update Client-Side Management*.)

Summary

Windows Server 2003 and Windows XP are the most accessible versions of Windows ever, at least in terms of script-based management. With the techniques you learned in this chapter, you can script numerous administrative tasks that are otherwise tedious or difficult, and make administration easier. To help ensure that future versions of Windows are even more open to script-based management, communicate with your regional Microsoft office and other Microsoft representatives, and let them know that you appreciate the work that went into making Windows XP and Windows Server 2003 more accessible to scripts. Tell them that you look forward to future versions going even further. Hopefully, a future version of this chapter covering scripting in the next version of Windows will be large enough to fill an entire book.

Part IV
Scripting for the Enterprise

Chapter 14
Group Policy Management Scripting

Group Policy management can be a full-time job in most medium to large enterprises. Fortunately, Microsoft Windows Server 2003 includes the Group Policy Management Console (GPMC). The GPMC was a boon to system administrators, and it had the added benefit of a scripting interface. Now Group Policy objects (GPOs) can be managed with VBScript. We'll explore GPMC scripting in this chapter.

Group Policy was one of the primary benefits most enterprises gained by moving to Microsoft Windows 2000. Unfortunately, the management tools for Group Policy were weak. With the arrival of Windows Server 2003, Microsoft introduced a totally new Group Policy Management Console. With it, you can create, back up, copy, move, and generate reports on all GPOs in the enterprise. As a bonus, almost all the functionality is also available through a scripting interface.

Note We're assuming you are already familiar with the Group Policy Management Console and Group Policy in general. This chapter focuses on managing Group Policy by using VBScript.

Introducing Group Policy Management Scripting

First of all, let's get the bad news out of the way. Microsoft does not offer a scripting interface for creating or editing a GPO. You cannot write a script to disable access to the control panel, remove the Run command from the Start menu, or disable registry editing tools. What you *can* do with GPMC scripting is back up and restore GPOs, set GPO permissions, build GPO reports, and get Resultant Set of Policy (RSOP) for users and computers.

When you install the Group Policy Management Console, a Scripts folder is created under %ProgramFiles%\GPMC. Microsoft provides over 30 excellent scripts that you can use immediately to manage Group Policy in your enterprise. These scripts are in WSF format, so they can take arguments like an organizational unit (OU) name at run time. We won't spend any time on these scripts, even though we might cover some of the same core functionality.

> **Note**   The Group Policy Management Console is included with Windows Server 2003, but it can also be freely downloaded from
>
> *http://www.microsoft.com/windowsserver2003/gpmc/default.mspx*
>
> (This link is included on the companion CD; click *Enterprise Management with Group Policy Management Console*.)

Group Policy Management Scripting Requirements

To use the GPMC, you must be running Windows Server 2003 or Microsoft Windows XP and have the Microsoft .NET Framework installed. If you are still running XP SP1, you should install the patch referenced in Knowledge Base article Q326469. The GPMC will not run on Microsoft Windows 2000 Professional or Microsoft Windows 2000 Server. However, you can use the console on an XP desktop to manage Group Policy in a Windows 2000 domain. Of course, you need appropriate credentials either as a domain administrator or through delegation. It is possible to delegate Group Policy management rights.

> **Best Practices**   Install the GPMC on an a secure Windows XP SP2 desktop that is in the same site as the domain controller that holds the PDC Emulator role.

Group Policy Management Console Object Model

The GPMC object model is a bit complex, but fortunately, it is pretty well documented. Figure 14-1 illustrates the object model. There is plenty of information in the Help file as well as MSDN Library. Unfortunately, much of the documentation is aimed at application developers, not administrators hoping to develop VBScript. We won't go over the complete object model, but we will explore the basics.

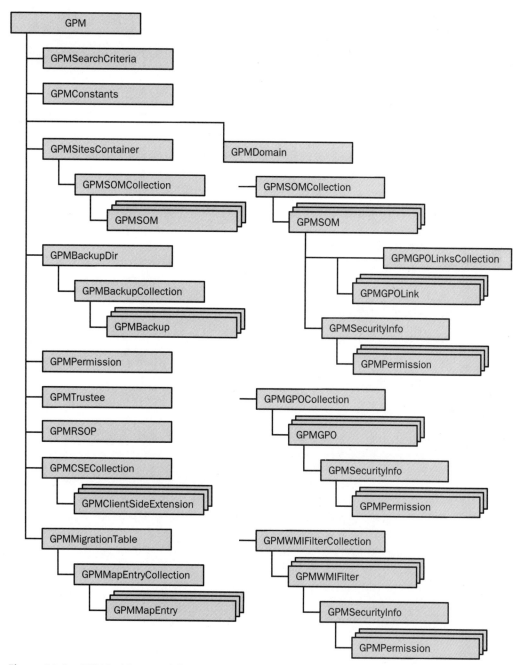

Figure 14-1   GPMC object model

> **More Info**   The GPMC object model is documented in the Help file gpmc.chm, and at
>
> *http://msdn.microsoft.com/library/default.asp?url=/library/en-us/gpmc/gpmc/gpmc_object_model.asp*
>
> (This link is on the companion CD; click *GPMC Object Model*).

You will primarily be working with the *GPM* object, which is instantiated like this.

```
set GPM=CreateObject("GPMGMT.GPM")
```

All other objects are created from the *GPM* object. With this object model, you can do the following:

- Back up, restore, import, and copy GPOs.

- Create and delete GPOs and WMI filters.

- Link GPOs and WMI filters to organizational units, domains, and sites.

- Search for GPOs.

- Report GPO settings.

- Manage GPO permissions and delegations.

- Get Resultant Set of Policy for a GPO.

- Create and modify GPO migration tables.

We'll cover some of the basics that most administrators will want to understand.

Constants

As you can probably judge from the object model, GPMC scripting is a complex topic, especially in regards to security permissions and access control lists. The object model requires numerous constants that define both properties, such as *PermGPOApply*, and methods, such as *get_ProcessSecurity*. Fortunately, you don't have to define every constant in the beginning of your script. The object model includes an object called *GPMConstants*. You will need to instantiate this object at the beginning of your script by using the *GetConstants* method.

```
Set GPM=CreateObject("GPMGMT.GPM")
set gpmConstants=GPM.GetConstants
```

As you work through the sample scripts and read the documentation, you will see where different constant values are required. Having a script editor that shows COM object properties and methods as you code will be invaluable when working with GPMC scripting. Table 14-1 defines the method constants, and Table 14-2 defines the property constants. This information is also available through MSDN and the GPMC documentation.

Table 14-1   GPMC Method Constants

Method Constant	Description
get_DestinationOptionByRelativeName	Retrieves the constant value corresponding to the *GPMDestinationOption* of *opDestinationByRelativeName*
get_DestinationOptionNone	Retrieves the constant value corresponding to the *GPMDestinationOption* of *opDestinationNone*
get_DestinationOptionBySameAsSource	Retrieves the constant value corresponding to the *GPMDestinationOption* of *opDestinationSameAsSource*
get_DestinationOptionSet	Retrieves the constant value corresponding to the *GPMDestinationOption* of *opDestinationSet*
get_EntryTypeComputer	Retrieves the constant value corresponding to the *GPMEntryType* of *typeComputer*
get_EntryTypeGlobalGroup	Retrieves the constant value corresponding to the *GPMEntryType* of *typeGlobalGroup*
get_EntryTypeLocalGroup	Retrieves the constant value corresponding to the *GPMEntryType* of *typeLocalGroup*
get_EntryTypeUniversalGroup	Retrieves the constant value corresponding to the *GPMEntryType* of *typeUniversalGroup*
get_EntryTypeUNCPath	Retrieves the constant value corresponding to the *GPMEntryType* of *typeUNCPath*
get_EntryTypeUnknown	Retrieves the constant value corresponding to the *GPMEntryType* of *typeUnknown*
get_EntryTypeUser	Retrieves the constant value corresponding to the *GPMEntryType* of *typeUser*
get_PermGPOApply	Retrieves the constant value corresponding to the *permGPOApply* permission type
get_PermGPOCustom	Retrieves the constant value corresponding to the *permGPOCustom* permission type
get_PermGPOEdit	Retrieves the constant value corresponding to the *permGPOEdit* permission type
get_PermGPOEditSecurityAndDelete	Retrieves the constant value corresponding to the *permGPOEditSecurityAndDelete* permission type
get_PermGPORead	Retrieves the constant value corresponding to the *permGPORead* permission type
get_PermSOMGPOCreate	Retrieves the constant value corresponding to the *permSOMGPOCreate* permission type

Table 14-1   GPMC Method Constants

Method Constant	Description
get_PermSOMLink	Retrieves the constant value corresponding to the *permSOMLink* permission type
get_PermSOMLogging	Retrieves the constant value corresponding to the *permSOMLogging* permission type
get_PermSOMPlanning	Retrieves the constant value corresponding to the *permSOMPlanning* permission type
get_PermSOMWMICreate	Retrieves the constant value corresponding to the *permSOMWMICreate* permission type
get_PermSOMWMIFullControl	Retrieves the constant value corresponding to the *permSOMWMIFullControl* permission type
get_PermWMIFilterCustom	Retrieves the constant value corresponding to the *permWMIFilterCustom* permission type
get_PermWMIFilterEdit	Retrieves the constant value corresponding to the *permWMIFilterEdit* permission type
get_PermWMIFilterFullControl	Retrieves the constant value corresponding to the *permWMIFilterFullControl* permission type
get_SearchPropertyBackupMostRecent	Retrieves the constant value corresponding to the *backupMostRecent* search property
get_SearchPropertyGPODisplayName	Retrieves the constant value corresponding to the *GPODisplayName* search property
get_SearchPropertyGPODomain	Retrieves the constant value corresponding to the *GPODomain* search property
get_SearchPropertyGPOEffectivePermissions	Retrieves the constant value corresponding to the *GPOEffectivePermissions* search property
get_SearchPropertyGPOID	Retrieves the constant value corresponding to the *GPOID* search property
get_SearchPropertyGPOPermissions	Retrieves the constant value corresponding to the *GPOPermissions* search property
get_SearchPropertyGPOUserExtensions	Retrieves the constant value corresponding to the *GPOUserExtensions* search property
get_SearchPropertyGPOWMIFilter	Retrieves the constant value corresponding to the *GPOWMIFilter* search property
get_SearchPropertySOMLinks	Retrieves the constant value corresponding to the *somLinks* search property
get_SearchOpContains	Retrieves the constant value corresponding to the *opContains* search operator
get_SearchOpEquals	Retrieves the constant value corresponding to the *opEquals* search operator
get_SearchOpNotContains	Retrieves the constant value corresponding to the *opNotContains* search operator
get_SearchOpNotEquals	Retrieves the constant value corresponding to the *opNotEquals* search operator

Table 14-1   GPMC Method Constants

Method Constant	Description
get_SOMDomain	Retrieves the constant value corresponding to the somDomain SOM type
get_SOMOU	Retrieves the constant value corresponding to the somOU SOM type
get_SOMSite	Retrieves the constant value corresponding to the somSite SOM type
get_DoNotValidateDC	Retrieves the value of the DoNotValidateDC property
get_SecurityFlags	Retrieves the value of the SecurityFlags property
get_UseAnyDC	Retrieves the constant value corresponding to the UseAnyDC property
get_DoNotUseW2KDC	Retrieves the constant value corresponding to the DoNotUseW2KDC property
get_UsePDC	Retrieves the constant value corresponding to the UsePDC property
get_SearchhPropertyGPOComputerExtensions	Retrieves the constant value corresponding to the GPOComputerExtensions search property
get_ReportHTML	Retrieves the constant value corresponding to the ReportHTML property
get_ReportXML	Retrieves the constant value corresponding to the ReportXML property
get_RSOPModeUnknown	Retrieves the constant value corresponding to the RSOPModeUnknown property
get_RSOPModePlanning	Retrieves the constant value corresponding to the RSOPModePlanning property
get_RSOPModeLogging	Retrieves the constant value corresponding to the RSOPModeLogging property
get_RSOPLoggingNoComputer	Retrieves the constant value corresponding to the RsopLoggingNoComputer property
get_RSOPLoggingNoUser	Retrieves the constant value corresponding to the RsopLoggingNoUser property
get_RSOPPlanningAssumeSlowLink	Retrieves the constant value corresponding to the RSOP_PLANNING_ASSUME_SLOW_LINK property
get_RSOPPlanningLoopbackOption	Retrieves the constant value corresponding to the RsopPlanningLoopbackOption property
get_RSOPPlanningAssumeUserWQLFilterTrue	Retrieves the constant value corresponding to the RsopPlanningAssumeUserWQLFilterTrue property

Table 14-1   GPMC Method Constants

Method Constant	Description
get_RSOPPlanningAssumeCompWQLFilterTrue	Retrieves the constant value corresponding to the *RsopPlanningAssumeCompWQLFilterTrue* property
get_MigrationTableOnly	Retrieves the constant value corresponding to the *MigrationTableOnly* property
get_ProcessSecurity	Retrieves the constant value corresponding to the *ProcessSecurity* property

Table 14-2   GPMC Property Constants

Property Constant	Description
DestinationOptionByRelativeName	Value corresponding to the *GPMDestinationOption* of *opDestinationByRelativeName*
DestinationOptionNone	Value corresponding to the *GPMDestinationOption* of *opDestinationNone*
DestinationOptionSameAsSource	Value corresponding to the *GPMDestinationOption* of *opDestinationSameAsSource*
DestinationOptionSet	Value corresponding to the *GPMDestinationOption* of *opDestinationSet*
DoNotUseW2KDC	Constant value corresponding to the DoNotUseW2KDC property
DoNotValidateDC	Constant value corresponding to the *DoNotValidateDC* property
EntryTypeComputer	Value corresponding to the *GPMEntryType* of *type-Computer*
EntryTypeGlobalGroup	Value corresponding to the *GPMEntryType* of *type-GlobalGroup*
EntryTypeLocalGroup	Value corresponding to the *GPMEntryType* of *type-LocalGroup*
EntryTypeUNCPath	Value corresponding to the *GPMEntryType* of *type-UNCPath*
EntryTypeUniversalGroup	Value corresponding to the *GPMEntryType* of *type-UniversalGroup*
EntryTypeUnknown	Value corresponding to the *GPMEntryType* of *type-Unknown.*
EntryTypeUser	Value corresponding to the *GPMEntryType* of *typeUser*
MigrationTableOnly	Value corresponding to the *GPM_MIGRATIONTABLE_ONLY* constant
PermGPOApply	Constant value corresponding to the *permGPOApply* permission type
PermGPOCustom	Constant value corresponding to the *permGPOCustom* permission type

Table 14-2   GPMC Property Constants

Property Constant	Description
PermGPOEdit	Constant value corresponding to the *permGPOEdit* permission type
PermGPOEditSecurityAndDelete	Constant value corresponding to the *permGPOEditSecurityAndDelete* permission type
PermGPORead	Constant value corresponding to the *permGPORead* permission type
PermSOMGPOCreate	Constant value corresponding to the *permSOMGPOCreate* permission type
PermSOMLink	Constant value corresponding to the *permSOMLink* permission type
PermSOMLogging	Constant value corresponding to the *permSOMLogging* permission type
PermSOMPlanning	Constant value corresponding to the *permSOMPlanning* permission type
PermSOMWMICreate	Constant value corresponding to the *permSOMWMICreate* permission type
PermSOMWMIFullControl	Constant value corresponding to the *permSOMWMIFullControl* permission type
PermWMIFilterCustom	Constant value corresponding to the *permWMIFilterCustom* permission type
PermWMIFilterEdit	Constant value corresponding to the *permWMIFilterEdit* permission type
PermWMIFilterFullControl	Constant value corresponding to the *permWMIFilterFullControl* permission type
ProcessSecurity	Value corresponding to the *GPM_PROCESS_SECURITY* constant
ReportHTML	Constant value corresponding to the *ReportHTML* property
ReportXML	Constant value corresponding to the *ReportXML* property
RSOPLoggingNoComputer	Value corresponding to the *RSOP_NO_USER* constant
RSOPLoggingNoUser	Value corresponding to the *RSOP_NO_USER* constant
RSOPModeLogging	Constant value corresponding to the *RSOPModeLogging* property
RSOPModePlanning	Constant value corresponding to the *RSOPModePlanning* property
RSOPModeUnknown	Constant value corresponding to the *RSOPModeUnknown* property
RSOPPlanningAssumeCompWQLFilterTrue	Value corresponding to the *RSOP_PLANNING_ASSUME_COMP_WQLFILTER_TRUE* constant
RSOPPlanningAssumeSlowLink	Value corresponding to the *RSOP_PLANNING_ASSUME_SLOW_LINK* constant

Table 14-2   GPMC Property Constants

Property Constant	Description
RSOPPlanningAssumeUserWQLFilterTrue	Value corresponding to the RSOP_PLANNING_ASSUME_USER_WQLFILTER_TRUE constant
RSOPPlanningLoopbackOption	Value corresponding to either the RSOP_PLANNING_ASSUME_LOOPBACK_MERGE constant if vbMerge is VARIANT_TRUE, or the RSOP_PLANNING_ASSUME_LOOPBACK_REPLACE constant if vbMerge is VARIANT_FALSE
SearchOpContains	Constant value corresponding to the opContains search operator
SearchOpEquals	Constant value corresponding to the opEquals search operator
SearchOpNotContains	Constant value corresponding to the opNotContains search operator
SearchOpNotEquals	Constant value corresponding to the opNotEquals search operator
SearchPropertyBackupMostRecent	Constant value corresponding to the backupMost-Recent search property
SearchPropertyGPOComputerExtensions	Constant value corresponding to the GPOComputer-Extensions search property
SearchPropertyGPODisplayName	Constant value corresponding to the GPODisplayName search property
SearchPropertyGPODomain	Constant value corresponding to the GPODomain search property
SearchPropertyGPOEffectivePermissions	Constant value corresponding to the GPOEffective-Permissions search property
SearchPropertyGPOID	Constant value corresponding to the GPOID search property
SearchPropertyGPOPermissions	Constant value corresponding to the GPOPermissions search property
SearchPropertyGPOUserExtensions	Constant value corresponding to the GPOUser-Extensions search property
SearchPropertyGPOWMIFilter	Constant value corresponding to the GPOWMIFilter search property
SearchPropertySOMLinks	Constant value corresponding to the somLinks search property
SecurityFlags	Representation of the portions of the security descriptor to retrieve or set for a GPO. These values are required to call the IGPMGPO::GetSecurityDescriptor and IGPMGPO::SetSecurityDescriptor functions (the GPMGPO.GetSecurityDescriptor and GPMGPO.SetSecurityDescriptor methods).
SOMDomain	Constant value corresponding to the somDomain SOM type

Table 14-2   GPMC Property Constants

Property Constant	Description
SOMOU	Constant value corresponding to the *somOU* SOM type
SOMSite	Constant value corresponding to the *somSite* SOM type
UseAnyDC	Constant value corresponding to the *UseAnyDC* property
UsePDC	Constant value corresponding to the *UsePDC* property

Listing 14-1 demonstrates GPMC constants. This script searches the current domain and lists all the Group Policy objects.

Listing 14-1 List All Group Policy Objects

```
Dim GPM,gpmConstants,gpmDomain
dim collGPOS,gpmSearchCriteria,gpo,gpmResult
dim RootDSE,objDomain

set GPM=CreateObject("GPMGMT.GPM")
set gpmConstants=GPM.GetConstants
strFQDN=GetDomainFQDN

set gpmDomain=GPM.GetDomain(strFQDN,"",gpmConstants.UseAnyDC)

set gpmSearchCriteria=GPM.CreateSearchCriteria
set collGPOS=gpmDomain.SearchGPOs(gpmSearchCriteria)
wscript.Echo "Found " & collGPOS.Count & " group policy objects in " &_
gpmDomain.Domain & "(" & gpmDomain.DomainController & ")"
For Each gpo In collGPOS
    WScript.Echo gpo.Displayname & " [" & gpo.path & "]"
Next

WScript.Quit

'*****************************************************
Function GetDomainFQDN()
  set RootDSE=GetObject("LDAP://RootDSE")
  DomainPath= RootDSE.Get("DefaultNamingContext")
  DomainPath=Replace(DomainPath,"DC=","")
  GetDomainFQDN=Replace(DomainPath,",",".")
End Function
```

The script starts by instantiating the *GPM* and *GPMConstants* objects.

```
set GPM=CreateObject("GPMGMT.GPM")
set gpmConstants=GPM.GetConstants
```

To search the domain, we need to know the fully qualified name of the domain, for example, *company.pri*. We've written a function that takes the domain path from the default naming context and converts it to a fully qualified domain name (FQDN). In other words, the function will convert *DC=company,DC=pri* to *company.pri*.

```
Function GetDomainFQDN()
 set RootDSE=GetObject("LDAP://RootDSE")
 DomainPath= RootDSE.Get("DefaultNamingContext")
 DomainPath=Replace(DomainPath,"DC=","")
 GetDomainFQDN=Replace(DomainPath,",",".")
End Function
```

With this information, we can use the *GetDomain* method to connect to the domain and create a *gpmDomain* object.

```
set gpmDomain=GPM.GetDomain(strFQDN,"",gpmConstants.UseAnyDC)
```

As you can see, the method takes several parameters. The first is the FQDN of the domain, which we got from the function. The second parameter, which is blank in our example, is used to specify a specific domain controller to connect to. Because we want the script to run in any domain, we leave this blank. However, this means we can use the third parameter to specify how we will find a domain controller. This flag is set by a constant. We can use *gpmConstants.UseAnyDC* to reference the *GPM_USE_ANYDC* constant, which we would otherwise have to define. By the way, we could have also used *gpmConstants.UsePDC* to specify a connection to the PDC emulator.

The script next instantiates a *gpmSearchCriteria* object (which we'll cover later in this chapter). We then call the *SearchGPOS* method to instantiate a *GPO* collection object.

```
set gpmSearchCriteria=GPM.CreateSearchCriteria
set collGPOS=gpmDomain.SearchGPOs(gpmSearchCriteria)
```

With this collection object, we can now loop through and display information about the collection members, which will be *GPO* objects from the object model.

```
wscript.Echo "Found " & collGPOS.Count & " group policy objects in " &_
gpmDomain.Domain & "(" & gpmDomain.DomainController & ")"
For Each gpo In collGPOS
    WScript.Echo gpo.Displayname & " [" & gpo.path & "]"
Next
```

When you run the script from a command prompt with CScript, you should see output like this.

```
Found 5 group policy objects in company.pri(DC02.company.pri)
Test Security [cn={20029756-EC91-44FB-B57C-
87A9A5584880},cn=policies,cn=system,DC=matrix,DC=local]
Default Domain Policy [cn={31B2F340-016D-11D2-945F-
00C04FB984F9},cn=policies,cn=system,DC=matrix,DC=local]
New Group Policy Object [cn={4962C921-BCFC-4B22-BF39-
8746D9CD8536},cn=policies,cn=system,DC=matrix,DC=local]
Default Domain Controllers Policy [cn={6AC1786C-016F-11D2-945F-
00C04FB984F9},cn=policies,cn=system,DC=matrix,DC=local]
Desktop Restrictions [cn={B171DED9-C308-45C5-A1B5-
48494C0B6DB5},cn=policies,cn=system,DC=matrix,DC=local]
```

Scope of Management

The other important concept in GPMC scripting is *Scope of Management (SOM)*. A SOM is a site, domain, or OU that has one or more GPOs linked to it. A single GPO can be linked to one or more SOMs. Listing 14-2 expands on the script in Listing 14-1 to find all the SOMs a specific GPO is linked to, and display that information.

Listing 14-2 List All Group Policy Objects and SOM Links

```
Dim GPM,gpmConstants,gpmDomain
dim collGPOS,gpmSearchCriteria,collSOMs
dim RootDSE,objDomain

Set GPM=CreateObject("GPMGMT.GPM")
set gpmConstants=GPM.GetConstants
strFQDN=GetDomainFQDN

set gpmDomain=GPM.GetDomain(strFQDN,"",gpmConstants.UsePDC)
set gpmSearchCriteria=GPM.CreateSearchCriteria
set collGPOS=gpmDomain.SearchGPOs(gpmSearchCriteria)

wscript.Echo "Found " & collGPOS.Count & " group policy objects in " &_
gpmDomain.Domain & "(" & gpmDomain.DomainController & ")"
For Each gpo In collGPOS
    WScript.Echo gpo.Displayname & " [" & gpo.id & "]"
    gpmSearchCriteria.Add gpmConstants.SearchPropertySOMLinks,_
    gpmConstants.SearchOpContains,gpo
    Set collSOMs=gpmDomain.SearchSOMs(gpmSearchCriteria)
    WScript.Echo "Linked to " & collSOMs.Count & " container(s)"
    If collSOMs.Count>0 Then
        For Each gpmSOM In collSOMs
            Select Case gpmSOM.Type
                Case gpmConstants.SOMSite
                    WScript.Echo vbtab & "Site:" & gpmSOM.Name

                Case gpmConstants.SOMDomain
                    WScript.Echo vbTab & "Domain:" & gpmSOM.Name

                Case gpmConstants.SOMOU
                    WScript.Echo vbTab & "OU:" &gpmSOM.Name
            End Select
        Next
    End if

Next

WScript.Quit

'*************************************************
Function GetDomainFQDN()
  set RootDSE=GetObject("LDAP://RootDSE")
  DomainPath= RootDSE.Get("DefaultNamingContext")
  DomainPath=Replace(DomainPath,"DC=","")
  GetDomainFQDN=Replace(DomainPath,",",".")
End Function
```

Because this script is very similar to Listing 14-1, let's focus on what's new. After we get the GPO collection, we can enumerate the collection and get an individual *GPO* object. We're displaying the GPO display name and its GUID.

```
For Each gpo In collGPOS
    WScript.Echo gpo.Displayname & " [" & gpo.id & "]"
```

We will search for SOM links by using the *searchSOMS* method of the *gpmDomain* object. However, this requires search criteria. Although search criteria weren't required to find GPOs, we need to specify criteria to find SOM links by using the *Add* method. When we add search criteria, the format is *Property,Operation,Value*. The first two parameters are specified with a *gpmConstant*.

```
For Each gpo In collGPOS
    WScript.Echo gpo.Displayname & " [" & gpo.id & "]"
    gpmSearchCriteria.Add gpmConstants.SearchPropertySOMLinks,_
    gpmConstants.SearchOpContains,gpo
    Set collSOMs=gpmDomain.SearchSOMS(gpmSearchCriteria)
```

This snippet adds criteria to search for SOM links by using a *contains* operation. We create a collection of SOMs with the *searchSOMS* method of the *gpmDomain* object. We can now enumerate the collection of SOMs.

```
WScript.Echo "Linked to " & collSOMs.Count & " container(s)"
    If collSOMs.Count>0 Then
        For Each gpmSOM In collSOMs
            Select Case gpmSOM.Type
                Case gpmConstants.SOMSite
                    WScript.Echo vbtab & "Site:" & gpmSOM.Name
                Case gpmConstants.SOMDomain
                    WScript.Echo vbTab & "Domain:" & gpmSOM.Name
                Case gpmConstants.SOMOU
                    WScript.Echo vbTab & "OU:" & gpmSOM.Name
            End Select
        Next
    End if
```

Each member of the collection is a SOM object, and we can return the SOM name as well as the type of SOM—OU, Domain, or Site. Here's another example of where we can use *gpm-Constants*. The *gpmSOM.Type* property returns a numeric constant that is pretty meaningless unless you know what it means. We can use the *SOMSite*, *SOMDomain*, and *SOMOU* constant property in a *Select Case* statement. Here is sample output from Listing 14-2.

```
Found 5 group policy objects In company.pri(DC02.company.pri)
Test Security [{20029756-EC91-44FB-B57C-87A9A5584880}]
Linked to 1 container(s)
    OU:TestingOU
Default Domain Policy [{31B2F340-016D-11D2-945F-00C04FB984F9}]
Linked to 1 container(s)
    Domain:company.pri
New Group Policy Object [{4962C921-BCFC-4B22-BF39-8746D9CD8536}]
```

```
Linked to 0 container(s)
Default Domain Controllers Policy [{6AC1786C-016F-11D2-945F-00C04fB984F9}]
Linked to 1 container(s)
   OU:Domain Controllers
Desktop Restrictions [{B171DED9-C308-45C5-A1B5-48494C0B6DB5}]
Linked to 1 container(s)
   OU:TestingOU
```

Scripting GPO Permissions

The GPMC object model provides access to GPO permissions through a permissions object. The *gpmGPO* object has a *GetSecurityInfo* method that returns a collection of *gpmPermission* objects. These objects have an interface for returning information about the trustee; that is, the account that holds particular permissions.

The script in Listing 14-3 adds a section to display permissions to the script we've been using to show all GPOs in a domain.

Listing 14-3 List GPO Permissions

```
Dim GPM,gpmConstants,gpmDomain
dim collGPOS,gpmSearchCriteria,gpo
Dim gpmResult,gpmSecurityInfo,gpmPerm
dim RootDSE,objDomain

set GPM=CreateObject("GPMGMT.GPM")
set gpmConstants=GPM.GetConstants
strFQDN=GetDomainFQDN

set gpmDomain=GPM.GetDomain(strFQDN,"",gpmConstants.UseAnyDC)

set gpmSearchCriteria=GPM.CreateSearchCriteria
set collGPOS=gpmDomain.SearchGPOs(gpmSearchCriteria)
wscript.Echo "Found " & collGPOS.Count & " group policy objects in " &_
gpmDomain.Domain & "(" & gpmDomain.DomainController & ")"

For Each gpo In collGPOS
    WScript.Echo gpo.Displayname
    set gpmSecurityInfo=gpo.GetSecurityInfo
    wscript.Echo gpmSecurityInfo.Count & " permission objects"
  For Each gpmPerm In gpmSecurityInfo
    Select Case gpmPerm.permission
        Case gpmConstants.permGPOApply
            WScript.Echo vbTab & "GPO Applies"
            wscript.Echo vbTab & vbTab & ListTrustees(gpmPerm)
        Case gpmConstants.permGPOCustom
            WScript.Echo vbTab & "GPO Custom"
            wscript.Echo vbTab & vbTab & ListTrustees(gpmPerm)
        Case gpmConstants.permGPOEdit
            WScript.Echo vbTab & "GPO Edit"
            wscript.Echo vbTab & vbTab & ListTrustees(gpmPerm)
        Case gpmConstants.permGPORead
            WScript.Echo vbTab & "GPO Read"
```

```
                    wscript.Echo vbTab & vbTab & ListTrustees(gpmPerm)
              Case gpmConstants.permGPOEditSecurityAndDelete
                    WScript.Echo vbTab & "GPO Edit Security"
                    wscript.Echo vbTab & vbTab & ListTrustees(gpmPerm)
              Case Else
                    WScript.Echo vbTab & gpmPerm.Permission
                    wscript.Echo vbTab & vbTab & ListTrustees(gpmPerm)
        End select
        next
Next


WScript.Quit


'*************************************************
Function GetDomainFQDN()
set RootDSE=GetObject("LDAP://RootDSE")
DomainPath= RootDSE.Get("DefaultNamingContext")
DomainPath=Replace(DomainPath,"DC=","")
GetDomainFQDN=Replace(DomainPath,",",".")
End Function


'*************************************************
Function ListTrustees(gpmPerm)
On Error Resume Next
  If gpmPerm.Trustee.TrusteeDSPath="" Then
   ListTrustees= gpmPerm.Trustee.TrusteeName
  Else
     ListTrustees= gpmPerm.Trustee.TrusteeName & " [" &_
     gpmPerm.Trustee.TrusteeDSPath & "]"
  End If
End Function
```

With each GPO object, we create a *gmpSecurityInfo* object by invoking the *GetSecurityInfo* method.

```
set gpmSecurityInfo=gpo.GetSecurityInfo
```

Next, we go through each permission object in *gpmSecurityInfo* by first figuring out what type of permission it is by looking at the *Permission* property.

```
Select Case gpmPerm.permission
```

As you can see in the *Select Case* statement, we again use the *gpmConstants* object to compare values that correspond to the different types of permissions. If we didn't, all we would see would be a number like 6547, and that would be pretty meaningless.

```
Case gpmConstants.permGPOApply
          WScript.Echo vbTab & "GPO Applies"
          wscript.Echo vbTab & vbTab & ListTrustees(gpmPerm)
        Case gpmConstants.permGPOCustom
          WScript.Echo vbTab & "GPO Custom"
          wscript.Echo vbTab & vbTab & ListTrustees(gpmPerm)
```

```
        Case gpmConstants.permGPOEdit
            WScript.Echo vbTab & "GPO Edit"
            wscript.Echo vbTab & vbTab & ListTrustees(gpmPerm)
        Case gpmConstants.permGPORead
            WScript.Echo vbTab & "GPO Read"
            wscript.Echo vbTab & vbTab & ListTrustees(gpmPerm)
        Case gpmConstants.permGPOEditSecurityAndDelete
            WScript.Echo vbTab & "GPO Edit Security"
            wscript.Echo vbTab & vbTab & ListTrustees(gpmPerm)
        Case Else
            WScript.Echo vbTab & gpmPerm.Permission
            wscript.Echo vbTab & vbTab & ListTrustees(gpmPerm)
    End select
```

To get trustee information for each permission, we called a function that returns the name of the trustee and the directory service path, if it exists. When you run the script, you get output like this.

```
Found 5 group policy objects in company.pri(DC02.company.pri)
Test Security
5 permission objects
    GPO Edit Security
        Domain Admins [CN=Domain Admins,CN=Users,DC=company,DC=pri]
    GPO Edit Security
        Enterprise Admins [CN=Enterprise Admins,CN=Users,DC=company,DC=pri]
    GPO Edit Security
        SYSTEM
    GPO Applies
        Authenticated Users
    GPO Read
        ENTERPRISE DOMAIN CONTROLLERS
Default Domain Policy
5 permission objects
    GPO Edit Security
        Domain Admins [CN=Domain Admins,CN=Users,DC=company,DC=pri]
    GPO Edit Security
        Enterprise Admins [CN=Enterprise Admins,CN=Users,DC=company,DC=pri]
    GPO Edit Security
        SYSTEM
    GPO Applies
        Authenticated Users
    GPO Read
        ENTERPRISE DOMAIN CONTROLLERS
New Group Policy Object
5 permission objects
    GPO Edit Security
        Domain Admins [CN=Domain Admins,CN=Users,DC=company,DC=pri]
    GPO Edit Security
        Enterprise Admins [CN=Enterprise Admins,CN=Users,DC=company,DC=pri]
    GPO Edit Security
        SYSTEM
    GPO Applies
        Authenticated Users
    GPO Read
        ENTERPRISE DOMAIN CONTROLLERS
```

```
Default Domain Controllers Policy
5 permission objects
    GPO Edit Security
        Domain Admins [CN=Domain Admins,CN=Users,DC=company,DC=pri]
    GPO Edit Security
        Enterprise Admins [CN=Enterprise Admins,CN=Users,DC=company,DC=pri]
    GPO Edit Security
        SYSTEM
    GPO Applies
        Authenticated Users
    GPO Read
        ENTERPRISE DOMAIN CONTROLLERS
Desktop Restrictions
5 permission objects
    GPO Edit Security
        Domain Admins [CN=Domain Admins,CN=Users,DC=company,DC=pri]
    GPO Edit Security
        Enterprise Admins [CN=Enterprise Admins,CN=Users,DC=company,DC=pri]
    GPO Edit Security
        SYSTEM
    GPO Applies
        Authenticated Users
    GPO Read
        ENTERPRISE DOMAIN CONTROLLERS
```

Setting permissions is relatively easy. You need to use the *CreatePermission* method to create a new permission object. The method requires three parameters.

- The trustee name you give permission to. Typically, this is something like *Company\SalesUsers*.

- The type of permission. Use the *gpmConstants* object so you can specify *permGPOApply*, *permGPORead*, *permGPOEdit*, or *permGPOEditSecurityAndDelete*.

- A Boolean value indicating whether the permission is inheritable.

You end up with a line of code like this.

```
Set GPM = CreateObject("GPMgmt.GPM")
set gpmConstants=GPM.GetConstants
Set gpmPermission=GPM.CreatePermission("Company\SalesUsers",_
gpmConstants.GPOApply,True)
```

> **Tip**   You can use this method to apply permissions to a GPO, SOM, or WMI filter. Check the documentation for details on the types of permissions you can set.

After the permission object has been created, use the *Add* method in the *gpmSecurityInfo* object to set the permission.

```
set gpmSecurityInfo=gpo.GetSecurityInfo
gpmSecurityInfo.Add gpmPermission
```

Scripting GPO Reports

A major improvement in GPO management is the addition of GPO configuration reports. You can configure many items with a GPO, but it was always difficult to see which settings had actually been configured. The Group Policy Management Console includes a report viewer and a menu command to save the report to a file. We can also perform those tasks from the command line very easily.

The GPO object has a method called *GenerateReportToFile*. The method takes a parameter indicating whether the report should be in HTML or XML format. Once again, we can use the *gpmConstants* object to specify the constant with a much easier-to-use name like *gpmConstants.ReportHTML* or *gpmConstants.ReportXML*. The other parameter is simply the filename and path where the report should be saved. Listing 14-4 takes our GPO enumeration script and generates an HTML report for each GPO using the GPO display name as part of the filename.

Listing 14-4 Generate GPO Report

```
'GPOMasterSummary.vbs
Dim GPM,gpmConstants,gpmDomain
Dim collGPOS,gpmSearchCriteria,gpo
dim RootDSE,objDomain

set GPM=CreateObject("GPMGMT.GPM")
set gpmConstants=GPM.GetConstants

strFQDN=GetDomainFQDN

set gpmDomain=GPM.GetDomain(strFQDN,"",gpmConstants.UseAnyDC)
set gpmSearchCriteria=GPM.CreateSearchCriteria
set collGPOS=gpmDomain.SearchGPOs(gpmSearchCriteria)

wscript.Echo "Found " & collGPOS.Count & " group policy objects in " &_
gpmDomain.Domain & "(" & gpmDomain.DomainController & ")"

For Each gpo In collGPOS
    WScript.Echo gpo.Displayname & " [" & gpo.path & "]"
    gpo.GenerateReporttoFile gpmConstants.ReportHTML, gpo.Displayname &_
    ".html"
Next

WScript.Quit

'***************************************************
Function GetDomainFQDN()
 set RootDSE=GetObject("LDAP://RootDSE")
 DomainPath= RootDSE.Get("DefaultNamingContext")
 DomainPath=Replace(DomainPath,"DC=","")
 GetDomainFQDN=Replace(DomainPath,",",".")
End Function
```

Scripting GPO Backups

A common GPO management task is to back up GPOs. This is an obvious best practice before editing a GPO; it ensures that you have a good version of the policy in case you need to revert to it. You might also want to run a job that periodically backs up GPOs. This is accomplished with the *Backup* method of the *gpmGPO* object.

The method requires the folder path for the backup. The folder must already exist or the method will fail. You can also specify a comment to associate with the backup.

```
Set gpmResult=gpmGPO.Backup("d:\backups\SalesDesktop-bkup","baseline")
```

When executed, the method creates a *gpmResult* object that you can use to check on the status of the backup by calling the *OverAllStatus* method. If there are no errors during the backup, the method returns an error code of 0; otherwise, it returns a failure error code.

```
gpmResult.OverAllStatus
if err.number<>0 then
  wscript.echo "Backup failed"
else
  wscript.echo "Backup successful"
end if
```

> **Troubleshooting**   If your backup command isn't working, make sure the folder path exists and that you have permissions. Do not include a trailing slash (\) in the path. If you don't include a comment, you must at least include two double quotation marks ("") for the second parameter.

The other useful feature of the *gpmResult* object is that its *Result* method will return information about the *gpmBackup* object that is implicitly created. Thus we can expand on our code snippet.

```
gpmResult.OverAllStatus
if err.number<>0 then
  wscript.echo "Backup failed"
else
  wscript.echo "Backup successful"
Set gpmBackup=gpmResult.Result
  WScript.Echo "Backed up " & gpmBackup.GPODisplayName &_
  "to " & gpmBackup.BackupDir & "\" & gpmBackup.ID
end if
```

Scripting GPO Restores

Restoring a GPO is a little more involved than backing one up. You must use the *RestoreGPO* method of the *gpmDomain* object. Additionally, you can only restore a GPO to the domain where it was created. The method requires a reference to the *gpmBackup* object to restore a flag for domain controller validation. If the value is 0, the method validates the domain controller to see if it can perform the restore. You could also use the *DoNotValidateDC* attribute of the *gpmConstant* object to skip validation.

> **Best Practices**   Microsoft recommends that you always validate, especially if you are using software policy settings. Group Policy objects with software policy settings should be restored to a Windows 2003 domain controller for minimal client impact. You can restore to a Windows 2000 domain controller, but users might have to reinstall software.

Of course, before you can restore the backup, you have to find it. You can use the *Search-Backups* method for the *gpmBackupDir* object.

```
strBackupDir="c:\backups"
Set gpmDomain=GPM.GetDomain(strFQDN,"",gpmConstants.UseAnyDC)
Set gpmSearchCriteria=GPM.CreateSearchCriteria
Set gpmBackupDir=GPM.GetBackupDir(strBackupDir)
Set collBackups=gpmBackupDir.SearchBackups(gpmSearchCriteria)
WScript.Echo collBackups.count & " Backups found in " & strBackupDir
For Each gpmBackup In collBackups
  WScript.Echo "ID:" & gpmBackup.ID
  WScript.Echo "  Name:" & gpmBackup.GPODisplayName
  WScript.Echo "  Comment:" & gpmBackup.Comment
  WScript.Echo "  Backed up:" & gpmBackup.TimeStamp
Next
```

This will return a collection of *gpmBackup* objects. The snippet just shown simply lists all the available backups. After you've added your code to identify the backup you want to restore, you simply add this code snippet.

```
Set gpmResult=gpmDomain.RestoreGPO(gpmBackup,0)
```

You can use the *gpmResult* object to validate the restore in much the same way we did for the backup method.

Scripting Resultant Set of Policy

The Group Policy Management Console includes an excellent planning and troubleshooting tool called Resultant Set of Policies (RSOP). This tool can calculate the end result of all the policies that might have been applied during a user session. You can use RSOP in two modes: planning and logging. In planning mode, RSOP simulates the result of some combination of user, computer, group membership, and SOM. In logging mode, RSOP examines the results of an actual user and computer session. In either mode, you can generate a nice looking HTML report to see what settings were applied and from what GPOs.

The GPMC object model has a *gmpRSOP* object that you can create from the *GPM* object with *GetRSOP*. The method requires several parameters. The first is whether RSOP will be in planning or logging mode. You can use *gmpConstant* to specify *RSOPModePlanning* or *RSOP-ModeLogging*. The second parameter is for a WMI namespace, which you can leave blank, and the last parameter must be 0.

```
Set GPM=CreateObject("GPMGMT.GPM")
set gpmConstants=GPM.GetConstants
set gpmRSOP=GPM.GetRSOP(gpmConstants.RSOPModePlanning,"",0)
```

In this snippet, we're going to do some RSOP planning. We define the user account and computer we want to test, as well as a domain controller. The *CreateQueryResults* method runs the RSOP in planning mode. We can then use the *GenerateReportToFile* method, as we did earlier in the chapter, to write the results to an HTML file.

```
gpmRSOP.PlanningComputer="company\XPDesk01"
gpmRSOP.PlanningUser="company\a.user"
gpmRSOP.PlanningDomainController="DC01"
gpmRSOP.CreateQueryResults
gpmRSOP.GenerateReportToFile gpmConstants.ReportHTML,".\rsop.htm"
```

There are additional planning parameters you could specify, such as *PlanningUserSecurityGroups* and *PlanningUserSOM*. They are explained in the GPMC Help file. You follow a similar approach for logging mode.

Viewing GPO Scripting in Action

Let's take everything we've covered in this chapter and roll it up into a single script. The script in Listing 14-5 generates an HTML document with information about every GPO in the domain including its permissions, SOM links, and the permissions on each SOM.

Listing 14-5 Generate GPO Master

```
Dim GPM,gpmConstants,gpmDomain
dim collGPOS,gpmSearchCriteria,collSOMs
Dim gpo
dim RootDSE,objDomain
Dim objFSO,objFile
Dim objDict
strFile="GPOMaster.htm"
WScript.Echo "Building GPO Master Report"

Set objDict=CreateObject("Scripting.Dictionary")
Set objFSO=CreateObject("Scripting.FileSystemObject")
Set objFile=objFSO.CreateTextFile(strFile,True)
'build the beginning of the html report"
objFile.Writeline "<html>"
objFile.Writeline "<head>"
objFile.WriteLine "<style type=text/css>"
objFile.WriteLine "body    {font-size:80%; font-family:Tahoma;}"
objFile.WriteLine "table   { font-size:100%; width:100%; }"
objFile.WriteLine "</style>"
objFile.WriteLine "</head>"
```

```
objFile.WriteLine "<body>"
objFile.WriteLine "<H3>Group Policy Master Report</H3><hr>"

'Create GPMC object
Set GPM=CreateObject("GPMGMT.GPM")
'Create GPMC constant object
Set gpmConstants=GPM.GetConstants
strFQDN=GetDomainFQDN

set gpmDomain=GPM.GetDomain(strFQDN,"",gpmConstants.UsePDC)

set gpmSearchCriteria=GPM.CreateSearchCriteria
set collGPOS=gpmDomain.SearchGPOs(gpmSearchCriteria)

objFile.WriteLine  "Found " & collGPOS.Count &_
 " group policy objects in " & gpmDomain.Domain & " (" &_
  gpmDomain.DomainController & ")"

For Each gpo In collGPOS
objFile.WriteLine "<Table border=0 cellpadding=3 cellspacing=3>"
objFile.WriteLine "<tr><td align=Center><B><a href=" & CHR(34) &_
 gpo.Displayname & ".htm" & Chr(34) & " target=_Blank>" &_
 gpo.Displayname & "</a></B></td><td>" & gpo.path & "</td></tr>"
objFile.WriteLine "<tr><td></td><td>Created " & gpo.CreationTime &_
"<br> Modified " & gpo.ModificationTime &"</td></tr>"

'Get SOM Links
gpmSearchCriteria.Add gpmConstants.SearchPropertySOMLinks,_
gpmConstants.SearchOpContains,gpo
Set collSOMs=gpmDomain.SearchSOMs(gpmSearchCriteria)
objFile.WriteLine "<tr><td>Linked to " & collSOMs.Count &_
 " container(s)</td></tr>"
If collSOMs.Count>0 Then
For Each gpmSOM In collSOMs
objDict.RemoveAll
  Select Case gpmSOM.Type
   Case gpmConstants.SOMSite
    objFile.WriteLine "<tr><td align=Right>[Site] " & gpmSOM.Name &_
     "</td><td>" & gpmSOM.Path &"</td></tr>"
    Set gpmSecurityInfo=gpmSOM.GetSecurityInfo
    objFile.WriteLine "<tr><td colspan=2>" & gpmSecurityInfo.Count &_
     " SOM permission objects</td></tr>"
    For Each gpmPerm In gpmSecurityInfo
        GetPerms(gpmPerm)
    Next
    k=objDict.Keys
    For i=0 To objDict.Count-1
     Select Case k(i)
        Case gpmConstants.permSOMLink
        objFile.WriteLine "<tr><td align=right>SOM Linking</td></tr>"
        tmpArray=Split(objDict.Item(k(i)),"||")
        For j=0 To UBound(tmpArray)
          objFile.WriteLine "<tr><td></td><td align=left>" &_
           tmpArray(j)&"</td></tr>"
        Next
     End Select
```

```
      Next
  Case gpmConstants.SOMDomain
    objFile.WriteLine "<tr><td align=Right>[Domain] " & gpmSOM.Name &_
    "</td><td>" & gpmSOM.Path &"</td></tr>"
    Set gpmSecurityInfo=gpmSOM.GetSecurityInfo
    objFile.WriteLine "<tr><td colspan=2>" & gpmSecurityInfo.Count &_
    " SOM permission objects</td></tr>"

    For Each gpmPerm In gpmSecurityInfo
      GetPerms(gpmPerm)
    Next
    k=objDict.Keys
    For i=0 To objDict.Count-1
      Select Case k(i)
      Case gpmConstants.permSOMLink
      objFile.WriteLine "<tr><td align=Right>SOM Linking</td></tr>"
      tmpArray=Split(objDict.Item(k(i)),"||")
      For j=0 To UBound(tmpArray)
        objFile.WriteLine "<tr><td></td><td align=left>" &_
        tmpArray(j)&"</td></tr>"
      Next
      Case gpmConstants.permSOMLogging
      objFile.WriteLine "<tr><td align=Right>RSoP Logging</td></tr>"
      tmpArray=Split(objDict.Item(k(i)),"||")
      For j=0 To UBound(tmpArray)
        objFile.WriteLine "<tr><td></td><td align=left>" &_
        tmpArray(j)&"</td></tr>"
      Next
      Case gpmConstants.permSOMPlanning
      objFile.WriteLine "<tr><td align=Right>RSoPPlanning</td></tr>"
      tmpArray=Split(objDict.Item(k(i)),"||")
      For j=0 To UBound(tmpArray)
        objFile.WriteLine "<tr><td></td><td align=left>" &_
        tmpArray(j)&"</td></tr>"
      Next
      End Select
    Next
  Case gpmConstants.SOMOU
      objFile.WriteLine "<tr><td align=Right>[OU] " &gpmSOM.Name &_
      "</td><td>" & gpmSOM.Path &"</td></tr>"
      Set gpmSecurityInfo=gpmSOM.GetSecurityInfo
      objFile.WriteLine "<tr><td colspan=2>" & gpmSecurityInfo.Count &_
      " SOM permission objects</td></tr>"
      For Each gpmPerm In gpmSecurityInfo
          GetPerms(gpmPerm)
      Next
      k=objDict.Keys
      For i=0 To objDict.Count-1
        Select Case k(i)
          Case gpmConstants.permSOMLink
          objFile.WriteLine "<tr><td align=right>SOM Linking</td></tr>"
          tmpArray=Split(objDict.Item(k(i)),"||")
          For j=0 To UBound(tmpArray)
            objFile.WriteLine "<tr><td></td><td align=left>" &_
            tmpArray(j)&"</td></tr>"
```

```
              Next
            Case gpmConstants.permSOMGPOCreate
            objFile.WriteLine "<tr><td align=right>Create GPO</td></tr>"
            tmpArray=Split(objDict.Item(k(i)),"||")
            For j=0 To UBound(tmpArray)
               objFile.WriteLine "<tr><td></td><td align=left>" &_
                tmpArray(j)&"</td></tr>"
            Next
            Case gpmConstants.permSOMLogging
            objFile.WriteLine "<tr><td align=right>RSoP Logging</td></tr>"
            tmpArray=Split(objDict.Item(k(i)),"||")
            For j=0 To UBound(tmpArray)
               objFile.WriteLine "<tr><td></td><td align=left>" &_
                tmpArray(j)&"</td></tr>"
            Next
            Case gpmConstants.permSOMPlanning
            objFile.WriteLine "<tr><td align=right>RSoPPlanning</td></tr>"
            tmpArray=Split(objDict.Item(k(i)),"||")
            For j=0 To UBound(tmpArray)
               objFile.WriteLine "<tr><td></td><td align=left>" &_
                tmpArray(j)&"</td></tr>"
            Next
            Case gpmConstants.permSOMWMICreate
            objFile.WriteLine "<tr><td align=right>Create WMI Filters</td></tr>"
            tmpArray=Split(objDict.Item(k(i)),"||")
            For j=0 To UBound(tmpArray)
               objFile.WriteLine "<tr><td></td><td align=left>" &_
                tmpArray(j)&"</td></tr>"
            Next
            Case gpmConstants.permSOMWMIFullControl
            objFile.WriteLine "<tr><td align=right>Full WMI Control</td></tr>"
            tmpArray=Split(objDict.Item(k(i)),"||")
            For j=0 To UBound(tmpArray)
               objFile.WriteLine "<tr><td></td><td align=left>" &_
                tmpArray(j)&"</td></tr>"
            Next
          End Select
        Next
    End Select
  Next
End If
'Get GPO permissions
'clear the dictionary
objDict.RemoveAll
Set gpmSecurityInfo=gpo.GetSecurityInfo
objFile.WriteLine "<tr><td colspan=2>" & gpmSecurityInfo.Count &_
  " GPO permission objects</td></tr>"
For Each gpmPerm In gpmSecurityInfo
GetPerms(gpmPerm)
Next
  k=objDict.Keys
  For i=0 To objDict.Count-1
    Select Case k(i)
        Case gpmConstants.permGPOApply
            objFile.WriteLine "<tr><td align=right>GPO Applies</td></tr>"
```

```
                tmpArray=Split(objDict.Item(k(i)),"||")
                For j=0 To UBound(tmpArray)
                  objFile.WriteLine "<tr><td></td><td align=left>" &_
                  tmpArray(j)&"</td></tr>"
                Next
            Case gpmConstants.permGPOCustom
                objFile.WriteLine "<tr><td align=right>GPO Custom</td></tr>"
                tmpArray=Split(objDict.Item(k(i)),"||")
                For j=0 To UBound(tmpArray)
                  objFile.WriteLine "<tr><td></td><td align=left>" &_
                  tmpArray(j)&"</td></tr>"
                Next
            Case gpmConstants.permGPOEdit
                objFile.WriteLine "<tr><td align=right>GPO Edit</td></tr>"
                tmpArray=Split(objDict.Item(k(i)),"||")
                For j=0 To UBound(tmpArray)
                  objFile.WriteLine "<tr><td></td><td align=left>" &_
                  tmpArray(j)&"</td></tr>"
                Next
            Case gpmConstants.permGPORead
                objFile.WriteLine "<tr><td align=right>GPO Read</td></tr>"
                tmpArray=Split(objDict.Item(k(i)),"||")
                For j=0 To UBound(tmpArray)
                  objFile.WriteLine "<tr><td></td><td align=left>" &_
                  tmpArray(j)&"</td></tr>"
                Next
            Case gpmConstants.permGPOEditSecurityAndDelete
                objFile.WriteLine "<tr><td align=right>GPO Edit Security</td></tr>"
                tmpArray=Split(objDict.Item(k(i)),"||")
                For j=0 To UBound(tmpArray)
                  objFile.WriteLine "<tr><td></td><td align=left>" &_
                  tmpArray(j)&"</td></tr>"
                Next
        End Select
    Next
'Generate HTML Report
 gpo.GenerateReporttoFile gpmConstants.ReportHTML, ".\" &_
 gpo.Displayname & ".htm"
objFile.WriteLine "</Table><br><br>"
Next
objFile.WriteLine "<I>Report run " & Now &  "</I>"
objFile.WriteLine "</Body>"
objFile.WriteLine "</html>"
objFile.Close
WScript.Echo "Finished building report page."
WScript.Quit


'*************************************************
Function GetDomainFQDN()
Set RootDSE=GetObject("LDAP://RootDSE")
DomainPath= RootDSE.Get("DefaultNamingContext")
DomainPath=Replace(DomainPath,"DC=","")
GetDomainFQDN=Replace(DomainPath,",",".")
End Function
'*************************************************
Function ListTrustees(gpmPerm)
```

```
On Error Resume Next
  If gpmPerm.Trustee.TrusteeDSPath="" Then
   ListTrustees= gpmPerm.Trustee.TrusteeName
  Else
    ListTrustees= gpmPerm.Trustee.TrusteeName & " [" &_
    gpmPerm.Trustee.TrusteeDSPath & "]"
  End If
End Function
'*************************************************
Sub GetPerms(gpmPerm)

If objDict.Exists(gpmPerm.Permission) Then
    strTemp=objDict.Item(gpmPerm.Permission)
    objDict.Remove gpmPerm.Permission
    'WScript.Echo "Adding " & strTemp & "," & ListTrustees(gpmPerm)
    objDict.Add gpmPerm.permission,strTemp & "||" & ListTrustees(gpmPerm)
Else
    objDict.Add gpmPerm.Permission,ListTrustees(gpmPerm)
End If

End Sub
```

We've simply taken some of the script samples from the chapter and written the results to an HTML table. We start by getting a connection to the domain and searching for all GPOs.

```
'Create GPMC object
Set GPM=CreateObject("GPMGMT.GPM")
'Create GPMC constant object
Set gpmConstants=GPM.GetConstants
strFQDN=GetDomainFQDN

set gpmDomain=GPM.GetDomain(strFQDN,"",gpmConstants.UsePDC)

set gpmSearchCriteria=GPM.CreateSearchCriteria
set collGPOS=gpmDomain.SearchGPOs(gpmSearchCriteria)
```

For each GPO, we write the display name, the path, and the creation and modification time to the table.

```
objFile.WriteLine "<Table border=0 cellpadding=3 cellspacing=3>"
objFile.WriteLine "<tr><td align=Center><B><a href=" & CHR(34) &_
 gpo.Displayname & ".htm" & Chr(34) & " target=_Blank>" &_
 gpo.Displayname & "</a></B></td><td>" & gpo.path & "</td></tr>"
objFile.WriteLine "<tr><td></td><td>Created " & gpo.CreationTime &_
"<br> Modified " & gpo.ModificationTime &"</td></tr>"
```

Next we get the SOM links for the GPO.

```
'Get SOM Links
gpmSearchCriteria.Add gpmConstants.SearchPropertySOMLinks,_
gpmConstants.SearchOpContains,gpo
Set collSOMs=gpmDomain.SearchSOMs(gpmSearchCriteria)
objFile.WriteLine "<tr><td>Linked to " & collSOMs.Count &_
 " container(s)</td></tr>"
```

We write information about the SOM to the table.

```
For Each gpmSOM In collSOMs
objDict.RemoveAll
  Select Case gpmSOM.Type
   Case gpmConstants.SOMSite
    objFile.WriteLine "<tr><td align=Right>[Site] " & gpmSOM.Name &_
    "</td><td>" & gpmSOM.Path &"</td></tr>"
```

For each SOM type, such as OU or Site, we get the permissions for the SOM.

```
Set gpmSecurityInfo=gpmSOM.GetSecurityInfo
    objFile.WriteLine "<tr><td colspan=2>" & gpmSecurityInfo.Count &_
    " SOM permission objects</td></tr>"
    For Each gpmPerm In gpmSecurityInfo
        GetPerms(gpmPerm)
    Next
```

We use a dictionary object to group the permission types together through a subroutine called *GetPerms*.

```
Sub GetPerms(gpmPerm)
If objDict.Exists(gpmPerm.Permission) Then
    strTemp=objDict.Item(gpmPerm.Permission)
    objDict.Remove gpmPerm.Permission
    'WScript.Echo "Adding " & strTemp & "," & ListTrustees(gpmPerm)
    objDict.Add gpmPerm.permission,strTemp & "||" & ListTrustees(gpmPerm)
Else
    objDict.Add gpmPerm.Permission,ListTrustees(gpmPerm)
End If
End Sub
```

The subroutine adds each new trustee, separated by two pipes (||). This is so we can later split the item into an array and write out each entry separately. We don't use a comma because the trustee information includes the Active Directory path, which has commas.

Each dictionary key corresponds to a particular permission type, and the item holds the trustees. We can then enumerate the dictionary and use *Select Case* to compare the permission types. Each dictionary item is split into an array so each trustee can be written separately.

```
k=objDict.Keys
    For i=0 To objDict.Count-1
      Select Case k(i)
        Case gpmConstants.permSOMLink
        objFile.WriteLine "<tr><td align=Right>SOM Linking</td></tr>"
        tmpArray=Split(objDict.Item(k(i)),"||")
        For j=0 To UBound(tmpArray)
          objFile.WriteLine "<tr><td></td><td align=left>" &_
          tmpArray(j)&"</td></tr>"
        Next
        Case gpmConstants.permSOMLogging
        objFile.WriteLine "<tr><td align=Right>RSoP Logging</td></tr>"
        tmpArray=Split(objDict.Item(k(i)),"||")
```

```
      For j=0 To UBound(tmpArray)
        objFile.WriteLine "<tr><td></td><td align=left>" &_
         tmpArray(j)&"</td></tr>"
      Next
      Case gpmConstants.permSOMPlanning
      objFile.WriteLine "<tr><td align=Right>RSoPPlanning</td></tr>"
      tmpArray=Split(objDict.Item(k(i)),"||")
      For j=0 To UBound(tmpArray)
        objFile.WriteLine "<tr><td></td><td align=left>" &_
         tmpArray(j)&"</td></tr>"
      Next
    End Select
  Next
```

This process is repeated for every SOM type, and then we use the same technique to get GPO permissions.

```
'Get GPO permissions
'clear the dictionary
objDict.RemoveAll
Set gpmSecurityInfo=gpo.GetSecurityInfo
objFile.WriteLine "<tr><td colspan=2>" & gpmSecurityInfo.Count &_
 " GPO permission objects</td></tr>"
For Each gpmPerm In gpmSecurityInfo
GetPerms(gpmPerm)
Next
  k=objDict.Keys
  For i=0 To objDict.Count-1
    Select Case k(i)
        Case gpmConstants.permGPOApply
            objFile.WriteLine "<tr><td align=right>GPO Applies</td></tr>"
            tmpArray=Split(objDict.Item(k(i)),"||")
            For j=0 To UBound(tmpArray)
              objFile.WriteLine "<tr><td></td><td align=left>" &_
               tmpArray(j)&"</td></tr>"
            Next
        Case gpmConstants.permGPOCustom
            objFile.WriteLine "<tr><td align=right>GPO Custom</td></tr>"
            tmpArray=Split(objDict.Item(k(i)),"||")
            For j=0 To UBound(tmpArray)
              objFile.WriteLine "<tr><td></td><td align=left>" &_
               tmpArray(j)&"</td></tr>"
            Next
        Case gpmConstants.permGPOEdit
            objFile.WriteLine "<tr><td align=right>GPO Edit</td></tr>"
            tmpArray=Split(objDict.Item(k(i)),"||")
            For j=0 To UBound(tmpArray)
              objFile.WriteLine "<tr><td></td><td align=left>" &_
               tmpArray(j)&"</td></tr>"
            Next
        Case gpmConstants.permGPORead
            objFile.WriteLine "<tr><td align=right>GPO Read</td></tr>"
            tmpArray=Split(objDict.Item(k(i)),"||")
            For j=0 To UBound(tmpArray)
              objFile.WriteLine "<tr><td></td><td align=left>" &_
```

```
                    tmpArray(j)&"</td></tr>"
              Next
        Case gpmConstants.permGPOEditSecurityAndDelete
              objFile.WriteLine "<tr><td align=right>GPO Edit Security</td></tr>"
              tmpArray=Split(objDict.Item(k(i)),"||")
              For j=0 To UBound(tmpArray)
                objFile.WriteLine "<tr><td></td><td align=left>" &_
                tmpArray(j)&"</td></tr>"
              Next
    End Select
  Next
```

The script generates an HTML report for each GPO.

```
'Generate HTML Report
gpo.GenerateReporttoFile gpmConstants.ReportHTML, ".\" &_
gpo.Displayname & ".htm"
```

When we wrote the GPO display name to the table, we included HTML code to link to the report.

```
objFile.WriteLine "<tr><td align=Center><B><a href=" & CHR(34) &_
gpo.Displayname & ".htm" & Chr(34) & " target=_Blank>" &_
gpo.Displayname & "</a></B></td><td>" & gpo.path & "</td></tr>"
```

When you run the script, you should get a result like the one shown in Figure 14-2.

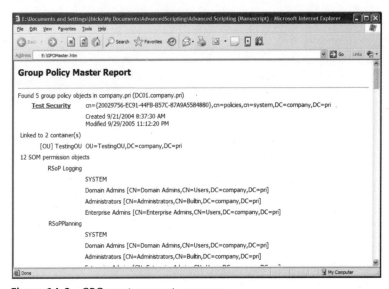

Figure 14-2   GPO master report summary

Summary

Scripting GPO management might not be something you do often. However, you'll find the Group Policy Management Console easy to use, especially for tasks such as RSOP planning. We think you'll find scripting with the GPMC especially useful for automating tasks such as backups and report generation. We demonstrated how the object model works, and how to work with the invaluable *Constants* object. GPMC scripting takes a little practice, but if you want something a little different than the scripts that are included with the tool, you'll be happy you took the time.

> **More Info**   We've included a number of helpful Web links about GPMC scripting on the companion CD. And don't forget to look at the Group Policy Management Console Help file (gpmc.chm) in the %ProgramFiles%\GPMC\Scripts folder.

Chapter 15

Exchange 2003 Scripting

Microsoft Exchange 2003 is the ideal platform for administrative scripting. If you have ever wished you could manage an Exchange environment with VBScript, Exchange 2003 is what you have been waiting for. In this chapter, we'll explore the various approaches to scripting with Exchange 2003. You will see how to manage Exchange servers, storage groups, and mail stores. As you'll see, there's no single scripting approach, and you will have to be well-versed in Active Directory Services Interface (ADSI), Windows Management Instrumentation (WMI), and more to get the most from Exchange 2003 scripting.

Exchange 2003 is by far the strongest enterprise mail platform Microsoft has ever introduced. One of its greatest strengths is that there are many ways to manage it; you no longer need to rely on the management console. Now you can create scripts for custom management tasks that you can't do with the management console or expensive third-party tools.

Introducing Exchange Scripting

Scripting with Exchange 2003 involves a variety of technologies. You use the Lightweight Directory Access Protocol (LDAP) ADSI provider to discover information about your Exchange organization from Active Directory. You use the WinNT ADSI provider to manage Exchange 2003 services. You use WMI to manage Exchange mailboxes and Exchange servers. Finally, you use Collaboration Data Objects (CDO) and Collaboration Data Objects for Exchange Management (CDOEXM) to manage storage groups and mailbox stores. One benefit of scripting with Exchange 2003 is that you can manage your Exchange organization remotely from your desktop. Assuming you have appropriate administrative credentials, you can perform most administrative tasks from a Microsoft Windows XP desktop with no additional software.

If you need to develop or run any scripts that use CDO or CDOEXM, though, you will need to install the Exchange 2003 management console on your desktop. If you are administering an Exchange server, chances are you have it installed already.

We also recommend that you install the Exchange 2003 Software Development Kit (SDK). The SDK is freely available for download from Microsoft at

http://www.microsoft.com/downloads/details.aspx?FamilyId=E7E34B5B-01B0-45ED-B91F-F7064875D379&displaylang=en

> **On the CD**   This link, like most of the links referenced in this book, is included on the companion CD. Click *Exchange 2003 SDK*.

The SDK is full of code samples and excellent documentation. Much of the SDK is targeted toward application developers, but you will find plenty of information about Exchange objects, properties, and methods.

Querying Active Directory

Starting with Exchange 2000, Microsoft began using Active Directory as the directory service for Microsoft Exchange. All configuration information about the Exchange organization, server, storage groups and more is now stored in Active Directory. This means we can use an ADSI query with the LDAP provider to discover information about our Exchange environment. For example, we can discover all the Exchange servers in our organization. Consider the script in Listing 15-1.

```
Listing 15-1 List Exchange Servers
'Get list of Exchange servers from AD
Dim objRootDSE
Dim objConfiguration
Dim cat
Dim conn
Dim cmd
Dim RS
Set objRootDSE = GetObject("LDAP://rootDSE")

strConfiguration = "LDAP://" & objRootDSE.Get("configurationNamingContext")
Set objConfiguration = GetObject(strConfiguration)

'select Exchange servers but not policies which happen to share the same class
strQuery="Select distinguishedname,name,serialnumber,whencreated from '"& _
objConfiguration.ADSPath & "' where objectclass='msExchExchangeServer' "&_
"AND objectclass<>'msExchExchangeServerPolicy'"

WScript.Echo strQuery & VbCrLf

Set cat=GetObject("GC:")
```

```
For each obj in cat
  Set GC=obj
Next

Set conn=Createobject("ADODB.Connection")
Set cmd=CreateObject("ADODB.Command")
conn.Provider="ADSDSOObject"
conn.Open

Set cmd.ActiveConnection=conn
Set RS=conn.Execute(strQuery)

Do While not RS.EOF
if isArray(RS.Fields("serialnumber")) Then tmpArray=RS.Fields("serialnumber")
 wscript.Echo rs.Fields("name") & " (Created " &_
  RS.Fields("whencreated") & ")" & vbTab & tmpArray(0)
 RS.movenext
Loop
RS.Close
conn.Close
```

On the CD   You will find this script, as well as other scripts listed in this chapter, on the CD that accompanies this book.

We start by defining a query to search the default configuration naming context of our Active Directory forest. We will search for objects in which the object class is equal to *ms-ExchExchangeServer* but not equal to *msExchExchangeServerPolicy*, because the *msExch-ExchangeServerPolicy* object inherits class settings from *msExchExchangeServer*. If we queried for *msExchExchangeServer* objects, we would also get a list of server policies. The script will display the query so you can see exactly what you are trying to find.

```
Set objRootDSE = GetObject("LDAP://rootDSE")

strConfiguration = "LDAP://" & objRootDSE.Get("configurationNamingContext")
Set objConfiguration = GetObject(strConfiguration)

'select Exchange servers but not policies which happen to share the same class
strQuery="Select distinguishedname,name,serialnumber,whencreated from '"& _
objConfiguration.ADSPath & "' Where objectclass='msExchExchangeServer' "&_
"AND objectclass<>'msExchExchangeServerPolicy'"

WScript.Echo strQuery & VbCrLf
```

By using simple ADODB code, we process the recordset and display the *name*, *whencreated*, and *serialnumber* properties.

Tip   Even though we don't display it, we query for the distinguished name of the server. You might want to add this to the script output as a learning aid to better understand how Exchange information is stored in Active Directory.

Notice that we process the *serialnumber* property as an array.

```
if isArray(RS.Fields("serialnumber")) Then tmpArray=RS.Fields("serialnumber")
```

That's because this attribute is a multi-lined value. If we just tried to use the following, we would get a type mismatch error.

```
wscript.echo RS.fields("serialnumber")
```

We knew *serialnumber* was multi-lined because we used ADSIEdit from Windows Support Tools to view the properties. Open the *Configuration* naming context and navigate to *CN=Services*. Expand this item, and you will see *CN=Microsoft Exchange*. This is where most Exchange information is stored in Active Directory. As you explore this hierarchy, you'll eventually find your administrative group and within that, your server. Right-click the server name, such as *CN=Mail01*, and click Properties to display all the property attributes. If you edit *serialnumber*, you will see that it is a multi-valued property.

If you continue exploring in ADSIEdit, you will see *CN=InformationStore*, which is where information about all the storage groups for a particular server is stored. The script in Listing 15-2 searches the default naming context in Active Directory for all storage groups.

Listing 15-2 List Exchange Storage Groups

```
'Get list of Storage Groups
Dim objRootDSE
Dim objConfiguration
Dim conn
Dim cmd
Dim RS

Set objRootDSE = GetObject("LDAP://rootDSE")
strConfiguration = "LDAP://" & objRootDSE.Get("configurationNamingContext")
Set objConfiguration = GetObject(strConfiguration)
strPath=objConfiguration.ADSpath

strQuery="Select distinguishedname,name,whencreated from '" & strPath &_
 "' WHERE objectclass='msExchStorageGroup'"

WScript.Echo strQuery & VbCrLf

set cat=GetObject("GC:")
for each obj in cat
 set GC=obj
Next

set conn=Createobject("ADODB.Connection")
set cmd=CreateObject("ADODB.Command")
conn.Provider="ADSDSOObject"
conn.Open

set cmd.ActiveConnection=conn
set RS=conn.Execute(strQuery)
```

```
do while not RS.EOF
  wscript.echo rs.Fields("distinguishedname")
  WScript.echo vbtab & rs.Fields("name") & "(Created " &_
 rs.fields("whencreated") & ")"
rs.movenext
Loop
rs.Close
conn.Close
```

The format of this script is essentially the same as that of Listing 15-1. The query is searching for any object of the *msExchStorageGroup* class.

```
strQuery="Select distinguishedname,name,whencreated from '" & strPath &_
 "' WHERE objectclass='msExchStorageGroup'"
```

When you run this script, you will get output like this.

```
Select distinguishedname,name,whencreated from 'LDAP://CN=Configuration,DC=company,DC=pri'
WHERE objectclass='msExchStorageGroup'

CN=First Storage Group,CN=InformationStore,CN=MAIL01,CN=Servers,CN=First Administrative
Group,CN=Administrative Groups,CN=company,CN=Microsoft
Exchange,CN=Services,CN=Configuration,DC=company,DC=pri
   First Storage Group(Created 12/1/2004 8:29:59 PM)
CN=Second Storage Group,CN=InformationStore,CN=MAIL01,CN=Servers,CN=First Administrative
Group,CN=Administrative Groups,CN=company,CN=Microsoft
Exchange,CN=Services,CN=Configuration,DC=company,DC=pri
   Second Storage Group(Created 4/27/2005 12:06:55 AM)
CN=ScriptingAnswers,CN=InformationStore,CN=MAIL01,CN=Servers,CN=First Administrative
Group,CN=Administrative Groups,CN=company,CN=Microsoft
Exchange,CN=Services,CN=Configuration,DC=company,DC=pri
   ScriptingAnswers(Created 8/9/2005 5:13:13 PM)
```

This code will return all storage groups for the entire Exchange organization. If you have only one Exchange server, all the storage groups will be on the same server. However, if you have multiple servers and you want to display only information about storage groups on a specific server, you have to search the storage group's distinguished name. Because the storage group is a child object of the Exchange server, the Exchange server name appears in the distinguished name. For example, a storage group on the server MAIL01 might have a distinguished name like *CN=First Storage Group,CN=InformationStore,CN=MAIL01,CN=Servers, CN=First Administrative Group,CN=Administrative Groups,CN=COMPANY,CN=Microsoft Exchange,CN=Services,CN=Configuration,DC=company,DC=pri*. If we want to see only storage groups for this server, we might modify the script like this.

```
strSrv="MAIL01"
do while not RS.EOF
  If InStr(rs.Fields("distinguishedname"),strSrv) then
    wscript.echo rs.Fields("distinguishedname")
    WScript.echo vbtab & rs.Fields("name") & "(Created " &_
    rs.fields("whencreated") & ")"
  end if
  rs.movenext
Loop
```

We can also get information about Exchange mailbox stores by querying Active Directory, as shown in the script in Listing 15-3.

Listing 15-3 List Exchange Mailbox Stores

```
'Get list of Mailbox Stores
Dim objRootDSE
Dim objConfiguration
Dim conn
Dim cmd
Dim RS

Set objRootDSE = GetObject("LDAP://rootDSE")
strConfiguration = "LDAP://" & objRootDSE.Get("configurationNamingContext")
Set objConfiguration = GetObject(strConfiguration)
strPath=objConfiguration.ADSpath

 strQuery="Select distinguishedname,name,whencreated from '" & strPath &_
  "' WHERE objectclass='msExchPrivateMDB' "

WScript.Echo strQuery & vbcrlf
set cat=GetObject("GC:")
for each obj in cat
 set GC=obj
Next

set conn=Createobject("ADODB.Connection")
set cmd=CreateObject("ADODB.Command")
conn.Provider="ADSDSOObject"
conn.Open

set cmd.ActiveConnection=conn
set RS=conn.Execute(strQuery)
do while not RS.EOF
   WScript.Echo RS.Fields("distinguishedname")
   WScript.Echo vbTab & RS.Fields("name") & "(Created " &_
   RS.fields("whencreated") & ")"
   rs.movenext
Loop
rs.Close
conn.Close
```

Again, the script hasn't really changed except for the object class in our query. Now we're searching for *msExchPrivateMDB* objects.

```
strQuery="Select distinguishedname,name,whencreated from '" & strPath &_
 "' WHERE objectclass='msExchPrivateMDB' "
```

Active Directory can't tell us much about the actual mailbox store. For example, it can't tell us how large it is, but it can tell us how it is defined, and this information can include the mailboxes within each mailbox store. The script in Listing 15-4 is very similar to Listing 15-3 except that it will also display every mailbox within the storage group.

Listing 15-4 List Mailbox Stores and Mailboxes

```
'Get list of Mailbox Stores
Dim objRootDSE
Dim objConfiguration
Dim conn
Dim cmd
Dim RS

Set objRootDSE = GetObject("LDAP://rootDSE")
strConfiguration = "LDAP://" & objRootDSE.Get("configurationNamingContext")
Set objConfiguration = GetObject(strConfiguration)
strPath=objConfiguration.ADSpath

strQuery="Select distinguishedname,name,homeMDBBL from '" & strPath &_
"' WHERE objectclass='msExchPrivateMDB' "

WScript.Echo strQuery & vbcrlf
set cat=GetObject("GC:")
for each obj in cat
 set GC=obj
Next

set conn=Createobject("ADODB.Connection")
set cmd=CreateObject("ADODB.Command")
conn.Provider="ADSDSOObject"
conn.Open

set cmd.ActiveConnection=conn
set RS=conn.Execute(strQuery)
do while not RS.EOF
    WScript.Echo RS.Fields("distinguishedname")
    WScript.Echo vbTab & "Mailboxes on " & RS.Fields("name")
    tmpArray=RS.Fields("homeMDBBL")
    For m=0 To UBound(tmpArray)
        WScript.Echo vbTab & " " & tmpArray(m)
    next
    rs.movenext
Loop
rs.Close
conn.Close
```

This script takes the script in Listing 15-3 and adds the *homeMDBBL* attribute to the query.

```
strQuery="Select distinguishedname,name,homeMDBBL from '" & strPath &_
"' WHERE objectclass='msExchPrivateMDB' "
```

The *homeMDBBL* attribute is multi-valued and contains the distinguished name of the account attached to each mailbox. Because the attribute is multi-valued, we treat it as an array.

```
do while not RS.EOF
    WScript.Echo RS.Fields("distinguishedname")
    WScript.Echo vbTab & "Mailboxes on " & RS.Fields("name")
    tmpArray=RS.Fields("homeMDBBL")
    For m=0 To UBound(tmpArray)
        WScript.Echo vbTab & " " & tmpArray(m)
    next
    rs.movenext
Loop
```

Understanding Exchange 2003 WMI Classes

Microsoft Exchange 2000 had a few new WMI classes, but Exchange 2003 introduces several more. You now have even more opportunities to use WMI classes in your scripts. Table 15-1 lists the new classes.

Table 15-1   Exchange 2003 WMI Classes

Exchange_FolderTree	Exchange_QueueSMTPVirtualServer
Exchange_Link	Exchange_QueueX400VirtualServer
Exchange_Logon	Exchange_ScheduleInterval
Exchange_Mailbox	Exchange_Server
Exchange_PublicFolder	Exchange_SMTPLink
Exchange_Queue	Exchange_SMTPQueue
Exchange_QueueCacheReloadEvent	Exchange_X400Link
Exchange_QueuedMessage	Exchange_X400Queue
Exchange_QueuedSMTPMessage	Exchange_QueuedX400Message

These classes are located in the *root\MicrosoftExchangev2* namespace. You can view them with a tool like Scriptomatic.

> **Important**   If you run Exchange 2003 on Microsoft Windows Server 2000, you likely won't see most of these classes. To use the new WMI classes, you need to run Exchange 2003 on Microsoft Windows Server 2003.

We won't go into detail about each new class, but let's take a quick look at the *Exchange_Server* class. Listing 15-5 is a script that uses this WMI class.

Listing 15-5 List Exchange Server Information

```
On Error Resume Next
strSrv="MAIL01"

Set objWMIService = GetObject("winmgmts:\\" & strSrv &_
 "\root\MicrosoftExchangev2")
Set colItems = objWMIService.ExecQuery("Select AdministrativeGroup,DN," &_
"ExchangeVersion,FQDN,Name,RoutingGroup,CreationTime,Name," &_
"IsFrontEndServer,MessageTrackingEnabled,SubjectLoggingEnabled," &_
"LastModificationTime  from Exchange_Server where name='" & strSrv &_
 "'",,48)

For Each objItem In colItems
    If objItem.FQDN="" Then
      wscript.echo "Failed to get Exchange server information from WMI." &_
      " Verify the Microsoft Exchange Management service is running on " &_
      strSRV
    Else
      wscript.echo UCase(objItem.FQDN) & " [" &_
      objItem.Exchangeversion & "]"
      wscript.echo "Administrative Group: " &_
       objItem.AdministrativeGroup
      wscript.echo "Last modified: " &_
       ConvertTime(objItem.LastModificationTime)
      wscript.echo "Front End Server: " & objItem.IsFrontEndServer
      wscript.echo "Message Tracking: " & objItem.MessageTrackingEnabled
      wscript.echo "Subject logging: " & objItem.SubjectLoggingEnabled
    End If
Next

Function ConvertTime(strTime)
On Error Resume Next

yr = Left(strTime,4)
mo = mid(strTime,5,2)
dy = mid(strTime,7,2)
tm = Mid(strTime,9,6)

ConvertTime=mo & "/" & dy & "/" & yr

End Function
```

We start by connecting to the Exchange namespace on the Exchange 2003 server.

```
strSrv="MAIL01"
Set objWMIService = GetObject("winmgmts:\\" & strSrv &_
 "\root\MicrosoftExchangev2")
```

This object class has many properties and we will query for several of them.

```
Set colItems = objWMIService.ExecQuery("Select AdministrativeGroup,DN," &_
"ExchangeVersion,FQDN,Name,RoutingGroup,CreationTime,Name," &_
"IsFrontEndServer,MessageTrackingEnabled,SubjectLoggingEnabled," &_
"LastModificationTime from Exchange_Server where name='" & strSrv &_
 "'",,48)
```

> **Troubleshooting**   You might find it odd that we have to specify the server name as part of a conditional clause in the query. It appears there is a minor bug. A query string of *Select * from Exchange_Server* will work just fine. But if you query *Select FQDN, ExchangeVersion,Name from Exchange_Server*, the query will fail. If you want a selective query, you need to use a qualifier, as we do here.

The query returns a WMI collection that we then enumerate.

```
For Each objItem In colItems
     If objItem.FQDN="" Then
       wscript.echo "Failed to get Exchange server information from WMI." &_
       " Verify the Microsoft Exchange Management service is running on " &_
       strSRV
     Else
       wscript.echo UCase(objItem.FQDN) & " [" &_
       objItem.Exchangeversion & "]"
       wscript.echo "Administrative Group: " &_
        objItem.AdministrativeGroup
       wscript.echo "Last modified: " &_
        ConvertTime(objItem.LastModificationTime)
       wscript.echo "Front End Server: " & objItem.IsFrontEndServer
       wscript.echo "Message Tracking: " & objItem.MessageTrackingEnabled
       wscript.echo "Subject logging: " & objItem.SubjectLoggingEnabled
     End If
Next
```

Here's another snippet showing what you can do with a WMI Exchange class. This code uses the *Exchange_PublicFolder* class to calculate the total size of all public folder messages.

```
strSrv="MAIL01"
iTotal=0
Set objWMIService = GetObject("winmgmts:\\" & strSrv &_
 "\root\MicrosoftExchangev2")
strPFQuery="Select * from Exchange_PublicFolder"
Set colItems = objWMIService.ExecQuery(strPFQuery,,48)
For Each objItem in colItems
  strFldrNAme=objItem.Name
  iFldrSize=objItem.TotalMessageSize
  iTotal=iTotal + iFldrSize
Next

Wscript.echo FormatNumber(iTotal/1048576,2) & " MB"
```

> **More Info**   For more information about using WMI with Exchange 2003, take a look at the excellent tutorials by Alain Lissoir at
>
> *www.microsoft.com/technet/scriptcenter/topics/exchange/ex03_wmi1.mspx*
>
> *www.microsoft.com/technet/scriptcenter/topics/exchange/ex03_wmi2.mspx*
>
> *www.microsoft.com/technet/scriptcenter/topics/exchange/ex03_wmi3.mspx*
>
> (These links are on the companion CD; click *Managing Exchange 2003 with WMI*, parts 1, 2, and 3, respectively.)

Scripting the Exchange Server State Class

The WMI class, *ExchangeServerState*, will give you information about the status of an Exchange server. For example, if you have an Exchange cluster, you can use this class to check the cluster state. Some key properties you can work with include the following:

- *ClusterState*   Indicates the condition of your Exchange cluster. This property returns a value of 0 (unknown), 1 (OK), 2 (warning), or 3 (error). This is a read-only property.

- *DiskState*   Indicates the condition of disk storage. This property returns a value of 0 (unknown), 1 (OK), 2 (warning), or 3 (error). This is a read-only property.

- *DN*   Returns the distinguished name of your Exchange server.

- *GroupDN*   Returns the distinguished name of the routing group to which the Exchange server belongs.

- *MemoryState*   Indicates the condition of memory on the Exchange server. This property returns a value of 0 (unknown), 1 (OK), 2 (warning), or 3 (error). This is a read-only property.

- *Name*   Returns the netBIOS name of the Exchange server.

- *QueueState*   Indicates the condition of Exchange mail queues. This property returns a value of 0 (unknown), 1 (OK), 2 (warning), or 3 (error). This is a read-only property.

- *ServerState*   Indicates the overall condition of the Exchange server. This property returns a value of 0 (unknown), 1 (OK), 2 (warning), or 3 (error). This is a read-only property.

- *Unreachable*   Returns a Boolean value that indicates whether the Exchange server can be contacted. It returns TRUE if the server is unreachable.

- *Version*   Returns version information for Microsoft Exchange.

The script in Listing 15-6 on the next page demonstrates this class. Unlike some of the other WMI classes we've looked at, this one is in the *root\cimv2\applications\exchange* namespace.

Listing 15-6 List Exchange Server Information

```
On Error Resume Next
Dim strComputer
Dim objWMIService
Dim propValue
Dim objItem
Dim SWBemlocator
Dim UserName
Dim Password
Dim colItems

strComputer = "MAIL01"
UserName = ""
Password = ""
Set SWBemlocator = CreateObject("WbemScripting.SWbemLocator")
Set objWMIService = SWBemlocator.ConnectServer(strComputer,_
"\root\cimv2\applications\exchange",UserName,Password)
strQuery="Select * from ExchangeServerState"
Set colItems = objWMIService.ExecQuery(strQuery,,48)
For Each objItem in colItems
    WScript.Echo "ClusterState: " & objItem.ClusterState
    WScript.Echo "ClusterStateString: " & objItem.ClusterStateString
    WScript.Echo "CPUState: " & objItem.CPUState
    WScript.Echo "CPUStateString: " & objItem.CPUStateString
    WScript.Echo "DisksState: " & objItem.DisksState
    WScript.Echo "DisksStateString: " & objItem.DisksStateString
    WScript.Echo "DN: " & objItem.DN
    WScript.Echo "GroupDN: " & objItem.GroupDN
    WScript.Echo "GroupGUID: " & objItem.GroupGUID
    WScript.Echo "GUID: " & objItem.GUID
    WScript.Echo "MemoryState: " & objItem.MemoryState
    WScript.Echo "MemoryStateString: " & objItem.MemoryStateString
    WScript.Echo "Name: " & objItem.Name
    WScript.Echo "QueuesState: " & objItem.QueuesState
    WScript.Echo "QueuesStateString: " & objItem.QueuesStateString
    WScript.Echo "ServerMaintenance: " & objItem.ServerMaintenance
    WScript.Echo "ServerState: " & objItem.ServerState
    WScript.Echo "ServerStateString: " & objItem.ServerStateString
    WScript.Echo "ServicesState: " & objItem.ServicesState
    WScript.Echo "ServicesStateString: " & objItem.ServicesStateString
    WScript.Echo "Unreachable: " & objItem.Unreachable
    WScript.Echo "Version: " & objItem.Version
Next
```

Scripting Exchange Storage Groups

To work with Exchange storage groups, you must have CDO for Exchange Management (CDOEXM) installed. After you install the Exchange management console on your desktop, you have everything you need. CDOEXM includes several objects you will instantiate in your script. Take a look at the script in Listing 15-7.

Listing 15-7 List Storage Groups

```
On Error Resume Next
strTitle="Storage Group Report"
strServer=InputBox("What is the name of the Exchange Server?",_
strTitle,"MAIL01")
If strServer="" Then
    WScript.Quit
else
    'Call report subroutine
    SGReport strServer
End if
WScript.Quit
'///////////////////////////////////////////////////////////////
Sub SGReport(strServer)
Dim iServer
Dim iSGs
Dim iMBS

Set iServer=CreateObject("CDOEXM.ExchangeServer")
Set iSGs=CreateObject("CDOEXM.StorageGroup")
'connect to Exchange server with CDOEXM
iServer.DataSource.Open strServer

'return array of storage groups
arrSGs=iServer.StorageGroups

'enumerate the array
For i=0 To UBound(arrSGs)
    'get the URL for each storage group
    strSGUrl=arrSGs(i)
    'connect to each storage group
    iSGs.DataSource.Open "LDAP://" & iServer.DirectoryServer & "/" &_
 strSGUrl
    strData=strData & iSGs.Name & VBCRLF
    strData=strData & vbTab & "LogPath: " &iSGs.LogFilePath & VBCRLF
    strData=strData & vbTab & "SystemPath:" & iSGs.SystemFilePath & VBCRLF
Next

'display the data
WScript.Echo strData

End sub
```

This script simply lists the name of each storage group as well as its log and database paths for a specified Exchange server. The heart of the script is the creation of two CDOEXM objects. We need one for the Exchange server object, and one for the storage group object.

```
Set iServer=CreateObject("CDOEXM.ExchangeServer")
Set iSGs=CreateObject("CDOEXM.StorageGroup")
```

With these objects, we can now connect to the Exchange server specified by the *strServer* variable and return an array of all the storage groups.

```
'connect to Exchange server with CDOEXM
iServer.DataSource.Open strServer
'return array of storage groups
arrSGs=iServer.StorageGroups
```

Then it is just a matter of enumerating the array. We do this by establishing a connection to each storage group by using the group's URL, which is essentially its distinguished name.

```
'get the URL for each storage group
    strSGUrl=arrSGs(i)
    'connect to each storage group
    iSGs.DataSource.Open "LDAP://" & iServer.DirectoryServer & "/" &_
strSGUrl
```

The storage group object has several properties of interest, including the path for the storage group's log files and the path for system transaction logs.

```
strData=strData & iSGs.Name & VBCRLF
    strData=strData & vbTab & "LogPath: " &iSGs.LogFilePath & VbCrLf
    strData=strData & vbTab & "SystemPath:" & iSGs.SystemFilePath & VBCRLF
```

There is a *MailboxStoreDBs* property that can be used to get mailbox store information. We'll look at this property later in this chapter.

Although it is a relatively simple task to create a new storage group on a single Exchange server, if you would like to automate the build process or have to provision many Exchange servers, you might want to script this process. The script in Listing 15-8 can be used to create a new storage group.

```
Listing 15-8 Create Storage Group
'CreateNewSG.vbs
strTitle="Create New Storage Group"
strServer=InputBox("What is the name of the Exchange Server?",strTitle,_
"MAIL01")
strNewSG=InputBox("What is the name of the new storage group?",strTitle,_
"ScriptingAnswers")

CreateNewStorageGroup strNewSG,strServer
WScript.Echo "Done!"

WScript.quit

Sub CreateNewStorageGroup(strSGName,strComputerName)

  On Error Resume Next
  Dim iServer
  Dim iStGroup
  Dim strTemp
```

```
Set iServer=CreateObject("CDOEXM.ExchangeServer")
Set iStGroup=CreateObject("CDOEXM.StorageGroup")

  ' Set the name of the StorageGroup
  iStGroup.Name = strSGName

  ' Bind to the Exchange Server
  iServer.DataSource.Open strComputerName

   For Each sg In iServer.StorageGroups
    strTemp = sg
    Exit For
  Next
   'cut out the Storage Group name from URL
  strTemp = Mid(strTemp, InStr(2, strTemp, "CN"))
  ' Build the URL to the StorageGroup
  strSGUrl = "LDAP://" & iServer.DirectoryServer & "/CN=" & strSGName &_
  "," & strTemp
  WScript.Echo "Creating " & strSGUrl
  ' Save the StorageGroup
  iStGroup.DataSource.SaveTo strSGUrl

End Sub
```

The subroutine creates the storage group. We need to specify a name for the storage group and the name of the Exchange server where it will be created. Like we did in Listing 15-7, we create the CDOEXM objects for the Exchange server and storage group.

```
Set iServer=CreateObject("CDOEXM.ExchangeServer")
Set iStGroup=CreateObject("CDOEXM.StorageGroup")
```

Given the name of the storage group, we can set the name of the storage group object.

```
  ' Set the name of the StorageGroup
  iStGroup.Name = strSGName
```

We bind to the Exchange server by using the *DataSource* property of the *Exchange CDOEXM* object.

```
' Bind to the Exchange Server
  iServer.DataSource.Open strComputerName
```

To create the new storage group, we need to know the full URL of the storage group. We could enter the long string as a parameter, but that would be too much work. Instead, we look at the URL of any existing storage group on the Exchange server, and save the parts of it that we need. We loop through all the storage groups, grab the first one, and exit the loop.

```
  For Each sg In iServer.StorageGroups
    strTemp = sg
    Exit For
  Next
```

We use the *Mid* function to strip out the name of the storage group, which will leave us with the base URL.

```
 'cut out the Storage Group name from URL
strTemp = Mid(strTemp, InStr(2, strTemp, "CN"))
```

Then we can create the URL of the new storage group.

```
' Build the URL to the StorageGroup
strSGUrl = "LDAP://" & iServer.DirectoryServer & "/CN=" & strSGName & "," & strTemp
```

Armed with the URL, we can use the *SaveTo* method to create the new storage group.

```
WScript.Echo "Creating " & strSGUrl
 ' Save the StorageGroup
iStGroup.DataSource.SaveTo strSGUrl
```

The log and database files for the new storage group will use their default settings. You can use the *MoveLogFiles* and *MoveSystemFiles* methods to change the location after the storage group has been created.

Deleting a storage group is very easy, as demonstrated in Listing 15-9.

Listing 15-9 Delete Storage Group

```
'Delete Storage Group
strTitle="Delete Storage Group"
strServer=InputBox("What is the name of the Exchange Server?",_
strTitle,"MAIL01")
strSG=InputBox("What is the name of the storage group to delete?",_
strTitle,"ScriptingAnswers")

DeleteSG strServer,strSG

Sub DeleteSG(strServer,strSGName)

Dim iServer, iSTGroup
Dim arrSGs

strSGUrl=""
Set iServer=CreateObject("CDOEXM.ExchangeServer")
Set iSTGroup=CreateObject("CDOEXM.storagegroup")

iServer.DataSource.Open strServer

arrSGs=iServer.StorageGroups

For i=0 To UBound(arrSGs)
If InStr(1, UCase(arrSGs(i)), UCase(strSGName)) <>    0 Then
   strSGUrl = arrSGs(i)
 End If
Next
```

```
If strSGUrl <> "" Then
  ' Bind to the StorageGroup
  iSTGroup.DataSource.Open "LDAP://" & iServer.DirectoryServer & "/" &_
  strSGUrl

  rc=MsgBox("Are you sure you want to delete" & VbCrLf &_
  strSGurl & "?",vbYesNo,strTitle)
   If rc=vbYes Then
     ' Delete the StorageGroup
     iSTGroup.DataSource.Delete
   End If
End If

End sub
```

Structurally, this script is very similar to Listing 15-8. After we connect to the Exchange server and storage groups, we simply look at each storage group's name until we find the one we want to delete.

```
arrSGs=iServer.StorageGroups

For i=0 To UBound(arrSGs)
 If InStr(1, UCase(arrSGs(i)), UCase(strSGName)) <>   0 Then
   strSGUrl = arrSGs(i)
 End If
Next
```

After we have the storage group's URL, we can bind to it.

```
If strSGUrl <> "" Then
 ' Bind to the StorageGroup
 iSTGroup.DataSource.Open "LDAP://" & iServer.DirectoryServer & "/" & strSGUrl
```

It's always a good idea to verify with the user when deleting something as major as a storage group. But assuming the user confirms the deletion, we simply call the *Delete* method and the storage group is gone.

```
rc=MsgBox("Are you sure you want to delete" & VbCrLf &_
   strSGurl & "?",vbYesNo,strTitle)
   If rc=vbYes Then
   ' Delete the StorageGroup
  iSTGroup.DataSource.Delete
```

Scripting Exchange Mailboxes

Working with mailbox stores and individual mailboxes requires several technologies. We will use CDOEXM to manage mailbox stores in much the same way we manage storage groups. We will use WMI to manage individual mailboxes within each storage group. We will also use ADSI to manage the connection between mailbox and security account. Let's start with the script in Listing 15-10 on the next page, which will list all the mailbox stores for a given Exchange server.

Listing 15-10 List Mailbox Stores

```
strTitle="Mailbox Storage DB Report"
strServer=InputBox("What is the name of the Exchange Server?",_
strTitle,"MAIL01")

MBReport strServer
WScript.Quit

Sub MBReport(strServer)
Dim iServer
Dim iSGs
Dim iMBs

Set iServer=CreateObject("CDOEXM.ExchangeServer")
Set iSGs=CreateObject("CDOEXM.StorageGroup")
Set iMBs=CreateObject("CDOEXM.MailboxStoreDB")
iServer.DataSource.Open strServer

arrSGs=iServer.StorageGroups

For i=0 To UBound(arrSGs)
    strSGUrl=arrSGs(i)
    'WScript.Echo strSGUrl
    iSGs.DataSource.Open "LDAP://" & iServer.DirectoryServer &_
     "/" & strSGUrl
    strData=strData & iSGs.Name & vbcrlf
    arrMBStores=iSGs.MailboxStoreDBs
    For j=0 To UBound(arrMBStores)
        iMBS.DataSource.open "LDAP://" & arrMBStores(j)
        strData=strData & vbTab & iMBs.Name& VbCrLf
        strData=strData & vbTab & iMBs.Status & VbCrLf
        strData=strData & vbTab & " DBPath:" & iMBs.DBPath& VbCrLf
        strData=strData & vbTab & " Streaming DB Path:" &_
         iMBs.SLVPath & vbcrlf
        strData=strData & vbTab & " Last Backup:" &_
         iMBs.LastFullBackupTime & vbcrlf
        strData=strData & vbTab & " StorageQuotaWarning:" &_
         iMBs.StoreQuota & vbcrlf
        strData=strData & vbTab & " StorageQuotaLimit:" &_
         iMBs.OverQuotaLimit & VbCrLf    Next
Next

WScript.Echo strData

End sub
```

The format of this script should look pretty familiar now, so we won't spend much time re-analyzing it. Each storage group object has a *MailboxStoreDBs* property that returns a collection of mailbox stores for a given storage group.

```
arrMBStores=iSGs.MailboxStoreDBs
```

Like storage groups, each mailbox store is defined with a URL. We can use this URL to establish a connection to each mailbox store.

```
For j=0 To UBound(arrMBStores)
        iMBs.DataSource.open "LDAP://" & arrMBStores(j)
```

After we are connected, we can display property information about each mailbox store.

```
        iMBS.DataSource.open "LDAP://" & arrMBStores(j)
        strData=strData & vbTab & iMBs.Name& VbCrLf
        strData=strData & vbTab & iMBs.Status & VbCrLf
        strData=strData & vbTab & " DBPath:" & iMBs.DBPath& VbCrLf
        strData=strData & vbTab & " Streaming DB Path:" &_
         iMBs.SLVPath & vbcrlf
        strData=strData & vbTab & " Last Backup:" &_
         iMBs.LastFullBackupTime & vbcrlf
        strData=strData & vbTab & " StorageQuotaWarning:" &_
         iMBs.StoreQuota & vbcrlf
        strData=strData & vbTab & " StorageQuotaLimit:" &_
         iMBs.OverQuotaLimit & VbCrLf
```

If you want to mount or dismount the store, you use the *Mount* or *Dismount* methods, respectively.

```
iMBs.Dismount
```

You have to use the *Mount* method if you create a new mailbox store, as we do in Listing 15-11.

Listing 15-11 Create Mailbox Store

```
strTitle="Create New MailBox Store"
strServer=InputBox("What is the name of the Exchange Server?",_
strTitle,"MAIL01")
strSG=InputBox("What is the name of the storage group to create the" &_
" new mailstore under?",strTitle,"First Storage Group")
strMDBName=InputBox("What is the name of the new mail store?",_
strTitle,"ScriptingAnswers Mail")

CreateNewMailStoreDB strMDBName,strServer,strSG
WScript.Quit

Sub CreateNewMailStoreDB(strMDBName,strServer,strSG)

Dim iServer
Dim iMDB

Set iServer=CreateObject("CDOEXM.ExchangeServer")
Set iMDB=CreateObject("CDOEXM.MailboxStoreDB")
' Set the name of the MailboxStoreDB
iMDB.Name = strMDBName
```

```
' Bind to the Exchange Server
iServer.DataSource.Open strServer

' Start to build the URL to the MailboxStoreDB - first part
strTemp = "LDAP://" & iServer.DirectoryServer & "/" & "cn=" & strMDBName &_
",")"

arrStGroup = iServer.StorageGroups

' Look in the StorageGroups array if the StorageGroup with strSG exists
If strSG = "" Then
 ' Finish to build the URL to the MailboxStoreDB - add last part
 strMDBUrl = strTemp & iServer.StorageGroups(0)
Else
 For i = 0 To UBound(arrStGroup)
     If InStr(1, UCase(arrStGroup(i)), UCase(strSG)) <> 0 Then
         strMDBUrl = arrStGroup(i)
     End If
 Next
 If strMDBUrl <> "" Then
     ' Finish to build the URL to the MailboxStoreDB - add last part
     strMDBUrl = strTemp & strMDBUrl
 End If
End If

' Save the New MailboxStoreDB
iMDB.DataSource.SaveTo strMDBUrl

' Mount the MailboxStoreDB
 iMDB.Mount
WScript.Echo "Finished creating " & strMDBName
End Sub
```

To create a mailbox store, we need to know the names of the Exchange server, the storage group, and the new mailbox store.

```
strServer=InputBox("What is the name of the Exchange Server?",_
strTitle,"MAIL01")
strSG=InputBox("What is the name of the storage group to create the" &_
" new mailstore under?",strTitle,"First Storage Group")
strMDBName=InputBox("What is the name of the new mail store?",_
strTitle,"ScriptingAnswers Mail")
```

Creating the mailbox store requires CDOEXM objects for the Exchange server and mailbox store, but interestingly enough, not for the storage group.

```
Set iServer=CreateObject("CDOEXM.ExchangeServer")
Set iMDB=CreateObject("CDOEXM.MailboxStoreDB")
```

Just as we did when we created a storage group, we can set the flat name of the mailbox store and create the mailbox store URL. We will need the URL when we commit the change to the Exchange server.

```
' Set the name of the MailboxStoreDB
iMDB.Name = strMDBName

' Bind to the Exchange Server
iServer.DataSource.Open strServer

' Start to build the URL to the MailboxStoreDB - first part
strTemp = "LDAP://" & iServer.DirectoryServer & "/" & "cn=" &_
 strMDBName & ","
```

Because the mailbox store is contained within the storage group, we need to get the storage group's URL because that will be part of the final mailbox store's URL, which is the *strMDBUrl* variable.

```
arrStGroup = iServer.StorageGroups

' Look in the StorageGroups array if the StorageGroup with strSG exists
If strSG = "" Then
 ' Finish to build the URL to the MailboxStoreDB - add last part
 strMDBUrl = strTemp & iServer.StorageGroups(0)
Else
 For i = 0 To UBound(arrStGroup)
     If InStr(1, UCase(arrStGroup(i)), UCase(strSG)) <> 0 Then
         strMDBUrl = arrStGroup(i)
     End If
 Next
If strMDBUrl <> "" Then
     ' Finish to build the URL to the MailboxStoreDB - add last part
     strMDBUrl = strTemp & strMDBUrl
 End If
End If
```

After we have the mailbox store's URL, we can commit the change to the Exchange server and the mailbox store will be created.

```
' Save the New MailboxStoreDB
iMDB.DataSource.SaveTo strMDBUrl
```

After we mount the store, it will be ready to be used.

```
' Mount the MailboxStoreDB
 iMDB.Mount
```

As the script in Listing 15-12 on the next page shows, to delete a mailbox store, we first need its URL. After we have that, we can connect to the mailbox store and call the *Delete* method.

Listing 15-12 Delete Mailbox Store

```
strTitle="Delete MailBox Store"
strServer=InputBox("What is the name of the Exchange Server?",_
strTitle,"MAIL01")
strSG=InputBox("What Storage Group is the mail db in?",strTitle,_
"First Storage Group")
strMDBName=InputBox("What is the name of the mail store to deletee?",_
strTitle,"ScriptingAnswers Mail")

DeleteMDBStore strServer,strSG,strMDBName
WScript.Quit

Sub DeleteMDBStore(strServer,strSG,strMDBName)

Dim iServer,iMDB

Set iServer=CreateObject("CDOEXM.ExchangeServer")
Set iMDB=CreateObject("CDOEXM.MailboxStoreDB")

iServer.DataSource.Open strServer

strTemp = "LDAP://" & iServer.DirectoryServer & "/" & "cn=" & strMDBName &_
","

arrStGroup = iServer.StorageGroups

' Look in the StorageGroups array if the StorageGroup with strSGName exists
If strSG = "" Then
    ' Add last part to the URL to the MailboxStoreDB
    strMDBUrl = strTemp & iServer.StorageGroups(0)
Else
    For i = 0 To UBound(arrStGroup)
        If InStr(1, UCase(arrStGroup(i)), UCase(strSG)) <> 0 Then
            strMDBUrl = arrStGroup(i)
        End If
    Next
    If strMDBUrl <> "" Then
        ' Add last part to the URL to the MailboxStoreDB
        strMDBUrl = strTemp & strMDBUrl
    End If
End If

' Bind to the MailboxStoreDB
iMDB.DataSource.Open strMDBUrl

' Delete the MailboxStoreDB
iMDB.DataSource.Delete

WScript.Echo "Deleted " & strMDBName

End Sub
```

To create an individual mailbox within a specific mailbox store, we need to use ADSI. Each mailbox is connected to a user or group SID in Active Directory, so we use ADSI to modify the user object in Active Directory. To create the mailbox, you need to know the distinguished name of the mailbox store. This will be something like this.

```
"CN=Mailbox Store (MAIL01),CN=First Storage Group,CN=InformationStore," &_
"CN=MAIL01,CN=Servers,CN=First Administrative Group,CN=Administrative " &_
 "Groups,CN=MATRIX,CN=Microsoft Exchange,CN=Services, CN=Configuration," &_
 "DC=COMPANY,DC=PRI"
```

You could hard-code this into a script if you had a single mailbox store. But for something more dynamic, you might want to search Active Directory for a list of mailbox stores, present the list to the administrator, and let him or her choose. The script in Listing 15-13 demonstrates this.

Listing 15-13 Create a Mailbox

```
Dim objUser
On Error Resume Next
strUserDN="CN=Jeff Hicks,OU=Employees,DC=Company,DC=Pri"

Set objUser=GetObject("LDAP://" & strUserDN)
If objUser.HomeMDB="" Then
    strMailDN=SelectMailStore()
    WScript.Echo "Creating mailbox For " & objUser.cn & " on " &_
     strMailDN
    objUser.CreateMailbox strMailDN
    objUser.SetInfo
    If Err.Number <>0 Then
        strMsg="Error creating mailbox for " & objUser & " on " &_
         strMailDN & vbcrlf & Err.Number & " " & Err.Description
        WScript.Echo strMsg
    Else
        WScript.Echo "Successfully created mailbox for " & strUserDN
    End If
Else
    WScript.Echo objuser.cn & " already has a mailbox"
End If
WScript.Quit
'//////////////////////////////////////////////////
Function SelectMailStore()
On Error Resume Next
Dim objRootDSE
Dim objConfiguration
Dim cat
Dim conn
Dim cmd
Dim RS
Dim objDict

Set objDict=CreateObject("scripting.dictionary")
Set objRootDSE = GetObject("LDAP://rootDSE")
x=1
```

```
strConfiguration = "LDAP://" & objRootDSE.Get("configurationNamingContext")
Set objConfiguration = GetObject(strConfiguration)

strQuery="Select name,cn,distinguishedname from '" & _
objConfiguration.ADSPath & "' Where objectclass='msExchPrivateMDB'"

set cat=GetObject("GC:")
for each obj In cat
 set GC=obj
Next

AdsPath=GC.ADSPath

set conn=CreateObject("ADODB.Connection")
set cmd=CreateObject("ADODB.Command")
conn.Provider="ADSDSOObject"
conn.Open

set cmd.ActiveConnection=conn
set RS=conn.Execute(strQuery)

do while not RS.EOF
    DN=rs.Fields("distinguishedname")
    CN=RS.Fields("cn")
    NM=RS.Fields("name")
   objDict.Add x,DN
   strResults=strResults &"(" & x & ") " &DN & VbCrLf
   x=x+1
    rs.movenext
Loop
rs.Close
conn.Close
t=1

a=objDict.Items
   For i=0 To objDict.Count-1
   c=c & "(" & i+1 & ")" & a(i) & VbCrLf
   'display available mailbox stores in groups of 4
       If t<>4 AND i<>objDict.count-1 Then
         t=t+1
       Else
       MsgBox c,vbOKOnly,"Available Mailbox Stores"
       t=1
       c=""
       End If
    Next
iDN=Inputbox("Enter in the number of the mail store you want to use.",_
"Select Mail Store","0")
   If iDN = "" Then
       WScript.Echo "Nothing entered or you cancelled."
       WScript.Quit
   End If

If objDict.Exists(Int(iDN)) Then
   SelectMailStore=objDict.Item(Int(iDN))
```

```
    Else
        rc=msgBox ("You selected an invalid number.  Try again.",_
        vbOKCancel+vbExclamation,"Select Mail Store")
        if rc=vbCancel Then
            wscript.Quit
        Else
            Main()
        End If
    End If
End If

End Function
```

The script needs the distinguished name of a user object. In this script, we hard-coded a name for simplicity. We then connect to the user object in Active Directory and check if a mailbox already exists by examining the *HomeMBD* property.

```
strUserDN="CN=Jeff Hicks,OU=Employees,DC=Company,DC=Pri"

Set objUser=GetObject("LDAP://" & strUserDN)
If objUser.HomeMDB="" Then
```

If the property is empty, we call the function to list available mailbox stores.

```
    strMailDN=SelectMailStore()
```

The function searches the global catalog for all object classes that are of the type *msExch-PrivateMDB* in the configuration naming context.

```
Set objDict=CreateObject("scripting.dictionary")
Set objRootDSE = GetObject("LDAP://rootDSE")
x=1
strConfiguration = "LDAP://" & objRootDSE.Get("configurationNamingContext")
Set objConfiguration = GetObject(strConfiguration)

strQuery="Select name,cn,distinguishedname from '" & _
objConfiguration.ADSPath & "' where objectclass='msExchPrivateMDB'"
```

The function puts the results into a dictionary object.

```
set cmd.ActiveConnection=conn
set RS=conn.Execute(strQuery)

Do while not RS.EOF
    DN=rs.Fields("distinguishedname")
    CN=RS.Fields("cn")
    NM=RS.Fields("name")
    objDict.Add x,DN
    strResults=strResults &"(" & x & ") " &DN & VbCrLf
    x=x+1
    'WScript.Echo vbcrlf
    rs.movenext

Loop
```

The dictionary object items are the distinguished names of all the mailbox stores. We enumerate the dictionary and present a numbered list to the administrator.

```
a=objDict.Items
    For i=0 To objDict.Count-1
    c=c & "(" & i+1 & ")" & a(i) & VbCrLf
    'display available mailbox stores in groups of 4
        If t<>4 AND i<>objDict.count-1 Then
          t=t+1
        Else
          MsgBox c,vbOKOnly,"Available Mailbox Stores"
          t=1
          c=""
        End If
    Next
```

This is followed by an *InputBox* function, where the administrator can enter the number of the mailbox store he or she wants to use. The function returns the distinguished name of the mailbox store. After we have this piece of information, creating the mailbox is very simple.

```
objUser.CreateMailbox strMailDN
objUser.SetInfo
```

> **Note**   You can run the script in Listing 15-13 from your desktop provided you have the administrator tools (adminpak.msi) installed in addition to the Exchange management console. You can create mailboxes on a domain controller, but it must also have the Exchange management console installed. Without it, you won't get the Exchange management tabs for the user object in Active Directory.

If you want to move a user's mailbox, you need to know the name of the mailbox store where it will be relocated. Consider the script in Listing 15-14. It is very similar to Listing 15-13 except that we use the *MoveMailbox* method.

Listing 15-14 Move Mailbox
```
On Error Resume Next
Dim objUser
strTitle="Move Mailbox Demo"
strDefault="LDAP://CN=Jeff Hicks,CN=Users,DC=Company,DC=Pri"
strUserDN=InputBox("Enter the full distinguished name of the user:",_
strTitle,strDefault)

Set objUser=GetObject(strUserDN)

if objUser.HomeMDB="" Then
    MsgBox "User has no mailbox defined"
    WScript.Quit
Else
    MsgBox "The user's current mailbox is on " & vbcrlf & objUser.HomeMDB
End If
```

```
'Call a function to list available mailbox stores
strNewMailDN=SelectMailStore

MsgBox "Moving the mailbox may take a few minutes depending on size"

objUser.MoveMailBox "LDAP://" & strNewMailDN
objUser.SetInfo
WScript.Echo "Finished."

WScript.quit

Function SelectMailStore()
On Error Resume Next
Dim objRootDSE
Dim objConfiguration
Dim cat
Dim conn
Dim cmd
Dim RS
Dim objDict

Set objDict=CreateObject("scripting.dictionary")
Set objRootDSE = GetObject("LDAP://rootDSE")
x=1
strConfiguration = "LDAP://" & objRootDSE.Get("configurationNamingContext")
Set objConfiguration = GetObject(strConfiguration)

strQuery="Select name,cn,distinguishedname from '" & _
objConfiguration.ADSPath & "' where objectclass='msExchPrivateMDB'"

set cat=GetObject("GC:")
for each obj in cat
 set GC=obj
Next

AdsPath=GC.ADSPath

set conn=CreateObject("ADODB.Connection")
set cmd=CreateObject("ADODB.Command")
conn.Provider="ADSDSOObject"
conn.Open

set cmd.ActiveConnection=conn
set RS=conn.Execute(strQuery)

do while not RS.EOF
    DN=rs.Fields("distinguishedname")
    CN=RS.Fields("cn")
    NM=RS.Fields("name")
   objDict.Add x,DN
   strResults=strResults &"(" & x & ") " &DN & vbcrlf
   x=x+1
    rs.movenext
Loop
```

```
    rs.Close
    conn.Close
    t=1

a=objDict.Items
    For i=0 To objDict.Count-1
    c=c & "(" & i+1 & ")" & a(i) & vbcrlf
    'display available mailbox stores in groups of 4
        If t<>4 And i<>objDict.count-1 Then
          t=t+1
        Else
        MsgBox c,vbOKOnly,"Available Mailbox Stores"
        t=1
        c=""
        End If
    Next

iDN=Inputbox("Enter in the number of the mail store you want to" &_
" use.","Select Mail Store","0")
    If iDN = "" Then
        WScript.Echo "Nothing entered or you cancelled."
        WScript.Quit
    End If

If objDict.Exists(Int(iDN)) Then
    SelectMailStore=objDict.Item(Int(iDN))
Else
    rc=msgBox ("You selected an invalid number.  Try again.",_
vbOKCancel+vbExclamation,"Select Mail Store")
    if rc=vbCancel Then
        wscript.Quit
    Else
        Main()
    End If
End If

End Function
```

To delete a mailbox, which actually just severs the association between the mailbox and the user's SID, we simply need to establish a connection to the user object in Active Directory and invoke the *DeleteMailbox* method.

```
strUserDN="CN= Jeff Hicks,OU=Authors,DC=company,DC=pri"
set objUser=GetObject("LDAP://" & strUserDN)
objUser.DeleteMailbox
```

To gather information about a specific mailbox, we return to WMI and the *Exchange_Mailbox* class. Listing 15-15 enumerates properties for a given user's mailbox.

Listing 15-15 Get Mailbox Information

```
On Error Resume Next
Dim strComputer
Dim objWMIService
Dim propValue
Dim SWBemlocator
Dim UserName
Dim Password
Dim colItems

strComputer = "MAIL01"
'specify alternate credentials if necessary
UserName = ""
Password = ""
strTitle="Mailbox Query"
strMailBox=InputBox("Enter the display name of the mailbox",_
strTitle,"Administrator")
Set SWBemlocator = CreateObject("WbemScripting.SWbemLocator")
Set objWMIService = SWBemlocator.ConnectServer(strComputer,_
"\root\microsoftexchangev2",UserName,Password)
Set colItems = objWMIService.ExecQuery("Select * from Exchange_Mailbox " &_
"WHERE MailboxDisplayName='" & strMailbox & "'",,48)
For Each objItem in colItems
  If UCase(objItem.MailboxDisplayName)=UCase(strMailBox) Then
    WScript.Echo "AssocContentCount: " & objItem.AssocContentCount
    WScript.Echo "Caption: " & objItem.Caption
    WScript.Echo "DateDiscoveredAbsentInDS: " &_
     objItem.DateDiscoveredAbsentInDS
    WScript.Echo "DeletedMessageSizeExtended: " &_
     objItem.DeletedMessageSizeExtended
    WScript.Echo "Description: " & objItem.Description
    WScript.Echo "InstallDate: " & objItem.InstallDate
    WScript.Echo "LastLoggedOnUserAccount: " &_
     objItem.LastLoggedOnUserAccount
    WScript.Echo "LastLogoffTime: " & objItem.LastLogoffTime
    WScript.Echo "LastLogonTime: " & objItem.LastLogonTime
    WScript.Echo "LegacyDN: " & objItem.LegacyDN
    WScript.Echo "MailboxDisplayName: " & objItem.MailboxDisplayName
    WScript.Echo "MailboxGUID: " & objItem.MailboxGUID
    WScript.Echo "Name: " & objItem.Name
    WScript.Echo "ServerName: " & objItem.ServerName
    WScript.Echo "Size: " & objItem.Size
    WScript.Echo "Status: " & objItem.Status
    WScript.Echo "StorageGroupName: " & objItem.StorageGroupName
    WScript.Echo "StorageLimitInfo: " & objItem.StorageLimitInfo
    WScript.Echo "StoreName: " & objItem.StoreName
    WScript.Echo "TotalItems: " & objItem.TotalItems
  Else
    WScript.Echo "Could not find mailbox for " & strMailbox
  End if
Next
```

The script uses a query to return all properties for an Exchange mailbox object where the display name matches the name provided in the input box.

```
Set colItems = objWMIService.ExecQuery("Select * from Exchange_Mailbox " &_
"WHERE MailboxDisplayName='" & strMailbox & "'",,48)
```

If you want information on more than one user, simply query for all of them. Look at the script in Listing 15-16.

Listing 15-16 Create Mailbox Report

```
Dim SWBemlocator
Dim objWMIService
Dim colItems
Dim objFSO
Dim objFile
strTitle="Mailbox Report"
strComputer ="MAIL01"
UserName = ""
Password = ""
strLog="MailboxReport.csv"
Set objFSO=CreateObject("Scripting.FileSystemObject")
Set objFile=objFSO.CreateTextFile(strLog,True)

strQuery="Select * from Exchange_Mailbox"
objFile.WriteLine "Server,StorageGroup,MailStore,User,Size(KB),TotalItems"
WScript.Echo "Examining " & strComputer
Set SWBemlocator = CreateObject("WbemScripting.SWbemLocator")
Set objWMIService = SWBemlocator.ConnectServer(strComputer,_
"\root\MicrosoftExchangeV2",UserName,Password)
Set colItems = objWMIService.ExecQuery(strQuery,,48)

For Each objItem in colItems
 objFile.writeline objItem.ServerName & "," &objItem.StorageGroupName &_
 "," & objItem.StoreName & "," & Chr(34) & objItem.MailboxDisplayName &_
 Chr(34) & "," & objItem.Size & "," & objItem.TotalItems
Next

objFile.close

WScript.Echo "See " & strLog & " for results."
```

This script creates a report for all Exchange mailboxes on a given Exchange server. The results are written to a comma-separated value (CSV) file, so you can easily review the file in Microsoft Excel.

Viewing Exchange Server Scripting in Action

Before we wrap up this chapter, let's take a look at one more scripting example that pulls a lot of the material together in a single script. The script in Listing 15-17 will produce a master report for all Exchange servers in our organization with version information, service information, queue status, storage groups, mailbox stores, mailboxes, and public folders.

Listing 15-17 Create Master Exchange Report

```
'MasterExchange.vbs
'usage: cscript MasterExchange.vbs
'You must have Exchange Management tools installed in order
'to run this script.

arrServers=GetExchangeServers

For s = 0 To UBound(arrServers)-1
    WScript.Echo "*****Server Information*****"
    ExchangeServerInfo arrServers(s)
    WScript.Echo "*****Server Status*****"
    ExchangeServerState arrServers(s),"",""
    WScript.Echo "*****Service Status*****"
    GetServiceStatus arrServers(s)
    WScript.Echo "*****Queue Status*****"
    GetQueueInfo arrServers(s)
    WScript.Echo "*****Storage Groups*****"
    GetStorageGroups arrServers(s)
    WScript.Echo "*****Public Folders*****"
    GetPublicFolderInfo arrServers(s),"",""
Next
WScript.quit
'/////////////////////////////////////////////////////////
Function GetExchangeServers()
' Find all servers in AD
'Returns an array of Exchange server names
WScript.Echo "Querying Active Directory for Exchange servers"
Dim objRootDSE
Dim objConfiguration
Dim cat
Dim conn
Dim cmd
Dim RS
Set objRootDSE = GetObject("LDAP://rootDSE")

strConfiguration = "LDAP://" & objRootDSE.Get("configurationNamingContext")
Set objConfiguration = GetObject(strConfiguration)

'select Exchange servers but not policies which share the same class
strQuery="Select distinguishedname,name from '" & _
objConfiguration.ADSPath & "' Where objectclass='msExchExchangeServer' " &_
"AND objectclass<>'msExchExchangeServerPolicy'"

strResults=""
Set cat=GetObject("GC:")
For each obj In cat
 Set GC=obj
Next

AdsPath=GC.ADSPath

Set conn=CreateObject("ADODB.Connection")
Set cmd=CreateObject("ADODB.Command")
```

```
conn.Provider="ADSDSOObject"
conn.Open

Set cmd.ActiveConnection=conn
Set RS=conn.Execute(strQuery)
Do while not RS.EOF
 strResults=strResults & rs.Fields("name")&  ";"
 RS.movenext
Loop
RS.Close
conn.Close
GetExchangeServers=Split(strResults,";")

End Function

Sub GetStorageGroups(strServer)
'Get list of Storage Groups on specified server
Dim objRootDSE
Dim objConfiguration
Dim conn
Dim cmd
Dim RS

Set objRootDSE = GetObject("LDAP://rootDSE")
strConfiguration = "LDAP://" & objRootDSE.Get("configurationNamingContext")
Set objConfiguration = GetObject(strConfiguration)
strPath=objConfiguration.ADSpath

strQuery="Select distinguishedname,name,whencreated from '" & strPath &_
 "' WHERE objectclass='msExchStorageGroup'"

set cat=GetObject("GC:")
for each obj in cat
 set GC=obj
Next

set conn=Createobject("ADODB.Connection")
set cmd=CreateObject("ADODB.Command")
conn.Provider="ADSDSOObject"
conn.Open

set cmd.ActiveConnection=conn
set RS=conn.Execute(strQuery)
do while not RS.EOF
 If InStr(UCase(RS.Fields("distinguishedname")),UCase(strServer)) then
   WScript.echo RS.Fields("name") & "(Created " &_
    rs.fields("whencreated") & ")"
   SGReport strServer,RS.Fields("name")
 End If
 rs.movenext
Loop
rs.Close
conn.Close

End Sub
```

```
Sub ExchangeServerInfo(strSrv)
Set objWMIService = GetObject("winmgmts:\\" & strSrv &_
 "\root\MicrosoftExchangev2")
Set colItems = objWMIService.ExecQuery("Select AdministrativeGroup,DN," &_
"ExchangeVersion,FQDN,Name,RoutingGroup,CreationTime,Name," &_
"IsFrontEndServer,MessageTrackingEnabled,SubjectLoggingEnabled," &_
"LastModificationTime from Exchange_Server where name='" & strSrv &_
 "'",,48)

For Each objItem In colItems
  If objItem.FQDN="" Then
 WScript.echo "Failed to get Exchange server information from WMI." &_
 " Verify the Microsoft Exchange Management service is running on " &_
 strSRV
Else
 wscript.echo UCase(objItem.FQDN) & " [" &_
 objItem.Exchangeversion & "]"
 wscript.echo "Administrative Group: " &_
  objItem.AdministrativeGroup
 wscript.echo "Last modified: " &_
  ConvertTime(objItem.LastModificationTime)
 WScript.echo "Front End Server: " & objItem.IsFrontEndServer
 wscript.echo "Message Tracking: " & objItem.MessageTrackingEnabled
 WScript.echo "Subject logging: " & objItem.SubjectLoggingEnabled
End If
Next
End Sub


Function ConvertTime(strTime)
On Error Resume Next

yr = Left(strTime,4)
mo = mid(strTime,5,2)
dy = mid(strTime,7,2)
tm = Mid(strTime,9,6)


ConvertTime=mo & "/" & dy & "/" & yr


End Function


Sub ExchangeServerState(strComputer,UserName,Password)
Dim objWMIService
Dim propValue
Dim objItem
Dim SWBemlocator
Dim colItems

Set SWBemlocator = CreateObject("WbemScripting.SWbemLocator")
Set objWMIService = SWBemlocator.ConnectServer(strComputer,_
"\root\cimv2\applications\exchange",UserName,Password)
strQuery="Select * from ExchangeServerState"
Set colItems = objWMIService.ExecQuery(strQuery,,48)
For Each objItem in colItems
  WScript.Echo "ClusterState: " & objItem.ClusterState
  WScript.Echo "ClusterStateString: " & objItem.ClusterStateString
```

```
    WScript.Echo "CPUState: " & objItem.CPUState
    WScript.Echo "CPUStateString: " & objItem.CPUStateString
    WScript.Echo "DisksState: " & objItem.DisksState
    WScript.Echo "DisksStateString: " & objItem.DisksStateString
    WScript.Echo "DN: " & objItem.DN
    WScript.Echo "GroupDN: " & objItem.GroupDN
    WScript.Echo "GroupGUID: " & objItem.GroupGUID
    WScript.Echo "GUID: " & objItem.GUID
    WScript.Echo "MemoryState: " & objItem.MemoryState
    WScript.Echo "MemoryStateString: " & objItem.MemoryStateString
    WScript.Echo "Name: " & objItem.Name
    WScript.Echo "QueuesState: " & objItem.QueuesState
    WScript.Echo "QueuesStateString: " & objItem.QueuesStateString
    WScript.Echo "ServerMaintenance: " & objItem.ServerMaintenance
    WScript.Echo "ServerState: " & objItem.ServerState
    WScript.Echo "ServerStateString: " & objItem.ServerStateString
    WScript.Echo "ServicesState: " & objItem.ServicesState
    WScript.Echo "ServicesStateString: " & objItem.ServicesStateString
    WScript.Echo "Unreachable: " & objItem.Unreachable
    WScript.Echo "Version: " & objItem.Version
Next

End Sub

Sub GetServiceStatus(strSrv)
On Error Resume Next
Set objWMIService = GetObject("winmgmts://" & strSrv)
strQuery="Select displayname,startmode,status,state from Win32_service " &_
"where displayname LIKE 'Microsoft Exchange%'"

Set colSvcs=objWMIService.ExecQuery(strQuery,,48)

For Each svc In colSvcs
 WScript.Echo svc.DisplayName & vbTab & svc.state & vbTab &_
  svc.startmode
Next

End Sub

Sub SGReport(strServer,strSG)
Dim iServer
Dim iSGs
Dim iMBS

Set iServer=CreateObject("CDOEXM.ExchangeServer")
Set iSGs=CreateObject("CDOEXM.StorageGroup")
Set iMBS=CreateObject("CDOEXM.MailboxStoreDB")
iServer.DataSource.Open strServer

arrSGs=iServer.StorageGroups

For i=0 To UBound(arrSGs)
 strSGUrl=arrSGs(i)
 'WScript.Echo strSGUrl
 If InStr(UCase(strSGUrl),UCase(strSG)) Then
```

```
   iSGs.DataSource.Open "LDAP://" & iServer.DirectoryServer &_
     "/" & strSGUrl
   'strData=strData & iSGs.Name & VbCrLf
   WScript.Echo vbTab & "LogPath: " &iSGs.LogFilePath
   WScript.Echo vbTab & "SystemPath:" & iSGs.SystemFilePath
   WScript.Echo "  MailBox Stores:"
   arrMBStores=iSGs.MailboxStoreDBs
   For j=0 To UBound(arrMBStores)
    iMBS.DataSource.open "LDAP://" & arrMBStores(j)
    WScript.Echo  vbTab & iMBS.Name
    WScript.Echo  vbTab & " DBPath:" & iMBS.DBPath
    WScript.Echo  vbTab & " StreamingPath:" & iMBS.SLVPath
    WScript.Echo  vbTab & " Last Backup:" & iMBS.LastFullBackupTime
    WScript.Echo  vbTab & " StorageQuotaWarning:" & iMBS.StoreQuota
    WScript.Echo  vbTab & " StorageQuotaLimit:" & iMBS.OverQuotaLimit
    ListMailboxes iMBS.Name
   Next
  End If
Next
End Sub


Sub ListMailboxes(strMailStore)
On Error Resume Next
Dim objRootDSE
Dim objConfiguration
Dim conn
Dim cmd
Dim RS

Set objRootDSE = GetObject("LDAP://rootDSE")
strConfiguration = "LDAP://" & objRootDSE.Get("configurationNamingContext")
Set objConfiguration = GetObject(strConfiguration)
strPath=objConfiguration.ADSpath

strQuery="Select distinguishedname,name,homeMDBBL from '" & strPath &_
"' WHERE objectclass='msExchPrivateMDB' AND name='" & strMailStore & "'"

set cat=GetObject("GC:")
for each objcat in cat
 set GC=objcat
Next

set conn=CreateObject("ADODB.connection")
set cmd=CreateObject("ADODB.Command")
conn.Provider="ADSDSOObject"
conn.Open
set cmd.ActiveConnection=conn
set RS=conn.Execute(strQuery)

do while not RS.EOF
 WScript.Echo RS.Fields("distinguishedname")
 WScript.Echo vbTab & "Mailboxes on " & RS.Fields("name")
 tmpArray=RS.Fields("homeMDBBL")
 For m=0 To UBound(tmpArray)
     WScript.Echo vbTab & " " & tmpArray(m)
 Next
```

```
   RS.movenext
Loop
rs.Close
conn.Close

End Sub

Sub GetQueueInfo(strSrv)
On Error Resume Next
Set objWMIService = GetObject("winmgmts:\\" & strSrv &_
 "\root\MicrosoftExchangev2")
strQuery="Select * from Exchange_Queue"
Set colItems = objWMIService.ExecQuery(strQuery,,48)

wscript.Echo "Queue (Protocol)" & vbTab & "Size (MsgCount)"

For Each objItem In colItems
wscript.Echo objItem.LinkName & "(" & objItem.ProtocolName & ")" &_
vbTab & FormatNumber(objItem.Size/1024,2) & "(" &_
 objItem.MessageCount & ")"
Next

End Sub

Sub GetPublicFolderInfo(strComputer,UserName,Password)
On Error Resume Next
Dim objWMIService
Dim propValue
Dim objItem
Dim SWBemlocator
Dim colItems

Set SWBemlocator = CreateObject("WbemScripting.SWbemLocator")
Set objWMIService = SWBemlocator.ConnectServer(strComputer,_
"\root\microsoftexchangev2",UserName,Password)
strQuery="Select * from Exchange_PublicFolder"
Set colItems = objWMIService.ExecQuery(strQuery,,48)
For Each objItem in colItems
 WScript.Echo "AddressBookName: " & objItem.AddressBookName
 WScript.Echo "CreationTime: " & ConvertTime(objItem.CreationTime)
 WScript.Echo "DeletedItemLifetime: " & objItem.DeletedItemLifetime
 WScript.Echo "Description: " & objItem.Description
 WScript.Echo "FolderTree: " & objItem.FolderTree
 WScript.Echo "FriendlyUrl: " & objItem.FriendlyUrl
 WScript.Echo "HasChildren: " & objItem.HasChildren
 WScript.Echo "HasLocalReplica: " & objItem.HasLocalReplica
 WScript.Echo "InstallDate: " & ConvertTime(objItem.InstallDate)
 WScript.Echo "IsMailEnabled: " & objItem.IsMailEnabled
 WScript.Echo "IsNormalFolder: " & objItem.IsNormalFolder
 WScript.Echo "IsSecureInSite: " & objItem.IsSecureInSite
 WScript.Echo "LastAccessTime: " & ConvertTime(objItem.LastAccessTime)
 WScript.Echo "LastModificationTime: " &_
  ConvertTime(objItem.LastModificationTime)
 WScript.Echo "MaximumItemSize: " & objItem.MaximumItemSize
 WScript.Echo "MessageCount: " & objItem.MessageCount
```

```
    WScript.Echo "MessageWithAttachmentsCount: " &_
     objItem.MessageWithAttachmentsCount
    WScript.Echo "Name: " & objItem.Name
    WScript.Echo "NormalMessageSize: " & objItem.NormalMessageSize
    WScript.Echo "OwnerCount: " & objItem.OwnerCount
    WScript.Echo "ParentFriendlyUrl: " & objItem.ParentFriendlyUrl
    WScript.Echo "Path: " & objItem.Path
    WScript.Echo "ProhibitPostLimit: " & objItem.ProhibitPostLimit
    WScript.Echo "PublishInAddressBook: " & objItem.PublishInAddressBook
    WScript.Echo "ReplicaAgeLimit: " & objItem.ReplicaAgeLimit
    for each propValue in objItem.ReplicaList
        WScript.Echo "ReplicaList: " & propValue
    Next
    WScript.Echo "ReplicationMessagePriority: " &_
     objItem.ReplicationMessagePriority
    for each propValue in objItem.ReplicationSchedule
        WScript.Echo "ReplicationSchedule: " & propValue
    Next
    WScript.Echo "ReplicationStyle: " & objItem.ReplicationStyle
    WScript.Echo "RestrictionCount: " & objItem.RestrictionCount
    for each propValue in objItem.SecurityDescriptor
        WScript.Echo "SecurityDescriptor: " & propValue
    Next
    WScript.Echo "Status: " & objItem.Status
    WScript.Echo "StorageLimitStyle: " & objItem.StorageLimitStyle
    WScript.Echo "TotalMessageSize: " & objItem.TotalMessageSize
    WScript.Echo "Url: " & objItem.Url
    WScript.Echo "UsePublicStoreAgeLimits: " &_
     objItem.UsePublicStoreAgeLimits
    WScript.Echo "UsePublicStoreDeletedItemLifetime: " &_
     objItem.UsePublicStoreDeletedItemLifetime
    WScript.Echo "WarningLimit: " & objItem.WarningLimit
    WScript.Echo VbCrLf
  Next
  End Sub
```

The main part of the script gets an array of all the Exchange servers in the organization by calling the *GetExchangeServers* function, and then it simply enumerates each server.

```
arrServers=GetExchangeServers

For s = 0 To UBound(arrServers)-1
    WScript.Echo "*****Server Information*****"
    ExchangeServerInfo arrServers(s)
    WScript.Echo "*****Server Status*****"
    ExchangeServerState arrServers(s),"",""
    WScript.Echo "*****Service Status*****"
    GetServiceStatus arrServers(s)
    WScript.Echo "*****Queue Status*****"
    GetQueueInfo arrServers(s)
    WScript.Echo "*****Storage Groups*****"
    GetStorageGroups arrServers(s)
    WScript.Echo "*****Public Folders*****"
    GetPublicFolderInfo arrServers(s),"",""
Next
```

We've broken the script into subroutines and functions that are called from the main part of the script. Most of these take the Exchange server's name as a parameter. As you look through the script, you will see that we use ADSI, WMI, CDOEXM, and ADO. We won't go through this script because we've covered most of the sections earlier in the chapter. We hope you will use portions of this script as building blocks for your own Exchange administrative scripts.

Summary

In this chapter, we showed you how to manage an Exchange 2003 server. There is no single scripting technology, but rather a collection of technologies that you must master depending on what you want to manage. You need to use ADSI, ADO, CDOEXM, and WMI to fully master your Exchange environment. We demonstrated how to manage servers, storage groups, mailbox stores, and mailboxes. There is a great deal more to scripting with Exchange 2003, enough to fill a book on its own. We encourage you to download and use the Exchange 2003 SDK, which will make script development much easier. Finally, we urge you to establish a test environment if you don't already have one. You can easily bring down an Exchange server or lose data through a poorly developed and tested script. We always stress testing, but given the business critical nature of e-mail, this is even more important.

On the CD   Included on the companion CD is an HTA that can be used to monitor an Exchange 2003 server. It utilizes much of the code we've demonstrated in this chapter. You will also find links to some helpful Web sites for scripting with Exchange 2003.

Chapter 16

Microsoft Operations Manager 2005 Scripting

Microsoft Operations Manager 2005 (MOM) keeps a close eye on your enterprise and can react, repair, or restore based on detected events. The MOM toolbox includes an extensive script library. These scripts are executed remotely on enterprise servers. In this chapter, we'll examine how MOM uses scripts, how those scripts are constructed, and how you can add your own scripts to MOM.

MOM 2005 is an enterprise-management application. MOM deploys management agents that monitor the health and status of a server. These agents report back to MOM where information is consolidated and reported to network administrators. In this chapter, we assume that you have at least a passing familiarity with the product.

> **More Info** For more information about Microsoft Operations Manager 2005 and to download an evaluation version, visit the Microsoft Web site at
>
> *http://www.microsoft.com/mom/default.mspx*
>
> (This link is on the companion CD; click *Microsoft Operations Manager Home*.)

MOM includes a number of scripts, and most of the management packs that you install with MOM also include scripts. After installing a few key management packs, such as Exchange 2003, Active Directory, Group Policy, and Windows Operating System, you will have quite a few scripts at your disposal, as shown in Figure 16-1 on the next page. Many of these scripts use WMI.

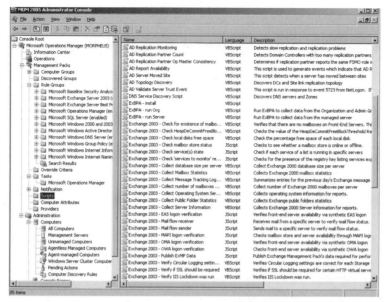

Figure 16-1   MOM scripts in the Administrator console

You might come across some scripts that you'd like to run on your own, or perhaps that you'd like to include as part of a MOM event. Don't try copying and pasting code just yet. Scripts for MOM are a little bit different than traditional scripts. We'll go through the differences and show you how to convert traditional scripts to MOM scripts.

Introducing MOM Scripting

One of the biggest differences between the scripts we've been working with so far and the scripts in MOM is how scripts are executed and processed. In traditional scripting, a script is executed on a host computer, and even if the target of the script is a remote system, the results can be returned to the host computer by using *wscript.echo*.

In a MOM environment, all scripts are executed on the remote machine by the MOM agent. There is absolutely no user interaction. The scripts run silently in the background. This means that no script intended for MOM can require user input, such as through an input or message box. MOM scripts also can't use *wscript.echo* because there is no administrator to receive the message. In fact, when scripting with MOM, we don't use the WScript environment at all. Instead, MOM uses a new scripting host called *ScriptContext*. In MOM, scripts run in the context of the MOM agent and report back to the MOM server. That's a pretty simplified explanation, but it should suffice for our purposes.

> **Note**   You don't have to instantiate the *ScriptContext* object because it is implicitly created by MOM. In much the same way that you never have to instantiate WScript, it's just there.

This means that commands like *wscript.echo* and *wscript.sleep* will no longer function when the script is executed by MOM. Equivalent methods are available, but we use the *ScriptContext* object instead. Tables 16-1 and 16-2 list the methods and properties for *ScriptContext*.

Table 16-1 *ScriptContext* Methods

Name	Description
CreateAlert	Generates a new *Alert* object
CreateDiscovery-Data	Generates a new *DiscoveryData* object
CreateEvent	Generates a new *Event* object
CreatePerfData	Generates a new *PerfData* object
Echo	Writes messages to a text file for debugging purposes
GetOverride	Gets the specified override for the current rule
GetScriptState	Gets the *ScriptState* object
IsAlert	Determines whether the object provided to the script by MOM is an *Alert* object
IsEvent	Determines whether the object provided to the script by MOM is an *Event* object
IsPerfData	Determines whether the object provided to the script by MOM is a *PerfData* object
Quit	Stops the running of the script and exits
Sleep	Suspends the running of the script for the specified number of seconds
Submit	Submits an *Alert*, *Event*, *PerfData*, or *DiscoveryData* object to the MOM data stream

Table 16-2 *ScriptContext* Properties

Name	Description
Alert	Gets the *Alert* object that caused MOM to invoke the script
Event	Gets the *Event* object that caused MOM to invoke the script
IsTargetAgentless	Checks whether the computer is monitored without a MOM agent
IsTargetVirtual-Server	Gets a Boolean value indicating whether the computer is running as a Windows Server Cluster server
ManagementGroup-Name	Gets the name of the management group that deployed the current response
Name	Gets the name of the current script
ProcessingRule	Returns the processing rule that invoked the current response script
Parameters	Gets a *VarSet* object that contains the parameters sent from MOM when the script was invoked
PerfData	Gets the *PerfData* object that caused MOM to invoke the script
TargetComputer	Gets the name of the computer being monitored
TargetComputer-Identity	Gets the identity of the target computer for the current script response

Table 16-2 *ScriptContext* Properties

Name	Description
TargetNetbios-Computer	Gets the target computer's NetBIOS name
TargetNetbios-Domain	Gets the target computer's NetBIOS domain name
TargetFQDN-Computer	Gets the target computer's fully qualified domain name

You will probably recognize some of the methods. Some will behave just as they do in WScript, but others are a little different.

Keep in mind that the purpose of MOM is centralized management, and that scripts run where no human can watch. We can still echo information from the script, but it won't appear in a command window or message box. When we call *ScriptContext.Echo*, it will send the message to the MOM server. If the script is called as part of a response script, the message will be written to the MOM log file. If the script is part of a MOM task, the message will be written to the task event window. We cover response scripts and task scripts later in this chapter.

Adding Scripts

Because MOM stores everything in a SQL database, you can't simply copy a script file to the MOM server. You need to create an entry for it in the database and then insert the contents of the script. Unfortunately, there isn't an elegant way to insert code. Follow these steps.

1. Open the MOM Administrator console on the MOM server.

2. Open your script in Microsoft Notepad. Select and copy the script.

3. Navigate to the Scripts folder.

4. Right-click the Scripts folder, and click Create Script.

5. Enter a script name and description. If your script is not written in VBScript, select the appropriate language. Click Next.

6. Press Ctrl+V to paste your copied script into the window. Click Next.

7. To define run time parameters, click Add, and then enter a name, a description, and a default value. Click Finish, and your script will be added to the list. It is now available for any MOM task, event, or response that you would like to create.

8. To edit a script, right-click it in the right pane, and click Properties. Click the Script tab. Select the text, and copy and paste it into Notepad or your script editor.

Defining Script Parameters

In traditional VBScript, we use the *wscript.arguments* property to get run-time parameters. However, the *wscript* object is not available when running scripts under MOM. Instead, we use the *ScriptContext.Parameters* property. When you create a script in MOM, you define the required run time parameters, as illustrated in Figure 16-2.

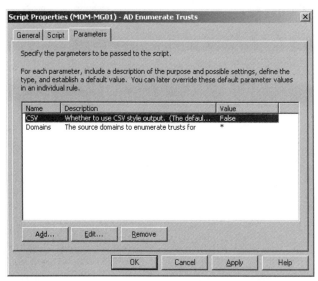

Figure 16-2   MOM script parameters

Within the script, you typically set an internal variable with the parameter value by using *ScriptContext.Parameters.Get*.

```
strDomainFilter = Trim(ScriptContext.Parameters.Get("Domains"))

On Error Resume Next
Dim strSeparator
If CBool(Trim(ScriptContext.Parameters.Get("CSV"))) Then
  strSeparator = ","
Else
  strSeparator = vbTab
End If
```

> **Best Practices**   As with any script, you should check for the existence of required parameters and validate them. If something isn't correct, use *ScriptContext.Echo* to write information to the event tab and gracefully terminate the script. This way, when you check the task status in the MOM Operator console, you have an indication of what went wrong.

Using Run Time Scripting Objects

The *ScriptContext* object is only one type of MOM run-time scripting object. However, as you can tell from Table 16-1, it is used to create several other objects that you will find useful.

Using the *PerfData* Object

Just as you can use the Performance Monitor management console or monitor counters in MOM, you can also create a *PerfData* object to work with performance counters that return the information to the MOM server. This means that you can create custom performance counters from just about anything you calculate as a number, such as the size of a file or the number of processes running at any given time.

To create performance data, you need a *PerfData* object, a name for your custom counter, a name of the instance, and the value you want to record. After you have this information, you use *ScriptContext.Submit* to send the information to the MOM server. The script in Listing 16-1 creates a new custom performance counter called *ProcessCount* that returns the number of processes running on the managed server. After you add the script to MOM, you create a task or a timed event to run the script on the managed computer.

Listing 16-1 Create Counter

```
On Error Resume Next
Dim strComputer
Dim objWMIService
Dim propValue
Dim objItem
Dim SWBemlocator
Dim colItems

strComputer = "."
iCount=0
Set SWBemlocator = CreateObject("WbemScripting.SWbemLocator")
Set objWMIService = SWBemlocator.ConnectServer(strComputer,"\root\CIMV2")
Set colItems = objWMIService.ExecQuery("Select caption from Win32_Process"_
,,48)
For Each objItem in colItems
  iCount=iCount+1
  ScriptContext.Echo "Caption: " & objItem.Caption
Next

ScriptContext.echo iCount & " Processes counted."

CreatePerfData "Processes","Process Count","ProcessInfo",iCount

Sub CreatePerfData(strObjectName,strCounterName,strInstanceName,numValue)
    Set objPerfData = ScriptContext.CreatePerfData
    objPerfData.ObjectName = strObjectName
    objPerfData.CounterName =strCounterName
    objPerfData.InstanceName = strInstanceName
    objPerfData.Value = numValue
    ScriptContext.Submit objPerfData
End Sub
```

On the CD   You will find this script, as well as other scripts listed in this chapter, on the CD that accompanies this book.

The first part of the script is basic WMI code that counts the number of processes running on the local computer.

```
Set SWBemlocator = CreateObject("WbemScripting.SWbemLocator")
Set objWMIService = SWBemlocator.ConnectServer(strComputer,"\root\CIMV2")
Set colItems = objWMIService.ExecQuery("Select caption from Win32_Process",,48)
For Each objItem in colItems
  iCount=iCount+1
  ScriptContext.Echo "Caption: " & objItem.Caption
Next
```

The *ScriptContext.Echo* command sends the output to the Properties tab of the event task, as shown in Figure 16-3.

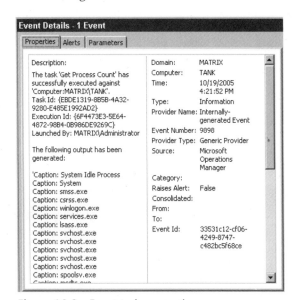

Figure 16-3   Event task properties

The counter we are creating is the number of current processes running, which is stored in the *iCounter* variable. We call the *CreatePerfData* subroutine, which creates the *PerfData* object and submits it to the MOM server. The subroutine needs to know the name of the performance object, the counter name, an instance name, and the value of the instance.

```
CreatePerfData "Processes","Process Count","ProcessInfo",iCount
```

Within the subroutine, we use *ScriptContext.CreatePerfData* to create the *PerfData* object. The subroutine then sets some object properties and submits it to MOM.

```
Sub CreatePerfData(strObjectName,strCounterName,strInstanceName,numValue)
    Set objPerfData = ScriptContext.CreatePerfData
    objPerfData.ObjectName = strObjectName
    objPerfData.CounterName =strCounterName
    objPerfData.InstanceName = strInstanceName
    objPerfData.Value = numValue
    ScriptContext.Submit objPerfData
End Sub
```

Depending on how often you execute the script, you can generate a nice performance graph in MOM, as shown in Figure 16-4.

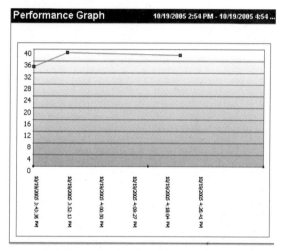

Figure 16-4   Customized performance graph

Using the *Alert* Object

The *Alert* object can be created or manipulated by the *ScriptContext.CreateAlert* method or *ScriptContext.Alert* property. Just as we did with the *PerfData* object, we can create a custom alert based on whatever scripted criteria we want. There are many alert properties that you can specify, but typically you will want to at least specify the following:

- *Name*   This property is the name you want to use to define the alert.
- *Level*   This property is the alert severity. The following values are used to indicate the severity level for the alert.
  - *10.* This value indicates success.
  - *20.* This value indicates information.
  - *30.* This value indicates a warning.
  - *40.* This value indicates an error.
  - *50.* This value indicates a critical error.

- *60*. This value indicates a security issue.

- *70*. This value indicates that the service is unavailable.

- *ResolutionState*   This property indicates the alert's resolution status. Typically, when creating a new alert, you will set this to 0.

- *Description*   This property is a brief description of the alert or problem.

- *Owner*   This property is the name of the user or group that will be responsible for the alert.

This short script in Listing 16-2 demonstrates how to create a new alert in MOM.

Listing 16-2 Create Alert

```
'Create the Alert object
Set objCreatedAlert = ScriptContext.CreateAlert()
'Set Alert properties
objCreatedAlert.Name = "Test Alert"
objCreatedAlert.AlertLevel = 20
objCreatedAlert.Owner = "[unassigned]"
objCreatedAlert.ResolutionState = 0
objCreatedAlert.Description="This is a test demonstration alert."
'Submit the Alert object to MOM
ScriptContext.Submit objCreatedAlert
```

Figure 16-5 shows the resulting alert in the MOM Operator console.

Figure 16-5   MOM test alert properties

Using the *Event* Object

The *Event* object is typically used in MOM to refer to any event-related element, such as an application log or NT event log. However, just as with *PerfData* and *Alert* objects, we can create our own events through a script, or we can handle events for which MOM doesn't have a provider. Just as with the previous objects, we use *ScriptContext* to create the object and define its properties, and we then use *ScriptContext.Submit* to commit the object to the MOM server. At minimum, you should set the properties shown on the next page.

- *EventNumber*   This is typically the Windows event ID number, but you can use any number you want when creating your own events.

- *EventSource*   This is the source of the event. It is typically the application, but you might want to set it to the name of the script that generated the event.

- *EventType*   This is a value that indicates the type of event, such as *Success*, *Failure*, or *Information*. The script in Listing 16-3 defines these values as constants.

- *Message*   This is the text you want to display as part of the event.

Listing 16-3 Create Event

```
Const EVENT_TYPE_SUCCESS = 0
Const EVENT_TYPE_ERROR   = 1
Const EVENT_TYPE_WARNING = 2
Const EVENT_TYPE_INFORMATION = 4
Const EVENT_TYPE_AUDITSUCCESS = 8
Const EVENT_TYPE_AUDITFAILURE = 16
'Create the Event object
Set objEvent = ScriptContext.CreateEvent()
'Define Event properties
objEvent.EventSource = "Demo Event Script"
objEvent.EventNumber = 9999
objEvent.EventType = EVENT_TYPE_INFORMATION
objEvent.Message="Your sample event has been raised."
'submit the Event object to MOM
ScriptContext.Submit objEvent
```

The graphic in Figure 16-6 illustrates the resulting event.

Figure 16-6   MOM test event results

Understanding Script Tracing and Debugging

Debugging scripts with MOM is much more complicated than traditional VBScript debugging because you can't "see" what the script is doing. If you need true debugging, you will need to use Microsoft Visual Studio .NET and remotely connect a debugger. (Debugging with Microsoft .NET is outside the scope of this book.) However, you can enable tracing on the managed server. When tracing is enabled, any *ScriptContext.Echo* commands will write to the trace log file. Here are the steps from the MOM SDK documentation.

1. Run Windows Registry Editor (Regedit.exe).

2. Browse to the HKEY_LOCAL_MACHINE\SOFTWARE\Mission Critical Software\ OnePoint registry key.

3. If *EnableActiveDebugging* does not already exist, create a new DWORD entry for it. Set the value of the *EnableActiveDebugging* entry to 1.

4. Tracing will begin the next time the MOM service starts. You can restart the service immediately, or wait until the next scheduled restart.

The file will be created in the %TEMP%\Microsoft Operation Manager folder and called something like AgentResponses-*MOMGroup*.log, where *MOMGroup* is the name of your management group.

To disable tracing, change *EnableActiveDebugging* to 0. The new settings will take effect the next time the MOM service starts. Be sure to turn off tracing when you are finished, because tracing can add significant overhead and will cause a performance penalty.

Note   You will need to install the MOM SDK in order to enable tracing.

Using Scripts in MOM

After a script has been defined in MOM, it can be used locally on the MOM server or on the managed server. When the script executes on the managed server, the MOM agent running on that server executes that script. Because the MOM agent service account is usually running under Local System, the script can only access local resources and information. MOM scripts generally fall into one of these four categories: response scripts, timed scripts, state variable scripts, and discovery scripts.

Using Response Scripts

This type of script is executed as a response to some event rule, performance counter value, or alert. For example, you might have a rule or timed event that checks the size of an event log and then defines a script that backs up the log to a file and then clears the log. You can have multiple scripts as part of a response. If you have more than one, scripts run synchronously. The script must also complete before the rest of the event or alert is processed by MOM.

Using Timed Scripts

A timed script is special type of response script. You can create your own timed events in MOM, and specify a script to run at the timed event interval. In the example just mentioned, the response script was responsible only for backing up and clearing the event log. You could just as easily create a script to run as part of a timed event that checks the size, reports the sizes back to MOM, and if the size exceeds some threshold, backs up and clears the log. This would be an ideal script in which to use parameters, such as the event log type, size threshold, and backup directory.

Using State Variable Scripts

Scripts that store state variables can help you correlate events across multiple managed servers. State variables are globally available to all scripts as long as the MOM service is running on the management server. If the service stops or restarts, the variables are reset. For example, you might run a script against an Exchange 2003 server as part of a timed event that checks the number of queues that have messages waiting to be delivered. If the number increases to a certain level within 15 minutes, it might indicate a problem with DNS, network connectivity, or a spreading virus. After 15 minutes, the script can be reset and start monitoring again.

The *ScriptState* object is used to store variable information across script sessions. Think of *ScriptState* as a type of global cache for information you want to access across multiple scripts. Within the *ScriptState*, create a *varSet* object for each piece of data you want to store.

This code snippet creates a new *varSet* object called *Queue Tracker*. Within the object, there is a *varSet* variable called *Number of Queues with messages*, and it will have some value that you specify, perhaps the result of a function that returns the number of Exchange queues with messages.

```
Const VARSET_NAME = "Queue Tracker"
Const QUEUE_COUNT = "Number of Queues with messages"
iCount=GetQCount 'some function to return the number of queues
                 'with messages.
'Create the ScriptState object
Set objScriptState = ScriptContext.GetScriptState()
'Create the VarSet object
Set objVarSet = objScriptState.CreateSet()

'save variable changes back to the VarSet
obVarSet.put QUEUE_COUNT, iCount

'save the VarSet by passing the name of the varSet
'object and the varSet object that was created in the script.
'You must do this to commit the change to the ScriptState.
objScriptState.SaveSet VARSET_NAME, objVarSet
```

> **Tip**   As an alternative to *CreateSet,* you can use *GetSet*(varSetName). If the specified *varSet* object exists, it will be returned; otherwise a new object will be created with the specified name.

To read the *varSet* object, we need to get the *ScriptState* object and then use its *GetSet* method to retrieve the specified *varSet.* After we have this object, we can get the variables that are stored within the object.

```
Const VARSET_NAME = "Queue Tracker"
Const QUEUE_COUNT = "Number of Queues with messages"
'Create the ScriptState object
Set objScriptState = ScriptContext.GetScriptState()
'Get the VarSet object
Set objVarSet = objScriptState.GetSet(VARSET_NAME)
'Retrieve the value of Number of Queues with messages variable
'and set iStoredCount to this value.
iStoredCount=objVarSet.Get(QUEUE_COUNT)
```

Here is a more complete sample that puts both pieces of the task in a single script.

```
Const VARSET_NAME = "Queue Tracker"
Const QUEUE_COUNT = "Number of Queues with messages"

'Create the ScriptState object
Set objScriptState = ScriptContext.GetScriptState()
'Create the VarSet object
Set objVarSet = objScriptState.GetSet(VARSET_NAME)

iCount=GetQCount 'some function to return the number of queues
                 'with messages.

'Get the stored value. Assuming this script runs every 15 minutes
'any value here will be the queue count from 15 minutes ago.
iStoredCount=objVarSet.Get(QUEUE_COUNT)

'compare the stored count with the current count
If iCount>iStoredCount Then
  'Count has increased
  'Execute some code to notify an administrator, write an event
  'or create an alert.
End If

'save variable changes back to the VarSet
obVarSet.put QUEUE_COUNT, iCount

'save the VarSet by passing the name of the varSet
'object and the varSet object that was created in the script.
'You must do this to commit the change to the ScriptState.
objScriptState.SaveSet VARSET_NAME, objVarSet
```

If you are trying to troubleshoot *ScriptState* code, you can use the *varSet* object's *DumpToFile* method to write the contents of a specified *varSet* object to a text file.

```
Const VARSET_NAME = "Queue Tracker"
dtmNow = Now()
'specify the filename
strFileName = Month(dtmNow) & "_" & Day(dtmNow) & "_" & _
              Hour(dtmNow) & "_" & Minute(dtmNow) & "_" & _
              Second(dtmNow) & ".dat"
'Get the ScriptState
Set objScriptState = ScriptContext.GetScriptState()
'Get the varSet object
Set objVarSet = objScriptState.GetSet(VARSET_NAME)
objVarSet.DumpToFile strFileName
```

You might create a script like this and run it as a task on the MOM server to provide additional monitoring capabilities for your Exchange 2003 servers.

> **Note**   If you don't specify a filename and path, the file will be created in the Microsoft Operations Manager 2005 folder.

Using Discovery Scripts

Discovery scripts are executed on either the MOM server or on the managed computer. These scripts discover information based on computer attributes that are defined on the MOM server. These attributes, such as operating system details, hardware, services, or applications, help group managed computers so that the appropriate management rules are applied. The *ScriptContext* object creates a *DiscoveryData* object by invoking the *CreateDiscoveryData* method.

```
Set objDiscData=ScriptContext.CreateDiscoveryData()
```

You can't directly add information to the *DiscoveryData* object. Instead, this object has collections that you populate. When finished, you must call *ScriptContext.Submit* to save the changes to the MOM server. Examine the script in Listing 16-4, which is from the IIS Management Pack. When this script is run against a managed computer, it is "discovered" as an IIS server, and added to the IIS server group in MOM.

Listing 16-4 Discover IIS Role

```
'-----------------------------------------------------------------
' <company>Microsoft Corporation</company>
' <copyright>Copyright (c) Microsoft Corporation. All rights reserved.
' </copyright>
' <name>
'  IIS Role Discovery
' </name>
' <summary>
```

```
'  Creates an IIS server role for this computer
' </summary>
'--------------------------------------------------------------------


Option Explicit

Const COMPUTER_CLASS_ID = "Computer"

Const COMPUTER_COMPUTER_NAME_ATTRIBUTE_ID = "ComputerName"
Const COMPUTER_TIME_ZONE_BIAS_ATTRIBUTE_ID = "Time Zone Bias"
Const COMPUTER_OPERATING_SYSTEM_VERSION_ATTRIBUTE_ID =_
   "Operating System Version"
Const COMPUTER_IP_ADDRESS_ATTRIBUTE_ID = "IPAddress"
Const COMPUTER_FQDN_ATTRIBUTE_ID = "FQDN"
Const COMPUTER_VIRTUAL_SERVER_TYPE_ATTRIBUTE_ID = "Virtual Server Type"

Sub Main()
  Dim oDiscData
  Dim oCollection
  Dim oInstance

  Set oDiscData = ScriptContext.CreateDiscoveryData()
  Set oCollection = oDiscData.CreateCollection()
  oCollection.AddScopeFilter COMPUTER_COMPUTER_NAME_ATTRIBUTE_ID,_
    ScriptContext.TargetComputerIdentity
  oCollection.ClassID = "IIS"

  Set oInstance = oCollection.CreateInstance()
  oInstance.AddKeyProperty "Server Name",_
    ScriptContext.TargetNetbiosComputer
  oCollection.AddInstance oInstance
  oDiscData.AddCollection oCollection

  ScriptContext.Submit oDiscData
End Sub
```

Discovery scripts need a *DiscoveryData* object after which we can instantiate a *DiscoveryCollection* object that will be used to hold information.

```
Set oDiscData = ScriptContext.CreateDiscoveryData()
Set oCollection = oDiscData.CreateCollection()
```

After we have a collection object, we need to add a scope filter.

```
oCollection.AddScopeFilter COMPUTER_COMPUTER_NAME_ATTRIBUTE_ID,_
  ScriptContext.TargetComputerIdentity
```

We set the class ID for our discovered data, in this case, *IIS*.

```
oCollection.ClassID = "IIS"
```

To add more information to the collection, we create a new instance and define a property.

```
Set oInstance = oCollection.CreateInstance()
oInstance.AddKeyProperty "Server Name",_
   ScriptContext.TargetNetbiosComputer
```

We then need to add the instance to the collection.

```
oCollection.AddInstance oInstance
```

We add the collection to the collection object.

```
oDiscData.AddCollection oCollection
```

Finally, we submit the *DiscoveryData* object to the MOM server.

> **Note**   The SDK documentation for discovery scripts is very light and, frankly, not too helpful. If you need to create custom discovery scripts, we recommend that you study some of the finished discovery scripts that come with MOM, and then modifying one of them to meet your needs.

Customizing MOM Scripts

Depending on the management packs you install, your MOM server could have quite a few scripts, some of which you might want to modify to better suit your purposes. Ideally, MOM scripts will use parameters to make them more flexible, but this isn't always the case. If you want to modify an existing MOM script, the best course of action is to do it manually. View the properties of the script, and then click the script source tab. Copy the script text, and paste it into Notepad to create a new script file. Edit the script file as necessary, and when finished, simply create a new script by following the steps we outlined earlier in this chapter under "Adding Scripts." You can then use the script however you want.

You might also find a MOM script that you would like to run as a separate script outside of the MOM environment. However, you can't simply paste the code into a new script and run it. First, you must remove any code related to *ScriptState*, *DiscoveryData*, *Alerts*, or *Events* because those objects don't exist in VBScript. When modifying a MOM script, you need to replace *ScriptContext* with *wscript*. Any *ScriptContext.Echo* statements should be replaced with *wscript.echo*. You will have to determine how to handle anything else with *ScriptContext*. If the script uses parameters, you will need to modify it to use *wscript.arguments*, or create the standalone version as a Windows Script File (.wsf) and use named arguments.

What you will probably find most useful are the portable WMI functions and subroutines. However, remember that MOM scripts are run locally on the managed server by the MOM service account. You will need to modify the WMI code to access remote machines, and pass credentials as necessary. To convert MOM scripts to standalone scripts, follow these steps.

1. Remove references to any MOM-specific objects, such as *ScriptState*.

2. Convert *ScriptContext.Echo* to *wscript.echo*.

3. Remove all other references to *ScriptContext*.

4. Convert parameters to *wscript.arguments* or used named arguments with a .wsf script.

5. Convert WMI code to access remote machines, passing alternate credentials if necessary.

Viewing MOM Scripting in Action

Let's put some of what we've covered in this chapter into a new MOM script. When creating your own MOM scripts, we recommend first developing and testing the core functionality with a traditional script. After you know the VBScript code is correct, you can begin modifying the script for use in a MOM environment, adding the MOM specific features as needed.

Listing 16-5 is a simple script that uses the *Scripting.FileSystemObject* to get the size of a specified folder. If the size exceeds a specified threshold, we want to raise an alert.

```
Listing 16-5 Check Folder Size
strFolder="e:\temp"
iThreshold=100000
iSize=GetFolderSize(strFolder)

If Int(iSize) > Int(iThreshold) Then
'folder size exceeds threshold so generate an alert
wscript.Echo "Alert!"
strDescription=strFolder & " has exceeded the specified threshold of " &_
FormatNumber(iThreshold,0,,True) & " bytes.  Folder size is " &_
FormatNumber(iSize,0,,True) & " bytes"
wscript.echo strDescription
Else
'folder size is OK
WScript.Echo "The size of " &strFolder & " (" & iSize &_
  ") is within the threshold of " & iThreshold
End If

Function GetFolderSize(strFolder)
dim objFSO,objFldr
set objFSO=CreateObject("Scripting.FileSystemObject")
set objFldr=objFSO.GetFolder(strFolder)
GetFolderSize=objFldr.Size
End Function
```

As written, this script would not work in a MOM environment because it utilizes the *wscript* object. We want to take advantage of some MOM benefits, such as using parameters, creating alerts, and capturing performance data. The latter is especially useful because a performance graph of folder size might help with capacity planning. The script in Listing 16-6 on the next page is fundamentally the same script as Listing 16-5, with the addition of MOM-related objects.

Listing 16-6 Monitor Folder Size

```
strFolder=ScriptContext.Parameters.Get("folder")
iThreshold=ScriptContext.Parameters.Get("threshold")
iSize=GetFolderSize(strFolder)

If Int(iSize)>Int(iThreshold) Then
'folder size exceeds threshold so generate an alert
ScriptContext.Echo "Alert!"
strDescription=strFolder & " has exceeded the specified threshold of " &_
 FormatNumber(iThreshold,0,True) & " bytes.  Folder size is " &_
 FormatNumber(iSize,0,True) & " bytes"
ScriptContext.echo strDescription
CreateAlert "Folder Size Exceeded",20,"[unassigned]",0,strDescription
Else
'folder size is OK
'write data to MOM event
ScriptContext.Echo strFolder & " is OK. Size=" &_
 FormatNumber(iSize,0,True) & " bytes"
End If

'create perfdata
CreatePerfData "Monitored Folder","FolderSize",strFolder,_
FormatNumber((iSize/1024000),2)

Function GetFolderSize(strFolder)
  dim objFSO,objFldr
  set objFSO=CreateObject("Scripting.FileSystemObject")
  set objFldr=objFSO.GetFolder(strFolder)
  GetFolderSize=objFldr.Size
End Function

Sub CreateAlert(strObjectName,iAlertLevel,strOwner,iResolutionState,_
strDescription)
  'Create the Alert object
  Set objCreatedAlert = ScriptContext.CreateAlert()
  'Set Alert properties
  objCreatedAlert.Name = strObjectName
  objCreatedAlert.AlertLevel = iAlertLevel
  objCreatedAlert.Owner = strOwner
  objCreatedAlert.ResolutionState = iResolutionState
  objCreatedAlert.Description=strDescription
  'Submit the Alert object to MOM
  ScriptContext.Submit objCreatedAlert
End Sub

Sub CreatePerfData(strObjectName,strCounterName,strInstanceName,numValue)
  'Create the PerfData object
  Set objPerfData = ScriptContext.CreatePerfData
  'Set PerfData properties
  objPerfData.ObjectName = strObjectName
  objPerfData.CounterName =strCounterName
  objPerfData.InstanceName = strInstanceName
  objPerfData.Value = numValue
  'Submit the PerfData object to MOM
  ScriptContext.Submit objPerfData
End Sub
```

Let's take a look at this script in more detail.

When we create a new script in MOM and paste this code, we have the option of defining parameters. By using parameters, we can reuse this script in a variety of scheduled tasks that can be run against a variety of managed servers with different parameters. The first two lines define script variables from the task parameters that launched the script.

```
strFolder=ScriptContext.Parameters.Get("folder")
iThreshhold=ScriptContext.Parameters.Get("threshold")
```

We next define a variable for the current size of the folder by calling the *GetFolderSize* function.

```
iSize=GetFolderSize(strFolder)
```

We've already tested this function in our VBS script, so we shouldn't have any problems. If the folder size is greater than the threshold, we want to record that information and generate an alert.

```
If Int(iSize)>Int(iThreshold) Then
'folder size exceeds threshold so generate an alert
ScriptContext.Echo "Alert!"
strDescription=strFolder & " has exceeded the specified threshold of " &_
 FormatNumber(iThreshold,0,True) & " bytes.  Folder size is " &_
 FormatNumber(iSize,0,True) & " bytes"
ScriptContext.echo strDescription
CreateAlert "Folder Size Exceeded",20,"[unassigned]",0,strDescription
```

The *ScriptContext.Echo* commands will write information to the event that is created when the task completes. That might be enough if someone is monitoring events. It would also be nice to create an alert object so that the problem can be addressed and resolved. We do this by calling the *CreateAlert* subroutine that creates an *Alert* object.

```
Sub CreateAlert(strObjectName,iAlertLevel,strOwner,_
iResolutionState,strDescription)
  'Create the Alert object
  Set objCreatedAlert = ScriptContext.CreateAlert()
  'Set Alert properties
  objCreatedAlert.Name = strObjectName
  objCreatedAlert.AlertLevel = iAlertLevel
  objCreatedAlert.Owner = strOwner
  objCreatedAlert.ResolutionState = iResolutionState
  objCreatedAlert.Description=strDescription
  'Submit the Alert object to MOM
  ScriptContext.Submit objCreatedAlert
End Sub
```

This code is very similar to the code we used earlier in the chapter. We call the *CreateAlert* method to create the object, set some properties, and use the *Submit* method to send the information to MOM.

If the folder size is within the threshold, we simply log that information to the MOM event.

```
Else
'folder size is OK
'write data to MOM event
ScriptContext.Echo strFolder & " is OK. Size=" & FormatNumber(iSize,0,True) & " bytes"
End If
```

The last thing we will do is capture the size information as a performance object. We call the *CreatePerfData* subroutine.

```
'create perfdata
CreatePerfData "Monitored Folder","FolderSize",strFolder,_
FormatNumber((iSize/1024000),2)
```

The subroutine creates a new performance object called *Folder Size*. This will appear as a performance counter for the managed server in the MOM Operator console. The instance is the name of the monitored folder, and the value is the current size in megabytes. The *GetFolder-Size* function returns a value in bytes, and we've simply formatted the number for megabytes.

```
Sub CreatePerfData(strObjectName,strCounterName,strInstanceName,numValue)
  'Create the PerfData object
  Set objPerfData = ScriptContext.CreatePerfData
  'Set PerfData properties
  objPerfData.ObjectName = strObjectName
  objPerfData.CounterName =strCounterName
  objPerfData.InstanceName = strInstanceName
  objPerfData.Value = numValue
  'Submit the PerfData object to MOM
  ScriptContext.Submit objPerfData
End Sub
```

Like the *CreateAlert* subroutine, all we need to do is create the *PerfData* object, set some properties, and submit the object to the MOM server.

As we've shown, you can easily take an existing administrative script and extend it to run in a MOM environment, often with enhanced functionality.

Summary

In this chapter, we discussed how to work with scripts in a Microsoft Operations Manager 2005 environment. We explained that the *ScriptContext* object replaces *wscript* as the script host on a MOM server, and we outlined how scripts execute on managed servers. We looked at the different types of script objects in MOM such as *Alerts, Performance Data,* and *Events.* You also learned various ways to use scripts, including as responses and scheduled tasks. Finally, we demonstrated how to use extend existing scripts to run in a MOM environment. Scripting with MOM is a bit more involved than traditional scripting, but it offers some tremendous benefits and value.

> **More Info**   For more information, visit the Technet script center or look at the Web links for this chapter on the companion CD.

Chapter 17
Virtual Server 2005 Scripting

Microsoft Virtual Server 2005 represents one of Microsoft's most script-accessible products ever. Designed to expose much of its functionality through Component Object Model (COM) objects, Virtual Server's scriptability makes it highly manageable. We'll explain the basics of the Virtual Server object model, and show you some examples of how scripts can make Virtual Server easier and more efficient to use.

When Microsoft purchased Virtual Server from its original creators, Connectix (*http:// www.connectix.com*), most industry watchers assumed that Microsoft would quickly release the nearly completed product. Instead, Microsoft surprised everyone by spending quite a long time improving Virtual Server's stability and performance, as well as making it easier to manage through the addition of a comprehensive Component Object Model (COM)-based application programming interface (API). That API ensures that other COM-compatible languages, including VBScript, can automate management tasks related to virtual disk drives, virtual machines, virtual networks, virtual server security, and more. Virtual Server comes with a programmer's guide that explains the complete API, so in this chapter, we focus on the core capabilities that a Windows administrator will find most useful.

> **Note** The techniques we demonstrate in this chapter only work with Virtual Server; they're not compatible with Virtual Server's sibling product, Virtual PC. Virtual PC is intended to run on client computers, and to run just a few virtual machines at once; Virtual Server is an enterprise-level application, intended to continuously run a larger number of virtual machines that act as actual production servers on your network.

Introducing Virtual Server Scripting

Virtual Server is designed to run one or more *virtual machines*. A virtual machine is a representation of a physical computer. The base server on which Virtual Server runs is often referred to as the *host*, and the copy of Microsoft Windows running on the host is referred to as the *host OS*, or *host operating system*. The host hardware is often a high-end, multiprocessor server, and the host OS is typically an edition of Microsoft Windows Server 2003. Each virtual machine runs its own independent operating system, referred to as a *guest OS*. Virtual machines running under Virtual Server can run almost any version of Windows—including Microsoft Windows NT—or almost any other operating system compatible with a 32-bit Intel processor, including variations of Linux, different brands of Unix, and so forth. Each virtual machine has one or more *virtual disks*, which are essentially files on the host computer that appear as storage devices to a virtual machine. For example, a virtual machine running Microsoft Windows 2000 Server might have two hard disks, C and D, which are virtual disks that exist as two independent files on the host computer. Similarly, a virtual network allows virtual machines to communicate with one another.

> **More Info**   A full discussion of Virtual Server's concepts and capabilities is beyond the scope of this book. However, you can learn more from the Virtual Server Web site at
>
> *http://www.microsoft.com/virtualserver*
>
> Another good source of information is John Howard's blog at
>
> *http://blogs.technet.com/howard/*

Virtual Server's API exposes five main categories of capabilities, each related to a specific functional component of Virtual Server.

- Virtual Server client capabilities, such as clicking a mouse button or pressing a key, which allow you to automate tasks within a guest OS. Virtual Server doesn't provide direct automation within a virtual machine (meaning you can't automate what goes on inside the virtual machine's guest operating system, although you can write scripts that run within the virtual machine), but it does provide the ability to send keystrokes, mouse clicks, and so forth into the virtual machine—essentially allowing you to automate the manual tasks that an on-site user would perform.

- Virtual disk drives, including removable media devices such as DVD drives, as well as virtual fixed storage such as virtual hard disks. The API also provides control over virtual SCSI controllers and drives.

- Virtual machine settings, including details of the virtual machine's hardware (such as ports), save states, and so forth.

- Virtual network configurations, including virtual network adapters, virtual networks that connect virtual machines, the built-in virtual DHCP server, and more.

- Virtual Server access rights and security, including the ability to search for and list access rights.

The Microsoft TechNet Script Center has a number of scripts designed to manage various aspects of Virtual Server. You can access the complete collection at

http://www.microsoft.com/technet/scriptcenter/scripts/vs/default.mspx

On the CD   This link is included on the companion CD. Click *Script Repository-Virtual Server*.

In fact, we use some of these scripts as the basis for our examples. We also show you how to extend these examples into scripts that perform more comprehensive administrative tasks.

Virtual Hardware

If you're planning to write scripts that run inside a virtual machine, your scripts will need to be compatible with the guest OS running inside the virtual machine. You might, however, be interested to know on what hardware the guest OS will be running, because that information can also affect how you write your scripts.

Each virtual machine emulates an Intel 440BX chipset and an AMI BIOS. The processor inside the virtual machine is exposed as the host computer's processor, meaning the processor isn't emulated in any way—it's simply passed through to the virtual machine. For graphics, each virtual machine emulates an S3 Trio 32/64 with 4MB of video memory. Virtual machines also emulate a standard 104-key, Windows-compatible keyboard with a PS/2 interface. (If you're using a physical USB keyboard, the virtual machine still sees it as a PS/2 keyboard; Virtual Server 2005 doesn't support USB devices inside virtual machines.) Similarly, the mouse inside each virtual machine is seen as a PS/2 mouse. No support is provided for sound or game controllers.

Each virtual machine can have up to two serial ports and one parallel port; again, USB devices aren't supported. Up to two 1.44-MB floppy drives can be attached. For hard drives, up to four IDE devices can be attached, including CD-ROM or DVD drives. Up to four SCSI host controllers can be emulated, as well; Virtual Server emulates an Adaptec 7870 SCSI controller chipset. Each controller can host up to seven virtual SCSI hard disks. Virtual IDE CD-ROM and DVD-ROMs are limited to 128 GB in size, although to store the maximum amount, you'll obviously need sufficient physical storage on the host computer. SCSI disk images can be up to 2 TB in size. SCSI CD-ROM or DVD-ROM drives are not supported.

For the network, Virtual Server emulates a single DEC 21140 10/100-MB multi-port Ethernet card, with up to four independent network connections on the card.

The important things to remember about Virtual Server's architecture—because they will come up while you are scripting the product—are:

- Virtual Server can contain one or more virtual machine configurations, which are all the settings that comprise a virtual machine. When the virtual machine is executing, it's referred to as a *session*.

- Each virtual machine has its own private, virtual resources, such as virtual disks, serial ports, and so forth. Some of these resources, such as a serial port, might map to a physical resource on the host computer.

- Virtual Server can contain one or more virtual networks, some of which might connect to the host computer's physical network. Each virtual machine can be connected to one or more virtual networks by means of virtual network adapters.

Understanding the Virtual Server Object Model

The Virtual Server object model starts with the *VirtualServer.Application* object, which implements a COM interface named *IVMVirtualServer*. This object provides the means to access all the other objects supported by the Virtual Server COM API. Some of the primary methods and properties of the *VirtualServer.Application* object include the following:

- *FindVirtualMachine*   This method returns a virtual machine object (*IVMVirtualMachine* interface) based on the configuration name you provide.

- *CreateVirtualMachine*   This method creates a new virtual machine configuration, and returns a *VirtualMachine* object that represents the new virtual machine. There's also a *DeleteVirtualMachine* method that deletes a virtual machine configuration.

- *RegisterVirtualMachine*   This method adds an existing virtual machine configuration to Virtual Server, allowing you to, for example, import virtual machines from another server. The *UnregisterVirtualMachine* method removes a virtual machine without deleting its configuration file from the disk.

- *FindVirtualNetwork, CreateVirtualNetwork, DeleteVirtualNetwork, RegisterVirtualNetwork,* and *UnregisterVirtualNetwork*   These methods all perform tasks similar to the above, but use virtual networks instead of virtual machines.

- *GetHardDisk, CreateFloppyDiskImage, GetFloppyDiskImageType, CreateDynamicVirtualHardDisk, CreateFixedVirtualHardDisk, CreateDifferencingVirtualHardDisk,* and *CreateHostDriveVirtualHardDisk*   These methods all work with virtual storage.

> **Note**   A *differencing* disk contains all the differences in a virtual machine's state. For example, you can create a virtual machine, and then create a new differencing disk based on the virtual machine's original virtual disk. Any changes to the virtual machine are stored on the differencing disk. By deleting the differencing disk and reverting to the original virtual disk, you effectively roll back all the changes made to the virtual machine. See the Virtual Server documentation for details.

- *GetConfigurationValue*, *RemoveConfigurationValue*, and *SetConfigurationValue* These methods allow you to work with virtual server configuration settings.

- *GetHardDiskFiles*, *GetVirtualMachineFiles*, *GetVirtualNetworkFiles*, *GetFloppyDiskFiles*, and *GetDVDFiles* These methods return arrays of the appropriate types of files.

- *AvailableSystemCapacity* This method returns a percentage of available capacity, based on the number of virtual machines currently running.

- *VirtualMachines* This method returns a collection of *VirtualMachine* objects. You can enumerate this collection to, for example, perform a task with each configured virtual machine.

- *VirtualNetworks* This method returns a collection of *VirtualNetwork* objects. You can enumerate this collection to, for example, examine the properties of each configured virtual network.

The Virtual Server API includes about 40 objects. In addition to the top-level *Virtual-Server.Application* object, the ones you're most likely to work with include the following (we're listing their COM interface names here):

- *IVMDHCPVirtualNetworkServer*

- *IVMDVDDrive*

- *IVMFloppyDrive*

- *IVMGuestOS*

- *IVMHardDisk*

- *IVMHostInfo*

- *IVMNetworkAdapter*

- *IVMSCSIController*

- *IVMSerialPort*

- *IVMVirtualMachine*

- *IVMVirtualNetwork*

For example, here's a quick script snippet that will display the name of all virtual machines configured under Virtual Server.

```
Set objVS = CreateObject("VirtualServer.Application")
For Each objVM In objVS.VirtualMachies
    WScript.Echo "VM: " & objVM.Name
Next
```

> **Note**   All the scripts in this chapter assume you're running the script directly on the Virtual
> Server computer, which is usually the only place the Virtual Server COM objects will be avail-
> able. In theory, you can use the VBScript *CreateObject* function to instantiate the *Virtual-
> Server.Application* object on a remote Virtual Server computer. We haven't had consistent suc-
> cess with this technique, though, and prefer to run our scripts directly on the Virtual Server
> host. If you want to write scripts on your Windows XP Professional computer by using a com-
> mercial script editor (such as PrimalScript or OnScript), you can install Virtual Server 2005 for
> development purposes. That'll give your computer the type libraries necessary to allow the
> editors' Intellisense-like code hinting features to work with the Virtual Server objects.

Writing Provisioning Scripts

Provisioning is the act of initially configuring a new virtual machine. Using a script to do this
can save time, and make the process of configuring multiple new virtual machines easier and
much more consistent. Creating a new virtual machine is straightforward.

```
Set objVS = CreateObject("VirtualServer.Application")
Set objVM = objVS.CreateVirtualMachine("MyMachine", _
    "D:\Virtual Machines\MyMachine")
```

After creating the new virtual machine, *objVM* will be a reference to the newly created virtual
machine object. Of course, a virtual machine by itself isn't very useful. You at least need a hard
disk attached, and you'll probably want to give the virtual machine a DVD-ROM drive so that
you can install an operating system. We usually prefer to create dynamic virtual hard disks,
which start out as smaller physical files and grow to the maximum size you specify (meaning
that a 4-GB disk won't take up 4 GB of storage until it's full). To create a new virtual machine,
assuming *objVS* is already instantiated as just shown, do the following:

```
errReturn = objVS.CreateDynamicVirtualHardDisk _
    ("D:\Virtual Machines\MyMachine\HardDisk.vhd", 10000)
```

This creates a new 10GB dynamic disk in the specified location. Let's suppose that we have an
ISO-formatted DVD-ROM image that contains our operating system installation media. We'll
now want to attach that DVD-ROM image, as well as the newly created hard disk, to the virtual
machine, which is represented by the variable *objVM*. First we'll attach the hard drive image as
an IDE image (zero) by using the first IDE bus (zero), and then we'll add the drive as device
zero. We'll get back a *HardDiskConnection* object, which we'll store in *objDrive*.

```
Set objDrive = objVM.AddHardDiskConnection _
    ("D:\Virtual Machines\MyMachine\HardDisk.vhd",0,0,0)
```

Now we'll add a DVD-ROM drive. Again, we'll attach it to the IDE bus (which is bus zero), but
this time, we make the DVD-ROM drive the first device (device zero) on the second bus.

```
Set objDVD = objVM.AddDVDROMDrive(0,1,0)
```

This returns a *DVDDrive* object, which we store in *objDVD*. To attach our ISO image, do the following:

```
errReturn = objDVD.AttachImage("D:\ISO\Win2003Standard.iso")
```

We might now want to adjust some of the properties of the hard disk. The *objDrive* variable represents the hard drive connection; to get the actual drive, we need to use the connection's *HardDisk* property.

```
Set objHDisk = objDrive.HardDisk
```

Right now, there's not much we can do with the disk because it doesn't contain any data, but it's useful to know how to access it.

Our virtual machine will probably be more useful if it has a network connection, too, so let's give it a network adapter.

```
Set objNIC = objVM.AddNetworkAdapter()
```

Right now, of course, we don't have a network to plug the adapter into, so let's create one.

```
Set objNetwork = CreateVirtualNetwork("MyNetwork", _
    "D:\Virtual Networks\MyNetwork\")
```

Now we can attach our virtual network adapter to the new virtual network.

```
objNIC.AttachToVirtualNetwork("MyNetwork")
```

All that's left to do is start the new virtual machine. If that DVD-ROM ISO image we attached is set up with an unattended installation script, the operating system installation can start by itself and get our new virtual machine up and running. To start the virtual machine, do the following:

```
objVM.Startup()
```

And that's it. We've created a new virtual machine and started it. Listing 17-1 is the entire script.

Listing 17-1 Create and Start a New Virtual Machine
```
Set objVS = CreateObject("VirtualServer.Application")
Set objVM = objVS.CreateVirtualMachine("MyMachine", _
    "D:\Virtual Machines\MyMachine")

'Create and attach the hard disk
errReturn = objVS.CreateDynamicVirtualHardDisk _
    ("D:\Virtual Machines\MyMachine\HardDisk.vhd", 10000)
Set objDrive = objVM.AddHardDiskConnection _
    ("D:\Virtual Machines\MyMachine\HardDisk.vhd",0,0,0)

'Attach DVD-ROM device and ISO image
```

```
Set objDVD = objVM.AddDVDROMDrive(0,1,0)
objDVD.AttachImage "D:\ISO\Win2003Standard.iso"

'Get a reference to the hard disk, even though we are
'not going to use it right now
Set objHDisk = objDrive.HardDisk

'Attach virtual network adapter, create a network,
'and connect adapter to the network
Set objNIC = objVM.AddNetworkAdapter()
Set objNetwork = CreateVirtualNetwork("MyNetwork", _
    "D:\Virtual Networks\MyNetwork\")
objNIC.AttachToVirtualNetwork("MyNetwork")
objVM.Startup()
```

On the CD   You will find this script, as well as other scripts listed in this chapter, on the CD that accompanies this book.

This is the basic pattern most provisioning scripts will follow.

1. Create the new virtual machine.

2. Create peripherals, such as network adapters and disks.

3. Attach the peripherals to the virtual machine.

4. Set peripherals' properties (such as attaching a DVD-ROM to an ISO image).

5. Start the virtual machine.

Prior to starting the virtual machine, you might want to configure other properties of the virtual machine itself. For example, we usually include some of the following:

```
objVM.Undoable = True
objVM.UndoAction = 1
objVM.Memory = 256
objVM.AutoStartAtLaunch = True
```

These lines configure the new virtual machine to be undoable, specify that the current state should be preserved when the virtual machine is shut down (as opposed to automatically committing or rolling back the current state), specify that the virtual machine is given 256 MB of memory, and configure the virtual machine to start when Virtual Server starts (that way, the virtual machine is always running and available).

Writing Management Scripts

Virtual Server management scripts are useful for performing regularly scheduled tasks, automating tedious tasks, or automating tasks that need to be performed against multiple virtual machines at once.

Obtaining Object References

Before you can work with a virtual machine, virtual network, virtual disk, or any other Virtual Server object, you need to obtain a reference to the object. The top-level *VirtualServer* object (using the *ProgID VirtualServer.Application*) provides methods that return references to various types of objects. For example:

- To obtain a reference to a virtual machine, use *FindVirtualMachine("machinename")*.

- To obtain a reference to a virtual network, use *FindVirtualNetwork("networkname")*.

- To obtain a reference to a virtual hard disk, use *GetHardDisk("disk_file_path")*.

You can also enumerate through most second-level objects. For example, the *VirtualServer* object includes a *VirtualMachines* property that is a collection of all virtual machines, and a *VirtualNetworks* property that is a collection of all virtual networks. For example, to work with a virtual machine named *Win2003Server*, you would execute the following:

```
Set objVS = CreateObject("VirtualServer.Application")
Set objVM = objVS.FindVirtualMachine("Win2003Server")
```

If you want to enumerate through all the virtual machines, execute the following:

```
Set objVS = CreateObject("VirtualServer.Application")
For Each objVM in objVS.VirtualMachines
    'objVM is a virtual machine object
Next
```

After you've obtained a reference to the appropriate object, you can work with its properties and methods to manage it.

Managing Multiple-Virtual-Machine Templates

Managing multiple virtual machines is pretty straightforward. Simply write a script that does whatever task you need for one virtual machine, being sure to refer to the virtual machine by using the object variable *objVM*. Then paste your script into a multiple-virtual-machine wrapper. Your script will perform whatever task you've scripted for each virtual machine targeted by the wrapper.

To get you started, we're providing two wrappers. Listing 17-2 on the next page is a wrapper that reads virtual machine names from a text file (C:\vmlist.txt by default, although you can easily modify that).

Listing 17-2 Target a List of Virtual Machines
```
Set objFSO = CreateObject("Scripting.FileSystemObject")
Set objTS = objFSO.OpenTextFile("C:\vmlist.txt")
Set objVS = CreateObject("VirtualServer.Application")
Do Until objTS.AtEndOfStream

    'Read the next VM name
    strVMName = objTS.ReadLine
    Set objVM = objVS.FindVirtualMachine(strVMName)

    'Insert your code here using objVM

Loop
objTS.Close
WScript.Echo "Complete"
```

Listing 17-3 targets every virtual machine configured in Virtual Server.

Listing 17-3 Target All Virtual Machines
```
Set objFSO = CreateObject("Scripting.FileSystemObject")
Set objVS = CreateObject("VirtualServer.Application")
For Each objVM In objVS.VirtualMachines

    'insert your code here using objVM

Next
```

We'll use Listing 17-2 at the end of this chapter, so you can see how inserting your own single-virtual-machine code creates a multiple-virtual-machine script. We'll use Listing 17-3 in Listing 17-4, again demonstrating how straightforward it is to script tasks against multiple virtual machines.

Performing Virtual Machine Tasks

There are a number of virtual machine management tasks that you can perform by using a script. We're not going to include provisioning tasks, such as attaching a new hard disk, that you'd usually only perform once; instead, we're focusing on management tasks that you might need to perform often

Several methods of the *VirtualMachine* object can be used to control the state of a virtual machine. (These examples assume you've obtained a *VirtualMachine* object reference in the variable *objVM*.)

```
objVM.Startup
objVM.TurnOff
objVM.Pause
objVM.Reset
objVM.Resume
objVM.Save
```

These methods perform tasks equivalent to the corresponding user interface controls:

- The *Startup* method activates a virtual machine.

- The *Pause* method temporarily suspends a virtual machine, but does not save its state. The virtual machine is suspended, essentially; Virtual Server leaves the virtual machine "turned on" but stops executing the virtual machine's guest OS.

- The *Resume* method brings a virtual machine out of Pause mode, returning it to the state it was in when you paused it.

- The *TurnOff* method cuts virtual power to the virtual machine, analogous to pulling the plug from a physical computer.

- The *Reset* method is similar to pressing the reset button on a physical computer, and it has an effect similar to running *TurnOff* and then *Startup* in quick succession.

- The *Save* method saves the current state of the virtual machine and then turns it off.

> **Note**   A virtual machine's *saved state* includes both the current condition of its virtual disks, as well as its entire memory, which is saved to a file on the host computer. The saved state represents the exact condition of a virtual machine at a point in time, similar to activating hibernate mode on a physical computer.

A few additional methods allow you to work with a virtual machine's saved state.

- The *DiscardSavedState* method destroys a virtual machine's saved state data, returning the virtual machine to the condition it was in before the session in which the saved state was created. For example, say you start a virtual machine, and then shut it down. Then you start it a second time, save its state, and then discard the saved state. The virtual machine would be in the same condition it was in after the first shutdown, which is the last time changes were committed to disk.

- The *DiscardUndoDisks* method is somewhat similar to *DiscardSavedState*. As we've explained, a virtual machine can be configured to be undoable, meaning its original virtual disks are untouched, and disk changes are written to a special undo file. Discarding that undo file (or *undo disk*) reverts the virtual machine to the condition of the original virtual disk. Alternately, you can use the *MergeUndoDisks* method to merge the undo disk's changes into the original virtual disk file, thus making the changes in the undo disk permanent.

  For example, suppose you have configured all your virtual machines to be undoable. Each evening, you want to merge the undo disks, and make the day's changes permanent. (Therefore, at any time prior to merging the disks, you could revert the virtual machine's state to that of the previous evening's merge.) To merge the undo disks with every virtual machine on your Virtual Server computer, you could run the short script in Listing 17-4 on the next page.

Listing 17-4 Merge All Virtual Machine Undo Disks

```
Set objFSO = CreateObject("Scripting.FileSystemObject")
Set objVS = CreateObject("VirtualServer.Application")
For Each objVM In objVS.VirtualMachines

    'insert your code here using objVM
    objVM.MergeUndoDisks

Next
```

You'll notice that we used one of our wrapper scripts to accomplish this task.

The *VirtualMachine* object exposes a number of properties that can be useful in various management tasks.

- *AutoStartAtLaunch*   When set to TRUE, this property causes Virtual Server to automatically start the virtual machine when Virtual Server itself starts (such as after a host computer reboot).

- *AutoStartAtLaunchDelay*   This property specifies a number of seconds that Virtual Server will wait to auto-start a virtual machine. This is useful because some virtual machines depend on others (such as domain controllers) to function.

- *GuestOS*   This property returns a *GuestOS* object that represents the guest OS running within a virtual machine. We'll discuss this object in more detail later in this chapter.

- *Keyboard*   This property returns a *Keyboard* object, which represents the virtual machine's keyboard. We'll discuss this property in more detail later in this chapter.

- *Memory*   This property allows you to examine or change the amount of memory, in megabytes, assigned to the virtual machine. Note that you cannot change this property unless the virtual machine is turned off.

- *Mouse*   This property returns a *Mouse* object, which represents the virtual machine's mouse. We'll discuss this property in more detail later in this chapter.

- *State*   This property lists the current state of the virtual machine. This property is read-only; you can't change the state by directly modifying this property. This property's possible values include the following:

  - *0: Invalid*

  - *1: Off*

  - *2: Saved*

  - *3: Turning on*

  - *4: Restoring*

  - *5: Running*

  - *6: Paused*

  - *7: Saving*

- *8: Turning off*

- *9: Merging drives*

- *10: Deleting VM*

- *Undoable*   When this property is set to TRUE, the virtual machine is set to undoable, when set to FALSE, it is not.

- *UndoAction*   This property sets the action that Virtual Server should take when the virtual machine's guest OS is shut down as usual. This property's possible values are:

  - *0* discards the undo drive (thus undoing any changes made to the virtual machine since it started).

  - *1* keeps the undo drive (persisting any changes but reserving the ability to undo them later).

  - *2* commits changes from the undo drive (merging the drives), making the changes permanent.

Listing 17-5 is an example of using the *VirtualMachine* object properties to produce an inventory list of virtual machines. Note that this only works if each virtual machine has a guest OS installed and functional.

Listing 17-5 Inventory Virtual Machines

```
Set objFSO = CreateObject("Scripting.FileSystemObject")
Set objVS = CreateObject("VirtualServer.Application")
For Each objVM In objVS.VirtualMachines

    If objVM.AutoStartAtLaunch Then
        strAuto = "Auto start"
    Else
        strAuto = "Manual start"
    End If


    strGuestOS = objVM.GuestOS.Name
    strDisks = objVM.HardDiskConnections.Count & " Disks"
    strNICs = objVM.NetworkAdapters.Count & " NICs"
    Select Case objVM.ShutdownActionOnQuit
        Case 0
            strAction = "Save state on quit"
        Case 1
            strAction = "Turn off on quit"
        Case 2
            strAction = "Shutdown on quit"
    End Select

    Select Case objVM.State
        Case 0
            strState = "Invalid"
        Case 1
            strState = "Off"
        Case 2
```

```
                strState = "Saved"
        Case 3
            strState = "Turning on"
        Case 4
            strState = "Restoring"
        Case 5
            strState = "Running"
        Case 6
            strState = "Paused"
        Case 7
            strState = "Saving"
        Case 8
            strState = "Turning off"
        Case 9
            strState = "Merging"
        Case 10
            strState = "Deleting"
    End Select

    If objVM.Undoable Then
        strUndo = "Undoable"
    Else
        strUndo = "Not undoable"
    End If

    WScript.Echo objVM.Name & ": " & _
     strUndo & "," & _
     strState & "," & _
     strAction & "," & _
     strGuestOS & "," & _
     strDisks & "," & _
     strNICs & "," & _
     strAuto

Next
```

Here's an example of this script's output when running under CScript.exe.

```
WinXP: Undoable,Running,Shutdown on quit,Windows XP Professional,1 Disks,1 NICs,Auto start
Win2003: Undoable,Running,Shutdown on quit,Windows Server 2003,1 Disks,1 NICs,Auto start
Linux: Not undoable,Turned off,Shutdown on quit,Red Hat Linux,2 Disks,1 NICs,Manual start
```

Performing Virtual Disk Tasks

The *HardDisk* object represents a virtual disk and includes a few methods useful for management, particularly periodic maintenance tasks.

- *Compact* For dynamic (as opposed to fixed-size) disks, this method reduces the disk file as much as possible, eliminating unused space.

- *Merge* This method merges a virtual disk's undo file with the parent file.

- *MergeTo*   This method merges an undo disk and its parent into a new, independent virtual disk file. You must pass two arguments to this method indicating the new virtual disk's filename, and the type (fixed-size or dynamic) to be used. For example, *objDisk.MergeTo("C:\Newdisk.vmdk",0)* will merge to a new dynamic disk (use 1 for fixed-size).

All these methods return a *Task* object; you can check that object's *IsComplete* method to see when the operation is completed. For example:

```
Set objTask = objDisk.Compact
Do Until objTask.IsComplete
    WScript.Sleep 5000
Loop
```

> **Note**   We refer to things like *undo disks* as though they were separate disks, but they're not. Any given virtual disk—that is, an instance of the Virtual Server *HardDisk* object—consists of one or more *base* files that contain the permanent portion of the disk. It can also include one or more *undo* or *differencing* files, which are commonly referred to as *undo disks*. However, all these files—base and undo—comprise the actual *HardDisk* object.

Performing Guest OS Tasks

The *GuestOS* object provides a few methods and properties that provide basic control over the guest OS running within a virtual machine. This object is accessible through the *GuestOS* property of a virtual machine. Note that some capabilities of the *GuestOS* object require that the Virtual Server Additions software be installed on the guest OS. Properties include the following:

- *AdditionsVersion*   This property is the version of the installed Virtual Server Additions. This can be Null if the Additions are not installed.

- *CanShutdown*   This property is set to TRUE if Virtual Server can trigger an ordinary guest OS shutdown.

- *OSName*   This property is the name of the guest OS.

- *IsHeartBeating*   This property returns TRUE if the Additions installed in the guest OS indicate that the guest OS is functioning. If the Additions are installed and *IsHeartBeating* is FALSE, the guest OS might have locked up or crashed.

Methods of the *GuestOS* object include the following:

- *InstallAdditions*   This method attempts to locate the ISO image (included with Virtual Server) that contains the appropriate Virtual Server Additions software for the guest OS. It attaches the ISO image to a DVD drive, and if the guest OS is a version of Windows, it launches the Additions installer.

- *ExecuteCommand*   We mention this method in case you run across it, and because its name is so enticing and promising. In Virtual Server 2005, unfortunately, it doesn't do anything.

- *ShutDown*   This method triggers an ordinary shutdown in the guest OS. It requires that the Additions be installed and running. It is only currently supported for Windows guest OSs.

Performing Mouse and Keyboard Tasks

You can use a virtual machine's *Mouse* and *Keyboard* objects (obtained through the virtual machine's *Mouse* and *Keyboard* properties, respectively) to automate sending keystrokes and performing other manual tasks within the virtual machine. The *Keyboard* object includes several methods.

- *PressKey*   This method simulates pressing a key within the virtual machine.

- *ReleaseKey*   This method simulates releasing a key within the virtual machine.

- *PressAndReleaseKey*   This method simulates pressing and releasing a key within the virtual machine.

- *TypeAsciiText*   This method simulates typing plain text within the virtual machine.

- *TypeKeySequence*   This method simulates typing a series of keys within the virtual machine.

For all but *TypeAsciiText*, you'll need to provide an appropriate key identifier. Regular characters—letters, numbers, and punctuation—are identified as *Key_A*, replacing *A* with the appropriate character. Special keys are identified differently. For example, the *F1* key is identified as *Key_F1*. The Virtual Server Programmer's Guide contains a complete reference of key identifiers. To send the *F1* keystroke to a virtual machine, where you have a reference to that virtual machine in the *objVM* variable, you'd do something like this.

```
Set objKey = objVM.Keyboard
objKey.PressAndReleaseKey("Key_F1")
```

Similarly, the *Mouse* object includes a *Click* method, which simulates clicking a mouse button inside the virtual machine. This method requires one argument, which indicates the mouse button to click: *1* for left, *2* for right, and *3* for center or mouse wheel click. For example, *objMouse.Click(1)* simulates a left button click inside the virtual machine (assuming the variable *objMouse* is referring to a virtual machine's *Mouse* object).

Viewing Virtual Server Scripting in Action

We have a Virtual Server 2005 computer that's running half a dozen virtual machines; each virtual machine contains a different version of Windows. We use them to test scripts and other projects. One of the virtual machines is a domain controller, on which we've configured various computer accounts to use in our tests. We've configured each virtual machine to be *undoable*, meaning that when we're done testing, we can roll each virtual machine back to its starting condition, ready for the next round of tests. Of course, because the virtual machines are in a domain, we like to roll them all back as a unit—that way, we know they're in a consistent state of readiness for our next test. Rolling back multiple virtual machines manually is a bit time-consuming, so we wrote a simple script to do it.

We start by opening a text file named TestVMs.txt. In this file, we've listed the name of each test virtual machine. By using this list, we can avoid any other virtual machines that Virtual Server might be running. (Once we accidentally turned off and rolled back a virtual machine that a SQL Server developer was using—he got pretty mad.)

```
Set objFSO = CreateObject("Scripting.FileSystemObject")
Set objTS = objFSO.OpenTextFile("C:\TestVMs.txt")
```

Next, we instantiate the Virtual Server COM object.

```
Set objVS = CreateObject("VirtualServer.Application")
```

We use a loop to read through the text file until we reach its end.

```
Do Until objTS.AtEndOfStream
```

We read a virtual machine name into a string variable, and then ask Virtual Server to find that virtual machine and return a *VirtualMachine* object.

```
'Read the next VM name
strVMName = objTS.ReadLine
Set objVM = objVS.FindVirtualMachine(strVMName)
```

Because we don't care about the virtual machine's contents at this point, we just turn it off. This is the virtual equivalent of flipping the power switch, rather than doing a clean operating system shutdown. Again, we're rolling back the virtual machine, so any damage done by an improper shutdown won't be retained.

```
'Turn off the VM
Set objTask = objVM.TurnOff
```

The *TurnOff* method returns a *Task* object. Virtual Server uses *Task* objects to keep track of tasks that might require some time to complete. We can't roll back the virtual machine until it's completely turned off, which might take a second or two, so we'll check the task's *IsComplete* property every five seconds or so. After the *IsComplete* property is TRUE, we'll move on.

```
Do Until objTask.IsComplete
    WScript.Sleep 5000
Loop
```

Because we configured the virtual machine to be undoable, Virtual Server doesn't touch the virtual machine's original hard disks (where we've installed Windows). Instead, changes to the guest OS caused by our tests are written to a special *undo disk*. We always have the option to commit the undo disk, thus making the changes to that point a permanent part of the virtual machine. Instead, we're discarding the undo disks, reverting the virtual machine back to its original condition.

```
'Discard undo disks
objVM.DiscardUndoDisks
```

We then start the virtual machine again so that it's ready for our next round of tests. This technique also returns a *Task* object, but we're not capturing that in a variable. That's because we know the virtual machine will take a while to start, but we don't care; we can move on to the next virtual machine and let this one do whatever it needs to do.

```
'restart VM
objVM.Startup
Loop
```

Finally, we close the input text file and display a message indicating that the script is complete.

```
objTS.Close
WScript.Echo "Complete"
```

Listing 17-6 is the complete script.

Listing 17-6 Roll Back a List of Virtual Machines

```
Set objFSO = CreateObject("Scripting.FileSystemObject")
Set objTS = objFSO.OpenTextFile("C:\TestVMs.txt")
Set objVS = CreateObject("VirtualServer.Application")
Do Until objTS.AtEndOfStream

    'Read the next VM name
    strVMName = objTS.ReadLine
    Set objVM = objVS.FindVirtualMachine(strVMName)

    'Turn off the VM
    Set objTask = objVM.TurnOff
    Do Until objTask.IsComplete
        WScript.Sleep 5000
    Loop

    'Discard undo disks
    objVM.DiscardUndoDisks

    'restart VM
    objVM.Startup

Loop
objTS.Close
WScript.Echo "Complete"
```

This is a great example of a script that can save time for a Virtual Server administrator. For example, we have one client who uses a script to routinely shut down—meaning a clean shutdown of the operating system, not just turning off the virtual power—their virtual machines every night. They then back up the virtual hard disk files to tape, and then restart the virtual machines. This gives them a complete, point-in-time backup of the entire set of virtual machines, without having to install backup software or agents within the guest OSs.

Summary

Virtual Server 2005 scripting can help make Virtual Server management easier and more effective. Certainly, it can help automate mundane tasks, such as setting up new virtual machines or rolling back virtual machines in a group. But beyond the specific applications to Virtual Server, we've shown you a whole new area of scripting and hopefully helped you realize how extensible scripting really is. Provided you can find documentation on them, the many, many COM objects present on every Windows computer can provide a broad array of administrative capabilities. Becoming comfortable scripting COM objects—such as the Virtual Server API—is the cornerstone to becoming a more successful and flexible Windows administrative scripter.

Part V
Appendix

Appendix A
Advanced Script Editor Features

An amateur carpenter can get by with a simple hammer, but a true professional uses a nail gun—an advanced tool for advanced work. The same holds true for scripting: Although Microsoft Notepad is fine for beginners, as an advanced scripter, you should be using a commercial script editor that makes scripting easier and more efficient. We'll introduce you to several, and we'll highlight the features we think are the most useful.

Most Microsoft Windows administrators start scripting in Notepad. It's free, readily available on almost any computer running any version of Windows, and easy to use. Unfortunately, using Notepad to script is a bit like using scissors to trim a hedge—you can do it, but it certainly doesn't do anything to make your job easier. Notepad lacks line numbering, which is crucial in scripting because the error messages you get from VBScript will all reference the line where the error occurred. Notepad also doesn't format your scripts, or add indentations within loops, properly capitalized keywords, and so forth. Of course, your scripts will run without those fancy extras. VBScript is extremely forgiving in that regard. However, your scripts will be harder to read, which means they'll be harder to debug, and harder, in the long term, to maintain.

That's why we recommend that serious scripters—and because you're reading a book on advanced scripting, you qualify as "serious"—invest in a commercial scripting tool. That means you'll have to make a financial investment; but we think the investment is well worth it in terms of the time and effort you'll save in creating, debugging, and maintaining your scripts over the long term.

> **Note**   There are several free script editors that provide basic features. Enter **VBScript Editor** in a search engine like Google or MSN, or visit a download site like Download.com, and see what turns up.

Of course, all the fancy features in the world are useless if you don't utilize them. The purpose of this Appendix is to help you recognize which features are truly useful in Windows administrative scripting, and to give you an idea of how these features work and how they can help you. You can train yourself to use these features in whatever tool you eventually purchase. We're going to focus on four commercial editors, each of which provides a variety of features that are designed specifically for Windows administrative scripting.

The four commercial scripting applications we examine are PrimalScript, AdminScriptEditor, OnScript, and VBSEdit. We don't directly compare these editors and we don't provide a comprehensive list of all their features. Instead, we point out some of the features they offer that have helped us write better scripts faster. You should evaluate these and other tools on your own to decide which ones best meet your needs.

Universal Features

There are a few features that any good commercial script editor should include. The first is syntax color-coding, which means the editor colors VBScript keywords, variables, literals, and other language elements. Typically, you can customize the coloring to suit your preferences or visual requirements. Color-coding is often accompanied by case correction, which allows the editor to change, for example, *msgbox* to *MsgBox*. VBScript, unlike languages such as JScript, is not case-sensitive, but having everything properly cased does make your scripts a bit easier to read and more professional-looking. That's really the ultimate purpose of color-coding and case correction: making your scripts easier to read. Ease of reading is a big deal when you're looking at a hundred lines of VBScript code and trying to find a bug. In fact, you'll be surprised at how a neatly formatted script can help make even basic debugging easier. You don't need to learn how to use the color-coding feature because the editors do it automatically.

Another automatic feature is indenting. This allows you to type your script without having to worry much about the formatting. That way, when you begin a new construct—a *Do...Loop* construct, for example—you simply press the *Tab* key inside the construct. That indents the next line of code, like this.

```
Do Until objTS.AtAndOfStream
    strName = objTS.ReadLine
```

Subsequent lines of code are automatically indented to the same level. When you're done with the loop, just press *Backspace*, and type the loop's closing statement. The result is something like this.

```
Do Until objTS.AtAndOfStream
    strName = objTS.ReadLine
    If strName = "Server1" Then
        WScript.Echo "Skipping Server1"
    Else
        ConnectToServer(strName)
    End If
Loop
```

Each construct is nicely indented, allowing you to visually identify where each loop or other construct begins and ends. This is tremendously useful in debugging scripts, and makes long-term maintenance easier. Indenting like this is considered an industry best practice (and has been for years, in fact), and automatic indenting in a script editor makes it much easier to follow this best practice in your own scripts.

Keyboard Shortcuts

This is going to seem like a silly thing to point out, but keyboard shortcuts are incredibly important, and surprisingly, not every script editor has a lot of them. Think about it: you create scripts by typing, not by using the mouse. Therefore, the more time your hands spend on the keyboard, the more productive you're likely to be. We can probably type an average line of script in three or four seconds. That's about the amount of time it takes to reach for the mouse and click a toolbar button. Pressing a keyboard shortcut to activate that toolbar button's feature, however, takes probably less than a second, and that's enough time to write an extra line of code. Multiply that savings by the several dozen or so toolbar buttons you might click in the course of writing a script, and you could be losing a substantial amount of time. Yes, you do have to train yourself to remember and use keyboard shortcuts, but it's worth the initial investment in time.

As a technical professional, you've probably experienced some frustration over folks who don't use keyboard shortcuts. For example, how often have you stood behind a user with a technical problem, and asked him or her to copy and paste a small amount of text? An inexperienced user will grab the mouse, highlight the text (maybe taking one or two tries to do that), right-click the text, and click Copy on the shortcut menu. Meanwhile, your fingers are twitching to take over, highlight the text with the keyboard, and press *Ctrl+C* to copy it to the clipboard. You'd be back to your other duties that much quicker. That is the sort of thing we're talking about when it comes to keyboard shortcuts in script editors. Find an editor that provides shortcuts for as many of its key functions as possible, including running scripts, setting debugging breakpoints, launching wizards, inserting code snippets, and so forth. Then train yourself to use the keyboard shortcuts, and keep your hands off the mouse as much as possible.

Script Snippets

A year or so ago, PrimalScript was pretty much the only script editor to feature *snippets*, which are short pieces of code that you can reuse in your scripts. Today, almost everyone includes snippets, or something like them, in their editor. AdminScriptEditor from iTripoli calls them ScriptBits, OnScript from XLnow simply has a code library, and VBSEdit from Adersoft has a menu that provides access to snippets. We still like PrimalScript (from SAPIEN) best, though. As shown in Figure A-1, PrimalScript displays a Snippets Browser pane on the right side of the screen. You can browse through dozens of snippets (the company even sells add-on packs on their Web site), and drag them directly into your script. Snippets can include fill-in areas where you complete statements to customize the snippet for your script.

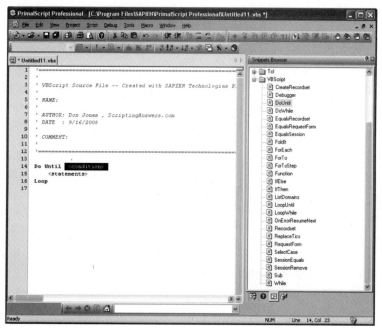

Figure A-1 Using snippets within PrimalScript

This is functionality that all the editors we're discussing provide. The reason we like Primal-Script's snippets best, however, is that snippets are also accessible through a keyboard short-cut. For example, if you need to create an ActiveX Data Objects (ADO) recordset, you can just type **createrecordset**–the name of a snippet–and press *Ctrl+J*. The entire snippet–a dozen lines of code, in this case–instantly appears in your script in place of the snippet's name.

Why are snippets so useful? Think about how long it might take you to write the dozen or so lines of code needed to, for example, open a recordset and enumerate through its records. Two minutes? Maybe five? With snippets, you can accomplish that in a couple of seconds. The trick is to train yourself to use these snippets, instead of writing code from scratch, whenever possible. Extending your snippets library helps, too. For example, PrimalScript can turn any section of code into a reusable snippet. Just select the code, right-click it, and click Save As Snippet from the shortcut menu. That's a really useful feature, because it essentially means you never have to type the same code twice. Type it the first time, save it as a snippet, and use the snippet from then on. Windows administrative scripts often need to open text files to read names, or even enumerate objects in Active Directory. There's no reason not to make that code into a snippet, allowing you to easily reuse it whenever you need to.

Code Hinting and Completion

All four of the editors we're discussing—PrimalScript, VBSEdit, AdminScriptEditor, and OnScript—offer some form of code hinting and completion. Microsoft's trade name for this feature is Intellisense, and if you've ever seen a developer working in Microsoft Visual Studio, you'll recognize the feature immediately. As shown in Figure A-2, OnScript displays a menu of options to complete the code you're typing. You can usually press an action key—*Spacebar*, *Tab*, and so forth—to accept the currently highlighted choice and complete your statement.

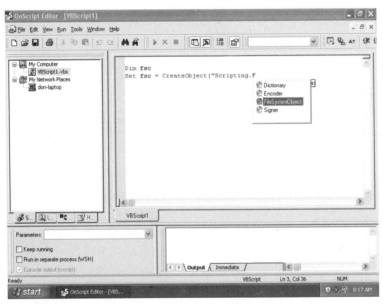

Figure A-2   Using code completion in OnScript

Code completion can often save you the time it would take to look in the documentation to find out what method, property name, or object *ProgID* to use. With all your choices alphabetically listed in a menu, you can just scroll down to the selection you want—using the *Arrow* keys, of course, because reaching for the mouse wastes time—press the action key, and finish your code.

Code hinting is a similar feature that serves the same purpose: avoiding the need to turn to the documentation. Figure A-3 on the next page shows PrimalScript's code hinting feature. A

ScreenTip reminds you of the proper syntax for functions and statements—even the ones you define yourself in your script. With this quick, unobtrusive reminder, you can figure out which argument comes first in, for example, the *InStr* function—something we always have a tough time remembering—without wasting time looking up the function's syntax in the VBScript documentation.

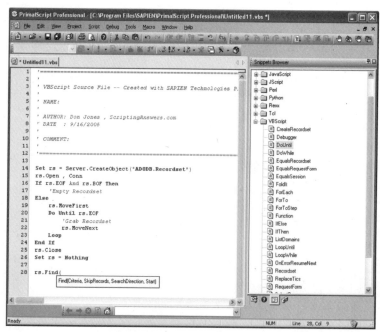

Figure A-3 Using code hinting in PrimalScript

Wizards

Wizards are small, built-in tools that a script editor provides to make scripting easier. A great example of a wizard is AdminScriptEditor's MessageBox Wizard. The VBScript *MsgBox* statement (or function, depending on how you're using it) has a lot of flexibility. You can specify a variety of button combinations, icons, and so forth. Unfortunately, remembering all the available options, and the values that select them, is tough, and often requires a quick look at the VBScript documentation. The MessageBox Wizard provides you with an easy graphical user interface for selecting the options you want, as shown in Figure A-4. When you're done, the correct VBScript code is inserted into your script for you.

Other wizards can perform more complicated tasks. For example, VBSEdit, AdminScript Editor, and PrimalScript all include a Windows Management Instrumentation (WMI) Wizard, which produces short WMI scripts for you. Figure A-5 shows PrimalScript's wizard, which allows you to browse the WMI classes on your computer, as well as the classes on any remote computer to which you have permissions.

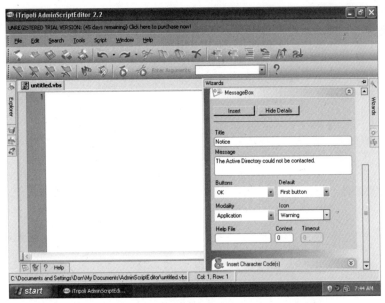

Figure A-4   Using the MessageBox Wizard in AdminScriptEditor

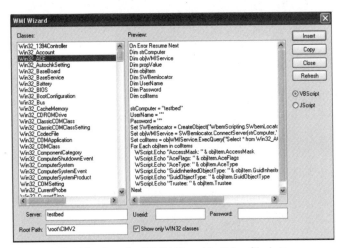

Figure A-5   Viewing the WMI Wizard in PrimalScript

More Info   Chapter 12, "Better Scripting with WMI Tools," covers the PrimalScript WMI Wizard in more detail, and provides suggestions for using it to write more complex scripts in less time.

The wizard-generated script can be inserted in your own script, and then adjusted to meet your needs. Using a wizard like this is often much easier than manually creating the code to query certain WMI information, and the wizard also provides a convenient way to browse the available WMI classes. Some WMI wizards, such as the one in AdminScriptEditor, also display sample data from the WMI class you select, helping you to confirm that the class is correct.

Sometimes, wizards go beyond writing simple sample scripts and actually extend the functionality of your script. A good example is PrimalScript's ADSI Wizard (only available in the Professional Edition). Figure A-6 shows the wizard in action. There's no preview—as wizards often provide—of the script the wizard will generate. What the wizard is doing, however, is much more complex than just creating some sample code. It's creating entirely new object classes within your script. Each class represents an Active Directory object, such as a user or computer.

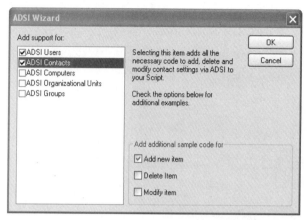

Figure A-6   Running the PrimalScript ADSI Wizard

After this is added to your script, you'll be able to create new instances of these object classes to represent ADSI users, computers, or whatever. As shown in Figure A-7, PrimalScript can provide full code completion and hinting for these objects, making ADSI scripting much more straightforward.

```
549   Dim objADSI
550   Dim objADSIUser
551   Dim objADSIContact
552
553   Set objADSI = New ADSIConnection
554   Set objADSIUser = New ADSIUser
555   Set objADSIContact = New ADSIContact
556
557   if False Then
558       ' Additional Wizard Sample Code
559       Call objADSI.GetUser(objADSIUser,"cn=Users","Hooten")
560       call objADSI.GetContact(objADSIContact,"ou=HR,ou=Depts",
561       objADSI.CreateContact("ou=HR,ou=Depts","Gates")
562   End If
563   ' End sample ADSI Wizard code
564
565   ' ************ End ADSI Wizard generated code. Do not modif
566
567   objADSIUser.|
568                    ADUser
                        AppendItem
                        ClearItem
                        GetItem
                        GetItemEx
                        PrintItems
                        PutItem
                        PutItemEx
```

Figure A-7   Testing code completion for the new ADSI-related objects

The lesson here is that code wizards can save time, make scripting easier, and provide functionality that might otherwise take you hours or even days to write on your own. Learning to use these wizards can save you a lot of time, especially in complex scripting tasks, even if you have to adjust their output a bit to suit your precise needs.

> **Tip**   Some editors—such as AdminScriptEditor and PrimalScript—are extensible, meaning that you can add wizards into the product. SAPIEN, for example, publishes the specification needed to write your own wizards in almost any COM-compatible language (including Visual Basic). The manufacturers of these editors sometimes release add-in packages of additional wizards, adding functionality and value to their tool.

The nice thing about wizards is that they give you the scripting capabilities of a more experience developer—namely, the person or people who wrote the wizard. As long as you know the basics and keep things simple, wizards can often write two-thirds or more of the scripts you need to automate Windows administration.

Debugging

Debugging is an unfortunate fact of life when you're writing scripts. Unless you're writing the simplest possible script with just a few lines of code, you're likely to run into a bug at some point. Three of the editors we're discussing—OnScript, AdminScriptEditor, and VBSEdit—provide integration with the Microsoft Script Debugger, which is a free download at

http://msdn.microsoft.com/library/default.asp?url=/library/en-us/sdbug/Html/sdbug_1.asp

> **Tip**   This link, like most of the links referenced in this book, is included on the companion CD. Click *Introducing Microsoft Script Debugger.*

This integration allows you to set debugging breakpoints within the editor's code window, and then launch the script debugger (often by using a toolbar button or menu command) from within the editor. If you're using one of these editors, take the time to download and install the Microsoft Script Debugger so that you'll have some basic debugging functionality available to you.

> **More Info**   A full discussion of debugging techniques and concepts is beyond the scope of this book. If you'd like to learn more about VBScript debugging, we suggest viewing the *VBScript Debugging* training video, available at these two Web sites:
>
> *www.ScriptingAnswers.com*
>
> *www.ScriptingOutpost.com*

PrimalScript Standard Edition includes this same style of integration, but PrimalScript Professional Edition includes a customized debugger named PrimalScope. PrimalScope is much more functional than the Windows Script Debugger, and makes it a lot easier to get inside your scripts as they're running to see what they're doing—a key to successful, efficient debugging. Like the other editors, PrimalScript allows you to set breakpoints—places where script execution will pause so that you can examine the script's operation to that point—within the code window. When you begin debugging, though, everything takes place within the PrimalScript window, as shown in Figure A-8.

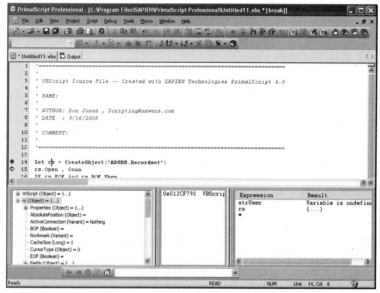

Figure A-8   Debugging in PrimalScript Professional

The lower-left pane displays all the current variable and object property values, so you can see at a glance which values your script is using in loops and logical comparisons. On the right, an expressions evaluator displays the current result of any expression. You can highlight even complex expressions in your script and drag them into the evaluator. PrimalScript will continually update the result of the expression as your script executes so you can see the values that your script is producing and using. Pressing *F11* advances your script by one line of code, enabling you to step through the script one line at a time, examining the script's values after each line of code executes. Using these tools, you can quickly see where your script is producing values you didn't expect, taking improper actions, and so forth. This is the fastest way to find and eliminate bugs.

Enterprise Features

Scripting is often seen as a rogue operation, and is something that many information technology managers don't like. Although scripting has obvious benefits to an administrator, company managers often worry that the company will become dependent on the scripts, and that when the administrator leaves, these scripts will create a maintenance nightmare.

One way to help alleviate this fear is through the use of enterprise best practices for software development; that is, by treating scripts as though they are a regular, full-size software-development project. We've already discussed some of these best practices, such as proper code formatting. Another best practice is the use of source-control software, such as Microsoft Visual SourceSafe, Borland StarTeam, and so forth. This software enables you to check in scripts, keeping them in a central repository that can be backed up and treated as an asset of the company. When you need to modify a script, you check it out, make your modifications, and check in the modified version. Every version you check in is retained, so that past versions can be easily retrieved, compared to other versions, and so forth. Although we're not aware of any script editors that include source-control software, PrimalScript provides a means for integrating with source-control software that you've acquired separately. (Almost any company that has internal software developers will already have a source control solution of some kind.) PrimalScript provides a source-control toolbar through which you can access the source-control software, and check scripts in and out. Figure A-9 shows the Checkin File(s) dialog box, where you can enter a comment about the version of a script you're checking in.

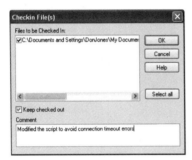

Figure A-9   Checking in scripts through PrimalScript

Although using source control won't alleviate every potential objection to administrative scripting, it will show that you're serious about using scripting as a tool for achieving your organization's goals more efficiently. Source control also provides a valuable backup and version-control resource as your library of scripts grows. Accessing source control through your scripting environment makes it more convenient, and that means you're more likely to use the source-control system.

Security Features

In Chapter 2, "Script Security," we discussed how script security is a concern for most businesses, and how Windows Script Host (WSH) can be configured to have a TrustPolicy that makes scripting safer. We believe that a properly secured scripting environment is a must for any environment, and we appreciate that some scripting-related tools are adopting that same belief. Of the four editors we're looking at in this Appendix, only PrimalScript provides full integration with WSH TrustPolicy. Figure A-10 shows PrimalScript's Options dialog box, and you can see that there's an entire section devoted to security. You can specify the name of a code-signing certificate, which enables PrimalScript to digitally sign scripts on demand, or automatically sign scripts each time you save them. Because WSH TrustPolicy relies on digital signatures to identify trusted scripts, the ability to easily and automatically sign scripts is a crucial part of a more secure scripting environment.

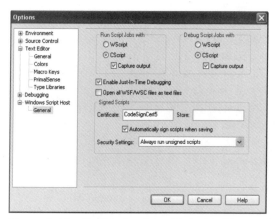

Figure A-10   Configuring PrimalScript's WSH security integration options

In the Security Setting drop-down list, you can select the WSH TrustPolicy level you want, potentially allowing you to override a domain-wide TrustPolicy configuration so that you can test scripts without interference from the TrustPolicy restrictions.

Script Deployment and Remote Scripting

Sometimes the best way to run a particular script is to run the script directly on one or more remote computers. We discussed remote scripting in Chapter 6, "Remote Scripting," but often the *WshController* object doesn't provide sufficient control or feedback for a particular situation. That's when you can turn to your scripting tools to provide deployment and remote scripting capabilities that are superior to the capabilities built into WSH.

Both AdminScriptEditor and PrimalScript provide script packaging capabilities. Admin-ScriptEditor's is called the Script Packager, and PrimalScript's is called ESP (Evolved Script Packager). Both tools essentially bundle a VBScript file into a standalone executable and allow you to apply alternate security credentials so that the executable can be run by a user who doesn't necessarily have permission to perform the tasks that the script performs. Figure A-11 shows PrimalScript's packager, which allows you to specify a custom icon for the final executable, and also allows you to include multiple script files, data files, and even COM components in the package. The package will automatically unpack the data files and COM components, register the COM components, and then execute your scripts sequentially or in parallel (you decide which). It can even remove the data files after your scripts have finished executing. As part of PrimalScript's focus on scripting security, scripts in the package can be digitally signed, making them compatible with WSH TrustPolicy.

Figure A-11   Packaging scripts using PrimalScript's ESP

Packaging scripts in this fashion makes it easier to deploy them as standalone tools to less technically proficient users, or even to deploy them as applications by using Group Policy objects or other software-deployment mechanisms.

Another way to deploy your scripts to remote computers is through remote scripting, very much along the lines of what *WshController* does. Both PrimalScript (Enterprise Edition) and OnScript (Network Edition) include remote scripting capabilities. PrimalScript's feature is called the Remote Script Execution Engine (RSEE); OnScript simply incorporates the feature as part of its feature set. OnScript's remote scripting requires that you install a small COM component on each remote computer on which you want to manage and execute remote scripts. The product then allows you to connect to any computer containing that COM component and maintain a repository of scripts on that remote computer. Any remote script can be executed, which causes the COM component to run the script locally on the remote computer. Basic status information is fed back to your copy of OnScript so that you can see when the script concludes. PrimalScript's RSEE is somewhat more robust, providing the ability to deploy a script to multiple computers, rather than executing remote scripts one at a time.

Remote scripting is a great way to spread the processing load of a major scripting effort. For example, rather than writing one script that connects to each of a thousand computers to make some configuration change, you can deploy the script directly to each of those computers, allowing the script to execute in parallel. It's a great time-saver, and having the ability built into your scripting tool makes it more convenient and easier to manage.

WSF and WSC Support

In Chapters 3 and 4, we showed you how to use Windows Script Files (WSFs) and Windows Script Components (WSCs) to package your script into more modular, standalone files. Both the WSF and WSC format require fairly complex XML formatting, and although most scripting tools and editors can display the files, they don't provide any means of simplifying the formatting. PrimalScript is an exception. It provides a graphical user interface that enables you to configure various options supported by the WSF or WSC format, while handling the complex XML formatting entirely behind the scenes. We like these features because they make it much more practical to use these powerful script file formats. Having to manually format the XML is intimidating and error prone, and often results in administrators simply abandoning the formats and doing without their valuable benefits.

> **More Info**   For more information about the WSF format, see Chapter 3, "Windows Script Files." The WSC format is covered in Chapter 4, "Windows Script Components."

Other Features

Commercial script editors can provide additional features that make scripting more efficient. Some of our favorite features include:

- The ability to capture output from WSH, displaying script output within the editor itself.

- Options for adding other tools, such as tools for working with databases, other scripting languages, and so forth. Some editors allow you to integrate existing tools that are already installed on your computer, whereas others sell or provide add-in tools that accomplish specific tasks.

- Integration of documentation, such as the downloadable VBScript documentation or Microsoft MSDN Library. The best form of integration lets you highlight a language keyword, press a hotkey such as *F1*, and then view help for that keyword in a pop-up box.

- Browsers that enable you to view the properties and methods of COM objects installed on your computer. These browsers often make it easier to locate and work with COM objects.

- Code folding, which is a feature that defines *regions* in your script. These regions can represent a subroutine or function, or regions of script that you define. Regions can then be collapsed (or *folded*) and expanded, helping you hide portions of the script so that you can focus on other portions.

- Block formatting features, such as the ability to indent or unindent blocks of code, turn blocks of code into comments, or turn blocks of comments into active code. These features help save time when you're writing longer, complex scripts.

The list goes on and on. As you use the editor you've selected, you'll find yourself becoming more and more efficient and effective, and your scripting efforts will require less time and produce even better results.

Where to Get the Software

You can obtain evaluation copies of the four products we've discussed, and of course, the products themselves, from their manufacturers' Web sites:

- AdminScriptEditor is available from the following two Web sites:

  http://www.itripoli.com

  http://www.adminscripteditor.com

  We worked with version 2.2 for this book.

- OnScript is available at

  http://www.onscript.com

  We worked with version 1.0 for this book.

- PrimalScript is available at

  http://www.sapien.com

  http://www.primalscript.com

  We worked with version 4 for this book, focusing primarily on the Professional Edition (although we did mention a couple of features that are only in the Enterprise Edition).

- VBSEdit is available at

  http://www.vbsedit.com

  We worked with version 3 for this book.

We want to once again acknowledge that there are a *huge* number of other editors out there. Some are free, and others require you to purchase them. The reason we've focused on these four products is that they provide the most functionality specific to Windows administrative scripting. Many other products are just fancy text editors, perhaps providing line numbering and a few other useful features. Others are specifically designed for Web development, although they might provide a few other VBScript development features. Although all these tools are certainly useful, they're nowhere near as useful as an editor that's specifically designed to make Windows administrative scripting easier. Of course, the most powerful and feature-filled tools cost more—in fact, our experience is that you really do get what you pay for in terms of functionality. Almost every professional in any trade will tell you that spending a bit to get an excellent set of tools will pay off in the time and effort it saves you.

We're often asked which scripting editor we prefer and recommend. We've tried all the ones we cover in this Appendix, and we both use PrimalScript as our daily editor. However, we can't say what's best for you. That's why we're so glad the manufacturers of these products offer trial versions, most in the 30-day to 45-day range, and most offering full product functionality for the duration of the trial. That gives you the opportunity to download each one, test it for a month or so, and decide which one has the features that work best for you. Of course, as we said at the beginning of this Appendix, be sure you're training yourself to *use* those features, so that you're getting the full benefit of whatever tool you eventually decide to use.

Index

Symbols

3-D scrollbars, displaying in HTAs, 142

A

aborting scripts, 20, 292
AbsolutePage property (ADO Recordset object), 249
AbsolutePosition property (ADO Recordset object), 249
Access. *See* Microsoft Access
accounts. *See* user accounts
ACEs (access control entries), 241
activating ODBC DSNs, 184
Active Directory
  alternate credentials, connecting through, 53
  configuring with WMI classes, 373–374
  connecting to, shortcut for, 255
  as database, 248–251
  Exchange information, viewing, 428
  mappings, list of, 248
  objects, retrieving LDAP path to, 254
  querying, and arrays, 428
  querying default configuration naming context, 427
  querying Exchange mailbox stores, 430
  querying Exchange storage groups, 428–429
  querying, with homeMDBBL attribute, 431–432
  Schema snap-in, registering, 251
  searching, 257
  trust provider, modifying, 373–374
Active Directory Browser (ADSVW), 217–218
  connecting to domain root, 218
  graphical interface, 218
  navigating, 218
Active Directory Services Interface (ADSI). *See* ADSI (Active Directory Services Interface)
ActiveConnection property (ADO Recordset object), 249
ActiveX, 96. *See also* COM objects
ActiveX Data Objects (ADO). *See* ADO (ActiveX Data Objects)
Add method (Dictionary object), 23
AddAsString method (SwBemPrivilegeSet object), 275

AdditionsVersion property (GuestOS object), 497
AddPrinterDriver method, 384
administrator password, changing with script, 26
AdminScriptEditor MessageBox Wizard, 510
AdminScriptEditor WMI Wizard, 349, 350
ADO (ActiveX Data Objects), 179–180
  advantages of, 180
  alternate credentials, connecting with, 247
  closing connection, 255
  Command objects. *See* Command objects (ADO)
  connecting to ADSI with, 247
  Connection objects, 181–182
  connection strings. *See* connection strings
  data sources. *See* specific data sources
  documentation, 191
  flexibility of, 180
  large result sets and, 245
  ODBC DSN connections, 182–184
  pages, 245
  queries, filtering with string variables, 258
  Recordset objects. *See* Recordset objects (ADO)
  testing for group membership, in conjunction with ADSI, 256–259
ADSCmd, 220–225
ADSI (Active Directory Services Interface), 24–29
  ADO Recordset object properties in, 249–251
  alternate credentials for, 53
  case sensitivity of, 25
  closing connections, 253
  command-line tools, 220–225
  ConnectionString property, vs. Provider property, 247
  data return limits, 227–229
  directory service types. *See* LDAP provider; WinNT provider
  paging, enabling automatic, 250
  permissions and, 167
  providers. *See* LDAP provider; WinNT provider
  queries. *See* ADSI queries

  recordsets, methods supported in, 250–251
  Scriptomatic. *See* ADSI Scriptomatic
  setting changes, 26
ADSI Provider, 246–247
ADSI queries
  Attributes portion of syntax, 252
  filter portion of syntax, 251–252
  filtering, 251–252, 253
  making changes with, 254–256
  remote, 163
  specifying scope, 253
  syntax, proprietary, 251–254
ADSI Scriptomatic, 207–209. *See also* Scriptomatic
  creating user account with, 207–208
  downloading, 209
  reusing code from, 209
ADSI Software Development Kit (SDK), 217. *See also* Active Directory Browser (ADSVW); ADSCmd; ADSIDump
ADSIDump, 222–225
ADSVW. *See* Active Directory Browser (ADSVW)
Alert object, 470–471
Alert property (ScriptContext object), 465
alerts, creating in MOM (Microsoft Operations Manager), 481
aliases, WMIC, 326–328
  determining which properties returned by get command, 333
  target classes, 329–331
  viewing information on, 331
alternate credentials, 52
  with Active Directory Services Interface (ADSI), 53
  with ADO, 247
  CIM Studio and, 344–345
  remote scripting with, 165
  with RunAs command, 52
  unavailable for local system, 344
  with Windows Management Instrumentation (WMI), 54
  with Windows Task Scheduler, 53
  with WMI Event Registration, 301
  with WMIC (WMI Command Line), 332
applicationname attribute (HTAs), 141
applications, authorizing in Windows Firewall, 361

About the Authors

Don Jones is an independent author, consultant, and trainer. He is also one of the industry's leading experts on Windows scripting. Don owns and operates ScriptingAnswers.com. He is a Microsoft Certified Systems Engineer (MCSE) and a Microsoft Most Valued Professional (MVP). Don is the author of *Microsoft Windows Administrator's Automation Toolkit* (Microsoft Press, 2005), *VBScript and WMI for Windows Administrators* (Addison-Wesley Professional, 2004), and *Managing Windows with VBScript and WMI* (Addison-Wesley Professional, 2004). He is also a co-author of the *Microsoft Windows Server 2003 Resource Kit* (Microsoft Press, 2005), and is a regular columnist for *Redmond Magazine* (formerly *Microsoft Certified Professional Magazine*).

Jeffery Hicks (MCSE, MCT, MCSA) is a Senior Network Engineer with Visory Group, a Microsoft Gold Partner. He is also President and Principal Consultant of JDH Information Technology Solutions. He has been in the IT industry for 15 years, doing everything from help desk support to project management. He is a freelance technology writer and has developed several training videos on administrative scripting. Jeff has been a frequent contributor to several online IT community Web sites, as well as an invited speaker at computer conferences and seminars. He is currently a Contributing Editor for ScriptingAnswers.com.